COMPLEX COGNITION

COMPLEX COGNITION

THE PSYCHOLOGY OF HUMAN THOUGHT

Robert J. Sternberg
Yale University

Talia Ben-Zeev
Williams College

New York ◆ Oxford
Oxford University Press
2001

Oxford University Press

Athens   Auckland   Bangkok   Bogotá   Buenos Aires   Calcutta
Cape Town   Chennai   Dar es Salaam   Delhi   Florence   Hong Kong   Istanbul
Karachi   Kuala Lumpur   Madrid   Melbourne   Mexico City   Mumbai
Nairobi   Paris   São Paulo   Shanghai   Singapore   Taipei   Tokyo   Toronto   Warsaw

and associated companies in
Berlin   Ibadan

Published by Oxford University Press, Inc.
198 Madison Avenue, New York, New York, 10016
http://www.oup-usa.org

Oxford is a registered trademark of Oxford University Press.

Library of Congress Cataloging-in-Publication Data

Sternberg, Robert J.
  Complex cognition : the psychology of human thought / Robert J. Sternberg, Talia Ben-Zeev.
     p. cm.
  Includes bibliographical references and indexes.
  ISBN 0-19-510771-3 (cloth : alk. paper)
  1. Cognition. I. Ben-Zeev, Talia. II. Title.

BF311 .S67775 2001
153.4—dc21   00-032411

Printing (last digit) 10 9 8 7 6 5 4 3 2 1

Printed in the United States of America
on acid-free paper

This book is dedicated to
Alexander J. Wearing and Henry Kaufman

Contents

Preface

On December 31, 1999, Boris Yeltsin resigned as president of Russia. What exactly did he mean by "resign": Was he going to disappear, or was he going to try to run things from behind the scenes? What problems would the country and the world face as a result of his resignation? How did he decide to resign, anyway? Would the next president of Russia, Vladimir Putin, be any better than Yeltsin was: Would he be a more expert head of state or a less expert one? Would he show the practical intelligence and wisdom that Yeltsin seemed to lack in his later years? These are the kinds of questions addressed by scientists who study complex cognition. They deal with these issues of concepts and meaning, problem solving, decision making, expertise, intelligence, and much more.

The goal of this book is to provide a thorough review of the field of complex cognition. Toward this end, the book contains chapters in virtually all the areas that are usually viewed as central to this field, including an overview and description of methods, history of the field, concepts, the representation and acquisition of knowledge, deductive reasoning, inductive reasoning, problem solving, decision making, the nature of language, language and thought, intelligence, creativity, expertise, the development of complex cognition, and the teaching of thinking.

The book is intended as an update on the field for psychologists, other social scientists, and educators or as a textbook for upper-division undergraduate or beginning graduate students who are taking courses in such areas as complex cognition, psychology of human thought, higher processes of cognition, complex processes of cognition, or thinking.

Historically, the dominant point of view in this field was one of normative reference. According to this view, people are rational thinkers who thoroughly consider alternatives and how to weigh them. "Economic-person" models and utility models represent this point of view. A more recent and contrasting point of view was introduced by Herbert Simon in his model of bounded rationality and has been carried forward by Amos Tversky and Daniel Kahneman in their model of heuristics and biases. The basic idea of these models is that people are surprisingly irrational or, at best, arational, in their thinking and often think in ways that lead them to wrong conclusions derived from ill-conceived shortcuts. More recently, Gerd Gigerenzer and others have suggested that people do use heuristics, but that the use of such heuristics makes perfect sense and often leads to better decisions than does the use of more complicated strategies.

The point of view of this book is a different synthesis from other syntheses of the thesis and antithesis just described. We suggest that from their own subjective point of view, people think sensibly, if not always wholly rationally; from an outside point of view, their thinking may not appear to be rational. From the point of view of this book, there is no "objective" stance; rather, different points of view lead to different conclusions about what is rational. In taking this points-of-view analysis, we use a dialectical perspective, showing how at different times in our attempts to understand complex cognition, different preferred points of view have prevailed.

The book is divided into 15 chapters. The first two chapters, "The Field of Complex Cognition: Overview and Methods" (chapter 1) and "History of the Field of Complex Cognition" (chapter 2), present an introduction to the field. These chapters discuss the kinds of things that are studied, why they are studied, and how they have been studied in the past. The next two chapters, "Concepts: Structure and Acquisition" (chapter 3) and "Knowledge Representation and Acquisition" (chapter 4), discuss how single concepts are represented and how they are integrated into larger representations of knowledge. The following two chapters, "Deductive Reasoning" (chapter 5) and "Inductive Reasoning" (chapter 6), cover the two main types of reasoning studied in the field of complex cognition. The subsequent two chapters, "Problem Solving" (chapter 7) and "Decision Making" (chapter 8), cover how people use their concepts and reasoning processes to confront the kinds of problems and decisions that face them, both in the laboratory and in the everyday world. The next two chapters, "The Nature of Language" (chapter 9) and "Language and Thought" (chapter 10), provide a comprehensive introduction to the study of language and how it influences thinking. The subsequent two chapters, "Human and Artificial Intelligence" (chapter 11) and "Creativity" (chapter 12), cover complex processes that integrate all the processes covered previously and consider in more detail issues of individual differences between people. The next chapter, "Expertise" (chapter 13), integrates much of what has been presented, discussing what characterizes experts in complex cognition of various kinds. The final two chapters, "Development of Complex Cognition" (chapter 14) and "Teaching Thinking" (chapter 15), cover development, both over the life span and through specific attempts to build complex cognitive skills.

Taken as a whole, the book covers most of the major topics that constitute the field of complex cognition. The book may help readers understand, at some level, the complex cognition that went into Boris Yeltsin's resignation, or Richard Nixon's, for that matter. Of course, the book does not cover everything. We do not include a chapter on the topic of memory, whose separate coverage we view as central to courses on cognitive psychology, but as less so to courses on complex cognition, as we believe that because memory is essential to all aspects of complex cognition, it needs to be referred to throughout the book as necessary. Emotional, social, and personality variables that affect complex cognition are also not covered separately in the book. Nor is there any claim that all the principles we cover are universal. Although we discuss a number of studies conducted around the world, most of the studies we include were conducted in developed countries, primarily in the United States. Although we do not cover all possible topics, we believe that those we do present will prepare readers to go beyond what we have reviewed and to learn the further information that makes the field of complex cognition an exciting one to study.

Preparation of this book was supported, in part, by Grant R206R950001 under the Javits Act Program from the Office of Educational Research and Improvement, U.S. Department of Education. The positions taken in this book do not, however, necessarily reflect those of the Department of Education or the U.S. government. We are thankful to Paul Allopenna and Karen Adler for their thoughtful ideas and contributions to this book. Many thanks are also due to Steven Sloman, Joachim Krueger, Quix Lezine, Christine Pacheco, and Winnie Eng for their useful suggestions. We are grateful to Sai Durvasula for assistance in preparing the manuscript.

Credits

Figure 3.1. Reprinted with permission from J. G. Snodgrass and the American Psychological Association.

Snodgrass, J. G., & Vanderwart, M. (1980). A standardized set of 260 pictures: Norms for name agreement, image agreement, familiarity, and visual complexity. *Journal of Experimental Psychology: Human Learning & Memory, 6*(2), 174–215.

Figure 4.5. Reprinted with permission from J. R. Anderson.

Anderson, J. R. (1993). *Rules of the mind.* Hillsdale, NJ: Lawrence Erlbaum Associates.

Figure 4.11. Reprinted with permission from J. L. McClelland.

McClelland, J. L., Rumelhart, D. E., & the PDP Research Group (1986). *Parallel distributed processing: Explorations in the microstructure of cognition. Vol. 2. Psychological and biological models.* Cambridge, MA: MIT Books.

Figure 7.3. Reprinted with permission from J. R. Anderson.

Anderson, J. R. (Ed.) (1980). *Cognitive psychology and its implications.* New York: W. H. Freeman.

Table 8.5. Reprinted with permission from M. Charge.

Loomes, G. (1987). Testing for regret and disappointment in choice under certainty. *Economic Journal, 97,* 118–129.

Figure 14.1. Reprinted with permission from Harcourt, Inc.

Sternberg, R. J. (1996). *Cognitive psychology.* Orlando, FL: Harcourt, Inc.

Table 14.1. Reprinted with permission from Harcourt, Inc.

Sternberg, R. J. (1996). *Cognitive psychology.* Orlando, FL: Harcourt, Inc.

Table 14.2. Reprinted with permission from Harcourt, Inc.

Sternberg, R. J. (1996). *Cognitive psychology.* Orlando, FL: Harcourt, Inc.

COMPLEX COGNITION

The Field of Complex Cognition
Overview and Methods

◆ Complex Cognition Defined
◆ Research Methods in Complex Cognition
◆ Key Issues and Fields in the Study of Complex Cognition
◆ Chapter Previews
◆ Summary

On December 28, 1999, the mayor of Seattle, Washington, decided to cancel the city's millennium celebration because of a fear of terrorist acts. Anyone listening to the newscast of this announcement might have wondered how the mayor decided that the threat was real and serious enough to cancel the celebration. To make his decision, the mayor used complex cognition, and to understand his decision requires complex cognition as well.

COMPLEX COGNITION DEFINED

Complex cognition deals with how people mentally represent and think about information. For example, people may mentally represent information in the form of sentences or conceptual propositions underlying sentences or in the form of images. They may think about sentences by converting a sentence in the active voice to the passive voice or by mentally rotating an image in their minds. A psychologist who is interested in complex cognition may study how people learn language, decide which one of several computers to buy, or think when they play chess or politics. Why do people find it easier to reason when content is familiar than when it is unfamiliar? Why do people view a robin as more like a bird than an ostrich, even though both are birds? Why are many people more afraid of traveling in airplanes than in automobiles, when the chances of injury and death are so much higher in an automobile than in an airplane? These are some of the kinds of questions that can be answered through the study of complex cognition.

This chapter introduces the field of complex cognition by describing the major methods, issues, and content areas of cognitive psychology. The ideas presented here will provide a foundation on which to build an understanding of the topics in complex cognition covered in the remaining chapters.

A key theme of this book is the role of the dialectic in the study of complex cognition, in particular, and in psychology, in general. One pattern that emerges from a study of intellectual history is the observation that the progression of ideas often involves a *dialectical process.* In a dialectic, a *thesis* (statement of belief) is proposed. For example, one school of thought has long held that many aspects of human behavior (e.g., intelligence or personality) are entirely governed by human nature. Other people consider the thesis, and if it seems plausible, the idea may be accepted. After a while, however, some people notice apparent flaws in the thesis, and eventually (or perhaps even soon), an *antithesis* (a statement that counters the previous statement of belief) emerges. For example, an alternative school of thought has postulated that many aspects of human behavior are determined almost entirely by our nurture—the environmental contexts in which we are reared and in which we later function as adults.

Sooner or later, the debate between the thesis and the antithesis leads to a *synthesis,* which integrates the most credible features of each of the two views. For instance, in the debate over nature versus nurture, many psychologists believe that various aspects of human behavior are governed by an interaction between our nature (innate) and our nurture (environment). If this synthesis seems to advance our understanding, it then serves as a new thesis, which is followed by a new antithesis, then a new synthesis, and so on. This observation of the dialectical progression of ideas was advanced by George Hegel (1770–1831), a German philosopher who came to his ideas by synthesizing some of the views of his intellectual predecessors and contemporaries.

An example of the dialectic is highly relevant to the field of complex cognition and to this book. At one time, many psychologists believed in models of "economic man and woman," a uniformly rational thinker who solves problems in a logical way whenever possible. An antithesis of this view arose out of the work of Herbert Simon (1957), who proposed a model of men and women as "satisficing"—that is, as choosing the first minimally satisfactory option available to them. For example, consider the choice of a new car. According to the model of economic man and woman, a person is likely carefully to consider each potential feature of a car, decide how important that feature is, and then find a car that somehow optimally combines the desired features. According to the satisficing model, a person is likely to choose the first car he or she encounters that meets his or her basic requirements, whether or not the automobile is, in any sense, optimal.

Today, many psychologists believe that people are sometimes rational and sometimes not, although people often perceive themselves as rational when they are not. Thus, the original thesis of economic man and woman gave way to an antithesis of satisficing man and woman, which, in turn, has given way to a mixed model in which people are viewed as sometimes rational and sometimes not.

RESEARCH METHODS IN COMPLEX COGNITION

Goals of Research

Suppose you worked in the marketing department of an automobile company and wanted to figure out how people decide what car to buy. What do they care about in this regard, and how do they weigh the different features on which cars differ? To answer these questions, you would have to do research on people's complex cognition. What kinds of goals do researchers have, in general, when they initiate a research project?

Before we describe some of the specific methods used by researchers in the field of complex cognition, it may help to highlight some of the goals of research in the field. Briefly, these goals include theory development, hypothesis formulation, hypothesis testing, data collection, data analysis, and perhaps even application of the research to settings outside the research environment. Often, researchers seek simply to gather as much information as possible about a particular phenomenon. They usually, although not always, have preconceived notions about what they may find while they are gathering the data. In any case, their research focuses on describing particular cognitive phenomena, such as how people learn concepts or how they develop expertise.

Data collection reflects an empirical aspect of the scientific enterprise. Once there are sufficient data on the cognitive phenomenon of interest, psychologists who study complex cognition use various methods for drawing inferences from the data. Ideally, they use converging types of evidence to support their hypotheses. Sometimes, just a quick glance at the data leads to intuitive inferences regarding patterns that have emerged. More commonly, however, researchers use various statistical means of analyzing the data.

Data collection and statistical analysis help researchers describe complex cognitive phenomena. No scientific pursuit could get far without such descriptions. However, most psychologists who study complex cognition want to understand more than the *what* of complex cognition; they also seek to understand the *how* and the *why* of thinking. That is, researchers seek ways to explain complex cognition, as well as to describe it. To move beyond descriptions, cognitive psychologists must use reasoning to leap from what is observed directly to what can be inferred regarding observations.

Suppose that we wish to study an aspect of complex cognition, such as how people comprehend technical information in computer manuals. We usually start with a **theory** (an organized body of general explanatory principles regarding a phenomenon), as well as some reasonable **hypotheses** (tentative proposals of expected empirical consequences of the theory, such as of the outcomes of research) derived from the theory on how people comprehend technical information in computer manuals. Then we seek to test the theory and thereby to see whether it has the power to predict certain aspects of the phenomenon in question. In other words, our thought process is, "If our theory is correct, then whenever X occurs, outcome Y should result."

Next, we test our hypotheses through experimentation. Even if particular findings appear to confirm a given hypothesis, the findings must be subjected to statistical analysis, to determine their statistical significance. Measures of *statistical significance* indicate the likelihood of obtaining a set of findings only by chance. For example, a finding that is significant at the 5% level is one that would occur only 5% of the time if chance was operating alone.

Once our hypothetical predictions have been experimentally tested and statistically analyzed, the findings from those experiments may lead to further data collection, data analysis, theory development, hypothesis formulation, and hypothesis testing. In addition, many psychologists who study complex cognition hope to use insights gained from research to help people use complex cognition in real-life situations. Thus, basic research may lead to everyday applications. And some research in complex cognition is applied from the start, to help people improve their lives and the conditions under which they live. For each of these purposes, different research methods offer different advantages and disadvantages.

Consider an example. Suppose we had a theory that when people make complex decisions, they consider only the factor that really matters the most to them and ignore the rest—what Gigerenzer and his colleagues (1999) referred to as the "take the best" heuristic. So the theory is that people consider just one major factor when they make decisions. In studying how people decide what car to buy, we hypothesize that the best predictor of what car people will buy will be which car is optimal on the one factor each person in a sample of people believes to be the most important to his or her decision. If our hypothesis is correct, that factor should be a better predictor of what cars people by than any other single factor or weighted combination of multiple factors. Gigerenzer and his colleagues found that, in general, the take-the-best heuristic provides prediction–that is better than that of many much more complex alternative models of how people make decisions.

Distinctive Methods of Research

Psychologists in the field of complex cognition use various methods to explore how humans think. These methods include, among others, (1) laboratory or other controlled experiments, (2) psychobiological research, (3) self-reports, (4) case studies, (5) naturalistic observation, and (6) computer simulations and artificial intelligence. Sometimes these various methods are combined in a research project.

Experiments on Human Behavior

Controlled laboratory experiments are probably the method most people think of when they think of scientific research. In controlled experimental designs, an experimenter conducts research in a laboratory setting in which he or she controls as many aspects of the experimental situation as possible. The experimenter then manipulates the independent variables, controlling for the effects of suspected irrelevant variables, and observes the effects on the dependent variables (outcomes).

In implementing the experimental method, the experimenter must use a representative sample of the population of interest and must exert rigorous control over the experimental conditions, randomly assigning participants to the treatment and the control conditions. If these requisites for the experimental method are fulfilled, the experimenter may be able to infer probable causality—the effects of the independent variable (the treatment) on the dependent variable (the outcome). If the outcomes in the treatment condition show a statistically significant difference from the outcomes in the control condition, the experimenter can infer the likelihood of a causal link between the independent variable and the dependent variable. Because the researcher can establish a likely causal link between the given independent variables and the dependent variables, controlled laboratory experiments are an excellent means of testing hypotheses.

For example, suppose that we wanted to see whether hearing music by Mozart in the background influences the ability to perform a particular cognitive task (e.g., reading a technical passage from a computer manual and responding to comprehension questions) well. Ideally, we would first select a random sample of participants from within our total population of interest. We would then randomly assign each participant to a treatment condition or a control condition. We would then introduce some representative music by Mozart to the participants in the treatment condition, but not to the participants in the control condition. We would present the cognitive task to participants in both the treatment condition and the control condition, measuring their performance by some means (e.g., the speed and accuracy of their responses to comprehension questions). Finally, we would statistically analyze our results, to see whether the difference between the two groups reached statistical significance. If the performance of the participants in the treatment condition was different from the performance of the participants in the control condition at a statistically significant level, we might then infer that listening to music by Mozart did, indeed, influence the ability to perform well on this particular cognitive task.

In cognitive-psychological research, the dependent variables may be diverse, but they often involve various outcome measures of accuracy (e.g., frequency of errors), of response times, or of both. Among the myriad possibilities for independent variables are the characteristics of the situation, of the task, or of the participants. For example, the characteristics of the situation may involve the presence versus the absence of particular stimuli, such as hints during a problem-solving task; characteristics of the task may involve reading versus listening to a series of words and then responding to comprehension questions; and characteristics of the participants may include age, educational status, and test scores.

Although the characteristics of the situation or of the task may be manipulated through the random assignment of participants to either the treatment or the control group, the characteristics of the participant are not easily manipulated experimentally. For instance, if the researcher wants to study the effects of aging on the speed and accuracy of problem solving, he or she cannot randomly assign participants to various age groups. In such situations, researchers often use other kinds of studies, such as those involving *correlation*, a statistical relationship between two (or more) attributes (characteristics of the participants, of a situation, and so forth), expressed as a number on a scale that ranges from -1.00 (a negative correlation) to 0 (no correlation) to 1.00 (a positive correlation). For example, we may expect a negative correlation between fatigue and alertness, no correlation between intelligence and length of ear lobe, and a positive correlation between vocabulary size and reading comprehension.

Findings of correlational relationships are highly informative, and their value should not be underrated. Also, because correlational studies do not require the random assignment of participants to treatment and control conditions, these methods may be flexibly applied. However, correlational studies generally do not permit unequivocal inferences regarding causality, so many psychologists who study complex cognition strongly prefer experimental data to correlational data.

An example of a correlational study was one that looked at whether a widely used test for admission to graduate school, the Graduate Record Examination, predicted aspects of performance in a graduate school in a particular university (Sternberg & Williams, 1997). In other words, what is the correlation between success on this high-level test of thinking skills and success in graduate school? It was found that the test was modestly to moderately predictive of first-year grades but less predictive of other criteria of success in graduate school. Prediction was somewhat better for men than for women.

Psychobiological Research

In *psychobiological research*, investigators study the relationship between cognitive performance and cerebral events and structures. The specific techniques that are used in psychobiological research generally fall into three categories: (1) techniques for studying an individual's brain *postmortem* (after the death of an individual), relating the individual's cognitive function prior to death to observable features of the brain; (2) techniques for studying images showing structures of or activities in the brain of an individual who is known to have a particular cognitive deficit; or (3) techniques for obtaining information about cerebral processes during the normal performance of a cognitive activity.

Postmortem studies offered some of the first insights into how specific *lesions* (areas of injury) in the brain may be associated with particular cognitive deficits, and such studies continue to provide useful insights into how the brain influences cognitive function. Recent technological developments have also enabled researchers increasingly to study individuals with known cognitive deficits *in vivo* (while the individual is alive). The study of individuals with abnormal cognitive functions, linked to cerebral pathologies, often enhances our understanding of normal cognitive functions.

In addition, psychobiological researchers investigate some aspects of normal cognitive functioning by studying cerebral activity in animals. Researchers often use animals for experiments involving neurosurgical procedures that cannot be performed on humans because such procedures would be difficult, unethical, or impractical. For example, studies that have mapped neural activity in the cortex have been conducted on cats and monkeys.

Consider an example of psychobiological research related to complex cognition. In one set of studies, researchers used a brain-scanning technique, called positron emission tomography (PET), to show how association areas in the brain integrate information from various parts of the cerebral cortex (Petersen, Fox, Posner, Mintun, & Raichle, 1988; Peterson, Fox, Posner, & Mintun, 1989). They were investigating cerebral blood flow during several activities involving the reading of single words. When the participants in their studies looked at a word on a screen, areas of the visual cortex showed high levels of activity; when they spoke a word, their motor cortex was highly active; and when they heard a word spoken, their auditory cortex was activated. And when they were asked to produce words related to the words they had seen, the association areas of the cortex showed the greatest amount of activity. In other words, complex cognition was occurring primarily in the association areas.

Some psychologists who are interested in complex cognition have questioned whether findings based on the cognitive and cerebral functioning of animals and of abnormal individuals may be generalized to apply to the cognitive and cerebral functioning of normal humans. Psychobiologists have responded to these questions in various ways, most of which go beyond the scope of this chapter. As just one example, however, for some kinds of cognitive activity, the available technology permits researchers to study the dynamic cerebral activity of normal human participants during cognitive processing.

Self-Reports, Case Studies, and Naturalistic Observation

Individual experiments and psychobiological studies often focus on the precise specification of discrete aspects of cognition across individuals. To obtain richly textured information about how particular individuals think in a broad range of contexts, researchers may use *self-reports* (individuals' own accounts of cognitive processes), *case studies* (in-depth studies of individuals), and *naturalistic observation* (detailed studies of cognitive performance in everyday situations and nonlaboratory contexts). Whereas experimental research is most useful for testing hypotheses, research that is based on self-reports, case studies, and naturalistic observation is perhaps more useful for the formulation of hypotheses.

The reliability of data based on various kinds of self-reports depends on the candor of the participants who provide the reports. Even if one assumes that participants are completely truthful in their reports, reports involving recollected information (e.g., diaries, retrospective accounts, questionnaires, and surveys) are notably less reliable than are reports provided during the cognitive process under investigation because participants sometimes forget what they did. In studying complex cognitive processes, such as problem solving or decision making, researchers often use a *verbal protocol,* in which the participants describe aloud all their thoughts and ideas during the given cognitive task (Ericsson & Simon, 1980). (For example, "I like the apartment with the swimming pool better, but I can't really afford it, so I might choose . . .")

An alternative to a verbal protocol is for participants to report specific information regarding a particular aspect of their cognitive processing. For instance, in a study of insightful problem solving, participants were asked, at 15-second intervals, to report numerical ratings indicating how close they thought they were to reaching a solution to a given problem. Unfortunately, even these self-report methods have limitations because cognitive processes may be altered by the act of giving the report and cognitive processes may occur outside conscious awareness (processes that do not require conscious attention or that take place so rapidly that we fail to notice them).

Case studies (e.g., the study of exceptionally gifted individuals) and naturalistic observations (e.g., the observation of individuals operating in nuclear power plants) may be used to complement findings from laboratory experiments because these two methods of cognitive research offer high **ecological validity,** which refers to the degree to which particular findings in one context may be considered relevant outside that context (as in the generalization of results from a laboratory to the everyday world). Many researchers seek to understand the interactive relationship between complex human thought processes and the environments in which humans are thinking. Sometimes, complex cognitive processes that are commonly observed in one setting (e.g., in a laboratory) are not identical to those observed in another setting (e.g., in an air-traffic control tower or a classroom).

An example of naturalistic observation can be found in a study of street children in Caracas, Venezuela (Márquez, 1999). The researcher, an anthropologist, was trying to understand the thoughts and feelings of children who live on the streets. What kinds of thinking do they do to enable them to survive? For these children, every moment harbors potential danger, so they must become extremely adept at recognizing potential danger and deciding how to deal with it. One boy, Elvis, was confronted by other street children and told to "take off your shoes and your jacket" (p. 195). Should he take off the shoes and jacket? Were the other street children just bluffing, or were they serious? On the one hand, if one gave in to every threat, one would soon find oneself with no possessions. On the other hand, if one did not give in at appropriate times, one would not live long. Elvis guessed wrong. He refused to give up the shoes and jacket, and another street child shot him. Fortunately, the gun misfired, and Elvis, still very much alive, ran away.

Computer Simulations and Artificial Intelligence

Digital computers played a fundamental role in the emergence of the study of complex cognition. Their influence has been both indirect—through models of complex human cognition based on models of how computers process information—and direct—through computer simulations and artificial intelligence.

In *computer simulations*, researchers program computers to model a given human function or process, such as humans' performance on particular cognitive tasks (e.g., solving a chess problem) or of particular cognitive processes (e.g., concept formation). Some researchers even have attempted to create computer models that simulate the entire cognitive architecture of the human mind, and their models have stimulated heated discussions regarding how the human mind may function as a whole. In **artificial intelligence**, researchers attempt to build systems that show intelligence, often the maximal level of intelligence the researchers can create within the systems. Sometimes, the distinction between simulation and artificial intelligence is blurred, as in the case of certain programs that are designed simultaneously to simulate human performance and to maximize functioning.

An example of a computer simulation is a computer program designed to play jazz improvisations (Johnson-Laird, 1993). The program can play as well as a decent (but not outstanding) jazz musician. It does so by generating simple, harmonically sensible chord sequences, then creating complications of these sequences, and then applying a set of rules to create variations. Johnson-Laird's goal in designing the program was not merely to simulate jazz, but to show that aspects of human creativity could be modeled by a computer.

Putting It All Together

Psychologists often broaden and deepen their understanding of complex cognition through research in **cognitive science,** a cross-disciplinary field that uses ideas and methods from cognitive psychology, neuroscience, artificial intelligence, philosophy, linguistics, and anthropology to study how humans acquire, store, represent, and utilize information. Psychologists who study complex cognition also profit from collaborations with other kinds of psychologists, such as social psychologists (e.g., in the cross-disciplinary field of social cognition), psychologists who study motivation and emotion, and engineering psychologists (psychologists who study human-machine interactions). Collaborations with engineering psychologists illustrate the interplay between basic complex cognitive-psychological research and applied psychological investigation.

KEY ISSUES AND FIELDS IN THE STUDY OF COMPLEX COGNITION

Throughout this chapter, we have alluded to some of the key issues that arise in the study of complex cognition. Many of these issues have a long history, starting with early philosophical analysis, but others arise largely as a result of recent work in the field. It may help to summarize these issues because they appear again and again in the various chapters of this book. Some of these questions go to the very core of the nature of the human mind.

Underlying Themes in the Study of Complex Cognition

If we review the major ideas in this chapter, we discover some of the major themes that underlie all complex cognition. What are some of these themes? Here are seven of them, which are also summarized in Table 1.1 for handy reference as you read the rest of the book:

1. *Nature versus nurture.* One major issue in the study of complex cognition is the respective influences of nature and nurture on human cognition. If we believe that innate characteristics of human cognition are more important, we may focus our research on the innate characteristics of complex cognition. If we believe that the environment plays an important role in cognition, we may explore how distinctive characteristics of the environment seem to influence complex cognition.

2. *Rationalism versus empiricism.* How should we discover the truth about ourselves and about the world around us? Should we do so by trying to reason logically, on the basis of what we already know, or by observing and testing our observations of what we can perceive through our senses?

3. *Structures versus processes.* Should we study the structures (contents, attributes, and products) of the human mind, or should we focus on the processes of human thinking?

4. *Domain generality versus domain specificity.* Are the processes we observe limited to single domains, or are they general across a variety of domains? Do observations in one domain (e.g., mathematics) apply also to all domains, or do they apply only to the specific domain observed?

5. *Validity of causal inferences versus ecological validity.* Should we study thinking by using highly controlled experiments that increase the probability of valid inferences regarding causality, or should we use more naturalistic techniques, which increase the likelihood of obtaining ecologically valid findings, but possibly at the expense of experimental control?

6. *Applied versus basic research.* Should we conduct research on fundamental complex cognitive processes, or should we study ways in which to help people use complex cognition effectively in practical situations?

7. *Biological versus behavioral methods.* Should we study the brain and its functioning directly, perhaps even by scanning the brains of people while they are performing complex cognitive tasks? Or should we study people's behavior in complex cognitive tasks by looking at measures, such as percentage correct and reaction time?

TABLE 1.1   Seven Major Themes in the Study of Complex Cognition

1. *Nature versus nurture*
2. *Rationalism versus empiricism*
3. *Structures versus processes*
4. *Domain generality versus domain specificity*
5. *Validity of causal inferences versus ecological validity*
6. *Applied versus basic research*
7. *Biological versus behavioral methods*

Although many of these questions are posed in either-or form, it is important to remember that a synthesis of views or methods often proves more useful than one extreme position or another (Sternberg, 1999a). For example, nature may provide an inherited framework for our distinctive characteristics and patterns of thinking and acting, but nurture may shape the specific ways in which we realize that framework. We may use empirical methods for collecting data and testing hypotheses, but we may use rationalist methods for interpreting data, constructing theories, and formulating hypotheses based on theories. Our understanding of complex cognition deepens when we consider both basic research into fundamental complex cognitive processes and applied research on effective uses of complex cognition in real-world settings. Syntheses are constantly evolving: What today may be viewed as a synthesis may tomorrow be viewed as an extreme position, or even vice versa.

Before this chapter ends, it is useful to think about some of the fields of complex cognition, described in the remaining chapters, to which these key issues may apply.

CHAPTER PREVIEWS

Psychologists have been involved in studying a wide range of psychological phenomena. In fact, almost any topic of psychological interest may be studied from a perspective of complex cognition. Nonetheless, there are some main areas of interest to psychologists in this field. In this volume, we attempt to describe some of the preliminary answers to questions asked by researchers in the main areas of interest.

• Chapter 2, "History of the Field of Complex Cognition." How has the field of complex cognition evolved? What are its roots in philosophy and early psychology? What are the main questions that have been addressed historically in this field?

• Chapter 3, "Concepts: Structure and Acquisition." How do we acquire new concepts? How do we represent concepts in our minds? How do we link concepts together?

• Chapter 4, "Knowledge Representation and Acquisition." How do we mentally organize what we know? How do we manipulate and operate on knowledge? Do we have multiple forms of representation?

• Chapter 5, "Deductive Reasoning." What makes a deduction valid? How do we make logically valid deductions from information we are given? What effects does the content of the information have on our deductive reasoning?

• Chapter 6, "Inductive Reasoning." How do we make inferences in the face of information that cannot give us a logically certain answer? What gives us confidence in our inductive inferences? What are the different types of inductive inferences we can make?

• Chapter 7, "Problem Solving." How do we represent and then solve problems? What processes aid and impede us in reaching solutions to problems? What makes some people better problem solvers than others?

• Chapter 8, "Decision Making." How do we make decisions? Do we make practical decisions that affect our lives in a way that is different from the way we make inconsequential decisions? What kinds of factors do we take into account when we make decisions? What kinds of biases do we have?

• Chapter 9, "The Nature of Language." How do we derive and produce meaning through language? How do we acquire language—both our primary language and additional languages?

• Chapter 10, "Language and Thought." How does our use of language interact with our ways of thinking? How does our social world interact with our use of language?

• Chapter 11, "Human and Artificial Intelligence." What mental processes are used in intelligent thinking? Why do we consider some people more intelligent than others? Why do some people seem better able to accomplish whatever they want to accomplish in their chosen fields of endeavor?

• Chapter 12, "Creativity." Why are some of us more creative than others? How do we become and remain creative? What are the mental processes involved in creative thinking?

• Chapter 13, "Expertise." What are the factors that underlie expertise in an area? How does a person become an expert? Are there costs to expertise?

• Chapter 14, "Development of Complex Cognition." How does our thinking change across the life span? What factors contribute to these changes?

• Chapter 15, "Teaching Thinking." How can we teach people to think better? Are interventions effective? Are they more effective for some individuals than for others?

In this book, we try to emphasize the underlying and common ideas across various aspects of complex cognition, rather than simply to state the facts. In addition, we try to convey some idea of how psychologists in the field of complex cognition think and how they structure their field in their day-to-day work. We hope that this approach will convey the nature of problems in complex cognition at a deeper level than otherwise would be possible. We also try to present the field of complex cognition as a dynamic discipline, rather than one that comprises a static set of facts that we can only pretend will never change or be viewed from a different perspective. The discipline evolves as it follows a dialectical process of thesis leading to antithesis leading to synthesis.

◆ SUMMARY

The study of complex cognition examines how people think about information. Psychologists in this field use a broad range of methods, including experiments, psychobiological techniques, self-reports, case studies, naturalistic observation, and computer simulations and artificial intelligence. Some of the major issues in the field have centered on how to pursue knowledge by using both *rationalism* (which is the basis for theory development) and *empiricism* (which is the basis for gathering data), by underscoring the importance of cognitive structures and cognitive processes, by emphasizing the study of domain-general and of domain-specific processing, by striving for a high degree of experimental control (which better permits causal inferences) and for a high degree of *ecological validity* (which better allows findings to be generalized to settings outside the laboratory), and by conducting basic research seeking fundamental insights about cognition and applied research seeking effective uses of cognition in real-world settings. Although positions on these issues may seem to be diametrical opposites, apparently antithetical views are often synthesized into a form that offers the best of each of the opposing viewpoints.

History of the Field of Complex Cognition

◆ The Dialectical Progression of Ideas

◆ A Brief Intellectual History: Western Antecedents of the Psychology of Complex Cognition

◆ The Diverging Perspectives of Modern Studies of Complex Cognition

◆ Twentieth-Century Perspectives on Complex Cognition

◆ Summary

How does a student learn that "Me gusta la psicología" means "I like psychology" in Spanish? It depends, of course, on whom you ask. At one time, many psychologists might have said that a student would do so by being rewarded, or reinforced, for making the right connection—and some psychologists would still take this point of view. Today, more psychologists may say that a student makes this connection by having a propositional network that, in the past, has represented the idea "I like psychology" in terms of those English words at a node within the propositional network and that now incorporates "me gusta la psicología" into this node. Other contemporary psychologists may view the information as being encoded into a connection between two nodes, rather than at a node. And still others may reject all these explanations, arguing that we learn what the phrase means when we are engaged in the activity represented by the phrase. All these attempts to understand how people learn what a sentence means represent alternative ways of studying complex cognition.

The way in which we attempt to understand ideas (such as "I like psychology"), interpret ideas, and determine what seems reasonable (or unreasonable) about these concepts is shaped by our contemporary context of ideas (our Zeitgeist) and by the past ideas that have led up to the present ones. Today, we may consider many psychological ideas that were proposed recently to be outrageous, many other ideas proposed millennia ago to be reasonable, and still other intervening ideas to be surprising but appealing in some ways. This chapter presents both the historical and the more contemporary context for many of the current perspectives in the study of the nature of complex cognition and discusses how these perspectives have come and gone through a process of dialectical evolution (Kalmar & Sternberg, 1988; Sternberg, 1995, 1998b).

Why even bother to study the history of theory and research on complex cognition, rather than just deal with contemporary theory and research? There are three major reasons to study the history of a field. First, many current ideas can be better understood if we grasp their historical context. The debate between rationalists, who emphasize a priori theory, and empiricists, who emphasize data, for example, goes back a long way. By understanding the history of the argument, we are better able to understand all the issues involved. Second, we can credit scholars of the past who often had ideas that we merely reinvent. In any field, people have ideas they believe are new but that scholars recognize as quite old. Part of good scholarship is crediting those who had ideas before we did. We are better able to go beyond these past ideas if we know what they are. Third, understanding history can help prevent us from making mistakes made in the past. We save ourselves the trouble of following blind alleys that others already have followed.

Consider an example. At one time, investigators who studied concept formation were likely to use experimental materials that enabled them to study this process in what appeared to be a relatively pure form. So the investigators might show participants a series of chips of different colors, sizes, textures, and so forth and ask them to try to figure out what the chips in a given series had in common (see Bruner, Goodnow, & Austin, 1956). The idea of studying such simplified concepts was that one could study pure concept formation, unimpeded by individual and group differences in prior knowledge. Presumably, everyone in the experiments knew color names, sizes, and so forth equally well.

Why bother to study what Jerome Bruner and his colleagues did roughly a half century ago? The reason is that it was later found that how people form concepts about abstract items, such as these chips, bears little resemblance to how people form concepts about natural kinds, such as kinds of animal or plant life (Rosch, 1975). Someone who seeks to understand how people form concepts can learn from the past so as not to repeat errors that are easy to make, in the present as well as in the past. So it is important to understand the history of our field or any field.

First, we discuss some of the ideas that were historical precursors to the study of complex cognition as a discipline. We then turn to some major schools of thought in the history of modern complex cognitive theory and research.

THE DIALECTICAL PROGRESSION OF IDEAS

Much of psychological thinking about complex cognition or anything else proceeds in cycles, spiraling through the centuries of human thought. Philosophers, psychologists, and other people may propose and believe strongly in one view for a while (a thesis) and then a contrasting view comes to light (an antithesis); after a while, the most attractive or reasonable elements in each are melded into a new view (a synthesis), which then gains acceptance. This new integrated view then serves as the springboard (thesis) for a new contrasting view (antithesis) and eventually yet another melding (synthesis) of views (as discussed in chapter 1). This evolution of ideas through theses, antitheses, and syntheses was termed a *dialectic* by Georg Hegel (1807/1931).

A BRIEF INTELLECTUAL HISTORY: WESTERN ANTECEDENTS OF THE PSYCHOLOGY OF COMPLEX COGNITION

Where and when did the study of complex cognition begin? Arguably, however far back historical records may go, these documented accounts do not trace the earliest human efforts to understand the ways in which humans think. In a sense, the mythical origins of psychology are in the ancient Greek myth of *Psyche*, whose name was synonymous with the vital "breath of life," the soul, believed to leave the body at death. The Greek term *thymos* was a motivational force generating feelings and actions, and to this day, the Greek root thym- is used as a combinative form to mean feelings and motivations. The Greek word *nous* (an organ responsible for the clear perception of truth) is an uncommon English word for the mind, particularly for highly reasoned or divinely reasoned mentation. Thus, according to the archaic Greeks, the body and the mind are somewhat distinct, although the mind, perhaps influenced by external causes, does cause activity of the body. The dialectic of mind versus body has its roots, at the very latest, in ancient Greece.

Ancient Classical Greece and Rome (600–300 B.C.E.)

The roots of the study of complex cognition can be traced to two different approaches to human behavior: philosophy and physiology. In the contemporary world, these two fields seem dialectically opposed—philosophy tending to use armchair speculation and physiology tending to use more systematic empirical investigation through laboratory science. In ancient Greece, however, the approaches of these two fields did not differ much. Both fields used the more philosophical approach of introspective contemplation and speculation in seeking to understand the nature of the body and the mind—how each works and how they interact. In ancient Greece, many philosophers and physiologists believed that understanding could be reached without having or even pursuing supporting observations.

As the fields of philosophy and physiology diverged, they continued to influence the way in which psychology was to develop. Several strands intertwine as important philosophical precursors to the dialectics of modern psychological thought about complex cognition: whether the mind and body are separate entities; whether knowledge is innate or is acquired through experience; what contributes to learning and the acquisition of knowledge; and how speculation and theory development, on the one hand, and observation and data gathering, on the other hand, are used in seeking an understanding of the truth.

The ancient Greek physician (and philosopher) Hippocrates (ca. 460–377 B.C.E.), commonly known as the father of medicine, left his mark on the then-overlapping fields of physiology and philosophy. What sharply distinguished him from archaic Greek philosophers and physicians was his unorthodox idea that disease was not a punishment sent by the gods. Hippocrates also used unorthodox methods—empirical observations—to study medicine. Contrary to the mode of the day, he studied animal anatomy and physiology directly, using both dissection and vivisection. Thus, he moved the study of living organisms toward the empirical. He was not entirely empirical in his methods, however, for he often assumed that what he had observed in animals could be generalized to apply to humans. Despite his assumption, he did not confirm that the animal and human structures and functions were indeed parallel (Trager, 1992).

Hippocrates was particularly interested in discovering the source of the cognizing mind, which he thought was a separate, distinct entity that controlled the body. This belief that the body and the mind (or "spirit," or "soul") are qualitatively different, **mind-body dualism**, is the view that the body is composed of physical substance, but the mind is not. Unlike his archaic Greek ancestors, Hippocrates proposed that the mind resides in the brain; he induced this conclusion by observing that when either side of the head was injured, spasms were observed in the opposite side of the body (Robinson, 1995). Thus, with regard to the dialectic of the causes of thought and behavior, Hippocrates held that the agent of control was within the body, not in external forces, whether gods or demons. He also presaged modern psychology by speculating that physiological malfunctions, rather than demons, cause mental illness—again, turning away from divine intervention as a cause of human behavior.

Two younger contemporaries of Hippocrates also considered the location of the mind to be within the body: Plato (ca. 428–348 B.C.E.), who agreed that the mind resides in the brain, and his student Aristotle (384–322 B.C.E.), who thought that the mind is in the heart. These two philosophers profoundly affected modern thinking about complex cognition. Of the many, far-reaching aspects of Platonic and Aristotelian philosophies, there are three key areas in which the dialectics between these two philosophers are particularly relevant to modern psychology: the relationship between mind and body, the use of observation versus introspection as a means for discovering truth, and the original source for our ideas.

Plato and Aristotle differed in their views of mind and body because of their different views of the nature of reality. According to Plato, reality resides not in the concrete objects of which we are aware through our senses, but in the abstract forms that these objects represent. These abstract forms exist in a timeless dimension of pure abstract thought. Thus, reality is not inherent in any particular chair we see or touch, but in the eternal abstract idea of a chair that exists in our minds.

The objects that our bodies perceive are only transient and imperfect copies of these true, pure, abstract forms. Plato's reason for locating the mind in the head was based on his introspective reflections on these abstract forms, rather than on any observations of physiology or behavior: The head must contain the seat of the mind because the head resembles a sphere—a perfect abstract form. Hence, to Plato, body and mind are interactive and interdependent but are essentially different, with the mind superior to the body. We reach truth not via our senses but via our thoughts.

Aristotle, in contrast, believed that reality lies only in the concrete world of objects that our bodies sense. To Aristotle, Plato's abstract forms—such as the idea of a chair—are only derivations of concrete objects.

Aristotle's concrete orientation set the stage for monism, a philosophy of the nature of the body and mind, based on the belief that reality is a unified whole, existing in a single plane, rather than the two planes specified by dualism. According to monism, the mind (or soul) does not exist in its own right, but is merely an illusory by-product of anatomical and physiological activity. Therefore, the study of the mind and the study of the body are one and the same. We can understand the mind only by understanding the body.

Their different views of the nature of reality led Plato and Aristotle to disagree about how to investigate their ideas. Aristotle's view that reality is based on concrete objects led him to research methods based on the observation of concrete objects—and of actions on those objects. Thus, Aristotle (a naturalist and biologist, as well as a philosopher) was an **empiricist**, believing that we acquire knowledge via empirical evidence, obtained through experience and observation. The Aristotelian view is associated with empirical methods, by which we conduct research—in laboratories or in the field—on how people think and behave. Aristotelians tend to induce general principles or tendencies, on the basis of observations of many specific instances of a phenomenon.

Plato's views lay at the opposite end of the dialectical continuum. For Plato, empirical methods have little merit because true reality lies in abstract forms, not in the imperfect copies of reality observable in the world outside our minds. Observations of these imperfect, nonreal objects and actions would be irrelevant to the pursuit of truth. Instead, Plato suggested a **rationalist** approach, using philosophical analysis to understand the world and people's relations to it. For him, rationalism was consistent with his dualistic view of the nature of body and mind: We find knowledge only through using the mind—through reason and speculation about the ideal world, not about the corporeal world of the body. Hence, rationalists tend to be much less drawn to inductive methods and usually tend to deduce specific instances of a phenomenon on the basis of general principles.

Aristotle's view, then, leads directly to empirical psychological research, whereas Plato's view foreshadows theorizing that may not be grounded in extensive empirical observation. Each approach has merit, of course, and thus a synthesis of the two views is necessary in scientific and other forms of thought. Rationalist theories without any connection to observations have little validity, but mountains of observational data without an organizing theoretical framework have little meaning and therefore little use.

In addition to differing in both their views of the relationship between mind and body and their methods for finding truth, Plato and Aristotle differed in their views of the dialectic of the origin of ideas. Where do ideas come from? Aristotle believed that ideas are acquired from experience, whereas Plato believed that ideas are innate and need only to be dug out from the sometimes-hidden nooks and crannies of the mind.

In the dialogue *Meno*, Plato claimed to show that the rules of geometry already resided within the mind of a slave boy, who needed only to be made aware of these innate ideas, not to be taught these ideas from the world outside his mind. That is, through dialogue, Socrates (the protagonist in this and other Platonic dialogues) helped the boy become aware of his innate mental concepts of these pure forms. Today, many people still debate whether abilities and dispositions, such as language or intelligence, are innate (a thesis) or are acquired through interactions with the environment (an antithesis). The most plausible solution is that a synthesis of both experience and innate ability contributes to many aspects of cognition and other psychological constructs.

The Early Christian Era (200–450 c.e.) and the Middle Ages (400–1300 c.e.)

The dialectics of monism versus dualism, empiricism versus rationalism, and innate versus acquired abilities continued in Europe, even throughout the early Christian era and the Middle Ages. These epochs were not, however, a golden age for empirical science, and even some rationalists did not thrive during this time. The basis of philosophical discourse was faith in a Christian God and in scriptural accounts of phenomena. Neither empirical demonstrations nor rationalist arguments were considered valid or even permissible unless they illustrated what was already dictated to be true on the basis of religious faith and official doctrine. Whatever contradicted these beliefs was heretical and unacceptable—to the point where the free-dom and even the life of the doubter were at risk.

Great Christian philosophers of this era, such as St. Augustine of Hippo (354–430 C.E.; a bishop in Roman Africa), were much more interested in and hence urged people to seek a de-sirable afterlife, rather than a desirable life. Unlike Plato, they were relatively doctrinaire and not fully open to the critical tradition. However, they agreed with Plato that the main basis for thought is introspection, not observation. Like Plato, they considered the concrete, material objects and phenomena of the world to be of interest primarily for what they symbolically rep-resent, not for any empirical value that might lead to knowledge.

The critical tradition is widely accepted in most societies today, but dogmatists of all kinds—political extremists, jingoists, chauvinists, and other ideologues—continue to accept as true only those ideas and observations that conform to their prior and often rigid beliefs, and people continue to die for opposing their rigid beliefs. Such attitudes diverge from most contemporary notions of science, in which it is believed that, ultimately, the truth will come out, whether or not it conforms to our present convictions and beliefs.

It is easy to believe that only extremists fall prey to the neglect or rejection of the criti-cal tradition. Unfortunately, we are all susceptible to such tendencies. For example, everyone is susceptible to the phenomenon of **confirmation bias**, whereby one seeks only the infor-mation that confirms ideas one already has. In fact, although most of us, including scientists, cherish the belief that we are open to new ideas and are willing to change our minds when faced with contradictory evidence, most of us hesitate to embrace ideas that challenge some of our core beliefs. We see confirmation bias in dictators and their mindless subjects, but of-ten not in ourselves.

After centuries of medieval dogmatism, some thinkers tried to provide a synthesis that in-tegrated empiricism and faith. St. Thomas Aquinas (1225–1274), the theologian and philoso-pher, was an avid student of and commentator on Aristotle and his works. He attempted to synthesize a sort of "Christian science," in which empiricist philosophy was bounded by the dictates of Christian theology. According to Aquinas, reasoning is also important and accept-able because it can lead to God. Aquinas's acceptance of reason as a route to truth opened the way for those who followed him but did not share his religious dogma.

According to Aquinas's precariously perched empirical–rational–religious approach, hu-mans are at the juncture of two universes, the corporeal and the spiritual (an idea similar to Plato's idea of mind-body dualism). The goal for humans is to understand the life of the body through the life of the spirit; therefore, science must take a backseat to religion. As the Mid-dle Ages drew to a close, particularly in the 11th and 12th centuries, many changes heralded the arrival of the Renaissance: The first modern universities were founded, ancient Greek medical and natural-science texts were translated, and some experimental techniques were advanced.

The Renaissance of Criticism (1300s to 1600s) and the Nascence of Science

As critical thought was reborn throughout Europe, modern views of science were born. Dur-ing the Renaissance (rebirth), the focus of philosophical thinking shifted from God to hu-mankind and from the afterlife to the present life. The established Roman Catholic Church remained a strong force both philosophically and politically, but the focus of philosophical thinking veered away from Christian doctrine's emphasis on God and the afterlife to a renewed interest in humankind and the here and now. Science as we know it was born, and direct observation was established as the basis of knowledge.

Another name for the Renaissance is the Awakening, and during this period, the intellectual movement known as humanism awoke after centuries of slumber. Renaissance humanism investigated the role of humans in the world, centering on humans "as the measure of all things." Humanists exalted the role of humans in nature, in contrast with the previous exaltation of God. Humanism grew out of the rediscovery and revival of ancient classics of Greek and Roman philosophy, literature, mathematics, medicine, and the natural sciences, which had been ignored, submerged, or even destroyed during the Middle Ages.

Revolutionary thinkers in mathematics and physics led the way toward empirical science as we know it today. Modern astronomy was heralded when Polish astronomer Nicolaus Copernicus (1473–1543) proposed his heliocentric theory, which argued that the sun, not the earth, is at the center of our solar system. This theory contracted the traditional Ptolemaic geocentric theory and the then-official Church doctrine. Later in this era, Italian astronomer, mathematician, and physicist Galileo Galilei (1564–1642) was branded a heretic and placed under lifelong house arrest by the Roman Catholic Church because of his unorthodox use of scientific observation, rather than religious faith, as the basis for his conclusions.

During the Middle Ages, Christian religious theory was the engine that drove all attempts to understand human nature. Today, the guidance by theory that sometimes occurs in science differs from the extreme guidance by theory that occurred during the Middle Ages: With moderate guidance by theory, the theory forms a path, from which it is hard to swerve. However, with some effort, we can leave a path that has ended in a blind alley. In the Middle Ages, however, the role of theory was more like that of a train track, any departure from which could lead to sheer disaster and sometimes even death.

During the Renaissance, strict guidance by religious theory came under attack. Francis Bacon (1561–1626) proposed an antithesis to the medieval point of view: Scientific thinking must be purely empirical—not guided by theory at all. Bacon believed that theories color our vision and thereby get in the way of our perceiving the truth. He therefore asserted that studies of nature and of humankind must be wholly unbiased and atheoretical.

Many contemporary scientists who study cognition and other phenomena seek to synthesize the two extreme views on the role of theory. Theories should guide and give meaning to our observations; yet they should be formed, modified, and perhaps even discarded as a result of our observations. Progress in the study of complex cognition or of any other phenomenon depends on a continual interaction between theory and data.

The Beginnings of the Modern Period (1600s to 1800s)

Descartes and Locke (1600s to 1750)

The dialectic of theory versus data continued in the 17th century, when René Descartes (1596–1650) sharply disagreed with the glorification of the empirical methods espoused by Bacon and his intellectual predecessor Aristotle. Descartes agreed with Plato's rationalist belief that the introspective, reflective method is superior to empirical methods for finding truth. Cartesian rationalist philosophy contributed much to the modern philosophy of mind (thus

Descartes served as a grandparent of psychology), and Descartes's views had numerous other implications for psychology.

Like Plato, Descartes (1662/1972) believed in both mind–body dualism (that the mind and the body are qualitatively different and separate) and innate (versus acquired) knowledge. According to Descartes, the dualistic nature of mind (nonmaterial, incorporeal, spiritual) and body (material) separates humans from animals. For humans, the mind and its powers are supreme: *Cogito ergo sum* ("I think, therefore I am"). According to Descartes, the mind has great influence over the body, but the body still has some effect on the mind. Thus, Descartes is considered both mentalistic, in that he viewed the body as subordinate to the mind, and in-teractionistic, in that he held that there is a two-way interaction between mind and body.

On the other side of the dialectic, the British empiricist philosopher John Locke (1632–1704) believed that the interaction between mind and body is a symmetrical relationship be-tween two aspects of the same unified phenomenon. The mind depends on sensory experience processed by the body for its information, whereas the body depends on the mind for the stor-age and later usage of processed sense experience (Locke 1690/1961). Locke and other British empiricists also shared Aristotle's and Bacon's reverence for empirical observation. Locke's Aristotelian (and perhaps anti-Cartesian) valuing of empirical observation naturally accompa-nied his view that humans are born without knowledge—and must therefore seek knowledge through empirical observation. Locke's term for this view is *tabula rasa*, meaning "blank slate" in Latin: Life and experience "write" knowledge upon us. David Hume also advocated a re-lated empiricist position.

Mill and Kant (1750 to 1870)

Locke's philosophical successor was John Stuart Mill (1806–73), who took British empiricism to its philosophical extreme. As a radical associationist, Mill believed that events occurring close to one another in time become associated in our minds, so that they can later be recalled in tan-dem by memory. Mill (1843) suggested that the mind can be viewed in entirely mechanistic terms. According to him, the laws of the physical universe can explain everything, including the activity of the mind. The idea of a separate mind or soul that exists independent of the body is thus both unnecessary and wrong. This extreme version of monism is sometimes referred to as *reductionism*, in that it reduces the role of the mind to the status of a mere cog in a larger phys-iological machine. The important thing is therefore the environment and how the sensory organs of the body—eyes, ears, and so on—perceive it. In one form of reductionism, the individual re-sponds mechanistically, with all knowledge starting at the level of sensations and working up to the mind, which is merely the next step in the "intellectual assembly line" (Schultz, 1981).

In the 18th century, the debates about dualism versus monism and empiricism versus ra-tionalism had peaked. German philosopher Immanuel Kant (1724–1804) began the process of dialectical synthesis for these questions. He redefined the mind–body question by asking how mind and body are related, rather than whether the mind is in control (Kant, 1781/1987).

Instead of phrasing the problem in terms of duality or unity, Kant proposed a set of fac-ulties, or mental powers: the senses, understanding, and reason. He believed that the faculties, working in concert, control and provide a link between mind and body, integrating the two. Loosely speaking, Kant's faculty of the senses is closest to the idea of body, his faculty of reason parallels the concept of mind, and his faculty of understanding bridges the two. Fac-ulties of mind also figured prominently in psychology later on, when early 20th-century psychologists tried to define and understand more clearly what the faculties of the mind might be. The debate lives on today.

In terms of rationalism versus empiricism and whether knowledge is innate or passively acquired through experience, Kant declared that a synthesis of both rationalism and empiricism is needed in which the two ways of thinking work together in the quest for truth. Kant called empirically acquired experiential knowledge *a posteriori knowledge* (from the Latin meaning "from afterward"); we gain this knowledge after we have experience.

On the other hand, Kant recognized that some knowledge ("general truth") exists, regardless of individual experience. Kant referred to this "general truth" as *a priori knowledge*; such knowledge exists whether or not we become aware of it through our experiences. A key example of a priori knowledge is knowledge of time. We know a priori to link our fleeting sensations over time into a seemingly continuous stream of experience. However, for us to observe any cause–effect relationship over time, we must have a posteriori knowledge of the related preceding and consequent events. According to Kant's synthesis, understanding requires both a posteriori, experience-based knowledge (thesis) and a priori, innate concepts (antithesis), such as knowledge of the concepts of time and causality, which permit us to profit from our experiences. In this way, understanding evolves both through nature (innate) and through nurture (experience).

Of course, Kant did not settle these debates once and for all. Questions about the nature of complex cognition and reality have not been and probably never will be settled for good. In fact, two influential books that appeared since the late 1980s have continued the dialectic about the mind-body issue. Dennett (1991) took a reductionist view, saying that there is no mind without the physical body, whereas Penrose (1989) allowed for a consciousness not linked to the physical realm.

Scholars will probably always wrestle with aspects of these problems. However, Kant effectively redefined many of the issues with which philosophers before him had grappled. His enormous impact on philosophy interacted with 19th-century scientific exploration of the body and how it works to produce profound influences on the eventual establishment of psychology as a discipline in the 1800s.

The Merger of Philosophy and Physiology Into Modern Psychology (1800s to 1900s)

The issues that philosophers, physicians, and other scholars have faced and continue to face also confront all those who study complex cognition. We have seen this confrontation in dialectics described earlier on the nature of mind and body and on the sources of knowledge. So intertwined are the issues that philosophers, physicians, and psychologists have confronted that, in the 1800s (about the same time that Georg Hegel proposed his idea of the dialectic), when psychology was starting out as a field, it was viewed by some as a branch of philosophy and by others as a branch of medicine. As psychology increasingly became a scientific discipline focused on the study of mind and behavior, 19th-century philosophy merged increasingly with the study of physiological issues pertaining to sensory perception.

Gradually, the psychological branches of philosophy and of medicine diverged from the two parent disciplines and then merged to form the distinct unified discipline of psychology. Today, although psychology, philosophy, and medicine are essentially discrete, they are not completely so, for many psychological questions remain rooted in both philosophy (such as the nature of the mind and its relation to the body) and medicine (such as the biological causes of behavior).

THE DIVERGING PERSPECTIVES OF MODERN STUDIES OF COMPLEX COGNITION

Building on dialectics of the past, the study of complex cognition has utilized a wide variety of intellectual perspectives on the human mind and how it should be studied. To understand complex cognition as a whole, one needs to be familiar with the schools of thought that are precursors to and that have evolved as bases in psychology for the field of complex cognition. The main early psychological perspectives built on and reacted to those perspectives that came before. The dialectical process that appeared throughout the history of thought about complex cognition also threads through modern psychology, starting with approaches that focus on mental structures and continuing with approaches that focus on mental functions or mental associations. The main schools of thought are summarized in Table 2.1.

Structuralism, Functionalism, Pragmatism, and Associationism: Early Dialectics in Psychology

Structuralism

The goal of **structuralism**, generally considered to be the first major school of thought in psychology, was to understand the structure (configuration of elements) of the mind by analyzing the mind in terms of its constituent components or contents. When structuralism was a dominant school of psychological thought, scientists in other fields were similarly analyzing materials in terms of basic elements and then studying combinations of these basic elements. For example, chemists were analyzing substances in terms of their constituent chemical elements, biologists were analyzing the biochemical constituents of cells, and physiologists were analyzing physiological structures. Although structuralism is no longer a dynamic force in psychology, it is important because it took the first steps toward making psychology a systematic, empirical science. It also established some of the dialectics of contemporary psychology,

TABLE 2.1   Some Main Historical Schools of Thought in the Psychological Study of Complex Cognition

School of Thought	Main Emphasis
Structuralism	Analysis of consciousness into constituent components
Functionalism and pragmatism	Mental operations and practical use of consciousness
Associationism	Mental connections between events and ideas
Behaviorism	Study of observable emitted behavior
Gestaltism	Study of holistic concepts, not merely as sums of parts
Cognitivism	Understanding how people think

such as the dialectic between molecular analysis of behavior, on the one hand (the position of structuralism), and global analysis, on the other hand.

An important influence on structuralism was German psychologist Wilhelm Wundt (1832–1920). Wundt believed that psychology and the study of cognition should focus on immediate and direct, as opposed to mediated (interpreted), conscious experience. For example, suppose that one looks at a green, grassy lawn. To Wundt, the concepts of lawn or even of grass would be irrelevant. Even one's awareness of looking at a grassy lawn would not have particularly interested Wundt. These conceptually mediated experiences are too far removed from the mental elements of one's experience, which one infers from the more important (to Wundt) immediate experience of seeing narrow, vertical, spiky, green protrusions of varying lengths and widths, amassed closely together on a two-dimensional surface. It was to these elementary sensations that Wundt gave his attention.

For Wundt, the optimal method by which a person could be trained to analyze these sensory experiences is introspection, looking inward at pieces of information passing through consciousness—a form of self-observation. Today, we would call introspection subjective, but it did not seem so to the structuralists of the time.

Wundt's student, Edward Titchener (1867–1927), held views that we would consider generally similar to Wundt's. Titchener (1910) believed that all consciousness could be reduced to three elementary states: sensations—the basic elements of perception; images—the pictures we form in our minds to characterize what we perceive; and affections—the constituents of emotions, such as love and hate.

During most of his life, Titchener was a strict structuralist and used structuralist principles in his teaching, research, and writings at Cornell University. Toward the end of his life, however, Titchener began to diverge from Wundt. He open-mindedly listened to alternative views (particularly the criticisms by functionalists, described in the following section), which suggested that structuralists had proposed too many sensations. Titchener eventually came to argue that psychology should study not merely the basic elements of sensation, but the categories into which these sensations can be grouped (Hilgard, 1987).

Titchener's change of mind illustrates an important point about psychologists, in particular, and scientists, in general. Outstanding scientists do not necessarily adopt a specific viewpoint in the dialectical cycle and then stick with it for the rest of their lives. The thinking of most scientists and other good thinkers (see, e.g., Basseches, 1984; Labouvie-Vief, 1980, 1990; Pascual-Leone, 1984; Riegel, 1973, 1979) evolves dialectically; these scientists and other thinkers reject or build on their earlier work (and the work of others) in the creation of what they hope will be their lasting contributions to scientific or other kinds of thinking. Truly outstanding scientists or other thinkers are not immune to criticism and change; instead, they consider antitheses to their own theses and formulate their own syntheses, incorporating the alternative views into their own thinking. Early in his career, Titchener had been considered dogmatic, but he had the intellectual strength and fortitude to allow his thinking to evolve and change.

In any case, structuralism has been criticized on a number of grounds. First, it posited too many elementary sensations. There seemed to be no limit to the number that could be generated. Second, it did not explain many complex aspects of human behavior, especially those of complex cognition, such as the use of language. Third, its key technique, the method of introspection, is probably useful when used in conjunction with other methods, but is often not adequate when used by itself. Finally, it was found that no matter how much people are trained, their introspections are different, so that it is difficult to get reliable data by relying on this method alone.

Functionalism: An Alternative to Structuralism

The roots of structuralism were in Germany, but its countermovement, functionalism, was rooted in the United States—the first American-born movement in psychology. The **functionalist** addresses the broad question of how and why the mind works as it does, by seeking functional relationships between specific earlier stimulus events and specific subsequent response behaviors. It could be said that the key difference between structuralists and functionalists lay not in the answers they found, but in the fundamentally different questions they asked. Whereas structuralists asked, "What are the elementary contents (structures) of the human mind?" functionalists asked, "What do people *do*, and *why* do they do it?" Structure versus function thus constituted the basis of the dialectic that distinguished the two schools of thought.

Another way of viewing the difference between structuralism and functionalism is to say that structuralists viewed the human or other organism as an object to be analyzed that passively receives sensations. Functionalists, in contrast, viewed humans and others as more actively engaged in their sensations and actions. Psychologist and educator James Rowland Angell (1869–1949), whose criticism of structuralism was instrumental in swaying Titchener to change his views, suggested three fundamental precepts of functionalism (Angell, 1907): (1) the study of mental processes, (2) the study of the uses of consciousness, and (3) the study of the total relationship of the organism to its environment.

Even given these precepts, the functionalist school of thought never had the unity that structuralism had. Functionalists were unified by the kinds of questions they asked, but not necessarily by the answers they found or the methods they used to find those answers. They may even have been unified in believing that a diversity of methods could be used, as long as each method helped to answer the particular question being probed.

Functionalism, like structuralism, has been criticized on a number of grounds. First, there were so many definitions of the term *function* that it became extremely unclear what it meant. Second, functionalists used so many different approaches and techniques that it was not clear just what held the whole school of thought together. Third, the techniques that were used lacked the quantitative precision that later established psychology as a science.

Functionalists' openness to diverse methodologies broadened the scope of psychological methods. Among the various approaches used by functionalists was animal experimentation, perhaps prompted by Charles Darwin's revolutionary ideas on evolution.

Pragmatism: An Outgrowth of Functionalism

Because functionalists believed in using whichever methods best answered the researcher's questions, it seems natural for functionalism to have led to pragmatism. **Pragmatists** believe that knowledge is validated by its usefulness: What can you do with it? Pragmatists are concerned not only with knowing what people do, but with what scholars can do with our knowledge of what people do.

A leader in guiding functionalism toward pragmatism was William James (1842–1910)— a physician, philosopher, psychologist, and brother of author Henry James. James's chief functional contribution to the field of psychology was a single book: the landmark *Principles of*

Psychology (James, 1890). Today, many regard James as among the greatest psychologists ever, although James seems to have rejected psychology later in his life.

James minced no words in his criticism of structuralism's detail-oriented approach, snidely commenting that structuralism's nit-picking approach "taxes patience to the utmost, and could hardly have arisen in a country whose natives could be *bored*" (p. 192). James is particularly well known for his pragmatic theorizing about consciousness, emphasizing that the function of consciousness is to enable people to adapt to the environment and to give them choices for operating within it.

Another of the early pragmatists has profoundly influenced our own evolution of thinking about psychology, as well as the thinking of many others. John Dewey (1859–1952), along with Angell, mentioned earlier, is credited with laying out the formal defining principles of the philosophical school of functionalism. Dewey was important to psychology for his contribution to functionalism, as well as for his stimulation of new ideas in others. However, he is remembered primarily as a philosopher of education; his pragmatic functionalist approach to thinking and schooling heralded many of the current notions in cognitive and educational psychology. Much of what cognitive and educational psychologists say today reiterates what Dewey said early in the 20th century.

Dewey (1910, 1913, 1922), ever the pragmatist, emphasized motivation in education. If no one inspires you to learn, the chances are that you will not learn well. To learn effectively, you need to see the point of your education—the practical use of it. One way to interest you in education is to give you more opportunity to select your own problems, rather than always to tell you what problems to solve. What is perhaps most important, you should learn by experimentation and by doing, not by merely being told facts, so that you can learn to think for yourself and to use information intelligently. Dewey also practiced what he preached: He opened an elementary school at Columbia University that taught according to his precepts (Hilgard, 1987).

Dewey's practical applications of psychological principles were not universally well received, owing to one of the many dialectics underlying the study of complex cognition and other aspects of the mind. Many psychologists thought that true scientists should avoid diverting their attention from the study of underlying principles merely to address some immediate applications of those principles. Other scientists believed, and still do, that basic research ultimately leads to many of the most practical applications. To this day, scientists disagree on how much of scientific research should be basic research and how much should be applied research. Ideally, there would be a synthetic balance between basic and applied research.

In addition to the question of applied versus basic research, many of the dialectics that first emerged via functionalism and structuralism were fundamental to the development of the psychology of complex cognition. In particular, functionalism expanded the scope of the fledgling academic discipline to comprise a range of methodological techniques far wider than the structuralists would have ever permitted. Although functionalism, like structuralism, did not survive as an organized school of thought, its influence remains widespread in psychological specializations that stress both the flexibility of research methods and the practicality of applications.

Pragmatism did not survive in its original form partly because it was so oriented toward applied issues that it neglected fundamental, basic issues in psychological research. Many of the most practical findings in science derive, in the long term, from basic research. As a result, it is often more pragmatic not to start with applied questions, but to start with basic ones and to work one's way up to the applied questions with the fundamental knowledge gained through the basic research.

Associationism: An Integrative Synthesis

Associationism, like functionalism, was less a rigid school of psychology than an influential way of thinking. In general, associationists are mainly interested in the middle-level to higher-level mental processes, such as those of learning. **Associationism** deals with how events or ideas can become associated with one another in the mind, to result in a form of learning. This focus on high-level mental processes runs exactly counter to Wundt's insistence on studying elementary sensations.

For example, with repetition, concepts, such as *thesis, antithesis,* and *synthesis*, will become linked in one's mind so often that they will become inextricably associated with one another. To put it another way, one will have learned that the dialectical process involves a thesis, an antithesis, and a synthesis. Learning and remembering thus depend on mental association.

Associationism itself has been linked with many other theoretical viewpoints. Traveling backward in time, its principles can be traced directly to Mill; even further back, we find Locke's view that the mind and the body are two aspects of the same unified phenomenon, a view rooted in Aristotle's ideas. Subsequent contemporary views were also founded on associationism. Consequently, it is difficult to categorize associationism as belonging strictly to one era.

An influential associationist was the German experimenter Hermann Ebbinghaus (1850–1909), the first experimenter to apply associationist principles systematically. Ebbinghaus prided himself on using much more rigorous experimental techniques (counting his errors, recording his response times, and so forth) than Wundt used during introspection. On the other hand, he used himself as his only experimental subject, just as Wundt had done. In particular, Ebbinghaus used his self-observations to study and quantify the relationship between rehearsal and recollection of material.

Psychologists' views about introspection have evolved since the days of Ebbinghaus and Wundt, but there are still many dialectical controversies regarding its use. Some psychologists discount most self-observations as being fruitless for gathering empirical data because many of our thought processes are unconscious or at least not available to our conscious minds (Nisbett & Wilson, 1977). Others consider self-observations valuable for generating hypotheses but useless in evaluating hypotheses. Still others view subjects' introspective self-analyses while they perform a task to be an invaluable source of empirical data (Ericsson & Simon, 1980). Even those who value self-observations as a tool for empirical study disagree on when to obtain the observational data. Some contend that if observations are obtained during the performance of a task, the very act of observing the performance changes the task. Others argue that inaccurate (or at least imperfect) recall interferes with self-observations obtained after the task performance has ended.

Ebbinghaus's ideas were elaborated by Edwin Guthrie (1886–1959), who observed animals instead of himself. Guthrie proposed that two observed events (a stimulus and a response) become associated through their close temporal contiguity. That is, the stimulus and the response behaviors/events become associated because they continually occur at about the same time. In contrast, Edward Lee Thorndike (1874–1949) held that the role of "satisfaction," rather than of Guthrie's temporal contiguity, was the key to forming associations. Thorndike (1905) termed this principle the *law of effect*: A stimulus tends to produce a certain response (*effect*) over time if an organism is rewarded (*satisfaction*) for that response.

Associationism as a school of thought has not survived in its original form because it was overly simplistic. The idea that complex behavior could be explained just on the basis of simple associations generally has not been found to work in the study of complex cognition. Eventually, psychologists recognized the need to supplement associationist explanations with more complex explanations of thought and behavior.

In considering the methods of Ebbinghaus, Guthrie, and Thorndike, we see that the associationists followed the functionalist–pragmatic tradition of using various methods in their research. In fact, Thorndike can be tied directly back to his functionalist mentor, William James. James even encouraged Thorndike to conduct his experiments on animals, offering his own house as the locale for some of Thorndike's earliest studies of animals learning to run through mazes.

TWENTIETH-CENTURY PERSPECTIVES ON COMPLEX COGNITION

Origins of Behaviorism

Other researchers, who were contemporaries of Thorndike, used animal experiments to probe stimulus–response relationships in ways that differed from those of Thorndike and his fellow associationists. These researchers straddled the line between associationism and the emerging field of behaviorism. Some of them, like Thorndike and other associationists, studied responses that were voluntary (though perhaps lacking any conscious thought, as in Thorndike's work), but others studied responses that were involuntarily triggered, in response to what appear to be unrelated external stimuli.

In Russia, Nobel prize–winning physiologist Ivan Pavlov (1849–1936) studied involuntary learning behavior of this sort, beginning with his observation that dogs salivated in response to the sight of the laboratory technician who fed them before the dogs even saw whether the technician had food. To Pavlov, this response indicated a form of learning, termed *classically conditioned learning*, over which the dogs had no conscious control. In the dogs' minds, some type of involuntary learning was linking the technician with the food (Pavlov, 1955).

Behaviorism

Behaviorism, an American school of psychology, may be considered an extreme version of associationism that focuses entirely on the association between environmental contingencies and emitted behavior. Behaviorism was born as a dialectical reaction against the focus on personally subjective mental states found in both structuralism and functionalism. Instead, **behaviorism** asserts that the science of psychology should deal only with observable behavior. According to strict, extreme ("radical") behaviorists, any conjectures about internal thoughts and ways of thinking are nothing more than speculation, and although they may belong within the domain of philosophy, they certainly have no place in psychology. This behaviorist view originates in the philosophical tradition of logical positivism, which contends that the only basis for knowledge is sensory perceptions; all else is idle conjecture.

Watson's Groundwork

The man who is usually acknowledged as the father of radical behaviorism was American psychologist John Watson (1878–1958). Watson, like British empiricist John Stuart Mill, had no use for internal mental contents or mechanisms. Still, although Watson disdained key aspects of functionalism, he was clearly influenced by the functionalists in his emphasis on what people do and what causes their actions. In fact, behaviorism depends more on the study of functions in behavior than functionalism ever did!

Behaviorism also differed from previous movements in psychology by shifting the emphasis of experimental research from human to animal participants (although animal studies have been used since the days of Hippocrates). Historically, much behaviorist work has been conducted (and still is) with laboratory animals, such as rats. Watson himself preferred animal participants, believing that with animal participants, it was easier to ensure behavioral control, to establish stimulus-response relationships, and to minimize external interference. Indeed, the simpler the organism's emotional and physiological makeup, the less the researcher needs to worry about any of the interference that can plague psychological research with human participants. Many nonbehavioral psychologists wonder whether animal research can be generalized to humans (i.e., applied more generally to humans instead of just specifically to the animals that were studied). In response, some behaviorists would argue that the study of animal behavior is a legitimate pursuit in its own right, and all behaviorists would assert that we can learn useful principles that generalize to other species, including humans.

Hull's Synthesis With Pavlovian Conditioning

An American behavioral psychologist who tried to connect the involuntary learning studied by Pavlov with the voluntary learning studied by Watson and Thorndike was Clark Hull (1884–1952). Hull had always shown a predilection for synthesis; even his dissertation synthesized strict experimental psychology with theoretical analyses of thought processes, particularly in regard to learning concepts. Although Hull's work was virtually ignored for nearly a decade, during which he became quite discouraged (see Hilgard, 1987), his research on learning eventually became among the most widely cited work of his time. Hull's ideas also enriched the field of psychology with ideas from such diverse fields as physiology and evolutionary biology (see Robinson, 1995).

Above all, Hull was particularly influential for his belief that the laws of behavior could be quantified, as are laws in other scientific disciplines like physics. Hull's (1952) final presentation of his theory of behavior contained numerous mathematical postulates and corollaries. Hull's interest in mathematical precision also led to his development of an early computational device, which he used in his psychological research, that used punch cards for statistical calculations.

Skinner's Radicalism

In modern times, radical behaviorism has seemed almost synonymous with one of its most radical proponents, B. F. Skinner (1904–1990). For Skinner, virtually all human behavior, not just learning, could be explained by behavior emitted in response to environmental contingencies, which can be studied effectively by observing animal behaviors. Skinner applied the behaviorist model to almost everything, from learning to the acquisition of language to problem solving and even to the control of behavior in society. As a consequence, he has been criticized for overgeneralizing the applicability of his data by making pronouncements about what would be good for society as a whole, based largely on data from learning in animals.

Skinner also entered domains typically reserved nowadays for philosophers. For example, in his novel, *Walden Two* (Skinner, 1948), he depicted a utopian society run entirely on behaviorist principles. He also argued that "ought" and "should" are meaningless concepts outside a specific environment. The environment controls behavior, and thus, the setting in which a person is raised determines what he or she should do. The following passage illustrates how behaviorists view social interactions in terms of the specific observable rewards that may be derived from a conversational interchange and avoid references to the elusive, unobservable aspects of social relationships:

> The [Walden] Code [by which the utopia's members agree to abide] even descends to the level of the social graces, . . . We've tried a number of experiments to expedite and improve personal relations. For example, introductions in Walden Two are solely for the purpose of communicating information; we don't wait to be introduced before speaking to a stranger, nor do we bother to make introductions if no relevant information is to be communicated. (Skinner, 1948, p. 163)

This deterministic view calls to mind the original radical conception of behaviorism, proposed by Watson, which stated that any behavior can be shaped and controlled:

> Give me a dozen healthy infants, well-formed, and my own specified world to bring them up in, and I'll guarantee to take any one at random and train him to become any type of specialist I might select—doctor, lawyer, artist, merchant–chief and yes, even beggarman and thief, regardless of his talents, penchants, tendencies, abilities, vocations, and race of his ancestors. (Watson, 1930, p. 104)

Many psychologists disagree with the behaviorist view. For example, in a debate between Watson and psychologist William McDougall (1871–1938), McDougall said:

> I come into this hall and see a man on this platform scraping the guts of a cat with hairs from the tail of a horse; and, sitting silently in attitudes of rapt attention, are a thousand persons who presently break out into wild applause. How will the Behaviorist explain these strange incidents: How explain the fact that the vibrations emitted by the cat-gut stimulate all the thousand into absolute silence and quiescence; and the further fact that the cessation of the stimulus seems to be a stimulus to the most frantic activity? (Watson & McDougall, 1929, p. 63)

Today, relatively few scholars who study complex cognition are strict behaviorists. A major reason is that behaviorism ignored or did not adequately address internal causes of behavior. It also failed to explain many interesting aspects of complex cognition, such as problem solving and language acquisition.

Gestalt Psychology

Of the many dialectical critics of behaviorism, Gestalt psychologists may be among the most avid. According to **Gestalt psychology**, we best understand psychological phenomena when we view them as organized, structured wholes, not when we break them down into pieces; the whole differs from the sum of its parts. Actually, this movement was an antithetical reaction not only against the behaviorist tendency to analyze behaviors in terms of stimulus-response units, but against the structuralist tendency to analyze mental processes into elementary sensations. The name of the approach comes from the German word *Gestalt* (now an English word). The German word does not have an exact synonym in English, although it is something close to "whole unitary form," "integral shape," or "fully integrated configuration" (Schultz, 1981). The movement originated in Germany, the fount of structuralism, and later spread to the United States, the fount of behaviorism, and to other countries.

Gestalt psychology is usually traced to the work of German psychologist Max Wertheimer (1880–1943), who collaborated with compatriots Kurt Koffka (1886–1941) and Wolfgang Köhler (1887–1967) to form a new school of psychology, with an emphasis on understanding wholes in their own right. The Gestaltists applied this framework to many areas in psychology. For example, they proposed that problem solving cannot be explained simply in terms of automatic responses to stimuli or to elementary sensations. Instead, new insights emerge in problem solving; people simply form entirely new ways to see problems.

Given some of the criticisms of the vagueness of the Gestalt perspective and of its tendency to label, rather than explain, many psychologists now believe that the most fruitful approach to understanding psychological phenomena is to synthesize analytic and holistic strategies. Cognitivists are among the many who use both analytic and holistic strategies.

Cognitivism

Finally, we reach cognitivism, the conceptual basis of this book. **Cognitivism** is the belief that much of human behavior can be understood if we understand first how people represent and process information. The contemporary cognitivist examines the elementary structuralist contents of thought, the functionalist processes of thought, and the Gestaltist holistic results of thinking. The cognitivist, like the Gestaltist, may well conclude that the whole is indeed different from the sum of its parts. At the same time, however, cognitive psychologists attempt to determine precisely which mental mechanisms and which elementary elements of thought make that conclusion true. Cognitivists would study the way in which we understand the Gestalt of this chapter or of a Seurat painting, but they also would want to determine precisely how we understand it as such.

Early cognitivists (e.g., Miller, Galanter, & Pribram, 1960) argued that traditional behavioristic accounts of behavior were inadequate precisely because they said nothing about—indeed ignored—how people think. Subsequent cognitivists Newell and Simon (1972) proposed detailed models of human thinking and problem solving from the most basic levels to the most complex (such as playing chess). Ulric Neisser (1967) was especially critical in bringing cognitivism to prominence. Neisser defined **cognitive psychology** as the study of how people learn, structure, store, and use knowledge. The cognitive approach has been applied in a variety of areas of psychology—including everything from thinking to emotion to the treatment of various psychological syndromes, including depression. Cognitive psychologists use a variety of methods to pursue their goal of understanding human thought, such as the study of reaction times, the study of people's subjective reports as they solve problems, and computer simulations.

Today, cognitivism incorporates many aspects of the biological approach to cognition. For example, a direct descendant of evolutionary theory is behavioral genetics, which attempts to account for behavior by attributing it to the synthetic influence of particular combinations of genetic and environmental influences. A behavioral geneticist may attempt to explain, for instance, the genetic and environmental elements that contribute to general or specific cognitive abilities.

Another psychobiological approach is to determine which specific regions of the brain are responsible for the origination, learning, or expression of particular behaviors, feelings, or kinds of thoughts. For example, Roger Sperry (1920–94) tried to determine what kinds of thinking occur in each of the two halves of the brain. These and other insights into our minds and bodies—and the interactions between the two—have synthesized the methods and data from cognitive psychology and biological psychology.

In the 1960s, cognitivism was just coming of age, and behaviorism seemed to be on its way out. Today, cognitivism is popular, and many fields within psychology have adopted a cognitive perspective. It is the primary perspective used in this book for analyzing complex cognition. This perspective, too, may someday fade in importance and yield to other perspectives. The dominant perspective of the future may be unimaginable today. Psychology is a dynamic science, precisely because it is ever evolving in its dialectical perspectives on the puzzles of human behavior.

◆ SUMMARY

Ideas in psychology, as in many other disciplines, evolve in a dialectical fashion. An idea is proposed, which serves as a thesis. Then an idea is proposed that seems to contradict or otherwise be inconsistent with the earlier idea; this second idea serves as an antithesis. Over time, people begin to realize that neither extreme position is quite correct, so one or more people formulate a synthesis that captures the best aspects of both of the earlier ideas.

The study of complex cognition originated in ideas derived from philosophy and physiology. Hippocrates, in ancient Greece, proposed mind-body dualism, the idea that the body is composed of physical substance but the mind is not. Plato, an ancient Greek philosopher, took a largely rationalist approach to thinking about complex cognition, whereas Aristotle took a largely empiricist approach. Much later, Descartes espoused a rationalist philosophy, Locke, an empiricist philosophy. Kant synthesized many of their seemingly disparate ideas.

The first major school of psychological thought was structuralism, which sought to understand the mind by analyzing it into its constituent parts. Functionalism later concentrated more on processing and the functions that psychological events serve. Pragmatism was an outgrowth of functionalism. Associationism concentrated on associations of ideas and later gave rise to behaviorism, which concentrated on observable behavior. This book represents largely the perspective of cognitivism, which seems to elucidate the mental representations and processes underlying complex and other mental processes.

3 Concepts

Structure and Acquisition

> From the first dawn of life, all organic beings are found to resemble each other in descending degrees, so that they can be classed in groups under groups.
>
> —CHARLES DARWIN, *On the Origin of Species*, 1859

How do we decide that the animal lurking in our neighbor's backyard belongs to the category dog, or worse, belongs to the more specific category dangerous dog? How do we determine whether a new object is edible, hazardous, fun to play with, or useful as a tool? The processes people use for judging whether a certain entity belongs to a certain category and for inferring the nature of new from familiar entities have been the primary areas of study in research on concepts and categorization.

A **concept** is a mental representation of a class of entities (e.g., Medin & Smith, 1984). The class of entities that are embodied in the concept is referred to as a **category** (Medin & Ross, 1992). Forming a concept is useful because it allows for "cognitive economy" (Rosch, 1978). That is, by using a single word to denote a whole class, one avoids the effortful and often impossible task of placing a label on every new entity.

There are fundamental questions about the categorization process: What makes a category cohere? What is the effect of context on categorization? Finally, do different kinds of concepts (e.g., living things and inorganic objects) require different explanations? These questions are examined in light of the different theoretical approaches to the nature of categorization.

The first theory of categorization to appear in the psychological literature was the classical view. This view is based on the Aristotelian notion that every object is composed of defining features that are individually necessary and jointly sufficient. For example, a square is defined as a two-dimensional object with four equal sides and 90-degree angles at its corners. Every square must have each and every one of these attributes. If a geometric figure has all these attributes, then one must conclude that the object is a square. This view was compelling at first, but ultimately proved to be narrow in scope and applicability.

There are two main current approaches to the study of concepts and categories: the similarity- and explanation-based views. The similarity-based view holds that instances of a category are represented mentally by the degree to which they are similar to other known instances of the category (e.g., deciding that an unfamiliar object is a chair because it resembles familiar chairs in important characteristics, such as having four legs). In this chapter, we examine two such theories, the probabilistic and exemplar. The explanation-based view, on the other hand, argues that instances of a category are related by an explanatory structure; by a person's naive theories and background knowledge (e.g., deciding that an unfamiliar object is a chair because it serves a function, such as providing a place to sit).

Which has the upper hand: the similarity- or rule-based approach? As is usually the case, the truth most likely lies somewhere in between. Explanation-based theories are based on more well-defined rules. They are more exact but apply to more narrow cases. Similarity-based approaches are less precise but are more flexible and better equipped to handle ill-defined situations. In sum, similarity and explanation may act together in the process of concept acquisition.

Concepts play important roles in reasoning and inference making. Categorizing a new object or entity allows people to understand better how to interact with it (e.g., if you are told that an unfamiliar animal is a kind of a dog, then you probably can assume that it likes to play fetch and be petted), as well as to make future predictions about it (e.g., the animal will probably bite if you play too aggressively with it). Representing a category of objects allows people to instantiate goals in planning (e.g., objects belonging to the category toiletries are useful for taking on a trip) (Medin & Heit, 1994). In sum, concepts are useful because they promote a cognitive economy (Rosch, 1978), expressing the maximum amount of essential information about a category with a minimum-length description. Without the ability to form concepts, it would be difficult to make sense of most of the information that we encounter daily, and doing so would require a great deal of cognitive effort. Concepts allow us to organize knowledge gained in the past in such a way that we can use it to understand and make predictions about new experiences.

How do we acquire the concepts that we have? There are several theories of concepts that can be divided broadly into **similarity**- versus **explanation**-based views (Komatsu, 1992; E. E. Smith & Medin, 1981). Before we define and discuss these views in detail, however, we would like you to bear several fundamental questions in mind.

CATEGORIZATION: SOME FUNDAMENTAL QUESTIONS

A theory of categorization should answer fundamental questions about the nature of concepts in a fulfilling way. These questions examine the conditions that make objects in a category cluster or cohere, the possible effects of context on categorization, and the existence of different types of concepts.

What Makes a Category Cohere?

What makes objects in a category cluster or cohere? Why are dissimilar entities, such as penguins, eagles, and robins, often perceived as belonging to the same category (birds), whereas similar sea animals, such as sharks and whales, are usually grouped in different categories? (B. H. Ross & Spalding, 1984). The question of coherence is crucial to the answer because, as Goodman (1972) noted, every object bears some similarity to every other object in the world (e.g., both animate and inanimate objects are made of matter). For a theory of categorization to be adequate, it needs to be able to explain how objects are partitioned into particular sets from a (functionally) infinite set of possibilities. To be useful as a psychological explanation, a theory must specify adequate constraints on both concept-acquisition processes and on the structure of a category.

What Is the Effect of Context on Categorization?

Concepts may be tied to context. Normally, people will not categorize the objects, children, cash, and important papers, as part of the same concept, but these seemingly disparate concepts cohere when one thinks of "things to take out of the house in case of a fire" (Barsalou, 1983). Context is also a factor in communication. For example, the same concept may bring to mind different instances depending on the context in which it is used. If a person is asked to think about a typical example of a bird, she would most likely respond with "robin." However, when the person is told that "the holiday bird looks delicious," it would be more likely for her to think of "turkey" (Roth & Shoben, 1983). A general theory of concepts should be able to explain the interaction between contextual factors and the acquisition and use of concepts.

Do Different Types of Concepts Require Different Explanations?

Concepts can be divided into various types. **Artifacts** and **nominal concepts** (e.g., chair, road, and bachelor) refer to entities that are defined by convention, as opposed to **natural kinds** (e.g., dogs, flowers, trees) that are first "discovered" and only then labeled (Medin & Heit, 1994). **Ad hoc concepts** encompass entities (e.g., passport, money, medicines) that are unified by an underlying principle or explanation (e.g., "things to take on a trip") and are goal derived and transient. **Abstract concepts** involve ideas or events that are not perceived at a perceptual level (e.g., acts of kindness). **Social concepts** refer to social types, such as introvert and extrovert. In addition, concepts may also be divided along a continuum of complexity, ranging from **simple** (e.g., fish) to **complex** (pet fish). Finally, many concepts are thought to be organized in a hierarchy. **Basic-level concepts**, such as chair and dog, lie at an intermediate level, above **subordinate concepts** that are more specific, like a bar stool and Dalmatian, but below **superordinate concepts** that are more general, such as furniture and animal (Rosch, Mervis, Gray, Johnson, & Boyes-Braem, 1976). For a theory of concepts to be robust, it needs to account for the representation of as many types of concepts as possible. At the least, the theory should specify its ability to generalize to some or all types of concepts.

What kind of theory would answer these fundamental questions in a satisfying way? The first attempt to create a modern psychological theory of categorization became known as the "classical view."

THE CLASSICAL VIEW

The **classical view** is based on an Aristotelian taxonomy, in which every object is composed of **defining features** that create clear and stable category boundaries. That is, all objects, in any given category, share all the defining features of that category. The defining features are **individually necessary** and **jointly sufficient** for inclusion in the category (Bruner, Goodnow, & Austin, 1956; Katz, 1972; Katz & Fodor, 1963). For example, a circle is defined as the set of all points that are a fixed distance from a fixed point in the plane. Every circle must have each and every one of these attributes. If a geometric figure has all these attributes, then one must conclude that the object is a circle. In addition, the classical view argues that the structure of a category is hierarchical: Subcategories must have all the features of their superordinate categories (E. E. Smith & Medin, 1981). Thus, if a square is a kind of rectangle, then it must possess all the features of a rectangle (e.g., four sides and 90-degree angles).

There are two main implications of the classical view. The first is that membership boundaries are clear-cut and mutually exclusive. That is, Macho, the German shepherd, is either a dog or is not a dog. The second implication is that membership has no gradedness because all members of a category are equally good examples of the category (Medin & Ross, 1990). Thus, Macho the German shepherd is no more of a dog than is Fluffy the poodle.

The advantage of the classical view is that it is powerfully simple. It provides a single representation for describing a whole category of objects. Nevertheless, this advantage is also its main limitation: It causes the classical view to apply to only a narrow set of concepts. Many arguments have been leveled against the classical view's lack of generality and explanatory power.

Criticisms of the Classical View

The classical view appeals to common sense but fails to provide a broad account of categorization for several reasons. First, because the classical view assumes that objects have defining features, it implies that objects fall into distinct and well-defined categories. Instead, many categories are "fuzzy," that is, instances of one category often share features with instances of other categories. For example, McCloskey and Glucksberg (1978) showed that people tend to (1) disagree on whether some objects belong to one category or another, such as whether a tomato is a kind of fruit or vegetable, and (2) change some of their initial classifications over time. Therefore, defining features cannot offer a sufficient basis for classification (Bellezza, 1984; Hampton, 1998; McCloskey & Glucksberg, 1978).

Second, the classical view may be useful for classifying well-defined objects, such as a square, but it is often impossible to specify a set of features that are singly necessary and jointly sufficient for classifying most concepts, such as a tiger (Medin & Smith, 1984; Rosch & Mervis, 1975; McNamara & Sternberg, 1983). As E. E. Smith (1989) pointed out, the concept of tiger is often assigned the attributes of being striped and carnivorous. However, most people would agree that if one paints a tiger so as to cover its stripes and if the tiger eats only vegetables because it had surgery of the digestive tract, it is still a tiger. Therefore, the at-

Figure 3.1 Are these animals both tigers?

tributes of having stripes and eating meat cannot serve as defining features. This argument holds true for many other types of natural kinds (e.g., dog, human, and tree) and a subset of artifacts (e.g., furniture, odd number).

You will surely agree that the striped animal in Figure 3.1 is a tiger, but is the white animal also a tiger? (adapted from Snodgrass & Vanderwart, 1980).

Third, the classical view would predict that an instance belonging to a subordinate category (robin) would be judged as more similar to the basic level category (bird) than to the superordinate category (animal) because it shares more common properties with the former and less common properties with the latter. However, people do not always abide by this prediction, as when they judge the similarity of hierarchically nested categories, such as chicken, bird, animal (McCloskey, 1980; Roth & Mervis, 1983).

Fourth, the classical view cannot explain **typicality effects**, in which people are faster to agree that a typical example of a particular category is a member of that category, but are slower to establish category membership when presented with an atypical instance (Murphy & Brownell, 1985; Rips, Shoben, & Smith, 1973; Rosch & Mervis, 1975; Smith, Shoben, & Rips, 1974). Typicality is expressed in terms of ratings (Rosch & Mervis, 1975) and reaction times. For example, people are faster to agree that "A robin is a bird" than that "A penguin is a bird" (Rips et al., 1973). People also retrieve typical versus atypical instances from memory first when asked to generate a list of instances that belong to a particular category (Rosch, 1978) and are faster to determine that a picture of a typical instance belongs to a category (a robin is a bird) than they are for a nontypical instance (a penguin is a bird) (Murphy & Brownell, 1985).

Why do typicality effects pose a threat to the classical view? They do so because the classical view posits that every instance in a category is defined by the same necessary and sufficient features and should thus be categorized just as quickly and easily as any other instance. Furthermore, typicality effects often result from frequent but nonnecessary features of instances in a group (e.g., sweet is a typical but not a necessary feature of fruit) (Rosch & Mervis, 1975).

The classical view cannot account for the effect of the frequency of nonnecessary attributes on judgments of categories.

Any one of these criticisms alone is not completely damning to the classical view but together they make a strong case against it. As Medin and Smith (1984, p. 117) so elegantly put it, these arguments "reveal a picture not unlike Cinderella's stepsisters trying on the glass slipper—even if they could have gotten it on, certainly they would not have walked very gracefully."

If the classical view does not provide a satisfying account of categorization, then where should we look for one? More recently, researchers have focused on two main constructs: similarity and explanation.

SIMILARITY- VERSUS EXPLANATION-BASED VIEWS

When we are confronted with a new object, how do we categorize it? For example, imagine that you are taking an art history test. You are presented with a painting that you fail to recognize and are then asked to try to determine the art movement with which it was associated. If the artist used vibrant, soft brush strokes, the shapes lost focus and became more abstract as you approached the painting, and the picture reminded you of works by Monet and Renoir, then you might be tempted to say that the painting was generated during the impressionistic period. In this case, you would be using a similarity-based approach, by comparing the painting to known exemplars (familiar paintings) of a familiar category (impressionism). On the other hand, imagine that you were using some acquired expertise from what you have learned in your art history class to conclude that although the painting seems similar to other impressionist works, it would have to be from a different period because the brush strokes are too wide and the color scheme is not quite representative of impressionism. In this case, you would use an explanation-based approach, by relying on a set of principled rules.

Sloman and Rips (1998) delineated four viewpoints on how central the role of similarity is in reasoning and concept acquisition:

Strong similarity. This viewpoint, termed "original sim," argues that similarity is fundamental to cognitive judgments. Strong similarity is thought to be quick, perceptual, and relatively automatic in nature. In other words, similarity is an atomic unit on which judgments are based.

Weak similarity. This perspective argues that similarity is computed by means of a fixed algorithm that compares two entities to each other; however, the set of properties that are compared between the two entities is not necessarily fixed. In this view, similarity has less explanatory power than in the first case, but it is still a considerable force because it can be calculated and applied in a systematic and explicit fashion. Here, the process by which similarity is determined is the same in all cases, but the actual features that are compared (the inputs to the algorithm) differ from case to case.

Feeble similarity. Here, similarity can be thought of as being synonymous with property-based cognitive processing. Comparisons are made in which two different mental representations are analyzed for overlapping features, but both the computational algorithms used and the actual features compared can differ from case to case.

No-Similarity. This is the view that judgments are dependent not on similarity, per se, but on independent cognitive processes from which someone may form the impression that two items are similar. However, similarity itself is not a fundamental attribute that plays any special role in the process of comparing two entities. Thus, the identity of features may be computed independently for several features of the two objects in question. If there are enough identical features, one may decide that the two objects are similar, but similarity itself is not basic to the comparison process.

The alternative to the similarity-based approach is that cognition, in general, and categorization, in particular, are based on systematic rules. In the chapter on knowledge representation (chapter 4), we discuss the ACT theory (J. R. Anderson, 1983, 1993) as an example of a rule-based architecture of cognition. ACT and other rule-based models are based on production rules of the form If C then A (If Condition then Action). As Sloman and Rips (1998) pointed out, rules do not necessarily exclude similarity, in that they could use similarity as an input (the condition) for performing computations or could produce a judgment of similarity as a result of those computations. The major topic of debate is whether similarity is an essential or "special" cognitive process, or whether it is governed by a set of more general and fundamental rules.

Fodor and Pylyshyn (1988) argued that the two most important features of rule-based systems are that (1) there are no theoretical limits on the number of new representations that rule-based systems can produce by legally combining old information in new ways and (2) rules do not apply only to specific and concrete instances, but can apply to a whole class of relations. For example, Sloman and Rips (1998) contended that if a rule combines A and B, and B' belongs to the same class of objects that B does, then it is safe to assume that one can combine A and B' by the same rule. These features are made possible by the abstract and logical internal structure of rule systems, in which the fundamental constituents are not specific instances but, rather, variables that represent an entire class of objects. In contrast, similarity-based models do not include abstract classes of objects but are based on specific instances. In the following sections, we discuss similarity- versus explanation-based views of categorization in detail.

SIMILARITY-BASED VIEWS

The idea that most concepts may be based on similarities, rather than on a set of defining features, was captured elegantly by the philosopher Ludwig Wittgenstein (1953; aphorism 66):

> Consider for example the proceedings that we call "games." I mean board-games, card-games, ball-games, Olympic games, and so on. What is common to them all?—Don't say: "There *must* be something common, or they would not be called 'games' "—but *look and see* whether there is anything common to all.—For if you look at them you will not see something that is common to *all*, but similarities, relationships, and a whole series of them at that. . . . And the result of this examination is: we see a complicated network of similarities overlapping and criss-crossing: sometimes overall similarities, sometimes similarities of detail.

The similarity-based accounts of categorization encompass the probabilistic and exemplar views. These views hold that instances of a category are represented mentally by the degree to which they are similar to (have overlapping attributes with) either an abstract representation of the category or other known instances of the category. These views, however, disagree on the ways in which similarity is used for forming representations of categories and for acquiring concepts.

The Probabilistic View

The failure of the classical approach universally to account for concept formation led to the development of the **probabilistic view**. This view suggests that features are neither necessary nor sufficient for categorization, but that they are made up of objects that have similar features in common. An object is judged to be a member of a category if it shares some proportion of the typical features of other members of the category. Thus, the probabilistic view can account for typicality effects that the classical view cannot (Rosch & Mervis, 1975).

The probabilistic model of categorization was introduced by Eleanor Rosch and Carolyn Mervis (Rosch, 1975; Rosch & Mervis, 1975). Its fundamental idea is that concepts are organized by a **family resemblance** (Wittgenstein, 1953). A family-resemblance structure (e.g., bird) contains a set of instances (e.g., robin, penguin, blue jay, crow, canary, and humming bird) in which each instance has at least one overlapping attribute with one or more of the other instances in the set (e.g., has wings, flies, or sings). Thus, at the heart of the probabilistic view is the notion that instances within a category differ in terms of their typicality, where the degree of typicality is determined by family resemblance. In contrast to the classical view, membership in a category is judged not by defining features, but by characteristic features.

One class of probabilistic models, known as **prototype theory** (e.g., Posner & Keele, 1968), was designed to show that people create a representation of a category's central tendency in the form of a **prototype**. An instance is judged to be prototypical of the whole set in proportion to the extent to which it has family resemblance to, or shares overlapping attributes with, other members of that set (e.g., a robin shares the highest number of features with other birds). The prototype is therefore the instance that embodies the most characteristic attributes with members of its own category (e.g., robin). On this view, people's classification judgments result from a comparison between the similarity of a new instance and a prototype (e.g., a sparrow would be classified as a bird, not as an insect, because it is more similar to a prototypical bird than to a prototypical insect). Similarity, in turn, is a function of the number, salience, and psychological "weight" (the perceived importance) of features that the object and prototype have in common.

Contrast Model of Similarity

In probabilistic models, not all properties or attributes have the same weight. Each attribute is weighted according to how much it contributes to the concept's coherence. For instance, the attribute of having feathers may be more diagnostic of the category bird than of being small. An instance is said to belong to a category if it exceeds a critical number of properties or sum of weighted properties. The instance that has the most frequent properties and the largest weighted sum is considered to be the prototype.

The weights of an instance's attributes can be combined by using different methods (see, e.g., Medin & Schaffer, 1978). The most common method, based on Tversky's (1977) **contrast model of similarity**, assumes that sets of features are independent and can be combined linearly by adding. The contrast rule is given in the following equation (where I refers to instance and P to prototype):

$$Sim(I,P) = af(I \cap P) - bf(P - I) - cf(I - P)$$

The $(I \cap P)$ refers to the set of features that the instance and the prototype have in common. For example, if the instance is penguin and the prototype is robin, then the $(I \cap P)$ may be lays eggs. The $(P - I)$ refers to the set of features that belong only to and are distinctive of the prototype, such as flies, sings, builds nests in trees, and is small. The $(I - P)$ refers to the set of features that belong only to and are distinctive of the instance, such as swims and is large. The f denotes a function that scales the salience of each of the three sets: common set $(I \cap P)$, distinctive set for prototype $(P - I)$, and distinctive set for instance $(I - P)$. If all three sets have equal salience (importance), then $f = 1$. The a, b, and c, are parameters that measure the weight or contribution of each of the three sets. If the distinctive and common features have the same weights or contribute equally to the judgment of similarity, then $a = b = c = 1$. The underlying principle behind the contrast model is that the more features the instance and prototype have in common and the greater the salience and weight of these features, the higher the perceived similarity between them.

The implication of the contrast model of similarity, and prototype approaches in general, is that judging an instance's similarity to a prototype involves adding weighted attributes together until they pass (or fail to pass) some critical criterion. If an instance has the critical sum of weighted attributes (sparrow), then it will be classified as belonging to the category (bird). Categorizations are consequently influenced by the degree of instance typicality, in which typicality is a direct function of the additivity of features.

Thus, a major constraint on the categorization process is that some additive combination of (weighted) attributes must exist that can accurately discriminate members of one category from members of a different category. In other words, instances of a category can be differentiated from noninstances by a linear discriminant function that distinguishes two groups of objects on the basis of the combined weights of their attributes (Medin & Schaffer, 1978; Medin & Schwanenflugel, 1981; Nakamura, 1985; Wattenmaker, Dewey, Murphy, & Medin, 1986). Therefore, categories must be **linearly separable**, such that there is a clear dividing line between members of one category and members of another category. Consider the graphical representation of linear separability in Figure 3.2. The right graph shows linear separa-

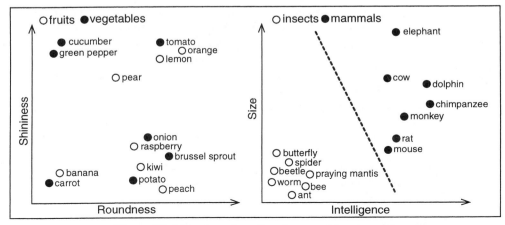

Figure 3.2 Linearly and nonlinearly separable categories.

bility between insects and mammals with respect to the features, size and intelligence. That is, on the basis of these features, we can draw a line that would separate insects from mammals. The left graph, in contrast, provides an example of two nonlinearly separable categories, fruits and vegetables, with respect to the features of roundness and shininess.

Any categorization model that is based on the idea of adding attributes to exceed a criterion implies that people would find it easier to learn linearly separable categories than to learn nonlinearly separable categories (Wattenmaker et al., 1986). However, there is no evidence that this is indeed the case. Most notably, Medin and Schwanenflugel (1981) manipulated different variables (e.g., category size) in tasks that had both linearly and nonlinearly separable categories. They found that the similarity of instances to each other had the most effect on people's performance, whereas linear separability did not have any effect.

Furthermore, Wattenmaker et al. (1986) showed that under certain conditions (when people have a guiding schema), linearly separable categories can be more or less easy to acquire than can nonlinearly separable categories. For example, our schemas for a house painter versus a construction worker most likely include a representation of a person who likes to work inside versus outside, in a small versus a large crew, and all year round versus not in winter. On the basis of these features, the house painter versus construction worker categories seem linearly separable. However, if we are reminded of the subgroup of exterior painters, then these two categories no longer can be seen as linearly separable (try graphing these categories and drawing a dividing line between them). Wattenmaker et al. showed that people use their background knowledge in a way that can facilitate learning either linearly or nonlinearly separable categories. This finding is hard to accommodate in a similarity-based framework.

Advantages and Disadvantages of the Probabilistic View

There are several advantages to the probabilistic view. First, in contrast to the classical view, it provides an explanation of typicality effects in categorization judgments. Second, because the probabilistic view allows for probable, rather than defining, properties, it can apply to a larger set of concepts than can the classical view, including both natural kinds and artifacts. In fact, the prototype work has been extended to social and personality types as well, such as to the concepts of introvert and extrovert (Cantor & Mischel, 1979). Third, the probabilistic view helps explain the "fuzzy boundary" issue. For example, the problems associated with classifying tomato as belonging to either the fruit or vegetable category can be explained by the fact that tomato shares similar properties with both categories (it lies close to each of their boundaries, at a similar distance from both prototypes).

The probabilistic view, however, has been criticized on several grounds. First, when people form natural categories, they are often aided by the fact that particular attributes tend to covary (having feathers is correlated positively with having a beak, whereas having feathers is not correlated with having fur) (Mervis & Rosch, 1981). Malt and Smith (1984) extended this idea by demonstrating that attributes that correlate or co-occur with one another within a category provide additional internal structure for that category (e.g., small birds tend to sing whereas large birds tend to squawk). This finding poses a difficulty for the probabilistic view because even though a new entity may share a highly diagnostic or heavily weighted attribute (e.g., sings) with the prototype (e.g., robin), the weight of this attribute tends to be mitigated by a correlation violation (e.g., the animal sings and is large).

Furthermore, the probabilistic view does not seem to take *context* into account (Medin & Schaffer, 1978; Roth & Shoben, 1983). As was mentioned previously, when one is told that "the holiday bird looks delicious," one usually thinks of a turkey instead of the more prototypical robin. Probabilistic theories have difficulty in accommodating such context-dependent factors.

In addition, a prototype-based approach cannot explain clearly how a single concept that is a poor instance of two categories can be a good instance of the combined categories. For instance, a guppy is a relatively poor example of either the category "pet" or "fish," but is a representative example of the complex category "pet fish" (for a discussion, see Hampton, 1993).

There are also empirical counterexamples to the probabilistic view's predictions. Notably, two instances that are equally similar to the prototype (have the same weighted shared features) may be classified differentially with respect to both speed and accuracy (Whittlesea, 1987).

Some of the categorization effects that the probabilistic view cannot account for, such as context and correlated category features, have led to the development of an alternative theory of similarity-based categorization known as the exemplar view.

The Exemplar View

The **exemplar view** argues that novel objects are classified by comparison to specific exemplars of a particular category that are stored in memory. More specifically, it suggests that people use the most similar exemplar or exemplars in their knowledge base to determine the category membership of a new object. For example, Fluffy the poodle may elicit the exemplar of a small dog (e.g., a spaniel), whereas Macho the German shepherd may elicit the exemplar of a larger dog (e.g., a Laborador retriever). In either case, the sufficient similarity between a given novel entity (Macho or Fluffy) and the retrieved exemplar (spaniel or retriever) may enable the person to categorize both entities correctly (Macho and Fluffy are both dogs).

Thus, the exemplar view holds that concepts are formed on the basis of separate descriptions of individual exemplars that are stored in memory. A new instance is classified as belonging to a particular category according to on-line comparisons with known exemplars of the category (see, e.g., Brooks, 1978; Medin & Schaffer, 1978). In contrast to the probabilistic view, in the exemplar view, there is no constraint that requires an instance of a category to share at least one attribute with one or more members of the same category.

The family-resemblance view assumes that there is an already stored abstracted prototype in memory and that a new object is compared to the prestored prototype during classification (see Medin & Smith, 1981). The exemplar view, on the other hand, does not require storing an abstract representation of any sort. The only abstraction that may take place occurs when a person encounters a new entity and then proceeds to make computations for determining the degree of similarity that the new entity shares with familiar instances.

The exemplar view can account for typicality effects because it assumes that when a person attempts to categorize a novel object, he or she will draw on all past exemplars of a category weighted by similarity to the new object (Hintzman, 1986). A more typical exemplar (e.g., chair as a member of the category furniture) will have more overlapping features with stored exemplars, whereas a more atypical exemplar (e.g., vase as a member of the category furniture) will have fewer overlapping features. Thus, a person will give a higher typicality rating to an exemplar with high-frequency features, without the need to match that exemplar to a prestored prototype.

If all the exemplar view could do was to explain typicality effects, then the exemplar and probabilistic views would come out even. In fact, a number of authors have argued this very point (see, e.g., E. E. Smith and Medin, 1981). However, the explanatory power of the exemplar view extends beyond that of the probabilistic view because it is able to account for a variety of effects that the probabilistic view cannot adequately explain. For example, the exemplar view can help explain why categorization judgments are frequently affected by context because it allows exemplars to have different degrees of activation at different times. In particular, exemplar theory maintains that instances will differentially activate stored exemplars at different times, depending on the situational context. Sitting at a Thanksgiving dinner, for instance, may activate turkey from preceding holiday gatherings. On such an occasion, bird will become associated more with turkey than with robin.

The exemplar approach also can help explain why people's typicality judgments are affected by correlational structure (e.g., Malt & Smith, 1984). As we previously discussed, in the category bird, there is a correlation between being small and singing and between being large and squawking. When people are given information about an animal that is large and sings, even though singing is a highly diagnostic attribute of bird, they will not rate that instance as a typical member of the bird category because it violates the correlation of being large and squawking. Since exemplar models assume that an individual instance of a category and all its features are stored together as a unit, information about what specific attributes tend to correlate with one another is retained. This method of representing information on attributes accounts for people's ability to make detailed predictions about the features of a particular member of a category. To return to our earlier example, if you see a large, unfamiliar bird, you are able to predict that it will squawk because all the stored examples of large birds you were able to retrieve happened to squawk, not sing.

Criticisms of the Exemplar View

The exemplar view encounters difficulties, however, in explaining why people seem to have knowledge about the prototypes of categories, even when they are not presented directly with examples of these prototypes (Franks & Bransford, 1971; Knapp & Anderson, 1984; Posner & Keele, 1968). For example, Posner and Keele presented participants with dot patterns distorted by statistical rules from their prototype. During testing, the prototype elicited higher recognition rates than did other new patterns at the same distance from the trained dot patterns. After its first presentation, the prototype was recognized just as well as the original dot patterns. The fact that people have an idea of what the prototype is, without having been explicitly presented with it, is more consistent with the probabilistic view than with the exemplar view. Figure 3.3 presents a graphical illustration of similar stimuli to the type used by Posner and Keele and Knapp and Anderson. The upper-left panel shows a randomly generated prototype pattern of 9 points on a 100×100 array. Each of the exemplars was created by randomly displacing the prototype by some maximum number of pixels. For the "close exemplar," points could be moved in a random direction in distances ranging from 0 to 3 points away from the prototype. For the "moderate exemplar," the range was 0 to 10 points away from the prototype, and for the "distant exemplar," the range was 0 to 20 points.

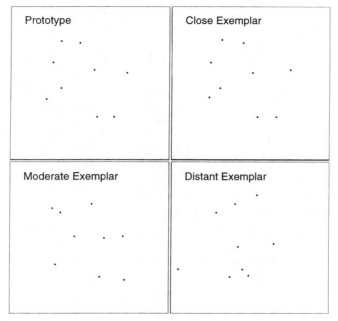

Figure 3.3 Dot patterns distorted by statistical rules from their prototype.

Even more troubling for the exemplar view is the finding that people provide higher confidence ratings in response to prototypes versus prior instances during classification (How confident are you that this object belongs to a given category?) but give higher confidence ratings in response to prior instances versus prototypes during recognition (How confident are you that you have seen this object before?) (Hayes-Roth & Hayes-Roth, 1977). The dissociation between classification and recognition may suggest that people use both the prototype and specific representations during categorization (see also Metcalfe & Fisher, 1986). However, proponents of the exemplar view have argued that this dissociation can be explained within the framework of exemplar-based models as well (e.g., Nosofsky, 1988). The explanation is as follows: The prototype shares a large number of features with many of the stored exemplars and is seen as highly similar to those exemplars, producing a confident categorization judgement. In contrast, the prior instance, although familiar, shares fewer features with a smaller number of stored exemplars and is seen as less similar to members of the category in question. There is no need to assume that a prototype was abstracted and represented.

A more general theoretical problem for the exemplar-based view is the lack of representational economy (Komatsu, 1992). If all instances were to be stored in memory, then that could lead to a combinatorial explosion or, at the least, to an extremely laborious memory-retrieval process. Admittedly, only a few models contend that all information is retained in memory (see, e.g., Reed, 1972). Others argue that information often decays over time or is only partially encoded in the first place (Hintzman, 1986; Hintzman & Ludlam, 1980; Nosofsky, 1988, 1989, 1991). The challenge, in the latter case, is to specify exactly what details of instances will and will not be retained in memory, and why.

THE SIMILARITY-BASED VIEW: A FEW THORNY PROBLEMS

The probabilistic and exemplar views have provided useful frameworks for understanding categorization and concept formation. However, these models have been criticized on several grounds (Medin & Ortony, 1989; Murphy & Medin, 1985; Schank, Collins, & Hunter, 1988). Researchers have argued that similarity-based models (1) are hard to distinguish from each other; (2) are inadequate for explaining the full range of categorization judgments and inferences that people make; and (3) ignore information, other than similarity, that is critical to the categorization process.

It is difficult to distinguish between prototype- and exemplar-based models. Barsalou (1989) argued that trying to determine whether people create abstract- or exemplar-based representations may be fruitless because these models cannot be differentiated on the basis of either their theoretical assumptions or the behavioral data that have been used to support these assumptions. Specifically, Barsalou contended that in contrast to common assumptions, prototype-based models can contain idiosyncratic information and co-occurrence or correlational information and be dynamic and changing. Therefore, their abstracted representations may support the kind of processing that is usually associated with exemplar-based representations.

There could also be alternative accounts of similarity effects that do not require either exemplar- or prototype-based models. Such an example comes from the **rule-plus-exception model** (RULEX) (Nosofsky, Palmeri, & McKinley, 1994). RULEX suggests that ill-defined categories (categories that cannot be formed by singly necessary and jointly sufficient rules) can be learned by forming "imperfect" rules and then storing exceptions to these rules. This account is vastly different from exemplar accounts of categorization because classification in RULEX is assumed to be driven by hypothesis testing: the extraction of simple rules and their exceptions, when the exceptions are often not complete exemplars. The hypothesis-testing process is idiosyncratic, leading to large individual differences in the extracted rules and the stored exceptions.

Consider, for instance, two categories: A and B. Exemplars in each category have four dimensions that are binary: Each dimension can have a value of either 1 (e.g., lives near water) or 2 (e.g., lives away from water). Category A contains exemplars that tend to have a logical value of 1 on each of their four dimensions: A1 = 1112, A2 = 1212, A3 = 1211, A4 = 1121, A5 = 2111. Category B contains exemplars that tend to have a logical value of 2 on each of their four dimensions: B1 = 1122, B2 = 2112, B3 = 2221, B4 = 2222. There is no single rule that can divide the exemplars into categories A or B. According to exemplar-based theories (e.g., Medin & Schaffer, 1978), all the exemplars are stored in memory, and during classification, people compute a similarity function between the new instance and the stored exemplars. On the other hand, RULEX assumes that people use an imperfect rule, for example, "If there is a value of 1 on the first dimension, then the exemplar most probably belongs to Category A, whereas if there is a value of 2, it belongs to category B." When the person encounters the exemplar A5 (2111) and learns that it also belongs to Category A, he or she attempts to create an exception to the rule, allowing for exemplars of the form 211* (where * denotes a wild card that can take any value) also to be members of Category A. The person may then learn that the exception does not work (2112 belongs to Category B) and thus will continue to update and modify the exception until it seems to work. Different people may adopt different hypothesis-testing approaches but are similarly expected to go through the steps of creating rules and storing and updating exceptions.

Similarity, itself, is often underconstrained (Goldstone, 1994; Goodman, 1972; Komatsu, 1992; Ross & Spalding, 1994). Most models adopt, either implicitly or explicitly, Tversky's (1977), Tversky and Gati's (1982), and Gati and Tversky's (1984) contrast model of similarity (see, E. E. Smith, 1989). The contrast model, however, does not explain how the particular attributes that determine similarity are selected. In other words, this model does not answer the question, What makes an attribute psychologically salient? Many objects in the world share the attribute of weighing less then 200 tons, but people do not appear to use such attributes as a basis for performing judgments of similarity (Goodman, 1972; Murphy & Medin, 1985). The main challenge, then, is to identify a set of constraints, beyond similarity, that provides more explanatory power (Medin, 1989).

Yet another challenge for similarity-based accounts is that similarity judgments change as a function of which attributes are perceived to be psychologically relevant in a given situation. For example, when people are asked to judge the similarity between a raccoon and a snake, they tend to produce relatively low ratings. However, if people receive the additional word *pets*, their similarity ratings increase (Barsalou, 1982). These ad hoc kinds (see also Barsalou, 1983) cannot be based on a simple similarity matrix. Ross and Spalding (1994) argued that, in general, similarity-based theories do not provide adequate descriptions of the interrelationships between types of concepts, such as the relationships between basic (Rosch et al., 1976), superordinate, and subordinate types. Similarity-based views leave open the question of whether different kinds of concepts are categorized differently.

Finally, the measurement of similarity also poses a threat to the reliability of similarity-based views because different measures of similarity do not always converge. For example, similarity that is measured by rating scales (e.g., Likert-type scales) does not always produce identical results to similarity that is measured by other manipulations (see, Goldstone, 1994, for a discussion). This finding implies that similarity may vary as a function of the characteristics of tasks.

Another alternative to a straightforward probabilistic or exemplar-based account is that categorization involves a combination of rules and similarity. For example, the Two-Stage Model (Ahn & Medin, 1992) suggests that people first create categories based on simple rules, but when faced with exceptions to these simple rules, they are forced to rely on similarity. In the model's first stage, people sort exemplars into categories by using a single-most-salient dimension. This stage is consistent with Medin, Wattenmaker, and Hampson's (1987) findings that people do not readily create categories that form a family-resemblance structure when asked to sort exemplars into different groups. Instead, people often tend to sort categories on the basis of a single salient dimension (e.g., having a long or short tail). During the second stage, they classify the remaining exemplars that do not obey the initial rule perfectly (that are exceptions) by similarity to their initially created groups. These exceptions may consist of exemplars that do not have an extreme value on the dimension (e.g., having a tail of medium length) or exemplars that do not have common values. In this second stage, people can use a variety of strategies, such as judgment by overall similarity or judgment by similarity along a single dimension.

Even if people demonstrate behavior that is consistent with the probabilistic or family-resemblance view, does that mean that they are relying only on similarity? What makes people rely on the particular similarity metric that they use? Lassaline and Murphy (1996) demonstrated that when people were asked to perform inductive inferences ("Given that this animal has a short tail, what kind of teeth would you expect it to have?"), they tended to create family-resemblance categories. This finding suggests a modified view of the role that family resemblance may play in categorization. Rosch and Mervis (1975) hypothesized that family resemblance motivates categorization decisions. In contrast, as the data from Lassaline and Murphy imply, family-resemblance structures may result from people's theories and inductive hypotheses. As Lassaline and Murphy stated: "family resemblance stimuli are said to be useful because they support inferences" (p. 96). Drawing inductive inferences may render certain attribute relationships salient and thus give rise to the simultaneous use of multiple attributes.

In addition to similarity, there appear to be a number of factors that play a critical role in the categorization process. These factors include context (Medin, & Schaffer, 1978), prior knowledge (Wisniewski, 1995; Wisniewski & Medin, 1994), theory (Medin & Ortony, 1989; Medin, Wattenmaker, & Hampson, 1987), and function (Medin & Ortony, 1989; Putnam, 1988; Rips, 1989b). As a response to these criticisms, more recent research has taken a "top-down" approach to explaining categorization judgments in the form of an explanation-based view.

THE EXPLANATION-BASED VIEW

The explanation-based view argues that instances of a concept are related by an explanatory structure. Consider an example from Murphy (1993): A physician determines that the results from two different kinds of tests (a blood test and a CAT scan) show support for the presence of a particular disease. Even though the results of these tests are different from one another, the physician perceives them as being similar because she uses a theory of what kinds of results to expect for the given disease and then groups these results as being part of the same category.

The explanation-based view has been strongly supported by the dissociation between classification and similarity judgments. Rips (1989b) presented participants with stories about natural kinds and artifacts that had undergone some change. The change was either (1) "essential," that is, one that involved a fundamental change in the entity's natural development, genetic makeup, or function (e.g., a bird had been transformed, through exposure to toxic waste, into a creature that looked like an insect) or (2) "accidental," that is, one that involved a superficial change that left the entity's natural development, genetic makeup, or function intact (e.g., a bird had been transformed, through exposure to toxic waste, into a creature that more closely resembled an insect, but left its "essence" intact, such that the bird could have normal offspring, for example).

Rips (1989b) found that for both natural kinds and artifacts, essential changes affected classification more than they affected similarity judgments (e.g., the bird was rated as being more similar to a bird than to an insect but was less likely to be classified as belonging to the category bird). The reverse was true for accidental changes. Accidental changes affected similarity more than they did classification judgments (e.g., the bird was rated as being more similar to an insect and less similar to a bird but was more likely to be classified as belonging to the category bird). The participants' similarity judgments were influenced by surface-structural properties, whereas their categorization judgments were based on what seemed to be a naive theory of biology and genetics.

Rips was able to demonstrate further evidence for the dissociation between similarity judgments and classification. He instructed the participants to form a mental image of a 3-inch-round object and then asked them to determine whether the object they had imagined was more similar to a quarter or to a pizza and whether it was more likely to be a quarter or a pizza. The participants tended to rate the object as being more similar to a quarter but more likely to be a pizza, on the basis of their background knowledge that pizzas versus quarters are more variable in size. This finding suggests that judgments of categorization may be orthogonal to judgments of similarity (however, see E. E. Smith & Sloman, 1994, for contrasting evidence).

A subset of explanation-based models are **theory-based accounts**. These theories' main tenet is that explanatory structures are derived from global theories. For example, Carey (1985) contended that categorization is driven by a naive theory of living beings (e.g., living things can move on their own and are composed of internal biological matter). Carey showed that even though most children believed that a toy monkey is more similar to a human being than to a worm, they often decided that the worm, rather than the toy monkey, shared biological matter with people (e.g., both have spleens). S. A. Gelman (1988a, 1988b) and S. A. Gelman and Markman (1987) also provided evidence that young children use naive causal theories for performing judgments that transcend surface-structural similarities.

Keil (1986) provided evidence of a theory-based account by demonstrating the central role of explanatory-based rules in people's judgments of category mutability. Specifically, he presented participants with artifacts and animals that had altered physical appearances (e.g., a raccoon that looked like a skunk) as a result of an accidental event (e.g., "cosmetic surgery"). Upon being asked what they would call the mutated entity, both children (in the fifth grade and above) and adults referred to the mutations on the basis of their nonmutable genetic structure and ignored physical similarity. Keil concluded that explanation was a necessary element of the categorization process.

Keil (1989) provided further support for the theory-based view. In his study, children and adults were asked to categorize a novel stimulus, either an artifact or a natural kind, that looked like a familiar entity (e.g., a horse) but had the innards of a different familiar entity (e.g., a cow). In the discovery condition, the children were told that scientists found that the entity's innards were those of a different entity, whereas in the transformation condition, they were told that the original entity was converted into the second entity by changing its external features. In both the discovery and the transformation conditions, younger children tended to categorize an entity on the basis of its external features, whereas older children and adults tended to base their decisions on internal structure. However, Keil found that participants of all ages categorized cross-ontological transformations (from artifact to natural kind, or vice versa) on the basis of internal structure. This last finding supports the view that people have naive theories that cause them to categorize entities and objects in predictable ways. Categorization therefore may be sensitive to theoretical relations among features (when features of a natural kind, such as a heart, have a specific purpose).

In the following sections, we review a range of variants of explanation-based theories. They include **psychological essentialism** (Keil, 1989; Malt, 1990; Medin & Ortony, 1989; Wattenmaker, Nakamura, & Medin, 1988), **idealized cognitive models** (Lakoff, 1987a;

1987b), the **two-tier approach** (Michalski, 1989), and **causal models** (Waldmann, Holyoak, & Fratianne, 1995).

Psychological Essentialism

Do objects and entities in the world have real or perceived essences? An **essence** is an elusive construct that refers to a hidden aspect of an object that determines the object's identity. S. A. Gelman and Hirschfeld (1996) argued that there are three distinct types of essences:

Sortal essence. A **sortal essence** is made up of defining characteristics that are common to all members of a category. It is based on the Aristotelian notion that an object has an essence by virtue of having defining, nonaccidental properties. For example, the concept of a grandmother involves having the essential attribute of being a parent's mother, but does not include the accidental characteristics of wearing eyeglasses and having gray hair (Landau, 1982). This conceptualization of categorization is similar to the classical view's.

Causal essence. A **causal essence** is the causal entity that leads to all other, secondary properties. For example, the essence of water is typically conceived of as being H_2O.

Ideal essence. An **ideal essence** does not have an objective existence in the world, but is a mental construct. For example, the essence of romantic love is an idealized notion of positive feeling toward another that is manifested by overt behavior and verbal expressions. The latter are indications of the underlying emotion, but exist independently of it.

Several psychologists (P. Bloom, 1996; Medin & Ortony, 1989; Rips, 1989b) have argued that people *believe* that concepts have essences that play a role in determining what instances will be classified as members of a concept. This view has been termed psychological essentialism. Psychological essentialism is different from metaphysical essentialism (the philosophical view that an object has an essence by virtue of being that object) because it focuses on perceptions of essences, rather than on the "objective" properties of objects in the world. Psychological essentialism is, thus, a descriptive theory of concepts.

Medin and Ortony (1989) contended that attributes of concepts range on a continuum of accessibility from being deeply hidden in the background, or abstract (e.g., the biological composition of an entity), to being more surface-structural and easily perceived (e.g., the color or shape of an entity). Central to their theory of psychological essentialism is the idea that people attend to particular surface-structural features that are constrained by the more central properties of concepts. For example, two entities that are surface-structurally different (a whale and a bear) are often grouped together as members of the same concept (mammals) because they may share the same central representation.

Medin and Ortony (1989) claimed that surface-structural information plays a larger role earlier in development, whereas more abstract attributes are acquired later. Deep-structural attributes in categorization judgments, however, may be used earlier than was previously thought. S. A. Gelman and Markman (1987) found that children as young as 4 years judge membership of objects in different categories on the basis of theoretical principles, rather than surface-structural features. For example, they showed children pictures of a flamingo and a bat. The children were told that the flamingo gives its young mashed-up food, whereas the bat gives its babies milk. The children were then presented with a picture depicting a blackbird that was surface-structurally similar to the bat. They were asked what the blackbird feeds its young, and most often answered on the basis of category membership (bird), rather than surface structure (bat) (see also P. Bloom, 1996; Carey, 19852; Keil, 1989; Kelemen & Bloom, 1994; Markman, 1989; D. J. K. Nelson, 1995; Spelke, von Hofsten, & Kestenbaum, 1989).

The development of the continuum of accessibility, from reliance on surface-structural features to reliance on deep-structural features, according to Medin and Ortony (1989), is adaptive and mirrors the evolution of the cognitive system. Their idea is that the cognitive system is tuned to superficial characteristics that are causally linked to deeper attributes, in accordance with the ecological constraints proposed by Neisser (1987).

Psychological essentialism has had particular success in accounting for human-made objects, or artifacts. For example, Rips (1989b) presented participants with descriptions of objects that looked like a given object (e.g., an umbrella) but that were designed to have a function associated with a different object (e.g., the umbrella was originally designed to be a lampshade). He found that the participants considered the target object to be more similar to the predicted object (umbrella), but that they nevertheless named the object on the basis of its perceived function (lampshade). The conclusion is that the object's function was more essential than its form.

Research has shown that people tend to focus on function versus form when making artifact category judgments. For example, Kelemen and Bloom (1994) had participants view different sized and colored circular objects (adapted from E. E. Smith, 1989) and then sort them into groups. They found that only when the objects were described as artifacts did the participants ignore their form and instead attend to their function. Furthermore, P. Bloom (1996) argued that an instance is perceived to be a member of a specific artifact kind if its form and potential function are explained as resulting from deliberate intention.

Psychological essentialism may correspond to our intuitions about the way in which we tend to treat an object as a whole, instead of breaking it down into independent features. However, what makes something an essence is far from clear.

Idealized Cognitive Models

Lakoff (1987a, 1987b) suggested that concepts correspond to idealized cognitive models (ICMs). For example, the concept of bachelor appears to be well defined: an adult male who is not married. But the definition of *bachelor* does not capture its connotative properties, namely, that a bachelor is eligible for marriage. Another way of stating this idea is that the definition of bachelor is idealized and does not necessarily correspond to attributes that signal marriagibility in the real world. Although the pope fits the definition, for instance, he would not typically be labeled a bachelor. Similarly there are many instances of priests, homosexuals, or people who live with life-long partners out of wedlock for which this definition is not accurate.

Lakoff also argued that some categories, which he termed **radial categories**, require the formation of multiple related models. A good example is the concept mother. In contrast to bachelor, the concept mother gives rise to different conceptualizations, such as, birth mother, mother-in-law, stepmother, and so forth. The central idea underlying Lakoff's theory is the importance of taking *context* into account in explaining the categorization process. That is, concepts can be understood not in a vacuum, but through an interaction between the ICM and world knowledge.

The Two-Tier Approach

Michalski (1989) distinguished between the base concept representation (BCR) and the inferential concept interpretation (ICI). The BCR involves both specific and general information stored in long-term memory. The specific information consists of examples, counterexamples, and exceptions to general rules, and the general type includes "typical" or easily defined beliefs about the nature of a concept that may be context independent and result either from an inferential process or from adapting other people's beliefs directly (e.g., teacher-defined beliefs). The BCR does not capture information about relationships between objects, which is inferred via the ICI.

The ICI interprets knowledge in the BCR by using background information and context that is specific to the BCR. It uses metaknowledge about which attributes of the concept are relevant in a given context, the kinds of transformations that can be done on the BCR (e.g., possible physical transformations), and specific information regarding the effect of transformations on various instances of a concept. For example, the kinds of transformations that are perceived as permissible for a chair may be to alter its shape, color, and material but not its function; in other words, the chair should still enable a person to sit on it.

Michalski contended that to match an entity to a concept representation, one needs to take into account both context and background knowledge. Michalski illustrated this idea by using the concept fish. If one learns about this concept by reading a description and seeing a few exemplars, then one's background knowledge consists of these experiences. A visit to the aquarium may reveal a new kind or exemplar of fish, for example, a horse-shaped fish that then becomes incorporated into a revised version of one's background knowledge of fish. However, if during the visit a person were told that a particular fish was sick, the person would not insert that exemplar into her background knowledge. Instead, she would reason about the nature of the sick fish on the basis of her knowledge of sick animals in general. This contextual processing allows concepts, such as horse-shaped fish and sick fish, to elicit two different representations within the framework of the two-tier approach.

Causal Models

Waldmann and colleagues (Waldmann & Holyoak, 1992; Waldmann et al., 1995) argued for an integration between bottom-up and top-down accounts of categorization learning. They suggested that in the majority of learning episodes, concept acquisition is guided by bottom-up information from environmental input, combined with expectations based on *causal models*. Waldmann et al. noted that people construct two basic kinds of causal models: **common cause** and **common effect** that affect how they encode the structural properties of a given category. In common-cause models, several effects (E1, E2, and E3) are connected by a single cause (C) (see Figure 3.4). For example, a single virus can cause multiple effects, such as sneezing, a runny nose, and fever. These symptoms may be correlated with each other, but there are no direct causal links among them. In the common-effect model, a single effect (E) is brought about by the presence of multiple causes (C1, C2, and C3) (see Figure 3.5). For example, a house (E) is built from numerous sources, such as materials (e.g., bricks and mortar), architects, builders, and money, among others.

There are two general properties that affect causal models: the direction of the causation and the amount of variation in the causal variables. If a common-cause model can take on

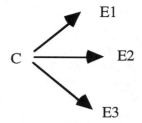

Figure 3.4 A common-cause model.

multiple values, then we should see that, for example, in a population of persons who have the same disease, strong symptoms correlate with a strong virus whereas weak symptoms correlate with a weak virus.

Waldmann et al. (1995) conducted experiments that manipulated participants' causal models to be either of the common-cause or the common-effect type. The type of model was crossed with two types of category structure: either linearly separable (composed of additive features or a list of properties connected by the logical operator *and*) or nonlinearly separable (composed of features that interact or correlate with each other and that are connected by the operators *and* and *or*: A housepainter can either "work inside" *and* "work year round" *or* can "work outside" *and* "not work year round"). Waldmann et al. showed that by manipulating the kind of causal model a participant acquired, a participant was biased to acquire a particular category structure (linearly separable or nonlinearly separable) on otherwise identical learning materials. For example, when people were given the common-effect model, they found the nonlinearly separable structure harder to learn than the linearly separable structure.

Waldmann et al. distinguished their causal-model explanation from other theory-based accounts by arguing that general causal structures do not require domain-specific knowledge. This idea has met with the criticism that their theory may have limited explanatory power because in real-world situations, there may be only a few instances in which people do not use their prior specific knowledge to acquire new concepts (see Ahn, 1999). Furthermore, Ahn found that when people were provided with either common-effect or common-cause models and subsequently were asked to generate categories, the structure of these categories did not differ by linear or nonlinear separability, contrary to what the causal-model theory would predict.

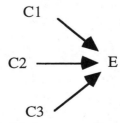

Figure 3.5 A common-effect model.

The Explanation-Based View and Its Variants: Open Questions

The explanation-based view provides valuable accounts of categorization that take people's naive theories, beliefs, and context into account. However, explanation-based accounts must specify the exact constraints that delineate the kinds of theories or beliefs that people hold (Komatsu, 1992). They should specify how a theory arises as well as identify what particular factors constrain theory structure. For example, how is Medin and Ortony's (1989) essence placeholder constrained in the first place? And what are the constraints on information contained in Michalski's (1989) ICI or Lakoff's (1987a, 1987b) ICM? Specifying constraints would strengthen explanation-based models by making them more testable and therefore more rigorously adherent to the scientific method.

In addition, naive theories and explanations can be hard to differentiate from general knowledge (Komatsu, 1992). Does the fact that we know how people usually interact with cars come from our background knowledge, or is this fact specifically stored in our concept of car? Taken to an extreme, this lack of differentiation between beliefs about concepts and general knowledge leads to the conclusion that almost any piece of knowledge a person acquires can get stored as part of a conceptual representation.

SIMILARITY VERSUS RULES: WHICH HAS THE UPPER HAND?

As we have seen, there has been ample evidence to support the role of both similarity (instance-based) and explanation-based (rule-based) views in categorization. We are left in the perplexing position of deciding on which view we should believe. According to Sloman and Rips (1998), rule-based systems are easier to analyze and to test because they are discrete, logical, and explicit in nature. However, similarity-based models are more nearly immune to error and more flexible in their usage because the computations they make are widely distributed across the system. In addition, they can respond to stimuli that they were not explicitly programmed to handle because they generalize automatically on the basis of similarity and do not need to be explicitly instructed as to class membership. In other words, rule-based approaches are more precise and better able to deal with certainty and generativity, whereas similarity-based approaches are more flexible and more able to handle uncertainty. The conclusion? The logical one is to believe both. That is, similarity and explanation may function in a combined way to support knowledge representation and concept acquisition.

Toward this end, there have been recent attempts to integrate top-down explanation-based approaches that emphasize people's naive theories with a more bottom-up similarity approach that focuses on how people learn experientially by interacting with new instances and using concepts (Ross & Spalding, 1994; Sloman & Rips, 1998; Waldmann et al., 1995). The idea is to create models of categorization and concept formation that account for the interaction between similarity, on the one hand, and knowledge or theory, on the other hand.

The need to create hybrid models of similarity and explanation was highlighted by Keil, Smith, Simons, and Levin (1998), who argued that the widespread success that similarity models have been able to achieve in predicting categorization has been somewhat misleading because in natural kinds, typical attributes often have an underlying causal significance. For example, people may identify having webbed feet as a typical feature of a duck, but it is not clear if that judgment is made primarily on the basis of a repeated perceptual association or because having webbed feet is a fundamental feature that allows a duck to survive in its habitat. In general, typicality and casual structure tend to be correlated for most real-world categories, making it somewhat difficult to distinguish which mechanism is driving category judgments. However, it is doubtful that category judgments are based on non-theory-driven similarity computations that involve keeping track of the frequency of feature associations. First, the range of possible features that could be used to determine similarity is too large because any two objects could be judged as being similar (Goodman, 1972; Keil, 1989; Murphy & Medin, 1985). Thus, some level of theory is necessary to explain why certain features are psychologically relevant and why others are not. In Keil et al.'s view, a feature's salience corresponds to its perceived functional significance according to people's intuitive notions of causality. This idea has been supported empirically. Murphy and Wisniewski (1989) showed that adults do a relatively poor job of identifying correlations between attributes when learning artificially constructed categories in which there is no functional relationship between the correlated attributes. A study by Murphy and Allopenna (1994) further illustrates this point. In that study, the participants were taught about novel animals who had features that were either causally or noncausally associated. An animal that has sharp teeth and eats meat has causally related attributes, whereas an animal with pointed ears and spots has attributes that are not causally related. Murphy and Allopenna found that the causally related categories were learned faster than were those that were not causally related. Also, when causally related features that occurred infrequently were presented, the participants judged them to be as typical as were the more frequently mentioned features of that category. In contrast, the participants who learned categories whose features were not causally related rated infrequently mentioned features as being atypical of the category. Thus, how typical a feature is judged to be is influenced by its perceived functional significance. These findings do not suggest that we should abandon similarity altogether but, rather, that similarity and explanation operate simultaneously to produce a categorization judgment.

Keil et al. (1998) objected to hybrid models that presume that a reliance on similarity precedes a reliance on casual mechanisms during concept formation, either from the perspective of novices versus experts or from a developmental standpoint. Instead, they argued that many hybrid models assume that new categories initially are learned by calculations of similarity and only later, once knowledge of the category has accumulated, can people make explanatory-based judgments. There is evidence that even people's earliest category judgments are not completely devoid of causal attribution. In fact, there may be a tendency toward the opposite pattern: that causal explanations dominate initially and that similarity plays a larger role once expertise has been acquired. For example, when asked to make diagnoses from case reports, medical students made a greater use of biomedical reasoning than did their mentors, who relied more heavily on similarities to previous cases (Boshuizen & Schmidt, 1992). This finding held true even when the teaching philosophy of the medical school emphasized learning through specific examples (Norman & Schmidt, 1992).

Keil et al. (1998) applied similar criticisms to models that presume that children initially classify according to the similarity of features and only later apply causal reasoning when making category judgments. As we discussed earlier, even young children seem to have naive causal theories for grouping natural kinds (see, e.g., Keil, 1986). Some researchers (e.g., E. J. Gibson & Walker, 1984; Leslie, 1995a, 1995b) have even made the case that infants have some notion of causality and are able to distinguish between movement that is biological and movement that is nonbiological in origin (see, e.g., Fox & McDaniel, 1982). In summary, although it is clear that both similarity and rules govern people's determinations of category membership, the two approaches do not appear to be related in a linear sequence. In other words, it cannot be said unequivocally that similarity-based approaches predominate when knowledge of an area is minimal and that explanatory-based approaches take over after knowledge has been acquired. Rather, it appears that the two approaches function in concert to determine category judgments at all stages of cognitive development and knowledge acquisition.

THE CATEGORIZATION FIELD: CURRENT AND FUTURE DIRECTIONS

The field of categorization has been moving in several directions. One recent direction is to view categorization as a kind of problem solving (B. H. Ross, 1996), in which representations of problems change as a result of the learner's experience and interaction with the structure of problems. Traditionally, there has been much emphasis on how people classify new instances, not on how people interact with and use them. Ross, however, contended that interactions with instances occur frequently and that these interactions can affect later representations and further classifications of instances in the same category. To support this idea, Ross showed that people who solved mathematics equations after classifying them were able to use the mathematical structure of these problems to categorize new problems, in contrast to people who learned only to classify the problems.

An associated line of research has been concerned with how concepts are learned in *unsupervised learning* tasks in which people learn categories naturally without explicit labeling or feedback (J. R. Anderson, 1991; Billman & Heit, 1988; Billman & Knutson, 1996; Clapper & Bower, 1994; Heit, 1992; Lassaline & Murphy, 1996; Wattenmaker, 1992, 1993). Similar to B. H. Ross's (1996) findings, this research has also shown that experiences with certain instances may affect how people form categories later on. The difference between these two lines of research is that classification learning is integrated with use, whereas in unsupervised learning, no explicit classification is involved.

Other questions of current focus are how some categories are used to make inferences about other categories and how relations among members of the same category affect subsequent learning of concepts. For example, given that robins have a particular characteristic, how much can one be certain that sparrows have that same characteristic? These questions have been addressed in work on category-based induction (e.g., Osherson, Smith, Wilkie, Lopez, & Shafir, 1990; Rips, 1975). Osherson et al. showed that the inductive strength of an argument is a function of the similarity between the premises and the conclusion of that argument and the extent to which the premise categories are similar to the lowest-level category that includes both the premise and conclusion categories.

We illustrate these ideas here by using examples of two phenomena demonstrated empirically in Osherson et al.'s studies (pp. 186–187). The first is that when people are given a premise (P) and are asked to judge the strength of the conclusion (C), the more typical P is of C, the stronger the perceived strength of the conclusion. For example, people would most often rate example 1 as being a stronger argument than example 2:

Robins have a higher concentration of potassium in their blood than humans.
$$\overline{\text{All birds have a higher concentration of potassium in their blood than humans.}} \quad (1)$$

$$\frac{\text{Penguins have a higher concentration of potassium in their blood than humans.}}{\text{All birds have a higher concentration of potassium in their blood than humans.}} \quad (2)$$

The second phenomenon is that the more similar the premise categories (P1 - Pn) are to the conclusion category, the more they tend to confirm the conclusion. For example, people would most often rate example 3 as being a stronger argument than example 4:

$$\frac{\begin{array}{l}\text{Robins use serotonin as a neurotransmitter.}\\ \text{Bluejays use serotonin as a neurotransmitter.}\end{array}}{\text{Sparrows use serotonin as a neurotransmitter.}} \quad (3)$$

$$\frac{\begin{array}{l}\text{Robins use serotonin as a neurotransmitter.}\\ \text{Bluejays use serotonin as a neurotransmitter.}\end{array}}{\text{Geese use serotonin as a neurotransmitter.}} \quad (4)$$

Category-based induction thus goes beyond similarity-to-prototype effects (either prestored or on-line), and, instead, considers categorization an integral part of a more general framework of induction. However, this work has not gone unchallenged. Sloman (1998) found that people do not apply the category-inclusion principle consistently when they evaluate categorical arguments (e.g., all electronic equipment has parts made of germanium; therefore all stereos have parts made of germanium) even when they endorse the relevant categorical relation (e.g., stereos are electronic equipment).

In addition, the concepts field has shifted toward focusing on more abstract concepts. The emphasis in the literature, so far, has been on object concepts (Komatsu, 1992; Ross & Spalding, 1994). However, there are many examples of concepts that are more abstract and represent, for example, social and emotional categories (e.g., E. R. Smith & Zarate, 1992). Examining how people represent and categorize social and emotional events may lead to more nearly complete theories of categorization.

The field has also been moving toward asking questions about domain specificity versus domain generality: Do children start out by having domain-specific concepts and then generalize their specific knowledge to other domains, or do they develop general theories and then constrain their assumptions as a result of acquiring domain-specific knowledge (Medin & Heit, 1994)? A related question is whether people have domain-specific causal theories or generalized causal structures (Waldmann et al., 1995). An even more fruitful question may be this: Under what circumstances does knowledge that supports concept acquisition appear to be domain specific and under what circumstances does it tend to be more domain general?

In a related line of research, cognitive psychologists have begun to ask a question that has been traditionally studied in the field of anthropology: To what degree is categorization affected by environmental structure, and to what degree does it occur as a result of constructive processes in people's minds (Malt, 1995; Medin, Lynch, Colely, & Atran, 1997; Walker, 1992)? There has been little intersection, so far, between the kinds of studies that psychologists and anthropologists have conducted to investigate this question. As both Malt and Walker pointed out, however, cognitive psychologists may gain valuable information by carrying out cross-cultural studies because such methods (1) can be helpful in distinguishing between cultural-specific and universal aspects of categorization, (2) are especially appropriate for studying natural kinds, and (3) can be useful for examining the effects of different levels of abstraction on category formation. The anthropological studies that have been completed thus far have shown that conceptions of essences and similarity may not be consistent across ethnic, cultural, and religious lines (Walker, 1992).

Concepts are central to the way we reason about and understand ourselves and our environment. There is an infinite number of ways we can parse the world into concepts. What is special about our categorization schemes? Why do we create the dividing lines we impose on instances in the world? The answers most likely lie in a synthesis of similarity and explanation.

◆ SUMMARY

A concept allows for cognitive economy, that is, it enables us to use one word to denote a whole class, to avoid the impossible task of placing a label on every new entity we encounter.

The first theory of categorization to emerge in the modern psychological literature was the classical view. This view is based on the Aristotelian notion that every object is composed of defining features that are individually necessary and jointly sufficient.

The advantage of the classical view is also its biggest limitation. It provides a single representation for describing an entire category of objects but can therefore apply only to a narrow set of concepts. Criticisms of the classical view are that (a) it assumes that objects fall into distinct and well-defined categories, whereas group membership is often "fuzzy"; (b) it may be useful for classifying well-defined objects, such as a "square," but it is often impossible to specify a set of features that are singly necessary and jointly sufficient for classifying most natural kinds, such as a "tiger"; (c) it makes false predictions, such as that an instance belonging to a subordinate category (robin) will always be judged as being more similar to the basic-level category (bird) than to the superordinate category (animal); and, most important, (4) it cannot explain typicality effects.

An alternative to the classical view was first presented in terms of similarity-based accounts of categorization, which encompass the probabilistic and exemplar views. These views suggest that instances of a category are represented mentally by the degree to which they are similar to (have overlapping attributes with) either an abstract representation of the category or other known instances of the category.

The probabilistic view holds that features are neither necessary nor sufficient for categorization, but are made up of objects that have characteristic features in common. An object is judged to be a category member if it shares some proportion of the typical features of other category members. The probabilistic view's fundamental assumption is that concepts are organized by a family resemblance (Wittgenstein, 1953), such that a concept contains a set of instances, each of which has at least one overlapping attribute with one or more of the other instances in the set.

One class of probabilistic models, known as prototype theory, argues that people create a representation of a category's central tendency in the form of a prototype. The prototype is the instance that embodies the most characteristic attributes with members of its own category (e.g., robin). In this framework, categorization results from a comparison between the similarity of a new instance and a prototype. Similarity, in turn, is a function of the number, salience, and psychological "weight" (perceived importance) of features that the object and prototype have in common. We have demonstrated this conception of similarity by using the contrast model.

There are several advantages to the probabilistic view: First, in contrast to the classical view, it explains typicality effects in categorization judgments. Second, because the probabilistic view allows for probable, rather than defining properties, it can apply to a larger set of concepts, including both natural kinds and artifacts, than can the classical view.

The probabilistic view, however, has been criticized on several grounds: (a) People make use of correlated features (or the lack thereof) at the expense of highly typical features; (b) the probabilistic view does not seem to take context into account; and (c) the probabilistic view cannot explain clearly how a single concept that is a poor instance of two categories can be a good instance of the combined categories (e.g., "pet fish").

Criticisms of the probabilistic view led to the development of the exemplar view. The exemplar view contends that objects are classified by comparison to specific exemplars that are stored in memory. It suggests that people use the most similar exemplar or exemplars in their knowledge base to determine the category membership of a novel object. In contrast to the probabilistic view, it does not constrain an instance of a category to share at least one attribute with one or more members of the same category.

The exemplar view can account for typicality effects because it suggests that when a person categorizes a new object, he or she will draw on all past exemplars of a category weighted by similarity to the new object. However, it, too, has shortcomings: (a) it has difficulty explaining why people seem to have knowledge about prototypes of categories, even when they are not presented directly with examples of these prototypes; (b) it has a hard time explaining why people provide higher confidence ratings in response to prototypes versus prior instances during classification, but give higher confidence ratings in response to prior instances versus prototypes during recognition; (c) it lacks representational economy.

A major challenge to the similarity-based view comes from the explanation-based view. The explanation-based view argues that instances of a concept are related by an explanatory structure. Strong evidence for this idea comes from the observed dissociation between classification and similarity judgments. A subset of explanation-based models are theory-based accounts. These theories' main tenet is that explanatory structures are derived from global theories, such as naive biological theories.

We reviewed different variants of explanation-based theories, which include psychological essentialism, idealized cognitive models, causal models, and the two-tier approach. These theories differ from each other but embrace the shared viewpoint that people's categorizations are sensitive to context, prior knowledge, theory, and function.

Which should we believe in: explanation- or similarity-based views? Perhaps, as is most often the case, the truth lies somewhere in between. Explanation-based views are based on rules that are more precise and better able to deal with well-defined situations, whereas similarity-based approaches are more flexible and can handle more ill-defined concepts. In sum, similarity and rules may function together to support knowledge representation and concept acquisition.

4 Knowledge Representation and Acquisition

◆ Meaning-Based Knowledge Representations
◆ The Representation of Semantic Knowledge With Schemas, Frames, and Scripts
◆ Rule-Based Versus Instance-Based Theories: The Controversy Over Representation
◆ Summary

> If the human mind were simple enough to understand, we'd be too simple to understand it.
>
> —EMERSON PUGH

Every day we absorb an enormous amount of information from the environment. How does our brain organize this information into coherent representations? This question lies at the foundation of human cognition: It is a fundamental question about the architecture of the mind.

Researchers have made a distinction between **perception-based representations** and **meaning-based representations**. The former preserve the original perceptual qualities of our experiences, whereas the latter maintain the semantics of an event but often discard many of its surface-structural details. Meaning-based representations tend to be retained longer in memory than do perception-based representations. This is a descriptive answer to the fundamental question we raised: Knowledge representations strip off peripheral details and preserve the essence of our experiences.

How do we retain meaning? Meaning-based representations can be divided into two kinds: (1) **propositional structures**, which preserve specific information about an event (e.g., what kind of food you ate today for breakfast), when propositions are the smallest units of knowledge about which one can make true or false judgments, and (2) *schemas,* which are general knowledge structures that aid in comprehending information (e.g., what sequence of steps one should go through while ordering food in a restaurant).

Schemas are fairly high-level constructs. How do they capture the meanings of experiences and events? The main issue is whether knowledge is represented by a system of rules or is encoded in specific instances of events. Central to rule-based models of knowledge representation is the proposal that people store information via abstract rules that have general applicability, such as *production rules,* consisting of an *if* clause followed by a *then* clause.

We use J. R. Anderson's (1983, 1993) ACT-R model as a prime example of this approach. In contrast, instance-based theories are able to exhibit rulelike behavior by incorporating a set of exemplars or instances. Our focus is on a class of **instance-based models**, known as neural networks, that are inspired by neural processing in the brain. If you are looking for an answer to the fundamental question of mind, you will not find it here. What we hope you find are ways to explore this question from a variety of empirical, computational, and neuropsychological perspectives.

How does our brain make sense of the immense amount of data that we encounter in our environment daily? In other words, how do we organize and represent knowledge? In this chapter, we tackle the fundamental question of the architecture of the mind. Before we introduce theories and experimental approaches to the study of knowledge representation, we invite you to read the following passage and to try to decide what it describes (from Bransford & Johnson, 1972, p. 722):

> The procedure is actually quite simple. First you arrange things into different groups. Of course, one pile may be sufficient depending on how much there is to do. If you have to go somewhere else, due to lack of facilities, that is the next step, otherwise you are pretty well set. It is important not to overdo things. That is, it is better to do too few things at once than too many. In the short run this may not seem important but complications can easily arise. A mistake can be expensive as well. At first the whole procedure will seem complicated. Soon, however, it will become just another facet of life. It is difficult to foresee any end to the necessity for this task in the immediate future, but then one never can tell. After the procedure is completed one arranges the materials into different groups again. They can be put into their appropriate places. Eventually they will be used once more and the whole cycle will then have to be repeated. However, that is part of life.

What is this passage about? If we told you that it was about washing clothes, would you be convinced? With this subject matter in mind, the passage may make more sense. Bransford and Johnson discovered that people could remember twice as many details about the passage when they were cued about its subject matter with an appropriate title than if the passage was given to them untitled. Although all the participants were given the same information, those who were also provided with knowledge about the meaning of the passage remembered more, indicating that as they read, they mentally represented the information in a different way than did those who did not have access to the meaning of the passage. In sum, these results suggest that people may use cues to activate knowledge structures that, in turn, help them to organize new information more sensibly and therefore to make it more easily committed to memory.

Traditionally, researchers have distinguished between perception-based and meaning-based representations. *Perception-based representations* preserve the original perceptual experiences fairly well, whereas *meaning-based representations* extract the semantics of an event but often discard many of the surface-structural or perceptual details (e.g., J. R. Anderson, 1995). How are different representations retained in memory over time?

Meaning-based representations tend to be retained longer in memory than are perception-based representations. Although we initially encode perceptual details of both verbal and visual stimuli, we tend to forget many of these details quickly. This phenomenon may be illustrated by memory for spatial orientation. For example, Gernsbacher (1985) showed participants pictures of various scenes (e.g., a boy opening a present) and then gave them pairs of pictures, in which one picture in each pair was the mirror image of the other. The participants' task was to recognize correctly which picture they had seen previously. The participants were 79% accurate at a 10-second delay between studying the pictures and the test, demonstrating a fairly high level of retention for the picture's orientation. However, their accuracy dropped to almost chance performance (57% correct identification) after a 10-minute delay.

Another demonstration can be found in the verbal domain. In J. R. Anderson's (1974b) study, the participants were instructed to listen to a narrative that contained sentences, such as "The missionary shot the painter." During the test phase, they were given new sentences that involved either a stylistic change (e.g., "The painter was shot by the missionary") or a meaning change (e.g., "The painter shot the missionary"). Participants were asked to determine which sentence they had heard previously, either immediately after hearing the test narrative or after a two-minute delay. When the test sentence had been changed stylistically, participants were 99% correct when there was no delay, but were only 56% correct after the short delay. In contrast, the delay condition had little impact on the participants' accuracy in recognizing the original sentence when the meaning of the test sentence had been changed (98% accuracy in the immediate condition and 96% accuracy with the delay). In sum, our memory for perceptually driven details seems to fade at a relatively more rapid pace than does our memory for meaning. What, then, enables the nature of meaning-based representations to be retained over a long period?

MEANING-BASED KNOWLEDGE REPRESENTATIONS

Meaning-based representations can be divided into two kinds: *propositional structures*, which preserve specific information about an event, and *schemas*, which are knowledge structures that aid in understanding information and result in a general and more abstracted description of a typical event. We now turn to a more detailed description of these two theories of knowledge representations. We also discuss some recent alternative proposals for representing knowledge, embodied by a class of computational models known as *neural networks,* in which events and concepts are linked by weighted connections whose association strengths can increase with experience.

Propositional Representations

Propositional-representation theories (J. R. Anderson & Bower, 1973; H. H. Clark, 1974; Frederiksen, 1975; Kintsch, 1974; Norman & Rumelhart, 1975) assert that knowledge representations comprise **propositions**, which are the smallest units of knowledge about which one can make true or false judgments. For example, consider the following sentence:

> Marilyn Monroe, a famous Hollywood actress during the wholesome 1950s, became a legend.

The information in this sentence can be broken down into the following simple sentences:

> Marilyn Monroe was a famous Hollywood actress during the 1950s.
> The 1950s were wholesome.
> Marilyn Monroe became a legend.

TABLE 4.1 Kintsch's System for Representing Propositions

Proposition	Notation
Marilyn Monroe was a famous Hollywood actress during the 50s.	(actress, Marilyn Monroe, Hollywood, 50s)
The 50s were wholesome.	(wholesome, 50s)
Marilyn Monroe became a legend.	(became, Marilyn Monroe, legend)

Each sentence corresponds to a proposition that contains a unit of meaning. If any of these simple sentences is false, then the larger, complex proposition must also be false.

J. R. Anderson (1974b) showed that people do not remember the exact wording of such simple sentences (for example, the participants tended to confuse a sentence like "Lincoln freed the slaves" with one like "The slaves were freed by Lincoln"), but preserve the meaning of the more atomic assertions.

Kintsch (1974) developed a convenient formal notational system to represent these propositions in which each proposition is represented as a list containing a **relation** and a set of **arguments** (marked by parentheses). The relation usually corresponds to a verb (*became*), adjective (*wholesome*), and another relational term (*Marilyn Monroe, 1950s, legend*) that helps form connections between the arguments. The arguments usually correspond to nouns, such as times, places, and people (see Table 4.1). Note that a set of propositions can be formed into sentences that share the same building blocks and have the same meaning but that have slightly different stylistic forms, such as "During the wholesome 1950s, Marilyn Monroe, a famous Hollywood actress, became a legend."

Bransford and Franks (1971) provided empirical evidence for the idea that propositions have psychological validity and are not merely convenient formal notations. In their study, the participants were asked to learn sentences, such as the following:

The ants ate the sweet jelly which was on the table.
The rock rolled down the mountain and crushed the tiny hut.
The ants in the kitchen ate the jelly.
The rock rolled down the mountain and crushed the hut at the edge of the woods.
The ants in the kitchen ate the jelly which was on the table.
The tiny hut was at the edge of the woods.
The jelly was sweet.

These sentences were created from two sets of four propositions (see Table 4.2).

Bransford and Franks examined recognition memory for old (e.g., "The ants in the kitchen ate the jelly"), new (e.g., "The ants ate the sweet jelly"), and "noncase" sentences that were created from studied words from both sets 1 and 2 in Table 4.2 (e.g., "The ants ate the jelly at the edge of the woods"). The results indicated that the participants had difficulty distin-

TABLE 4.2 The Two Sets of Propositions

Set 1	Set 2
(eat, ants, jelly, past) (sweet, jelly) (on, jelly, table, past) (in, ants, kitchen, past)	(roll-down, rock, mountain, past) (crush, rock, hut, past) (at the edge, hut, woods, past) (tiny, hut)

guishing between old and new sentences, but determined that they were not given the non-case sentences during study. In sum, the participants were more inclined to judge a test sentence as old when there was a greater degree of overlap between the original propositions and the given test sentence.

Furthermore, the participants often "recognized" sentences they were not given during study (false alarms) if these sentences contained familiar propositions. This result was especially true if the test sentences were composed of all four propositions (e.g., "The ants in the kitchen ate the sweet jelly which was on the table"). Thus, the participants seem to have represented propositional information contained in the sentences they were given without retaining the sentences' specific surface-structural information.

Propositional Networks

One way to represent propositions is by constructing a list of propositions, as we just discussed. Another approach is to create a network representation that shows the connections within and among propositions (J. R. Anderson, 1995). In a **propositional network**, each proposition is represented by a circle, connected by labeled arrows to the relation and argument terms. The propositions, relations, and arguments are referred to as the **nodes**, and the arrows are called the **links**. There are many spatial ways to create such networks, but the important part is to preserve the elements and their relations. For example, the sentence, "Marilyn Monroe, a famous Hollywood actress during the wholesome 1950s, became a legend" can be represented as in Figure 4.1.

The nodes in propositional networks can be thought of as ideas and the links between the nodes as associations between these ideas (J. R. Anderson, 1995). A study that supports this view was conducted by Weisberg (1969). Weisberg asked the participants to try to memorize sentences such as "Children who are slow eat bread that is cold." This sentence can be represented as in Figure 4.2 by combining its three propositions. After the participants were presented with the sentence, they were given a word from the sentence and asked to respond with the first word from the sentence that came to mind. Those who were presented with the tar-

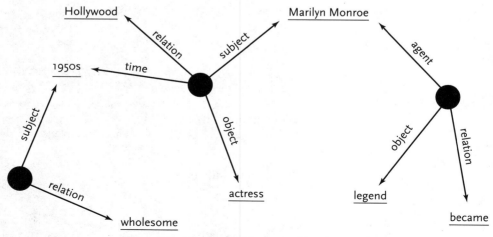

Figure 4.1 An example of a propositional network.

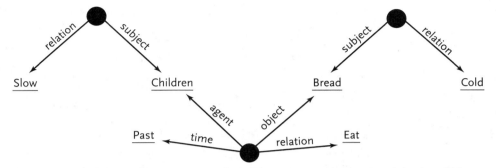

Figure 4.2 A propositional network of "Children who are slow eat bread that is cold."

get word *slow* almost always responded with *children* and rarely with *bread*. Even though *bread* is physically closer to *slow* in the actual sentence than it is to *children*, it traverses fewer nodes to *children* in the network representation.

More evidence for the existence of propositional representations was provided by Ratcliff and McKoon (1978). In their study, people were instructed to examine a series of sentences, such as "The driver bruised a hip and the passenger strained a knee." The propositional network for this sentence can be represented as in Figure 4.3.

After reading a set of such sentences, the participants were given a list of words, presented one at a time, and were asked to determine which ones they had previously encountered. The analysis consisted of measuring the participants' reaction times to particular words (e.g., *passenger*) that followed certain other words in the list (e.g., *hip* or *knee*). Reaction times were then compared to the distance between the two words in the propositional network. The participants' response times agreed with the network representation of the propositional structure of the sentences, reflecting shorter response times for words that had shorter distances in the network from the previously presented word (*passenger*, *knee*) and longer response times for words that had longer distances in the network from the previously presented word (*passenger*, *hip*).

Ratcliff and McKoon's study provides evidence for **associative priming**. If sentences are represented within propositional networks, then a target word should be processed faster when it is primed by a word in the same proposition (short distance) than when it is primed by a word in a different proposition (longer distance).

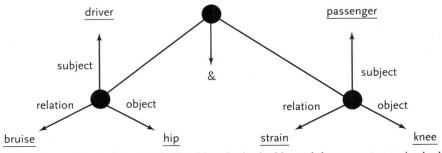

Figure 4.3 A propositional network of "The driver bruised a hip, and the passenger strained a knee."

In sum, propositions and propositional networks are powerful in that they extract the meaning of a sentence or set of sentences while letting go of more peripheral information, such as surface-structural style. Although propositions can represent information well and priming effects have provided some empirical corroboration for their validity, propositional representations lack intrinsic constraints. In other words, there is an unspecified number of ways to represent a given sentence in the form of a propositional network. In a given experiment, if people's reaction-time data do not match the propositional model constructed a priori by the experimenter, it would be unclear whether the propositions simply needed to be represented in a different way or if the general model was inaccurate. That is, given a set of human data, at least one propositional network model can be applied to them post hoc. Therefore, propositional models are, to a large degree, unfalsfiable, which makes it difficult to assess their validity.

Semantic Networks

Whereas propositional networks represent specific sentences or instances, **semantic networks** organize general knowledge into categories of information. Semantic networks are structured similarly to propositional networks in that they consist of nodes (concepts) and links (associations) and the concepts separated by the fewest links are predicted to be the most strongly associated with each other. An early semantic network was proposed by Quillian (1966) and A. M. Collins and Quillian (1969, 1972), who argued that people store information about categories in a network structure of the form shown in Figure 4.4.

This semantic network suggests that people represent a hierarchy of categories (e.g., a fish has fins or a tuna is a fish) by connecting the nodes for the two categories. In this hierarchy, low-level categories inherit the attributes of high-level categories (e.g., animals eat, therefore fish eat, therefore tuna eat). There is room for exceptions in this model, however, that are stored at the subordinate level (e.g., the Mexican hairless dog). According to Quillian and Collins, to determine the truth of a statement, such as "A tuna is a fish," the information contained in a semantic network is accessed by using a parallel search that begins from the node in question (tuna) and fans out in all directions until it intersects with the node that is to

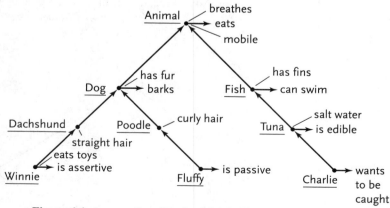

Figure 4.4 A semantic network of the Collins and Quillian model.

be confirmed (fish). According to the predictions of this model, people should be fastest at recognizing the validity of a statement when it is separated by the fewest number of links. The example sentence "A tuna is a fish" (one link) should elicit a faster response than "A tuna is an animal" (two links). To test this model, A. M. Collins and Quillian (1969) measured the reaction time of a group of participants who were asked to assess the truth of similar simple sentences. Their findings were in line with the structure of the model (e.g., the participants responded more quickly to the sentence "A canary can fly" than to the sentence "A canary has skin"). However, later studies have cast doubt on how hierarchical these representations actually are.

Take a moment to decide if the following sentences are true or false:

1. A dog is a mammal.
2. A dog is an animal.

According to Collins and Quillian's model, you should have been able to decide more quickly that a "dog is a mammal" than that "a dog is an animal" because mammals are subordinate to the category animal and would intersect earlier with the node dog. However, Rips et al. (1973) demonstrated that sentence 2 is actually verified faster.

Why does the hierarchical structure not hold in this case? One possibility is that the associations that we make more frequently (e.g., a dog is more often associated with being an animal than with being a mammal) are stronger and are more quickly verified. Collins and Quillian's model can accommodate such frequency or typicality effects by hypothesizing that commonly encountered facts become stored with a concept at some intermediate level. This modification to the model implies that in most cases, lower-level categories inherit properties from higher-level ones, with some exceptions.

However, the hierarchical model has difficulty accommodating other findings. Notably, the model does not make accurate predictions regarding people's response times to false statements. For instance, people are faster to disagree that "A bat is a plant" than that "A bat is a bird." According to Collins and Quillian's model, it should take an equivalent amount of time to respond to both statements because links from the node bat to all its associated superordinate nodes would be explored. Then, only when the top of the hierarchy is reached, without confirmation, can the sentence be rejected as false. In reality, the similarities between bats and birds may cause people's response times to slow down, a phenomenon known as the **relatedness effect** (Medin & Ross, 1992).

A different model that has been more successful in accounting for effects such as frequency and relatedness was proposed by A. M. Collins and Loftus (1975). In their model, related concepts are once again connected by associative links, but instead of being connected by a rigid hierarchical structure, concepts are connected by direct links of various lengths. The shorter the link between two concepts, the stronger the association, and the faster the two concepts are judged to be related to each other.

In this framework, frequently associated concepts, such as dog and animal, are joined by shorter links than are less frequently encountered associations like dog and mammal. The model operates on the basis of **spreading activation**, such that presenting a concept (e.g., red) will first activate strongly linked concepts (e.g., fire), followed by slightly weaker associations (e.g., roses). Activation continues to spread to the more distal links, including associates of associates (e.g., fire engine and flowers). As activation spreads out, it also becomes more diffuse and weak, but still allows for the possibility that many different associations will be triggered.

An alternative representation for meaningful knowledge is captured by schemas, frames, and scripts, which are mental mechanisms that help organize incoming information in a summary form. We discuss these constructs in depth next.

THE REPRESENTATION OF SEMANTIC KNOWLEDGE WITH SCHEMAS, FRAMES, AND SCRIPTS

Schemas are useful mental structures that aid in organizing incoming information from the environment in a meaningful way and thereby help to represent the essential qualities of an object or an event (Bartlett, 1932; Piaget, 1965; Rumelhart & Ortony, 1977; Schank & Abelson, 1977). The concept of a schema as a representative general knowledge structure was first introduced by Bartlett (1932). Bartlett was interested in what kinds of things people remember about a given event and how their past knowledge influences the kind of information people retain in memory. Toward this end, he presented the participants (who were his friends and students) with several short folktales and legends and then asked them to reproduce these stories from memory. He used the method of *serial reproduction*, in which the same material is repeatedly reproduced orally by one participant and passed on to another participant at a series of fixed time intervals. In some cases, he would test people's retention at intervals as great as 10 years from the original study session. By having participants reproduce the stories over a long period, Bartlett was able to analyze what kinds of information were remembered, what kinds were forgotten, and what kinds were altered. An interesting finding was that people reconstructed the stories with details that were never present in the original tale but that were congruent with their own experiences.

For instance, in one of Bartlett's stories, the "War of the Ghosts," two Native American men are hunting seals by the river when they are approached by some canoes. Most participants "remembered" that the men were busy fishing and referred to the canoes as "boats." To people of British culture, in particular, an activity that involves obtaining food, a sailing vessel, and a body of water also involves fishing. Bartlett proposed that specific details of an instance are mapped onto a general schema at the time of encoding and then become impossible to separate from memory at the time of retrieval.

Most contemporary views of schemas have built on Bartlett's work. For example, Rumelhart and Ortony (1977) conceived of schemas as structures that incorporate typical facts about a category or an event in a flexible way that allows for some variation, can encompass other schemas (e.g., a schema for good food may include a schema for French cuisine), and may have different levels of abstraction (e.g., a schema for happiness is more abstract than is a schema for squares).

In artificial intelligence, schemas have been used as a basis for creating computer models that simulate how knowledge is represented and used. Minsky (1975) developed a theory of knowledge representation by way of schemas. In this view, a schema can be thought of as a **frame** that contains several *slots* to hold specific information about the situation. The slots specify the general categories that hold true for every instance of the schema; for example, in a schema for going to a party, there would be slots for the host, the occasion, the type of party, and the size of the party. To use the schema to understand a situation, the slots are filled in with the particular values for that instance. For example, the host could be your mother, the occasion could be a birthday, the type of party could be a family gathering, and the size could be large. It is important to remember that the schema itself is general and does not contain any specific values. Those values must be mapped onto the schema at the time it is activated.

Consider the following sentences (from Schank & Abelson, 1977, p. 39):

> John went to Bill's birthday party.
> Bill opened his presents.
> John ate the cake and left.

Although these are only three short sentences, you can infer a great deal more from them than what they explicitly state. For example, we automatically understand that John brought Bill a present, there was at least one other guest at the party, and that the cake was a birthday cake. These appear to be rather mundane conclusions, but none of that information is stated directly in the passage. Schank and Abelson proposed that people's ability to make such inferential leaps with ease is due to the existence of special kinds of schemas called **scripts.** Scripts provide a template for the ordered sequences of events that characterize certain everyday situations, such as going to a restaurant, grocery store, or doctor's office. Scripts differ from schemas and frames in that they are applicable only to a limited number of stereotyped situations and are structured as an ordered series of causally linked events. The highly structured causal nature of scripts allows people to make predictions from partial information, as well as to understand the reasons for deviations from the normal script routines. For example, the script for going to a restaurant typically includes entering a restaurant, being seated, ordering food, eating food, paying, and leaving. However, if you entered a restaurant and were seated, but then had to leave unexpectedly before you had a chance to order, it is understood automatically that you did not eat or pay because those actions are causally dependent on having ordered a food item.

Bower, Black, and Turner (1979) provided empirical evidence for the use of scripts. They had participants generate important events in a stereotyped script, such as going to the doctor or eating at a restaurant. Even though there was some variability in the descriptions that the participants generated, there were strong commonalties. Almost all the participants (73%) agreed that first you are asked to be seated; then you look at the menu, order the meal, eat the food, and pay your bill; and then you leave. Almost half (48%) agreed on actions, such as entering, ordering drinks, discussing the menu with others, ordering dessert, and leaving a tip.

Bower et al. (1979) gave the participants stories that incorporated some of these common events. They then asked the participants either to recall the stories from memory (in one experiment) or to judge whether particular statements had appeared in the stories (in another experiment). The participants tended to recall events that were consistent with the story's script but had not been present in the stories themselves. For example, when given a story about someone's visit to the doctor, many participants later recalled that the main character had to lie down on the examination table, although that fact was never mentioned in the story.

This last issue shows that schemas and scripts can lead to the reconstruction of false memories. Further corroboration for this idea is illustrated in R. C. Anderson and Pichert's (1977, p. 310) study, in which the participants were asked to read the following story, from the perspective of either a burglar or a prospective home buyer.

◆ **The House Passage**

The two boys ran until they came to the driveway. "See, I told you today was good for skipping school," said Mark. "Mom is never home on Thursday," he added. Tall hedges hid the house from the road so the pair strolled across the finely landscaped yard. "I never knew your place was so big," said Pete. "Yeah, but it's nicer now than it used to be since Dad had the new stone siding put on and added the fireplace."

There were front and back doors and a side door which led to the garage which was empty except for three parked 10-speed bikes. They went in the side door, Mark explaining that it was always open in case his younger sisters got home earlier than their mother.

Pete wanted to see the house so Mark started with the living room. It, like the rest of the downstairs, was newly painted. Mark turned on the stereo, the noise of which worried Pete. "Don't worry, the nearest house is a quarter of a mile away," Mark shouted. Pete felt more comfortable observing that no houses could be seen in any direction beyond the huge yard.

The dining room, with all the china, silver and cut glass, was no place to play so the boys moved into the kitchen where they made sandwiches. Mark said they wouldn't go to the basement because it had been damp and musty ever since the new plumbing had been installed.

"This is where my Dad keeps his famous paintings and his coin collection," Mark said as they peered into the den. Mark bragged that he could get spending money whenever he needed it since he'd discovered that his Dad kept a lot in the desk drawer.

There were three upstairs bedrooms. Mark showed Pete his mother's closet which was filled with furs and the locked box which held her jewels. His sisters' room was uninteresting except for the color TV which Mark carried to his room. Mark bragged that the bathroom in the hall was his since one had been added to his sisters' room for their use. The big highlight in his room, though, was a leak in the ceiling where the old roof had finally rotted.

After being assigned the perspective of either the burglar or the prospective home buyer, the participants read the story and then were asked to remember as many details about it as possible. The majority (64%) of the information that the participants recalled was germane to their perspective (e.g., those who were thinking like burglars were more likely to remember the coin collection than the leaky roof). In a subsequent part of the experiment, the participants were asked to think of the story again, only this time, from the opposite point of view, and to see whether they could remember any additional details. They were able to remember 10% more details from the story when they were asked to switch from one perspective to another. Most of those details were relevant to the new perspective they had assumed. For example, when the participants were asked to think like burglars, their schemas for robbery may have been activated, facilitating the process of accessing information related to stealing valuables. When they switched perspectives, their home-buying schemas may have been triggered, resulting in an ability to retrieve "forgotten" details related to purchasing a home.

This study suggests that remembering is a process of reconstructing an experience or event using information contained in one's schemas. Thus, schemas may guide our expectations about the nature of events. These findings, taken together with those of Bower et al. (1979) and Bartlett (1932), show that people not only remember selectively but may construct false memories. This issue has strong implications for the legal system, which relies heavily on the accuracy of eye witnesses' testimony, for example (Loftus, 1997; Schacter, 1995).

In sum, schemas seem useful for understanding new events or objects in comparison to a typical description in memory. The main controversy that surrounds the representation of schemas is whether they are made up of abstract rules or whether they are composed of exemplars or instances. We compare the exemplar- versus instance-based perspectives in detail next.

RULE-BASED VERSUS INSTANCE-BASED THEORIES: THE CONTROVERSY OVER REPRESENTATION

Rule-based theories suggest that people abstract general attributes from exemplars and then store them in some summary form, such as schemas. In contrast, instance-based theories suggest that people encode specific instances or exemplars and perform "on-line" computations on these instances, such as judging whether a new instance belongs to a particular category by determining how many features it shares with other known exemplars of that category (see chapter 3 for more details on the exemplar-based view). Here, we exemplify the rule- versus instance-based approaches by discussing knowledge representation models that are founded on their contrasting architectures: production systems and neural networks, respectively.

Rule-Based Theories of Knowledge Representation

Central to rule-based models of knowledge representation is the idea that people store information in abstract rules that have general applicability. One type of rule is a **production rule**, consisting of an *if* clause followed by a *then* clause (Newell & Simon, 1972). The *if* clause specifies the condition or conditions that must be met for the action specified in the *then* clause to be executed or "fired." These rules are also known as condition-action rules.

A large number of production rules form a **production system**. In this system, production rules are structured around a set of goals and subgoals, in which one goal is always active. To satisfy the goals, the condition of a production rule responds to information stored in working memory. In this framework, **working memory** refers to the knowledge that the production system is attending to at a given point in time (J. R. Anderson, 1993).

Production systems share the following important features: (1) they engage in a process of **pattern matching**, in which the system determines if a production's conditions match the contents of a rule stored in memory; (2) when more than one production rule provides a match, the system performs a process of **conflict resolution**, deciding on which production rules to perform on the basis of different criteria, such as the success with which the rule has performed in the past; and (3) the matched production rule gets executed or **fired**. The sequence of matching production rules, performing conflict resolution, and then executing a production is termed a **cycle**.

To illustrate how production systems work, consider, for example, the following system for performing multicolumn addition (J. R. Anderson, 1993, p. 5), which contains five production rules (denoted in CAPS) (where c1, d1, d2, and d3 are variables that can assume different values).

The first production rule, NEXT-COLUMN, attends to the rightmost unprocessed column, resulting in processing the ones column as the first step in solving a multicolumn addition problem. NEXT-COLUMN then activates a subgoal in working memory, namely, to write an answer in the first column (c1). In response to this subgoal, PROCESS-COLUMN becomes activated because an element in its condition ("the goal is to write an answer in c1") matches the current subgoal. PROCESS-COLUMN retrieves the digits in that column (d1 and d2) and then matches the sum of these digits (d3). It then creates a subgoal of writing the sum of these digits (d3) in the answer column. This subgoal becomes activated in working memory. If the

NEXT-COLUMN
IF   the goal is to solve an addition problem
            and c1 is the rightmost column without an answer digit
THEN set a subgoal to write out an answer in c1

PROCESS-COLUMN
IF   the goal is to write out an answer in c1
            and d1 and d2 are the digits in that column
            and d3 is the sum of d1 and d2
THEN set a subgoal to write out d3 in c1

WRITE-ANSWER-CARRY
IF   the goal is to write out d1 in c1
            and there is an unprocessed carry in c1
            and d2 is the number after d1
THEN change the goal to write out d2
            and mark the carry as processed

WRITE-ANSWER-LESS-THAN-TEN
IF   the goal is to write out d1 in c1
            and there is no unprocessed carry in c1
            and d1 is less than 10
THEN write out d1
            and the goal is satisfied

WRITE-ANSWER-GREATER-THAN-NINE
IF   the goal is to write out d1 in c1
            and there is no unprocessed carry in c1
            and d1 is 10 or greater
            and d2 is the ones digit of d1
THEN write out d2
            and note a carry in the next column
            and the goal is satisfied

Figure 4.5 Anderson's production rules for multicolumn addition.

sum of the digits is greater than 9, WRITE-ANSWER-GREATER-THAN-NINE will become activated; otherwise, WRITE-ANSWER-LESS-THAN-TEN will be activated.

In sum, the critical features of a production system are that (1) each production rule is a modular piece of knowledge that is an independent unit, (2) cognitive processes are carried out by setting goals and activating information in working memory, and (3) production rules are abstract and therefore can generalize to different situations. For example, the rules in the production system for multicolumn addition are not specific to particular digits. This kind of generality results from using variables in the production-system formalism.

The ACT Model and Its Variants

ACT theory (adaptive control of thought) and its more recent formulations, ACT* and **ACT-R** (J. R. Anderson, 1983, 1990, 1993), suggest that cognitive skills are realized by production rules organized into production systems. It divides knowledge into two kinds: declarative and procedural. Procedural knowledge is represented in the form of a production system (such as the one for multicolumn addition described above) whereas declarative knowledge is represented in the form of propositional networks. Both **declarative memory** and **procedural memory** write to and read from elements in working memory. For example, when one starts doing a multicolumn addition problem, one activates the goal of "solve an addition problem" in working memory. The condition of the NEXT-COLUMN production in procedural memory matches that goal, which then fires the subgoal: "Write an answer in the first column" and writes it in working memory. This subgoal then activates PROCESS-COLUMN, which, in turn, retrieves numbers and number facts (adding two digits) from declarative memory (see Figure 4.6).

The early instantiation of declarative knowledge in the ACT model comprised propositions only, but subsequent models were expanded to include networks of spatial configurations and images, as well as temporal information about the sequencing of actions. These declarative networks contain mechanisms for retrieving and storing information. Concepts are stored at nodes within the network that are either active or inactive at a particular time. A node can be activated directly by stimuli in the external environment, such as through receiving input through the sensory system, or by internal stimuli, such as memories. A node also can be activated indirectly through stimulation from other nodes in a semantic network, resulting in a process of spreading activation (see, e.g., A. M. Collins & Loftus, 1975). As more nodes become activated, the spread of activation weakens as a result of traveling a greater distance from the original source of activation. Specific links become stronger with repeated activation

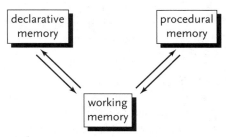

Figure 4.6 Anderson's ACT model.

over time, such that with frequent use, declarative knowledge is learned and maintained through the strengthening of particular connections. For example, if you work as a bank teller and someone tells you that she is going to the bank, you are much more likely to think that she means a savings bank than a river bank. The association between the ambiguous word *bank* and "a place that deals with money" is typically repeated many times and thus becomes much stronger than the less frequent association between *bank* and "a strip of land alongside a river."

The acquisition of procedural knowledge is suggested to occur in three separate stages (J. R. Anderson, 1980): (1) during the **cognitive stage**, people engage in learning explicit rules for implementing a specific procedure (e.g., learning how to type); (2) during the **associative stage**, people practice using these explicit rules, which results in strengthening the procedures that are instantiated by these rules (e.g., becoming more familiar with which fingers to use for typing certain letters); and (3) during the **autonomous stage**, people learn to use the rules automatically, improving in speed and accuracy (e.g., typing becomes automatic in a way that does not require thinking about what actions to do, looking down at the keyboard, and so forth).

The ACT-R Theory: Are Production Rules Psychologically Real?

Are production rules psychologically real? J. R. Anderson (1993) claimed that they are. At an informal level, he argued that production rules are intuitively appealing (e.g., the productions involved in a task like addition seem reasonable and correspond to people's intuitions about their experiences). His more formal argumentation is based on attempts to pit the performance of the model against human data and then show that the model fits the data well.

A study along these lines involved creating an ACT-R model of navigation (J. R. Anderson, 1993). Participants were presented on a computer screen with maps that included a road system, a starting point, a destination point, and a number of intermediate locations. They were able to "drive," "walk," or use a combination of the two to reach their destination, which could not be reached by a direct route. The number of steps required to reach the destination and the total distance from start to finish were highly correlated between human problem solvers and the computer algorithms ($r = .94$ and $.83$, respectively). These results, as well as those from similar studies (e.g., J. R. Anderson, 1976, 1983, 1993; Kintsch, 1988; Newell & Simon, 1972), show that the ACT-R model may be successful at modeling human cognition.

However, Anderson and his colleagues also have found consistent differences between human and computer performance. For example, in the navigation study, when the participants were presented with "backup" maps that included a route that led near, but not directly to, the destination, ACT-R reached the destination in fewer moves and in shorter distances. The participants, on the other hand, tended to overemphasize the importance of reducing the difference between their current position and their final destination without considering the possibility that going a little out of their way initially might lead them to a more direct route to the destination eventually. This approach is known as *difference reduction* (see also chapter 7 for a discussion of *means-ends analysis*). In sum, ACT-R failed to incorporate an important aspect of human problem solving: the tendency to use a straightforward difference-reduction strategy, even when it is not optimal.

In addition, ACT-R does not provide a mechanism for generating a complete theory of cognitive errors (J. R. Anderson, 1990). ACT-R models errors of omission (when people forget to carry out a problem-solving step) by preventing a production rule from being executed. However, it cannot accommodate more complex errors that stem from overgeneralization from examples (see e.g., Ben-Zeev, 1995, 1996; Tatsuoka & Baillie, 1982; VanLehn, 1986, 1988, 1990). (The nature and origin of problem-solving errors are discussed in detail in chapter 7 on problem solving.)

Another, more general, source of difficulty, which is not limited to ACT-R, is that it is often hard to ascertain the validity of computer models by comparing their performance to human data because even though a model can predict people's problem-solving steps at the algorithm level, it may not capture the cognitive architecture at the implementation level. The **algorithm level** involves the rules that are actually firing, whereas the **implementation level** is a lower level of processing that specifies exactly when a particular rule will fire and with what speed. In other words, although computer models may correctly predict a person's problem-solving steps, they may arrive at these steps by using different processes from those the person uses. In the ACT* and ACT-R models, computations at the implementation level are carried out by brainlike neural processes in which rules compete via inhibitory processes, memory processes are executed in parallel (e.g., the matching of production rules is done in parallel, rather than serially), and declarative memory structures vary in their level of activation and availability. The implementation level, in turn, is used to support operations that are more symbolic and abstract at the algorithm level.

Behaviors at the algorithm level are relatively easy to identify and match with human behavior (e.g., examine when people choose to carry a 10 in the multicolumn addition algorithm). However, it is much harder to ascertain what the processes at the implementation level are. There may be more than one model consistent with the data at the implementation level, giving rise to what J. R. Anderson calls the **discovery problem**, which refers to the process of trying to find an implementation that is consistent with present and future data.

In ACT-R, J. R. Anderson (1990) tried to solve the discovery problem by appealing to a rational analysis. In general terms, a **rational analysis** is an attempt to understand a particular facet of human behavior on the basis of the idea that it has been optimized to fit the structure of the environment over time (see also J. R. Anderson, 1991; Marr, 1982). This conception is useful because it allows researchers to make inferences about the human cognitive architecture by studying the structure of the environment. Once a formal model of the environment has been developed, it becomes possible to identify the constraints on the kinds of mental mechanisms that could be operating in the performance of a given algorithm. The number of potential implementations that could fit a set of data is greatly reduced by this technique, but obviously cannot be distilled into just one implementation. Thus, there is always some uncertainty about the chosen implementation. It is therefore important to use **converging operations**, or multiple studies with different methodologies, that together can show stronger support for a particular theory.

Instance-Based Models

In contrast to ACT-R and other rule-based models, instance-based models do not operate on the basis of explicit rules. Instead, they are able to exhibit rulelike behavior by being exposed to a series of examples. Our focus in this chapter is on a class of instance-based models known as neural networks.

What Is a Neural Network?

The term **neural network** describes a class of computational models that are inspired by neural processing in the brain. Much of the neurophysiological detail is ignored in computational neural networks in favor of constructing models that capture the essence of neural interactions and behavior.

Before we describe neural models formally, it may be helpful to provide some background about the ways in which information is processed by the nervous system. **Neurons** send signals by emitting chemical transmitters. The signal propagated by one neuron is accepted by other neurons that are connected to the signaling neuron. Receptor sites on the receiving neurons are located in treelike structures called **dendrites**. Dendrites pass information to the cell body, or **soma**, which accumulates and integrates input signals. All neurons have an electrical charge when at rest. Incoming neural transmitters change the **electric potential** of the receptor neuron. If a neuron's electrical potential is raised above a specific **threshold**, the neuron sends an **action potential** (in the form of a **firing** pulse) down its **axon**—a long transmission line—to **synapses**, which are gaps connecting axons to other dendrites or cell bodies of other neurons. Synapses vary in how strongly they are connected to other neurons. Variations in synaptic strength therefore affect the amount of influence that one neuron has on its neighbors. **Synaptic transmission** involves the propagation of particular neural transmitters from a *presynaptic* neuronal junction to a *postsynaptic* junction. Signals are sent from one neuron to another by the propagation of action potentials. Given the large number of neurons in the brain (approximately 10^{14}), the flow of information in a biological neural network can best be described as a pattern of firing that reflects the strength of the synaptic connections among neurons.

In comparison to biological networks, a computational neural network contains a number of simple processing units (called **nodes**) that are linked by **connections** or **weights**. A node corresponds approximately to a neuron's cell body. The weights carry information about the strength of connections between nodes. An abstract representation of a model neuron is shown in Figure 4.7. In this simplified model, a processing unit receives input from other units by multiplying each input by its connecting weight. All of the inputs are summed together, and

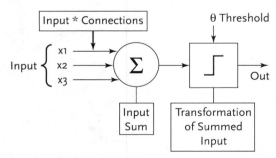

Figure 4.7 The basic processing unit in an artificial neural network. Processing occurs in two stages. The first stage consists of input accumulation. Each input is multiplied by its connection into the unit. All of the inputs are then summed together. In the second stage, this summed input is transformed by an activation function that outputs in the final activity value of the unit. The activation function can take many different forms, as discussed in the text.

the result of the summation passed on to a transformation (or **activation function**). The activation function determines the final response of a node to a particular pattern of input.

It is important to remember that neural network models of the type used in modeling psychological processes are inspired by neural structures in the brain, but no attempt is generally made to model biological function accurately. Instead, it is the basic approach to computation that drives interest in neural network research. As a consequence, neural networks of cognitive behaviors are frequently termed **connectionist networks** to distinguish them from detailed biological models. In a connectionist network, information flows into one unit from all of the units that are connected to it. The term *information* here simply means some positive or negative real number that represents the output of a connecting unit (see Figure 4.7).

To illustrate some of the computational properties of connectionist networks, let us examine a case in which a network is constructed to behave like a binary threshold device (see Figure 4.7). In this type of network, each unit has a fixed threshold value. If the sum of the unit's total input equals or exceeds this threshold, the unit emits a 1. If the summed input into the unit does not reach the threshold value, then the unit emits a 0. This can be mathematically expressed by the following equation (see Figure 4.8).

$$output = \begin{cases} 1 \text{ if } \sum_{i=1}^{n} connection_i \cdot input_i \geq \text{threshold} \\ 0 \text{ otherwise} \end{cases}$$

Binary threshold devices can model certain first-order logical functions, such as *and* and *or*. For an **and function** to be true, both conditions have to be met, whereas for an **or function** to be true, either one of the conditions must be true, or both can be true, but it is not necessary. Consider the following sentence, which illustrates the *or* function:

If it is raining or if I have to walk to work, then I will wear sturdy shoes.

In this case, if either of the stated conditions are met, then the outcome in the predicate (wearing sturdy shoes) will result. Clearly, if it is both raining and I have to work, the result is the same: I will wear sturdy shoes. In the case of the *and* function, both the conditions have to be met for the statement to be true, as in this example:

If the weather is nice and my hayfever is not bothering me, then I will go camping.

Here, it is obvious that simply meeting one of the stated conditions is not enough to allow the statement "I will go camping" to be true. If either one of the conditions is not met, then the predicate of the sentence is false. Figure 4.8 illustrates a threshold unit that can realize the logical function *and*, given binary {1 = true, 0 = false} inputs and the truth table (see Table 4.3).

Connectionist networks have certain characteristics that distinguish them from other processing models. For example, they do not explicitly encode symbolic or propositional knowledge. Instead they represent knowledge as a pattern of unit activities at a particular point in time. The concept of an activity pattern representing a knowledge state implies that knowledge is stored across the entire network, rather than in one particular node. Knowledge in a connectionist system is therefore referred to as being **distributed** across the network. For a

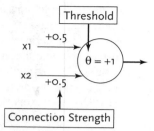

Figure 4.8 A simple network that provides the result of the *and* function as output. This connectionist network unit takes either a **1** or a **0** as input and provides the result of the *and* function as output. Notice that if the threshold is lowered to +0.5, the behavior of the unit is changed such that it now computes the *or* function.

network to represent distributed knowledge, information must flow through the entire network at all times, not in a step-by-step fashion. This is a second important characteristic of connectionist networks: **parallelism**. The combination of parallel processing with distributed representations led early researchers to refer to connectionist models as **parallel distributed processing** models (Rumelhart & McClelland, 1986).

Although the qualities of distributed representations and parallel processing are fundamental to connectionist networks, perhaps their most intriguing quality is that networks can develop their knowledge over time. In other words, part of the makeup of a connectionist network is that it learns knowledge representations from experience. Learning involves adjusting the connections (or weights) between units in proportion to a learning parameter. Over time, weight adjustments enable the network to produce a desired output (given a particular input). There are generally two phases of network learning—a training phase and a testing phase. Training involves computing the difference between the desired output of the network and its actual output; this difference produces an **error** term. The goal of the training phase is to reduce the average error (the error term computed for all input-output pairs) over time to some low number, typically close to zero. The testing phase consists of presenting the network with both new and old examples of inputs and recording (without adjusting connections) the network's output. If the average error of the testing set of inputs is close to zero, a network can be said to have "learned" a solution to a modeling problem.

What are the implications of this style of learning for theories of knowledge representation? One implication of learning in connectionist networks is that the system as a whole (i.e.,

TABLE 4.3 A Logical Truth-Table for the *And* and *Or* Functions

Input 1	Input 2	*And* (1 *and* 2)	*Or* (1 *or* 2)	XOR (1 *or* 2) but not (1 *and* 2)
0	0	0	0	0
0	1	0	1	1
1	0	0	1	1
1	1	1	1	0

Note: In this table, 1 stands for true and 0 stands for false. This version of the *or* function is sometimes referred to as the "inclusive-or-function" because it includes the *and* truth-conditional. The last function—XOR—is discussed in the text.

the network weights) must evolve in response to local problems (i.e., specific input-output pairs). A second, closely related, implication was stated earlier, namely, that networks can produce rulelike, or patternistic, behavior without explicitly encoding rules or propositions. In the next two sections we look at two basic architectures for connectionist models and discuss both their advantages and limitations.

Architecture of Connectionist Networks: Linear Networks

In general, connectionist networks are composed of separate layers of units. Each layer in a network represents a group of units that handle information in a particular way. In the binary threshold networks mentioned earlier, input units are directly connected to output units. A network with direct connections between input and output is called a **single-layer network** (that is, there is a single layer of connecting weights in the network). It learns to associate a particular pattern of input (e.g., [1 0]) with a particular output (e.g., [1]). There are several different methods by which this type of associative system can learn. Most of these procedures involve presenting a pattern to the network, producing an output, and then comparing the output with a target output, computing an *error* signal, and then adjusting the connections between units to reduce the error by an amount specified by a learning parameter.[1]

It is possible to show that binary threshold units can learn to compute any function that is *linearly separable*. The term *linear separability* means that given, for example, a unit square, two distinct clusters of points can be separated by a single line. To clarify the idea of linear separability, imagine a unit square in which each vertex is labeled according to its X and Y coordinates. This is a two-dimensional system (pairs of {x, y} coordinates can delineate any point in the square). In two dimensions, a line can be drawn such that it will divide the vertices of the square into two separate classes. If a function can be specified this way, it is known as a **linearly separable function**. Illustrations of how logical *and* and *or* functions are linearly separable is shown in Figure 4.9.

Although binary threshold networks are successful at linear classification, there are classes of functions that these networks cannot solve (Minsky & Papert, 1969). An example of the type of function that is not computable by a linear classifier is the **XOR** (exclusive *or*) function (either A or B, but not both). The XOR function means that for the sentence to be true, either one but *not both* of the conditions must be met. If both or neither of the conditions are met, then the statement is false. To look at this function in a concrete way, imagine that you are told the following:

Either John or Bill left the party.

---

[1]There is an extremely fundamental and important method of pattern association that does not involve explicit error correction. This technique—Hebbian Learning—is based on correlational learning. If two units in a Hebbian network are "on" at the same time, their connections are strengthened, but if either or both units are "off" no changes in connection strength are made. Hebbian learning has an important biological basis; however, the most common connectionist networks use some form of error correction. For this reason, we do not consider Hebbian networks here. The interested reader should refer to J. A. Anderson (1995) and J. R. Anderson (1993).

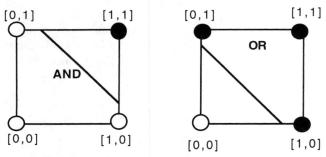

Figure 4.9 An illustration of how *and* and *or* can be represented as linear discriminant functions. The black circles represent the **True** values for each function, while the white circles represent the **False** values. Notice that for each function a straight line can divide the true and false conditions from each other. Any straight line that separates the two conditionals is considered to be a linear discriminant. This implies that there are many acceptable solutions to the problems that could be learned by a network.

You would gather from this sentence that either John or Bill, but not both, left the party. If both left or neither one left, you would understand the statement to be false. Because the function is true when one, but not both or neither, of the conditions is satisfied, the XOR function is not linearly separable, and thus cannot be modeled by a binary threshold network. The XOR function is shown geometrically in Figure 4.10. Since it is not possible to find a single line that can be drawn to separate the true from the false values of the function, it is a non-linearly separable function. A severe restriction on linear networks, then, is that they can compute only a limited range of functions. Given the limits of the networks we have discussed so far, is there a network architecture that could learn to solve a problem like the XOR function? One possibility is to build a network that has an intermediate layer of units that both receive information from network inputs and send information to network outputs. We now have a network that connects inputs to outputs, inputs to intermediate units, and intermediate units to output units (see Figure 4.11).

We illustrate how to solve the XOR problem by using the previous example: "Either John or Bill left the party," but not both. We start with two input nodes, one representing "John left the party" and the other representing "Bill left the party." Each node produces a value of 1

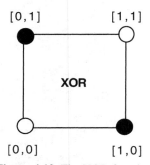

Figure 4.10 The XOR function.

when it is true (T) and a value of 0 when it is false (F). We also have an output node that has a threshold activation of 0.5. When the summed activation from the input nodes exceeds the threshold level, the output node returns a value of T, whereas when the summed activation from the input nodes is below the threshold level, the output node returns a value of F. A simple input-to-output connection, with no intermediate nodes, will work well for situations when either input node is true (e.g., Bill left the party or John left the party). In this case, one node will produce a 1, and the other will produce a 0, which together would sum to a 1 in the output unit (exceeding the 0.5 threshold), causing the network to output a T. This simple network will also work in the case when neither input node is true (both nodes produce 0, which sum to a 0 in the output node, causing the network to return an F).

However, this simple model fails when both nodes are true. In this case, each node will produce a 1, which would exceed the threshold of the output node. This activation forces the model to return a T even though it should return an F (because if both Bill and John left the party, then the XOR is false). What would happen if we set the weights of both input nodes to 0? In this situation, when both inputs are true (or false), the system will return a false value, as it should. However, now it would not work when one input node is true and the other is false. In fact, it is impossible to solve the XOR problem without introducing an additional layer of nodes.

To solve the XOR problem, therefore, we add one layer (see Figure 4.11). In the new network, both input nodes send activation to both the output node and an intermediate or hidden node (that has a threshold activation level of 1.5), which, in turn, projects to the output layer node (which, as before, has a threshold activation level of 0.5). The weights from the input nodes to the hidden node remain at 1, whereas the weight of the intermediate node is set to −2. Thus, the "trick" is that the hidden node connects to the output node with a weight that is equal in magnitude but opposite in sign to the sum of the two input nodes. Now, when the two input nodes are true, they sum to a value of 2 (each produces a 1), but they also exceed the activation of the hidden unit, which, in turn, outputs a value of a −2, resulting in a summation of 0 at the output unit. This activation causes the network to return an F, as it should. Does this model work for all other cases? When one input node is true and the other is false, then the true node produces a 1, the false node produces a 0, the summation fails to activate the hidden unit, so that the final summation at the level of the output unit is 1, resulting in the value T. This pattern of results is exactly the one we expected on the basis of the truth table for XOR.

In sum, for a problem, such as XOR, the thresholds and connection strengths do not need to be learned; they can be determined by analytical techniques. The network shown in Figure 4.11 demonstrates that the inclusion of intermediate units allows a network to learn a more complex function than would be possible for a simple linear associator that has only input-output connections.

For more complicated (and larger) problems than XOR, an analytical solution for setting network weights and thresholds may not be possible. In the linear networks discussed earlier, there is a proof that states that for any linearly discriminable function—a problem that can be solved by a network without intermediate units—there is a learning rule that guarantees that the network will arrive at a correct solution. This proof, known as the **perceptron convergence theorem** (Rosenblatt, 1959), is important to neural network theory. However, until the 1980s, no such equivalent proof existed for networks that contained intermediate units. As a

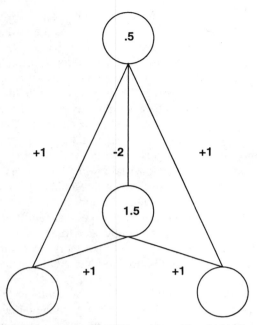

Figure 4.11 A simple network that solves the XOR problem. Thresholds for each unit are inside the circles. Connection strengths are marked next to the lines drawn between units (after Rumelhart & McClelland, 1986). The presence of an intermediate unit makes it possible for the network to solve a non-linearly discriminable function.

consequence, there was no guarantee that a multilayered network that had to arrive at a solution from training examples would necessarily do so.

One of the seminal advances in neural network research came with the development of mulitlayered network architectures that could learn complex nonlinearly separable problems. It was with the advent of such networks that some of the unique possibilities for knowledge representation began to emerge. We consider this type of network in the next section.

Architecture of Connectionist Networks: Multilayered Perceptrons

In the XOR network shown in Figure 4.11, input units were connected to output units, as well as to the intermediate unit. In one sense, the role of the intermediate unit in this network is to provide information over and above what is available from just the input-output connections themselves. Let us consider an alternative network architecture to accomplish the same task. The goal of this network is also to learn the XOR function, but now we would like the network to develop its own representation of the problem without any direct links between the input and the output of the network. This type of network is illustrated in Figure 4.12.

This two-layered network shows what has become the most common type of neural network architecture—known as a **backpropagation network** (Rumelhart & McClelland, 1986). Backpropagation networks have at least two layers of weights, which means that there are

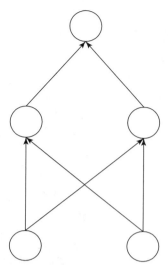

Figure 4.12 A backpropagation network architecture.

weights that connect input to intermediate units (from here on, we call these units **hidden units**) and weights that connect hidden units to output units. Input and output layers are fairly self-explanatory. The **input layer** presents a signal that is presumably derived from an external source. The **output layer** displays the time-dependent explicit "behavior" of the network. The behavior of the hidden layer (or layers) is somewhat more complicated. Units in a hidden layer take weighted input from the input layer, transform it, and pass a weighted version of that transformation on to the output layer. Transformation functions can vary from a linear response (the output is equal to the sum of the input) to the threshold functions discussed earlier. In most backpropagation networks, the transfer function is usually a nonlinear S-shaped function, which tends to squash either very small or very large responses and behaves like a linear function for medium responses. This type of transformation function, known as a **sigmoid** function—formally, a logistic function—is useful because it limits the output range of a network (see Figure 4.13).

From a computational point of view, the development of backpropagation learning rules represents an algorithmic solution to learning for networks that contain hidden units. Networks with hidden units are important because they develop representations that encode **microinferences** (Hinton, 1989) of input-output pairs. In other words, hidden units learn to represent the knowledge of relationships between inputs and outputs, rather than directly encode stimulus-response patterns.

To illustrate how the presence of hidden units helps a network to represent problems, let us look at another network that solves what is known as the **encoding problem**. In this problem, the network is presented with an input pattern, and its job is to output the exact same pattern (known as an *autoassociative problem*). We are interested in a specific feature of how a backpropagation network arrives at a representational solution to this problem. In particular, we want to see how hidden units can compress input-output relationships to arrive at a more compact representation of the problem.

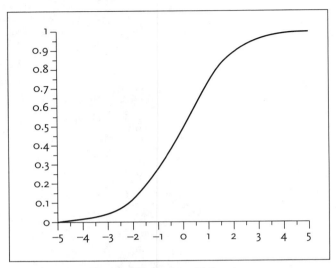

Figure 4.13 A sigmoid function.

In the example we are using, the input and output patterns are arrays of four numbers, with one of the array units assigned a 1 and the rest of the units are assigned a 0 (e.g., [1 0 0 0]). The hidden layer, by contrast, contains only two units. To arrive at a solution, the network must learn to represent four-dimensional number strings in two dimensions. The network architecture is illustrated in Figure 4.14 (note that this is a 4 × 2 × 4 encoder network. Only one set of connections is shown).

Figure 4.15 is a graphic illustration of one network's final state after learning. Each square in the graph represents a connection between two units. The top of the graph shows the connections between input and hidden units, and the bottom area shows the connection between hidden and output units. Black squares represent negative (or inhibitory) connections; white squares represent positive (or excitatory) connections. The size of each square is scaled to show the relative strength of connection between two units (note that the *bias* units are

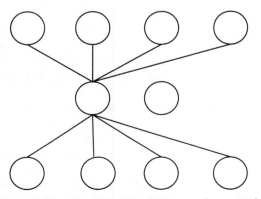

Figure 4.14 A simplified 4 × 2 × 4 encoder network.

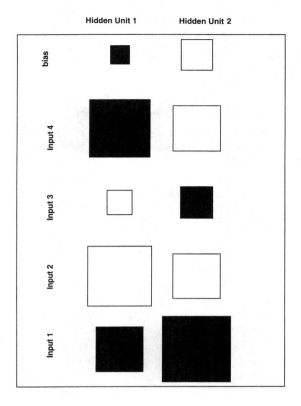

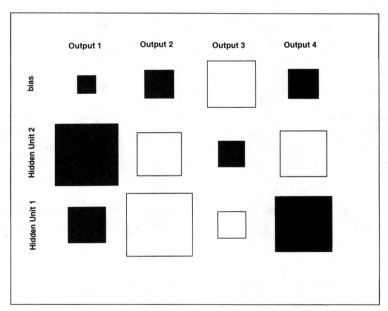

Figure 4.15 An illustration of a network's weights after learning.

additional nodes that have a constant input of 1. They are essentially an alternative way of representing thresholds).

What can we say about how this network has learned to represent the encoding problem? Two important aspects of the network's performance stand out. First, it is clear that the information coded in the weights is distributed. This ability of networks to distribute their knowledge makes them fault tolerant. In other words, the network should be able to respond reasonably well in degraded situations, including the presentation of partial input (i.e., incomplete input patterns) or the loss of a specific connection. Because the information for any input-output pair is represented by multiple connections, the network should be able to complete patterns and give the appropriate output in most cases.

The second important point is that for this type of learning to be successful, the network has to be able to recognize patterns present in the input; that is, it is learning by computing input statistics. If the input to a network does not contain the appropriate information (i.e., does not capture the essential properties of the problem being modeled), then the network cannot successfully learn. Thus, it is critical that the input and output representations capture the relevant aspects of a problem to allow the network to represent a solution successfully. The previous sentence notwithstanding, it is possible for networks to arrive at final representations that capture information that is not explicitly represented during training.

Hinton (1989) reported the performance of a network that was to learn relationships among extended family members. Two family trees were constructed. The network was at two sets of inputs. The first input layer simply denoted a family member (by marking a 1 in a string of zeros). The second input layer denoted a relationship (e.g. "is the son of . . .") in a similar fashion. The output layer denoted the person in the family tree for whom the relationship held. The network had a fully connected and distributed hidden layer. It was trained by random presentation of specific family members. What was interesting about the final outcome of the network was that although the model was trained only on specific instances, it made generalizations that captured elements of the family tree's hierarchical structure; that is, it distinguished one generation from another. In addition, one set of connections completely separated the two family trees from one another. Although this network was constructed for demonstration purposes, it showed that networks can generalize over instances to capture some of the global higher-order structure that is present in the input.

We have only touched briefly on some of the basic properties of neural networks and their ability to represent knowledge. There are many representational domains that are just beginning to be explored using a connectionist paradigm. For example, an important aspect of human cognition is the ability to represent an object (or event) as playing a different role in different contexts. Thus, a car could be the focus of a sentence ("That's my car she's driving"), or it could be a feature in a larger environment (e.g., things to see in Los Angeles). It remains a challenge for connectionist models to capture such cognitive flexibility. The extent to which neural networks can solve these problems will determine their success in the future as explanatory devices of cognitive behavior.

RULE-BASED VERSUS INSTANCE-BASED THEORIES: WHO WINS?

The answer to the question of which theory of knowledge representation, rule- or instance-based, has the upper hand, is difficult to ascertain at this time. The main advantage of instance-based models over rule-based models is that they can produce what seems to be rule-governed behavior by learning implicitly. That is, instance-based models are adept at exploiting statistical patterns that exist in the data and therefore provide an alternative to the idea that knowledge representation is symbolic and abstract. However, instance-based models incur difficulties in modeling particular cognitive processes. Consider the case of learning language. All adults become fluent speakers of their native language and can effortlessly understand sentences that they have never heard before. What is striking about these phenomena is that no two adults grow up hearing the same sentences spoken. The paradox of language learning is that people obtain the same level of linguistic understanding even though they have been trained on different sets of instances. For this reason, it has been argued that there must be a system of grammatical rules that all people are genetically born with, which are thought to behave similarly to the kind of production rules we discussed in this chapter (e.g., Fodor & Pylyshn, 1988). In response to this argument, advocates of instance-based theories have contended that it is possible to extract similar patterns from different sets of data (e.g., Elman et al., 1996). For example, different sets of exemplars can give rise to the same prototypes in categorization learning (Posner & Keele, 1967). We hope that the growing research efforts to produce sound and compelling computational models of knowledge representation will be able to provide us with more insights regarding the advantages and disadvantages of rule- versus instance-based approaches in the future.

◆ SUMMARY

To organize the enormous amount of information one takes in from the environment, the brain must somehow retain the essence of events and experiences and rid itself of more superficial details. How is it possible to accomplish such a daunting task?

How does the brain retain meaning over time? In general, meaning-based representations can be divided into two kinds: *propositional structures* that preserve specific information about an event and *schemas* that provide a more general and description of a typical event.

Propositions are the smallest units of knowledge about which one can make true or false judgments. For example, the following sentence, "Marilyn Monroe, a famous Hollywood actress during the wholesome 1950s, became a legend," is made up of the propositions:

> (actress, Marilyn Monroe, Hollywood, 1950s)
> (wholesome, 1950s)
> (became, Marilyn Monroe, legend)

These propositions can be combined into stylistically different sentences that retain the original meaning of the sentence, such as "During the wholesome 1950s, Marilyn Monroe, a famous Hollywood actress, became a legend." Bransford and Franks (1971) showed empirically that participants often "recognized" sentences they were not given during study if the sentences contained familiar propositions.

There has also been empirical support for the use of schemas. For example, Bower et al. (1979) gave participants stories that incorporated common events. They then asked the participants either to recall the stories from memory or to judge whether particular statements had appeared in the stories. Often the participants recalled events that had not been present in the stories themselves, but that were consistent with the kinds of schemas that they held.

The main controversy over the architecture of knowledge representation is between rule-based and instance-based theories. On the one hand, rule-based theories suggest that people abstract general rules from exemplars and then store them in some summarized form, such as schemas. On the other hand, instance-based theories suggest that people encode specific instances or exemplars and perform on-line computations on these instances.

Central to rule-based models of knowledge representation is the idea that people store information in abstract rules. One kind of rule is a *production rule*, consisting of an *if* clause followed by a *then* clause. The *if* clause specifies the condition or conditions that must be met for the action specified in the *then* clause to be executed. A large number of production rules forms a production system, in which rules are structured around a set of goals and subgoals and one goal is always active.

Anderson's (1983, 1990, 1993) ACT theory model and its more recent formulations, ACT* and ACT-R, suggest that cognitive skills are realized by production rules organized into production systems. The model divides knowledge into two kinds: declarative and procedural. Procedural knowledge is represented in the form of a production system, whereas declarative knowledge is represented in the form of propositional networks. Both declarative and procedural memory write to and read from elements in working memory.

In contrast to ACT-R and other rule-based models, instance-based models are able to exhibit rule-like behavior by being trained on a set of exemplars. Our focus in this chapter has been on a class of instance-based computational models, known as neural networks, that are inspired by neural processing in the brain. Neural networks contain a number of imple processing units (called *nodes*) that are linked by connections or weights. The weights carry information about the strength of connections between nodes. Because the connections between nodes are crucial to knowledge representation, neural networks have also become known as connectionist networks.

Neural networks do not explicitly encode symbolic or propositional knowledge. Instead, they represent knowledge as a pattern of unit activities at a particular point in time. The concept of an activity pattern representing a knowledge state implies that knowledge is stored across the entire network, rather than in one particular node. Knowledge in a connectionist system is therefore referred to as being *distributed* across the network. For a network to represent distributed knowledge, information must flow through the entire network at all times, not in a step-by-step fashion. This characteristic of parallel processing is an important feature of neural networks. The combination of parallel processing with distributed representations led early researchers to refer to these models as parallel distributed processing models.

The question of which theory of knowledge representation, rule- or instance based, "wins," is hard to assess at this time. Instance-based theories are better at learning implicitly by exploiting statistical patterns that exist in the environment and thus provide an alternative to the conceptualization that knowledge representation is symbolic and abstract. However, they have difficulty modeling particular cognitive phenomena, such as language acquisition. In the future, we hope that research on computational modeling will provide more insights into the advantages and disadvantages of rule- versus instance-based approaches.

5   Deductive Reasoning

"Then you should say what you mean," the March Hare went on.
"I do," Alice hastily replied; "at least I mean what I say, that's the same thing, you know."
"Not the same thing a bit!" said the Hatter. "Why, you might just as well say that 'I see what I eat' is the same thing as 'I eat what I see!' "

—Lewis Carroll, *Alice in Wonderland*

If we are told that all planets revolve around the sun, can we then conclude that all objects that revolve around the sun are planets? The answer is no (a counterexample would be a moon or a meteorite). We can be 100% confident in this answer, not only because we can think of a counterexample, but because we have available to us the rules of *deductive reasoning* that allow us to reason with certainty whether a conclusion follows from a statement or a set of statements that are assumed to be true.

We make a distinction between two types of deductive reasoning: syllogistic and conditional. Syllogistic reasoning involves evaluating or generating statements with exactly two premises followed by a conclusion, such as this: All A are B (premise 1) and all C are A (premise 2); therefore, all C are B (conclusion). The study of syllogisms has historical roots in the Aristotelian conception of logic. Conditional reasoning involves making inferences from statements that have an *if-then* form, such as "If Charley eats a seven-course meal, then Charley is full." We examine conditional reasoning with respect to an (in)famous task that has generated much research and controversy: the Wason selection task.

We make a distinction (following Rips, 1994) between rule-based and ruleless accounts of deductive reasoning. **Rule-based theories** suggest that people generate a variety of mistakes but may nevertheless have a "mental logic" that requires a special logical structure, abstract specifications of rules, and discrete inferential steps that derive a conclusion from a delimited set of premises. **Ruleless theories**, on the other hand, argue that people have not evolved special structures for deductive reasoning, but that reasoning is linked more directly to a person's available experience and the context in which the reasoning takes place.

Finally, we discuss cross-cultural research on the effects of everyday experience on deductive reasoning and question whether people think deductively in the real world.

In *Alice in Wonderland*, Alice is berated by the March Hare for being evasive: "Then you should say what you mean." Alice, in a defensive retort, answers that she does: "at least I mean what I say, that's the same thing, you know." In her response, Alice commits a logical fallacy, much to the March Hare's delight, who reprimands her some more: "Not the same thing a bit! . . . Why, you might just as well say that 'I see what I eat' is the same thing as 'I eat what I see!' Like people in the real world, Alice had difficulty with **deductive reasoning**. Formally, deductive reasoning involves making inferences about arguments that consist of a set of sentences called **premises** and a **conclusion**. A **deductively correct argument** is one in which the conclusion is true in any state of affairs in which the premises are true (Rips, 1994). Consider the following example, which contains two premises and a conclusion, separated by a dividing line:

$$
\frac{\text{If Charley eats a seven-course meal, then Charley is full.}}{\text{Charley eats a seven-course meal}} \tag{1}
$$
$$
\text{Charley is full.}
$$

This inference is an example of **modus ponens**, in which given the two premises: "if p then q" and "p," one can correctly deduce that "q" is true:

$$
\frac{\text{If p then q.}}{\text{p.}} \tag{2}
$$
$$
\text{q}
$$

Note that a deductively valid inference may or may not correspond to real-life knowledge. For example, even though the following deduction seems nonsensical, it is still logically valid:

$$
\frac{\text{If the cat has a hat, then pigs can fly.}}{\text{The cat has a hat.}} \tag{3}
$$
$$
\text{Pigs can fly.}
$$

In an experimental setting, a researcher typically provides participants with an argument and then (1) asks them whether the conclusion is true; (2) gives them a set of conclusions and asks them to choose the valid one; or (3) asks them to generate their own conclusion, given a set of premises.

A robust finding is that people uniformly find modus ponens arguments to be valid. Rips (1990, 1994) contended that this finding provides support for the idea that deduction may be a natural schema for people to reason by, a form of a **mental proof**. To illustrate this point, Rips (1994) argued that people cannot help but reason by modus ponens and cannot accept that there may be sentient creatures who would endorse an equally simple but contrary inference, such as "modus shmonens":

> If Charley eats a seven-course meal, then Charley is full.
> $$\underline{\text{Charley eats a seven-course meal.}} \qquad (4)$$
> Charley is not full.

Another example that shows that people have strong deductive intuitions is the knights-and-knaves problem. Knights and knaves look alike but are distinguished by whether they tell the truth or lie. Knights always tell the truth and knaves always lie. Consider the following problem adapted from Smullyan (1978, p. 22):

> Suppose there are three people: A, B, and C, each of whom is either a knight or a knave. Two people are of the same type if they are both knights or they are both knaves.
> A says: "B is a knave."
> B says: "A and C are of the same type."
> What type is C?

Rips (1989a) asked participants to solve this problem out loud and later analyzed their problem-solving protocols. He found that most participants were systematic: They started out by assuming that A is a knight and concluded that because B is lying, C must be of a different type than A, making C a knave. They then turned to examine the second possibility that A is a knave, concluding that this time B must be a knight who is telling the truth, and because A and C are of the same type, they must both be knaves. This line of thinking leads to the correct conclusion that C must be a knave. The problems that the participants encountered in correctly executing this task were due mainly to working-memory overload—they often forgot parts of their previous answers and had to backtrack and reconstruct these parts. These studies show that people are capable of representing the information in a deductive problem, transforming it into a sequence of steps, and using the transformed information for answering the problem at hand.

However, does people's ability to reason systematically entail an internal mental logic; a special structure for reasoning deductively? Rips and others (Braine, Reiser, & Rumain, 1984; Osherson, 1975) supported the view that people have evolved an internal rule-based logic system. In contrast, Johnson-Laird (1997) suggested that people's reasoning relies on *mental models* (Johnson-Laird & Byrne, 1991, 1993) that contain semantic information based on a person's linguistic and general knowledge. These models allow people to rely on and use available instances instead of formal rules. We devote a considerable part of this chapter to this debate between rule-based and contextually driven ruleless theories of deductive reasoning. Before we do so, however, we introduce two major types of deductive reasoning, **syllogistic** and **conditional**, and examine the kinds of systematic errors that people tend to make in using them.

SYLLOGISTIC REASONING

All men are mortal
Socrates was mortal
All men are Socrates
—WOODY ALLEN

Almost all the early studies on deduction were centered on syllogisms, arguments with exactly two *premises* (a major and a minor one), followed by a *conclusion*. **Linear syllogisms**, which have been used primarily in intelligence tests, involve a comparison among terms, where each term shows either more or less of a given quantity or quality. For example, consider the following linear syllogism (Sternberg, 1996b):

$$\text{You are smarter than your best friend (major premise).}$$
$$\underline{\text{Your best friend is smarter than your roommate (minor premise).}} \quad (5)$$
$$\text{——— is the smartest (conclusion: fill in the blank).}$$

One can deduce with certainty that the answer is: "you!"

The more widely investigated kind of syllogisms are **categorical syllogisms**, which have the following abstract (6) or concrete (7) form:

$$\text{All A are B.}$$
$$\underline{\text{All C are A.}} \quad (6)$$
$$\text{All C are B.}$$

$$\text{"All men are mortal}$$
$$\underline{\text{Socrates is a man}} \quad (7)$$
$$\text{Socrates is mortal"}$$

Because categorical syllogisms have been the main focus of work in deductive reasoning, we use the term **syllogism** from now on as an abbreviation for *categorical syllogism*. As can be seen in the foregoing example, a syllogism contains three terms (A, B, C) and their possible relations. The **middle term** (A), which is used once in each premise, is related to the **predicate term** (C), the second term in the minor premise, and to a **subject term** (B), the first term of the major premise, in the premises, yielding four possible syllogistic figures (see Table 5.1).

The relationship between the terms in a deductive argument is expressed by the quantifiers "all" (the universal quantifier) or "some" (the existential or particular quantifier) and may

TABLE 5.1 The Four Syllogistic Figures

Figure 1	Figure 2	Figure 3	Figure 4
A-B	B-A	A-B	B-A
C-A	C-A	A-C	A-C
C-B	C-B	C-B	C-B

contain negative or positive sentences. The **universal affirmative** consists of statements, such as "All A are B," in which members of the category of the first term (A) are also all members of the category of the second term (B) (e.g., "all women are human beings"). The **particular affirmative** consists of statements like "Some A are B," in which some members of the category of the first term (A) are also members of the category of the second term (B) (e.g., "some women are doctors"). The **universal negative** consists of statements, such as "All A are not B" or "No A are B," in which no members of the category of the first term (A) are members of the category of the second term (B) (e.g., "no women are men"). Finally, the **particular negative** consists of statements like "Some A are not B," in which some members of the category of the first term (A) are not members of the category of the second term (B) (e.g., "some women are not doctors").

Syllogistic arguments may be valid or invalid. Decide whether the following argument is valid or not before you read on:

$$\frac{\begin{array}{l}\text{All A are B.}\\ \text{All C are B.}\end{array}}{\text{All A are C.}} \qquad (8)$$

This argument is invalid because it rests on the belief that two terms that are either a subset of or coincident with a third term (All A are B and All C are B) must also be a subset of or coincident with each other (All A are C). This inference is formally known as the **fallacy of the undistributed middle.** It can be seen easily to be false when you substitute "men" for "A," "women" for "C," and "human beings" for "B":

$$\frac{\begin{array}{l}\text{All men are human beings.}\\ \text{All women are human beings.}\end{array}}{\text{All men are women.}} \qquad (9)$$

Now, judge the validity of the following syllogism (Wilkins, 1928):

$$\frac{\begin{array}{l}\text{No oranges are apples.}\\ \text{No lemons are oranges,}\end{array}}{\text{No apples are lemons.}} \qquad (10)$$

If you decided that this argument was valid (it is not) then, again, you are in good company. Willkins found that 31% of the participants judged this argument to be true.

Early research on syllogistic reasoning sought to ascertain why people made deductive mistakes such as the one just illustrated (e.g., assuming that [8] and [10] are true). A classic explanation was provided by Woodworth and Sells's (1935) **atmosphere hypothesis**, which suggests that people match the quantifier type of the conclusion (whether it is positive or negative, universal or existential) with the quantifier type of either or both of the premises. In both (8) and (10), the conclusion is matched with both premises, universal and positive in (8), and universal and negative in (10). When the quantifiers in the premises are of varied types (all, some, not), the atmosphere hypothesis predicts that a combination of a universal premise and an existential premise produces an existential atmosphere, and a combination of an affirmative premise and a negative premise creates a negative atmosphere. Consider the following:

$$
\begin{array}{l}
\text{All x are y.} \\
\underline{\text{Some z are not x.}} \\
\text{Some z are not y.}
\end{array}
\qquad (11)
$$

Here, because the second premise is existential and negative, it would create the "atmosphere" or predilection toward endorsing an existential and negative conclusion.

Sells (1936) tested the atmosphere hypothesis by giving participants 180 syllogisms in the abstract form, such as this:

$$
\begin{array}{l}
\text{If all z are y} \\
\text{And all x are y} \\
\text{Are all x then z?}
\end{array}
\qquad (12)
$$

The participants had to decide whether the conclusion was definitely true, probably true, false, or indeterminate. As predicted, their ratings of the correctness of the invalid syllogisms could primarily be attributed to the atmosphere hypothesis. Sells and Koob (1937) demonstrated that when people were given premises and asked to generate their own conclusions, erroneous responses could be explained largely by the atmosphere hypothesis.

When the content of the syllogisms is concrete, rather than abstract, people's patterns of errors may be prone to a **belief-bias effect**, or the extent to which there seems to be a relationship between the real-world truth of the premises and that of the conclusion (Janis & Frick, 1943; Lefford, 1946; Morgan, 1945; Morgan & Morton, 1944). This effect suggests that people tend to endorse conclusions that are consistent with their prior beliefs and to reject conclusions that are not. For example, Wilkins (1928) showed that whereas the participants had a tendency to endorse (10) as valid, only 16% accepted the following argument (13) as true:

$$
\begin{array}{l}
\text{No x are y.} \\
\underline{\text{No z are x.}} \\
\text{No y are z.}
\end{array}
\qquad (13)
$$

Note that the atmosphere hypothesis would have predicted the same response for both (10) and (13)! However, there have been many critiques of the belief-bias effect, on the grounds that the work suffered from inadequate methodological controls (e.g., Henle, 1962; Revlin & Leirer, 1978).

A more serious challenge to the atmosphere hypothesis was proposed by Chapman and Chapman's (1959) **conversion hypothesis**. This hypothesis suggests that people convert "all x are y" into "all y are x" and "some x are y" into "some y are x." For example, consider argument (11). If people believe that "all x are y" is equivalent to "all y are x," then if some z are not x, it follows that some z are not y (because x and y constitute either overlapping sets or have a set-subset relation owing to conversion).

To pit the predictions of the atmosphere versus the conversion hypotheses, one needs to find items for which these theories would make differential predictions. For example, decide what would be the correct conclusion for the following syllogism (14):

$$\frac{\text{All y are x.}}{\text{No y are z.}} \tag{14}$$

Chapman and Chapman (1959) found that when people were asked to select the correct conclusion in a multiple-choice format (in contrast to the method of asking people to provide true-false judgments in the original Sells, 1936, article), people tended to choose "No z are x" (conversion) over "Some z are not x" (atmosphere). Begg and Denny (1969), however, conducted a comprehensive analysis of the atmosphere versus conversion theories and found that the former predicted most of the data obtained by Chapman and Chapman (1959) and the earlier study by Sells (1936) (but see Wason and Johnson-Laird, 1972, and Henle, 1962, for attacks on the atmosphere hypothesis).

These early explanations of errors are informative, but they do not constitute theories of syllogistic reasoning. Even if error patterns are more compatible with the predictions of the atmosphere hypothesis, for example, it does not necessarily mean that the mental processes underlying these errors were generated by the atmosphere "formula" (Gilhooly, 1988). In general, these early accounts of errors were more descriptive than explanatory. Attempts to provide theoretical accounts came later (e.g., Erickson, 1974; Guyote & Sternberg, 1981; Johnson-Laird & Bara, 1984; Revlis, 1975), after the rise of information-processing psychology (Rips, 1994).

Erickson (1974) provided a set-theory account of deductive reasoning. He argued that people represent premises as combinations of Euler circles (shown in Figure 5.1 and explained later). Consider the following argument:

$$\frac{\begin{array}{l}\text{All x are y.}\\ \text{Some z are x.}\end{array}}{\text{Some z are y.}} \tag{16}$$

According to Erickson's prediction, a correct representation of the first premise, "all x are y," is done with two different models, one in which the set of x is a subset of y and the other in which the two sets are coincident (see Figure 5.1).

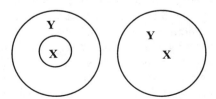

Figure 5.1 A model of "all x are y."

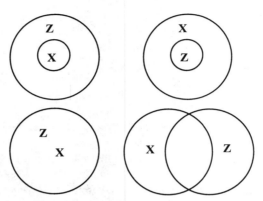

Figure 5.2 A model of "some z are x."

The premise "some z are x" can be represented by four different models (the set of x is a subset of z, the set of z is a subset of x, the two sets are coincident, the two sets overlap) (see Figure 5.2).

To decide whether a conclusion is valid or not, a person has to combine the representations of the syllogism as a whole. There are, of course, many possible combinations that can be generated. If a conclusion is true in all possible combinations, then the conclusion is deemed valid. Erickson found that people tended to generate Euler diagrams that were consistent with the premises and possible valid conclusions of arguments in which both premises were affirmative universals. More specifically, he found that 40% of the responses conformed to the subset interpretation and 60% conformed to the coincident interpretation. However, people had more trouble reasoning with arguments that had particular quantifiers. Erikson's model could explain these inferential errors by positing that people often fail to represent or combine all possible combinations of premises or fail adequately to check a hypothesized conclusion with regard to all the combinations to examine whether it holds. Erikson's model is compelling, but it may not generalize to deductive tasks other than syllogistic reasoning (Rips, 1994).

A different set-theoretic account was offered by Guyote and Sternberg (1981). These researchers distinguished between a **competence model**, which represents the deductions of an ideal reasoner, and a **performance model**, which outlines the constraints on the competence model imposed by the cognitive system, such as working-memory capacity. The first step in the competence model involves a correct encoding and set-theoretic representation of the terms in the premises. The second step involves creating all combinations of possible diagrammatic representations. For example, if the two premises are existential (e.g., "some x are y" and "some z are x"), then there are four different interpretations of the premises, resulting in 16 different combinations (see Figures 5.1 and 5.2). These combinations form "transitive chains" that link the end terms of the syllogism (e.g., the predicate term "y" and the subject term "z") by their relation to the middle term ("x").

The performance model, on the other hand, involves four separate stages. The first is identical to that of the competence model and involves a correct encoding of the premises. The second is a combination stage that is subject to error, such as the inability to form more than four combinations of pairs because of working-memory constraints, in which the choice of pair combination depends on the simplicity or ease of combination. The third stage involves assigning a label for the resulting combinations (positive, negative, universal, particular, or no valid conclusion). Finally, the conclusions that a person is supposed to evaluate are pitted against the assigned labels, resulting in either matches or mismatches. Even though the Guyote and Sternberg model provided a fairly good fit to accuracy and reaction-time data, it has elicited two criticisms: (1) people often do not perfectly encode the premises (e.g., Ceraso & Provitera, 1971) and (2) the model puts what may be an unreasonable limit on the number of combinations that people can make (Johnson-Laird, 1983).

Another criticism that has been launched at diagrammatic accounts of deductive reasoning, in general, has been that they do not explain **figural effects** in syllogistic reasoning. Figural effects occur when people generate conclusions with a particular order of terms (subject-predicate or predicate-subject) in response to the figural form of the syllogism (see Table 5.1) (Johnson-Laird, 1983; Johnson-Laird & Steedman, 1978):

$$\frac{\text{Some of the parents are scientists.}}{\text{All the scientists are drivers.}} \tag{17}$$

Common answer: Some of the parents are drivers
(versus the equivalent: Some of the drivers are parents).

$$\frac{\text{Some of the scientists are parents.}}{\text{All the drivers are scientists.}} \tag{18}$$

Common answer: Some of the drivers are parents
(versus the equivalent: Some of the parents are drivers).

The first argument elicits a subject-predicate response (see syllogistic figure 4 in Table 5.1), whereas the second argument tends to elicit a predicate-subject response (see syllogistic figure 1 in Table 5.1). In sum, the order of the terms in the premises seems to make a psychological difference in how people approach syllogistic reasoning tasks.

As Rips (1994) argued, the psychological explanations of syllogistic reasoning have failed to provide more general accounts of deductive reasoning because they were centered on a small number of syllogistic forms that provided a convenient tool for conducting research. For example, to examine what makes syllogisms easy or hard to solve, an experimenter can manipulate easily the type of quantifiers used, the order of terms in the premises, and the order of the premises themselves. In an attempt to explore generalizations, researchers have gone beyond syllogistic reasoning to include conditional and other forms of reasoning (e.g., C. Clement & Falmagne, 1986; Cummins et al., 1991; Evans, 1977; Marcus & Rips, 1979; Markovits, 1988; Taplin, 1971; Taplin & Staudenmayer, 1973).

CONDITIONAL REASONING

On a conditional reasoning task, a person is given a proposition of the form: *if* p, *then* q, where p is the **antecedent** and q is the **consequent**, and is asked to generate or evaluate a given conclusion. Consider argument (1) presented at the outset of the chapter, now renumbered (19):

If Charley eats a seven-course meal (p), then Charley is full (q).
Charley eats a seven-course meal (p).   (19)
Charley is full (q).

We have already discussed the correct inference of modus ponens (given "if p, then q," and "p," one can correctly deduce "q"). This inference also is called **affirmation of the antecedent**. Another correct inference is **modus tollens**, or *denial of the consequent*:

If p then q.
not q.   (20)
not p.

Modus tollens can be illustrated more concretely by applying it to the rule about Charley:

If Charley eats a seven-course meal (p), then Charley is full (q).
Charley is not full (not-q).   (21)
Charley did not eat a seven-course meal (not-p).

In addition to modus ponens and modus tollens, there are two incorrect or fallacious deductions that one can draw. The first fallacy is the **denial of the antecdent:**

If p then q.
not p.   (22)
not q.

or

If Charley eats a seven-course meal (p), then Charley is full (q).
Charley does not eat a seven-course meal (not p).   (23)
Charley is not full (not q).

The second fallacy is the **affirmation of the consequent:**

If p, then q.
q.   (24)
p.

or

If Charley eats a seven-course meal (p), then Charley is full (q).
Charley is full (q).   (25)
Charley ate a seven-course meal (p).

Note that affirming the consequent and denying the antecedent are deductively correct when a statement is a **biconditional** of the form: "If and only if p, then q." However, unless

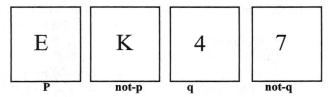

Figure 5.3 The Wason selection task.

an if-and-only-if (Iff) relationship is specified explicitly, even if it is consistent with our real-world knowledge (e.g., If I am over 21 years old, then I can legally drink alcohol), we cannot assume that such a relationship exists in formal logic (e.g., inferring that "I can legally drink alcohol if I am over 21," based on the statement: "If I am over 21 years old, then I can legally drink alcohol," would be logically false, unless the statement has an Iff relation).

A conditional reasoning task that has generated much work and controversy is the **Wason selection task** (WST) (Wason, 1966, 1968). In the original abstract version of this task, participants are presented with four cards. On one side of each card is a letter, and on the other side is a number. The participants are then given a conditional rule, such as this:

If there is a vowel on one side of the card, then there is an even number on the other side.

They are then asked to check whether the cards conform to this rule by deciding which card or cards they definitely need to turn over. In Figure 5.3 (and in others that follow), the cards are lying flat, so you can see only one side of each card.

If the task is understood according to propositional logic, people should turn the p and not-q cards (the E and the 7), which would allow them to apply the arguments of modus ponens and modus tollens. However, only a small percentage of people choose this selection of cards (between 4%–10%, on average). They instead opt to select either the p and q cards (46%) or only the p card (33%) (Oaksford & Chater, 1994).

THE WASON SELECTION TASK: ARE PEOPLE SPECIALIZED DEONTIC REASONERS?

Whereas the abstract version of the WST has shown people to be fairly "irrational" in terms of selecting cards (but see the ensuing discussion of Oaksford & Chater, 1994), there seems to be much improvement when they are given several **deontic** versions of the task, in which a rule is expressed as a social obligation or a right (see Griggs & Cox, 1982; Johnson-Laird, Legrenzi, & Legrenzi, 1972). A classic example involves the "drinking-age rule" (Griggs & Cox, 1982):

If a person is drinking beer, then that person must be over 21 years of age.[1]

---

[1]In the original article, the rule was: "If a person is drinking beer, then that person must be over 19 years of age." We modified the age to be 21, to be consistent with drinking rules in most of the United States.

To perform this task, participants are asked to assume the role of a police officer entering a bar who wants to uphold the drinking rule. Then, they are given four cards depicting four different people who are either "drinking beer," "drinking Coke," "22 years old," or "16 years old." This manipulation causes the majority of the participants to select the logically correct cards: "drinking beer" (p) and "16 years old" (not-q) cards.

In the following subsections we discuss two main theories of deontic reasoning on the WST: pragmatic reasoning schemas and social-contract theory. We then provide an alternative interpretation of why people show improvement on deontic tasks. We claim that this improvement has to do more with the availability of counterexamples in memory than with the deontic context per se.

Pragmatic Reasoning Schemas

Cheng and Holyoak (1985) argued that deductive reasoning is based on **pragmatic reasoning schemas** involving rules of permission and obligation. A pragmatic reasoning schema is an abstract knowledge structure incorporating a set of rules that are sensitive to context and are goal directed.

The permission schema is applied to all conditionals of the type: "If an action is to be taken (p), then a precondition must be satisfied (q)" and includes four rules:

P1: If the action is to be taken (p), then the precondition must be satisfied (q).

P2: If the action is not to be taken (not-p), then the precondition need not be satisfied (q or not-q).

P3: If the precondition is satisfied (q), then the action may be taken (p or not-p).

P4: If the precondition is not satisfied (not-q), then the action must not be taken (not-p).

The obligation schema is applied to all conditionals of the type: "If the precondition is satisfied (p), then the action must be taken (q)" and includes the following rules:

O1: If the precondition is satisfied (p), then the action must be taken (q).

O2: If the precondition is not satisfied (not-p), then the action need not be taken (q or not-q).

O3: If the action is to be taken (q), then the precondition may have been satisfied (p or not-p).

O4: If the action is not to be taken (not-q), then the precondition must not have been satisfied (not-p).

Theses schemas explain people's behavior on the WST as follows. The abstract version of the task does not elicit permission or obligation. However, the drinking-age rule, for example, evokes a permission schema. Specifically, P1 is evoked first because it matches the given conditional rule (If a person is drinking beer, then the person must be over 21). In turn, P4 is also activated because permission entails that if the precondition is not satisfied (the person is under 21), then the action must not be taken (the person is not permitted to drink beer). Note that both P1 and P2 contain the imperative "must" (as do O1 and O2), making them crucial components of the schema. Rules P2 and P3, on the other hand, are deemed irrelevant because their consequents imply that something may or may not be true (if a person is drinking

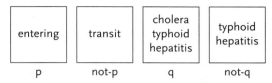

Figure 5.4 Cheng and Holyoak's (1985) task.

Coke, then the person may or may not be over 21, and if a person is over 21, then the person may be drinking either Coke or beer). Similar explanations are involved in situations in which the obligation schema is elicited.

To test their predictions empirically, Cheng and Holyoak (1985) asked the participants to imagine that their task was to check whether passengers' vaccination forms at an airport upheld the following rule: "If the form says 'entering' on one side, then the other side includes cholera among the list of diseases." The participants were presented with the following four cards (on one side of the card is information about whether a passenger is entering the country or is in transit, and on the other side is information about which diseases the passenger was vaccinated for), corresponding to four different passengers. The participants were asked to turn over only those cards that would help them to determine whether the rule was upheld or not (see Figure 5.4).

To evoke the use of a permission schema, Cheng and Holyoak gave half their participants the following rationale for checking the rule: The cholera inoculation would protect the entering passengers from the disease. In this way, the rule was not just arbitrary but reflected a societal contract. The other half were not given this rationale. The results showed that participants who were given this rationale tended to outperform the others by selecting the p (entering) and not-q (typhoid, hepatitis) cards more often.

Cheng and Holyoak (1995) argued that the specific interpretation of a conditional as either a permission or obligation rule may lead to what are known as **perspective effects**. Perspective effects occur when some people choose the correct p and not-q cards whereas others select the reverse pattern, the not-p and q cards, for solving the same selection task rule because they have different viewpoints. As an illustration of a perspective effect, consider the "day-off rule" (Gigerenzer & Hug, 1992): "If an employee works on the weekend, then that person gets a day off during the week." The employee interprets the rule as an obligation for the employer: "If an employee works on the weekend, then the employer must grant a day off during the week." The employer interprets the rule as permission: "If an employee works on the weekend, then that person may take a day off during the week." The employee will therefore check the cards corresponding to the antecedents of O1 and O4 ("worked on the weekend" and "did not get a day off"), whereas the employer would select the cards corresponding to the antecedents of P1 and P4 ("gets a day off" and "did not work on the weekend"). Pragmatic reasoning schemas explain perspective effects by appealing to deontic contracts that involve both duties and rights (Holyoak & Cheng, 1995).

Social-Contract Theory

Social-contract theory (Cosmides, 1989; Cosmides & Tooby, 1996) proposes that people have evolved domain-specific skills for reasoning in situations of social exchange. The main idea is that an environment in which individuals cooperate for mutual benefit leads to the development of social contracts whereby each individual has to pay a cost to receive a benefit. These contracts are thought to give rise to Darwinian algorithms, such as the "look for cheaters" algorithm that detects individuals who take a benefit without paying the cost. This algorithm is suggested to have the following social contract form: "If you take a benefit, then you must pay a cost."

To show that people abide by this algorithm, Cosmides (1989) provided the participants in some of her experiments with novel scenarios depicting cultural norms of fictitious societies, such as the following:

> You are a Kaluame, a member of a Polynesian culture found only on the Maku Island in the Pacific. The Kaluame have many strict laws which must be enforced, and the elders have entrusted you with enforcing them. To fail would disgrace you and your family.
>
> Among the Kaluame, when a man marries, he gets a tattoo on his face; only married men have tattoos on their faces. A facial tattoo means that a man is married, an unmarked face means that a man is a bachelor.
>
> Cassava root is a powerful aphrodisiac—it makes the man who eats it irresistible to women. Moreover it is delicious and nutritious—and very scarce.
>
> Unlike Cassava root, molo nuts are very common, but they are poor eating—molo nuts taste bad, they are not very nutritious, and they have no other interesting "medicinal" properties.
>
> Although everyone craves cassava root, eating it is a privilege that your people closely ration. You are a very sensual people, even without the aphrodisiacal properties of cassava root, but you have very strict sexual mores. The elders strongly disapprove of sexual relations between unmarried people, and particularly distrust the motives and intentions of bachelors.
>
> Therefore, the elders have made laws governing rationing privileges. The one you have been entrusted is as follows:
>
> "If a man eats cassava root, then he must have a tattoo on his face."
>
> Cassava root is so powerful an aphrodisiac, that many men are tempted to cheat on this law whenever the elders are not looking. (p. 264)

The participants were asked to imagine that they were part of the Kaluame tribe and that their job was to catch men whose sexual desires might make them break the rule when the elders are not around. They were reminded that if any such man was to get past them, they would bring disgrace to themselves and to their families.

The rules that the participants had to check followed two general forms: the *standard social contract* ("If you take a benefit, then you must pay a cost") and the *switched social contract* ("If you pay a cost, then you must take the benefit"). In the Kaluame example, the standard social-contract rule was: "If a man eats cassava root, then he must have a tattoo on his face," as presented in the scenario just quoted. The switched social-contract rule was: "If a man has a tattoo on his face, then he must eat cassava root." The participants in each group (standard or switched) were asked to check whether their respective rule was upheld, with respect to four men, depicted in four cards. On one side of the card was information about what the man was eating, and on the other side was information about whether the man had a tattoo on his face (see Figure 5.5). In the versions with the standard social contract, the participants selected the p and not-q cards, whereas in the versions with the switched social contract, the participants chose the not-p and q cards. This last result is consistent with social-contract theory because the selected cards always corresponded to "takes the benefit" and "did not pay the cost," which are the constituent parts of the look-for-cheaters algorithm.

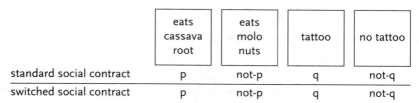

	eats cassava root	eats molo nuts	tattoo	no tattoo
standard social contract	p	not-p	q	not-q
switched social contract	p	not-p	q	not-q

Figure 5.5 Cosmides' (1989) task.

IS DEONTIC REASONING SPECIAL?

Facilitation on the selection task (choosing the p and not-q cards) has been demonstrated in nondeontic contexts as well (Almor & Sloman, 1996; Green, 1995; Green & Larking, 1995; Sperber, Cara, & Girotto, 1995). For example, Almor and Sloman gave their participants the quality-control rule, "If the product breaks, then it must have been used under abnormal conditions" and found that the participants were more likely to choose the correct p and not-q cards (the product broke, and it was used under normal conditions), even though the rule was clearly nondeontic. Their study showed that when people have an available counterexample, they will use it, whether it is in a deontic context or not.

Researchers who advocate a special-deontic view of reasoning have used perspective effects to argue for the importance of social context (e.g., Cheng & Holyoak, 1985). Perspective effects, remember, are ones in which some people are primed to choose the correct p and not-q cards, whereas other people can be induced to select the reverse pattern, the not-p and q cards, on the same rule. For example, Manktelow and Over (1991) presented participants with the following rule (a statement made by a mother to her son): "If you tidy your room, then you may go out to play." If the participants were instructed to take the son's perspective and to check whether the mother violated the rule, they tended to select the p card ("tidied the room") and the not-q card ("did not go out to play"). However, if they were asked to take the mother's perspective and to check whether the son has violated the rule, they opted for turning the not-p card ("did not tidy the room") and the q card ("went out to play") instead. The deontic explanation for people's behavior would be that this rule elicits a different aspect of permission or obligation for the parent versus the child, which, in turn, leads to perspective effects.

Staller, Sloman, and Ben-Zeev (2000) provided evidence that perspective effects can occur in a nondeontic context as well. The main idea is that perspective effects arise whenever different perspectives elicit different counterexamples to a rule with a biconditional interpretation. In one of Staller et al.'s experiments, the participants were assigned to either the "p and not-q" condition or the "not-p and q" condition. People in the "p and not-q" were given the following nondeontic scenario to read:

> A friend of yours complains about the weather, saying "If it's a weekday, then the sun is shining."
> You think your friend may be wrong because you seem to remember that last Monday it was raining. Circle the newspaper or newspapers below that you would need to turn over to verify conclusively whether your friend's rule is true or not for these four days.

The four newspapers are identified by what you can see on them (see Figure 5.6). The "not-p and q" version was identical except that the third sentence read: "You think your friend may be wrong because you seem to remember that last Sunday the sun was shining."

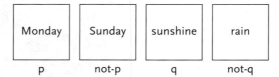

Figure 5.6 Staller, Sloman, and Ben-Zeev's (2000) task.

The predicted perspective effects were obtained, such that the majority of people in the "p and not-q" and in the "not-p and q" conditions made more "p and not-q" and "not-p and q" selections, respectively. This pattern of results was also obtained with abstract materials. Altogether, these findings show that human reasoning may not give special status to rule violators in a social context. Rather, rule violators may serve as just one kind of counterexample for people's reasoning about conditional rules.

A different nondeontic interpretation of performance on the WST was provided by Kirby (1994). According to Kirby, people's reasoning is motivated by a subjective analysis of costs and benefits associated with turning each card in deontic and nondeontic contexts. To demonstrate this point, Kirby gave participants two versions of the WST that varied in the sizes assigned to the p and not-p sets. In one version, the p set was small (one member) and the not-p set was large (1,000 members). In the second version, the reverse was true—the p set was large (1,000 members) and the not-p set was small (one member). The q and not-q sets had one member each in both conditions. The task was as follows:

A computer was given the task of printing out cards with an integer from zero to one thousand (0, 1, 2, . . . 1000) on one side of the card, and one of two arithmetic symbols (+ or −) on the other side of the card. For each card, the computer first printed an integer on one side, and was then instructed to print the other side so the following statement would be true:

If the card has a 0 on one side, then it has a + on the other side. [Small P Set Condition]

If the card has a number from 1 to 1000 on one side, then it has a + on the other side. [Large P Set Condition]

The computer has made 1 mistake after 100 cards. Below are four new cards that were just printed. Please circle those cards, and only those cards, that you would need to turn over to determine whether the computer made a mistake and violated the statement. (p. 7)

The four cards are shown in Figure 5.7.

The prediction was that if people are paying attention to the utilities (costs and benefits) of the cards, then the proportion of participants that will select the not-q card will in-

Figure 5.7 Kirby's (1994) task.

crease with a larger p set. It is more useful to turn over the not-q card in the larger p-set condition because the probability of finding a not-p card behind the not-q card would decrease substantially and would thus be informative. The results confirmed this prediction and demonstrated that people can produce the correct response on a nondeontic task. They suggest that social-context effects may be caused not by specialized reasoning processes but by an association with larger p sets (e.g., there are more beer drinkers in a bar than non-beer drinkers, which may facilitate people's selection of "p and not-q" on the drinking-age rule).

Kirby's (1994) analysis implies that the best formal model to use as a standard against which to measure people's performance on the WST may be a probabilistic or inductive model instead of a deductive one (see also Evans & Over 1996). A probabilistic model would reflect the utility of turning a card, given the likelihood that the card would convey important information.

IS THE WASON SELECTION TASK A DEDUCTIVE TASK?

Oaksford and Chater (1994) challenged the use of deductive logic as the normative standard to which people's performance should be compared. They argued that the appropriate model for reasoning on this task is an information-theoretic model of optimal data selection in inductive hypothesis testing. Induction, in contrast to deduction, involves reasoning from a specific to a more general conclusion with a certain degree of likelihood or confidence.

Oaksford and Chater's model suggests that people's reasoning on the WST may be rational, rather than erroneous. For example, people's reasoning may obey the **rarity assumption**, which suggests that given that p and q are rare (there are many more not-p and not-q cases), then their intersection is even more rare, and thus it may be beneficial to flip over the p and the q cards. If both p and q are true, then there is probabilistic evidence that supports a positive relationship between the two. Let us give a more concrete example. Suppose that you are to evaluate the truth of the conditional: "If a person eats a mango, then the person develops a rash." The probability of eating mango is small and so is the probability of getting a rash. If both cooccur, then your confidence in the link between them would be strengthened.

Oaksford and Chater's work highlights an important question regarding research on human cognition. To create **descriptive models** of reasoning that describe how people think, one needs to pit these models against **normative models** that prescribe how people should be thinking to achieve optimal performance. However, it is not always clear just what the relevant normative models are. For many years, the assumption was that for the WST, the normative model is deductive logic. According to this model, it is a fallacy to choose the p and the q cards (affirmation of the consequent). However, if the relevant normative model is probabilistic, rather than deductive, then the choice of p and q may be rational, not erroneous.

Have people evolved specialized rule systems for making deductive inferences that are analogous to the rules of formal logic? If not, how do they represent knowledge in such a way as to allow them to make deductions, such as modus ponens? What does the nature of errors tell us about the cognitive architecture underlying deduction? These questions lie at the core of the ensuing discussion on the nature of deductive reasoning.

RULE-BASED VERSUS RULELESS THEORIES OF DEDUCTIVE REASONING

Rips (1994) divided theories of deductive reasoning into rule-based and ruleless accounts. Rule-based theories attribute special status to the logical form of an argument, whereas ruleless theories build on other factors, such as people's background knowledge and available examples.

Rule-Based Theories of Deductive Reasoning

The idea that people generate a variety of mistakes, but may nevertheless have a "mental logic" can be traced to the developmental writings of Piaget (see, e.g., Beth & Piaget, 1966). More recent theories of deduction also incorporate the notion that people have a set of internal deductive rules (see, e.g., Braine et al., 1984; Osherson, 1975; Rips, 1983, 1994). The core idea underlying mental-logic models is that people store information in memory in the form of statements and then treat these statements as premises to which one can apply inferential rules, such as modus ponens.

Mental-logic theories assume a **strict view** of deductive reasoning (versus a *loose* one; see chapter 6). A strict view (Rips, 1990) suggests that reasoning requires a special logical structure that represents formal structure, abstract specifications of rules, and discrete inference steps that derive a conclusion from a delimited set of premises.

In this section, we review three main rule-based theories in chronological order: Osherson's (1976) model of deduction, Braine et al.'s (1984) theory of natural logic, and Rips's (1994) PSYCOP. As Rips (1994) admitted, these theories are difficult to contrast with each other because they cover somewhat different domains of deduction. However, because together they make a case for a natural cognitive deduction system, it is worthwhile to discuss each theory's contribution.

Osherson's Model of Deduction

Osherson (1976) suggested that people have an internal list of inference rules that they apply in a rigid order to the premises of a deductive argument, starting with the first rule at the top of their mental list. This process continues until either a conclusion is generated or the list is exhausted but no appropriate rule has been found. These rules operate in a forward direction only, but there are "helping conditions" that check the validity of the conclusion and of any intermediate assertions that are generated during the deductive reasoning process.

Osherson made two predictions regarding the validity of this model: the inventory and additivity requirements. The **inventory requirement** posits that for a person to reason correctly, he or she must possess all the relevant rules. A person who reasons incorrectly lacks at least one rule. For example, in solving argument (26), one needs to have rules (27) and (28):

> If Paul is working, then Karen either reads a book or listens to music.
>
> If Karen does not read a book and does not listen to music, then Paul is not working. (26)

$$\frac{\text{Not (p or q)}}{\text{(Not p) and (Not q)}} \qquad (27)$$

$$\frac{\text{If p, then q}}{\text{If (not q), then (not p)}} \qquad (28)$$

The **additivity requirement** posits that multistep arguments, such as (26), are related to the level of difficulty of the single-step arguments they are composed of (27 and 28). The prediction here is that there would be a positive correlation between the difficulty of an argument and its constituent one-step arguments. Osherson presented support for this prediction by demonstrating a positive correlation between the overall difficulty ratings that people provide in response to multistep arguments and their perceived difficulty of the pertinent single-step arguments. (However, for a criticism that Osherson's inventory and additivity requirements may not fit the experimental data all that well, see Rips, 1994).

The use of a natural logic may be dependent on language development. Osherson and Markman (1976) investigated the reasons underlying children's inability to evaluate correctly logical contradictions (p AND not-p) and tautologies (p OR not-p). Second graders were asked to asses whether statements about the physical characteristics of stimuli (poker chips) were true or false. The chips were in clear view of the children or were hidden. The statements that children were asked to judge were either contradictions (e.g., "Either this chip is white and it is not white") or tautologies (e.g., "Either this chip is white or it is not white"). When the chips were in clear view, the children were asked to judge the validity of empirical statements (e.g., "This chip is green and it is not blue").

The children had difficulty evaluating the truth of nonempirical statements, that is, statements that are true or false on the basis of their linguistic structure alone, and tended to evaluate the statements by relying on empirical considerations, such as searching for evidence by looking at the chip itself. On trials in which the chips were hidden from the children's view, the majority of the answers to nonempirical statements were "can't tell," indicating a reluctance to evaluate a statement on the basis of its linguistic properties alone. On the other hand, the children had little difficulty evaluating the truth of empirical statements, such as "Either this chip is blue or it is not green," whether the chip was hidden or in view. This study suggests that children have difficulty with nonempirical statements, partly because they lack the ability to evaluate language objectively, that is, to regard language as independent from its referent. These results are consistent with the Piagetian claim that certain linguistic skills are a prerequisite for a facility with propositional logic.

Braine et al.'s Theory of Natural Logic

Similar to Osherson's approach, Braine et al. (1984) argued that people create **inference schemas** that are the mental representations of logical arguments that are made up of a set of premises and a conclusion (e.g., p or q; not-p, therefore q). They propose that such schemas are formed via a *comprehension mechanism* that decodes the verbal information in a logical argument into the representation used in the schemas (the set of semantic elements, such as *and*, *or*, and *if-then*, among others, have to be translated from their linguistic meaning into the semantics of logic and then represented internally). The second component is a **heuristic reasoning program** that has both routines and strategies for constructing sets of inferences and deciding on which schema should be applied at each step of the deductive process. Braine et al. suggested that there may also be a third component, which consists of nonlogical fallback procedures that determine which response to generate when the heuristic reasoning program fails or comes to a halt.

To examine their theories, Braine et al. presented participants with reasoning problems, consisting of one or more premises and a conclusion, and asked them to evaluate whether the conclusion was valid or not. They predicted that heuristic inadequacy errors would occur when the heuristic reasoning program failed to find a solution (the problem may have been too difficult) and processing errors would result from attention lapses and working-memory limitations.

To predict errors a priori, Braine et al. manipulated the kinds of problems to require either **direct reasoning** or **indirect reasoning**. Direct-reasoning problems were of low to moderate difficulty and could be solved by making inferences in a forward direction (e.g., if a conclusion is an *if-then* proposition, then the antecedent is considered the new premise, and the consequent is the conclusion). This process continues until either a contradictory result is found (the answer is false) or until no new results can be produced (the answer is true). Direct reasoning was predicted to elicit processing errors only.

Indirect-reasoning problems, on the other hand, are more difficult and may require making inferences that lie outside the problem's premises, for example. These problems were expected to elicit heuristic-inadequacy errors. The following is an example of a problem that requires indirect reasoning to evaluate its conclusion (to infer that the conclusion is true, one must reason from the **lemma:** If there is a T, then there is a T):

$$
\begin{array}{l}
\text{If there is a P, then there is a K.} \\
\underline{\text{There is a P or a T.}} \\
\text{There is a K or a T.}
\end{array}
\qquad (29)
$$

Overall, error patterns were supportive of the authors' predictions. In addition, Braine et al. asked the participants to rate the difficulty of individual steps in solving a problem. They then showed that the sum of the rated difficulties of the individual steps could predict fairly well the difficulty of the problems in which they were used. These results support Braine et al.'s idea that people use inference schemas that correspond to logical arguments and go through the mental steps that are required to solve them.

Rips's PSYCOP

The main tenet of Rips's (1994) theory, **PSYCOP** (psychology of proof), is that people solve deduction problems by constructing *mental proofs*. A mental proof consists of a set of sentences in working memory that link the premises of an argument with its conclusion via inference rules. For example, the mental proof for modus ponens is roughly as follows:

a. If sentences of the form if p then q, and p hold in some domain D,

b. and p holds in D,

c. and q does not yet hold in D,

d. then add q to D.

Rips recognized that people are not always optimal reasoners and attributed failures on deductive tasks to limitations of the cognitive system, such as exceeding the capacity of working memory. The idea is that whether successful or not, people, at the least, attempt to construct mental proofs.

The main strategy used in PSYCOP for evaluating whether a conclusion is valid or not is to work from the outside in, by using **forward-directed rules** to deduce inferences from the premises and **backward directed rules** for generating subgoals based on the conclusion. Forward rules work from the premises to the conclusion, whereas backward rules work from the conclusion to the premises. For example, a forward rule for modus ponens looks for such assertions as "If p then q" and "p" to deduce that "q" is the correct conclusion, whereas a backward rule for modus ponens takes "q" (the conclusion) as input and then searches for "If p then q." If that assertion is found, then a search ensues for "p" in the givens. The backward procedures are inspired by the problem-solving literature on goal-oriented heuristic search (e.g., "p" is the subgoal for "q") (see chapter 7).

Rips provided empirical support for PSYCOP. He was able to show, for instance, that PSYCOP's distinction between backward and forward rules could predict people's reaction times. Specifically, people's reaction times were faster when the model anticipated a forward rule than when it anticipated a backward rule. These reaction-time data are consistent with PSYCOP because forward rules are assumed to be used automatically, whereas backward rules are carried out in response to particular goals.

Summary

Rule-based models share the assumption that people have a natural-logic system. Osherson (1976) argued that people mentally store inference rules that they then apply to the premises of a deductive argument. Braine et al. (1984) claimed that people create inference schemas that are the mental representations of logical arguments. Finally, Rips's (1994) PSYCOP theory suggests that people solve deduction problems by constructing *mental proofs*. These proofs involve creating a set of sentences in working memory that link the premises of an argument with its conclusion by the application of inference rules.

In contrast to this rule-based view, Johnson-Laird (1997) suggested that people's reasoning relies on mental models (Johnson-Laird & Byrne, 1991, 1993), rather than on formal proofs. Mental models contain semantic information that is based on a person's linguistic and general knowledge. A person then may use this semantic information to generate and evaluate conclusions.

Mental Models: A Ruleless Theory of Deductive Reasoning

Johnson-Laird and colleagues (e.g., Johnson-Laird, 1983, 1989; Johnson-Laird & Bara, 1984; Johnson-Laird & Byrne, 1991; Johnson-Laird & Steedman, 1978) proposed that people form **mental models** of the information contained in the premises of a logical argument and then generate a possible conclusion based on these models. A mental model is a knowledge structure that represents information contained in the premises by relating it to available examples and real-life knowledge. Optimally, people seek to construct alternative mental models, in which the hypothesized conclusion does not hold. If such a model is not found, then the conclusion is endorsed. This process can lead to both correct and faulty beliefs in the validity of a conclusion. Consider the following example:

$$\underline{\begin{array}{l} \text{All mailmen are dog haters.} \\ \text{All dog haters are cat lovers.} \end{array}} \qquad (30)$$

The mental model corresponding to the first premise is created by generating a few examples of mailmen (denoted each by the letter M) and then tagging the mailmen as dog haters (M = D). Because the set of mailmen may be smaller than or equal to the set of dog haters, one also needs to represent the possibility of a dog hater who is not a mailman (denoted by a parenthesis):

$$\begin{array}{c} \text{M} = \text{D} \\ \text{M} = \text{D} \\ \text{(D)} \end{array}$$

The model that corresponds to the second premise in the argument (all dog haters are cat lovers) is created in a similar fashion (cat lovers are each denoted by the letter C):

$$\begin{array}{c} \text{D} = \text{C} \\ \text{D} = \text{C} \\ \text{(C)} \end{array}$$

The final step is to combine the two premises by combining the two mental models they entail:

$$\begin{array}{c} \text{M} = \text{D} = \text{C} \\ \text{M} = \text{D} = \text{C} \\ \text{(D)} = \text{C} \\ \text{(C)} \end{array}$$

It is then clear from the combined model that all mailmen are cat lovers. In the context of this argument, there is only one possible model. But that is not always the case. Consider, for example, the following syllogism:

$$\underline{\begin{array}{l} \text{Some mailmen are dog haters.} \\ \text{Some dog haters are cat lovers.} \end{array}} \qquad (31)$$

What kinds of models can you think of that would describe this argument? Often, people create the following model on the basis of the assumptions that some of the M are D and some of the D that are M are also C. This model entails the incorrect deduction that some M are C:

$$\begin{array}{c} \text{M} = \text{D} = \text{C} \\ \text{(M) (D) (C)} \end{array}$$

Mental-models theory allows for both correct and erroneous reasoning. Erroneous conclusions frequently occur when a person forms just a single model out of a set of two or three models and fails to construct the others (Johnson-Laird & Bara, 1984; Johnson-Laird & Steedman, 1978). The failure to create alternative models may result from working-memory load, when people try to hold too much explicit information in memory (Johnson-Laird, Byrne, & Schaeken, 1992). Other factors that affect the use of an exhaustive set of mental models include ease of imagery and the relatedness of premises. For example, C. A. Clement and Falmagne (1986) showed that people's performance on deduction tasks is helped more when terms lend themselves to high imagery and the propositions are highly related (e.g., "Some artists are painters. Some painters use black paint.") than when they are not (e.g., "Some texts are prose. Some prose is well written").

Mental-models theory can be applied to more general forms of deductive logic that extend beyond syllogistic reasoning (Johnson-Laird & Byrne, 1991). The general theory is based on a fundamental representational principle, which states that people avoid placing heavy demands on working memory by representing explicitly only what is true, not what is false, about a deductive argument (referred to as the **principle of truth**). For example, consider the following case of a **conjunction** (a statement of the form p *and* q) (taken from Johnson-Laird & Savary, 1999):

There was a king in the hand, and there was an ace.

In this case, people would construct one true model:

King   Ace

Consider another case of an **inclusive disjunction** (a statement of the form p *or* q or both):

There was a king in the hand, or there was an ace or both.

The mental model for this argument contains three true possibilities:

King

           Ace

King   Ace

For a more complete set of mental models, see Johnson-Laird et al. (1992).

Given the principle of truth, how do people represent a situation in which assertions are false? Johnson-Laird and Savary (1999) argued that people must infer these cases from the true cases contained in their mental models. For example, the mental models for the conditional "If there was a king, then there was an ace" are these:

King   Ace

. . .

The second (implicit) model leaves room for more possibilities (denoted by the ellipses). It results from a situation in which people may not immediately appreciate the relevance of cases in which the antecedent is false. In this situation, it implies that the king cannot occur with a nonace. When needed, people can elaborate on their initial representations, as follows (where ¬ stands for a negation, or "not"):

$$\begin{array}{ll} \text{King} & \text{Ace} \\ \text{King} & \neg\text{Ace} \end{array}$$

The mental-models theory does not a necessitate a reliance on formal rules. Instead, it posits that deductive reasoning can lead to either necessary, probable, or possible conclusions. A **necessary conclusion** must be true if it holds in all the models of the premises; a **probable conclusion** is likely to be true if it holds in most of the models of the premises; Finally, a **possible conclusion** may be true if it holds in at least one model of the premises (Johnson-Laird, Legrenzi, Girotto, Legrenzi, & Caverni, 1999).

There are a variety of inferential strategies that people can apply to mental models. For example, given the premises and respective models:

$$\begin{array}{lll} \text{If A, then B:} & \text{A} & \text{B} \\ & & \ldots \\ \text{If B, then not C:} & \text{B} & \neg\text{C} \\ & & \ldots \end{array}$$

A person can integrate them into the following set of mental models:

$$\begin{array}{lll} \text{A} & \text{B} & \neg\text{C} \\ & \ldots & \end{array}$$

The combined models support the correct conclusion: "If A, then not C." This conclusion is valid, as can be seen from the full set of possibilities:

$$\begin{array}{lll} \text{A} & \text{B} & \neg\text{C} \\ \neg\text{A} & \text{B} & \neg\text{C} \\ \neg\text{A} & \neg\text{B} & \text{C} \\ \neg\text{A} & \neg\text{B} & \neg\text{C} \end{array}$$

There is robust empirical evidence for the mental-models theory (see Johnson-Laird & Byrne, 1991) and the principle of truth (see Johnson-Laird & Barres, 1994). The main finding is that the difficulty of a solution is a function of the number of models that people are suggested to create. A conditional or syllogism that requires only one model, for example, is generally easier than a conditional or syllogism that requires two.

In sum, mental-models theory argues that people reason on the basis of their mental models and, under certain circumstances, can flesh out their models to make them more nearly complete. Theories based on formal rules, like PSYCOP, on the other hand, suggest that people first extract the logical form of the premises and apply inferential rules to these logical forms. The mental-models theory, in contrast, suggests that interpreting the premises leads to a set of mental models, which, in turn, serves as a basis for evaluating or generating a conclusion.

MENTAL PROOFS OR MENTAL MODELS?

In the *Psychology of Proof*, Rips (1994) presented a study that provides counterevidence to the predictions of mental-models theory. Rips gave the participants either a disjunctive (p *or* q) (32) or a conjunctive (p *and* q) (33) inference to evaluate:

$$
\begin{array}{c}
\text{p } or \text{ q} \\
\text{If p, then r} \\
\underline{\text{If q, then r}} \\
\text{r}
\end{array}
\tag{32}
$$

$$
\begin{array}{c}
\text{p } and \text{ q} \\
\text{If p, then r} \\
\underline{\text{If q, then r}} \\
\text{r}
\end{array}
\tag{33}
$$

Mental-models theory predicts that conjunctive inferences, such as (33), should be easier to evaluate than disjunctive inferences, such as (32), because conjunctive inferences require only one model, whereas disjunctive inferences require multiple models. The disjunctive (32′) and conjunctive (33′) are as follows:

$$
\begin{array}{ccc}
\text{p} & \text{q} & \text{r}
\end{array}
\tag{32′}
$$

$$
\begin{array}{ccc}
\text{p} & \neg\text{q} & \text{r} \\
\neg\text{p} & \text{q} & \text{r} \\
\text{p} & \text{q} & \text{r}
\end{array}
\tag{33′}
$$

Rips discovered, however, that people found the disjunctive inferences just as easy to evaluate as the conjunctive ones (both elicited a relatively high accuracy rate). These results are more consistent with PSYCOP and other formal rule-based models because the number and difficulty level of both types of inferences are fairly equivalent.

However, in a later study, García-Madruga et al. (2000) were able to show that conjunctive inferences are easier than disjunctive inferences when people were allowed to generate their own conclusions and when the conjunction and disjunction came last in the premises. They also demonstrated that people spent less time reading the premises and generating conclusions in response to conjunctions versus disjunctions and provided higher ratings of difficulty in response to the disjunctions compared with the conjunctions. The results of this study show further support for the mental-models theory despite Rips's findings.

The mental-models theory suggests that people create models of the situations presented in the premises that make explicit only what is true about the premises. As a result, it predicts an unintuitive result that cannot easily be accommodated by mental-proof theories: the occurrence of **illusory inferences**, or inferences that are false as a result of ignoring information that is false. Johnson-Laird and Savary (1999) provided evidence for the existence of these illusory inferences. In their study, the participants received problems that were predicted to elicit illusory inferences, as well as control problems that were not expected to do so. For example, they were expected to draw an illusory conclusion (there is an ace in the hand) on the following problem.

Suppose you know the following about a specific hand of cards:

> If there is a king in the hand, then there is an ace in the hand, or else if there isn't a king in the hand, then there is an ace in the hand.
>
> There is a king in the hand.

What, if anything, follows?

The expected answer, that there is an ace in the hand, is false, because the first premise could be false. In contrast, the participants were expected to perform well on the control problems, such as the following.

Suppose you know the following about a specific hand of cards:

> There is a king in the hand, and there is not an ace in the hand, or else there is an ace in the hand and there is not a king in the hand.
>
> There is a king in the hand.

What, if anything, follows?

The first premise yields the mental models:

$$K \qquad \neg A$$
$$\neg K \qquad A$$

The premise: "There is a king in the hand" eliminates the second model, leaving people with the correct conclusion that "There is not an ace."

The results of Johnson-Laird and Savary's (1999) study showed that every participant performed more accurately on the control problems than on the illusions. The participants made the illusory inferences in every case (i.e., 100% of their conclusions on the illusions were the predicted false conclusions), whereas they were almost always correct in their conclusions for the control problems.

Johnson-Laird and Savary found that people committed illusory inferences even when they were given premises based on disjunctions or were provided with a rubric that made explicit an exclusive disjunction of conditionals, such as the following.

Suppose you are playing cards with Billy and you get two clues about the cards in his hand. You know that one of the clues is true and that one of them is false, but unfortunately you don't know which one is true and which one is false:

If there is a king in his hand, then there is an ace in his hand.

If there is not a king in his hand, then there is an ace in his hand.

Please select the correct answer:

a. There is an ace in Billy's hand.

b. There is not an ace in Billy's hand.

c. There may or may not be an ace in Billy's hand.

Johnson-Laird and Savary argued that given the limitations of human cognition, such as working-memory constraints, people cannot possibly develop the fully explicit formal models that would allow them to avoid illusory inferences. Furthermore, the principle of taking into account what is true while ignoring what is false may be a sensible strategy for everyday inferences because truth is often more useful than falsity. Only in relatively few situations does truth alone lead people to the illusion that they have a grasp of a set of logical possibilities when they do not.

Johnson-Laird and his colleagues have provided an alternative explanation of deductive reasoning to Rips's PSYCOP, which is based on the use of instances or mental models instead of on formal rules. However, the question of which theory has the upper hand is hard to ascertain. Mental-models theory makes a strong case for the importance of context and interpretation in deductive reasoning but leaves open the question of just what defines a mental model (or, rather, what is not a mental model). The answer may be that people rely on both instances and rules in making inferences (see, e.g., E. E. Smith, Langston, & Nisbett, 1992). Yet a third perspective on deductive reasoning can be gleaned from cross-cultural studies.

WHAT DOES IT MEAN TO REASON CORRECTLY, ANYWAY? A CROSS-CULTURAL PERSPECTIVE

Cross-cultural studies on reasoning show that people question the assumptions of whether arguments that are given to be true are really true. Consider the following transcript of a discourse between a Kpelle man and his Western interviewer (Scribner, 1975, p. 155).

EXPERIMENTER: All Kpelle men are rice farmers. Mr. Smith (this is a Western name) is not a rice farmer. Is he a Kpelle man?

PARTICIPANT: I don't know the man in person. I have not laid eyes on the man himself.

EXPERIMENTER: Just think about the statement.

PARTICIPANT: If I know him in person then I can answer that question, but since I do not know him in person I cannot answer that question.

EXPERIMENTER: Try and answer from your Kpelle sense.

PARTICIPANT: If you know a person, if a question comes up about him you are able to answer. But if you do not know the person, if a question comes up about him, it's hard for you to answer it.

In the Kpelle people's world, the question takes on a different meaning than what the experimenter intended. Thus, the participant produces what seem to be "inappropriate" responses that nevertheless make sense (the man indeed never met Mr. Smith). In fact, in the eyes of the Kpelle man, the experimenter must have looked pretty dim-witted.

The following anecdote from Cole and Scribner (1974, p. 162) shows even more clearly that to reason, people prefer using concrete information that agrees with their everyday reasoning.

EXPERIMENTER: At one time spider went to a feast. He was told to answer this question before he could eat any of the food. The question is: Spider and black deer always eat together. Spider is eating. Is black deer eating?

PARTICIPANT: Were they in the bush?

EXPERIMENTER: Yes.

PARTICIPANT: Were they eating together?

EXPERIMENTER: Spider and black deer always eat together. Spider is eating. Is the black deer eating?

PARTICIPANT: But I was not there. How can I answer such a question?

EXPERIMENTER: Can't you answer it? Even if you were not there, you can answer it. (Repeats the question).

PARTICIPANT: Oh, oh, black deer is eating.

EXPERIMENTER: What is your reason for saying that black deer is eating?

PARTICIPANT: The reason is that black deer always walks about all day eating green leaves in the bush. Then he rests for a while and gets up again to eat.

These findings suggest that there may be another theoretical approach to the study of deduction, in addition to mental proofs and mental models. This approach claims that few, if any, people engage in deductive reasoning at all in the real world. Thus, even when people are given deductive arguments to evaluate, they will not treat the task as a deductive one. As in the case of the Kpelle man, we may not trust the truth of the given premises and instead consult our theories and ideas about the world. As reasoning on the WST has shown, people's judgments may have more of a probabilistic than a deductive nature.

◆ SUMMARY

The study of deduction involves examining how people reason about arguments that consist of a set of sentences called *premises* and a *conclusion*. A *deductively correct argument* is one in which the conclusion is true in any state of affairs in which the premises are true. In an experimental setting, a researcher typically provides the participants with an argument and then asks them whether the conclusion is true, presents them with a set of conclusions and asks them to choose the valid one, or asks them to generate their own conclusion given a set of premises.

Syllogistic reasoning tasks consist of arguments with exactly two *premises* (a major premise and a minor premise) followed by a *conclusion*. Linear syllogisms, which have been used primarily in intelligence tests, involve a comparison between terms, in which each term shows either more of a given quantity or quality or less of it. The other, more widely used, type of syllogism is the categorical syllogism, which has the following form: All A are B, and all C are A; therefore all C are B.

A syllogism contains three terms (A, B, C) and their possible relations. The relationship between the terms are expressed by quantifiers, either "all" (the universal quantifier) or "some" (the existential or particular quantifier). The argument may contain negative or positive sentences, such as "No A are B," "Some A are not B," or "Some A are B." Syllogistic arguments may be valid or invalid.

There have been attempts to explain errors in syllogistic reasoning. For example, Woodworth and Sells's (1935) *atmosphere hypothesis* suggests that people match the quantifier type of the conclusion (whether it is positive or negative, universal, or existential) with the quantifier type of either or both premises. An alternative to the atmosphere hypothesis was proposed by Chapman and Chapman's (1959) conversion hypothesis. These researchers showed that erroneous responses on categorical syllogisms would often be explained by converting: "all x are y" into "all y are x" and "some x are y" into "some y are x."

More theoretical accounts of syllogistic reasoning came after the rise of information-processing psychology (Rips, 1994). Erickson (1974, 1978) provided a set-theory account of deductive reasoning. He argued that people represent premises as combinations of Euler circles. A different set-theoretic account was offered by Guyote and Sternberg (1981). A general criticism that has been launched at these diagrammatic accounts of deductive reasoning has been that they do not explain *figural effects* in syllogistic reasoning.

Conditional-reasoning tasks involve providing a person with a proposition of the form: if p, then q, where p is the *antecedent*, and q is the *consequent*, and then asking him or her to generate or evaluate a given conclusion (e.g., If Charley eats a seven-course meal, then Charley is full). The correct inferences on this task are modus ponens (given "If p, then q" and "p," one can correctly deduce "q"), also called the *affirmation of the antecedent*. Another correct inference is modus tollens, or *denial of the consequent*: (given "If p, then q" and "not q," one can correctly deduce "not p"). The two incorrect or fallacious deductions are *denial of the antecdent* ("If not-p, then not-q") and *affirmation of the consequent* ("If q, then p").

An extensively studied task in conditional reasoning has been the WST. People do not perform well deductively on the abstract version of this task, but do so on several deontic versions of the task in which a rule is expressed as a social obligation or a right. Deontic theories include pragmatic reasoning schemas (Cheng & Holyoak, 1985) and social-contract theory (Cosmides, 1989). These theories propose that that people have evolved domain-specific skills for reasoning in situations of social exchange. In contrast, other theories have held that facilitation may occur as a result of using available counterexamples in deontic or nondeontic contexts (e.g., Almor & Sloman, 1996; Staller et al., 2000).

A major debate is whether people have evolved abstract rule systems or whether they reason by mental models. Rule-based models suggest that people store information in memory in the form of deductive arguments and then apply rules, such as modus ponens, to perform inferences on the premises of these arguments. Ruleless theories, such as mental models, emphasize the importance of context and are linked more directly to a person's available experience.

What does it mean to reason correctly, anyway? Cross-cultural studies on reasoning have provided support for yet a third approach to deductive reasoning. This approach suggests that people do not engage in deductive reasoning in the real world. Instead, their judgments may have more of a probabilistic than a deductive quality.

6 Inductive Reasoning

> The world will not stop and think—it never does, it is not its way; its way is to generalize from a single sample.
>
> —MARK TWAIN, *The United States of Lyncherdom*

After having a fight with his partner, a man concludes that the partner is under a lot of pressure and is therefore acting defensively. A college student is unhappy with her grade in a statistics class and decides that she is lacking quantitative skills. A man notices that a female colleague at work has been paying him a lot of attention and is certain that she has developed a crush on him. A scientist discovers that when people get stressed, they tend to produce higher levels of a certain hormone. These are all examples of inductive reasoning.

Whereas deductive reasoning entails making inferences from a set of premises to a certain conclusion, inductive reasoning involves a continuous adjustment to and updating of one's confidence in a belief or the strength of a belief. Inductive reasoning is the most common form of everyday and scientific reasoning. We hardly ever can conclude anything with complete certainty. At the extreme, some philosophers would argue that we cannot even prove that we are alive.

This chapter is concerned with the question of how people perform inductive inferences.

There are many possible inductions to any given situation. Why do people make certain inductive inferences over others? To answer this question, researchers have attempted to identify constraints on the inductive process that guarantee that inferences made by the cognitive system are both plausible and relevant to the system's goals (Holland, Holyoak, Nisbett, & Thagard, 1986). This kind of a *pragmatic approach* advocates the idea that to study induction, one must examine how knowledge is relevant to the aims and experience of an individual and examine how it gets modified through use.

The pragmatic approach is part of a more general "loose" view of reasoning (Rips, 1990). This view holds that inductive reasoning is a process of constantly updating the strength of beliefs on the basis of the availability of concrete instances, without the need for special logical structure, abstract specifications, or discrete inference steps. We contrast this view with the opposing syntactic view, which argues for the importance of special reasoning structures.

We then discuss how people evaluate the inductive inferences that they generate by processes of hypothesis testing and evaluation, often leading to what has been known as a "confirmation bias"—a tendency to look for evidence that confirms hypotheses, rather than to search for disconfirming evidence.

The remainder of this chapter is devoted primarily to probabilistic and correlational reasoning. The main question we address is, What are the appropriate normative models for these kinds of reasoning, and how does people's reasoning deviate from these models? Instead of deciding whether people are rational or irrational, we take the view that it is more productive to identify the circumstances under which people exhibit correct or fallacious reasoning.

Finally, we end with a discussion of the role of the self in inductive reasoning and if it is erroneous to generalize from the self to others. We highlight the importance and difficulty of finding the appropriate normative models for evaluating what is known as the "false-consensus effect," in particular, and biases in inductive reasoning, in general.

Whereas deductive reasoning entails making inferences from a set of premises to a conclusion, with certainty, **inductive reasoning** involves a continuous adjustment to and updating of one's confidence in a belief or the strength of a belief (Rips, 1990). To illustrate this distinction more concretely, imagine that you just found the following tidbit in your local newspaper:

> Olga, dubbed the funniest woman in the world, lives in a little village in Iceland. Olga performs in local entertainment shows, making her audience laugh for up to five hours straight. People are often forced to leave her show early, in fits of uncontrollable giggling, to prevent bodily harm.

Assuming that this article is true and that Olga is indeed the funniest woman in the world, you can conclude with deductive certainty that the funniest woman in the world, at the time that the article was written, lived in Iceland. Where will the funniest woman in the world be tomorrow? You would be wise to infer, with a high degree of certainty, that she will still be in Iceland. However, you cannot be completely sure of this fact. Immediately after the newspaper item, appeared, there could have been a natural disaster in the little Icelandic village, wiping it off the map. Alternatively, Olga may have been immediately asked to take her act on the road.

Formally, a *logical argument* (deductive or inductive) is composed of sentences called premises, followed by a conclusion. Using the example of Olga, we can write three types of arguments:

$$\frac{\text{The funniest living woman in the world today lives in Iceland.}}{\text{Olga is the funniest woman in the world.}}$$ (1)
Olga currently lives in Iceland.

$$\frac{\text{The funniest living woman in the world today lives in Iceland.}}{\text{Olga is the funniest woman in the world.}}$$ (2)
The funniest living woman in the world tomorrow will live in Iceland.

$$\frac{\text{The funniest living woman in the world today lives in Iceland.}}{\text{Olga is the funniest woman in the world.}}$$ (3)
The oldest cow in Holland is called Gretchen.

The first argument is deductively valid, the second is *inductively strong*, the third is neither deductively valid nor inductively strong. An argument is inductively strong when the conclusion is likely to be true, given that the premises are true (Skyrms, 1966).

INDUCTION: THE SCANDAL OF PSYCHOLOGY

Induction has been referred to as the scandal of philosophy and, more recently, as the scandal of psychology and artificial intelligence (Holland et al., 1986). The reason is that unless induction is constrained, it can lead to an infinite number of fruitless hypotheses in the search for useful hypotheses. Consider, for example, the possible solutions to the following problem.

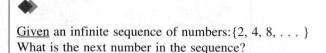

Given an infinite sequence of numbers: {2, 4, 8, . . . }
What is the next number in the sequence?

One possible answer is "16," based on adding exponents of 2 to each number in the series. There are many other possibilities for completing this sequence. In fact, there are an infinite number of them. Some are more likely to be generated by people (e.g., "14," by adding multiples of 2) whereas others are much less likely to be generated (e.g., "11111111"). The telling question is why do people choose to create certain inductions over others?

The main challenge is to identify constraints on the inductive process that will guarantee that the inferences made by the cognitive system are both plausible and relevant to the system's goals (Holland et al., 1986). This kind of an approach advocates that to study induction, one must examine how knowledge is relevant to the goals and experience of an individual and how knowledge gets modified through its use. In such a framework, induction is highly context dependent and is affected by real-world knowledge (also see Johnson-Laird, 1993).

Holland et al. (1986) suggested that the constraints on the acquisition of new rules may come from **triggering conditions**; for example, when a rat gets shocked for the first time in a Skinner box, that shock serves as a triggering condition for learning new associations. Similarly, when we notice a change in someone's behavior, that change may trigger an inference about the cause of the new behavior. Holland et al. also argued that the inferences people make are constrained by people's ability to perceive and represent the variability in the environment. That is, people tend to create default hierarchies for representing the variability of a particular kind of object with respect to a given property. Objects that are perceived to be less variable will create stronger inductions than will objects that are perceived to be more variable. For instance, we know that birds within the same family tend to share similar colors. Thus, when we are told that a new bird, referred to as a "shreeble," is blue, we will have a high degree of confidence in assuming that all shreebles are blue. However, if we are told that a man, referred to as a "Barrato," is obese, we will not readily assume that all Barratos are obese because we know that people tend to be variable with respect to weight (Nisbett, Krantz, Jepson, & Kunda, 1983) (for more discussion on how variability affects belief revision, see Rehder & Hastie, 1996).

Holland et al.'s (1986) position is an example of a **pragmatic approach** to inductive reasoning that emphasizes the role of the system's goals and the context in which induction takes place. It suggests that people use inferential rules for making analyses but have few abstract rules that are analogous to the rules of formal logic. The pragmatic position is part of what Rips (1990) referred to as a **loose view of reasoning**.

STUDYING INDUCTION WITHIN A LOOSE VIEW

Rips (1990) stated that it is useful to examine induction within the context of a **loose view of reasoning**. This view assumes that inductive reasoning is a process of constantly updating the strength of beliefs based on the availability of concrete instances. Inductive reasoning, within a loose view, does not require special logical structure, abstract specifications, or discrete inference steps. To illustrate this idea, consider the following inductive argument:

$$\frac{\text{Bill Clinton had at least one affair.}}{\text{All presidents had at least one affair.}} \qquad (4)$$

The knowledge that Bill Clinton had at least one affair may increase one's confidence that all presidents had at least one affair and may decrease one's confidence in other assertions, such as that from now on, Clinton will abstain from having sexual liaisons, without requiring a special structure that needs updating.[1] To make a stronger case for this idea, one needs to find two arguments that share the same logical form, but elicit different inductive strengths. Such a case would demonstrate that inductive strength is independent of formal structure. Rips (1990) provided evidence for this distinction by using Goodman's (1955) New Riddle of Induction:

> Let grue be the color of an object at time t if and only if the object is green and t is before the beginning of the year 2,000, or the object is blue and t is on or after the beginning of the year 2,000.

---

[1]This view is contrasted with a strict view, in which parts or characteristics of beliefs would be important in the inductive process, such as making the leap from "Clinton had at least one affair" to "Someone had at least one affair" by assuming that the expression "someone" is essential but the predicate "had at least one affair" could stand for any other predicate. The inference can thus be said to have the form: c is P, therefore, someone is P (Rips, 1990).

Arguments 5 and 6 have the same logical form, but people tended to judge argument 5 as being inductively stronger than argument 6:

$$\frac{\text{All emeralds so far observed have been green.}}{\text{The first emerald to be observed after the beginning of the year 2000 will be green.}} \quad (5)$$

$$\frac{\text{All emeralds so far observed have been grue}}{\text{The first emerald of the year 2000 will be grue.}} \quad (6)$$

The differential degrees of confidence that people tended to generate in response to (5) versus (6) show that inductive strength cannot simply be attributed to the logical or deductive form of an argument (for similar arguments, see Osherson, Smith, & Shafir, 1986; Sternberg, 1982). Instead, people's confidence in an argument may depend on their theories about objects and categories in the world.

The loose and the pragmatic views lie at odds with the strict or **syntactic view of reasoning**. The latter view advocates that inductive reasoning has a special structure that involves processes and representations that operate in the abstract, without regard to real-life or pragmatic constraints. One kind of inductive reasoning, analogical reasoning, has generated research that supports the syntactic view. We now define analogical reasoning and examine whether it requires a special structure.

ANALOGICAL REASONING: A ROLE FOR SPECIAL STRUCTURE?

Analogical reasoning is a special case of inductive reasoning. In the process of solving a new problem (the "target problem") by analogy, a person may retrieve a similar problem that he or she has solved successfully in the past (the "source problem") and then may proceed to perform a *mapping* between the two problems to reach a solution (e.g., Gentner, 1983; Holyoak & Thagard, 1989a, 1995). Finding an adequate source problem is a nontrivial task. To use a problem as a source analog, one needs to recognize the old problem's relevance to the target problem at hand. Analogical reasoning is a challenging task when the source and target share an underlying *deep similarity* (i.e., they operate on the same principles) but have different surface-structural features (e.g., different content).

For example, Gick and Holyoak (1980, 1983) asked college students to solve Duncker's (1945) problem that describes a patient with an inoperable stomach tumor. The students were told that there are rays that can destroy the tumor, but that a ray with sufficient intensity will destroy both the healthy and unhealthy tissue. They were then asked to think of a way to destroy the tumor without causing damage to the healthy tissue that surrounds it. In the experimental condition, the students were first given a story analog that had a different content (different surface-structure) but operated on the same underlying principles (same deep structure). One version of the story describes a general who is planning to conquer a fortress. The general's problem is that the roads leading to the fortress are mined such that they explode when a large group of soldiers passes over them, but do not explode if the group is small. The general then decides to solve the problem of attacking the fortress with a big-enough army by sending many small groups of soldiers along the different roads that lead to the fortress and having them meet at the fortress. This story serves as a source analog for solving the tumor problem, namely, that one needs to emit several weaker rays that, together, converge on the tumor with the intensity of a single, strong ray.

The findings indicated that only 10% of the students in the control group who were given only the radiation problem were able to solve the problem, versus 30% of those in the experimental group who had been given the solution to the fortress problem as well. However, 70% of the students in the experimental group solved the problem when given a hint to use the fortress problem as a source analog. When the source and target have dissimilar surface-structure, one needs to make the connection between them explicit.

The analogical reasoning process can be captured by the following four stages (Thagard, 1996):

1. A person is presented with a target problem to solve (e.g., the radiation problem).

2. The person recalls a similar source problem for which a solution has been computed (e.g., the fortress problem).

3. The source and target problems are compared; their relevant components are put in correspondence with each other. This correspondence enables a mapping between the target and source components (e.g., "A fortress was located in the center of the country" is mapped to "A tumor was located in the interior of the patient's body").

4. The person adapts the source problem to produce a solution for the given target (converging small forces onto a single object results in a force with a sufficient intensity to destroy the object without causing unnecessary harm).

In her **structural mapping theory**, Gentner (1983) argued that analogical mapping relies primarily on *relational* or *structural similarity*, not as much on the actual *object attributes* involved.[2] To illustrate this idea, consider how relational similarity may be crucial to interpreting an analogy such as this:

The hydrogen atom is like our solar system.

Structural mapping theory suggests that people interpret this analogy by positing that the electron *revolves around* the nucleus in the same way that the planets *revolve around* the sun. The analogical mapping process is suggested to proceed as follows: (1) set up a correspondence between two domains (e.g., an atom and the sun); (2) discard the attributes (sun is *yellow*); (3) map the relations from the source or base domain (the sun) onto the target domains (atom); and, finally, (4) observe which relations are preserved (the electron *revolves around* the nucleus in the same way that the planets *revolve around* the sun), also called the **systematicity principle**. Gentner's structural mapping theory has received both empirical and computational support (Falkenhainer, Forbus, & Gentner, 1990; Gentner, 1989; Gentner, Rattermann, & Forbus, 1993; Gentner & Rattermann, 1991).

Holyoak and Thagard (1989, 1995) developed a model of analogical reasoning that is based on similarity and relational structure but extends beyond them to include goal-directed

---

[2]For example, consider the following sentence: "x collides with y, x is larger than y." The attributes are predicates that only take one argument, such as *large* (x), whereas relations are predicates that take two or more arguments such as *collide* (x, y).

processes. Specifically, they argued that retrieving a source problem from memory is governed by three constraints: **similarity**, **structure**, and **purpose**. Consider the constraint of similarity first. Two analog problems are similar to the extent that they are based on similar concepts. For example, if you need to register for courses at the university for the first time, you will probably retrieve other similar instances of registering that belong to the more general concept of bureaucracy.

Strong analogs are ones that share a deep-structural similarity. Thagard (1996) gave the following example: If registering for courses this year will cause you to miss your favorite TV show, it will cue you to remember a different instance that also caused you to miss your favorite TV show (e.g., paying tuition). Then you may realize that (1) both events involve bureaucracy and missing a show, leading you to infer a higher-order relation that (2) the bureaucracy *caused* you to miss a show. To create this higher-order causal inference, the "miss" and "cause" must align perfectly, as follows (Thagard, 1996, p. 81):

Target	Source
Cause: register (you)	Cause: pay tuition (you)
miss (you, TV-show)	miss (you, TV-show)

The **purpose** of making the analogy in the first place is also relevant to determining the nature of the analogical reasoning process. For example, if the analogy between registering and paying tuition serves to help you write a term paper on the effects of bureaucracy on people's emotional states, then that goal may lead to a different retrieval and mapping process than if it were to help you gain practical information on how to increase the efficiency of carrying out bureaucratical operations. The constructs of structure and purpose go beyond the work of Gentner and her colleagues (e.g., Forbus, Gentner, & Law, 1995), which focuses more heavily on the role of similarity in retrieval (see Hummel & Holyoak, 1997, for a computational model of analogical access and mapping, called LISA, which is sensitive to structural relations).

The work on analogical reasoning supports the view that inductive reasoning may rely, in part, on a special relational structure. However, as Rips (1990) pointed out, people often create analogies in situations in which the causal relations are unclear or in which more than just one source problem is available. Therefore, there may be a need for more than a logical structure to understand the processes involved in creating and using analogies.

ABSTRACT RULES OR INSTANCES: WHAT IS INDUCTIVE REASONING BASED ON?

Holland et al. (1986) and Holyoak and Thagard (1989b) argued that the end result of analogical mapping is the induction of a schema, or a set of more-abstract rules that embodies the relationship between the source and target problems. For example, Holyoak and Thagard suggested that the resulting schema from forming an analogy between the fortress and radiation problems is a general principle (i.e., converging small forces onto a single object results in a force with a sufficient intensity to destroy the object without causing unnecessary harm).

Proponents of the loose view reject the use of abstraction and point instead to the role of instances in reasoning, much like exemplar views in categorization (e.g., Hintzman, 1986; Medin & Schafer, 1978; Nosofsky, 1986; see also chapter 3). To illustrate why logical structure may not suffice for performing analogies, Rips (1990) provided the following demonstration (based on Davies, 1988):

Say that instance a has property p, denoted $p(a)$, and we want to know whether instance b also has property p, denoted $p(b)$. An inductive analogy would be to find a property or set of properties P that both a and b share, denoted $P(a)$ and $P(b)$. The inference would then be this:

$$\frac{p(a) \quad P(a) \ \& \ P(b).}{p(b)} \tag{7}$$

There must be constraints on P because it cannot be just any property or set of properties. For example, if a is a brown dog [$p(a)$ & $P(a)$] and b is a dog [$P(b)$], we cannot assume that b is brown. We may then want to consider using a similarity function of some sort to determine how similar a and b are. However, even if they are similar (both are Labrador retrievers), we still cannot be certain about the validity of the conclusion (one can be brown and the other black). Similar to the case of categorization, we may need to have some knowledge about the variability of p (the color brown) across P (dogs) to have a certain degree of confidence in the conclusion.

One way to resolve the controversy between the loose camp, which argues for the importance of real-world context, and the strict camp, which argues for specialized abstract structures, is to posit the existence of both. Sloman (1996) made a strong case for two complementary systems of reasoning: the associative and the rule based.

The **associative system** operates on similarity and contiguity, draws on personal experiences with exemplars, and is largely automatic. This system is consistent with the loose view. The **rule-based system**, on the other hand, operates by manipulating symbols that have a logical structure and a set of variables; draws on language, culture, and formal systems (such as formal logic and mathematics); and is largely conscious or strategic (although conscious processing is neither necessary or sufficient for the rule-based system). This system is consistent with the strict or syntactic view.

Sloman illustrated the distinction between the associative and rule-based systems in diverse areas of reasoning, such as deduction, induction, and categorization. In the area of deduction, he cited work that shows that people's error rates, reaction times, or both are proportional to the number of rules required for making a logical inference (e.g., determining whether an argument is true or not) (see Braine et al., 1984; Osherson, 1975; Rips, 1983, 1989a, 1994). In the case of categorization, Sloman argued that even though similarity is clearly important, there is also a place for a rule-based system because similarity alone cannot determine how people infer that an object is an instance of a particular category.

Sloman used an example from Murphy (1993) to illustrate this last point: Imagine that you are looking at a new animal in a zoo, called a Zork. Assuming that this is the first Zork you encounter, which of its features would you generalize to other Zorks? People are usually willing to make generalizations about attributes, such as size and weight, but not about age or sex, for example. There is more than similarity operating here because if it were the only factor, one should be willing to generalize from all attributes, giving them the same psychological weight. Theory-based views of categorization use rules to provide explanations for inductive inferences (see chapter 3 for more details).

So far, we have discussed general issues regarding the nature of inductive reasoning: Is it constrained by pragmatic or syntactic factors? Is it based on similarity judgments or on rules? We now examine the specifics of induction by discussing processes involved in the formation and evaluation of hypotheses.

HYPOTHESIS TESTING

One of the classic areas in which cognitive psychology emerged as an independent discipline was concept identification or concept formation. The main question it addressed was how people form concepts by consciously testing hypotheses about the nature of these concepts. A historical set of studies on concept formation was conducted by Bruner et al. (1956). We first detail their approach and its impact on current theories and then discuss more recent work on hypothesis testing.

Concept Formation

Bruner et al. (1956) used a **concept-identification task** to examine how people form hypotheses. Their paradigm consisted of showing participants a set of stimuli, comprising geometric figures on rectangular cards, and asking them to discover whether these stimuli followed a predetermined concept or rule. Each stimulus was formed by combinations of four dimensions, each having three different values. Specifically, figures appeared as one of four distinct shapes (a circle, square, triangle, or cross) and as one of three set sizes (single, dou-

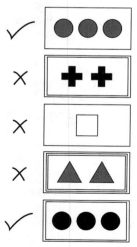

Figure 6.1 An example of a concept-identification task (1).

ble, or triple) and colors (black, green, or red). The borders of the cards were either single, double, or triple. A particular concept could be defined by the joint presence of the stimulus features (e.g., *two green circles*), by the presence of either of several features (e.g., *three borders or crosses*), or by the presence of a certain relationship between different dimensions (e.g., *the number of figures equals the number of borders*). These concepts are termed conjunctive, disjunctive, and relational, respectively.

The cards depicted in Figure 6.1 are positive and negative exemplars of a concept, indicated by a check mark or by an "X" respectively. Can you identify the concept or rule in Figure 6.1? The rule is the conjunctive concept "three circles." Now try to discover the concept depicted in Figure 6.2. It is a bit more difficult. In this case, it is the disjunctive concept "white shapes or three borders." The problem is similar to those used by Bruner et al. (1956).

In the **reception paradigm**, the participants were shown cards, in succession, that were either positive or negative exemplars of a particular concept. After each card was presented, they provided a tentative hypothesis about the correct concept it represented without receiving any feedback from the experimenter. For disjunctive concepts, in particular, the participants tended to rely on positive instances (that conformed to their hypothesized rule) and to disregard negative instances (that disconfirmed their hypothesized rule).

In the **selection paradigm**, the participants were allowed to control the sequence of cards they received. The experimenter began by providing a participant with a card that was a positive exemplar of a particular concept from the entire array of available stimuli. The participant then was asked to decide what the concept was by choosing cards, one at a time. As each card was chosen, the experimenter provided feedback on whether the card was a positive or

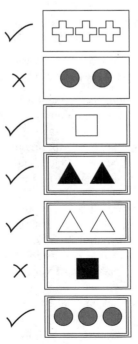

Figure 6.2 An example of a concept-identification task (2).

a negative exemplar of the concept, and then the participant was allowed to guess what the concept was.

An efficient strategy for performing the task is **focusing**. In this strategy, a positive exemplar of the correct concept is used as a focus card against which the next card is compared. The person selects a card with features that differ from the focus card by either one (in conservative focusing) or several (in focus gambling) attributes at a time. For example, if the focus card contains two red squares with a single border, then the next card chosen may be one with two red squares with a double border. If the new exemplar is classified by the experimenter as being a positive exemplar of the concept, then the number of borders can be eliminated as a relevant attribute. With each subsequent card selected, the relevant attributes of the correct concept can be retained or eliminated in this fashion. The corresponding hypothesis can then be either strengthened or weakened. This strategy provides a direct test of the hypothesis and is also cognitively efficient.

Most participants, however, tended to engage in a **successive scanning** strategy: They tested cards that would confirm a single hypothesis at a time. For example, if the hypothesis was *green*, then the participants tended to select only cards with green objects for subsequent testing. If a subsequent card was a negative exemplar that falsified the person's hypothesis, then a different hypothesis was selected and tested. The testing of the new hypothesis was usually conducted with no reference to the information already attained through tests of prior hypotheses. As in the reception paradigm, the participants tended to avoid testing cards that may have turned out to be negative exemplars.

Bruner et al. concluded that people tend to commit a **verification bias**. In the process of testing hypotheses, people tend to try to confirm their initial hypotheses, rather than to seek disconfirmation. That is, they tend to test cases that would support and strengthen their hypotheses, rather than cases that would weaken these beliefs. This bias has been referred to as *confirmation bias* (e.g., Fischhoff & Beyth-Marom, 1983).

Confirmation Bias in Hypothesis Testing

A classic demonstration of confirmation bias can be illustrated by people's behavior on Wason's (1960) 2-4-6 problem: You are provided with a set of three numbers: 2, 4, and 6. These numbers conform to a rule. Your task is to discover the rule by creating new triples that conform to your inferred rule. The experimenter will respond yes if your triple conforms to the real rule and no if it does not. Once you feel confident that you have discovered the rule, please state your hypothesis. What is the first triple that you would generate to test your inferred rule?

People show a strong tendency to generate triples that are consistent with their initial hypotheses. For example, participants who assumed that the rule was "numbers increasing by 2" tended to provide confirming triples, such as 4, 6, and 8 over disconfirming instances, such as 4, 6, and 7. Wason's rule was simply "any three ascending numbers." The participants demonstrated a strong bias toward verifying their hypothesis, which resulted in their overconfidence in their erroneous inferred rule. As it happens, if a person keeps on generating triples that conform to the inferred rule—"numbers increasing by 2"—the experimenter will always say yes.

The tendency to seek positive instances that confirm one's initial hypothesis, rather than to seek negative instances that will not, has been replicated in many studies following Wason's 2-4-6 task (e.g., Dunbar, 1993; Mynatt, Doherty, & Tweney, 1977, 1978; Tweney et al., 1980; Wason & Johnson-Laird, 1972). For example, Mynatt et al. (1978) provided undergraduate science majors with computer-generated displays that depicted geometric shapes with various degrees of brightness, shape, and size. They asked the participants to fire a particle across the screen and then to discover the laws of the particle's motion in that artificial universe. Half the participants were assigned to the "strong inference" condition, in which they were instructed on the value of falsification and multiple hypothesis testing. The other half were not given any instruction. Mynatt et al. found that the participants in both groups relied heavily on confirmation strategies (such as temporarily abandoning a hypothesis that did not seem to work, only to return to it later). The participants permanently abandoned falsified hypotheses only 30% of the time.

Snyder and Swann (1978) provided evidence for confirmation bias in the area of social cognition. They asked participants to place themselves in a situation in which they were interviewing another person. The participants' task was to discover whether the interviewee was an introvert or an extrovert by selecting what they perceived to be the most diagnostic questions from a set of questions they were handed. The participants tended to select questions that were consistent with their stereotype of an introverted or an extroverted person. For example, if the task was to assess whether a person was an extrovert, the participants tended to ask **confirmatory questions**, such as "What would you do if you wanted to liven up a party?" rather than **disconfirmatory questions**, such as "What factors make it hard for you to really open up to people?" or neutral questions, like "What are your career goals?" Snyder and Swann claimed that if the answer to a question is predictable, then the question is nondiagnostic and leads to an inefficient interviewing process.

Fischhoff and Beyth-Marom (1983) criticized studies of confirmation bias on several grounds. The first is that participants may be behaving in accordance with social norms, rather than committing inferential errors per se. They criticized Snyder and Swann's study on the grounds that the participants may have treated the hypothesis as true (the person is an introvert or an extrovert) and then decided to ask the person questions that would be the least awkward socially.

A second criticism is that what appears to be a confirmation bias may actually reflect consideration of *source credibility*. For example, Mahoney (1977) found that when scientists were asked to review a fictitious manuscript, their comments were more favorable when the manuscript's results confirmed a dominant hypothesis in their field than when the manuscript's results disconfirmed an accepted viewpoint. However, as Fischhoff and Beyth-Marom (1983) pointed out, the reviews may have reflected a belief that investigators who report disconfirming results for an established hypothesis tend to use inferior or biased research methods.

Finally, Fischhoff and Beyth-Marom (1983) attacked the interpretation of the Wason 2-4-6 task as demonstrating confirmation bias. They argued that the modal response pattern that participants give (e.g., sequential even numbers, such as 8, 10, and 12) illustrates affirmation rather than confirmation. Because of the vast number of potentially correct hypotheses in the 2-4-6 task, people may tend to construct triples to which an affirmative answer would serve to falsify one of their hypotheses. For example, say a person selects the triple 8, 10, and 12 for testing. This triple could be diagnostic if the person held two corresponding hypotheses: "sequential even numbers" (the person's first guess) and "numbers less than 7" (the person's second guess). If this triple gets corroboration from the experimenter, then the person increases her confidence in the "sequential even numbers" rule while dismissing the "num-

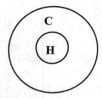

Figure 6.3 The hypothesized rule as a subset of the correct rule.

bers less than 7" rule. The triple is nondiagnostic on the 2-4-6 task because of the specific nature of the correct rule: "numbers increasing in value." This rule belongs to a special case that cannot be ruled out by an affirmation strategy.

If an affirmative test strategy turns out to be helpful, is trying to confirm a hypothesis (rather than trying to falsify it) a bias after all?

Confirmation Bias Revisited: A Fallacy or a Rational Choice?

The "bias" in confirmation bias may be a misnomer. Klayman and Ha (1987) treated confirmation as a **positive test strategy**. They contended that such a strategy may not be unwise in many real-life circumstances. Let us use the 2-4-6 task as an example. Wason designed the "correct" rule—ascending numbers—on purpose, such that a positive test strategy for the subrule—consecutive even numbers—would always yield positive results and never meet with falsification. However, as Klayman and Ha pointed out, such a situation, in which the hypothesized rule is a subset of the correct rule, is only one instance of all possible relations between hypotheses and correct rules (where "C" stands for the set generated by the correct rule and "H" stands for the set generated by the hypothesized rule) (see Figure 6.3).

The hypothesized rule could also overlap with the correct rule or the incorrect rule. For example, assume that the hypothesized rule ("numbers increasing by 2") overlaps with the correct rule ("three even numbers") (see Figure 6.4). Here, positive instances of the hypothesized rule (1, 3, 5) would falsify the hypothesized rule, and some positive instances of the correct rule (4, 6, 2) would not be found in the set generated by the hypothesized rule. In this case, falsification would occur with either a positive or a negative test strategy.

Furthermore, consider a situation in which the correct rule is a subset of the hypothesized rule (see Figure 6.5). For example, the hypothesized rule could still be "numbers increasing by 2," but the correct rule may now be "consecutive even numbers." A person who would look only for negative instances would actually be hurt by using this "optimal" strategy of disconfirmation because there are no instances in which "increases by 2" gets violated but is found in the set generated by the correct rule (any triple that violates "increases by 2" will

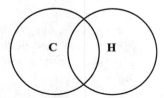

Figure 6.4 Overlap between the hypothesized rule and the correct rule.

Figure 6.5 The correct rule as a subset of the hypothesized rule.

also violate "consecutive even numbers"). The only way to obtain falsification in this situation is to look for positive instances that occur in the hypothesized set but that do not occur in the correct set (1, 3, and 5).

The main point is that a positive test strategy may be a good heuristic under many conditions. For example, Klayman and Ha (1987) pointed out that if you are a manufacturer trying to find out the best way to advertise your product and you are operating on the assumption that the best way to do so is through television, the target set that would correspond to the correct choice or rule is the one that has the most effective advertising strategies. Let the target set consist of a variety of methods (including TV commercials, magazine ads, and radio advertisements) that are all equally effective. Positive tests would never provide you with disconfirmation, similar to Wason's manipulation of the 2-4-6 rule. However, suppose that the correct rule for maximizing efficiency is to use humor. In this case, both positive and negative instances of the rule would yield falsification (for example, serious TV ads would not work, whereas humorous non-TV ads would). The crucial factor for hypothesis testing, therefore, seems to be which strategy would prove a hypothesis wrong, rather than whether people use a confirmation "bias" by testing only positive instances. In fact, testing positive instances may lead to falsification under many real-life circumstances.

Once people generate hypotheses, how do they evaluate them? In the next section, we discuss normative and descriptive theories of evaluating hypotheses by using probability.

HYPOTHESIS EVALUATION AND PROBABILISTIC REASONING

To evaluate a hypothesis, people form judgments on the basis of estimating probabilities. **Probability estimation** refers to a quantitative measure of the strength of or confidence in a particular proposition, such as the belief that one will get a tenured job in a university based on the number of one's publications (Baron, 1988). Probabilistic reasoning is challenging for most people. For example, try to solve the following three-card problem.

You are told that there are three cards in a hat. One card is red on both sides (the red-red card). One card is white on both sides (the white-white card). One card is red on one side and white on the other (the red-white card). You close your eyes, pick a single card randomly, and then toss it into the air. The drawn card lands on the floor with a red side up. What is the probability that this is the red-red card?

Think about the answer to this question before you read on. If your answer is "1/2," then you responded in accordance with the majority of people (Bar-Hillel & Falk, 1982). Most people reason as follows: The red face means that we can exclude the white-white card from consideration. This means that the cards can either be the red-red or the red-white ones; each with a 50-50 chance. However, this response is wrong. Why?

To demonstrate the process for arriving at the correct solution, let us construct a table of possible outcomes (see Table 6.1). As can be seen from this table, there are three possibilities when red lands on top: It either belongs to the red-white card (one out of three possible scenarios) or it belongs to the red-red card (two out of three possible scenarios). Thus, the probability of the card being the red-red one is two out of three, or .67.

Probability estimates can be done in response to objective problems, such as the one just described, and to more subjective problems, such as the previously mentioned one about the strength of or confidence in the belief that one will get tenure. To examine the validity of people's probabilistic judgments, we need to decide on a normative theory against which to pit these judgments. Baron (1988) identified three theories of probability: the **frequency**, **logical possibilities**, and **personal judgments** theories.

The **frequency theory** measures probability in terms of the relative frequencies of past events. In this framework, the probability of getting a tenured job if one has a certain number of publications, say, 30, corresponds to the proportion of tenured professors who had produced at least 30 publications at the time they were up for tenure. If there is no information about such a proportion, then a probability judgment would be meaningless. Such a theory is problematic. Baron illustrated this point by using the following example: Consider the case in which one flips a coin 10 times in a row, and it comes up Heads 7 times. What is the probability of getting Heads on the 11th flip? The frequentist would argue that it is .7, even though most mathematicians would argue that it is .5 (an independent toss of a fair coin can come up only heads or tails).

Proponents of the frequency theory would respond that probability is not the observed frequency but the limit that the observed frequency would approach if the coin were tossed repeatedly. A counterargument was made by Hacking (1965), who claimed that some sequences may not have a limit. Another problem is that the relative frequency of an event depends on how one classifies the event. Different classification schemes may result in different relative frequencies. For instance, in classifying publications, will just any publication do (even one in the *Journal of Irreproducible Results*), or would each publication have to be of a certain quality? If so, is there an unequivocal way to define quality?

TABLE 6.1   The Three-Card Problem

Type of Card	Outcome	
	Top of Card	Bottom of Card
White-white card	White	White
White-white card	White	White
Red-white card	Red	White
Red-white card	White	Red
Red-red card	Red	Red
Red-red card	Red	Red

The **logical theory** suggests that we can specify a set of events or propositions that are exchangeable and thus have independent and identical probabilities (e.g., drawing a particular card from a deck, say an ace of spades, has exactly the same probability as that of drawing a different card from the same deck, say the ace of hearts). More formally, the probability of a proposition is the proportion of exchangeable possible worlds in which that proposition is true (Carnap, 1950). For example, the set of possible worlds in which you would draw an ace of spades is exchangeable with the set of all the possible worlds in which you would draw a king. The logical view helps explain why when one flips a coin 10 times in a row and it comes up Head 7 times, then the probability of getting Heads on the 11th flip is .5 (not .7 as the frequentists would have us believe). However, as Baron pointed out, the disadvantage of this theory is that it is often impossible to identify the set of exchangeable events. This theory may apply better to coin tosses and card drawing than to real-life problems, such as trying to predict the probability of getting tenure.

The **personal theory** differs from both the frequency and logical theories in that it assumes that a probability estimate is a subjective judgment of the likelihood of an event (Savage, 1954). This theory holds that a probability judgment is based on beliefs and knowledge that may, in turn, include knowledge about frequencies and logical possibilities. It differentiates between how probability judgments should be constructed (the normative-prescriptive component) and how people actually make these judgments (the descriptive component). People who adhere to this theory argue that probability judgments can be made even in the face of uncertainty. For instance, if there is no reason to believe that one event is more probable than another, then we should assign each event the same likelihood (1/52 for drawing each card in a deck with replacement). Thus, the personal view can make use of logical possibilities.

Both the frequency theory and the logical theory treat probability statements as reflecting the objective likelihood of objects or events. The personal view, on the other hand, treats probability statements as subjective judgments. What are the rules or constraints that govern people's probability judgments? One kind of constraint is *coherence* (Baron, 1994). Coherence means that people's probability judgments must follow certain mathematical rules:

1. Any statement is either true or false. The probability that it is true and the probability that it is false both add up to a certainty, or a probability of 1.

2. Two statements are mutually exclusive if they cannot both be true simultaneously.

3. The conditional probability of a proposition P1, given proposition P2, is the probability that one can assign to P1, given that P2 is true. We denote this conditional probability as p(P1/P2), which reads as "the probability of P1 given P2" (where the slash stands for "given").

These coherence rules help us to evaluate the strength and consistency of probability judgements. One major formalism for capturing coherence is Bayes's theorem.

Bayes's Theorem

Bayes's theorem is a formal model for evaluating the coherence requirement embedded in the personal view. We demonstrate this theorem by using a problem, posed by Tversky and Kahneman (1982, pp. 156–157) first, and then by defining it more formally.

A cab was involved in a hit-and-run accident at night. Two cab companies, the Green and the Blue, operate in the city. You are given the following data:

(a) 85% of the cabs in the city are Green and 15% are Blue.

(b) A witness identified the cab as Blue.

The court tested the reliability of the witness under the same circumstances that existed on the night of the accident and concluded that the witness correctly identified each one of the two colors 80% of the time and failed 20% of the time.

What is the probability that the cab involved in the accident was Blue rather than Green?

What do you think the answer is? Try to compute the answer before you read on (this problem will be discussed again in the next section). Before we present the Bayesian analysis, let us think of this problem in terms of frequencies. Let us assume that there are 100 cabs in the city, so that 85 are green and 15 are blue. Out of 100 cases, if the cab involved was really blue, then the witness would identify 80% of all blue cabs as blue (12 blue cabs) but would erroneously classify 20% as green (3 blue cabs). If the cab involved in the accident was green, then the witness would correctly identify 80% of green cabs as green (68 green cabs) but erroneously judge the other 20% to be blue (17 green cabs). The ratio we are looking for is the number of cabs that the witness identified as blue when they were really blue (number of hits; see Table 6.2), out of the total number of cabs that the witness identified as blue that were either blue or were actually green (number of hits and false alarms) [when the witness says blue and cab is blue/ (says blue and cab is blue + says blue but cab is green)]. So we have: $12 / (12 + 17) = 12/29 = 41\%$.

In Bayesian terms, we are looking to find the probability that the cab was really blue (the hypothesis, or H), given that the witness said it was blue (the datum or D), denoted P(H/D), or the probability of the hypothesis, given the datum. The Bayesian odds formula is as follows:

$$\frac{P(H \mid D)}{P(\sim H \mid D)} = \frac{P(H) \cdot P(D \mid H)}{P(\sim H) \cdot P(D / \sim H)}$$

Rewritten, it reads as follows:

$$P(H \mid D) = \frac{P(H) \cdot P(D \mid H)}{P(H) \cdot P(D \mid H) + P(\sim H) \cdot P(D / \sim H)}$$

The P(H/D) is the probability of the hypothesis, given the datum (the probability that the car is really blue, given that the witness identifies it as blue). The P(D/H) is the probability of the datum, given the hypothesis (the probability that the witness will say "blue" when the cab is really blue). The P(H) is the base rate of the hypothesis, or its relative frequency (the relative frequency of blue cabs). The P(~H) is the base rate of an alternative hypothesis (~ stands for "not"), or the relative frequency of the alternative algorithm that has been used in past problem-solving episodes.

Table 6.2 The Cab Problem

| Type of Cab | Witness's Response | |
	Says Green	Says Blue
Green cab	68 (correct rejection)	17 (false alarm)
Blue cab	3 (MISS)	12 (HIT)

With respect to the cab problem, we have the following:

$$P(H) = .15$$

$$P(\sim H) = .85$$

$$P(D/H) = .8$$

$$P(D/\sim H) = .2$$

The Bayesian analysis yields the following probability:

$$P(H \: / \: D) = \frac{(.15)\cdot(.8)}{(.15)\cdot(.8) + (.85)\cdot(.2)} = \frac{.12}{.12 + .17} = \frac{.12}{.29} = .41$$

Usually, when people are given problems, such as the one just stated, they estimate the probability that the cab was indeed blue as .8. This reasoning process fails to take into account the P(H), or the base rate or relative frequency of the hypothesis (the relative frequency of blue cabs), a phenomenon that Tversky and Kahneman (1981) termed **base-rate neglect**. This finding suggests that, subjectively, people tend to overweigh the probability of the datum, given the hypothesis (e.g., the reliability of the witness) and ignore or underemphasize the probability of the hypothesis (the fact that the base rate of blue cars is small). Base-rate neglect has been shown in many different inductive reasoning tasks and has generated much research and controversy.

Deviations From Normative Probabilistic Reasoning: Base-Rate Neglect

Researchers have used Bayes's theorem as a normative model for examining base-rate neglect (Fischoff & Beyth-Marom, 1983; Slovic & Lichtenstein, 1971; von Winterfeldt & Edwards, 1986) in different domains, including clinical diagnosis (Eddy, 1982; Meehl & Rosen, 1955), accounting (Joyce & Biddle, 1981), and the law (Fienberg & Schervish, 1986; Finkelstein, 1978; Kaye, 1989). For example, Eddy (1982) demonstrated that physicians suffer from base-rate neglect, resulting in serious repercussions for diagnosis and treatment. Consider, for instance, the following problem by imagining that you are in the role of the physician (adapted from Eddy, 1982; see also Baron, 1988).

A woman in her 30s comes to see you. She has just discovered a small lump in her breast, and she is worried that it might be cancerous. After you examine her, you determine that the probability of cancer is about .05, or 1 in 20, in women who are her age and who have a similar medical history. You decide that the best course of action would be to have the woman undergo a mammogram. In women who have cancer, the mammogram indicates cancer 80% of the time. In women who do not have cancer, the mammogram indicates cancer falsely 20% of the time.

The mammogram for your patient comes out positive. What is the probability that she actually has breast cancer?

Most often, people, including physicians, tend to say that the probability that the woman actually has cancer corresponds to the reliability of the mammogram (in this case, it is is.8). However, conducting a Bayesian analysis on this problem shows that the probability is actually only .17! To convince yourself of this result, you can use the Bayesian formula, where P(cancer) = .05, P(~cancer) = .95, P(positive mammogram/cancer) = .8, and P(positive mammogram/~cancer) = .2.

Eddy (1982) argued that base-rate neglect is due to people's tendencies to confuse conditional probabilities, or the probability of X, given that Y is present (e.g., the probability of cancer, given the existence of a positive mammogram) with the probability of Y, given that X is present (e.g., the probability of getting a positive mammogram, given that the woman has breast cancer). In Bayesian terms, it is the confusion between P(H/D) and P(D/H). Eddy was able to show that conditional probabilities are confused, at times, even in medical research journals, leading to damaging effects on medical decision making. A physician who underestimates the possibility of a false positive (a woman with a positive mammogram who does not have cancer) may cause a patient to take more drastic measures than is realistically warranted and cause her undue stress.

Another example that has been frequently used to illustrate the phenomenon of base-rate neglect is the lawyer-engineer problem (Kahneman & Tversky, 1973, pp. 241–242). Kahneman and Tversky presented two groups of participants with the following scenario: An individual has been chosen at random from a set of 100 individuals. The first group was told that the set comprised 70 engineers and 30 lawyers (the engineer high group). The second group was told that the set comprised 70 lawyers and 30 engineers (the engineer low group). The participants in both groups were then asked to determine the probability that the randomly chosen individual was an engineer. They met this challenge by giving the correct probabilities: The engineer high group gave an estimate of .70, and the engineer low group gave an estimate of .30.

The participants were then told that another individual was randomly selected from the set. This time, they received a personality description of the individual:

Jack is a 45-year-old man. He is married and has four children. He is generally conservative, careful, and ambitious. He shows no interest in political and social issues and spends most of his free time on his many hobbies, which include home carpentry, sailing, and mathematical puzzles.

The participants in both groups gave a .90 probability estimate that Jack was an engineer, even though the base rates for engineers were different in the two groups. Another manipulation involved giving the participants the following personality description of a different randomly selected individual:

Dick is a 30-year-old man. He is married with no children. A man of high ability and high motivation, he promises to be quite successful in his field. He is well liked by his colleagues.

The participants in both groups estimated a .50 probability that Dick was an engineer. This time, even a completely uninformative description affected people's probability estimates. In conclusion, Kahneman and Tversky (1973) argued that when there is individuating information about an individual, regardless of its informativeness, people tend to rely on that information at the expense of using base rates. The fact that the more stereotypical description (Jack) elicited high probability estimates supports the use of a representativeness heuristic. The **representativeness heuristic** suggests that a sample looks representative if it is similar in important characteristics to the population from which it was selected (Kahneman & Tversky, 1972). We discuss this heuristic in more detail in chapter 8.

More recent research has shown, however, that there are many circumstances under which people's judgments are affected by base-rate information. What are these circumstances? One answer is when there is a clear relationship between the base rate and the outcome of the problem (e.g., Bar-Hillel & Fischhoff, 1981; Gigerenzer, Hell, & Blank, 1988). Consider the following example (Gigerenzer et al., 1988, p. 521):

In the 1978/79 season of the West-German soccer "Bundesliga," Team A won 10 out of the 34 games. The other games were either drawn or lost. We have selected some of the games of that season randomly and checked their final results as well as their half-time results. For instance, on the 7th day of the season the half time result was 2:1 in favor of Team A. What is your probability that this game belongs to those 10 games won out of 34?

Gigerenzer et al. varied the base rate of winning from a low of 7 to a high of 19 out of the 34 games. They found that as the base rate increased, so did the estimates of winning. People did use the base-rate information, as predicted.

Another factor that promotes the use of base-rate information is a direct experience with examples, rather than reasoning based on summary information only (Manis, Dovalinia, Avis, & Cardoze, 1980; Medin & Edelson, 1988). For example, in Manis et al.'s (1980) study, the participants were shown 50 yearbook pictures of male students and then were asked to infer these students' attitudes toward the legalization of marijuana and mandatory seat-belt legislation. After the participants made a prediction about each student in the yearbook, some were told that 20% of the students favored the given legislation (marijuana or seat-belt law), whereas other participants were told that 80% of the students favored the given legislation. After looking at pictures of 20 other students, many more participants in the high base-rate condition (80%) predicted that these students were likely to endorse the legislation, which showed a marked effect of the base-rate manipulation. Similarly, Christensen-Szalanski and Bushyhead (1981) and Christensen-Szalanski and Beach (1982) found that when physicians had direct experience with a base rate (e.g., for pneumonia) based on their clinical experience, they were affected by that base rate in making medical decisions.

Other sources of facilitation involve factors, such as representing problems in a formulation that involves a random and repeated selection of choices (Gigerenzer, 1991, 1996; Gigerenzer et al., 1988; Gigerenzer, Hoffrage, & Kleinboelting, 1991; Tversky & Kahneman, 1983). For example, Gigerenzer et al. (1988) showed that repeated random sampling of six informative personality descriptions on the lawyer-engineer problem increased the use of base-rate information (for a criticism of this study, see Kahneman & Tversky, 1996). For more details on this and other sources of base-rate facilitation see Koehler (1996).

We have seen that under some circumstances, people can behave more normatively, even when they have a general tendency to endorse certain biases, such as confirmation bias or base-rate neglect. A fruitful question may then be this: Under what circumstances do people display "rational" or "irrational" reasoning? We believe that rationality may be linked to people's ability to reason probabilistically with set-based representations. We define what we mean by a set-based representation by first discussing research on a difficult conditional probability problem, known as the *Monty Hall dilemma*.

WHEN ARE PEOPLE "RATIONAL" OR "IRRATIONAL": FACILITATING INDUCTIVE REASONING ON THE MONTY HALL DILEMMA

Under which conditions do people exhibit rational or irrational reasoning? We center this discussion on an extremely hard conditional probability problem, known as the Monty Hall dilemma. This problem stirred much controversy when it appeared in Marilyn Vos Savant's column in *Parade* magazine (September 9, 1990):

> Suppose you're on a game show, and you're given a choice of three doors. Behind one door is a car; behind the others, goats. You pick a door—say, No. 1—and the host, who knows what's behind the doors, opens another door—say, No. 3—which has a goat. He then says to you, 'Do you want to pick door No. 2?' Is it to your advantage to switch your choice?

The initial set of choices is captured by diagram A, whereas the final set of choices is captured by diagram B in Figure 6.6.

The solution to this problem is counterintuitive (e.g., Falk, 1992; Gilovich, Medvec, & Chen, 1995; Shimojo & Ichikawa, 1989). Almost always, people choose to stay with their first choice because they believe that the odds are 50:50 that the prize is behind either of the re-

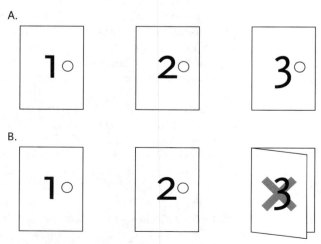

Figure 6.6 The Monty Hall dilemma.

maining doors. Instead, the correct answer is that switching increases the odds of winning. We demonstrate why the odds of switching are higher by using a Bayesian analysis. The prior probabilities (i.e., the probabilities that the prize is behind each door, before the contestant chooses a door) are as follows:

$$P(door1) = P(door2) = P(door3) = .33.$$

The next step is to calculate the conditional probabilities: $P(doori/doorj)$, namely, the probabilities that the prize is behind each one of the doors (door$j$), given that the host opens a particular door (door$i$). For ease of demonstration, suppose that the contestant chooses door 3, and the host opens door 2:

$$P(door2/door3) = .5$$

$$P(door2/door2) = 0$$

$$P(door2/door1) = 1$$

According to Bayes's theorem, the probability that the prize is in door$j$, given that the host chooses to open door$i$ is this:

$$P(doorj \mid doori) = \frac{P(doorj){\cdot}P(doori \mid doorj)}{P(door1){\cdot}P(doori \mid door1) + P(door2){\cdot}P(doori \mid door2) + P(door3){\cdot}P(doori \mid door3)}$$

Staying with door 3 thus results in the following probability that the prize is in door 3, given that the host chooses to open door 2:

$$P(door3 \mid door2) = \frac{(.33){\cdot}(.5)}{(.33){\cdot}(.5) + (.33){\cdot}(0) + (.33){\cdot}(1)} = .33$$

Switching to door 1, on the other hand, results in an increased probability:

$$P(door1 \mid door2) = \frac{(.33){\cdot}(1)}{(.33){\cdot}(1) + (.33){\cdot}(.5) + (.33){\cdot}(0)} = .67$$

Why does the incorrect answer to this problem—the odds that the prize is in either door are the same—seem right when it is wrong? Ben-Zeev, Dennis, Stibel, & Sloman (2000) posited that when people are asked to make a decision on three doors, they create individual mental models of each door with an assigned probability (.33) for each. When one door is discarded from consideration, the remaining "equally likely" alternatives maintain the same ratio (i.e., first, the chance of winning is 1:3 because there are three doors, but after one door is eliminated, the ratio becomes 1:2). People use what appears to be a "constant ratio" theorem (Falk, 1992; Shimojo & Ichikawa, 1989).

Ben-Zeev et al. argued that if people use a mental-model representation, then given 100 doors, they would be more likely to switch because representing 100 individual choices would exceed working memory capacity. The prediction, called *the collapsing-sets hypothesis*, is that memory overload would force people to create only two sets: one for their initial choice ("my choice") and one for the collapsed remaining set of choices ("the rest"). Whereas eliminating a choice from the three-choice condition would leave two seemingly equiprobable choices, removing 98 choices from the 100-choice condition would make the remaining choice inherit the higher probability associated with the set it belonged to.

After headlines that stated "Marilyn is wrong," Vos Savant argued for switching on the Monty Hall dilemma in a similar fashion:

> Yes, you should switch. The first door has a 1/3 chance of winning, but the second door has 2/3 chance. Here's a good way to visualize what happened. Suppose there are a million doors, and you pick door No. 1. Then the host, who knows what's behind the doors and will always avoid the one with the prize, opens them all except for door No. 777,777. You'd switch to that door pretty fast, wouldn't you?

However, Ben-Zeev et al. (2000) found that even though more people who were given 100 choices tended to switch (7 out of 22) than people who were presented with 3 choices (1 out of 22), the overwhelming majority still decided to stay!

Gilovich et al. (1995) argued that people usually tend to stay on the Monty Hall dilemma (rather than stay half the time and switch the other half) because of the effects of possible future regret. The idea is that people give more psychological weight *to errors of commission* than to *errors of omission*. That is, they are more willing to take the risk that their initial choice was wrong (error of omission) than to "tempt fate" by switching, only later to find out that their original choice was correct ("I would kick myself if I switched, and it turned out that my first choice was correct") (error of commission).

Ben-Zeev et al. (2000) showed, however, that the effects of the collapsing-sets hypothesis were stronger than the effects of regret. In one experiment, the participants were told that they were presented with two tables—one that had three boxes on it and one with no boxes. In one of the boxes was a cash prize. In this scenario, the host selected a box randomly and moved that box to the empty table. This way, the initial choice was clearly partitioned from the rest of the set (similarly, in the 100-choice condition, the host partitioned one box from the remaining 99). Then, the knowledgeable host opened one of the remaining two boxes on the original table (or 98 out of the 99 remaining boxes), and the participant had to decide whether to stay or to switch. If regret was the major force, then more people would stay in both the 3- and the 100-choice conditions. However, the results were consistent with the collapsing-sets hypothesis: half the people in the 3-choice condition switched, and so did an overwhelming majority (75%) of people in the 100-choice condition.

The conclusions from this study are that people's probabilistic reasoning may be facilitated when they are given an opportunity to generate set-based representations. Such representations may be created when either working-memory capacity is exceeded or when choices are explicitly partitioned. The idea that people use set-based representations is consistent with work in deductive reasoning, such as the set-theoretic accounts of deductive reasoning offered by Guyote and Sternberg (1981) and Erickson (1978) (see chapter 5).

A caveat about the Monty Hall dilemma is in order, however. Creating collapsed sets may improve people's performance but not necessarily people's understanding of the underlying probabilities. More experiments need to be done to show that people switch because they have developed meaningful representations. One such manipulation would be to use a simple transfer task, training people on the 100-box condition first and then giving them a 3-box problem to solve. These results would then be compared to those of a control group that would receive only the 3-box condition.

Future research may help elucidate the question of whether people did or did not develop an understanding of conditional probabilities on the Monty Hall dilemma. However, there have been demonstrations that people can be made to develop a better understanding of inductive-reasoning principles. Nisbett et al. (1983) claimed that the conditions that help elicit the correct use of probabilistic and inferential reasoning are (1) when the sample space and the process of sampling is made clear (i.e., tossing a coin or selecting a card from a deck), (2) when the role of chance is made salient (e.g., spinning a wheel of numbers), and (3) when there is a cultural prescription to reason inductively (e.g., taking a formal course in logical and inductive reasoning). The last condition has also been supported by other studies, such as Fong, Krantz, and Nisbett's (1986), which showed that with more instruction, people are able to improve the frequency and quality of their inductive inferences.

CORRELATIONAL REASONING AND JUDGMENTS OF CO-OCCURENCE

An important part of making inferences is determining the relationship between different variables or events. For example, we may want to determine the relationship between scores on the SAT and students' performance in undergraduate classes, between people's level of stress during a given week and the number of times they worked out (or failed to work out) that week, or between people's level of hunger and their amount of impulse buying at a supermarket. These examples require **correlational reasoning**: a type of reasoning that is conducted on repeated observations between two variables or events. For example, imagine that you are conducting a study about the relationship between people's level of hunger and their amount of impulse buying at a food store. There are three possibilities: The hungrier people get, the more they will buy impulsively (a positive correlation); the hungrier they get, the less they will buy impulsively (a negative correlation); or that there is no relation between hunger and levels of impulse shopping (zero or no correlation). In statistics textbooks, you would most often encounter Pearson's r, an index of correlation that ranges between (-1) and ($+1$).

Correlational reasoning should not be confused with causal reasoning. There could be multiple reasons why a correlation is positive, negative, or zero. Suppose you find a positive correlation in your study. It may then be tempting for you to conclude that the hungrier people get, the more they buy impulsively because they find food to be irresistible. However, the "reverse" interpretation of causality may also be true: The more impulsive people become, the more their physiological arousal levels may increase, leading to increased feelings of hunger.

Are people good at judging correlational data? To answer this question, Jennings, Amabile, and Ross (1982) asked participants to study a list of number pairs. After each list, the participants were asked to provide a measure of relational strength between two given numbers (how often these two numbers occurred together) on a scale ranging from -100 (never) to $+100$ (always). The true correlations ranged from 0 (no correlation) to 1 (perfect correlation). Jennings et al. found that people tended to give ratings of close to 100 for correlations of 1 and give -100 ratings for correlations of 0. For correlations of .5, however, people tended to give ratings of about 20 (closer to a perfect correlation than to a zero correlation). These results indicate that people have a sense of the strength of the co-occurence between variables, even if it does not completely match the data.

How does sensitivity to correlational information affect real-life inferences? In an early study, Smedslund (1963) asked a group of nurses to examine 100 cards that were supposedly taken from patients' records. On the basis of the information contained in the cards, the nurses were asked to determine whether there was a connection between a particular symptom and a given disease. Each card noted explicitly the presence or absence of the symptom and the disease, yielding four different combinations: symptom present–disease present, symptom present–disease absent, symptom absent–disease present, and symptom absent–disease absent.

A full 85% of the nurses said that there was a relation between the symptom and the disease, even though there was no correlation between the two in the cards they were given. About the same number of patients had the symptom but either had or did not have the disease, and about the same number of patients did not have the symptom but either had or did not have the disease. Smedslund found that the best predictor of performance was the symptom present–disease present relation. If there were many cases of this kind, then the nurses tended to focus on it and discount information about the other relations. These results suggest that people fall prey to an *attentional bias* by attending differentially to equally important relations.

The attentional bias can be found in everyday reasoning. For example, lay people who believe in God often endorse the following reasoning when asked: "Does God answer prayers?" (Nisbett & Ross, 1980, p. 92): " 'Yes,' such a person may say, 'because many times I've asked God for something, and He's given it to me." This reasoning is based on the present-present relation (the prayer was present, and the answer to the prayer was present). What people often fail to take into account are the times when they prayed for something but did not get it (the prayer was present, and the answer to the prayer was absent). It is difficult to convince people of this logic, however, because a possible retort is: "Well, I didn't pray hard enough." It may be that people are not considering all possible relations because they often create unfalsifiable hypotheses to begin with.

The idea that people overemphasize the co-occurence of two events but discount instances in which one event occurs without the other has been shown in more recent studies as well (e.g., Arkes & Harkness, 1983; Crocker, 1981; Nisbett & Ross, 1980; Schustack & Sternberg, 1981). However, Crocker (1981) argued that this result may be due, in part, to the ways in which questions are framed. She suggested that social judgments tend to be less accurate when the questions that researchers ask are biased toward focusing on positive co-occurences (e.g., Is there a relationship between *Event A* and *Outcome B*?). In contrast, judgments tend to be more accurate when questions are "neutral" and focus on the lack of co-occurences as well (e.g., Is there a relationship between *Event A* or the lack of *Event A* and *Outcome B* or the lack of *Outcome B*?).

Another bias in correlational reasoning involves people's prior beliefs about what the nature of a relation between two variables or events should be. This work was pioneered by Chapman and Chapman (1967, 1969). The Chapman and Chapman paradigm consists of giving naive observers a set of contrived responses to a projective test (an assessment technique in clinical interviews) paired with the alleged patient's list of symptoms. The typical finding is that participants report that certain responses were made by patients with particular symptoms, even though the materials are designed in such a way that all responses occur equally frequently with all symptoms. Thus, people seem to "find" confirming correlational information, even when it is absent. Chapman and Chapman referred to this phenomenon as the endorsement of an **illusory correlation**.

People's beliefs can also affect their perception of correlations between certain personality traits. One such example is the **halo effect**, in which A thinks that B has a favorable trait because of A's experiences with B (e.g., B is helpful). This inference, in turn, causes A to think that B has other favorable traits (e.g., is intelligent), regardless of whether B does or does not possess these traits. The halo effect was demonstrated by Shweder (1977) and by Shweder and D'Andrade (1979) with regard to counselors' perception of children's' extroversion and introversion traits at a summer camp. Both attentional bias and illusory correlations demonstrate that people tend to distort data in consistent ways. Overall, our prior beliefs make us less sensitive to counterevidence than we should be (Baron, 1993).

INDUCTIVE INFERENCE AND THE SELF

> No matter what you think you think you think you think like I think.
>
> —SPENCER TRACY in *Adam's Rib*

Our self is a continuous source of information about the physical and social world. To what extent should we use the self as a source of generalization? One pitfall of doing so is the danger of succumbing to a **False Consensus Effect** (FCE)—the tendency to see one's own behaviors and judgments as being more common and appropriate than those of others (L. Ross, Greene, & House, 1977). In a famous demonstration, Ross et al. asked college students whether they would help conduct a communication study by carrying a board around campus that said either "Eat at Joe's" or "Repent!" The participants exhibited FCEs in both cases, irrespective of whether the questions were hypothetical or real. That is, they estimated other students' responses to either request to be relatively common and unrevealing when these responses were similar to theirs. In general, the participants stated that most people would either agree or disagree to participate in the study, depending on whether the participants themselves had agreed to participate or not. This study spurred a multitude of subsequent studies, which corroborated the FCE in many areas of human reasoning.

Ross et al. explained that the FCE results from two cognitive factors and a motivational one. The first cognitive factor is **selective exposure**, which refers to a reality in which people usually have access only to biased samples of the population because they tend to socialize with people who are similar to them. The second cognitive factor is **resolution of ambiguity**, which refers to the fact that social events tend to be ill defined and subject to multiple interpretations (Griffin & Ross, 1991). Finally, the motivational factor is consistent with ego-protective mechanisms, such as the **actor-observer effect** (Jones & Nisbett, 1971, 1987), which is the tendency to externalize a negative behavior (e.g., yelling at an incompetent waiter) if it was committed by oneself ("I had a bad day") and to internalize the same behavior if it was committed by someone else ("She must be a mean person").

The FCE implies that people should underemphasize or even ignore their own responses. However, is the FCE an example of an inductive failure: an overgeneralization from a sample of one? Krueger (1998) argued that generalizing from oneself actually can be diagnostic. First, a person who dismisses one sample would have to dismiss all samples to be consistent (Dawes & Mulford, 1996). Second, single-case samples can be informative. To demonstrate this point, Krueger gave the following example: Suppose that you are given an opportunity to sample 100 colored chips from an urn of 1,000 chips. If two thirds of the chips came up blue and a one third turned out to be red, then you could be quite confident that this color distribution reflected the one in the urn. Now, say that you would mentally go back to the point where 99 chips were sampled. The reliability of the sample would still be fairly high, but less so. Reliability would decrease every time you took another step back. As the sample approached 0, the reliability would decrease, but would never become completely uninformative. However, imagine simulating this process in the reverse, in the direction of increasing the sample size. In this situation, the first observation would become extremely important, and each additional datum point would increase its reliability by a small increment.

The underlying question is, just what should the normative model be that we should compare people's reasoning against? Until recently, the FCE paradigm has chosen a standard that prescribed that people should ignore their own responses. However, this model may not be appropriate. It may lead people to place insufficient weights on small samples (Edwards, 1982). To ascertain to what extent (if at all) the FCE is a bias, we need to use better normative models to compare people's projections against. One such way to do so is to think of consensus estimation as a revision of probabilities and examine it within a Bayesian framework (see Krueger, 1998, for details).

ARE PEOPLE RATIONAL? IN SEARCH OF THE APPROPRIATE NORMATIVE MODEL

The idea of finding the appropriate normative model has important implications for reasoning in both the inductive and deductive domains. It points to the dangers of defining human rationality on the basis of models that may not be rational or appropriate. As Dawes and Mulford (1996, p. 201) so aptly put it:

> [A] belief in these particular systematic limitations of judgment arises not from the irrationality of experimental subjects allegedly demonstrate their existence, but from the cognitive limitations of the psychologists studying these subjects.

In sum, to identify both rational and irrational reasoning processes, we need first to identify the appropriate normative models against which to pit these processes. To find the relevant normative models, in turn, we must examine how knowledge is related to the goals and experience of the individual.

◆ SUMMARY

Inductive reasoning lies at the core of human cognition. It is the kind of reasoning that involves a continuous adjustment to and updating of one's confidence in a belief or the strength of a belief. Inductive reasoning is the most common form of everyday and scientific reasoning.

There are many possible inductions from any given situation. Why do people make certain inductive inferences over others? The pragmatic approach answers this question by positing that there are constraints on the inductive process that guarantee that inferences are both plausible and relevant to the person's goals (Holland et al., 1986). It suggests that to study induction, one must examine how knowledge is relevant to the goals and experience of an individual and how that knowledge gets modified through its use.

The pragmatic approach is part of a more general "loose" view of reasoning (Rips, 1990). It argues that inductive reasoning is a process of constantly updating the strength of beliefs on the basis of the availability of concrete instances, without the need for special logical structure, abstract specifications, or discrete inference steps. This view is contrasted with the syntactic view, which suggests that inductive reasoning, such as analogical reasoning, has a special relational structure.

How do people evaluate inductive inferences? They often do so by looking for positive instances that corroborate an inference, leading to what has been known as a confirmation bias, or the tendency of people to look for evidence that confirms their hypotheses, rather than to search for disconfirming evidence. This term may actually be a misnomer because, as Klayman and Ha (1987) showed, a positive test strategy may actually be beneficial in real-world environments.

Once people generate hypotheses, how do they evaluate them? To evaluate a hypothesis, they engage in *probability estimation*, assessing the likelihood that a particular proposition is true.

There are numerous normative models of probabilistic reasoning. One such model is presented by Bayes's theorem. People's reasoning tends to deviate from this model by ignoring base rates, for example. We demonstrated that there are circumstances, however, when people do use base rates, such as when they have direct experience with them.

People can be made to perform in accordance with Bayesian probability if they are allowed to develop set-based representations. The research we presented on the Monty Hall dilemma supports this view.

People can also demonstrate various degrees of accuracy on correlational reasoning problems. Deviations from correct performance occur when people fall prey to attentional bias or to illusory correlations.

Finally, the self is implicated in inductive reasoning. Our self is a continuous source of information about the physical and social environment. How much should we use the self as a source of generalization? One pitfall of doing so is the danger of succumbing to a FCE, or the tendency to see one's own behaviors and judgments as being more common and appropriate than those of others (Ross et al., 1977). A second look at this effect reveals, however, that it may be a useful strategy after all. To identify fallacies in human cognition, we need first to identify the appropriate normative models against which these fallacies should be compared.

7 Problem Solving

> When I am working on a problem I never think about beauty. I only think about
> how to solve the problem. But when I have finished, if the solution is not
> beautiful, I know it is wrong.
>
> —RICHARD BUCKMINSTER FULLER (1895–1983)

Problem solving is part of our everyday experience. Problems occur when we are trying to decide what the best route would be to get to a new location, create a solution strategy for a difficult mathematics equation on a homework assignment, or figure out how much money we would need in a loan from a bank to pay for college. In general, being confronted with a problem means that we want to achieve a certain goal but are uncertain about what steps to take. To solve the problem, we need to create mental representations of the current state we are in and the desired state we wish to achieve. We then need to search for ways to transform the current state into the solution state.

Problems have three general characteristics: (1) an **initial state**, or the state in which the problem solver sorts out the givens; (2) a **goal state**, or the solution state that the problem solver tries to achieve; and (3) the steps that the problem solver takes to transform the initial state into the goal state that are not obvious.

To decide on which steps to take, it is suggested that people conduct a search in a **problem space**, or a mental space consisting of symbolic representations of states and a set of operators that takes a state as input and produces a state as output. This search requires a person to apply operators, add new states, and evaluate the effectiveness of the operators.

People engage in many different methods for solving problems, including algorithms and heuristics. An **algorithm** is a method that will always produce a solution to the problem, whereas a **heuristic** is a rule of thumb that involves conducting a selective search that examines selected portions of the problem space that are most likely to produce a solution. We focus on the application of a commonly used heuristic called **means-end analysis**, which involves the general steps of (1) determining the goal state, (2) assessing the distance between the current problem-solving state and the desired goal state, and (3) choosing an operator for reducing the greatest difference between these states.

To conduct a successful search, it is crucial to create the right representation of the problem's givens. We highlight the importance of representation by using problems that have traditionally been referred to as insight problems, the solution to which becomes apparent suddenly (the Aha! experience) after a prolonged period of effortful and unsuccessful deliberation.

The remainder of this chapter is dedicated to understanding problem solving by examining the nature of systematic errors. Human problem solving is paradoxical. When people are faced with solving a new problem, they usually do not give up but construct rules or strategies to solve it. These strategies are frequently systematic and internally consistent, not random. However, they often lead to erroneous solutions. What goes wrong in the problem-solving process? At what point does a reasonable algorithm result in an error? What can rule-based errors tell us about the learning and problem-solving processes? We discuss the answers to these questions in detail here.

Every day, we are confronted with having to solve a multitude of different problems. These problems can be either **well defined** or **ill-defined**. Well defined problems have at least one clearly specified path to the solution (e.g., a logical syllogism), whereas ill-defined problems lack such specificity. For example, we all opt to make choices that will lead us to become happier and more fulfilled. Nonetheless, it is frequently hard to figure out how to get there—to understand what happiness or fulfillment entail. Researchers, for instance, are on a continuous quest to test theoretical assumptions and models. A large part of such endeavors involves the feeling of never being completely satisfied with one's current state of knowledge. Choosing a research problem also involves sifting relevant from irrelevant information. The challenge is to frame a research problem in a way that clarifies what the substantive information is. This chapter is centered on the nature of well-defined problems, whereas the chapters on inductive reasoning (chapter 6) and decision making (chapter 8) tackle reasoning on more ill-defined problems.

Well-defined problems can either be **knowledge-lean** or **knowledge-rich problems** (VanLehn, 1989). Knowledge-lean problems require little specific knowledge about a given domain. Knowledge-rich problems, on the other hand, require specialized knowledge about a domain, such as the ability to carry out mathematical procedures (e.g., performing long division by hand). Even though knowledge-lean problems do not require much domain knowledge, they may not be easier to solve than knowledge-rich problems. For example, try to solve the following *Tower of Hanoi* problem, which has generated much research and will serve as a basis for an ensuing discussion on the nature of problem solving (see also Figure 7.1).

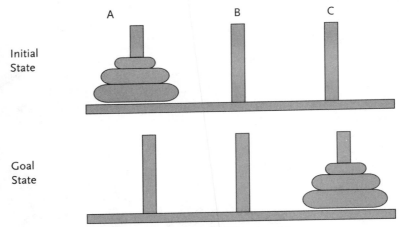

Figure 7.1 The Tower of Hanoi problem.

◆ The Tower of Hanoi Problem

You are presented with a board that has three pegs, A, B, and C (see the top part of the Figure 7.1). On Peg A are three disks of different sizes,[1] with the largest disk on the bottom and the smallest on the top. Your goal is to get all the disks onto Peg C in the same order, from the largest to the smallest (see the bottom part of Figure 7.1). A disk can be moved onto another peg with the following constraints: It is the top disk on its peg, and it is not placed on a disk smaller than itself.

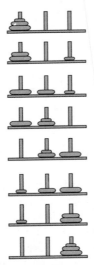

Figure 7.2 Solution to the Tower of Hanoi problem.

---

[1]This is a specific case of the more general Tower of Hanoi problem, which can contain *n* number of disks.

There are multiple solution paths to this problem, but a unique one for solving it with the minimum number of steps (seven steps) is presented in Figure 7.2.

The Tower of Hanoi problem illustrates three general characteristics of problems:

1. Problems have an *initial state*, or the state in which the problem solver sorts out the givens (the disks are on Peg A, arranged from the largest on the bottom to the smallest on the top).

2. They have a *goal state*, or the solution state that the problem solver tries to achieve (the disks should end up on Peg C, arranged from the largest to the smallest).

3. The steps that the problem solver takes to transform the initial state into the goal state are not obvious.

To decide on these steps, people need to conduct a search in a problem space.

PROBLEM SOLVING: A SEARCH THROUGH A PROBLEM SPACE

Newell (1990) proposed that any goal-directed activity involves a fundamental organizational unit called the *problem space*. The problem space is made up of symbolic structures (the **states** of the space) and a set of *operators*, or problem-solving actions that take a state as input and produce a state as output. The operators do not have to be defined for all the states. Applying sequences of operators creates solution paths in the problem space.

Both a problem space and a problem are constructs that require the mental representation of states and operators. These constructs can be exemplified by the Tower of Hanoi problem, as follows: The *problem space* consists of (1) states, which are the configurations of the pegs on the disk, and (2) operators, which consist of moving of a disk from one peg to another. The *problem* is composed of two states and a path constraint: an initial state (the configuration shown in the top part of Figure 7.1, the goal state (the configuration shown in the bottom part of Figure 7.1), and the path constraint (that no disk may be placed on a smaller disk).

Newell's conception of the problem space stemmed originally from the pioneering work of Newell and Simon (1972) in their book, *Human Problem Solving*. Newell and Simon used computer simulations to model people's problem-solving processes. They changed the cognitive psychological study of problem solving and knowledge representation not only by introducing innovative methods, but, more important, by emphasizing the merit of examining the interaction between the information-processing system (the cognitive architecture of the problem solver) and the given task environment (the problem at hand).

The search through the problem space requires a person to apply operators, add new states, and evaluate the effectiveness of the operators. To conduct a successful search, a person must apply a fixed set of functions repeatedly, such as deciding to quit the problem, deciding whether a goal state has been produced, selecting a state to become the current state, selecting an operator to become the current operator, and deciding to save the new state just created by applying the operator. These functions are part of a *search-control* process that operates within a cycle that repeats the three steps of assessing a given state and selecting an operator, applying the operator to the current state to create a new state, and deciding whether to quit or to continue.

How do people go about organizing search-control knowledge? To do so, they use different problem-solving methods that coordinate the selection of states and operators in different ways.

PROBLEM-SOLVING METHODS

People engage in different methods for solving problems, including algorithms and heuristics. An algorithm is a method that will always produce a solution to a problem. An example of an algorithm is an **exhaustive search**, which consists of trying out all possible methods in a brute-force manner. An algorithm guarantees a solution, but is often inefficient and unsophisticated.

A heuristic, in contrast, is a rule-of-thumb method that involves conducting a selective search by looking at particular portions of the problem space that are the most likely to produce a solution and ignoring the others. One of the more commonly used heuristic is means-end analysis, which involves the following steps: (1) determining what the goal state is, (2) assessing the distance between the current problem-solving state and the desired goal state, and (3) choosing an operator for reducing the greatest difference between these states. When an operator is applied and an obstacle occurs, the problem solver sets a subgoal of removing that obstacle. This process is called **subgoaling**. The subgoal then becomes the desired end goal (temporarily, until it is removed) and is solved again by the three steps of means-ends analysis just described. Subgoaling is a **recursive procedure**, that is, a procedure that repeats itself until a goal is reached. After all the subgoals are attained, then the end goal is met.

The use of means-ends analysis can be illustrated by the folk song *There's a Hole in the Bucket*. In this song, Liza asks Henry to fix a hole in the bucket by using different operators (e.g., plug the hole with a twig). Each time the operator fails (the twig is too long), the sub-goal is to search for a different operator that will enable the use of the previous one (cut the twig). The song depicts the process of infinite recursion because Liza eventually suggests the use of an operator (water) that can be made available only by using a bucket.

Research on the means-ends analysis heuristic shows that people often use subgoals to solve problems, but that they have difficulty applying subgoals that take them temporarily away from the desired end goal. A good example of this phenomenon is how people solve the Hobbits-and-Orcs problem (Greeno, 1974; Thomas, 1974). Try to solve this problem before you read on.

◆ The Hobbits-and-Orcs Problem

There are three hobbits and three orcs on one side of a river. Your goal is to ensure that the hobbits and orcs all arrive safely at the other side of the river by transporting them across the river with a boat. The boat can carry up to two creatures at a time. Orcs eat the hobbits, so the number of orcs cannot exceed the number of hobbits on either side of the river. What sequence of crossings will transport all six creatures across the river without causing harm to the hobbits?

The solution to this problem requires the 12 steps shown in Figure 7.3 (where ■ stands for the boat, the dividing line stands for the river, H = hobbit, and O = orc). The difficulty lies in step 6, in which one must send the boat back with both a hobbit and an orc. This step is counterintuitive because to achieve the end goal of having all creatures on the other side of the river, it is tempting to apply a simple **difference-reduction** strategy, which reduces the greatest difference between the current and goal state successively until the problem is solved,

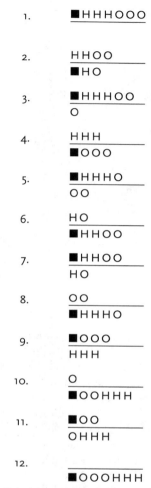

1. ■HHHOOO

2. HHOO
   ■HO

3. ■HHHOO
   O

4. HHH
   ■OOO

5. ■HHHO
   OO

6. HO
   ■HHOO

7. ■HHOO
   HO

8. OO
   ■HHHO

9. ■OOO
   HHH

10. O
    ■OOHHH

11. ■OO
    OHHH

12.
    ■OOOHHH

Figure 7.3 Solution to the Hobbits-and-Orcs problem.

by shipping two creatures to the far side and having only one creature return with the boat at all times. People have difficulty solving the Hobbits-and-Orcs problem because they are reluctant to move backward temporarily from their desired end goal (Jeffries, Polson, Razran, & Atwood, 1977).

Another helpful heuristic is the **working backward** method (Wickelgren, 1974). This method is commonly used when there are too many operators that can apply to the initial state of the problem. The person then starts at the desired end state and examines the possible conditions that would have to be true if the desired end state was true. This process is continued for each identified "prior-to-the-goal" state (one would have to determine again which states would be needed for the current state to be true). For instance, try to prove that the base angles of an isosceles triangle are equal (see Figure 7.4). The traditional solution is to construct

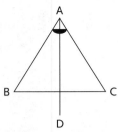

Figure 7.4 A geometry problem. *Task*: Given $\triangle ABC$, where AB = AC, prove that $\angle B = \angle C$.

an angle bisector AD, such that $\angle A1 = \angle A2$. Now we can show that $\triangle ABD \cong \triangle ADC$ by the SAS (side-angle-side) postulate because

$$AD = AD, \angle A1 = \angle A2, \text{ and } AB = AC \text{ (given)}.$$

Therefore,

$$\angle B = C. \text{ QED}$$

This solution is an example of working backward because to assume that the two base angles are equal, we look for the conditions that would have to be true if this desired state was true: that $\triangle ABD \cong \triangle ADC$. To assume that these triangles are congruent, we need to assume that $\angle A1 = \angle A2$. To assume that these two angles are equal, we need to construct an angle bisector AD (the initial step in creating the formal proof).

Can you prove that the base angles of an isosceles triangle are equal without constructing an angle bisector? A creative proof was offered by Pappus (see Boden, 1994): Imagine lifting $\triangle ABC$ into the third dimension, turning it about its y-axis, and then placing it back on itself such that its equal and opposite sides are flipped. This action results in $\triangle ACB$. We can now prove that $\triangle ABC \cong \triangle ACB$ because the two sides are equal by definition and $\angle A = \angle A$ (SAS).

Problem-solving methods are affected by memory constraints. Hunt (1994) argued that the working-memory system serves as a cue that triggers the execution of **pattern-action rules** (see also J. R. Anderson, 1983; Hunt & Lansman, 1986; Just & Carpenter, 1992; Newell, 1990; Newell & Simon, 1972). Pattern action rules are condition-action rules of the form If C, then A. **Forward pattern-action rules** provide instructions on what one should do from one's current state, such as in the following example (Hunt, 1994, p. 223):

> If the goal is to arrive at a European city, AND you are at a U.S. city, AND there is no flight from the U.S. city to the European city, THEN search for a flight to a U.S. airline hub city east of your current location, and set a goal to fly from that city to the European city.

Backward pattern-action rules prescribe what goals a person should set to get to a solution, such as in the following example (Hunt, 1994, p. 223):

> If the goal is to arrive at a European city, AND there is no flight between that city and a U.S. city, find a nearby larger European city and attempt to solve the problem of moving from the U.S. to the larger city.

For problem solving to be successful with either forward or backwards rules, problem solvers need to ensure that the representation of the problem does not overload the working-memory system and that they follow pattern-action rules that move the problem solver along a correct path through the problem space. In sum, it is crucial that problem solvers set up the right representation of the problem because knowing *when* to apply a rule or operator is often much harder than knowing *how* to apply that same rule or operator.

THE IMPORTANCE OF PROBLEM REPRESENTATION

To apply the correct operators, one needs to create a correct representation of the problem space. For example, to solve the Hobbits and Orcs problem, it is important to allow for the existence of states that take us temporarily away from our goals, so that we can eventually get to the desired goal state. The importance of representation can be illustrated especially well with problems that have been traditionally referred to as **insight problems**, in which the solution becomes suddenly apparent (the Aha! experience) after a prolonged period of effortful and unsuccessful problem solving, typically as a result of taking a new viewpoint on or approach to the problem at hand (e.g., Davidson, 1995; Gick & Lockhart, 1995; Seifert, Meyer, Davidson, Palatano, & Yaniv, 1995). For example, try to solve the following insight problem.

A man who lived in a small town married 20 women in that town. All of the women are still living, and he has never divorced any of them. Yet the man has broken no laws. How is this situation possible?

The solution to this problem is that the man has broken no laws because he was a priest. To arrive at this solution, a person has to represent the givens of the problem correctly by representing the meaning of "married" and "divorced" as referring to active, rather than passive, states.

Another classic demonstration of **insight** that requires a more spatially oriented representation is the nine-dot problem shown in Figure 7.5.

◆ The Nine-Dot Problem

Your task is to connect the nine dots in Figure 7.5 with four straight lines. You may not lift your pencil from the paper as you draw the four lines.

Figure 7.5 The nine-dot problem.

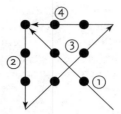

Figure 7.6 Solution to the nine-dot problem

To solve this problem, one needs to represent the possibility of extending lines beyond the square formed by the nine dots, as in Figure 7.6. If one does not create the right representation for this and other problems, one may end up searching the wrong problem space (Schooler & Melcher, 1994).

There is evidence to support the idea that insight and noninsight problems require different problem-solving processes. Metcalfe and Wiebe (1987) provided participants with insight problems, similar to the ones just described, and noninsight problems (e.g., the Tower of Hanoi). The participants were asked to judge, every 15 seconds, how close they thought they were to reaching a solution. The results showed that on the noninsight problems, the participants were fairly confident that they were close to the solution about 15 seconds before they solved the problem, whereas on insight problems, they had little idea they were close to a solution even seconds before they were able to produce it. Schooler, Ohlsson, and Brooks (1993) provided additional evidence for a dissociation between insight and noninsight problems by showing that requiring participants to verbalize their problem-solving steps interfered with the participants' ability to solve insight but not noninsight problems. Taken together, these findings suggest that insight problem solving is an "all-or-none" process in which one either achieves the solution or does not. Noninsight problem solving, on the other hand, may involve a more gradual process and can be self-monitored (for an opposing view, however, see Kihlstrom, 1990).

The role of representation in problem solving also can be seen in how content affects people's ability to create correct solution paths. An example of such an effect is in how people respond to isomorphs of the Tower of Hanoi problem. People show large variability on how difficult they find these isomorphs to be. For example, try to solve the Monster Move problem (K. Kotovsky, Hayes, & Simon, 1985, p. 290).

◆ The Monster Move Problem

Three five-handed extraterrestrial monsters were holding three crystal globes. Because of the quantum-mechanical peculiarities of their neighborhood, both monsters and globes come in exactly three sizes with no others permitted: small, medium, and large. The small monster was holding the large globe, the medium-sized monster was holding the small globe, and the large monster was holding the medium-sized globe. Since this situation offended their keenly developed sense of symmetry, they proceeded to transfer globes from one monster to another so that each monster would have a globe proportionate to its own size.

> Monster etiquette complicated the solution of the problem, since it requires that
>
> 1. only one globe may be transferred at a time;
> 2. if a monster is holding two globes, only the larger of the two may be transferred; and,
> 3. a globe may not be transferred to a monster who is holding a larger globe.
>
> By what sequence of transfers could the monsters have solved this problem?

The monsters are isomorphic to the pegs and the globes are isomorphic to the disks in the standard Tower of Hanoi problem. Even though the rules are exactly the same as those used to solve the Tower of Hanoi problem, the Monster Move problem takes about eight times longer to solve, on average, than the standard Tower of Hanoi problem. Why are some isomorphs harder than others? K. Kotovsky et al. (1985) argued that the relevant factors include (1) the degree of novelty of the given entities and relations (e.g., presenting people with unfamiliar objects), (2) the extent to which rules are counterintuitive, and (3) whether the content is abstract and therefore difficult to visualize. Conversely, problems are easier when the rules or constraints are consistent with people's everyday, real-world knowledge or, at the least, when a person has gained familiarity with the rules by practicing them in another domain.

Another difficulty may lie in the kinds of interpretations that people create regarding the relations between entities in a problem. Bassok, Wu, and Olseth (1995) found that problems involving different entities, such as objects and people, led the participants to abstract an asymmetric relational structure (in the Monster Move problem, globes would get assigned to monsters but not vice versa), whereas problems involving similar entities led the participants to abstract a symmetric relational structure (in the standard Tower of Hanoi problem, disks and pegs are both objects, such that a peg can get assigned to a disk and a disk can get assigned to a peg). The interpretation of unintended symmetry-asymmetry relationships shows that problems that are structurally isomorphic but have different cover stories can lead people to create different representations. We have seen examples of content effects in other domains as well, such as in the differential performance on isomorphs of the Wason selection task (WST) (see chapter 5). On the WST, familiar content may allow people to retrieve and use an available counterexample, resulting in facilitation.

Gestalt psychologists identified early several contextual factors that may hinder people from creating correct problem-solving representations. One such factor is **functional fixedness**—the tendency to represent objects as serving traditional problem-solving functions, resulting in an inability to use these objects in novel ways. A classic demonstration of this problem is the **two-string problem** (Maier, 1931). This problem presents a person with the task of tying together two strings that are hanging from the ceiling. The strings are so far apart that the person cannot grasp both at once. Among the objects in the room are a chair and a pair of pliers. The person's task is to use these tools to tie the strings. How is it possible to do so? The solution is to tie the pliers to one string and set that string swinging like a pendulum and then to get the second string, bring it to the center of the room, and wait for the first string to swing close enough to grasp. Maier found that only 39% of the participants were able to solve this problem because they had difficulty representing the pliers in a role of a weight that could be used as a pendulum.

Another classic demonstration of functional fixedness is the **candle problem** (Duncker, 1945): You have at your disposal a candle, a box of tacks, and matches. Your task is to mount the candle vertically on a plywood wall, so the candle will serve as a lamp. The solution to this problem is to (1) empty the box containing the tacks; (2) use some of the tacks to mount the box onto the plywood wall; and (3) use the box as a basis for mounting the candle by lighting the base of the candle with the matches until it forms drops of wax and then quickly attaching the candle to the mounted box while the wax is still warm. Duncker attributed people's difficulty in solving this problem to functional fixedness, or the tendency rigidly to associate primary functions to objects (e.g., a box of tacks is used for holding tacks). Functional fixedness impedes the creation of representations that allow for multiple purposes (e.g., a box of tacks can also be used to support the candle in the process of creating a makeshift lamp).

The crucial role of representation in problem solving also can be exemplified by the phenomenon of set effects. A **set effect** refers to a situation in which a problem solver becomes biased toward using a certain problem-solving operator when the operator is more available than other, more efficient operators. People's performance on the **water-pitcher problem** illustrates this phenomenon well (Luchins, 1942; Luchins & Luchins, 1959).

 The Water-Pitcher Problem

Your goal is to measure exactly 100 units of water from an unlimited source. The only tools you have at your disposal are three pitchers: A, B, and C. Pitcher A holds 21 units, Pitcher B holds 127 units, and Pitcher C hold 3 units. Describe the sequence of filling and pouring steps that you would use to measure the 100 units.

Now try to solve the additional problems presented in Table 7.1 (Luchins & Luchins, 1959, p. 109).

TABLE 7.1 The Water-Pitcher Problem

Problem	Pitcher A	Pitcher B	Pitcher C	Desired Goal
1	3	29	3	20
2	21	127	3	100
3	18	43	10	5
4	9	42	6	21
5	20	59	4	31
6	23	49	3	20
7	15	39	3	18
8	28	76	3	25
9	18	48	4	22
10	14	36	8	6

The optimal solution to the original water-pitcher problem is Fill Pitcher B (127 units), then pour the water out from Pitcher B to Pitcher A, leaving 106 units in Pitcher B. Then pour water from Pitcher B to Pitcher C twice, subtracting 3 units each time for a total of 6 units. This process leaves 100 units in Pitcher B, as requested. The solution is captured by the rule: $B - A - 2C$. Many people use this rule correctly on the original problem and the first few problems in the additional problem set (see Table 7.1), but then continue to use it on other problems, such as numbers 9 and 10 in the additional problem set, that require much simpler solutions (79% of the participants in Luchins & Luchins's, 1959, study used the $B - 2C - A$ method for solving numbers 9 and 10, instead of using the rules $A + C$ and $A - C$, respectively). In short, the first few problems created a bias for a particular solution that then hurt people's performance on subsequent problems.

The water-pitcher problem shows that people can overly routinize strategies for solving problems. This phenomenon is related to the finding that the representation of problems is affected by the kinds of schemas that people develop while learning. *Schemas* are mental structures that organize information from the environment in a useful way (Bartlett, 1932; Piaget, 1965; Schank & Abelson, 1977). For instance, Greeno (1980) and Riley, Greeno, and Heller (1983) argued that children develop three types of schemas for solving arithmetic word problems: (1) **change** (Joe had some marbles. Then Tom gave him 5 marbles. Now Joe has 8 marbles. How many marbles did Joe have at the beginning?), (2) **combination** (Joe has 3 marbles. Tom has 5 marbles. How many marbles do they have together?), and (3) **comparison** (Joe has 3 marbles. Tom has 5 marbles more than Joe. How many marbles does Tom have?). These three schemas are based on children's ability to distinguish the whole from its parts.

Older students are aided by schemas in learning to solve more advanced problems as well. For example, Hinsley, Hayes, and Simon (1977) showed that high school and college students could categorize mathematics problems into different types by using information contained in the first few words of the problem (e.g., problems that began with "In a sports car race . . . " cued the retrieval of formulas associated with the distance-rate-time category). The particular content of the problems cued specific solution algorithms.

The same schemas that facilitate performance may also lead to predictable errors (Ben-Zeev, 1996). For example, Hinsley et al. (1977) were able to "fool" their participants into assigning a nonsense problem (e.g., "Chort and Frey are stimpling 150 fands. Chort stimples at the rate of four fands per yump and Frey at the rate of six fands per yump") to a certain category (e.g., "proportion problem") because of surface-structural cue words (e.g., "rate of " and "per").

The use of schemas affects memory for problems as well. Mayer (1982) presented students with a variety of word problems that were either frequently or less frequently encountered in textbooks. Mayer asked the students first to read and later to recall a set of these problems. He found that when students tried to recall the less frequent problems, they often changed these problems' forms to make them similar to the more common versions. These results show that people tend to remember material that is consistent with their schemas (see also chapter 4).

A set of studies conducted by Reusser (1988) illustrated some of the negative effects of the use of schemas as early as the first grade. Reusser provided first- and second graders with the following problem: "There are 26 sheep and 10 goats on a ship. How old is the captain?" The majority of students were content to respond that the captain was 36 years old. In a similar vein, Reusser asked fourth- and fifth graders to solve the following problem: "There are

125 sheep and 5 dogs in a flock. How old is the shepherd?" This time, the students performed more elaborate calculations to get to a "reasonable" solution. For instance, several students attempted to solve the problem by calculating $125 + 5 = 130$ and $125 - 5 = 120$, first. They realized, however, that these results were "too big" to be true. The students then decided to perform the more "meaningful" operation, "$125/5 = 25$," and concluded more confidently that the shepherd was 25 years old.

Other instances of the overuse of schemas can be seen in more advanced mathematical domains. A particularly striking example comes from Paige and Simon (1966). Paige and Simon gave college students problems that were logically impossible, such as the following (p. 79).

The number of quarters a man has is seven times the number of dimes he has. The value of the dimes exceeds the value of the quarters by two dollars and fifty cents. How many has he of each coin?

This problem is logically impossible because if the number of quarters exceeds the number of dimes, then the value of the dimes cannot exceed that of the quarters. The majority of college students who were tested, however, were content to set up the formal equations ($Q = 7D$ and $.10D = 2.5 + .25Q$) for "solving" the problem. This kind of performance results from applying a rote schema for identifying variables and expressing the relationship between them in a formal way, without paying attention to the actual meaning of the problem.

How does a person attain **expertise** in any given problem-solving domain? The transition from being a novice to becoming an expert in a domain requires more than just the accumulation of information. There are important differences between novice and expert problem solvers in both their ability to memorize and represent knowledge. Experts have a better memory for information that is relevant to their domain of expertise than for information for other domains (Chi et al., 1981). Moreover, their memory is attuned to meaningful information (de Groot, 1965; Simon & Chase, 1973; Vicente & de Groot, 1990). For example, Chase and Simon (1973) presented both a novice and a master chess player with a brief presentation of a chess board with a particular configuration of chess pieces. They then asked the players to try to recall the positions of the chess pieces in the configuration they had just viewed by rearranging them on a different board. The master chess player was able to reconstruct many more pieces of the board than was the novice. In a different variation of this experiment, Chase and Simon controlled the meaningfulness of the configuration. When the configuration was meaningful (a possible array of chess pieces that can occur during a match), then the experts exhibited greater recall than did the novices. When the configuration was random, however, there was no novice-expert difference in recall. Chase and Simon concluded that the experts had a different way of organizing knowledge in memory: They were able to remember different board positions by chunking them into meaningful units in memory.

More recent research has corroborated and extended these findings by showing that (1) novices often use surface, rather than deep-structural representations. For example, in the domain of physics, novices tend to categorize problems on the basis of their surface-structural content (e.g., whether they contain objects, such as blocks, pulleys, and toboggans), not on the problems' underlying principles (e.g., whether they require the application of Newton's second law) (Chi, Feltovich, & Glaser, 1981); (2) experts are better able to construct physical representations of abstract concepts, such as force and momentum (Larkin 1983); and (3) experts are more prone to use graphical depictions or diagrams to create meaningful representations (Larkin & Simon, 1987).

There may be an advantage, however, for both novices and experts to rely on surface-structural or contextual factors like the content of a given problem. Content that is similar to that of a familiar problem increases the likelihood that the solver will notice this similarity and proceed to use the familiar strategy (e.g., Gentner, Rattermann, & Forbus, 1993; Holyoak & Koh, 1987; Novick, 1988; Reeves & Weisberg, 1993; B. Ross, 1984). This behavior is advantageous when superficial and deep similarity are correlated positively, such as when problems with similar content (e.g., involving cars) have similar solution strategies (the distance-rate-time formula).

Experts also differ from novices in their use of problem-solving methods. Experts tend to use the means-ends heuristic more effectively in their area of expertise than do novices (Schraagen, 1993). Experts also engage in more efficient planning behavior. They spend more time devising a global problem-solving approach before delving into the specifics of the problem (Priest & Lindsay, 1992). In general, experts spend more time thinking about the initial states of a problem. Voss et al. (1991) presented experts and novices (on the subject of international relations) with a problem involving the Soviet response to German reunification. They found that the experts took some time to examine the historical background of the problem and the goals of the parties involved, whereas the novices immediately began generating responses to the problem without consulting prior knowledge or goals. The experts preferred to engage in forward-reasoning, rather than in backward-reasoning, heuristics in a variety of domains, including chess, physics, economics, medicine, and law (e.g., Chi, Glaser & Farr, 1988; Ericsson & Smith, 1991). Finally, there is also evidence that experts generally perform problem-solving faster than do novices (Bedard & Chi, 1992) and that experts' problem-solving steps become more automatic with time (Glaser & Chi, 1988).

In sum, experts rely more on explanation than do novices. The nature of the explanation is often captured in terms of goals, in a way that extracts meaning and transcends surface-structural content. Novices may not generate explanations spontaneously, but when they are asked to provide explanations, they often show improvements in both understanding and performance (Chi, de Leeuw, Chiu, & LaVancher, 1994).[2] Thus, to become an expert, a person must learn to provide explanations for problem-solving steps and to monitor his or her own actions in light of these explanations (Chi, Bassok, Lewis, Reimann, & Glaser, 1989; Pirolli & Recker, 1994). Explanations allow for more flexibility of thought. Understanding deep-structural principles enables one to adapt solutions from old to new problems (Catrambone, 1994; Novick & Holyoak, 1991; Reed, Dempster, & Ettinger, 1985).

---

[2]However, a caveat is in order. Chi et al. (1989) found that self-generated explanations led to improved performance for high- but not for low-ability problem solvers.

As can be seen from the discussion of problem representation and novice-expert differences, errors in human reasoning can be helpful in gaining insight into people's mental representations. In the remainder of this chapter, we examine people's problem-solving strategies by looking at systematic rule-based errors and what they can tell us about the way in which people represent and manipulate problem states.

RULE-BASED ERRORS: A WINDOW INTO PROBLEM SOLVING

Human problem solving is paradoxical. On the one hand, when people are faced with solving an unfamiliar problem, they usually do not give up but construct rules or strategies to solve it (Ashlock, 1976; Brown & VanLehn, 1980; Buswell, 1926; Cox, 1975; VanLehn, 1983). These strategies tend to be systematic and internally consistent, not random. They often make "sense" to the people who created them. On the other hand, the same procedures often lead to erroneous solutions. What goes wrong in the problem-solving process? At what point does a logically consistent algorithm result in an error? What can these rule-based errors (Ben-Zeev, 1995, 1996) tell us about learning and problem-solving processes?

Errors that are rule based, deliberate, and systematic open a window into the problem-solving process by pointing to principled (mis)understandings (Ben-Zeev, 1998). For example, try to decipher the following commonly observed subtraction error (VanLehn, 1986):

$$\begin{array}{r} 23 \\ -7 \\ \hline 24 \end{array}$$

What is the origin of this error? VanLehn (1986) argued that it results from applying a "smaller-from-larger" procedure. That is, the student subtracts the smaller digit (e.g., the "3") from the larger digit (e.g., the "7") instead of performing a borrow. This error may be *rational* because it makes probabilistic sense. In past problem-solving episodes, the student learned to subtract smaller from larger numbers (a student learns about single-digit subtraction first without being introduced to negative numbers). In the case of the smaller-from-larger procedure, the student simply may be applying a rule that worked successfully in a past problem-solving episode to a new and similar episode.[3]

Are there broad categories of systematic errors in problem solving? Can we explain a variety of seemingly different procedures by using only a few principles? As a possible answer to these questions, we discuss a taxonomy of errors presented by Ben-Zeev (1998). The taxonomy is focused on mathematical cognition but has implications for more general theories of problem solving and skill acquisition. For example, in language development, young children have been shown to make grammatical errors on verbs they previously used correctly,

---

[3]Rule-based errors do not include "fact errors," such as $3 \times 4 = 7$ that result from associations or priming effects, like the intrusion of an addition fact into a multiplication problem (Zbrodoff & Logan, 1986). Instead, these errors extend beyond simple memory effects.

such as erroneously adding the past form "-ed" to roots of familiar verbs (e.g., when children say "goed," although they previously said "went") (e.g., Karmiloff-Smith, 1986). This process of overgeneralization, or induction, is a main focus of the taxonomy.

As can be gleaned from the other chapters in this book, there are many examples of systematic errors in human cognition, captured most clearly by research on heuristics and biases (e.g., Kahneman & Tversky, 1973). The research on human error follows a historical tradition. For example, when Piaget (1972) was developing intelligence tests in Alfred Binet's laboratory, he noticed that children's erroneous answers to test problems were systematic, and therefore, were a useful way to gain access to children's understanding. Identifying categories of errors has educational implications as well. Instead of targeting myriad different errors, the teacher can focus on correcting the few principles that may underlie them (Hennessy, 1993).

Before we discuss the possible mechanisms underlying errors, we would like the reader to become familiar with a few common errors from different mathematical problem-solving domains.

RULE-BASED ERRORS IN PROBLEM SOLVING

Counting. Children quickly learn how to add single digits to a two-digit number (e.g., 21, 22, 23, 24 . . . 29). However, once they add on the 9 and are asked to name the next two-digit number, they often encounter difficulties (Ginsburg, 1996). Many children then decide that after 29, for example, comes "20-10." Although 20-10 is not the right linguistic label for 30, it captures its magnitude correctly.

Algebraic problem solving. Students commonly produce what is known as a "precedence error" (S. Payne & Squibb, 1990; Sleeman, 1984):

$$m\,X + n \Rightarrow (n + m)X$$

where ⇒ stands for erroneous equivalence, m and n are integers, and X is the unknown. Payne and Squibb (1990) contended that this error may have origins in forming an analogy to a familiar language constructions, such as "three apples plus another four give us seven apples."

Geometrical problem solving. In high school geometry classes, students are asked to match polynomials to functions (i.e., they are shown a graph and are asked to write its corresponding equation). One kind of error is to confuse the y-intercept of a parabola with its vertex (i.e., the "visual" center of the graph) (Dugdale, 1993). Dugdale explained that their confusion occurs because in the first set of examples that students tend to receive, a parabola is symmetric about the y-axis, resulting in a situation where the y-intercept always coincides with the vertex of the parabola. Students respond to this association by inventing a functional invariance between these two features. This error illustrates that students may pick up on feature correlations that the teacher had not intended them to learn.

Calculus. Students often exhibit a common misunderstanding of the concept of limit in calculus (e.g., Davis & Vinner, 1986; T. Dreyfus, 1990) by erroneously asserting that the terms in an infinite sequence get closer and closer to the limit but never reach it, such that for all n,

$a_n \neq L$ (where a_n is the nth term of the sequence and L is the limit value). This definition applies to the most commonly encountered examples of infinite sequences, namely, monotonic sequences, such as .1, .01, .001, .0001, . . . It fails, however, because it does not hold for all sequences, such as "1, 1, 1, 1, . . ." where $a_n = L$.

There is no single scheme that helps to explain the origin of the foregoing errors. The main contribution to understanding problem-solving errors comes from J. S. Brown and Van-Lehn's (1980) *repair theory* and its later version, *Sierra* (VanLehn, 1987, 1990). These theories provide an invaluable account of the production of errors, but they only cover a small subset of errors. We discuss the contribution of these theories and then present a more general taxonomy of problem-solving errors.

REPAIR THEORY AND SIERRA

Brown and VanLehn's (1980) **repair theory**, and its later development into **Sierra** (VanLehn, 1983, 1990), implements people's problem-solving behavior in computer algorithms made up of IF C *then* A rules, where C is the condition and A is the action (see Klahr, Langley, & Neches, 1987). For instance, when C corresponds to a situation in which the top digit is smaller than the bottom digit in a multicolumn subtraction problem, then A may correspond to a borrowing action.

Repair theory suggests that when a student attempts to solve a problem that requires adding new rules to his or her knowledge base, the student reaches an *impasse*, or a state of being deadlocked. The student then selects a *repair*—a set of actions that modifies the current knowledge base and gets the student unstuck. Sierra models how people select the set of actions that forms the solution strategy by a process of induction from worked-out examples. For instance, a student who has learned only how to borrow on two-column subtraction problems may induce that borrowing occurs just in the "adjacent and left-most digit," because in all the examples the student receives, borrowing occurs only in this digit. This overgeneralization leads to errors on problems that have more than two columns, such as the following (VanLehn, 1986):

$$
\begin{array}{r}
5 \\
\cancel{6}21 \\
-219 \\
\hline
312
\end{array}
$$

In this problem, the student has adequately borrowed a 10 in the units column ($11 - 9 = 2$), but instead of decrementing the top digit in the 10s column, the student opts to decrement the left-most top digit in the 100s column.

This type of induction is based on a syntactic process of manipulating symbols without regard to the procedure's underlying principles. The syntactic nature of induction occurs because arithmetic procedures are often taught as facts that are isolated from everyday knowledge and are, therefore, a "bane of teachers but a boon for psychologists" (VanLehn, 1990, p. 3). However, as VanLehn admitted: "The methodological advantages of these task domains are so great that all the major computational theories of skill acquisition address formal, common-sense-free task domains, *even though they risk lack of generality by doing so.*"

Thus, a more general explanation of error production should include components that encompass more than a process of syntactic induction. To accomplish this goal, Ben-Zeev (1998) created a taxonomy that categorizes errors and identifies the mechanisms underlying them by integrating findings from the problem-solving literature. This taxonomy is discussed next in some detail.

A TAXONOMY OF RULE-BASED ERRORS

A preliminary classification of rule-based errors is whether they result from either critic-related or inductive failures. **Critic-related failures** occur when a person fails to develop internal mechanisms for detecting violations in the problem-solving process. **Inductive failures** occur when the person overgeneralizes or overspecializes a rule from familiar examples. We discuss two kinds of inductive failures in subsequent sections: syntactic and semantic.

Critic-Related Failures

In artificial intelligence, a **critic** is a procedure that monitors a current problem state and signals when a constraint is violated (Rissland, 1985). The critic can be represented as a production rule with a condition that lacks an action (i.e., *if* C, *then* ?) and is executed when it reaches an unfamiliar problem state (C). Thus, the activation of a critic may cause the problem solver to reach an impasse at a particular problem state that leads to erroneous problem solving. In general, critic-related failures may result from the following three kinds of situations.

The critic is absent. The absence of a critic can lead to errors. For example, VanLehn (1990) discovered a common subtraction error in which students fail to decrement the digit from which they borrowed. This kind of error may be caused initially by a **slip**, or an unintentional overlooking of a step (Norman, 1981). A slip eventually may become a full-fledged erroneous rule if it is not adequately corrected and the student fails to develop an appropriate critic. Computationally, this account of error production can be modeled by deleting rules from a correct procedure (VanLehn, 1990; Young & O'Shea, 1981).

The critic is weak and is inhibited by a stronger prior-knowledge rule. Even if a critic exists, it can still be overwritten by a stronger prior-knowledge rule, when the strength of a rule is defined by how successfully it has performed in past problem-solving episodes (J. R. Anderson, 1993; Holland et al. 1986). For example, Ben-Zeev (1995) instructed college students to perform addition in a new number system called **NewAbacus**. The students were given a list of NewAbacus numbers and their representation in base-10. They were explicitly told that the digits 7 through 9 do not exist in NewAbacus. However, during a subsequent test, many students failed to convert these illicit numbers into their proper representations. A possible explanation is that because these numbers were valid in the old and familiar base-10 system, they inhibited the newly formed NewAbacus number-representation critics.

The condition that activated the critic is negated. When a person reaches an unfamiliar problem state (C) and the critic fires "If C then?" the person may attempt to fix the violation by simply removing it, thereby forcing the problem to assume its valid form. To remove the violation, people frequently negate the condition of the critic. That is, if the critic signals "If C then ?" people change the problem's form from C to ~C (i.e., not-C). The *negation* action makes the problem seem valid and therefore prevents the critic from refiring. In essence, one "fools" the critic by preventing it from refiring. For example, if an incorrect operation leads to an impossible answer (e.g., two adjacent multiplication signs in an algebraic expression), then negating the critic involves deleting the offending feature (e.g., the extra multiplication sign), and forcing the problem to assume a "correct" form.

Not all errors have this form of extreme constraint-satisfaction. Instead, many errors occur as a result of syntactic induction.

Syntactic Induction

In the process of **syntactic induction**, people overgeneralize or overspecialize algorithms from the surface-structural features of familiar examples (VanLehn, 1986). For instance, recall the previous example of an incorrect borrowing action from the left-most instead of the left-adjacent column in multicolumn subtraction. Overall, VanLehn (1986, 1990) discovered that only 33% of errors could be explained by this process of syntactic induction.[4]

More robust support for syntactic induction was provided by Ben-Zeev's (1995) empirical and computational work on rule-based errors in NewAbacus. After the participants were instructed in NewAbacus number representation, they were then divided into groups, each of which received an example of a certain part of the NewAbacus addition algorithm. Then, the participants were given a range of addition problems in NewAbacus, some of which were familiar and some of which were new. Those who received the same type of worked-out examples produced categories of similar errors. Similar errors were defined to be algorithmic variations on a single procedure. For example, one set of worked-out examples illustrated how to carry the digit 6 correctly. When participants in this condition reached impasses on new problems, they produced a variety of illicit carries of 6 in response. Overall, Ben-Zeev found that 67% of the participants' errors were induced from examples.

A more fine-grained analysis of syntactic induction reveals different processes of partial matching, misspecification, and spurious correlations.

Partial matching. On encountering a new problem state, a person may search for a familiar example or rule that shares some of the features of the current problem and has successfully

---

[4]VanLehn (1986) was able to explain 85% of second- through fifth-graders' subtraction errors as originating from induction from examples. He admitted, however, that this analysis is liberal because it involves some amount of guessing about which examples an individual student actually received while learning.

worked in the past. Once a familiar example is found, its procedure is performed. This process is called **partial matching** and is consistent with ACT* (J. R. Anderson, 1983). In condition-rule form, when a person reaches a new problem state (C) and the critic signals a violation of the form "If C then ?" where C itself is composed of conditions such that $C = C_1$ and C_2 and . . . and C_n," the person searches for a familiar example or rule that has one or more of the conditions. Once the familiar rule is found, its corresponding action (A) is executed.

Misspecification of constraints. Rule-based errors may also occur when people induce rules from examples but do not adequately constrain them. For example, Matz (1982) showed that problem solvers engage in a process of **linear decomposition**, in which they apply an operator to each subpart of a problem independently and then combine the partial results from each operation to form the solution. A correct use of linear decomposition is the distributive law of multiplication: $A (B + C) = AB + AC$. However, unless this law is constrained to apply only to linear functions, it can lead to errors, such as the commonly observed $\sqrt{(A + B)} = \sqrt{A} + \sqrt{B}$.

Spurious correlations. Either verbal or written worked-out examples may contain a misleading or spurious correlation between an irrelevant feature (a feature that is not essential for the solution) and a specific solution algorithm. People often detect these correlations and then abstract them into erroneous rules (given irrelevant feature *f*, then execute algorithm *a*). The vertex-intercept confusion, presented previously, illustrates this process well (people confuse the two because they lie on the same point in parabolas that are symmetrical about the y-axis).

A good illustration of experimental evidence for spurious correlations in problem solving comes from B. Ross (1984), who instructed college students how to solve elementary probability problems (e.g., permutation). Each problem was associated with a particular content (e.g., involving dice). When the students were tested on their knowledge of the probability principles, Ross found that they tended to use the particular problem content as a cue for applying a specific probability principle. When the same content appeared in a problem requiring a different probability principle, the students were reminded of the original principle the content was associated with and proceeded to execute it erroneously.

Relying on correlational structure may be adaptive because feature-algorithm correlations often lead to correct solutions (see C. Lewis & Anderson, 1985). For instance, teachers commonly instruct students to search explicitly for a "cue" word in a problem and then to associate that cue with a particular solution algorithm. Specifically, the word *left* is used as a cue word for performing subtraction on word problems like this: "Tom has 5 apples. Jerry takes away 3. How many apples are *left*?" However, Schoenfeld (1988) noted that this strategy may backfire because several children who are given the word *left* in nonsensical word problems (with premises, such as "Tom sits to the left of Jerry") proceed to subtract the given quantities in the problem in a rote fashion. Induction from examples does not always involve such a syntactic quality. It also can be semantically based.

Semantic Induction

Studies on intuitive physics have shown that people have a set of naive beliefs about the physical world. McCloskey, Caramazza, and Green (1980) found that when people were asked to draw the path of a moving object shot through a curved tube, they believed that the object would move along a curved (rather than a straight) path even in the absence of external forces. These naive beliefs may occur as a result of induction from everyday experience, such as drawing an incorrect analogy to the Earth's circular movement around the sun (one does not "see" the forces that sustain this movement).

People may also have a sense of "intuitive mathematics" akin to that of "intuitive physics" (Ben-Zeev, 1996; Ben-Zeev & Star, 2000; Chi & Slotta, 1993; diSessa, 1982,1993; McCloskey et al., 1980) that may also result from **semantic induction**—or a process of forming analogical mappings to real-life examples or concepts. For example, a common error among students who learn about exponents is that $n^0 = 0$, not $n^0 = 1$. Duffin and Simpson (1993) argued that the belief that doing nothing equals nothing is a "natural" argument that stems from real-world experience. The student may form the analogy that doing nothing : nothing :: n^0 :0.

Semantically driven misconceptions may also be affected by linguistic variables. For example, Davis and Vinner (1986) found that students tended to treat a limit in calculus as a boundary of an infinite sequence that could never be reached. They argued that this misconception may occur, in part, from the fact that in everyday language the word *limit* does imply a boundary that cannot not be reached, such as, "the outer-limit of the universe," and "the limits of our understanding." In sum, problem solving is strongly affected by a person's experience with real-world examples and linguistic affordances.

A Taxonomy of Rule-Based Errors: A Brief Summary

Problem solving involves internal critics, syntactic induction, and semantic induction. These processes can be beneficial but can also lead to predictable errors. Critic-related failures are dependent on whether people create a set of internal monitoring devices correctly. Syntactic induction can lead to overgeneralization as a result of symbol pushing without attention to the deeper structure of a problem. Finally, semantic induction is based on a person's experience with real-world examples and intuitive theories that may or may not hold in a given problem-solving domain.

Thus, a person often meets the challenge of solving a new problem state by creating rule-based but erroneous algorithms that lead to errors. These algorithms are the person's attempt to create a reasonable solution in a short time. This kind of problem solving can be characterized by a "bounded rationality" (Simon, 1957); one aims to achieve what seems to be a workable, rather than an optimal, solution. During this process, the same problem-solving strategies that lead to correct solutions (e.g., the various induction-from-examples procedures that we reviewed) can cause predictable errors as well.

THE IMPORTANCE OF EXAMPLES IN PROBLEM SOLVING

The nature of rule-based errors suggests that the acquisition of procedural knowledge is constrained by the surface-structural features of worked-out examples (e.g., Chi et al., 1981), as indicated by our previous discussion on syntactic induction. Examples provide a ready-made recipe that people can follow without attention to underlying deep structure. This problem is compounded by the fact that when people are given a choice between using worked-out examples or written instructions or explanations, they tend overwhelmingly to choose the former (J. R. Anderson, Farrell, & Sauers, 1984; LeFevre & Dixon, 1986; Pirolli, & J. R. Anderson, 1985). LeFevre and Dixon (1986) found that when participants were given a conflicting set of instructions (i.e., the written instructions asked them to perform a different procedure than the example illustrated), the majority of participants tended to follow the procedure illustrated by the worked-out example without realizing that the written instructions were different.

The pivotal role of examples in problem solving has been captured by research on *case-based reasoning* (e.g., Schank, 1982). Case-based reasoning suggests that problem solving proceeds by the use of specific examples, or cases, that are stored in memory. These cases are retrieved and adapted to fit a given problem. The adapted solutions are then stored in memory for future use (see Kolodner, 1993). This view of problem solving emphasizes the role of similarity over general knowledge. It thus predicts that people will use surface-structurally similar problems for solving a given target problem.

Blessing and Ross (1996) showed that even experienced problem solvers fall prey to the surface-structural features of problems. Specifically, they demonstrated that experienced problem solvers often use a problem's verbal content to categorize and solve the problem. When a problem's content (e.g., about investment) is inconsistent with the problem's underlying structure (e.g., a motion problem), experienced problem solvers become slower and less accurate in solving the problem than when the content is consistent (e.g., about driving).

The reason why both novice and experienced problem solvers are influenced by the surface-structural information in the examples they receive may be that superficial features are often causally linked to deeper structure. This argument has been advanced in the categorization literature (see chapter 3). For example, Medin and Ortony (1989) suggested that the attributes of concepts range on a continuum of accessibility from being deeply hidden or abstract (e.g., the biological composition of an entity) to being more surface structural and easily perceived (e.g., the color or shape of an entity). People frequently attend to the surface-structural features that are constrained by the more central properties of concepts. For instance, two entities that are surface-structurally different (a whale and a bear) are often grouped together in the same category (mammals) because they share the same central attributes. The main thesis is that the cognitive system becomes tuned to surface-structural characteristics that are causally linked to deeper attributes.

The constraining effect of examples on problem solving has educational implications. Teachers and textbooks often present students with worked-out examples that are confirmatory. That is, these examples illustrate how a particular algorithm solves a given problem but do not show when the algorithm is no longer appropriate for solving a similar but different problem. Confirmatory examples may lead people to create solution procedures that are underconstrained. It may be useful, therefore, to provide students with "negative" examples that illustrate when an algorithm no longer works, from early in the school years, to mitigate the process of overgeneralization. Teachers may wish to discuss the origin and nature of common rule-based errors as an integral part of teaching procedural skills. By acquiring meta-level knowledge about the conditions that may lead to errors, people can gain a deeper understanding of their own strategies, as well as of the structure of the given problem-solving domain.

◆ SUMMARY

Problems can be either well defined or ill defined. Well-defined problems (e.g., the Tower of Hanoi) have at least one clearly specified path to solution, whereas ill-defined problems (e.g., how to choose a lifelong partner) do not.

Problems have three general characteristics: (1) an *initial state*, or the state in which the problem solver examines the givens; (2) a *goal state*, or the desired end state; and (3) the operators that the problem solver applies to transform the initial state into the desired end state.

To solve problems, people are said to conduct a search in a *problem space.* The problem space is made up of symbolic structures (the *states* of the space) and a set of *operators*, or problem-solving actions that take a state as input and produce a state as output. The *problem* in the problem space consists of a set of initial states, a set of goal states, and a set of path constraints. The problem solver's challenge is to find a path through the space that starts at the initial state, passes along a clear path, and eventually reaches the desired goal state.

People use algorithms and heuristics for solving problems. An *algorithm* is a method that will always produce a solution to a problem, whereas a *heuristic* is a rule of thumb, a selective search of selected portions of the problem space that are most likely to lead to a solution. A commonly used heuristic, *means-end analysis*, involves the following steps: (1) determining what the goal state is; (2) assessing the distance between the current problem-solving state and the desired goal state; and (3) choosing an operator to reduce the greatest difference between these states. When an operator is applied and an obstacle occurs, the problem solver sets a subgoal of removing that obstacle. The subgoal then becomes the desired end goal and is solved again by the three steps of means-ends analysis just described.

Research on means-ends analysis shows that people can use subgoals for solving problems, but that they have difficulty applying subgoals that take them temporarily away from the desired end goal. An illustration of this phenomenon was demonstrated by the hardships that people experience on the Hobbits-and-Orcs problem.

The representation of the problem's givens is crucial to successful problem solving. We highlighted the importance of a correct representation on insight problems, in which the solution becomes suddenly apparent (the Aha! experience) after a prolonged period of effortful and unsuccessful deliberation and by the phenomenon of functional fixedness.

Functional fixedness refers to people's tendency to represent objects as serving traditional problem-solving functions, leading people to have difficulty using these objects in new ways. A classic demonstration of this phenomenon is the two-string problem which presents a person with the task of tying together two strings that are hanging from the ceiling, given that the strings are so far apart that the person cannot grasp both at once and among the objects in the room are a chair and a pair of pliers. The solution is made possible when one ties the pliers to one string and sets that string swinging like a pendulum, and then to get the second string, one brings it to the center of the room and waits for the first string to swing closely enough to grasp.

Another demonstration of functional fixedness is illustrated by the candle problem. This problem presents a person with a candle, a box of tacks, and matches and asks the person to mount the candle vertically on a plywood wall, such that the candle will serve as a lamp. The solution to this problem is to empty the box containing the tacks, use some of the tacks to mount the box onto the plywood wall, and use the box as a basis for mounting the candle by heating the candle so it drips warm wax onto the box.

Human problem solving is paradoxical. When people are faced with solving a new problem, they usually do not give up but construct rules or strategies to solve it. These strategies are often systematic and internally consistent but, nevertheless, may lead to predictable errors. Errors that are rule based, deliberate, and systematic open a window into problem solving by uncovering principled misunderstandings. Misunderstandings occur as a result of different mechanisms: (a) critic-related failures result from inadequate internal monitoring; (b) syntactic misinduction results from overgeneralization from the surface-structural features of worked-out examples; and (c) semantic misinduction is caused by a person's overrelience on his or her experience with real-world examples and intuitive theories.

Rule-based but erroneous algorithms are a person's attempt to create a reasonable solution in a short time. This kind of problem solving has the quality of "bounded rationality" (Simon, 1957), whereby one aims to achieve what seems to be a workable, rather than an optimal, solution.

8 Decision Making

◆ Normative Theories of Decision Making

◆ Human Decision Making: Deviations From Normative Models

◆ Descriptive Strategies and Theories of Decision Making

◆ Descriptive Theories of Decision Making

◆ Decision-Making Heuristics and Biases

◆ Decision Making: The Question of Rationality

◆ Summary

> Do you dare to go out? Do you dare to stay in?
> How much can you lose? How much can you win?
> And *IF* you come in, should you turn left or right . . .
> Or right-and-three-quarters? Or maybe not quite?
> Simple it's not, I am afraid you will find,
> for a mind-maker-upper to make up his mind.
>
> —Dr. Seuss, *Oh, the Places You'll Go!*

How do we make decisions, ranging from the mundane, such as what clothes to wear each day, to the important, such as what career to choose and with whom to spend the rest of our lives? In this chapter, we examine people's decision-making strategies in light of normative theories.

Normative theories of decision making provide prescriptions of how people *should* make decisions. They include expected value theory, expected utility theory, and subjective expected utility theory, which assign either an objective or subjective value to an option and then factor in the option's probability. Another approach is captured by multi-attribute utility theory (MAUT). MAUT first calculates the utility of different choice options (e.g., buying one of two houses) by breaking them down into independent dimensions (e.g., number of rooms, location, and price) and then weighs the importance of the dimensions relative to each other.

People's decision-making strategies deviate from the principles of normative models, which prescribe how people should make judgments, in systematic ways. For example, people are affected by the way in which a problem is framed verbally. They may violate fundamental assumptions of logic (transitivity) and behave inconsistently by using different strategies for solving the same kinds of problems on two different occasions.

Descriptive theories of decision making show how people *do* make decisions. Prospect theory suggests that people's choices deviate from the normative model of expected utility by overweighing low and high probabilities relative to intermediate probabilities. Regret theory claims that people overweigh the anticipated feelings of regret and joy when the differences between anticipated outcomes are large.

We discuss in detail several heuristics that have an impact on people's decision-making processes, including representativeness, availability, and anchoring and adjustments. Finally, we examine the question of whether people are rational thinkers. We argue that instead of trying to determine whether people are rational or irrational, it is more useful to identify the circumstances under which they exhibit correct or fallacious reasoning.

What made you decide to read this book? How did you choose which courses to take at your college or university? When you start thinking of making a new purchase, such as a car, how do you go about weighing your options? If a friend decided to get you a gift of your choice, say within a $100 price range, what would you ask for? How do you decide whether you want to be romantically involved with a particular person? How might you determine which name to give a pet dog, cat, or fish? These questions involve making decisions, often under conditions of some uncertainty. That is, we frequently are required to select among different options, even when we do not have all the relevant information accessible to us.

How do people make decisions, and are these decisions rational? To examine these questions, we need first to agree on what we mean by rational decision making. That is, we need to decide which normative models to compare to compare people's thinking. Thus, we discuss **normative theories** of decision making that prescribe how people should make decisions. We then compare people's actual behaviors to the standards set by these normative models. A caveat is in order, however. The normative theories are themselves founded on human intuitions about which assumptions are axiomatic, or true (L. J. Cohen, 1981).

NORMATIVE THEORIES OF DECISION MAKING

Normative theories of decision making provide prescriptions for how people *should* make decisions (versus how they actually make them). These models describe the behavior of an ideally rational decision maker. In this section, we discuss expected value theory, expected utility theory, subjective expected utility theory, and multi-attribute utility theory. At the core of all these theories is the idea that people should make a trade-off between the probability of an outcome and its utility, where **utility** is a measure of how well an outcome helps people achieve their goals. These theories are designed to help people choose an option that has the highest **expected utility**.

Expected Value Theory

When values of outcomes are objective and the probabilities of each outcome are known, one can calculate the **expected value** of an option or gamble using **expected value theory (EVT)**. For example, suppose that you agree to participate in the following gamble: You are randomly drawing a marble from an urn that contains four marbles, each of which is a different color (black, red, blue, or green). You will get $10 if you draw a black marble, $8 for a red, $6 for a blue, and $1 for a green. What would be the expected value of your average winnings over time? The general formula for expected value is

$$EV = \sum_i p_i \cdot v_i$$

where EV = expected value, i = each possible outcome, p(i) = the probability of the ith outcome, v(i) = the value of the ith outcome.

For the specific gamble just stated, the expected value (where, p(i) = .25 because each color has a 1 out of 4 chance [or .25 probability] of being drawn) is

$$EV = \sum_{i=1}^{4} .25 \cdot v_i = .25*\$10 + .25*\$8 + .25*\$6 + .25*\$1 = \$6.25$$

People, however, do not seem to take expected value into account when they make monetary gambles. Consider the **St. Petersburg paradox** (Bernoulli, 1738/1954, p. 31):

> Peter tosses a coin and continues to do so until it should land "heads" when it comes to the ground. He agrees to give Paul one ducat if he gets "heads" on the very first throw, two ducats if he gets it on the second, four if on the third, eight if on the fourth, and so on, so that with each additional throw the number of ducats he must pay is doubled. Suppose we seek to determine the value of Paul's expectation.

We can demonstrate that the expected value of playing this game is infinite by plugging it into the expected value formula:

$$EV = \sum_i p_i \cdot v_i = 1/2 \cdot 1 + 1/4 \cdot 2 + 1/8 \cdot 4 + 1/16 \cdot 8 + \ldots = 1/2 + 1/2 + 1/2 \ldots$$

As you can see, as the probability halves for longer sequences of consecutive tail tosses, the utility doubles. The sum of the expected value is infinite because the probability of arbitrarily long sequences approaches but never reaches zero. A person would have to play this game an infinite number of times to get an infinite sum of money. Does the infinite excepted value mean that you should be willing to pay a large sum of money to play this game? Bernoulli argued that any rational person would be willing to pay no more than 20 ducats for the rights of either playing this game or selling the rights to someone else because the subjective value or utility of monetary gain is not a simple linear function. Instead, Bernoulli suggested that the subjective utility of monetary gain may follow a logarithmic function, where the value of each additional ducat one makes diminishes as the amount of gain increases (see Figure 8.1).

This idea of diminishing returns is captured by the *law of diminishing marginal utility* (Bernoulli, 1738/1954; Savage, 1954). This law suggests that a fixed increment of cash wealth results in an ever smaller increment in utility as the basic cash wealth to which the increment applies is increased. In the St. Petersburg paradox, the additional utilities of winnings (e.g., heads on the 10th toss) are no longer large enough to compensate for their low probability. Here is another example that would make the law of diminishing marginal utility even clearer: If you increased the wealth you now have to reach $1 million, you probably would be very happy (assuming that you are not a millionaire already). However, adding yet another million would probably not make you as happy as getting the first million.

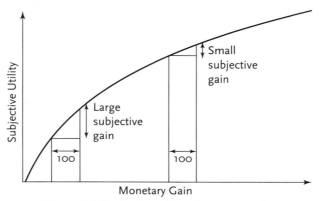

Figure 8.1 Subjective utility of monetary gain.

Expected Utility Theory and Subjective Expected Utility Theory

Expected utility theory (EUT) involves assigning subjective utilities (versus objective values) to events that may take on different values for different people (Von Neumann & Morgenstern, 1947). Expected utilities are calculated in a similar manner to expected values for different states, choice possibilities, and outcomes. A major extension of EUT is **subjective expected utility theory (SEUT)** (Savage, 1954). In contrast to EUT, SEUT allows for the consideration of subjective probabilities as well as subjective utilities.

We now apply SEUT to analyze an argument of why people should live religiously (called Pascal's wager). The argument is that there are two possible *states*: Either God exists or God does not exist. We therefore assign a probability of .50 to each of these states (note that these probabilities are subjective because there is no way to ascertain them normatively). Now let us examine the utilities of the two choices of either living secularly or religiously for each of these two states. First, say you choose to live secularly. If God does not exist, then you will end up living a normal life (we assign this choice a subjective utility of zero that will then set the standard for the magnitude and direction of all other choices). However, if God exists, you will go to hell (a very high negative utility). Alternatively, if you choose to live religiously, then you either will go to heaven if God exists (a very high positive utility) or you will inconvenience your life somewhat if God does not exist (a small-to-moderate negative utility). The **decision table**, a table that specifies the outcomes of all possible decision options crossed by all possible states of the world, is presented in Table 8.1. To compute the utility of an op-

TABLE 8.1 Pascal's Wager

Option	State	
	God Exists	**God Does Not Exist**
Live religiously	Go to Heaven	Make relatively small sacrifice
Live secularly	Go to Hell	Lead normal life

tion (e.g., living religiously or secularly), we multiply the utility of each of its outcomes by the probability of the state that leads to that outcome and then sum across the states:

$$SEU = EU = \sum_i p_i \cdot u_i$$

where EU = expected utility, i = all possible outcomes, p(i) = the probability of the ith outcome (objective if it is EU or subjective in the case of SEU), u(i) = the subjective utility of the ith outcome.[1]

To calculate the subjective utilities for Pascal's wager, let us choose specific numbers for the utilities of the four outcomes in the decision table. We have anchored on normal life as our reference point by assigning it a utility of 0 (note that this choice of reference point is arbitrary. It does not matter what units we choose. All that matters is their relative subjective magnitude). Our scale ranges from $-\infty$ to $+\infty$, where normal life = 0, heaven = $+\infty$, hell = $-\infty$, and the sacrifice for living religiously is an arbitrary cost of -100.

We can now compute the expected utilities for each choice possibility in the decision table by plugging it into the SEU formula:

Living religiously = $+\infty*.5$ (cell 11) + $-100*.5$ (cell 12) = ∞

Living secularly = $-\infty*.5$ (cell 21) + $0*.5$ (cell 22) = $-\infty$

According to EUT, one should live as though there is a God, regardless of whether one really believes that God exists. Now assign your own subjective utilities for each outcome and see which choice option wins. We suspect that you will get the same result. In fact, Pascal's wager would work as an argument for living a religious life even if we assigned a very small probability (e.g., .01) to the state in which God exists because the value of heaven is still infinitely larger than that of any of the other outcomes.

EUT and SEUT incorporate six axioms that an ideal decision maker should follow: The **ordering of alternatives** axiom suggests that rational decision makers should be able to compare any two alternatives and have a preference for either one or the other or decide that both are equally good, but should not decide that a preference is impossible. The **transitivity axiom** holds that if a person prefers choice A to B and choice B to C, she then ought to prefer choice A to choice C. The **dominance axiom** suggests that if one alternative is at least as good as another in every attribute and is better than it in at least one attribute, then that alternative should be preferred. The **cancellation axiom** suggests that if two options include identical and equally probable outcomes, then the utility of these outcomes should be ignored in deciding between these two options (such that their common factors cancel out). For example, if you are choosing between two business suits that have the same price tag, then the price factor should not influence which suit you choose. The **continuity axiom** entails that people should always prefer a gamble between the best and worst outcomes (for example, between winning $100 and losing $100) to a sure intermediate outcome (a guarantee of $10) if the probability of the best outcome is high enough (in this example, the probability of winning $100 has to be greater than .55 to make choosing the gamble worth it). Choosing the gamble is ideal because one comes out ahead by repeatedly choosing to gamble with favor-

---

[1]Note that SEUT is calculated the same way except that p(i) refers to the subjective instead of the objective probability of the ith outcome.

able odds than by always choosing the intermediate "sure thing." Finally, the **invariance axiom** suggests that people should not be affected by the way alternatives are presented or framed.

Multi-Attribute Utility Theory

Multi-attribute utility theory (MAUT) (Wright, 1984) is a type of normative decision analysis that (1) calculates the utility of a choice option (e.g., what kind of apartment to rent) by breaking it into psychologically *independent* dimensions (e.g., the number of rooms, location, and rent per month), (2) measures the utility of each dimension by weighing the dimensions relative to each another, and (3) sums across the utilities of each dimension to decide on the total utility of the option. For example, imagine that you are considering renting an apartment and have the four choices (each with three independent dimensions) listed in Table 8.2.

First, you would need to assign a utility of a particular dimension to each outcome, say 100 to the best outcome (central location) and 0 to the worst (peripheral location). If you simply summed across the utilities of each dimension, Apartment 3 would take the lead (resulting in the largest sum of 225). However, is Apartment 3 your best choice? It may not be if you are more concerned with rent than with location. To figure out which apartment is your best choice, when you have a differential preference for one dimension over another, you would need first to determine the relative importance of each of the dimensions involved.

Let us first compare rent to location. We start with the apartment that has the lowest price per month ($500). Given that it lies in a peripheral location, you can ask: "How much more would I pay for this apartment if it were in a central location?" Say the answer is $250. The scale for location, therefore, would weigh half as much as the scale for rent. When adding the utilities, we can use rent as a standard and multiply the utilities for the location dimension by .5. Let us assume that you have no preference for the number of rooms dimension versus the location dimension (they both weigh the same), so we multiply those utilities by .5 as well. Which apartment takes the lead now? Summing the new weighted utilities makes Apartment 2 (50 + 0 + 100 = 150) a better choice than Apartment 3 (50 + 50 + 25 = 125).

There are several difficulties with using MAUT as a normative theory. The set of all relevant dimensions cannot always be clearly determined, and people's weightings of dimensions may change over time (W. M. Goldstein, 1990). Also, in many real-life situations, it is often difficult to generate dimensions that are clearly independent.

A simplified alternative to MAUT is the **equal weights heuristic (EQW)** (J. Payne, Bettman, & Johnson, 1993). EQW ignores information on the relative importance of attributes. Instead, it prescribes that people sum the values for each option and then choose the alternative with the highest total. However, this method and others may not prove to be optimal under all circumstances (such as the rent problem presented). In essence, the choice of

TABLE 8.2 A Multi-Attribute Utility Theory for Choosing an Apartment

Apartment	Rooms (Ro)	R Utility	Location (L)	L Utility	Rent (Re)	Re Utility
1	2	0	Central	100	$1,000	0
2	3	100	Peripheral	0	$ 500	100
3	3	100	Central	100	$ 875	25
4	3	100	Peripheral	0	$ 750	50

which analysis to use boils down to a subjective, rather than an objective, decision, calling into question whether MAUT is really a normative theory after all or just a reasonable way to conduct a decision analysis (out of many possible analyses).

HUMAN DECISION MAKING: DEVIATIONS FROM NORMATIVE MODELS

What do people do when they make decisions? People frequently do not follow the guidelines of EVT, EUT, SEUT, or MAUT. Instead, they tend to violate these theories' principles in systematic ways. In this section, we examine such violations and their possible causes.

Intransitivity

People often violate the transitivity principle of utility theory by applying a decision rule to narrow down options. For example, in a business setting, a manager may apply a decision rule for hiring a job applicant in a manner that is similar to the following (Plous, 1993, p. 88):

> If the difference in IQ between any two applicants is greater than 10 points, choose the more intelligent applicant. If the difference between applicants is equal to or less than 10 points, choose the applicant with more experience.

Consider Table 8.3, which contains data from three applicants: A, B, and C. Let us first use the decision rule for comparing A and B. Given that the difference between their IQ scores is equal to or less than 10 points, we end up choosing the more experienced applicant, which is B. Now we compare B to C. By applying the same decision rule, we end up choosing C. Applicant C is thus our candidate of choice out of the three applicants. However, notice that A has 20 more IQ points than does C! Applying the decision rule for choosing among the three applicants led us to make an intransitive inference. Intransitivity may have occurred in this example because the decision was based on two separate attributes, intelligence and experience, that increase gradually and are inversely related (the applicants' IQ scores are inversely related to their years of experience) (see Table 8.3).

The Allais Paradox

Another axiom of utility theory is the cancellation principle. The violation of this axiom is well illustrated by the **Allais paradox** (Allais, 1953). To demonstrate this paradox, consider the following game, in which you are asked to decide between two alternatives, A and B (based on Plous, 1993, p. 85).

TABLE 8.3 The Applicants' Profiles

Applicants	Attributes	
	Intelligence (IQ)	Experience (Years)
A	120	1
B	110	2
C	100	3

Game 1

Alternative A: You win $1 million for sure.

Alternative B: You have a 10% chance of getting $2.5 million, an 89% chance of getting $1 million, and a 1% chance of getting $0.

Most people choose Alternative A, even though Alternative B has the greater expected value. Now consider the alternatives in Game 2.

 Game 2

Alternative A: You have an 11% chance of getting $1 million and an 89% chance of getting $0.

Alternative B: You have a 10% chance of getting $2.5 million and a 90% chance of getting $0.

In this case, most people choose Alternative B, which indeed has the greater expected value (EV = $250,000). But herein lies the paradox: If a person chooses Alternative A in Game 1, then if the person applies a consistent strategy (e.g., opting for the highest probability of gain versus the highest expected value), he or she should also choose Alternative A in Game 2.

We will demonstrate more formally why one should choose Alternative B in both games using the normative measure of expected value. Let us first compute the expected values of alternatives A and B [EV(A) and EV(B)] in Game 1:

$$EV(A) = (1.0)(\$1,000,000) \qquad\qquad = \$1,000,000$$

$$EV(B) = (.10)(\$2,500,000) + (.89)(\$1,000,000) + (.01)(\$0) = \$1,140,000$$

After summing the terms, we are left with is an overall positive difference of $140,000 in favor of alternative B. We now turn to compute the expected values of alternatives A and B [EV(A) and EV(B)] in Game 2:

$$EV(A) = (.11)(\$1,000,000) + (.89)(\$0) = \$110,000$$

$$EV(B) = (.10)(\$2,500,000) + (.90)(\$0) = \$250,000$$

Here, the sums of all the terms yield an overall positive difference of $140,000 in favor of alternative B. Diagrammatically, these differences are illustrated in Figure 8.2.

The Ellsberg Paradox

The cancellation principle is also violated by the **Ellsberg paradox** (Ellsberg, 1961, p. 653). Here is a paraphrase of the paradox.

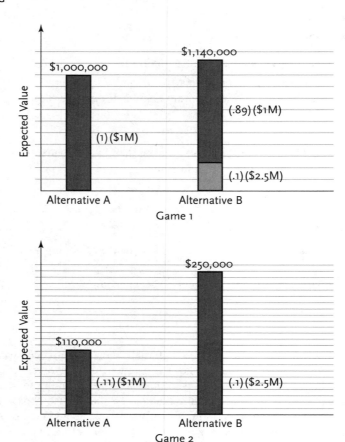

Figure 8.2 The Allais paradox.

 Imagine an urn that contains 30 red balls and 60 black balls and yellow balls, the latter in unknown proportion. One ball is to be drawn at random from the urn.

Consider the bets presented in Table 8.4. Which alternative would you choose? Most people choose red (Alternative 1.1) for Bet 1 but choose black or yellow (Alternative 2.2) over red or yellow for Bet 2. However, the yellow ball is worth the same amount in Alternatives 2.1 and 2.2, so the value of the yellow ball should cancel out and not influence a person's decision in choosing between bets. The switching behavior is an example of a violation of the axioms of *ordering*, *dominance*, and *cancellation*. In Bet 1, the red ball was preferred, but in Bet 2, all things being equal (the yellow ball is in both options), the black ball is preferred.

TABLE 8.4 The Ellsberg Paradox

	30 Balls	60 Balls	
Bet	Red	Black	Yellow
Bet 1			
Alternative 1.1: A red ball	$100	$0	$0
Alternative 2.1: A black ball	$0	$100	$0
Bet 2			
Alternative 2.1: A red or yellow ball	$100	$0	$100
Alternative 2.2: A black or yellow ball	$0	$100	$100

Preference Reversals

Imagine that you are playing a game in which you have to choose between two gambles, the P Bet and the $ Bet (Tversky, Sattath, & Slovic, 1988):

P Bet: 29/36 probability of winning $2

$ Bet: 7/36 probability of winning $9

Which game would you choose to play? If you decided on the P Bet, you are in good company because the majority of people prefer to play this bet. Now, decide how much each bet would be worth to you if you were to sell the rights for playing it. In this case, most participants give higher values to the $ Bet, showing what is known as a **preference reversal**.

Similarly, Lichtenstein and Slovic (1971, 1973) asked gamblers in a Las Vegas casino to choose a bet, from the following game, and to name a minimum price they would sell it for:

Bet A: 11/12 chance to win 12 chips
1/12 chance to lose 24 chips

Bet B: 2/12 chance to win 79 chips
10/12 chance to lose 5 chips

They found that Bets A and B were selected just as often, but that Bet B tended to receive a higher selling price. In fact, people who chose to play Bet A assigned Bet B a higher value 87% of the time.

Shafir (1993) elicited preference reversals for the same decision options by providing people with different instructions. People were asked either to pick their preferred option or to cancel their undesired option (p. 549).

◆ **Prefer Option**

Imagine that you are planning a week vacation in a warm spot over spring break. You currently have two options that are reasonably priced. The travel brochure gives only a limited amount of information about the two options. Given the information available, which vacation spot would you prefer?

Cancel Option

Imagine that you are planning a week vacation in a warm spot over spring break. You currently have two options that are reasonably priced, but you can no longer retain your reservation in both. The travel brochure gives only a limited amount of information about the two options. Given the information available, which reservation would you decide to cancel?

The spots, A and B, were described as follows:

Spot A	*Spot B*
average weather	lots of sunshine
average beaches	gorgeous beaches and coral reefs
medium-quality hotel	ultra-modern hotel
medium-temperature water	very cold water
	very strong winds
average nightlife	no nightlife

The results showed that people preferred Spot A 33% of the time and canceled Spot A 52% of the time. They preferred Spot B 67% of the time and canceled Spot B 48% of the time. Spot B was strongly preferred to Spot A, but was about as likely to be rejected as Spot A. These results stand in contrast to what EUT would predict, namely, that if a choice is preferred two thirds of the time, it should be rejected one third of the time.

Preference reversals violate the transitivity axiom of EUT. So why do they occur? One explanation of preference reversals is that people use **contingent weighting** (Tversky et al., 1988), treating each gamble as having a two-attribute outcome (probability and dollar amount). The probability of winning is important when people are choosing between gambles ("I prefer a sure bet to an iffy bet"). However, the dollar amount becomes more important when the focus is on the value of selling it ("How much is the gamble worth to me?"). Thus, the weighting of the same problem is contingent on the way in which a problem is framed to focus on one attribute (probability) or another (monetary reward). This explanation can be applied to Shafir's (1993) study: The possible reasons for the reversals between preferring Spot B more often, but canceling Spot A about as often as Spot B, is that the "prefer option" may focus people's attention on the positive aspects of an option, whereas the "cancel option" may bias people to attend to negative attributes.

Framing Effects

As was shown in the case of preference reversals, the way a problem is framed may affect people's decisions about it. Kahneman and Tversky (1979) argued that people's preferences are affected by whether problems are framed in terms of gains or losses. If an initial reference point is defined such that an outcome is perceived as a gain, then people become more risk averse, but if the reference point is defined such that an outcome is perceived as a loss, then people are more prone to become risk seekers. Consistent with this prediction, participants who were presented with Problem 1 tended to choose Alternative B (a sure option), whereas those who were presented with Problem 2 tended to choose Alternative C (a risky option) (the problems are paraphrases of the original, more terse versions, for clarity; see Kahneman & Tversky, 1979, p. 273).

◆ Problem 1

In addition to whatever you own, you have been given $1,000. You are now asked to choose between A: a 50% chance of gaining $1,000 and B: a sure gain of $500.

◆ Problem 2

In addition to whatever you own, you have been given $2,000. You are now asked to choose between C: a 50% chance of losing $1,000 and D: a sure loss of $500.

Note that in the two problems, both choices yield the same outcome (i.e., $1,000 or $2,000 for A and C and $1,500 for B and D).

Another problem that demonstrates the powerful results of the framing effect is the unusual Asian disease problem. This problem, in its two variations, is presented next (Tversky & Kahneman, 1982, p. 166). Try to solve them before you read on.

◆ Problem 1

Imagine that the United States is preparing for the outbreak of an unusual Asian disease, which is expected to kill 600 people. Two alternative programs to combat the disease have been proposed. Assume that the exact scientific estimates of the consequences of the program are as follows:

If Program A is adopted, 200 people will be saved.

If Program B is adopted, there is a one-third probability that 600 people will be saved, and two-thirds probability that no people will be saved.

Which of the two programs would you favor?

◆ Problem 2

Imagine that the United States is preparing for the outbreak of an unusual Asian disease, which is expected to kill 600 people. Two alternative programs to combat the disease have been proposed. Assume that the exact scientific estimates of the consequences of the program are as follows:

If Program C is adopted, 400 people will die.

If Program D is adopted, there is a one-third probability that no people will die, and two-thirds probability that 600 people will die.

Which of the two programs would you favor?

The results showed that for Problem 1, 72% of participants chose Program A and 28% chose Program B. Thus, even though both programs were statistically equivalent, the participants seemed to be averse to taking risks. For Problem 2, however, just the opposite result was found: 22% of the participants preferred Program C and 78% preferred Program D. In this case, the participants were more risk taking. In sum, the framing effect, among other examples detailed earlier, shows that people violate the different axioms of EVT in systematic ways. What are some explanations for people's judgments? We now discuss possible answers to this fundamental question.

DESCRIPTIVE STRATEGIES AND THEORIES OF DECISION MAKING

Descriptive theories of decision making delineate how people actually make decisions in the face of certain and uncertain events. Here, we discuss strategies that include satisficing (Simon, 1957), elimination by aspects (Tversky, 1972), and the more-important-dimension hypothesis (Slovic, 1975). We then examine two more broadly encompassing theories: prospect theory (Kahneman & Tversky, 1979), which suggests that people assign differential values to situations that are framed as either gains or losses, and regret theory (Loomes & Sugden, 1982), which argues that people's decision making is affected by their expectations of feelings of regret and rejoicing at having picked a specific choice over another.

Satisficing

Satisficing (Simon, 1957) refers to the process whereby people consider options, one at a time, and immediately select an option that fulfills their goals in an acceptable way, even though that choice may not be optimal. Inherent in this theory is the idea that people are rational within predictable limits—that they have a **bounded rationality**. People commonly engage in satisficing when they decide to purchase an item, such as a VCR, but do not have enough time to research the best deal for getting it. Imagine a typical scenario of buying a VCR. A person goes to a department store that she finds satisfactory (that has a range of high-quality electronics and is reasonably priced). Then she compares a few VCRs in terms of their brand names and prices and picks one that meets her level of acceptability. That particular VCR may not be the best choice (there could be a better deal down the road, or a different brand may have a higher price but would last longer), but her choice will serve her fairly well.

Elimination by Aspects

When facing complex problem situations that afford multiple alternatives, people often shift from one alternative to the next until they reach their final decision. Tversky (1972)'s **elimination by aspects** (EBA) heuristic is designed to explain why people find some decisions harder to make than others. EBA suggests that people attend to the favorable attributes of each alternative, one at a time. For example, imagine that you are trying to decide between spending your Sunday hiking in the woods or going to the beach (the choice set). You then would think of some favorable aspects of each decision, such as bathing or seeing beautiful trees, among others. Using EBA, you would focus on just one favorable attribute and eliminate all other alternatives in the choice set that do not have it. For example, if you decide on bathing as your favorable aspect, then you can proceed to eliminate hiking as the activity of choice. However, if you decide on an attribute that the options have in common, such as "being outdoors," you would then continue to search for other more distinguishing characteristics that would distill the decision process to just one option.

The disadvantage of EBA is that the decision maker may search for attributes that will eliminate better options, leading to nonoptimal decisions. For example, an alternative option may differ from the chosen option by only some small differences in some attributes. However, taken together, the total attributes of the alternative option may fulfill the person's goals better. In addition, EBA becomes unstable when a person decides to switch or to revise his or her initial attributes of choice. This situation occurs when the first attribute one thinks of is not the most important one (e.g., "I would like to bathe in the ocean, but, on second thought, it is more important that I get more strenuous exercise"). The main advantage of EBA, however, is that it is a reasonable method for making simple decisions while preventing a laborious process of optimal decision making.

The More-Important-Dimension Hypothesis

The more-important-dimension hypothesis (Slovic, 1975) suggests that if people are given a choice between two equally valued options, they will choose the option that has a greater value on what they perceive to be the most important dimension involved. To corroborate this idea, Slovic provided participants with a scenario that described two baseball players: Player 1 has hit 26 home runs and has a batting average of .273, and Player 2 has hit 20 home runs. The participants were asked to decide what Player 2's batting average would have to be to ensure that the two players would be of equal ability and value to their teams. After they gave their answers, they were asked to rate the importance of the dimensions (home-runs and batting averages) and to choose which player was better. As predicted by the more-important-dimension hypothesis, the participants often chose the player who had a higher value on the dimension that they deemed to be more important.

DESCRIPTIVE THEORIES OF DECISION MAKING

Prospect Theory

Prospect theory (Kahneman & Tversky, 1979) originated as an attempt to provide a general descriptive theory of decision making that explains how people's reasoning deviates from normative models, especially those that violate EUT. Similar to EUT, prospect theory assumes that people make decisions on the basis of utilities and probabilities. However, the assumptions of prospect theory are that (1) utilities are evaluated in terms of gains and losses or as deviations from a reference point. These utilities are referred to as "values"; (2) the reference point is affected by nonnormative factors, such as framing effects; and (3) people's estimations of probability are subjective.

One of the basic assumptions of the theory is that people choose options as if they were evaluating outcomes in reference to a zero point (a status quo point). This assumption is corroborated by people's violations of the **sure thing principle** (Dawes, 1998; Savage, 1954).

This principle suggests that if a person prefers one option (option x) to another (option y) if an event occurs or does not occur—"no matter what"—then that option (option x) will always dominate over the other option (option y).

Tversky and Shafir (1992) demonstrated how people violate the sure thing principle by offering them the opportunity to play the following gamble: Consider a gamble with a 50–50 chance of winning $200 or losing $100. About a third of the participants consented to play this gamble. Tversky and Shafir then told the participants to imagine that they had just played the game for the first time and were now being offered the opportunity to play it again. The participants were divided into three groups. Group 1 was told that they won the first gamble; Group 2 was told that they lost the first gamble; and Group 3 was told that the outcome for the first gamble had been determined by a coin toss, but that they would not be told the outcome until they decided whether they would play another round.

The findings showed that 69%, 59%, and only 36% of the participants in Group 1, Group 2, and Group 3, respectively, opted to play the second game. It is rational to want to play another round if you either won or lost on the first game because in the case of a win, you can end up with $400 or $100 the second time around, and in the case of a loss, you still have a 50% chance of coming out ahead. Another way to express this point is that if it was rational to bet the first time (the expected value of the bet is +$50), then it is rational to do so the second time as well.

Why did more people choose not to play the second round in Group 3? A compelling answer comes from prospect theory. Prospect theory suggests that people choose options as if they were evaluating outcomes in reference to a zero point, rather than in terms of total wealth (W). In other words, the values of choices in the gamble are not considered to be W + $200 and W − $100, but are considered as either a gain of $200 or a loss of $100. People's assessments of utilities or values are suggested to be based on an S-shaped subjective **value function** of gains and losses, shown in Figure 8.3.

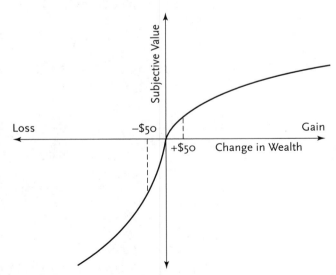

Figure 8.3 The value function for losses and gains based on prospect theory.

The value function gives more weight to losses than to gains (a given loss is more undesirable than the equivalent gain is desirable). The nature of this function can be used to explain why in Tversky and Shafir's (1992) experiment, two thirds of the people seemed to think that the prospect of losing $100 was much more unpleasant than the prospect of gaining $200 was pleasant, so they chose not to participate in the bet at all. Another property of this function is that the slope for gains decreases to the right, forming a concave (upward-curving) function, whereas the slope for losses increases to the right, forming a convex (downward-curving) function. This pattern suggests that people are willing to make more risky decisions in the context of losses but are more risk averse in the context of gains.

The shape of this function explains the decisions of the three groups in Tversky and Shafir's experiment. In the case of winning the first gamble (Group 1), the average of the value of $400 (winning the second time) and $100 (losing the second time) is greater than the $200 that the participants already won (even though the function for gains is concave). In the case of losing the first gamble (Group 2), the value of having a negative $100 is less than the average of −$200 (losing the second time) and $100 (winning the second time). However, for members of Group 3, who did not have information about whether they had won or lost, the anchor is the zero point (having nothing). From this vantage point, the gamble does not seem appealing (in fact, recall that only a third of all the participants agreed to play this game in the first place).

To show how the shape of the function (convex or concave) affects people's decision making, let us revisit Kahneman and Tversky's (1979) experiment that presented participants with either Problem 1 (In addition to whatever you own, you have been given $1,000. You can either choose a 50% chance of gaining $1,000 or a sure gain of $500) (concave function) or Problem 2 (In addition to whatever you own, you have been given $2,000. You can either choose a 50% chance of losing $1,000 or a sure loss of $500) (convex function). Prospect theory predicts that on Problem 1, people will be risk averse and choose Alternative B because of the underlying concave function (the subjective value increase is greater from $0 to $500 than from $500 to $1,000). Indeed, 84% of the participants chose this option of a sure gain on Problem 1. In contrast, prospect theory predicts that on Problem 2, people will choose Alternative C, the more risky alternative, because of the underlying convex value function (more subjective value is lost from $0 to $500 than from $500 to $1,000). Again, as predicted, 70% of the participants chose the more risky alternative.

Prospect theory has been applied to real-world decision making. For example, in a breast cancer study (Meyerowitz & Chaiken, 1987), women were given one of three pamphlets: a gain-frame pamphlet, a loss-frame pamphlet, and a no-frame pamphlet. In the gain-frame pamphlet, they were told that by doing a breast self-examination now, they would learn what their normal, healthy breasts feel like, so they would be prepared to notice any small abnormal changes that might occur with time. In the loss-frame pamphlet, the women were told that by not doing a breast self-examination now, they would not learn what their healthy breasts feel like, which, in turn, might prevent them from noticing any small abnormal changes that could occur in the future. Finally, in the no-frame pamphlet, these statements were omitted. Four months later, 57% of the women in the loss-frame group, 38% of the women in the gain-frame group, and 39% of the women in the no-frame group reported an increase in breast self-examinations.

Banks et al.'s (1995) study compared the effectiveness of gain- versus loss-frame messages to persuade women to undergo mammograms. Women were assigned randomly to view

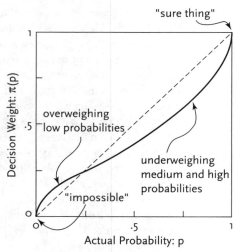

Figure 8.4 The π(p) function.

either gain-frame (emphasizing the benefits of obtaining mammography) or loss-frame (emphasizing the risks of not obtaining a mammogram) videotapes that contained the same medical facts. Consistent with predictions based on prospect theory, women who viewed the loss-frame message were more likely to have obtained a mammogram within 12 months of the intervention. These and Meyerowitz and Chaiken's (1987) findings suggest that loss-frame messages may have an advantage in promoting detection behaviors in real-world environments. Framing a health behavior in terms of losses increases one's involvement in preventive health behavior.

Prospect theory suggests that people's uses of probabilities deviate from the normative model of expected utility by overweighing low probabilities relative to intermediate and high probabilities. People who choose Alternative A in Game 1 of the Allais paradox, for example, overly attend to the .01 probability of winning nothing in Alternative B (comparing .00 of winning nothing in Alternative A to .01 of winning nothing in Alternative B). People who choose Alternative B in Game 2 ignore the fact that in both alternatives there is the same difference (.01) of winning nothing (they do not compare .89 of winning nothing in Alternative A to .90 of winning nothing in Alternative B).

Kahneman and Tversky modeled people's decisions by a π(p) function (called a **Pi function**), where instead of multiplying utilities by p (probability), they are multiplied by π(p), as illustrated in Figure 8.4.

The π(p) function represents the subjective perception of probability. People tend to overweigh small probabilities, greatly overweigh a probability of 1 (a sure bet), and greatly underweigh a probability of 0. The π(p) function is thus able to explain people's deviations from normative prescriptions. For example, The π(p) function can account for the **certainty effect** (McCord & de Neufville, 1985), which shows that people are attracted by the absolute certainty of a sure bet—an effect that EUT fails to explain. Consider the following example, taken from Baron (1988), of how EUT cannot account for the certainty effect. If a person prefers a sure bet ($50, $p = 1.00$) to a highly probable bet ($65, $p = .80$), then EUT would predict that

$$1.0 \cdot u(\$50) > .80 \cdot u(\$65)$$

If a person prefers ($65, $p = .20$) to ($50, $p = .25$), the equation changes to

$$.25 \cdot u(\$50) < .20 \cdot u(\$65)$$

Both these inequalities cannot be true at the same time because the first choice can be converted to the second choice by multiplying both probabilities by .25, yet the inequality sign should not change in the process. People's behavior seems to contradict a simple weighing of subjective utilities by their probabilities of occurring.

The $\pi(p)$ function, on the other hand, explains the certainty effect because $\pi(1.00)$ is much higher than $\pi(p)$ even for nearby values of p (i.e., $\pi(1)$ is much larger than $\pi(.99)$). In addition, $\pi(p)$ predicts that people tend to overweigh low probabilities much more than a probability of 0. Thus, it helps explain why in the Allais paradox, for example, the .01 difference between .01 and .0 in Game 1 seems larger than between .89 and .90 in Game 2.

In sum, prospect theory has been influential in providing a general descriptive theory of decisions based on subjective utilities and probabilities. Prospect theory shows that people's decision-making processes are prone to framing problems in terms of gains and losses in reference to a zero point. As we have seen, the implications of this theory extend to real-life decision making.

Prospect theory does not account for all of people's deviations from EUT. Other effects on the choice of decision strategies may come from people's emotional reactions to the choices they make. For example, people often imagine choosing one option and then considering what would have happened if they had chosen differently. This kind of thinking may lead them to experience emotions, such as regret or rejoicing, which, in turn, can further affect their decisions.

Regret Theory

Regret theory (Bell, 1982; Loomes & Sugden, 1982) suggests that people regret their decision if they realize or believe that the outcome would have been better had they made a different one. To illustrate this point, think about the decision of whether to take an umbrella with you on a cloudy day (Baron, 1994). You would feel regret if you left the umbrella at home and it rained that day or if you took the umbrella with you and it did not rain. You would feel relief if you left the umbrella at home and it did not rain that day or if you took it with you and it did rain. In any case, to make this or any other decision, people often take into account how they would feel. For example, one of us went on a recent trip to London and decided to leave her umbrella in the hotel. She then spent the day running between the rain drops and being absolutely adamant that if she had taken the umbrella, it would not have rained.

It is rational and adaptive to take emotional reactions into account. However, people tend to overweigh the anticipated feelings of regret and rejoicing when the differences between option outcomes is large. For example, Loomes (1987) presented participants with a scenario in which they would be given a randomly chosen ticket (from a set of 24 tickets). The participants then were asked to choose between two different sets of options: 1.1 and 1.2 or 2.1 and 2.2 (note that following Medin & Ross, 1992, we changed the units from pounds to dollars) (see Table 8.5). As you can see, Options 1.1 and 2.1 are identical, and options 1.2 and 2.2 both offer a 50% chance of winning $16. According to EVT, one should pick Options 1.1 versus 1.2 and 2.1 versus 2.2 because they both have a slightly higher expected value (prove it

TABLE 8.5 Loomes's (1987) Task

Game	Tickets 1–9	Tickets 10–21	Tickets 22–24
		Tickets	
Game 1			
Alternative 1.1	$24	$0	$0
Alternative 1.2	$0	$16	$0
Game 2			
Alternative 2.1	$24	$0	$0
Alternative 2.2	$16	$16	$0

to yourself by multiplying the probability of each option by its utility). However, Loomes found that in accordance with the predictions of regret theory, people tended to choose 1.1 slightly more often then 1.2, but tended overwhelmingly to choose 2.2 over 2.1.

DECISION-MAKING HEURISTICS AND BIASES

People's departure from normative theories is also expressed by the kinds of heuristics, or rules of thumb, that people follow to make decisions. Research on decision-making heuristics is based, in large part, on the theoretical writings and empirical work of Kahneman and Tversky. We review this work and its recent challenges and then conclude with a discussion of human rationality.

The Availability Heuristic

The **availability heuristic** suggests that people's estimation of frequency or probability is affected by the ease of retrieving examples from memory (Tversky & Kahneman, 1973). Try to answer the following problem, which was posed by Tversky and Kahneman (1973, p. 211), before you read on.

The frequency of appearance of letters in the English language was studied. A typical text was selected, and the relative frequency with which various letters of the alphabet appeared in the first and third positions in words was recorded. Words of less than three letters were excluded from the count.

You will be given several letters of the alphabet, and you will be asked to judge whether these letters appear more often in the first or in the third position, and to estimate the ratio of the frequency with which they appear in these positions.

After reading this description, the participants were asked to evaluate whether a letter, such as "K," was more likely to appear in the first or third position of a word and to determine the ratio of these two values. They tended to guess that twice as many words begin with *K* (that is, have *K* in the first position) as have *K* in the third position. In actuality, twice as many Ks occur in the third as in the first position. Because it is easier to retrieve words that start with K, people confuse the availability of these examples with their frequencies.

A related problem is the letter-frequency problem (Tversky & Kahneman, 1983, p. 295). This problem presents people with the task of rating the frequency with which they would expect words, taken from a sample of 2,000 words from a novel, to end with "-ing" or to have an "n" in the next-to-last position. The participants rated the occurrence of "-ing" as being more frequent than words with "n" in the next-to-last position, even though the latter generates a set of words that is subsumed by the prior. Thus, using the availability heuristic can lead to a violation of the extension law of probability, which suggests that if the extension of Set A includes the extension of Set B, then the probability of Set A must be greater than or equal to the probability of Set B.

The effects of the availability heuristic have been demonstrated in the areas of medical decision making and clinical diagnosis. A common finding in medical studies is that physicians' decisions are overly influenced by recent events. For example, physicians are more likely to make a particular diagnosis if they have just diagnosed someone else as having that disease, regardless of the base rate of that disease (Weber, Boeckenholt, Hilton, & Wallace, 1993). Physicians are also reluctant to recommend a medical procedure when another patient has just developed complications after undergoing that procedure, even though most patients recover from the procedure successfully (Pauker & Kopelman, 1992). Finally, physicians tend to exaggerate the dangers of diseases that are frequently discussed in journals (Christensen-Szalanski, Beck, Christensen-Szalanski, & Koepsell, 1983).

A closely related heuristic to availability is the **simulation heuristic** (Kahneman & Tversky, 1982). The simulation heuristic refers to how the ease with which people can imagine scenarios affects people's judgments. For example, Gregory, Cialdini, and Carpenter (1982) found that people who were asked to imagine a scenario about using a new cable TV service sold by a door-to-door salesman were more inclined to purchase the new service than were people who were given the same information about the service but were not asked to picture themselves using it. The effects of simulation can also be seen in people's responses to the following scenario (Kahneman & Tversky, 1982, p. 170).

Mr. Crane and Mr. Thomas were scheduled to leave the airport on different flights at the same time. They traveled from town in the same limousine, were caught in a traffic jam and arrived at the airport 30 minutes after the scheduled departure of their flights. Mr. Crane is told that his flight left on time. Mr. Thomas is told that his flight was delayed and just left five minutes ago. Who is more upset?

Kahneman and Tversky found that most people believed that Mr. Thomas would be more upset because he missed his goal by only 5 minutes versus 30 minutes for Mr. Crane. They argued that people make this attribution because they can more easily construct scenarios in which a person would have saved 5 minutes, rather than 30 minutes.

The Anchoring and Adjustment Heuristic

The **anchoring and adjustment heuristic** involves making a first approximation (an anchor) as a solution to a problem and then adjusting that value to fit new information (Tversky & Kahneman, 1982). For example, Tversky and Kahneman (1974) asked participants to estimate the percentage of UN delegates from African countries. First, they spun a wheel that randomly generated a number from 0 to 100. The participants had to say whether their answers were higher or lower than that random number. It is surprising that the arbitrary number served as an anchor for the participants' estimates, as evidenced by the fact that the participants tended to use this number or one that was similar in magnitude to it as a first guess for their answers, supporting the idea that highly available information is likely to serve as an anchor for making a judgment, even when it is clearly random.

In a different study, Tversky and Kahneman, (1974) asked people quickly to estimate the answer to either of the following multiplication problems:

a. 8 X 7 X 6 X 5 X 4 X 3 X 2 X 1

b. 1 X 2 X 3 X 4 X 5 X 6 X 7 X 8

They found that the median estimate for sequence a was 2,250, whereas the median estimate for sequence b was 512 (the correct answer is 40,320 for both). People seemed to be abiding by the anchoring and adjustment heuristic because their estimates were anchored on the product of the first few digits.

The Representativeness Heuristic

The **representativeness heuristic** suggests that a sample looks representative if it is similar in important characteristics to the population from which it was selected (Kahneman & Tversky, 1972). For example, Kahneman and Tversky asked participants to imagine a scenario in which they had an unbiased penny with one Head (H) and one Tail (T) that they tossed six times. The participants then had to determine which of two outcomes was more likely:

a. T H H T H T

b. T T T H H H

They most often chose Option *a* as the more likely outcome, even though both sequences are just as likely, because Option *a* resembles more closely what people perceive as being a random sequence.

According to the **law of large numbers** (see Tversky & Kahneman, 1971), large samples tend to be more representative of the population from which they were selected than are small samples. However, using the representativeness heuristic may cause people to ignore this law, as can be seen from the answers to the maternity-ward problem (Kahneman & Tversky, 1972, p. 443).

The Maternity-Ward Problem

A certain town is served by 2 hospitals. In the larger hospital, about 45 babies are born each day, and in the smaller hospital about 15 babies are born each day. As you know, about 50 percent of all babies are boys. The exact percentage of baby boys, however, varies from day to day. Sometimes it may be higher than 50%, sometimes lower.

For a period of 1 year, each hospital recorded the number of days on which (more/less) than 60% of the babies born were boys. Which hospital do you think recorded more such days?

a. the larger hospital

b. the smaller hospital

c. about the same (i.e., within 5 percent of each other)

Kahneman and Tversky (1972) found that most people tend to choose *Option c* (the number of days in which more than 60% of the babies born were boys was about the same in both hospitals), even though the correct answer is *Option a* (a smaller sample would have more aberrant recordings). They argued that people believe that the two events are the same because people treat these events as described by the same statistic and therefore as equally representative of the population.

Kahneman and Tversky have used the representativeness heuristic to explain *base-rate neglect*—the phenomenon whereby people overemphasize specific information about an item at the expense of how often the item occurs in the population (for details, see chapter 6). The lawyer-engineer problem, which depicts a scenario in which a group of 100 individuals is made up of 30 engineers and 70 lawyers (or vice versa). People are then asked to judge the likelihood that a person, drawn at random, whose personality description is more typical of an engineer (or a lawyer), is in actuality an engineer (or a lawyer). The modal finding is that people tend overwhelmingly to ignore the base-rate information they were given. Instead of realizing that the probability that the person belongs to the majority group is, by definition, greater than the probability that he or she belongs to the minority group, they tend to judge the person on the basis of how representative the person's description of the given profession is.

Representativeness has also been implicated in the **conjunction fallacy**. Before we define this fallacy formally, you may wish to work out the answer to the following problem (Tversky & Kahneman, 1983, p. 297).

Linda is 31 years old, single, outspoken, and very bright. She majored in philosophy. As a student, she was deeply concerned with issues of discrimination and social justice, and also participated in antinuclear demonstrations.

Tversky and Kahneman (p. 297) then gave participants a set of occupations and avocations and asked them to rank these options in terms of their likelihood of describing Linda.

Linda is a teacher at an elementary school.

Linda works in a bookstore and takes Yoga classes.

Linda is active in the feminist movement.

Linda is a psychiatric social worker.

Linda is a member of the League of Women Voters.

Linda is a bank teller.

Linda is an insurance salesperson.

Linda is a bank teller and is active in the feminist movement.

Tversky and Kahneman (1983) presented this problem to three group of participants: (1) statistically naive undergraduates, (2) first-year graduate students who had taken one or more statistics courses, and (3) doctoral students in a decision science program who had sophisticated statistical knowledge. They found that people in all three groups thought that "Linda is a bank teller and is active in the feminist movement" was a more likely description than "Linda is a bank teller." However, as in the letter-frequency example presented in the section on the availability heuristic, a conjunction rule entails that the probability of a conjunction of two events cannot be larger than the probability of its constituent events. Thus, the probability of the conjunction "Linda is a bankteller and a feminist" cannot be greater than the probability of its constituent event, "Linda is a bankteller." The representativeness heuristic explains why people judge the conjunction of "bank teller" and "feminist" as being more likely, on the basis of the fact that Linda's characteristics are more representative of a feminist than those of a bank teller.

One criticism of this study has been that people may interpret the statement "Linda is a bank teller" to mean that "Linda is a bank teller and is *not* active in the feminist movement" (Agnoli & Krantz, 1989). Restating the sentence as "Linda is a bank teller and is not active in the feminist movement" reduces the frequency with which people commit the conjunction fallacy, but does not make it disappear. A second manipulation that helps mitigate the conjunction fallacy is stating the problem in terms of frequencies, rather than probabilities. This manipulation involves presenting people with the same problem but changing the question to refer to how likely the different attributes are of "100 women like Linda" (Fiedler, 1988; Gigerenzer, 1996; Tversky & Kahneman, 1983).

What is the reason for this facilitation? Tversky and Kahneman (1983) argued that asking people to estimate frequencies (versus probabilities) allows them to appreciate the **inclusion rule**, If A includes B, then the p(A) ≤ p(B), by taking an **outside view** (perceiving the possible relationship of a subset to its superset). To test this hypothesis, they gave people the following problem (p. 309).

A health survey was conducted in a sample of 100 adult males in British Columbia, of all ages and occupations.

> Please give your best estimate of the following values:
>
> How many of the 100 participants surveyed have had one or more heart attacks?
>
> How many of the 100 participants both are over 55 years old and have had one or more heart attacks?

The results showed that only 25% of statistically naive participants made conjunction errors (gave higher estimates to the second question) versus 65% who were given percentages instead of frequencies. Reversing the order of the question further reduced the conjunction-fallacy rate in the frequency condition to 11%. The implication of this study is that a frequency formulation may help people create a spatial representation that makes the relation of set inclusion clearer.

Overconfidence

People tend to overestimate the degree of the accuracy of their judgments (e.g., Einhorn & Hogarth, 1978; Fischhoff, Slovic, & Lichtenstein, 1977; Gigerenzer et al., 1991; Kahneman & Tversky, 1996). For example, people tend to believe, in retrospect, that they could have predicted something before it occurred, when, in actuality, they probably could not have. This phenomenon has been referred to as a **hindsight bias**, and corresponds to people's intuitions that hindsight is 20-20. Slovic and Fischhoff (1977, pp. 545–546) demonstrated hindsight bias by providing participants with problems, such as the virgin-rat problem.

◆ The Virgin-Rat Problem

Several researchers intend to perform the following experiment: They will inject blood from a mother rat into a virgin rat immediately after the mother rat has given birth. After the injection, the virgin rat will be placed in a cage with the newly born baby rats, after the removal of the actual mother. The possible outcomes were (a) the virgin rat exhibited maternal behavior, or (b) the virgin rat failed to exhibit maternal behavior.

In the foresight condition, the participants were asked to imagine that the virgin rat either did or did not exhibit maternal behavior. In the hindsight condition, they were told that the virgin rat either did or did not exhibit maternal behavior. Then, the participants in both conditions were asked the following.

What is the probability that in a replication of this experiment with 10 additional virgin female rats,

    a. all will exhibit maternal behavior?

    b. some will exhibit maternal behavior?

    c. none will exhibit maternal behavior?

As predicted, the participants in the hindsight condition gave higher probabilities to the stated outcome (.55 on average) than did the participants in the foresight condition (.38 on average). Even though this study provides corroborating evidence for the hindsight bias, Christensen-Szalanski and Willham's (1991) meta-analysis of 122 studies on hindsight bias found that the overall magnitude of the bias was small and that it occurred more frequently when people were given unfamiliar as opposed to familiar tasks.

What may be the reasons for the existence of the hindsight bias? Hawkins and Hastie (1990) argued that once people know an outcome, they may anchor on it and reconstruct their previous judgment accordingly, without adjusting downward from that anchor. Other explanations for overconfidence, in general, are as follows:

1. People tend to focus on the instances when their judgments are, indeed, correct and either disregard or do not have access to instances when their judgments are false (Einhorn & Hogarth, 1978). This explanation is consistent with the phenomenon of confirmation bias; if one finds confirming examples, then one does not need to search for counterexamples (Baron, 1994).

2. People may not have access to whether their knowledge is based on tenuous and uncertain assumptions that come from unreliable sources (Carlson, 1995; D. Griffin & Tversky, 1992; Slovic, Fischhoff, & Lichtenstein, 1982).

3. People may have difficulty recalling alternative hypotheses because of limited memory capacity.

DECISION MAKING: THE QUESTION OF RATIONALITY

That research in decision making has focused on the many systematic biases that people tend to endorse has led some to argue that this research "has bleak implications for human rationality" (Nisbett & Borgida, 1975). Are people rational or irrational? What would you conclude from having read this book so far? To answer this question, one must first attempt to answer the following questions:

1. What is rationality anyway?
2. What are the appropriate normative models against which people's reasoning should be compared?
3. How does people's reasoning deviate from these models?
4. How is people's reasoning guided by their goals and environmental constraints?
5. Are systematic errors a proof of "irrationality?"
6. Is asking whether people are rational or not useful for understanding human cognition?

What is rationality anyway? It is hard to come up with a satisfying definition. Researchers (and laypeople) would probably agree that rationality involves making choices that have internal consistency (lack self-contradiction). An example is the "sure-thing principle" we discussed earlier (Savage, 1954). Recall that this principle suggests that if a person prefers one option (option x) to another (option y), if an event occurs or does not occur—"no matter what"—then option x should always be preferred to option y, whether an event occurs or not.

As we have seen, people tend to violate this principle. Does this violation mean that people are irrational?

What about the other biases that we discussed in this and other chapters, such as base-rate neglect, the conjunction fallacy, and overconfidence? Are they examples of human irrationality? To agree on irrationality, we have to agree on rationality first. We need to decide which normative model or models to endorse. L. J. Cohen (1981) argued that normative theories are founded on human intuitions about which assumptions are axiomatic, or true. The choice of the appropriate normative model is, therefore, a hard one to determine.

Another problem with normative models is that they often do not take into account the impossible processing demands that they place on the cognitive system, such as exceeding short-term memory capacity. For example, Evans and Over (1996) suggested that we would not consider a person to be irrational if she were unable to read a book that was placed beyond her level of visual acuity, recall one of several hundred customers' addresses upon request, or compute the square root of a large number mentally. People's processing limitations have led researchers, such as Baron (1995), to create *prescriptive* models that take processing demands into account.

One of the major debates on the use of correct normative models was spurred by Gigerenzer's (1996) attack on Kahneman and Tversky's work. Gigerenzer claimed that the correct normative model for human decision making is a frequentist one; that by presenting people with the same problems in a relative-frequency instead of a probability format, cognitive biases tend to "disappear." He presented an evolutionary argument regarding mental representation whose main thesis is that people have developed mental algorithms designed for dealing with natural frequencies. Gigerenzer argued that if the same problems that Kahneman and Tversky have used to demonstrate heuristics and biases are framed in terms of frequencies instead of probabilities, then people show better decision making. For example, by manipulating the Linda, the bank teller, problem to be about "100 Lindas," he contended, the conjunction fallacy "disappears" (a result that Kahneman and Tversky actually showed in their 1983 study, however). Gigerenzer argued that mental computations are simpler and more accurate when they correspond to information that is encountered in the same form (a frequency format) as in the environment in which we have evolved, in contrast to information that is more artificial or decontextualized (a probability format).

Gigerenzer et al. (1999) and Gigerenzer and D. G. Goldstein (1996) argued that humans and animals make inferences about the world under limited time and knowledge. They suggested that many other models of rational inference, in contrast, treat the mind as a "Laplacean Demon" that has at its disposal unlimited time, knowledge, and computational power. On the basis of Simon's (1957) idea of *satisficing*, Gigerenzer and D. G. Goldstein offered a family of algorithms that are based on a simple one-reason decision-making process that they call **fast-and-frugal heuristics**. In their study, Gigerenzer and Goldstein presented participants with a list of unfamiliar cities and asked them to guess which one had the largest population. The participants used the "take the best" heuristic, for example, by conducting an ordered search among these cities according to whether the cities had recognizable soccer teams. This heuristic search was based on previous knowledge that larger cities tend to have well-known soccer teams. The fast-and-frugal heuristics, such as take the best, do not satisfy the classical norms of rational inference but still can meet with real-world success. This critique of the biases research is consistent with L. J. Cohen's (1981) lament that laboratory experiments of reasoning and decision making are artificial and divorced from reasoning in the real-world and hence lead to "cognitive illusions."

Kahneman and Tversky (1996) addressed many of Gigerenzer's criticisms about their work on heuristics and biases. First, they argued that the correct normative model for their problems is a Bayesian one, which allows for judgments of single-event probabilities. Furthermore, they claimed that people make single-probability inferences in everyday life (e.g., stating who is more likely to win an election). This response was directed to Gigerenzer's criticism that "biases are not biases" and "heuristics are meant to explain what does not exist" (Gigerenzer, 1991, p. 102). Second, Kahneman and Tversky contended that even though biases can be mitigated with certain manipulations, they do not disappear. For example, in the case of base-rate neglect, such as on the lawyers and engineers problem, using a few personality descriptions facilitates the use of the base rate, but at a level that is still normatively suboptimal.

Evans and Over (1996) argued that human rationality can be assessed by either a personal or impersonal theory. The *personal theory* takes people's goals into account and whether people's reasoning helps fulfill these goals. The **impersonal theory** is based on normative theories that make use of principles of logic and probability. For example, a researcher who pits her hypothesis against one that she knows is untrue (the null hypothesis) is using a **strawman** argument (her results are bound to disconfirm the null hypothesis). From an impersonal viewpoint, she is committing a fallacy and being irrational. However, if her goal is to get people's attention, and she is clever enough to conceal her faulty reasoning, then from a personal viewpoint, she is rational.

From a pragmatic viewpoint, even if people fall prey to certain biases, it does not mean that they are irrational. Making mistakes can still be a part of a rational thinker's repertoire. This idea was captured eloquently by Evans (1989, p. 111):

> The view that I wish to argue here is that errors of thinking occur because of, rather than in spite of, the nature of our intelligence. In other words, they are an inevitable consequence of the way in which we think and a price to be paid for the extraordinary effectiveness with which we routinely deal with the massive information-processing requirements of everyday life.

Evans's view captures the essence of Kahneman and Tversky's research on heuristics and biases. These researchers have used systematic biases as a way of uncovering the kind of mechanisms and representations that underlie human reasoning and decision making. Their intention has been to further our knowledge of human cognition. We, therefore, contend that instead of trying to determine whether people are rational or irrational, it may be more useful to identify the circumstances under which people exhibit more or less useful reasoning.

◆ SUMMARY

How do we make decisions? To answer this question, we need to define normative theories of decision making. These theories include EVT, EUT, and SEUT, which prescribe that people assign either an objective or subjective value to an option and then factor in the option's probability. MAUT calculates the utility of a choice option by breaking it into independent dimensions and then weighing the importance of the dimensions relative to each other. This theory may be more descriptive than normative, however.

We have seen a variety of ways in which people deviate from the prescriptions of normative models. People often violate the transitivity (e.g., preference reversals) and cancellation principles (e.g., the Allais and Ellsberg paradoxes), and their preferences are affected by whether problems are framed in terms of gains or losses. If an initial reference point is defined such that an outcome is perceived as a gain, than people become more risk averse, but if the reference point is defined such that an outcome is perceived as a loss, then people are more prone to become risk seekers.

Prospect theory (Kahneman & Tversky, 1979) is a general descriptive theory of decision making that assumes that people make decisions on the basis of utilities and probabilities. In its framework, (a) utilities are evaluated in terms of gains and losses, or as deviations from a reference point; (b) the reference point is affected by nonnormative factors, such as framing effects; and (c) people's estimations of probability are subjective.

Regret theory (Bell, 1982; Loomes & Sugden, 1982) is another descriptive theory that suggests that people take their emotional reactions (regret or rejoicing) into account in making decisions. Even though it is rational to consider emotional reactions in choosing among options, people tend to overweigh the anticipated feelings of regret and rejoicing when the differences between option outcomes are large.

There are several heuristics and biases that have an impact on people's decisions. For example, the availability heuristic suggests that people's estimation of frequency or probability is affected by the ease of retrieving examples from memory; the simulation heuristic shows that the ease with which people can imagine scenarios affects their judgments; the anchoring and adjustment heuristic involves making a first approximation (an anchor) as a solution to a problem and then adjusting that value to fit new information; and, finally, the representativeness heuristic suggests that a sample looks representative if it is similar in important characteristics to the population from which it was selected.

Are people rational decision makers? We argue that instead of trying to determine whether people are rational or irrational, it is more useful to identify the circumstances under which people exhibit correct or incorrect reasoning.

The Nature of Language

◆ Properties of Language
◆ Processes of Language Comprehension
◆ Language Acquisition
◆ Summary

Because of language, we can tell our loved ones that we love them or tell people we detest to go to hell. **Language**—an organized means of combining words to communicate—makes it possible for us to communicate with those around us, as well as to think about things and processes we cannot currently see, hear, feel, touch, or smell, including ideas that may not have any tangible form. Not all **communication**—exchanges of thoughts and feelings—is through language. Communication encompasses such nonverbal means as gestures (e.g., to embellish or to indicate), glances (e.g., deadly or seductive), touches (e.g., handshakes, hits, and hugs), and the like.

Three areas of study have contributed greatly to an understanding of **psycholinguistics**—the psychology of people's use of language: (1) linguistics—the study of language structure and change; (2) neurolinguistics—the relationships among the brain, cognition, and language; and (3) sociolinguistics—the relationship between social behavior and language (D. W. Carroll, 1986). The first section of this chapter briefly describes some general properties of language. The next sections discuss the processes of language, including how we understand the meanings of particular words and how we structure words into meaningful sentences. The final section more fully elaborates the linguistic approach to language by describing how each of us has acquired at least one language. As you may expect, this discussion brings up the nature-nurture debate that often arises in regard to psychological issues, but focuses on how acquired abilities interact with experience. Chapter 10 describes the broader context within which we use language, including the psychological and social contexts of language.

PROPERTIES OF LANGUAGE

General Description

What are the principal properties that characterize language? There seems to be some consensus regarding six properties that are distinctive of language (e.g., R. Brown, 1965; H. H.

TABLE 9.1   Six Fundamental Properties of Language

Communicative
Arbitrarily symbolic
Regularly structured
Structured at multiple levels
Generative, productive
Dynamic

Clark & Clark, 1977; Glucksberg & Danks, 1975). They are communicative; arbitrarily symbolic; regularly structured; structured at multiple levels; generative, productive; and dynamic (see also Table 9.1).

Communicative. Language permits us to communicate with one or more persons who share our language. The communicative property of language is listed first because even though it is the most obvious feature, it is also the most remarkable one. For example, we can write what we are thinking and feeling, so that you may read and understand our thoughts and feelings. This is not to say that there are not occasional flaws in the communicative property of language—countless psychologists and others dedicate their lives to the study of how we fail to communicate through language. For instance we may tell someone, in anger, to get out of our life, and he or she may do so.

Arbitrarily symbolic. Language creates an arbitrary relationship between a symbol and its referent—an idea, a thing, a process, a relationship, or a description. We communicate through our shared system of *arbitrary symbolic reference* to things, ideas, processes, relationships, and descriptions. The *arbitrary* nature of the system alludes to the lack of any reason for choosing a particular *symbol*—something that represents, indicates, or suggests something else—to *refer* (point or allude) to a particular thing, process, or description, such as *carpenter, assist,* or *extraordinary.* By consensual agreement, a particular combination of letters or sounds may be meaningful to us, but the particular symbols do not themselves lead to the meaning of the word. The sound combination is arbitrary, as can be seen from the fact that different languages use different sounds to refer to the same thing (e.g., *happy, heureux, feliz*).

All words are *symbols.* A convenient feature of using symbols is that we can use them in so many ways. For example, we can use them to refer to things, ideas, processes, relationships, and descriptions that are not currently present (e.g., Mount Everest), that never existed (e.g., unicorns or Snow White), or that exist in a form that is not physically tangible (e.g., trigonometry, injustice, or peace). Without arbitrary symbolic reference, we would be limited to symbols that somehow resemble the things they are supposed to symbolize (e.g., a cowlike symbol to represent a cow).

Regularly structured. Language has a structure; only particularly patterned arrangements of symbols have meaning, and different arrangements yield different meanings. The *regular structure* of language makes our shared system of communication possible. Later in this chapter, we describe more specifically the structure of language. Here, it suffices that you know that (1) particular patterns of sounds and of letters form meaningful words, but random sounds and letters usually do not do so and (2) particular patterns of words form meaningful sentences, paragraphs, and discourse, whereas most others make no sense.

Structured at multiple levels. The structure of language can be analyzed at more than one level (e.g., in sounds, in meaning units, in words, in phrases). *Multiplicity of structure* refers to the fact that meaningful utterance can be analyzed at more than one level. Subsequent sections describe several levels at which we can analyze the structure of language. These various levels convey different degrees of meaningful content. Consider three such levels. First, psycholinguists study language at the level of sounds, such as "p" and "t"; at the level of words, such as *pat*, *tap*, *pot*, *top*, *pit*, and *tip*. They also study language at the level of sentences, such as "Pat said to tap the top of the pot, then tip it into the pit." Finally, they study language at the level of larger units of language, including this paragraph or even this book.

Generative, productive. Within the limits of a linguistic structure, language users can produce novel utterances, and the possibilities for creating new utterances are virtually limitless. The *productivity* (sometimes termed *generativity*) of language refers to our limitless ability to produce language creatively. That is, although our use of language has limitations—we have to conform to a particular structure and to use a particular shared system of arbitrary symbols— we can use language to produce an infinite number of unique sentences and other meaningful combinations of words. Although the number of sounds (e.g., "z" as in "zoo") used in a language may be finite, the various sounds can be combined endlessly to form new words and new sentences, among which are many *novel utterances*—language expressions that are brand-new—never spoken before by anyone. Thus, language is inherently creative, because it would never be possible for any of us to have previously heard all the sentences we are capable of producing that we actually produce in the course of our everyday lives. Moreover, it appears that any language has the potential to express pretty much any idea in it that can be expressed in any other language. However, the ease, clarity, and succinctness of expression of a particular idea may vary greatly from one language to the next. Thus, the creative potential of different languages appears to be roughly the same.

Dynamic. Languages are dynamic and constantly evolve. Individual language users coin words and phrases and modify language usage, and the wider group of language users either accepts or rejects the modifications. It is almost as incomprehensible to imagine that language would never change as it is to imagine that people and environments would never change. For example, today we speak modern English. This way of speaking evolved from Middle English, which, in turn, evolved from Old English.

To conclude, although there are many differences among languages, there are some common properties. Next, we consider how language is used in more detail.

Fundamental Aspects to Language

Essentially, there are two fundamental aspects of language: (1) receptive comprehension and decoding of language input and (2) expressive encoding and production of language output. *Decoding* refers to deriving the meaning from whatever symbolic reference system is being used (e.g., while listening or reading). Right now, as you read, you are decoding text. As applied to language, *encoding* involves transforming our thoughts into a form that can be expressed as linguistic output (e.g., speech, signing, or writing). If you write a paper based on this chapter, you will be encoding language to do so. In this chapter, we use the terms *encoding* and *decoding* to describe only semantic encoding and decoding. Sometimes, researchers use the terms **verbal comprehension**—the ability receptively to comprehend written and spoken linguistic input, such as words, sentences, and paragraphs—and **verbal fluency**—the ability expressively to produce such linguistic output. When we deal specifically with spoken communication, we can refer to vocal comprehension or fluency. People's verbal-comprehension skills are measured by tests of reading and vocabulary. People's verbal-fluency skills are measured by tests, such as those that ask them to write down as many names of animals as they can think of in two minutes.

Language can be broken down into many smaller units, much like chemists do in analyzing molecules into basic elements. The smallest unit of speech sound is the phone, which is simply a single vocal sound and may or may not be part of the speech system of a particular language. A click of your tongue, a pop of your cheek, or a gurgling sound may be a phone. The smallest unit of speech sound that can be used to distinguish one utterance in a given language from another is a **phoneme**. In English, phonemes are made up of vowel and consonant sounds; for example, we distinguish among *sit, sat, fat,* and *fit*, so the /s/ sound, the /f/ sound, the /I/ sound, and /ae/ sound are all phonemes in English (as is the /t/ sound). These sounds are produced by alternating sequences of opening and closing the vocal tract. Different languages use different numbers and combinations of phonemes. Hawaiian has about 13, whereas some African dialects have up to 60. North American English has about 40 phonemes, as shown in Table 9.2. The following set of examples highlight the difference between phones and phonemes.

In English, the difference between the /p/ and the /b/ sound is an important distinction. These sounds function as phonemes in English because they comprise the difference between different words. For example, English speakers distinguish between "they bit the buns from the bin" and "they pit the puns from the pin" (a well-structured but meaningless sentence). At

Table 9.2   North American English Phonetic Symbols

Consonants				Vowels		Diphthongs	
p	*p*ill	Θ	*th*igh	i	b*ee*t	ay	b*i*te
b	*b*ill	ŏ	*th*y	L	b*i*t	æw	ab*ou*t
m	*m*ill	š	*sh*allow	e	b*ai*t	oy	b*oy*
t	*t*ill	ž	mea*sure*	ε	b*e*t		
d	*d*ill	č	*ch*ip	æ	b*a*t		
n	*n*il		g*y*p	u	b*oo*t		
k	*k*ill	l	*l*ip	∪	p*u*t		
g	*g*ill	r	*r*ip	∧	b*u*t		
ŋ	si*ng*	y	*y*et	o	b*oa*t		
f	*f*ill	w	*w*et	ɔ	b*ou*ght		
v	*v*at	m	*wh*et	a	p*o*t		
s	*s*ip	h	*h*at	ə	sof*a*		
z	*z*ip			ɨ	m*a*rry		

Source: H. H. Clark & Clark (1997).

the same time, there are some phones that English speakers may produce, but that do not function to distinguish words and therefore do not serve as phonemes in English. These are often called *allophones*, or sound variants of the same phoneme.

To illustrate the difference between the allophones of the phoneme, /p/, put your open hand about one inch from your lips, and say aloud, "Put the paper cup to your lip." If you are like most English speakers, you felt a tiny puff of air when you pronounced the /ph/ in *Put* and *paper* and no puffs of air when you pronounced the /p/ in *cup* or *lip*. If you somehow manage to stifle the puff of air when saying, "Put" or "paper" or to add a puff of air when saying "cup" or "lip," you would be producing different (allo)phones, but you would not be making a meaningful distinction in the phonemes of English—there is no meaningful difference between /ph/ut and /p/ut in English, as opposed to the difference between /k/ut and /g/ut. However, in some languages (e.g., Thai), a distinction considered irrelevant in English is meaningful because in these languages, the difference between /p/ and /ph/ is phonemic, rather than merely allophonic (Fromkin & Rodman, 1988).

The study of the particular phonemes of a language is *phonemics*, and the study of how to produce or combine speech sounds or to represent them with written symbols is *phonetics*. Linguists, such as Peter Ladefoged, often travel to remote villages to observe, record, and analyze different languages, some of which are dying as members leave tribal areas in favor of more urban areas. The study of phonetic inventories of diverse languages is one way linguists gain insight into the nature of language (see Ladefoged & Maddieson, 1996).

At the next level of the hierarchy is the **morpheme**—the smallest unit that denotes meaning within a particular language. English courses may have introduced you to two forms of morphemes: (1) root words, to which we add (2) *affixes*—both *suffixes*, which follow the root word, and prefixes, which precede the root word. The word *affixes* itself comprises (a) the root *fix*; (b) the prefix *af-*, which is a variant of the prefix *ad-*, meaning "toward," "to," or "near"; and (c) the suffix *-es*, which indicates the plural form of a noun. The word *revisit* contains two morphemes, *re-* and *visit*.

Linguists analyze the structure of morphemes and words in a way that goes beyond the analysis of roots and affixes. They refer to the words that convey the bulk of the meaning as **content morphemes**. The morphemes that add detail and nuance to the meaning of the content morphemes or that help the content morphemes to fit the grammatical context are **function morphemes** (e.g., the suffix *-ist*, the prefix *de-*, the conjunction *and*, or the article *the*). A subset of function morphemes are inflections, the common suffixes we add to words to fit the grammatical context. For example, most American kindergartners know to add special suffixes to indicate the following:

- *Verb tense*—You walk to classes; yesterday you walked to class; and you probably are walking now.

- *Verb and noun number*—The professor talks incessantly; the professors talk only when they need to.

- *Noun possession*—The student's new car is striking.

- *Adjective comparison*—The younger of the two sisters did the dirty work in the house.

Linguists use the term **lexicon** to describe the entire set of morphemes in a given language or in a given person's linguistic repertoire. The average adult speaker of English has a lexicon of about 80,000 morphemes (G. A. Miller & Gildea, 1987). By combining morphemes, most adult English speakers have a **vocabulary** (repertoire of words) of hundreds of thousands of words. For example, by attaching just a few morphemes to the root content morpheme *study*, we have *student, studious, studied, studying*, and *studies*. One of the ways in which English has expanded to embrace an increasing vocabulary is by combining existing morphemes in novel ways. Some suggest that a part of William Shakespeare's genius lay in his creating new words by combining existing morphemes. He is alleged to have coined more than 1,700 words—8.5% of his written vocabulary—as well as countless expressions—including the word *countless* itself (Lederer, 1991).

For linguists, the next level of analysis is termed **syntax**, which refers to the way in which users of a particular language string words together to form sentences. A sentence comprises at least two parts: (1) a **noun phrase**, which contains at least one noun (often, the subject of the sentence) and includes all the relevant descriptors of the noun and (2) a **verb phrase**, which contains at least one verb and whatever the verb acts on, if anything. The verb phrase also may be termed the *predicate*, since it affirms or states something about the subject, usually an action or a property of the subject. Linguists consider the study of syntax to be fundamental to understanding the structure of language; the syntactic structure of language is specifically addressed later in this chapter.

Complementary to syntax is **semantics**, the study of meaning in a language. A semanticist would be concerned with how words express meaning (a topic also considered in chapters 7 and 8).

The final level of analysis is that of **discourse**, which encompasses the use of language at the level beyond the sentence, such as in conversations, paragraphs, stories, chapters, and entire books. Table 9.3 summarizes the various aspects of language.

TABLE 9.3 Description of Language Input and Output (All human languages can be analyzed at many levels.)

Language Input: Comprehension of Language	Language Output: Production of Language
Phonemes (distinctive subset of all possible phones)	. . . /t/ + /ā/ + /k/ + /s/ . . .
Morphemes (from the distinctive lexicon of morphemes)	. . . take (content morpheme) + s (plural function morpheme) . . .
Words (from the distinctive vocabulary of words)	It + takes + a + heap + of + sense + to + write + good + nonsense.
Phrases:	NP = It
Noun phrases (NP: a noun and its descriptors)	+
Verb phrases (VP: a verb and whatever it acts on)	VP = takes a heap of sense to write good nonsense.
Senses (based on the language's syntax—syntactical structure)	It takes a heap of sense to write good nonsense.
Discourse	"It takes a heap of sense to write good nonsense" was first written by Mark Twain (Lederer, 1991, p. 131) . . .

PROCESSES OF LANGUAGE COMPREHENSION

How do we understand language, given its multifaceted encoding? One approach to this question centers on the psychological processes involved in the perception of speech and how listeners deal with the peculiarities resulting from the acoustic (relating to sound) transmission of language. A more linguistically oriented approach focuses on descriptions of the grammatical structure of languages. Finally, a third approach examines the psycholinguistic processes involved in language comprehension at the discourse macrolevel of analysis. All three approaches overlap to some degree and offer interesting insights into the nature of language and its use. We consider here the more complex approaches, the second and third ones.

Semantics

Some people believe that the reason we have infantile amnesia—the inability to remember early experiences—is because we did not have adequate language as infants to attach verbal meanings to what was going on early in our lives. **Semantics** is the study of the meanings of words, as well as of larger units of language, such as phrases and sentences. We sometimes refer to the strict dictionary definition of a word as its **denotation**, whereas we refer to a word's emotional overtones, presuppositions, and other nonexplicit meanings as its **connotations**. Sometimes, the denotation and connotation of a word are the same, and sometimes they are different. For example, if you say that you are able to predict the future with astonishing accuracy, and someone replies to you, "Yeah, right," the denotation of the expression may suggest agreement, but the connotation suggests disagreement.

How do we understand word meanings in the first place? Recall from previous chapters that we encode meanings into memory through *concepts*—ideas (mental representations) to which we may attach various characteristics and with which we may connect various other ideas, such as through propositions—as well as through images and perhaps also through motor patterns for implementing particular procedures (Frazier, 1995). Here, we are concerned only with concepts, particularly in terms of words as arbitrary symbols for concepts.

Actually, with regard to words as concepts, words are economical ways in which to manipulate related information. For example, when you think about the single word *chair*, you may also conjure all these things:

- All the instances of chairs in existence anywhere
- Instances of chairs that exist only in your imagination
- All the characteristics of chairs
- All the things you may do with chairs
- All the other concepts you may link to chairs (e.g., things you put on chairs or places where you may find chairs)

Having a word for something helps us add new information to our existing information about that concept. For example, because you have access to the word *desk*, when you have new experiences related to desks or otherwise learn new things about desks, you have a word around which to organize all this related information. B. H. Ross and Spalding (1994) even suggested that having words as concepts for things helps us in everyday nonverbal interactions. For example, they noted that our concepts of skunk and of dog allow us more easily to recognize the difference between the two, even if we see an animal only for a moment. This rapid recognition enables us to respond appropriately, depending on which we saw. Clearly, being able to comprehend the conceptual meanings of words is important. Just how do words combine to convey meaning, though?

Syntax

An equally important part of the psychology of language is the analysis of linguistic structure—specifically, **syntax**, the systematic way in which words can be combined and sequenced to make meaningful phrases and sentences (D. W. Carroll, 1986). Whereas speech perception chiefly studies the phonetic structure of language, syntax focuses on the study of the grammar of phrases and sentences, in other words, the regularity of structure.

Although you have doubtless heard the word *grammar* before, in regard to how people *ought* to structure their sentences, psycholinguists use the word *grammar* in a slightly different way. Specifically, **grammar** is the study of language in terms of noticing regular patterns. These patterns relate to the functions and relationships of words in a sentence. In your English courses, you may have been introduced to *prescriptive grammar*, which prescribes the "correct" ways in which to structure the use of written and spoken language. Of greater interest to psycholinguists is *descriptive grammar*, in which an attempt is made to describe the structures, functions, and relationships of words in language.

Pinker (1994), a psycholinguist, gave this example of a sentence that illustrates the contrast between prescriptive and descriptive approaches to grammar: When Junior observes his father carrying an unappealing bedtime book upstairs, he responds, "Daddy, what did you bring that book that I don't want to be read to out of up for?" (p. 97). Whereas Junior's utterance would shiver the spine of any prescriptive grammarian, Junior's ability to produce such a complex sentence, with such intricate internal interdependencies, would please descriptive grammarians.

Why does syntax prompt such pleasure? Chiefly, for two reasons: First, the study of syntax allows language to be analyzed in manageable—and therefore relatively easily studied—units, and second, it offers limitless possibilities for exploration. There are virtually no bounds to the possible combinations of words that may be used to form sentences (the property of productivity of language). In English, as in any language, we can take a particular set of words (or morphemes, to be more accurate) and a particular set of rules for combining the items to produce a vast array of meaningful utterances. Barring intentional quotations, if you were to go to the U.S. Library of Congress, randomly select any sentence from any book, and then search for an identical sentence in the vast array of sentences in the books therein, you would be unlikely to find the identical sentence (Pinker, 1994).

The Syntax Tendency

Another reason that syntax intrigues cognitive psychologists, as well as linguists, is the remarkable degree to which people demonstrate a knack for understanding syntactical structure (no matter what your high school English teacher may have said). As the preceding demonstration showed, fluent speakers of a language can immediately recognize whether particular sentences and particular word orders are or are not grammatical (Bock, 1990; Pinker, 1994). People can do so even when the sentences are meaningless, as in Chomsky's (1972) sentence,

"Colorless green ideas sleep furiously," or are composed of nonsense words, as in Lewis Carroll's *Jabberwocky*, " 'Twas brillig and the slithy tove did gyre and gimble in the wabe."

Also, just as people show semantic priming of word meanings in memory, they show *syntactic priming* of sentence structures. That is, people spontaneously tend to use syntactic structures that parallel the structures of sentences they have just heard (Bock, 1990; Bock, Loebell, & Morey, 1992). For example, a speaker will be more likely to use a passive construction (e.g., "The student was praised by the professor") after hearing a passive construction, even when the topics of the sentences differ.

Other evidence of our uncanny aptitude for syntax is shown in the speech errors that people produce (Bock, 1990). Even when people accidentally switch the placement of two words in a sentence, they still form grammatical, if meaningless or nonsensical, sentences. People almost invariably switch nouns for nouns, verbs for verbs, prepositions for prepositions, and so on. For example, someone may say, "I put the oven in the cake," but the individual probably will not say, "I put the cake oven in the." People usually even attach (and detach) appropriate function morphemes to make the switched words fit their new positions. For example, when meaning to say, "The butter knives are in the drawer," they may say, "The butter drawers are in the knife," changing "drawer" to plural and "knives" to singular, to preserve the grammaticality of the sentence. Even among so-called agrammatic aphasics, who have extreme difficulty in both comprehending and producing language, substitution errors in speech seem to preserve syntactic categories (Butterworth & Howard, 1987; Garrett, 1992).

The preceding examples seem to indicate that humans have some mental mechanism for classifying words according to syntactical categories, and that this classification mechanism is separate from the meanings for the words (Bock, 1990). When people compose sentences, they seem to *parse* the sentences, assigning appropriate syntactic categories (often called "parts of speech," e.g., noun, verb, and article) to each component of the sentence. People then use the syntax rules for the language to construct grammatical sequences of the parsed components.

Early in this century, linguists who studied syntax largely focused on how sentences could be analyzed in terms of sequences of phrases (e.g., noun phrases and verb phrases, mentioned previously) and of how phrases could be parsed into various syntactical categories (e.g., nouns, verbs, and adjectives). Such analyses are termed **phrase-structure grammars** because they analyze the structure of phrases as they are used. The rules governing the sequences of words are termed *phrase-structure rules*. To observe the interrelationships of phrases within a sentence, linguists often use tree diagrams, such as the ones shown in Figure 9.1, although various other models have been proposed, including relational grammar (Perlmutter, 1983) and lexical-functional grammar (Bresnan, 1982).

Tree diagrams help to reveal the interrelationships of syntactic classes within the phrase structures of sentences (Bock, 1990; Wasow, 1989). In particular, they show that sentences are not merely organized chains of words, strung together sequentially, but are organized into hierarchical structures of embedded phrases. The use of tree diagrams helps to highlight many aspects of how people use language, including both their linguistic sophistication and their difficulties in using language. Look again at Figure 9.1, focusing on the two possible tree diagrams for one sentence, showing its two possible meanings. By observing tree diagrams of ambiguous sentences, psycholinguists can better pinpoint the source of confusion.

In 1957, Chomsky revolutionized the study of syntax by suggesting that to understand syntax, people must observe not only the interrelationships among phrases within sentences, but the syntactical relationships between sentences. Specifically, Chomsky observed that

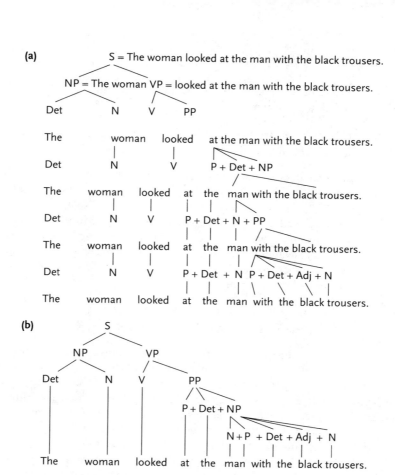

(a)

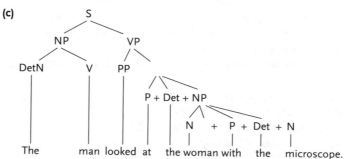

(b)

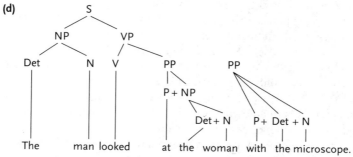

(c)

(d)

Figure 9.1 Tree diagrams of two phrase structures.

particular sentences and their tree diagrams show peculiar relationships. Consider, for example, the following sentences:

S_1: Susie greedily ate the crocodile.

S_2: The crocodile was eaten greedily by Susie.

Oddly enough, a phrase-structure grammar would not show any particular relation at all between sentences S_1 and S_2 (see Figure 9.2). Indeed, phrase-structure analyses of S_1 and S_2 would look almost completely different. Yet, the two sentences differ only in voice, the first sentence expressed in the active voice and the second in the passive voice. Propositions may be used to illustrate that the same underlying meanings can be derived through alternative means of representation. The preceding two sentences represent the same proposition: "ate (greedily)(Susie, crocodile)."

Consider another pair of paraphrased sentences.

S_3: The crocodile greedily ate Susie.

S_4: Susie was eaten greedily by the crocodile.

Phrase-structure grammar would similarly show no relationship between S_3 and S_4. What is more, it would show some similarities of surface structure between corresponding sentences in the first and second pairs (S_1 and S_3; S_2 and S_4)—which clearly have different meanings—particularly to Susie and the crocodile. It seems that an adequate grammar would address the fact that sentences with similar surface structures can have different meanings.

This observation and other observations of the interrelationships among various phrase structures led linguists to go beyond merely describing various individual phrase structures and to focus their attention on the relationships among different phrase structures. Principally, Chomsky (1957) suggested that linguists may gain a deeper understanding of syntax by studying the relationships among phrase structures that involve transformations of elements within sentences. Specifically, he suggested the study of **transformational grammar**, which involves augmenting the study of phrase structures with the study of transformational rules that guide the ways in which underlying propositions can be rearranged to form various phrase structures.

A simple way of looking at Chomsky's transformational grammar is to say that transformations are rules mapping tree structures onto other tree structures (Wasow, 1989). For example, transformational grammar is used to consider how the tree-structure diagrams in Figure 9.2 are interrelated. By applying transformational rules, one can map the tree structure of S_1 onto the tree structure of S_2, and the structure of S_3, onto the tree structure of S_4.

Chomsky used the term **deep structure** to refer to an underlying syntactic structure that links various phrase structures through the application of various transformation rules and the term **surface structure** to refer to any of the various phrase structures that may result from such transformations. Many casual readers of Chomsky have misconstrued his terms to suggest that deep structures signify profound underlying meanings for sentences, whereas surface structures refer only to superficial interpretations of sentences. Chomsky meant only to show that different phrase structures may have a relationship that is not immediately apparent by using phrase-structure grammar alone (as in the example of "Susie greedily ate the crocodile" and "The crocodile was eaten greedily by Susie"). To detect the underlying relationship between two phrase structures, transformation rules must be applied.

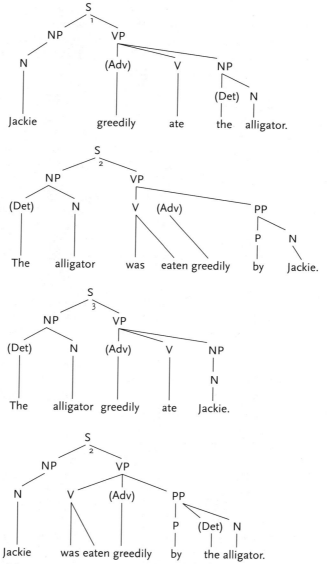

Figure 9.2 Tree diagrams and relationships among various phrase structrures.

Relationships Between Syntactical and Lexical Structures

Chomsky (1965, cited in Wasow, 1989) also addressed how syntactical structures may interact with lexical structures. In particular, he suggested that our mental lexicon contains more than the semantic meanings attached to each word (or morpheme). According to Chomsky, each lexical item also contains syntactic information. The syntactic information for each lexical item indicates (1) the syntactical category of the item (e.g., noun versus verb), (2) the appropriate syntactic contexts in which the particular morpheme may be used (e.g., pronouns as subjects versus pronouns as direct objects), and (3) any idiosyncratic information about the syntactical uses of the morpheme (e.g., the treatment of irregular verbs).

For example, there would be separate lexical entries for the word *spread* categorized as a noun and as a verb. Each lexical entry would indicate which syntactical rules to use for positioning the word, depending on which category was applicable in the given context. For example, as a verb, *spread* would not follow the article *the*, although as a noun, *spread* would be allowed to do so. Even the peculiarities of syntax for a given lexical entry would be stored in the lexicon. For instance, the lexical entry for the verb *spread* would indicate that this verb deviates from the normal syntactical rule for forming past tenses (i.e., "add -*ed* to the stem used for the present tense").

You may wonder why people would clutter up our mental lexicon with so much syntactical information. There is an advantage to attaching syntactical, context-sensitive, and idiosyncratic information to the items in their mental lexicon: If people add to the complexity of their mental lexicon, they can drastically simplify the number and complexity of the rules they need in their mental syntax. For example, by attaching the idiosyncratic treatment of irregular verbs (e.g., *spread* or *fall*) to their mental lexicon, they do not have to endure different syntactical rules for each verb. By making their lexicon more complex, they allow their syntax to be simpler, so that appropriate transformations may be simple and relatively context free. Once people know the basic syntax of a language, they can easily apply the rules to all items in their lexicon. They can then gradually expand their lexicon to provide increasing complexity and sophistication.

Not all psychologists agree with all aspects of Chomsky's theories (e.g., Bock et al. 1992; Garrett, 1992; Jackendoff, 1991). Many particularly disagree with his emphasis on syntax (form) over semantics (meaning). Nonetheless, several psychologists have proposed models of language comprehension and production that include the notion that lexical elements (morphemes) contain various kinds of syntactic information. These kinds of information indicate appropriate syntactic categories, idiosyncratic violations of syntactic rules (e.g., the treatment of irregular verbs or collective nouns), peculiarities regarding appropriate contexts for usage, and so on.

How do people link the elements in their mental lexicon to the elements in their syntactical structures? Various models for such bridging have been proposed (e.g., Bock et al., 1992; Jackendoff, 1991). According to some of these models, when people parse a sentence by syntactic categories, they create slots for each item in the sentence. For example, in the sentence, "Juan gave María the book from the shelf," there is a slot for a noun used as (1) a subject (Juan), (2) a direct object (the book), (3) an indirect object (María), and (4) an object of a preposition (the shelf). There are also slots for the verb, the preposition, and the articles.

In turn, lexical items contain information on the kinds of slots into which the items can be placed that is based on the kinds of **thematic roles** the items can fill. The thematic roles that have been identified include *agent* (the "doer" of any action), *patient* (the direct recipient of the action), *beneficiary* (the indirect recipient of the action), *instrument* (the means by which the action is implemented), *location* (the place where the action occurs), *source* (where the action originated), and *goal* (where the action is going) (Bock, 1990; Fromkin & Rodman, 1988). According to this view of how syntax and semantics are linked, the various syntactical slots (e.g., subject nouns) can be filled by lexical entries with corresponding thematic roles (e.g., agent). For example, nouns that can fill *agent* roles can be inserted into slots for subjects of phrases; *patient* roles correspond to slots for direct objects; *beneficiary* roles fit with indirect objects, and so on. Nouns that are objects of prepositions may be filled with various thematic roles (e.g., location—at the beach, source—from the kitchen, and goal—to the classroom). So far, we have concentrated on describing the structure and processes of language in its most developed state, but how do people acquire this remarkable ability?

Although it is possible to study syntax separately from semantics, the way people understand syntax is affected by semantics, and vice versa. Consider, for example, the sentence, "When he ran the show failed because of his disappearance." You are likely to have read one meaning for the word *ran* initially (*ran* as *managed*), only to replace it with another meaning (*ran* as *left quickly*) when the initial meaning did not work with the syntax of the sentence. A sentence such as this one is sometimes called a *garden-path* sentence because it initially deceives the reader or listener regarding its meaning (Tanenhaus & Trueswell, 1995). Clearly, semantics and syntax interact: A sentence cannot be understood syntactically in the absence of semantic considerations (Tanenhaus, Spivey-Knowlton, Eberhard, & Sedivy, 1995). Sometimes we make automatic inferences about meaning (Graesser & Kreuz, 1993; McKoon & Ratcliff, 1992a), only to have to replace them later.

LANGUAGE ACQUISITION

In the past, debates about the acquisition of language centered on the same theme as debates about the acquisition of any ability—the nature versus nurture theme. However, current thinking about language acquisition has incorporated the understanding that acquiring language really involves a natural endowment that is modified by the environment. Thus, the approach to studying language acquisition now revolves around discovering what abilities are innate and how these abilities are tempered by a child's environment—a process aptly termed "innately guided learning" (see Juszczyk, 1995, 1997).

Stages of Language Acquisition

Throughout the world, people seem to acquire their primary language in pretty much the same sequence and in just about the same way. Within the first years of life, humans seem to progress through the following stages in producing language:

1. Cooing, which comprises all possible phones
2. Babbling, which comprises only the distinct phonemes that characterize the primary language of the infant
3. One-word utterances
4. Two-word utterances and telegraphic speech
5. Basic adult sentence structure (present by about age 4), with the continuing acquisition of vocabulary.

In recent years, research on the development of speech perception has found the same overall pattern of progression—from more general to more specific abilities. That is, infants are initially able to distinguish among all possible phonetic contrasts, but, over time, people lose the ability to distinguish nonnative contrasts in favor of those used in their native language environment (see Jusczyk, 1997). Thus, some aspects of infants' speech perception and production abilities mirror each other, developing from more general to more specific abilities. It now appears that from day one, infants are programmed to tune into their linguistic environment with the specific goal of acquiring language.

For example, newborns seem to respond preferentially to their mothers' voices (DeCasper & Fifer, 1980) and seem to respond motorically in synchrony with the speech of the caregivers who interact with them directly (Field, 1978; J. A. Martin, 1981; Schaffer, 1977; Snow, 1977; Stern, 1977). Infants also prefer to listen to someone speaking in what will be their native language, rather than in a future nonnative language, and may focus on the rhythmic structure of the language (Bertoncini, 1993; Mehler, Dupoux, Nazzi, & Dehaene-Lambertz, 1996). If you were to videotape infants' motor responses while the infants were attending to someone speaking to them, their movements would seem to be dancing in time with the rhythm of the speech. The emotional expression of infants also seems to be matched to that of the infants' caregivers (Fogel, 1991).

Infants have also been known to produce sounds of their own; most obviously, the communicative aspect of crying—whether intentional or not—works quite well. In terms of language acquisition, however, it is the cooing of infants that most intrigues linguists. **Cooing** is the infant's oral expression that explores the production of all the possible phones humans can produce. The cooing of infants around the world, including deaf infants, is indistinguishable across babies and languages.

During the cooing stage, hearing infants can also discriminate among all phones, not just the phonemes that are characteristic of their own language. For example, during this stage, both Japanese and American infants can discriminate the /l/ from the /r/ phoneme. However, as infants move into the next stage, they gradually lose this ability, and by 1 year of age, Japanese infants—for whom the distinction does not make a phonemic difference—no longer make this discrimination (Eimas, 1985).

Loss of discrimination ability is not limited to Japanese infants. Werker and Tees (1984) found that infants who grow up in homes where English is spoken are able to distinguish between phonemes that are different in the Hindi language of India but are not different in English. In English, the phonemes are allophones of the *t* sound. In particular, the English-speaking infants are able to make the discrimination with roughly 95% accuracy at 6 to 8 months of age. By 8 to 10 months, their accuracy is down to 70%, and by 10 to 12 months, it is down to a mere 20%. As they grow older, infants clearly lose the capacity to make discriminations that are not relevant to their language.

At the babbling stage, deaf infants no longer vocalize, and the sounds produced by hearing infants change. **Babbling** is the infant's preferential production of only the distinct phonemes that are characteristic of the infant's own language (e.g., Locke, 1994; Petitto & Marentette, 1991). Thus, although the cooing of infants around the world is essentially the same, babbling distinctively characterizes the language an infant is acquiring. As suggested previously, the ability of the infant to perceive, as well as to produce, nonphonemic phones recedes during this stage.

Eventually, the infant utters his or her first word—followed shortly by one or two more and soon after yet a few more. The infant uses these one-word utterances—termed *holophrases*—to convey intentions, desires, and demands. Usually, the words are nouns describing familiar objects that the child observes (e.g., *car, book, ball, baby,* and *nose*) or wants (e.g., *Mama, Dada, juice,* and *cookie*).

By 18 age months, children typically have vocabularies of 3 to 100 words (Siegler, 1986). Because the young child's vocabulary cannot yet encompass all the child wishes to describe, the child deftly overextends the meaning of words in her or his existing lexicon to cover things and ideas for which a new word is lacking. For example, the general term for a man may be *Dada*—which can be distressing to a new father in a public setting—and the general term for any kind of four-legged animal may be *doggie*. The linguistic term for this adaptation is **overextension error**. Young children have to overextend the meanings of the words they know because they have few words in their vocabulary. How do they decide which words to use when they overextend the meanings of the words they know?

A *feature hypothesis* suggests that children form definitions that include too few features (E. V. Clark, 1973). Thus, a child may refer to a cat as a dog because of a mental rule that if an animal has the feature of four legs, it is a "doggie." An alternative *functional hypothesis* (K. Nelson, 1973) suggests that children first learn to use words that describe important functions or purposes: Lamps give light, and blankets make us warm. According to this view, overextension errors are due to functional confusions. A dog and a cat both do similar things and serve the same purposes as pets, so a child is likely to confuse them. Although the functional hypothesis has usually been viewed as an alternative to the feature hypothesis, it seems possible that both mechanisms are at work in children's overextensions.

Children overextend what they know in the grammatical as well as the semantic domain. Languages, such as English, with many exception words, are particularly susceptible to being overextended. Thus, young children who are learning English may say "He wented" in an attempt to regularize an irregular verb (Marcus et al., 1992).

Gradually, between $1\frac{1}{2}$ and $2\frac{1}{2}$ years of age, children start combining single words to produce two-word utterances. Thus begins an understanding of syntax. These early syntactical communications seem more like telegrams than conversations because the articles, prepositions, and other function morphemes are usually left out. Hence, linguists refer to these early utterances with rudimentary syntax as telegraphic speech. In fact, **telegraphic speech** can be used to describe three-word utterances and even slightly longer ones if they have these same characteristic omissions of some function morphemes.

Vocabulary expands rapidly, more than tripling, from about 300 words at about age 2 to about 1,000 words at about age 3. Almost incredibly, by age 4, children acquire the foundations of adult syntax and language structure (see Table 9.3). By age 5, most children can also understand and produce complex and uncommon sentence constructions, and by age 10, children's language is fundamentally the same as that of adults.

Nature and Nurture

If neither nature alone nor nurture alone adequately explains all aspects of language acquisition, just how may nature facilitate nurture in the process? Chomsky (1965, 1972) proposed that humans have an innate **language-acquisition device (LAD)**, which facilitates language acquisition. That is, we humans seem to be biologically preconfigured to be ready to acquire language. Given the complex neuropsychology of other aspects of human perception and thought, it is not absurd to consider that we may be neuropsychologically predisposed to acquire language.

Several observations of humans support the notion that we are predisposed to acquire language. For one thing, human speech perception is remarkable, given the nature of auditory-processing capacities for other sounds. Moreover, all children within a broad normal range of abilities and environments seem to acquire language at an incredibly rapid rate. In fact, deaf children acquire sign language in about the same way and at about the same rate as hearing children acquire spoken language. If you have ever struggled to acquire a second language, you can appreciate the relative ease and speed with which young children seem to acquire their first language. This accomplishment is particularly remarkable, given that children are offered a relatively modest quantity and variety of linguistic input (whether speech or signs) in relation to the highly sophisticated internalized language structures they create. Children seem to have a knack for acquiring an implicit understanding of the many rules of language structure, as well as for applying those rules to new vocabulary and new contexts.

Perhaps even more surprising, almost all children seem to acquire these aspects of language in the same progression and at more or less the same time. On the other hand, the linguistic environment clearly plays a role in the language-acquisition process. In fact, there seem to be *critical periods*—times of rapid development, during which a particular ability must be developed if it is ever to develop adequately—for acquiring these understandings of language. During such periods, the environment plays a crucial role. For example, the cooing and babbling stages seem to be a critical period for acquiring a native speaker's discrimination and production of the distinctive phonemes of a particular language; during this period, the child's linguistic context must provide those distinctive phonemes.

There seems to be a critical period for acquiring a native understanding of a language's syntax, too. Perhaps the greatest support for this view comes from studies of adult users of American Sign Language (ASL). Among adults who have signed ASL for 30 years or more, researchers could discernibly differentiate among those who acquired ASL before age 4, between ages 4 and 6, and after age 12. Despite 30 years of signing, those who acquired ASL later in childhood had a less profound understanding of the distinctive syntax of ASL (Meier, 1991; Newport, 1990).

Studies of linguistically isolated children seem to provide additional support for the notion of the interaction of both physiological maturation and environmental support. Of the rare children who have been linguistically isolated, those who are rescued at younger ages seem to acquire more sophisticated language structures than do those who are rescued when they are older. (The research on critical periods for language acquisition is much more equivocal for the acquisition of additional languages after the first one is acquired; see Bahrick, Hall, Goggin, Bahrick, & Berger, 1994; see also Chapter 10).

Two additional observations, which apply to all humans of all ages, also support the notion that nature contributes to language acquisition: First, humans have several physiological structures that serve no purpose other than to produce speech; second, myriad universal characteristics have been documented across the vast array of human languages. Since 1963, when a lone linguist documented 45 universal characteristics across 30 languages (e.g., Finnish, Hindi, Swahili, Quechua, and Serbian), hundreds of universal patterns have been documented across languages around the globe (see Pinker, 1994).

It appears that neither nature nor nurture alone determines language acquisition. One such postulate—**hypothesis testing**—suggests this integration of nature and nurture: Children acquire language by mentally forming tentative hypotheses regarding language on the basis of their inherited facility for language acquisition (nature) and then testing these hypotheses in the environment (nurture). The implementation of this process is said to follow several operating principles (Slobin, 1971, 1985). In forming hypotheses, young children look for and attend to these things:

1. Patterns of changes in the forms of words
2. Morphemic inflections that signal changes in meaning, especially suffixes
3. Sequences of morphemes, including both the sequences of affixes and roots and the sequences of words in sentences.

In addition, children learn to avoid exceptions and to figure out various other patterns that are characteristic of their native tongue. Although not all linguists support the hypothesis-testing view, the phenomena of overregularization (using and sometimes overapplying rules) and of language productivity (creating novel utterances based on some kind of understanding of how to do so) seem to support it.

Newport (1990) added a slightly different twist to the hypothesis-testing view, suggesting that while children are acquiring language, they do not pay attention to all aspects of language. Instead, they focus on the perceptually most salient aspects of language, which happen to be the most meaningful aspects in most cases. Although Newport's studies have focused on deaf children's acquisition of ASL, this phenomenon may apply to spoken language as well. Indeed, one study found that hearing infants attend to the salient acoustic cues in sentences that mark grammatically critical attributes of sentences (Hirsh-Pasek et al., 1987).

Although few (if any) psychologists have asserted that language is entirely a result of nature, some researchers and theoreticians have focused on the environmental mechanisms that children use to acquire language. Three such mechanisms are imitation, modeling, and conditioning.

Imitation and Modeling

In imitation, children do exactly what they see others do. Sometimes they imitate the language patterns of others, especially their parents. More often, though, children loosely follow what they hear, a phenomenon referred to as modeling.

Even amateur observers of children notice that children's speech patterns and vocabulary model the patterns and vocabulary of the persons in their environment. In fact, parents of infants and young children seem to go to great lengths to make it easy for the children to attend to and understand what they are saying. Almost without thinking, parents and other adults tend to use a higher pitch than usual, to exaggerate the *vocal inflection* of their speech (i.e., raising and lowering pitch and volume more extremely than normal), and to use simpler sentence constructions when speaking with infants and young children (Rice, 1989). This distinctive form of adult speech has been termed *motherese*, or perhaps more accurately, **child-directed speech**.

Through child-directed speech, adults seem to go out of their way to make language interesting and comprehensible to infants and young children. In this way, they also make it possible for the infants to model aspects of the adults' behavior. Indeed, infants seem to prefer listening to child-directed speech more than to other forms of adult speech (Fernald, 1985). These exaggerations seem to gain and hold infants' attention, to signal to them when to take turns in vocalizing, and to communicate affect (emotion-related information). Across cultures, parents seem to use this specialized form of speech, further tailoring it to particular circumstances: using rising intonations to gain children's attention; falling intonations to comfort them; and brief, discontinuous, rapid-fire explosions of speech to warn against prohibited behavior (Fernald et al., 1989).

Parents even seem to model the correct format for verbal interactions. Early caregiver-child verbal interactions are characterized by verbal turn taking, in which the caregiver says something and then uses vocal inflection to cue the infant to respond; the infant babbles, sneezes, burps, or otherwise makes some audible response; the caregiver accepts whatever noises the infant makes as valid communicative utterances and replies; and the infant further responds to the cue—and so on for as long as they both show interest in continuing.

Parents also seem to work hard to understand children's early utterances, in which one or two words may be used for conveying an entire array of concepts. As the children grow older and more sophisticated and acquire more language, parents gradually provide less linguistic support and demand increasingly sophisticated utterances from the children. It is as if they initially provide a scaffolding from which the children can construct an edifice of language, and as the children's language develops, the parents gradually remove the scaffolding.

Do parental models of language use provide the chief means by which children acquire language? The mechanism of imitation is appealing in its simplicity; unfortunately, it does not explain many aspects of language acquisition. For example, if imitation is the primary mechanism, why do children universally begin by producing one-word utterances, then two-word and other telegraphic utterances, and later complete sentences? Why not start out with complete sentences? In addition, perhaps the most compelling argument against imitation alone relates to our linguistic productivity. Shakespeare may have been more productive than most of us, but each of us is quite innovative in the speech we produce. Most of the utterances we produce are novel ones that we have not heard or read before.

Yet another argument against imitation alone is the phenomenon of **overregularization**, which occurs when young children have acquired an understanding of how a language usually works and then apply the general rules of language to the exceptional cases that vary from the norm. For example, instead of imitating her parents' sentence pattern, "The mice fell down the hole, and they ran home," the young child might overregularize the irregular forms and say, "The mouses falled down the hole, and they runned home."

Conditioning

The mechanism of conditioning is also exquisitely simple: Children hear utterances and associate those utterances with particular objects and events in their environment. They then produce those utterances and are rewarded by their parents and others for having spoken. Initially, their utterances are not perfect, but through successive approximations, children come to speak just as well as native adult speakers of their language. The progression from babbling to one-word utterances to more complex utterances would seem to support the notion that children begin with simple associations and that their utterances gradually increase in complexity and in the degree to which they approximate adult speech.

As with imitation, the simplicity of the proposed conditioning mechanism does not suffice to explain actual language acquisition fully. For one thing, parents are much more likely to respond to the *veridical content* of children's speech—that is, whether the statement is true or false—than to the relative correctness of the children's grammar and pronunciation (R. Brown, Cazden, & Bellugi, 1969). In addition, even if parents did respond to the grammatical correctness of children's speech, their responses might explain why children eventually stop overregularizing their speech but not why they begin doing so. Also, just as linguistic productivity argues against imitation alone, it contradicts conditioning: Children constantly use novel utterances, for which they have never previously been rewarded. That is, they consistently apply the words and language structures they already know to novel situations and contexts for which they have never before received reinforcement. Thus, through the combined effects of innately given linguistic abilities and exposure to a linguistic environment, infants acquire a language automatically and seemingly effortlessly.

Beyond the First Years

The foregoing theories offer explanations of how children acquire the foundations of adult language structure by age 4 or so. However, as remarkable as 4 year olds' language achievements are—and they truly are astonishing—few of us would have difficulty recognizing that the vocabulary and linguistic sophistication of 4 year olds differ from those of most older children and adults. What changes occur in children's use of language after age 4, and what do such changes imply regarding developmental changes in cognition?

To understand these changes, we explore both verbal comprehension and verbal fluency. In general, children's ability to comprehend language (and to process information) efficiently increases with age (e.g., Hunt, Lunneborg, & Lewis, 1975; Keating & Bobbitt, 1978). Older children also demonstrate greater verbal fluency than do younger children (e.g., Sincoff & Sternberg, 1988). In addition to the increases in verbal comprehension and fluency abilities that develop with age, we can best understand development by looking not simply at a child's age but at the strategies a child of a given age uses to comprehend or to generate verbal material. Much of what develops is not just verbal ability, but the ability to generate useful strategies for verbal comprehension and fluency. These strategies are at the intersection of language acquisition and metacognition and are important aspects of human intelligence (Sternberg, 1985).

An interesting aspect of research on strategies of verbal comprehension has been research on comprehension monitoring (Markman, 1977, 1979), which hypothesizes that one of the ways in which we enhance our understanding of verbal information is to monitor (check for accuracy, logic, and cohesiveness) what we hear and read. To study the influence of comprehension monitoring, researchers observed children and adults and attempted to correlate comprehension-monitoring skills with assessments of overall comprehension.

Consider a typical experiment. Children aged 8 to 11 heard passages containing contradictory information. This description of how to make the dessert baked Alaska is an example (Markman, 1979, p. 656):

> To make it they put the ice cream in a very hot oven. The ice cream in Baked Alaska melts when it gets that hot. Then they take the ice cream out of the oven and serve it right away. When they make Baked Alaska, the ice cream stays firm and does not melt.

Note that the passage contains a blatant internal contradiction, saying both that the ice cream melts and that it does not. Almost half the young children who saw this passage did not notice the contradiction. Even when they were warned in advance about problems with the story, many of the youngest children still did not detect the inconsistency. Thus, young children are not successful at comprehension monitoring, even when they are cued to be aware of inconsistencies in the text they read.

◆ SUMMARY

There are at least six properties of *language*, the use of an organized means of combining words to communicate: (1) Language permits us to *communicate* with one or more persons who share our language. (2) Language creates an *arbitrary* relationship between a *symbol* and its *referent*—an idea, a thing, a process, a relationship, or a description. (3) Language has a *regular structure*; only particular sequences of symbols (sounds and words) have meaning. Different sequences yield different meanings. (4) The structure of language can be analyzed at *multiple levels* (e.g., phonemic and morphemic). (5) Despite having the limits of a structure, language users can *produce* novel utterances; the possibilities for *generating* new utterances are virtually limitless. (6) Languages constantly *evolve*.

Language involves *verbal comprehension*—the ability to understand written and spoken linguistic input, such as words, sentences, and paragraphs—and *verbal fluency*—the ability to produce linguistic output. The smallest units of sound produced by the human vocal tract are *phones*; *phonemes* are the smallest units of sound that can be used to differentiate meaning in a given language. The smallest semantically meaningful unit in a language is a *morpheme*. Morphemes may be either roots or *affixes* (prefixes or suffixes), which may be either *content morphemes* (conveying the bulk of the word's meaning) or *function morphemes* (augmenting the meaning of the word). A *lexicon* is the repertoire of morphemes in a given language (or for a given language user). The study of the meaningful sequencing of words within phrases and sentences in a given language is *syntax*, and larger units of language are embraced by the study of *discourse*.

Syntax is the study of the linguistic structure of sentences. *Phrase-structure grammars* analyze sentences in terms of the hierarchical relationships among words in phrases and sentences. *Transformational grammars* analyze sentences in terms of transformational rules that describe interrelationships among the structures of various sentences. Some linguists have suggested a mechanism for linking syntax to semantics, in which grammatical sentences contain particular slots for syntactical categories; these slots may be filled by words that have particular *thematic roles* within the sentences. According to this view, each item in a lexicon contains information regarding appropriate thematic roles, as well as appropriate syntactical categories.

Humans seem to progress through the following stages in acquiring language: (1) cooing, which comprises all possible phones; (2) babbling, which comprises only the distinct phonemes that characterize the primary language of the infant; (3) one-word utterances; (4) two-word utterances and telegraphic speech; and (5) basic adult sentence structure (present by about age 4). This progression includes changes in perception that reduce the number of phonemes that can be distinguished, tuning in to those of the native language environment.

During language acquisition, children engage in *overextension errors*, in which they extend the meaning of a word to encompass more concepts than the word is intended to encompass. Neither nature alone nor nurture alone can account for human language acquisition. The mechanism of *hypothesis testing* suggests an integration of nature and nurture: Children acquire language by mentally forming tentative hypotheses regarding language (based on nature) and then testing these hypotheses in the environment (based on nurture). Children are guided in the formation of these hypotheses by an innate *language-acquisition device*, which facilitates language acquisition. Over the course of development, language complexity, vocabulary, and even strategies for acquiring vocabulary become increasingly sophisticated.

10 Language and Thought

"John's last girlfriend chewed him up and spit him out."

This statement is not literally true, yet fluent readers of English have little difficulty comprehending this metaphor and other nonliteral forms of language. How do people comprehend nonliteral language? One of the reasons that people can understand nonliteral uses of language is that they can interpret the words they hear within a broader linguistic, cultural, social, and cognitive context. In this chapter, we first focus on the cognitive context of language—how language and thought interact. Then, we discuss some uses of language in its social context and, finally, present some neuropsychological insights into language.

LANGUAGE AND THOUGHT

One of the most interesting areas in the study of language is the relationship between language and the thinking human mind. Many different questions have been asked about this relationship, only some of which we consider here. Of the many ways in which to study this relationship, one is by research that compares users of different languages and dialects. Such studies form the basis of this section.

Differences Among Languages

Why are there so many different languages around the world, and how does the use of language in general and the use of a particular language influence human thought? As you know, different languages comprise different lexicons and use different syntactical structures. These differences often reflect differences in the physical and cultural environments in which the languages arose and developed. For example, in terms of lexicon, the Garo of Burma distinguish among many different kinds of rice, which is understandable because they are a rice-growing culture. Nomadic Arabs have more than 20 different words for camels. These peoples clearly conceptualize rice and camels more specifically and in more complex ways than do people outside their cultural groups. As a result of these linguistic differences, do the Garo think about rice and Nomadic Arabs think about camels differently from the way you do?

The syntactical structures of languages differ, too. Almost all languages incorporate ways in which to communicate actions, agents of actions, and objects of actions (Gerrig & Banaji, 1994). What differs across languages is the order of subject, verb, and object in a typical declarative sentence, as well as the range of grammatical inflections and other markings that speakers are obliged to include as key elements of a sentence. For example, in describing past actions in English, people indicate whether an action took place in the past by changing (inflecting) the verb form (e.g., walked). In Spanish and German, the verb must also indicate whether the agent of action was singular or plural and is being referred to in the first, second, or third person. In Turkish, the verb form must indicate past action, singular or plural, and the person, and it must indicate whether the action was witnessed or experienced directly by the speaker or was noted only indirectly. Do these differences and other differences in obligatory syntactical structures influence—or perhaps even constrain—the users of these languages to think about things differently because of the languages they use while thinking?

Linguistic Relativity: The Sapir-Whorf Hypothesis

The concept relevant to this question is linguistic relativity, the assertion that the speakers of different languages have different cognitive systems and that these different cognitive systems influence the ways in which people who speak the various languages think about the world. Thus, according to the relativity view, the Garo would think about rice differently from the way you do. For example, the Garo would develop more cognitive categories for rice than would an English-speaking counterpart. When the Garo contemplated rice, they would purportedly view it differently—and perhaps with greater complexity of thought—than do English speakers, who have only a few words for rice. Thus, language would shape thought.

The **linguistic relativity hypothesis** is sometimes referred to as the Sapir-Whorf hypothesis, after the two men—Edward Sapir and Benjamin Lee Whorf—who were the most forceful in propagating it. Sapir (1941/1964, p. 69) said that "we see and hear and otherwise experience very largely as we do because the language habits of our community predispose certain choices of interpretation." Whorf (1956, p. 213) stated this view even more strongly:

> We dissect nature along lines laid down by our native languages. The categories and types that we isolate from the world of phenomena we do not find there because they stare every observer in the face; on the contrary, the world is presented in a kaleidoscopic flux of impressions which has to be organized by our minds—and this means largely by the linguistic systems in our minds.

The Sapir-Whorf hypothesis has been one of the most widely mentioned ideas in all the social and behavioral sciences (Lonner, 1989). However, some of its implications appear to have reached mythical proportions. For example, many social scientists have warmly accepted and gladly propagated the notion that Eskimos have multitudinous words for the single English word *snow*.—a myth that anthropologist L. Martin (1986) refuted. According to Pullum (1991, p. 160), "no one who knows anything about Eskimo (or more accurately, about the Inuit and Yupi'k families of related languages spoken from Siberia to Greenland) has ever said they do." Martin, who has done more than anyone else to debunk the myth, understands why her colleagues consider the myth charming, but she has been "disappointed in the reaction of her colleagues when she pointed out the fallacy; most, she says, took the position that true or not 'it's still a great example' " (quoted in Adler, 1991, p. 63). It appears that people must exercise caution in their interpretation of findings regarding linguistic relativity.

A milder form of linguistic relativism is that language may not *determine* thought, but it certainly may *influence* thought. People's thoughts and their language interact in myriad ways, only some of which psychologists now understand. Clearly, language facilitates thought, affecting even perception and memory. For one thing, people have limited means by which to manipulate nonlinguistic images (Hunt & Banaji, 1988). Such limitations make desirable the use of language to facilitate mental representation and manipulation. Even nonsense pictures ("droodles") are recalled and redrawn differently, depending on the verbal label given to the picture (e.g., Bower, Karlin, & Dueck, 1975).

To see how this phenomenon might work, look at Figure 10.1. If instead of being labeled as it is, it was entitled "beaded curtain," you might have perceived it differently. However, once a particular label has been given, it is harder to view it from another perspective (Glucksberg, 1988). Psychologists have used other ambiguous figures and have found similar results. Figure 10.2 illustrates three other figures that can be given alternative labels. When participants are given a particular label (e.g., either eyeglasses or dumbbells), they tend to draw their recollection of the figure in a way that is similar to the given label.

Language also affects how we encode, store, and retrieve information in memory in other ways. Loftus (e.g., Loftus & Palmer, 1974) has done extensive work showing that the testimony of eyewitnesses is powerfully influenced by the distinctive phrasing of questions posed to them. Schooler and Schooler (1990) found that even when the participants generated their own descriptions, the subsequent accuracy of their eyewitness testimony declined following an opportunity to write a description of an observed event, a particular color, or a particular face. When given an opportunity to identify statements about an event or the actual color or face, the participants were less able to do so accurately if they had previously described it. Paradoxically, when the participants were allowed to take their time in responding, their performance was even less accurate than when they were forced to respond quickly. That is, if

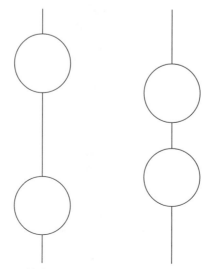

Figure 10.1 Bear climbing the far side of a tree.

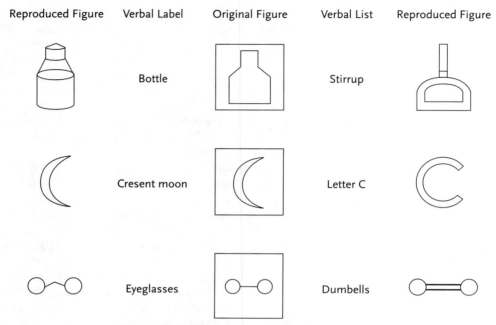

Reproduced Figure	Verbal Label	Original Figure	Verbal List	Reproduced Figure

Figure 10.2 Influence of verbal labels on memory.

given time to reflect on their answers, the participants were more likely to respond in accord with what they had said or written than with what they had seen.

Linguistic Universals

There has been some research that addressed **linguistic universals**—characteristic patterns across the languages of various cultures—and relativity. Linguists have identified hundreds of linguistic universals related to *phonology* (the study of phonemes), *morphology* (the study of morphemes), semantics, and syntax. An area that well illustrates much of this research focuses on color names. Words designating colors provide an especially convenient way of testing for universals because people in every culture can be expected to be exposed, at least potentially, to pretty much the same range of colors.

It turns out that different languages name colors quite differently, but in the languages, the color spectrum is not divided up arbitrarily. A systematic pattern seems universally to govern color naming across languages. Two anthropologists, Berlin and Kay (1969; see also Kay, 1975), who investigated color terms in a large number of languages, unearthed two apparent linguistic universals about color naming across languages. First, all the languages surveyed took their basic color terms from a set of just 11 color names: black, white, red, yellow, green, blue, brown, purple, pink, orange, and gray. Languages ranged from using all 11 color names, as in English, to using just 2. Second, when only some of the color names are used, the naming of colors falls into a hierarchy of five levels: (1) black, white; (2) red; (3) yellow, green, and blue; (4) brown; and (5) purple, pink, orange, and gray. Thus, if a language names only 2 colors, the colors will be black and white. If it names 3 colors, the colors will be black, white, and red. A fourth color will be taken from the set of yellow, green, and blue. The fifth and sixth will be taken from this set as well, and so selection will continue until all 11 colors have been labeled.

In addition to studying semantic differences, such as the use of color words, psycholinguists study how syntactical structural differences across languages may affect thought. For example, Spanish has two forms of the verb *to be—ser* and *estar;* however, they are used in different contexts. Sera (1992; *será* means "will be" in Spanish) studied the uses of *ser* and *estar* in adults and in children, both in highly structured situations (i.e., in response to patterned sentences in which *ser* or *estar* were used) and in relatively naturalistic situations (i.e., in response to open-ended requests to describe objects or situations).

When *to be* indicated the identity of something (e.g., in English, "This is José") or the class membership of something (e.g., "José is a carpenter"), both adults and children correctly used the verb form *ser*. Moreover, both adults and children correctly used different verb forms when *to be* indicated attributes of things: *Ser* was used to indicate permanent attributes (e.g., "María is tall"), and *estar* was used to indicate temporary attributes (e.g., "María is busy"). When using forms of *to be* to describe the locations of objects (including people, animals, and other things), both adults and children correctly used *estar*. However, when using forms of *to be* to describe the locations of events (e.g., meetings or parties), adults used *ser,* whereas children continued to use *estar*.

Sera (1992) interpreted these findings as indicating two things: First, *ser* seems to be used primarily for indicating permanent conditions (e.g., identity, class inclusion, and relatively permanent, stable attributes of things), and *estar* seems to be used primarily for indicating temporary conditions (e.g., temporary attributes of things and the location of objects, which are often subject to change from one place to another). That finding was in accord with other work and was relatively unsurprising. Her second finding was more intriguing. Children treat the location of events in the same way as the location of objects (i.e., as temporary, hence their use of *estar*), whereas adults differentiate between events and objects. In particular, adults consider the locations of events to be unchanging (i.e., permanent, thereby requiring the use of *ser*).

Sera (1992) noted that other researchers have suggested that young children have difficulty distinguishing between objects and events (e.g., Keil, 1979) and in recognizing the permanent status of many attributes (e.g., Marcus & Overton, 1978). Thus, the developmental differences in the use of *ser* to describe the location of events may indicate developmental differences in cognition. However, Sera's work leaves open the psychological question as to whether, as a result of language difference, native Spanish speakers have developed a more differentiated sense of the temporary and the permanent than have native English speakers, who use the same verb form to express both senses of *to be*. Thus far, the answer is unclear.

Other languages have also been used in investigations of linguistic relativity. For example, in the Navaho language, the choice of a verb depends on the shape of the object engaging in the action of the verb, whereas in English, it does not (J. B. Carroll & Casagrande, 1958). Might the use of different verb forms for different shapes suggest that Navaho children learn to perceive and organize information by shapes earlier than do children whose native language is English?

Early research indicated that young English-speaking children group objects by color before they group them by shape (Brian & Goodenough, 1929). In contrast, Navaho-speaking children are more likely than English-speaking Navaho children to classify objects on the basis of shape. However, these findings are problematic because English-speaking children from Boston perform more like the Navaho-speaking Navaho children than like English-speaking Navaho children (J. B. Carroll & Casagrande, 1958). Furthermore, more recent research comparing adults' and children's generalizations of novel nouns among novel objects found that young English-speaking children actually overuse shapes in classifying objects (L. B. Smith, Jones, & Landau, 1996). What would happen if people who speak both the languages were studied?

Hoffman, Lau, and Johnson (1986) conducted an intriguing experiment that was designed to assess the possible effects of linguistic relativity by studying persons who spoke more than one language. In Chinese, a single term, *shì gÈ,* specifically describes a person who is "worldly, experienced, socially skillful, devoted to his or her family, and somewhat reserved" (p. 1098), whereas English clearly has no comparable single term to embrace these diverse characteristics. Hoffman and his colleagues composed text passages in English and in Chinese describing various characters, including the *shì gÈ* stereotype (without, of course, specifically using the term *shì gÈ* in the descriptions). They then asked participants who were fluent in both Chinese and English to read the passages either in Chinese or in English and then to rate various statements about the characters in terms of the likelihood that the statements would be true of the characters. Some of these statements involved a stereotype of a *shì gÈ* person.

Hoffman et al.'s results seemed to support the notion of linguistic relativity, in that the participants were more likely to rate the various statements in accord with the *shì gÈ* stereotype when they had read the passages in Chinese than when they had read the passages in English. Similarly, when the participants were asked to write their own impressions of the characters, their descriptions conformed more closely to the *shì gÈ* stereotype if they had previously read the passages in Chinese. The authors did not suggest that it would be impossible for English speakers to comprehend the *shì gÈ* stereotype; rather, they indicated that having that stereotype readily accessible facilitates its mental manipulation.

The question of whether linguistic relativity exists, and if so, to what extent, remains an open question. Our reading of the evidence is that there may be a mild form of relativity, whereby language can influence thought. However, a stronger deterministic form of relativity, whereby language determines differences in thought among members of various cultures, is almost certainly inconsistent with the available evidence. Finally, it is probably the case that language and thought interact with each other throughout the life span (Vygotsky, 1986).

Bilingualism and Dialects

The research by Hoffman et al. (1986) raised a few questions that have fascinated psycholinguists: If a person can speak and think in two languages, does the person think differently in each language? In fact, do **bilinguals**—people who can speak two languages—think differently from **monolinguals**—people who can speak only one language? (*Multilinguals* speak at least two and possibly more languages.) What differences, if any, emanate from the availability of two languages versus just one? Might bilingualism affect intelligence, positively or negatively?

Hakuta (1986) reviewed much of the literature on this question and turned up some interesting findings. Consider some of the issues that arise in this field. First, does bilingualism make thinking in any one language more difficult, or does it enhance thought processes? Hakuta reviewed hundreds of studies and found the data to be self-contradictory. Different participant populations, different methodologies, and different language groups, as well as different experimenter biases, may have contributed to the inconsistency in the literature. Hakuta interpreted the literature as indicating that the question cannot be answered simply. He suggested that when bilinguals are *balanced bilinguals,* roughly equally fluent in both languages, and come from middle-class backgrounds, positive effects of bilingualism tend to be found, but under other circumstances negative effects may result. What may be the causes of this difference?

Cummins (1976) suggested that people must distinguish between what may be called additive versus subtractive bilingualism. In *additive bilingualism,* a second language is acquired in addition to a relatively well-developed first language. In *subtractive bilingualism,* elements of a second language replace elements of the first language. Cummins hypothesized that the additive form results in increased thinking ability, whereas the subtractive form results in decreased thinking ability. In particular, there may be something of a threshold effect: Individuals may need to be at a certain, relatively high, level of competence in both languages for a positive effect of bilingualism to be found. Children from backgrounds with lower socioeconomic status (SES) may be more likely to be subtractive bilinguals than are children from middle SES backgrounds; their SES may be the cause of their being hurt, rather than helped, by their bilingualism.

Another factor that is believed to contribute to the acquisition of a language is age. Some researchers have suggested that nativelike mastery of some aspects of a second language is rarely achieved after adolescence. Bahrick (1994) disagreed with this view, on the basis of their studies of bilingualism in both recent and long-term immigrants to the United States. They found that some aspects of a second language (e.g., vocabulary comprehension and fluency) seem to be acquired just as well after adolescence as before. Furthermore, contrary to previous findings (e.g., Johnson & Newport, 1989, 1991; Newport, 1990), these researchers found that even some aspects of syntax seem to be acquired readily after adolescence, although the mastery of nativelike pronunciation seems to depend on early acquisition (e.g., Asher & Garcia, 1969; Oyama, 1976). A surprising finding, by Flege (1991), is that it may be easier to learn completely novel phonemes in a second language than to learn phonemes that are highly similar to the phonemes of the first language.

What kinds of learning experiences facilitate the acquisition of a second language? Bialystok and Hakuta (1994) asserted that there is no single correct answer to that question. For one thing, each individual language learner brings distinctive cognitive abilities and knowledge to the language-learning experience. In addition, Bialystok and Hakuta suggested that the kinds of learning experiences that facilitate the acquisition of a second language should match the context of and uses for the second language once it is acquired.

Single Versus Dual System Hypotheses

One way of approaching bilingualism is to apply what we have learned from cognitive-psychological research to practical concerns regarding how to facilitate the acquisition of a second language. Another approach is to study bilingual individuals, to see how bilingualism may offer insights into the human mind. For example, some cognitive psychologists have been interested in finding out how the two languages are represented in the bilingual's mind. The **single-system hypothesis** suggests that the two languages are represented in just one system. Alternatively, **the dual-system hypothesis** suggests that the two languages are somehow represented in separate systems of the mind (Paradis, 1981). For instance, might German-language information be stored in a physically different part of the brain than English-language information?

One way to address this question is through the study of bilinguals who have had brain damage. If a bilingual has brain damage in a particular part of the brain, an inference consistent with the dual-system hypothesis would be that the individual would show different degrees of impairment in the two languages, whereas the single-system view would suggest roughly equal impairment in the two languages. The logic of this kind of investigation is compelling, but the results are not. When recovery of language after trauma has been studied, it has been found that sometimes the first language recovers first, sometimes the second language recovers first, and sometimes recovery is about equal for the two languages (M. L. Albert & Obler, 1978; Paradis, 1977). The conclusions that can be drawn on the basis of this methodology are equivocal, although the results seem to suggest at least some duality of structure.

A different method of study has led to an alternative perspective on bilingualism. Oje-mann and Whitaker (1978) mapped the region of the cerebral cortex relevant to language use in two bilingual patients who were being treated for epilepsy. Mild electrical stimulation was applied to the cortex of each patient. Electrical stimulation tends to inhibit activity where it is applied, leading to the reduced ability to name objects for which the memories are stored at the location being stimulated. The results for both patients were the same and may help explain the contradictions in the literature. Some areas of the brain showed equal impairments for naming objects in both languages, but other areas showed differential impairment in one or the other language. The results also suggested that the weaker language was more diffusely represented across the cortex than was the stronger language. In other words, the question of whether two languages are represented singly or separately may be the wrong one to ask. The results of this study suggest that some aspects of the two languages may be represented singly and other aspects may be represented separately.

To summarize, two languages seem to share some, but not all, aspects of mental representation. Learning a second language is often a plus, but it is probably the most advantageous if the individual is in an environment in which the learning of the second language adds to, rather than subtracts from, the learning of the first language. Moreover, for beneficial effects to appear, the second language must be learned well. The approach usually taken in schools, whereby students may receive as little as two or three years of second-language instruction spread out over a few class periods a week, is probably not sufficient for the beneficial effects of bilingualism to appear. However, schooling does seem to yield beneficial effects on the acquisition of syntax, particularly when a second language is acquired after adolescence. Furthermore, individual learners should choose specific kinds of language-acquisition techniques to suit both their abilities and preferences and their goals for using the second language.

Language Mixtures and Change

Bilingualism is not a certain outcome of linguistic contact between different language groups. Sometimes, when people of two different language groups are in prolonged contact with one another, they begin to share some vocabulary that is superimposed on each group's syntax, resulting in what is known as a *pidgin*. Over time, this admixture can develop into a distinct linguistic form, with its own grammar, becoming a *creole*. Bickerton (1990), a linguist, studied the similarities among different creoles and postulated that modern creoles may resemble an evolutionarily early form of language, which he termed *protolanguage*. The existence of pidgins and creoles and possibly a protolanguage support the universality notion discussed earlier. That is, linguistic ability is so natural and universal that given the opportunity, humans rapidly invent new languages.

Creoles and pidgins arise when two linguistically distinctive groups meet. The counterpart, a dialect, occurs when a single linguistic group gradually diverges toward distinctive variations. A **dialect** is a regional variety of a language that is distinguished by features, such as vocabulary, syntax, and pronunciation. Dialectical differences often represent harmless regional variations, which create few serious communication difficulties but can lead to some confusion. In the United States, for example, when national advertisers give 800 (toll-free) numbers to call, they often route the calls to the Midwest. They do so because they have learned that the Midwestern form of speech seems to be the most universally understood form in the country, whereas other forms, such as southern and northeastern ones, may be harder for people from diverse parts of the country to understand. Many radio announcers try to learn something close to a standard form of English, often called "network English," to maximize their comprehensibility to as many listeners as possible.

Sometimes, different dialects are assigned different social statuses, with *standard* forms having higher status than *nonstandard* ones. The distinction between standard and nonstandard forms of a language can be pernicious when speakers of one dialect start to view themselves as speakers of a superior dialect. Recall that none of the existing languages of the world is inherently better than any other language in terms of the ability to express thoughts. Moreover, virtually any thought can be expressed in any dialect.

Slips of the Tongue

Thus far, much of the discussion has assumed that people use (or, at least, attempt to use) language correctly. An area of particular interest to cognitive psychologists, however, is how people use language incorrectly. One way of using language incorrectly is through **slips of the tongue**, inadvertent linguistic errors in what we say, which may occur at any level of linguistic analysis: phonemes, morphemes, or larger units of language (Crystal, 1987; McArthur, 1992). In such cases, what we think and mean to say do not correspond to what we actually say. Freudian psychoanalysts have suggested that in *Freudian slips,* the verbal slip reflects some unconscious processing that has psychological significance, often indicating repressed emotions. For example, a business competitor may say, "I'm glad to beat you," when what he or she overtly intended was, "I'm glad to meet you."

In contrast to the psychoanalytic view, most psycholinguists and other cognitive psychologists are intrigued by slips of the tongue because of what the lack of correspondence between what is thought and what is said may tell us about how language is produced. In speaking, we have a mental plan for what we are going to say. Sometimes, however, this plan is disrupted when our mechanism for speech production does not cooperate with our cognitive one. Often, such errors result from the intrusions of other thoughts or by stimuli in the environment (e.g., a radio talk show or a nearby conversation) (Garrett, 1980). Slips of the tongue may be taken to indicate that the language of thought differs somewhat from the language through which we express our thoughts (Fodor, 1975). Often, we have the idea right, but its expression comes out wrong. Sometimes, we are not even aware of the slip until it is pointed out to us because in the language of the mind, whatever it may be, the idea is right, even though the expression is inadvertently wrong.

Fromkin (1973) and Fromkin and Rodman (1988) classified various kinds of slips that people tend to make in their conversations:

• In *anticipation,* the speaker uses a language element before it is appropriate in the sentence because it corresponds to an element that will be needed later in the utterance. For example, instead of saying, "an inspiring expression," a speaker may say, "an expiring expression."

• In *perseveration,* the speaker uses a language element that was appropriate earlier in the sentence but is not appropriate later on. For instance, a speaker may say, "We sat down to a bounteous beast" instead of a "bounteous feast."

• In *substitution,* the speaker substitutes one language element for another, for example, by warning someone to do something "after it is too late," rather than "before it is too late."

• In *reversal* (also called "transposition"), the speaker switches the positions of two language elements, such as the reversal that led *flutterby* to become *butterfly*—a reversal that captivated language users so much that the reversal is now the preferred form. Sometimes, reversals can be fortuitously opportune, creating *spoonerisms,* in which the initial sounds of two words are reversed and make two entirely different words. The term is named after the Reverend William Spooner, who was famous for them. Some of his choicest slips include, "You have hissed all my mystery lectures," and "Easier for a camel to go through the knee of an idol" (H. H. Clark & Clark, 1977).

• In addition, slips may be due to *insertions* of sounds (e.g., "mischievious" instead of "mischievous" or "drownded" instead of "drowned") or other linguistic elements. The opposite kind of slip involves *deletions* (e.g., sound deletions such as "prossing" instead of "processing"); such deletions often involve *blends* (e.g., "blounds" for "blended sounds").

Each kind of slip of the tongue may occur at a different hierarchical level of linguistic processing (Dell, 1986)—that is, at the acoustical level of phonemes (e.g., "bounteous beast" instead of "bounteous feast"), the semantic level of morphemes (e.g., "after it's too late" instead of "before it's too late"), or even higher levels (e.g., "bought the bucket" instead of "kicked the bucket" or "bought the farm"). The patterns of errors (such as reversals and substitutions) at each hierarchical level tend to be parallel (Dell, 1986). For example, in phonemic errors, initial consonants tend to interact with initial consonants (e.g., "tasting wime" instead of "wasting time"), final consonants with final consonants (e.g., "bing his tut" instead of "bit his tongue"), prefixes with prefixes (e.g., "expiring expression"), and so on.

Also, errors at each level of linguistic analysis suggest particular kinds of insights into how we produce speech. For example, in phonemic errors, a word that is stressed (emphasized through speech rhythm and tone) is more likely to influence other words than is a word that is not stressed (Crystal, 1987). Furthermore, even when sounds are switched, the basic rhythmic and tonal patterns are usually preserved (e.g., the emphasis on "hissed" and the first syllable of "mystery" in the first spoonerism quoted here).

Even at the level of words, the same parts of speech tend to be involved in the errors we produce (e.g., nouns interfering with other nouns, verbs with verbs) (Bock, 1990; Bock et al., 1992). For example, in the second spoonerism quoted here, Spooner managed to preserve the syntactical categories (the nouns *knee* and *idol*), as well as the grammaticality of the sentence, by changing the articles from "*a* needle" to "*an* idol." Even in the case of word substitutions, syntactic categories are preserved. In speech errors, semantic categories, too, may be preserved, as in naming a category when intending to name a member of the category (e.g., "fruit" for "apple"), naming the wrong member of the category (e.g., "peach" for "apple"), or naming a member of a category when intending to name the category as a whole (e.g., "peach" for "fruit") (Garrett, 1992). Data from studies of speech errors may help us better understand normal language processing. Another aspect of language that offers us a distinctive view is the study of metaphorical language.

Metaphorical Language

Until now, we have discussed primarily the literal uses of language. At least as interesting to poets and to us, as well as to many others, are its omnipresent figurative uses, particularly the use of metaphors as a way of expressing thoughts. **Metaphors** juxtapose two nouns in a way that positively asserts their similarities but does not disconfirm their dissimilarities; **similes** are similar to metaphors, except that they introduce the words *like* or *as* into the comparison.

Metaphors contain four key elements: the two items that are being compared, a tenor and a vehicle, and the two ways the items are related. The *tenor* is the topic of the metaphor, and the *vehicle* is what the tenor is described in terms of. For example, in saying that "billboards are warts on the landscape," the tenor is "billboards," and the vehicle is "warts." The similarities between the tenor and the vehicle are termed the *ground* of the metaphor, and the dissimilarities between the two are the *tension* of the metaphor. People may conjecture that a key similarity between billboards and warts is that they are both considered unattractive. The dissimilarities between the two are many, including that billboards appears on buildings, highways, and other impersonal public locations, but warts appear on diverse personal locations on an individual.

Of the various theories that have been proposed to explain how metaphors work, the main traditional views have highlighted either the ways in which the tenor and the vehicle are similar or the ways in which they differ. For example, the traditional *comparison view* highlights the importance of the comparison and underscores the comparative similarities and analogical relationship between the tenor and the vehicle (Malgady & Johnson, 1976; G. A. Miller, 1979; Ortony, 1979; cf. also Sternberg & Nigro, 1983). As applied to the metaphor, "Abused children are walking time bombs," the comparison view would underscore the similarity between the elements: their potential for explosion. In contrast, the *anomaly view* of metaphor emphasizes the dissimilarity between the tenor and the vehicle (e.g., Beardsley, 1962; Bickerton, 1969; H. H. Clark & Lucy, 1975; Gerrig & Healy, 1983; Lyons, 1977; Searle, 1979; van Dijk, 1975). The anomaly view would highlight the many dissimilarities between abused children and time bombs.

The *domain-interaction view* integrates aspects of each of the preceding views, suggesting that a metaphor is more than a comparison, as well as more than an anomaly. According to this view, a metaphor involves an interaction of some kind between the domain (area of knowledge, e.g., animals, machines, plants) of the tenor and the domain of the vehicle (Black, 1962; Hesse, 1966). The exact form of this interaction differs somewhat from one theory to another. According to Tourangeau and Sternberg (1981, 1982), the metaphor is more effective when the tenor and the vehicle share many similar characteristics (e.g., the potential explosiveness of abused children and time bombs), but the domains of the tenor and the vehicle are highly dissimilar (e.g., the domain of humans and the domain of weapons).

Glucksberg and Keysar (1990) suggested yet another view of how people understand metaphors, which they based on an extensive analysis of the metaphors cited in other research (e.g., some of the aforementioned studies: Black, 1962; H. H. Clark & Lucy, 1975; Ortony, 1979; Searle, 1979; Tourangeau & Sternberg, 1981). Glucksberg and Keysar asserted that metaphors are essentially a nonliteral form of class-inclusion statements, in which the tenor of each metaphor is a member of the class characterized by the vehicle of the given metaphor. That is, people understand metaphors not as statements of comparison but as statements of category membership, in which the vehicle is a prototypical member of the category.

For example, when we say, "Our colleague's partner is an iceberg," we are saying that the partner belongs to the category of things that are characterized by the lack of personal warmth, extreme rigidity, and the ability to produce a massively chilling effect on anyone in the surrounding environment. For a metaphor to work well, the reader should find the salient features of the vehicle ("iceberg") to be unexpectedly relevant as features of the tenor ("my colleague's partner"). That is, the reader should be at least mildly surprised that prominent features of the vehicle may characterize the tenor but, after consideration, should agree that those features do describe the tenor.

Metaphors enrich language in ways that literal statements cannot. It appears not only that people's understanding of metaphors requires some kind of comparison, but that the domains of the vehicle and of the tenor interact in some way. Reading a metaphor can change people's perception of both domains and therefore can educate them in a way that is perhaps more difficult to transmit through literal speech.

LANGUAGE IN A SOCIAL CONTEXT

The study of the social context of language is a relatively new area of linguistic research. Increasingly, however, students of language have become interested in **pragmatics**, the study of how people use language, including sociolinguistics and other aspects of the social context of language. Similarly, cognitive psychologists have become increasingly interested in the social context in which people acquire and use language.

Under most circumstances, you change your use of language in response to contextual cues without giving these changes much thought. Similarly, you usually un-self-consciously change your language patterns to fit different contexts.

For example, in speaking with a conversational partner, you seek to establish a *common ground*, or a shared basis for engaging in a conversation (H. H. Clark & Brennan, 1991). When you are with people who largely share a common background, knowledge, motives, or goals, establishing a common ground is likely to be easy and scarcely noticeable. But when little is shared, such a common ground may be hard to find.

Some sociolinguists and psycholinguists study the ways in which people use nonlinguistic elements in conversational contexts. For example, those who were interested in your use of language in context would observe your use of gestures and vocal inflections, as well as of other forms of nonverbal communication. One aspect of nonverbal communication is *personal space*—the distance between people in a conversation or other interaction that is considered comfortable for members of a given culture. The formal term for the study of interpersonal distance (or its opposite, *proximity*) is *proxemics* (the relative distancing and positioning of you and your fellow conversants). In the United States, 18 to 24 inches is considered about right (Hall, 1966). Scandinavians expect more distance, whereas Middle Easterners, southern Europeans, and South Americans expect less (Sommer, 1969; O. M. Watson, 1970).

When people are on their own turf, they take their cultural views of personal space for granted; only when they come into contact with persons from other cultures do they notice these differences. For example, when one of us was visiting Venezuela, he noticed his cultural expectations coming into conflict with the expectations of those around him. He often found himself in a comical dance, backing off from the person he was talking to while that person was trying to move closer. Within a given culture, greater proximity generally indicates that (1) the persons see themselves in a close relationship; (2) the persons are participating in a social situation that permits the violation of the bubble of personal space, such as close dancing; or (3) the "violator" of the bubble is dominating the interaction.

Speech Acts

Direct Speech Acts

Another key aspect of the way in which you use language depends on what purpose you plan to achieve with language. When you speak, what kinds of things can you accomplish?

The philosopher Searle (1975a) proposed a theory of **speech acts**, which addresses the question of what you can accomplish with speech. According to Searle, all speech acts fall into five basic categories, based on the purpose of the acts. Table 10.1 identifies these categories and gives examples of each.

• The first category of speech acts is representatives. A *representative* is a speech act by which a person conveys a belief that a given proposition is true. The speaker can use various sources of information to support the given belief, but the statement is simply a statement of belief. People can put in various qualifiers to show their degree of certainty, but they are still stating a belief, which may or may not be verifiable.

• A second category of speech act is a *directive,* which represents a speaker's attempt to get a listener to do something. Sometimes, a directive is quite indirect. For example, almost any sentence that is structured as a question is probably serving a directive function. Any attempt to elicit assistance of any kind, however indirect, falls into this category.

• A third category is a commissive. In uttering a *commissive,* the speaker is committing himself or herself to some future course of action. Promises, pledges, contracts, guarantees, assurances, and the like all constitute commissives.

• A fourth category of speech act is an *expressive,* which is a statement regarding the speaker's psychological state, such as delight or embarrassment.

• The fifth kind of speech act is a *declaration,* which is a speech act by which the very act of making a statement brings about an intended new state of affairs. When a cleric says, "I now pronounce you husband and wife," the speech act is a declaration because once the speech act is accomplished, the marriage rite is completed. Declarations are also termed *performatives* (H. H. Clark & Clark, 1977).

The appealing thing about Searle's taxonomy is that it classifies almost any statement that may be made. It shows exhaustively, at least at one level, the different kinds of things speech

TABLE 10.1 Speech Acts

Speech Act	Description	Example
Representative	A speech act by which a person conveys a belief that a given proposition is true	If I say "My math teacher is a sadist," I am conveying my belief that the math teacher enjoys seeing others feel pain. pain. I can use various sources of information to support my belief. Nonetheless, the statement is nothing more nor less than a statement of belief. Similarly, I can make a statement that is more directly verifiable, such as "As you can see here on this thermometer, the temperature outside is 20 degrees Celsius."
Directive	An attempt by a speaker to get a listener to do something, such as supply the answer to a question	I can ask someone to help me move furniture in various ways, some of which are more direct than others, such as, "Please help me move the furniture" or "It sure would be nice if you were to help me move the furniture" or "Would you help me move the furniture?" The different surface forms are all attempts to get him to help me. Some directives are quite indirect. If I ask, "Has it stopped snowing yet?" I am still uttering a directive, in this case seeking information, rather than physical assistance.
Commissive	A commitment by the speaker to engage in some future course of action	If the person responds, "I'm busy now, but I'll help you move the furniture later," he is uttering a commissive, in that he is pledging his future help. Promises, pledges, contracts, guarantees, assurances, and the like all constitute commissives.
Expressive	A statement regarding the speaker's psychological state	If I tell the person later, "I'm really upset that you didn't come through in helping me move the furniture," that, too, would be an expressive. If the person says, "I'm sorry I didn't get around to helping you out," he would be uttering an expressive.
Declaration (also termed *performative*)	A speech act by which the very act of making a statement brings about an intended new state of affairs	Suppose that you are called into your boss's office and told, "You're fired." The speech act results in your being in a new state—that is, unemployed. You might then tell your boss, "That's fine, because I wrote you a letter yesterday saying that I resign." You are again making a declaration.

can accomplish. It also shows the close relationship between the structure and function of language, such as the likelihood that a sentence that is structured as a question is serving a directive function.

Indirect Speech Acts

Sometimes, speech acts are indirect, meaning that people accomplish their goals in speaking in an oblique fashion. One way of communicating obliquely is through **indirect requests**, through which people make a request without doing so straightforwardly (Gordon & Lakoff, 1971; Searle, 1975b). There are four basic ways of making indirect requests: (1) asking or making statements about *abilities,* (2) stating a *desire,* (3) stating a future *action,* and (4) citing *reasons.* Examples of these forms of indirect requests are illustrated in Table 10.2.

TABLE 10.2   Indirect Speech Acts

Type of Indirect Speech Act	Example of Indirect Request for Information
Abilities	If you say, "Can you tell me where the pay telephone is?" to a staff member at a hotel, and she says, "Yes, of course I can," the chances are she missed the point. The question about her ability to tell you the location of the pay telephone was an indirect request for her to tell you exactly where it is.
Desire	"I would be grateful if you told me where the pay telephone is." Your statement of thanks in advance is really a way of getting someone to do what you want.
Future action	"Would you tell me where the pay telephone is?" Your inquiry into another person's future actions is another way to state an indirect request.
Reasons	You need not spell out the reasons to imply that there are good reasons to comply with the request. For example, you may imply that you have such reasons for the staff member to tell you where the pay telephone is: "I need to know where the pay telephone is."

When are indirect speech acts interpreted literally, and when is the indirect meaning understood by the listener? A study by Gibbs (1979) indicated that when an indirect speech act, such as "Must you open the window?" is presented in isolation, it is usually first interpreted literally (as, "Do you need to open the window?"). When the same speech act is presented in a story context that makes the indirect meaning clear, the sentence is first interpreted in terms of the indirect meaning. For instance, if a character in a story had a cold and asked, "Must you open the window?" it would be interpreted as an indirect request, "Do not open the window."

Subsequent work by Gibbs (1986) showed that indirect speech acts often anticipate the potential obstacles the respondent might pose and specifically address those obstacles. For example, the question, "May I have . . . " addresses potential obstacles of permission."

In speaking to each other, people implicitly set up a cooperative enterprise. Indeed, if people do not cooperate with each other when they speak, they often end up talking past, rather than to, each other, and they do not communicate what they intended. Grice (1967) proposed that conversations thrive on the basis of a **cooperative principle**, by which people seek to communicate in ways that make it easy for their listeners to understand what they mean. According to Grice, successful conversations follow four maxims: the maxim of quantity, the maxim of quality, the maxim of relation, and the maxim of manner. (Examples of these maxims are presented in Table 10.3).

According to the *maxim of quantity,* you should make your contribution to a conversation as informative as required, but no more informative than is appropriate. For example, suppose that someone says to you, "Hi, how are you?" and you enter into a three-hour soliloquy on how your life is not quite what you were hoping it to be. Here, you are violating the maxim of quantity. The social convention is to answer with a short response, even if you would like to go into greater detail. Sometimes, people violate the maxim of quantity for a specific end. If an instructor has been seeking a chance to tell the chairperson of the department about the

TABLE 10.3 Conversational Postulates

Postulate	Maxim	Example
Maxim of quantity	Make your contribution to a conversation as informative as required, but no more informative than is appropriate.	If someone asks you the temperature outside, and you reply, "It's 43.619287 degrees out there," you are violating the maxim of quantity because you are giving more information than was probably wanted
Maxim of quality	Your contribution to a conversation should be truthful; you are expected to say what you believe to be the case.	Clearly, there are awkward circumstances in which each of us is unsure of just how much honesty is being requested, such as for the response to, "Honey, do you think I'm eating too much?" Under most circumstances, however, communication depends on an assumption that both parties to the communication are being truthful.
Maxim of relation	You should make your contributions to a conversation relevant to the aims of the conversation.	Sometimes people at meetings go into long digressions that have nothing to do with purpose of the meeting and that serve only to hold up the meeting.
Maxim of manner	You should try to avoid obscure expressions, vague utterances, and purposeful obfuscation of your point.	Nobel prize–winning physicist Richard Feynman (1985) described how he once read a paper by a well-known sociologist and found that he could not make heads or tails of it. The sentence went something like this: "The individual member of the social community often receives information via visual, symbolic channels" (p. 281). Feynman concluded, in essence, that the sociologist was violating the maxim of manner when Feynman realized that the sentence meant, "People read."

problems he or she sees with the educational program, the chairperson is taking a big risk by asking, "How are things going?" while hoping for only a short reply.

According to the *maxim of quality,* your contribution to a conversation should be truthful. You are expected to say what you believe to be the case. If you have ever sought directions when in a strange city, you know the extreme frustration that can result if people are not truthful in telling you that they do not know where to find a particular location. Irony, sarcasm, and jokes may seem to be exceptions to the maxim of quality, but they are not: The listener is expected to recognize the irony or sarcasm and to infer the speaker's true state of mind from what is said. Similarly, a joke is often expected to accomplish a particular purpose, and it usefully contributes to a conversation when that purpose is clear to everyone.

According to the *maxim of relation,* you should make your contributions to a conversation relevant to the aims of the conversation. Sometimes, of course, people purposely violate this maxim. If a romantic partner says to you, "I think we need to talk about our relationship," and you say, "The weather sure is beautiful today," you are violating the maxim to make the point that you do not want to talk about the relationship. When you do so, however, you are being uncooperative, and unless the two of you can agree on how to define the conversation, you will talk past each other and have a frustrating conversation.

According to the *maxim of manner,* you should be clear and try to avoid obscure expressions, vague utterances, and purposeful obfuscation of your point. To these four maxims noted by Grice, we might add an additional maxim: Only one person speaks at a time (Sacks, Schegloff, & Jefferson, 1974). Given that maxim, the situational context and the relative social positions of the speakers affect turn taking (Sacks et al., 1974). Sociolinguists have noted many ways in which speakers signal to one another when and how to take turns; Harvey Sacks and his colleagues mentioned various *adjacency pairs*—invitations for the person to speak or self-selected requests to speak. Speakers also use several other strategies for guiding the conversational topics and determining who will speak, such as attention getters and interrupters, as well as conversational or topic openers and closings (Keller, 1976).

Gender and Language

Within our culture, do men and women speak a different language? Gender differences have been found in the content of what people say. For example, old adolescent and young adult males prefer to talk about political views, sources of personal pride, and what they like about the other person, whereas females in this age group prefer to talk about feelings toward parents, close friends, and classes and about their fears (Rubin, Hill, Peplau, & Dunkel-Schetter, 1980). Also, in general, women seem to disclose more about themselves than do men (Morton, 1978).

Tannen (1986, 1990, 1994) has done extensive sociolinguistic research on male-female conversation that has led her to view the conversations between men and women as cross-cultural communication. Tannen noted that young girls and boys learn conversational communication in essentially separate cultural environments through their same-sex friendships. As men and women, they then carry over the conversational styles they have learned in childhood into their adult conversations.

Tannen suggested that male-female differences in conversational style center largely on different understandings of the goals of conversation. These cultural differences result in contrasting styles of communication that can lead to misunderstandings and even breakups as each partner unsuccessfully tries to understand the other. According to Tannen (1990, 1994), men see the world as a hierarchical social order in which the purpose of communication is to negotiate for the upper hand, to preserve independence, and to avoid failure. Each man strives to one-up the other and to "win" the contest. Women, in contrast, seek to establish a connection between them and others, to give support and confirmation to others, and to reach a consensus through communication.

To reach their conversational goals, women use conversational strategies that minimize differences, establish equity, and avoid any appearances of superiority by one or another conversant. Women also affirm the importance of and their commitment to a relationship and handle differences of opinion by negotiating to reach a consensus that promotes the connection and ensures that both parties at least feel that their wishes have been considered, even if they are not entirely satisfied with the consensual decision.

Men enjoy connections and rapport, but because men have been raised in a gender culture in which status plays an important role, other goals take precedence in conversations. Tannen stated that men seek to assert their independence from their conversational partners to indicate clearly their lack of acquiescence to the demands of others (which would indicate their lack of power). Men also prefer to inform (indicating the higher status conferred by authority), rather than to consult (indicating subordinate status) with, their conversational partners. The male partner in a close relationship may thus end up informing his partner of their plans, whereas the female partner expected to be consulted on their plans. When engaging in cross-gender communications, the crossed purposes of men and women often result in miscommunication because each partner misinterprets the other's intentions.

Tannen suggested that when men and women become more aware of their cross-cultural styles and traditions, they may at least be less likely to misinterpret one another's conversational interactions. In this way, they may both be more likely to achieve their individual aims, the aims of the relationship, and the aims of the other persons and institutions affected by their relationship. Tannen may well be right, but at present, converging operations are needed in addition to Tannen's sociolinguistic case-based approach to pin down the validity and generality of her interesting findings.

Discourse and Reading Comprehension

The preceding sections discussed some of the more general aspects of the social uses of language. This section discusses more specifically the processes involved in understanding and using language in the social context of discourse. *Discourse* involves communicative units of language larger than individual sentences—in conversations, lectures, stories, essays, and even textbooks. Just as grammatical sentences are structured according to systematic syntactical rules, passages of discourse are structured systematically. By adulthood, most of us have a firm grasp of how sentences are sequenced into a discourse structure. From our knowledge of discourse structure, we can derive meanings of sentence elements that are not apparent by looking at isolated sentences.

Cognitive psycholinguists who analyze discourse are particularly intrigued by how people are able to answer the questions posed in the preceding example. When grasping the meanings of pronouns (e.g., *he, she, him, her, it, they, them, we, us*), how do people know to whom (or to what) the pronouns are pointing? How do people know the meanings of ellipsed utterances (e.g., "Yes, definitely")? What does the use of the definite article *the* (as opposed to the indefinite article *a*) preceding a noun signify to listeners regarding whether a noun was mentioned previously? How do people know what event is being referenced by the verb *do?* The meanings of pronouns, ellipses, definite articles, event references, and other local elements in sentences usually depend on the discourse structure within which these elements appear (Grosz, Pollack, & Sidner, 1989).

To understand discourse, people often rely on their knowledge not only of discourse structure, but of a broad physical, social, or cultural context within which the discourse is presented. For example, observe how your understanding of the meaning of a paragraph is influenced by your knowledge and expectations.

In discourse, your understanding at each point in the discourse is influenced by your knowledge and expectations that are based on your experiences within a particular context. Thus, just as prior experience and knowledge may aid us in the lexical processing of text, they may also aid us in comprehending the text itself. What are the main reading comprehension processes? The process of reading comprehension is so complex that many entire courses and myriad volumes are devoted exclusively to the topic, but we focus here on just a few processes: semantic encoding, acquiring vocabulary, comprehending ideas in text, creating mental models of text, and comprehending text based on context and point of view.

Semantic Encoding: Retrieving Word Meanings From Memory

Semantic encoding is the process by which people translate sensory information into a meaningful representation that they perceive, on the basis of their understanding of the meanings of words. In lexical access, they identify words, based on letter combinations, and thereby activate their memory in regard to the words, whereas in semantic encoding, they take the next step and gain access to the meaning of the words stored in memory. If people cannot semantically encode the words because the meaning of the words do not already exist in memory, they must find another way in which to derive the meanings of words, such as from noting the context in which they read them.

To engage in semantic encoding, the reader needs to know what a given word means. Knowledge of word meanings (vocabulary) is closely related to the ability to comprehend text: People who are knowledgeable about word meanings tend to be good readers, and vice versa. A reason for this relationship appears to be that readers simply cannot understand text well unless they know the meanings of the component words. For example, in one study, recall of the semantic content of a passage differed by 8% between two groups of participants who differed in their knowledge of passage-relevant vocabulary by 9% (I. L. Beck, Perfetti, & McKeown, 1982).

Hunt (1978) suggested that people with larger vocabularies are able to access lexical information more rapidly than are those with smaller vocabularies. Because verbal information is often presented rapidly—whether in listening or in reading—the individual who can gain access to lexical information rapidly is able to process more information per unit of time than can one who can gain access to such information slowly.

Acquiring Vocabulary: Deriving Word Meanings From Context

Another way in which having a larger vocabulary contributes to the comprehension of text is through learning from context. When people cannot semantically encode a word because its meaning is not already stored in memory, they must engage in some kind of strategy to derive meaning from the text. In general, they must either search for a meaning, using external resources (such as dictionaries or teachers), or formulate a meaning on the basis of existing information stored in memory and use context cues to do so.

Werner and Kaplan (1952) proposed that people learn most of their vocabulary indirectly, not by using external resources, but by figuring out the meanings of the fledges from the surrounding information. For example, if you tried to look up the word *fledges* in the dictionary, you would not find it there. From the structure of the sentence, you probably figured out that *flidges* is a noun, and from the surrounding context, you probably figured out that it is a noun having something to do with words or vocabulary. In fact, *flidges* is a nonsense word we used as a place holder for the word *words,* to show how you would gain a fairly good idea of a word's meaning from its context.

van Daalen-Kapteijns and Elshout-Mohr (1981; see also Sternberg & Powell, 1983) had adult participants learn meanings of words from sentence contexts and found that high- and low-verbal participants (i.e., people with large or small vocabularies, respectively) learned word meanings differently. The high-verbal participants performed a deeper analysis of the possibilities of a new word's meaning than did the low-verbal participants. In particular, the high-verbal participants used a well-formulated strategy for figuring out word meanings, whereas the low-verbal participants seemed to have no clear strategy at all.

Comprehension of Ideas in Text: Propositional Representations

Kintsch (1990; see also Kintsch & van Dijk, 1978) has been particularly interested in the factors that influence our comprehension of what people read and has developed a model of text comprehension based on his observations. According to Kintsch, as people read, they try to hold as much information as possible in working (active) memory, so they can understand what they read. However, they do not try to store the exact words they read in working (active) memory. Rather, they try to extract the fundamental ideas from groups of words and store those fundamental ideas in a simplified representational form in working memory.

The representational form for these fundamental ideas is the *proposition.* A proposition is the briefest unit of language that can be independently found to be true or false. For example, the sentence, "Penguins are birds, and penguins can fly" contains two propositions because you can verify independently whether penguins are birds and whether penguins can fly. In general, propositions assert either an action (e.g., flying) or a relationship (e.g., membership of penguins in the category of birds).

According to Kintsch and Keenan (1973), because working memory holds propositions, rather than words, its limits are taxed by large numbers of propositions, rather than by a particular number of words. Thus, when a string of words in text requires us to hold a large number of propositions in working memory, we have difficulty comprehending the text. When information stays in working memory a longer time, it is better comprehended and better recalled subsequently. Because of the limits of working memory, however, some information must be moved out of working memory to make room for new information.

According to Kintsch and Keenan (1973) propositions that are thematically central to the understanding of the text will remain in working memory longer than propositions that are irrelevant to the theme of the text passage. Kintsch and Keenan called the thematically crucial propositions, *macropropositions,* and the overarching thematic structure of a passage of text, the *macrostructure.* In an experiment testing the model, Kintsch and Van Dijk (1978) asked participants to read a 1,300-word text passage and then to summarize the key propositions in the passage immediately, at one month, or at three months after they read the passage. Even after three months, the participants recalled the macropropositions and the overall macrostructure of the passage about as well as could those who summarized it immediately after they read it. However, the propositions providing nonthematic details about the passage were not recalled as well after one month and not at all well after three months.

Representing the Text in Mental Models

Once words are semantically encoded or their meaning is derived from the use of context, the reader must still create a *mental model* of the text that is being read, which simulates the world being described, rather than the particular words being used to describe it (Craik, 1943; see Johnson-Laird, 1989). A mental model may be viewed as a sort of internal working model of the situation described in the text, as the reader understands it. In other words, the reader creates some sort of mental representation that contains the main elements of the text, preferably in a way that is relatively easy to grasp or, at least, that is simpler and more concrete than the text itself. For example, suppose that you read the sentence, "The loud bang scared Alice." You may form a picture of Alice becoming scared upon hearing a loud noise, or you may access propositions regarding the effects of loud bangs that you have stored in memory.

According to Johnson-Laird (1983), a given passage of text or even a given set of propositions (to refer back to Kintsch's, 1990, model) may lead to more than one mental model. For example, you may need to modify your mental model, depending on whether the next sentence is, "She tried to steer off the highway without losing control of the car" or "She ducked to avoid being shot." More than one mental model is possible to represent the loud bang that scared Alice, and if you start out with a different model than the one required in a given passage, your ability to comprehend the text will depend on your ability to form a new mental model.

Note that to form mental models, you must make at least tentative *inferences* (preliminary conclusions or judgments) about what is meant but not said. In the first case, you are likely to assume that a tire blew out; in the second case, you may infer that someone is shooting a gun, even though neither of these things is explicitly stated. The construction of mental models illustrates that in addition to comprehending the words themselves, people need to understand how words combine into meaningfully integrated representations of narratives or expositions. According to Johnson-Laird (1989), passages of text that lead unambiguously to a single mental model are easier to comprehend than are passages that may lead to multiple mental models.

Inferences can be of different kinds. One of the most important kind is what Haviland and Clark (1974) referred to as a *bridging inference*, which a reader (or listener) makes when a sentence seems not to follow directly from the sentence preceding it. In essence, what is new in the second sentence goes one step too far beyond what is given in the previous sentnece. Consider, for example, two pairs of two sentences:

1. John took the picnic out of the trunk. The beer was warm.
2. John took the beer out of the trunk. The beer was warm.

Readers took about 180 milliseconds longer to read the first pair of sentences than the second. Haviland and Clark suggested that the reason for this greater processing time was that information needed to be inferred (the picnic included beer) in the first pair that was directly stated in the second pair.

Although most researchers emphasize the importance of inference making in reading and forms of language comprehension (e.g., Graesser & Kreuz, 1993), not all reserchers do. According to the *minimalist hypothesis*, readers make inferences that are based only on information that is easily available to them and only when they need to do so to make sense of adjoining sentences (McKoon & Ratcliff, 1992a). We believe that the bulk of the evidence regarding the minimalist position indicates that it is too minimalist: Readers appear to make more inferences than this position suggests (Suh & Trabasso, 1993, Trabasso & Suh, 1993).

Comprehending Text Based on Context and Point of View

What we remember from a given passage of text often depends on our point of view. For example, suppose that you were reading a text passage about the home of a wealthy family that described many of the features of the house (e.g., a leaky roof, a fireplace, a musty basement), as well as its contents (e.g., valuable coins, silverware and a television set). How might your encoding and comprehension of the text be different if you were reading it from the viewpoint of a prospective purchaser of the home, as opposed to the viewpoint of a prospective burglar? In a study using just such a passage, people who read the passage from the viewpoint of a burglar remembered far more about the contents of the home, whereas those who read it from the viewpoint of a home buyer remembered more about the condition of the house (R. C. Anderson & Pichert, 1978). (For details see chapter 4.)

To summarize, our comprehension of what we read depends on the ability to (1) gain access to the meanings of words, either from memory or based on context; (2) derive meaning from the key ideas in what we read; (3) form mental models that simulate the situations about which we read; and (4) extract the key relevant information from the text, on the basis of the contexts in which we read and the ways in which we intend to use what we read.

Thus far, we have discussed the social and cognitive contexts of language. Language use interacts with, but does not completely determine, the nature of thought, and social interactions influence the ways in which language is used and comprehended in discourse and reading. Next, we highlight some of the insights that psychologists have gained by studying the physiological context for language. Specifically, how do our brains process language?

NEUROPSYCHOLOGY OF LANGUAGE

Through studies of patients with brain lesions, researchers have learned a great deal about the relationships between particular areas of the brain (the areas of lesions observed in patients) and particular linguistic functions (the observed deficits in the brain-injured patients).

Research on Brain Lesions and Event-Related Potentials

Many linguistic functions are located mainly in the areas of the brain identified by Paul Pierre Broca (1824–80) and Carl Wernicke (1848–1905), although it is now believed that damage to Wernicke's area (in the posterior of the cortex) entails more grim consequences for linguistic function than does damage to Broca's area (closer to the front of the brain) (Kolb & Whishaw, 1990). Also, studies of patients with brain lesions have shown that linguistic function is governed by a much larger area of the posterior cortex than just the area identified by Wernicke. In addition, other areas of the cortex also play a role, such as other association-cortex areas in the left hemisphere and a portion of the left temporal cortex. Moreover, recent imaging studies of the posttraumatic recovery of linguistic functioning have found that neurological language functioning appears to redistribute to other areas of the brain, including analogous areas in the right hemisphere and some frontal areas. Thus, damage to the major left hemisphere areas responsible for language functioning can sometimes lead to the enhanced involvement of other areas as language functioning recovers—as if previously dormant or overshadowed areas take over the duties left vacant (Cappa et al., 1997; Weiller et al., 1996). Finally, some subcortical structures (e.g., the basal ganglia and the posterior thalamus) are also involved in linguistic function (Kolb & Whishaw, 1990).

Geschwind (1970) proposed a model, sometimes known as the Geschwind-Wernicke model, of how language is processed by the brain. According to this model, speech sounds signaling language travel to the inner ear. The auditory nerve then carries these signals to the primary auditory cortex of the temporal lobe. From there, the signals travel to an association area of the brain at a region in which the temporal, occipital, and parietal lobes join. It is here that sense is made from what was said. In other words, meaning is assigned at this point. From there, the processed information travels to Wernicke's area and then to Broca's area. Although the model as originally formulated localized language comprehension in Wernicke's area and language production in Broca's area, it is now known that this veiw was an oversimplification, in that Wernicke's area seems to be involved in language production and Broca's area seems to be involved in language comprehension (Zurif, 1990).

Event-related potentials, or ERPs, can also be used to study the processing of language in the brain. For one thing, a certain ERP, called N400 (a negative potential 400 milliseconds after the onset of a stimulus), typically occurs when individuals hear an anomalous sentence (Kutas & Hillyard, 1980). Thus, if people are given sequences of normal sentences and anomalous sentences (such as "The leopard is a very good napkin"), the anomalous sentences will elicit the N400 potential. Moreover, the more anomalous a sentence is, the greater the response shown in another ERP, P600 (a positive potential 600 milliseconds after the onset of a stimulus; Kutas & Van Patten, 1994).

It appears that men and women may process language differently, at least at the phonological level (Shaywitz et al., 1995). An FMRI (functional magnetic resonance imaging) study of men and women asked the participants to perform one of four tasks:

1. Indicate whether a pair of letters was identical.
2. Indicate whether two words have the same meaning.
3. Indicate whether a pair of words rhymes.
4. Compare the lengths of two lines (a control task).

The researchers found that when both male and female participants were performing the letter-recognition and word-meaning tasks, they showed activation in the left temporal lobe of the brain. When they were performing the rhyming task, however, only the inferior (lower) frontal region of the left hemisphere was activated in men, whereas the inferior frontal region of both the left and right hemispheres was activated in women. These results suggested that the men localized their phonological processing more than did the women.

In studying brain-injured men and women, Kimura (1987) has observed some intriguing differences in the ways that linguistic function appears to be localized in the brains of men and women. The men she studied seemed to show more left-hemisphere dominance for linguistic function than did the women, whereas the women showed more bilateral, symmetrical patterns of linguistic function. Furthermore, the brain locations associated with aphasia seemed to differ for men and women: Most of the aphasic women had lesions in the anterior region, although some had lesions in the temporal region. In contrast, the aphasic men had more varied patterns of lesions and were more likely to have lesions in the posterior regions, rather than in the anterior regions. One interpretation of Kimura's findings is that the role of the posterior region in linguistic function may be different for women than for men. Another interpretation is that because women show less lateralization of linguistic function, they may be better able to compensate for any possible loss of function that is due to lesions in the left posterior hemisphere through functional offsets in the right posterior hemisphere. The possibility that there may also be subcortical sex differences in linguistic function further complicates the ease of interpreting Kimura's findings.

Sex differences are not the only individual differences that have interested Kimura. Kimura (1981) also studied hemispheric processing of language in persons who use sign language to communicate. She found that the locations of lesions that would be expected to disrupt speech also disrupt signing. Furthermore, the hemispheric pattern of lesions associated with deficits in signing is the same pattern found with speech deficits. (That is, all right-handers with signing deficits show left-hemisphere lesions, as do most left-handers, but some left-handers with signing deficits show right-hemisphere lesions.) This finding supports the view that the brain processes both signing and speech similarly, in terms of their linguistic function, and it refutes the view that signing involves spatial processing or some other nonlinguistic form of cognitive processing.

Despite the many findings that have resulted from studies of brain-injured patients, there are three key difficulties in drawing conclusions that are based only on these studies: (1) Naturally occurring lesions are often not easily localized to a discrete region of the brain with no untoward effects on other regions. For example, when hemorrhaging or insufficient blood flow (such as impairment that is due to clotting) causes lesions, the lesions may also affect other areas of the brain; thus, many patients who have cortical damage have also suffered some damage in subcortical structures, which may confound the findings of cortical damage. (2) Researchers are able to study the linguistic function of patients only after the lesions have caused damage, usually without having been able to document the linguistic function of patients prior to the damage. (3) Because it would be unethical to create lesions merely to observe their effects on patients, researchers are able to study the effects of lesions only in those areas where lesions happen to have occurred naturally, and therefore other areas are not studied.

Other Methods

Researchers have also investigated brain localization of linguistic function via methods other than those used with people who have brain lesions, such as by evaluating the effects on linguistic function that follow electrical stimulation of the brain (e.g., Ojemann, 1982; Ojemann & Mateer, 1979). They have found that electrical stimulation of particular points in the brain seems to yield discrete effects on particular linguistic functions (such as naming objects), across repeated, successive trials. For example, in a given person, repeated stimulation of one particular point may lead to difficulties in recalling the names of objects on every trial, whereas stimulation of another point may lead to the incorrect naming of objects. In addition, information on locations in the brain in a specific individual may not apply across individuals. Thus, for a given individual, a discrete point of stimulation may seem to affect only one particular linguistic function, but across individuals, these particular localizations of function vary widely. The effects of electrical stimulation are transitory, and linguistic function returns to normal soon after the stimulation has ceased. These brain-stimulation studies have also shown that many more areas of the cortex are involved in linguistic function than was thought previously.

Using electrical-stimulation techniques, Ojemann (1982) also studied sex differences in linguistic function and found a somewhat paradoxical interaction of language and the brain: Although women generally have superior verbal skills to men, men have a proportionately larger (more diffusely dispersed) language area in their brains than do women. Ojemann counterintuitively inferred that the size of the language area in the brain may be inversely related to the ability to use language. This interpretation seems to be bolstered by Ojemann and Whittaker's (1978) findings with bilinguals, mentioned earlier, regarding the diffuse distribution of the nondominant language versus the more concentrated localization of the dominant language.

Yet another avenue of research involves the study of the metabolic activity of the brain and the flow of blood in the brain during the performance of various verbal tasks. For example, preliminary metabolic and blood-flow studies of the brain (e.g., Petersen et al., 1988) have indicated that many areas of the brain appear to be involved simultaneously during linguistic processing. However, most studies have confirmed the left hemisphere bias indicated by studies of people with brain lesions (see Cabeza & Nyberg, 1997). Through these kinds of studies, researchers can examine multiple simultaneous cerebral processes that are involved in various linguistic tasks.

The diverse methods of studying the brain support the view that for all right-handed people and most left-handed people, the left hemisphere of the brain seems clearly implicated in the syntactical aspects of linguistic processing and is essential to speech and signing. The left hemisphere also seems to be essential to the ability to write. On the other hand, the right hemisphere seems capable of quite a bit of auditory comprehension, particularly in terms of semantic processing, as well as some reading comprehension, and in posttraumatic linguistic recovery. The right hemisphere also seems to be important in several of the subtle nuances of linguistic comprehension and expression, such as understanding and expressing vocal inflection and gesture and comprehending metaphors and other nonliteral aspects of language (e.g., jokes and sarcasm) (Kolb & Whishaw, 1990).

Finally, some subcortical structures, especially the basal ganglia and the posterior thalamus, seem to be involved in linguistic function. Starting more than a century ago, investigators noted that the thalamus seems to be involved in linguistic function (e.g., Hughlings-Jackson, 1866/1932), particularly in coordinating the activities of the cortical areas involved in speech (Penfield & Roberts, 1959). Since these early observations, Ojemann (1975) and others have linked lesions in the thalamus to specific difficulties in speaking (e.g., perseveration or impairment of speed, fluency, or naming). The thalamus may also play a role in activating the cortex for understanding and remembering language. Because of the difficulty of studying subcortical structures, the specific role of the thalamus and other subcortical structures is not yet well defined (Kolb & Whishaw, 1990).

◆ SUMMARY

According to the *linguistic relativity* view, cognitive differences that result from using different languages cause people who speak the various languages to perceive the world differently. However, the *linguistic universals* view stresses cognitive commonalities across different language users. No single interpretation explains all the available evidence regarding the interaction of language and thought.

Research on bilinguals seems to show that environmental considerations also affect the interaction of language and thought. For example, additive bilinguals have established a well-developed primary language; the second language adds to their linguistic and perhaps even their cognitive skills. In contrast, subtractive bilinguals have not yet firmly established their primary language when portions of a second language partially displace the primary language; this displacement may lead to difficulties in verbal skills. Theorists differ in their views of whether bilinguals store two or more languages separately (*dual-system hypothesis*) or together (*single-system hypothesis*). It is possible that some aspects of multiple languages are stored separately and others unitarily. Whereas creoles and pidgins arise when two or more distinct linguistic groups come into contact, a *dialect* appears when a regional variety of a language becomes distinguished by features, such as distinctive vocabulary, grammar, and pronunciation.

Slips of the tongue may involve inadvertent verbal errors in phonemes, morphemes, or larger units of language. They include anticipations, perseverations, reversals (including spoonerisms), substitutions, insertions, and deletions. Alternative views of *metaphor* include the comparison view, the anomaly view, the domain-interaction view, and the class-inclusion view.

Psychologists, *sociolinguists,* and others who study *pragmatics* are interested in how language is used within a social context, including various aspects of nonverbal communication. *Speech acts* comprise representatives, directives, commissives, expressives, and declarations. *Indirect requests,* ways of asking for something without doing so straightforwardly, may refer to abilities, desires, future actions, and reasons. *Conversational postulates,* which provide a means of establishing language as a cooperative enterprise, comprise several maxims, including the maxims of quantity, quality, relation, and manner. Sociolinguists have observed that people engage in various strategies to signal turn taking in conversations.

Sociolinguistic research suggests that male-female differences in conversational style center largely on men's and women's different understandings of the goals of conversation. It has been suggested that men tend to see the world as a hierarchical social order in which their communication aims involve the need to maintain a high rank in the social order. In contrast, women tend to see communication as a means of establishing and maintaining their connection to their communication partners; to do so, they seek ways to demonstrate equity and support and to reach a consensual agreement.

In *discourse* and *reading comprehension*, people use the surrounding context to infer the reference of pronouns and ambiguous phrases. The discourse context can also influence the semantic interpretation of unknown words in passages and aid in acquiring new vocabulary. *Propositional representations* of information in passages can be organized into *mental models* for comprehending text. Finally, a person's point of view likewise influences what will be remembered.

Neuropsychologists, cognitive psychologists, and other researchers have managed to link quite a few language functions with specific areas or structures in the brain, largely by noticing what happens when a particular area of the brain is injured, is electrically stimulated, or is studied in terms of its metabolic activity. Thus far, the various methods of studying the brain support the view that for most persons, the left hemisphere of the brain is vital to speech and affects many syntactical aspects of linguistic processing, as well as some semantic aspects. For most people, the right hemisphere handles a more limited number of linguistic functions, including auditory comprehension of semantic information, as well as the comprehension and expression of some nonliteral aspects of language use, such as vocal inflection, gesture, metaphors, sarcasm, irony, and jokes.

Human and Artificial Intelligence

◆ Implicit Theories of Intelligence

◆ Explicit Theories of Intelligence

◆ Factor Analysis of Intelligence

◆ Information Processing and Intelligence

◆ Alternative Approaches to Intelligence

◆ Artificial Intelligence

◆ Teaching Intelligence

◆ Summary

Societies are constantly evaluating the intelligence of their members. Some assessments are formal, as when a psychologist administers a standardized intelligence test. But most assessments are informal, occurring in everyday interactions. We assess the intelligence of new acquaintances and potential significant others and even of people whom we have known for a long time. What, exactly, are we assessing?

In some respects, intelligence integrates all higher cognitive processes and perhaps some lower ones as well. How may we know what intelligence is, though? One way is simply to ask people.

IMPLICIT THEORIES OF INTELLIGENCE

Implicit theories are people's beliefs about the nature of a construct. There have been a number of attempts to ascertain people's implicit theories of intelligence, some of which have involved experts and others of which have involved laypeople.

Experts' Theories

Early in the 20th century, the editors of the *Journal of Educational Psychology* asked 14 famous psychologists what they believed intelligence was ("Intelligence and Its Measurement," 1921). The responses varied, but two themes were common in many responses on the nature of intelligence: (1) the capacity to learn from experience and (2) the ability to adapt to the surrounding environment. Sixty-five years later (Sternberg & Detterman, 1986), 24 cognitive psychologists with expertise in research on intelligence were asked the same question. They, too, underscored the importance of learning from experience and adapting to the environment, but they broadened the definition to emphasize the importance of **metacognition**—people's understanding and control of their own thinking processes. In addition, these 24 experts more heavily emphasized the role of culture, pointing out that what is considered intelligent in one culture may be considered stupid in another culture. Thus, these experts defined **intelligence** as the capacity to learn from experience, using metacognitive processes to enhance learning, and the ability to adapt to the surrounding environment, which may require different adaptations within different social and cultural contexts.

Explicit definitions of intelligence also frequently take on an assessment-oriented focus. In fact, some psychologists, such as Boring (1923), have been content to define *intelligence* as whatever it is that intelligence tests measure. This definition has several drawbacks. The first drawback is that it is circular. According to the definition, tests define what intelligence is, but what goes on the tests must presuppose some definition of what should be tested, that is, intelligence. The second drawback of the definition is its conservatism. If we define intelligence in terms of what current tests test, there is no room for progress in developing new conceptions of intelligence. The third drawback is that the definition assumes all tests of intelligence measure more or less the same thing, but they do not (Daniel, 1997, 2000).

Laypeople's Theories

Studies have also been done of laypeople's implicit theories of intelligence. For example, Sternberg, Conway, Ketron, and Bernstein (1981) examined implicit theories of people in a train station, a supermarket, and a library. They found that three factors of intelligence accounted fairly well for their data: practical problem solving, verbal ability, and social competence. Note that only the second factor corresponds to an ability clearly measured on the modal intelligence test and that the third factor does not correspond at all. But implicit theories may vary across cultures. Chen (1994) found three factors that underlie Chinese conceptions of intelligence: nonverbal reasoning ability, verbal reasoning ability, and rote memory. Using a more elaborate methodology, Yang and Sternberg (1997) uncovered a more complex implicit theory among Chinese people in Taiwan: cognitive ability, interpersonal competence (understanding others), intrapersonal competence (understanding oneself), intellectual self-assertion (knowing when to show off one's intelligence), and intellectual self-effacement (knowing when not to show off one's intelligence). Other peoples' conceptions of the nature of intelligence can be found in Berry (1974) and Sternberg and Kaufman (1998).

Differences in implicit theories can emerge not only across cultures but in a single country. For example, Okagaki and Sternberg (1993) studied implicit theories of intelligence among Anglo, Asian, and Latino groups in California and found that Latino parents of schoolchildren emphasized social-competence skills more than did parents in the other two groups, both of which emphasized cognitive-competence skills. Teachers, however, had conceptions of intelligence that were similar to those of the Anglo and Asian parents and tended to reward students whose parents' conceptions of intelligence were similar to the teachers'.

People's implicit theories of intelligence do not develop in a vacuum. They are affected by explicit theories of intelligence that have been formally proposed by experts.

EXPLICIT THEORIES OF INTELLIGENCE

Early Theories and Measures of Intelligence

Contemporary theories and measures of intelligence can usually be traced to one of two different historical traditions. One tradition concentrated on lower-level, *psychophysical abili-*

ties (such as sensory acuity, physical strength, and motor coordination), and the other focused on higher-level, *judgmental abilities* (which are traditionally described as being related to thinking).

Psychophysical Abilities: The Theory of Sir Francis Galton

Sir Francis Galton (1822–1911) believed that intelligence is a function of psychophysical abilities. His theory, then, was that high-level intelligence derives from fairly low-level kinds of mental operations. For several years, Galton maintained a well-equipped laboratory at the Kensington Museum in London, where, for a fee, visitors could have themselves measured on a variety of psychophysical tests. These tests measured a broad range of psychophysical skills and sensitivities, such as *weight discrimination* (the ability to notice small differences in the weights of objects), *pitch sensitivity* (the ability to hear small differences between musical notes), and physical strength (Galton, 1883).

Galton's ideas were brought to the United States by James McKeen Cattell (1860–1944), a professor of psychology at Columbia University. An enthusiastic student of Cattell, Clark Wissler (1901), attempted to detect links among the assorted tests that would unify the various dimensions of psychophysically based intelligence. Much to Wissler's surprise, no unifying associations could be detected. Moreover, the psychophysical tests did not predict college grades. The impact on the field of intelligence was dramatic: The psychophysical approach to assessing intelligence soon faded almost into oblivion, although it would reappear many years later.

An alternative to the psychophysical approach to assessing intelligence was developed by Alfred Binet (1857–1911) and his collaborator, Theodore Simon, but their goal was much more practical than purely scientific. In response to a request from the minister for public instruction in France, who wanted to ensure that students would not be placed in special classes because they had behavioral problems but were incorrectly labeled "mentally retarded," they attempted to devise a procedure for distinguishing normal from mentally retarded learners (Binet & Simon, 1916).

Binet and Simon set out to measure intelligence as a function of the ability to learn within an academic setting. In their view, the key to intelligence was mental judgment, not psychophysical acuity, strength, or skill. They believed intelligence comprises three distinct elements: direction, adaptation, and criticism (Binet & Simon, 1916). *Direction* involves knowing what has to be done and how to do it; *adaptation* refers to customizing a strategy for performing a task and then monitoring it while implementing it; and *criticism* is the ability to critique one's own thoughts and actions. The importance of direction and adaptation certainly fits contemporary views of intelligence, and Binet's and Simon's notion of criticism actually seems prescient, considering the current appreciation of metacognitive processes as a key aspect of intelligence.

Initially, when Binet and Simon developed their intelligence test, they were interested in some means of comparing the intelligence of a given child with that of other children of the same chronological (physical) age. For their purposes, they sought to determine each child's *mental age*—the average level of intelligence for a person of a given age. Thus, a mental age of 7 refers to the level of thinking reached by an average 7 year old. Mental ages worked fine for comparing a given 7 year old with other 7 year olds, but the use of mental ages made it difficult to compare the relative intelligence in children of different chronological ages. For example, how does a mental age of 9 years for a 7 year old compare to a mental age of 7 years for a 5 year old?

William Stern (1912) suggested instead that people's intelligence should be evaluated by using an *intelligence quotient (IQ)*: a ratio of mental age (MA) divided by chronological age (CA), multiplied by 100. This ratio can be expressed mathematically as follows: IQ = (MA/CA) × 100. Thus, if Mary's mental age of 5 equals her chronological age of 5, then her intelligence is average, and her IQ is 100, because (5/5)(100) = 100. When mental age exceeds chronological age, the ratio will lead to an IQ score above 100, and when chronological age exceeds mental age, the ratio will lead to an IQ score below 100. Intelligence-test scores that are expressed in terms of a ratio of mental age to chronological age are termed *ratio IQs*.

For various reasons, ratio IQs, too, proved inadequate. One reason is that increases in mental age slow down at about age 16. It makes sense to speak of an 8 year old with a mental age of 12 years, but it is not clear what it means to speak of a 40 year old with a mental age of 60. Today, psychologists rarely use IQs based on mental ages. Instead, researchers have turned to measurement comparisons that are based on assumed normal distributions of test scores within large populations. Scores based on deviations from the middle score in a normal distribution of scores on an intelligence test are termed *deviation IQs*. Many cognitive theorists believe that IQs provide only incomplete measurement of intelligence, as will be discussed later.

Later Scales for Measuring Intelligence

Lewis Terman, of Stanford University, built on Binet and Simon's work in Europe and constructed the earliest version of what has come to be called the *Stanford-Binet Intelligence Scales* (Terman & Merrill, 1937, 1973; Thorndike, Hagen, & Sattler, 1986). This test measures skills, such as vocabulary, mental paper folding, mathematical problem solving, and understanding proverbs. For years, the Stanford-Binet test was the standard for intelligence tests, and it is still widely used. The competitive Wechsler scales, named for their creator, David Wechsler, are probably even more widely used, however.

There are three levels of the Wechsler intelligence scales, including the third edition of the *Wechsler Adult Intelligence Scale (WAIS-III)*, the third edition of the *Wechsler Intelligence Scale for Children (WISC-III)*, and the *Wechsler Preschool and Primary Scale of Intelligence (WPPSI)*. The Wechsler tests yield three scores: a verbal score, a performance score, and an overall score. The verbal score is based on tests like *vocabulary* and *verbal similarities*, in which the test taker has to say how two things are similar. The performance score is based on tests, such as *picture completion*, which requires the identification of a missing part in a picture of an object, and *picture arrangement*, which requires the rearrangement of a scrambled set of cartoonlike pictures into an order that tells a coherent story. The overall score is a combination of the verbal and the performance scores.

Wechsler (1939), like Binet, had a conception of intelligence that went beyond what his own tests measured. Although he clearly believed in the worth of attempting to measure intelligence, he did not limit his conception of intelligence to test scores. Wechsler believed that intelligence is central in our everyday lives and is not represented just by a test score or even by what we do in school. We use our intelligence not just in taking tests and doing homework, but in relating to people, in performing our jobs effectively, and in managing our lives in general.

Although Galton, Binet, and Wechsler all had theories of intelligence, they are most well known for their ideas about the testing of intelligence. Other measurement-oriented theorists, considered next, are more well known for their theories of intelligence based on psychometric measurements.

FACTOR ANALYSIS OF INTELLIGENCE

Psychologists who are interested in the structure of intelligence have relied on factor analysis as the indispensable tool for their research. **Factor analysis** is a statistical method for separating a construct—intelligence in this case, although other constructs also can be studied— into a number of hypothetical factors or abilities that the researchers believe form the basis of individual differences in test performance.

Factor analysis is based on patterns of correlation or covariation. The underlying idea is that the more highly two tests are correlated, the more likely they are to measure the same thing. In research on intelligence, a factor analysis may involve three basic steps. First, the investigator gives a large number of people a number of different tests of ability. Second, the investigator determines the correlations (or covariances) among all these tests. Third, the investigator statistically analyzes these correlations to reduce them to a relatively small number of factors that summarize people's performance on the tests.

Investigators in this area have generally agreed on and followed this procedure, yet various theorists have differed on the resultant proposed factorial structures of intelligence. Among the many competing factorial theories, the main ones have probably been those of Spearman, Thurstone, Guilford, Cattell, Vernon, and Carroll. Figure 11.1 contrasts four of these theories.

Spearman: The "g" Factor

Charles Spearman (1863–1945) is usually credited with inventing factor analysis (Spearman, 1927). Using factor-analytic studies, he concluded that intelligence can be understood in terms of both a single general factor that pervades performances on all tests of mental ability and a set of specific factors, each of which is involved in performance on only a single type of mental-ability test (e.g., arithmetic computations). In Spearman's view, the specific factors are of only casual interest because of their narrow applicability. To Spearman, the general factor, which he labeled **"g,"** provides the key to understanding intelligence. Spearman believed that g was due to "mental energy."

Spearman's theory, which is sometimes called the two-factor theory because it posits both a general factor and specific factors, is one of the most long-lived theories of any kind in psychology. Many investigators (e.g., Brand, 1996; Jensen, 1998) still support the theory's main contention, namely, that a general factor of intelligence exists. Other theorists, as we shall see, reject the notion of a general factor.

Spearman was not only the originator of the factor-analytic approach, but can be considered the originator of the cognitive approach to intelligence. In a cognitively oriented version of his theory, Spearman (1923) suggested that three cognitive processes underlie general ability. Imagine an analogy of the form A is to B as C is to D, for example, lawyer is to client as doctor is to patient. *Apprehension of experience* refers to the encoding of the various stimuli— A, B, C, and D, here, lawyer, client, doctor, and patient. *Eduction of relations* refers to infer-

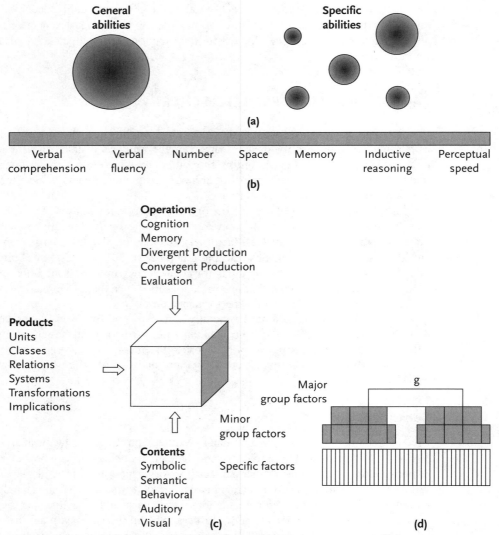

Figure 11.1 Comparisons among some of the structural approaches to intelligence. (a = Spearman; b = Thurstone; c = Guilford; d = Cattell–Vernon–Carroll)

ence of the relationship between A and B, here, lawyer and client. *Eduction of correlates* refers to application of the relationship from C to D, here, doctor to patient.

Renaming these processes and adding some others to the mix, Robert Sternberg and Michael Gardner (1983) argued that the same processes that apply to analogy items also apply to series completions (e.g., What number comes next in this series: 2, 7, 12, 17, ?) and classifications (e.g., Which word does not belong with the others? *dog, cat, gorilla, fish*). The idea was that to the extent that the processes are general, they are general because they apply to a wide range of problems that require inductive reasoning.

Thurstone: Primary Mental Abilities

In contrast to Spearman, Louis Thurstone (1887–1955) concluded that the core of intelligence resides not in a single factor but in seven factors, which he referred to as *primary mental abilities* (Thurstone, 1938). According to Thurstone, the primary mental abilities, and some examples of tests that measure them, are as follows:

1. *Verbal comprehension*—measured by vocabulary tests

2. *Verbal fluency*—measured by time-limited tests requiring the test taker to think of as many words as possible that begin with a given letter

3. *Inductive reasoning*—measured by tests, such as analogies and number-series completion tasks

4. *Spatial visualization*—measured by tests requiring the mental rotation of pictures of objects

5. *Number*—measured by computational and simple mathematical problem-solving tests

6. *Memory*—measured by picture and word-recall tests

7. *Perceptual speed*—measured by tests that require the test taker to recognize small differences in pictures or to cross out the *a*'s in strings of various letters.

Guilford: The Structure of Intellect

At the opposite extreme from Spearman's single g-factor model is J. P. Guilford's (1967, 1982, 1988) **structure-of-intellect (SOI)** model, which includes up to 150 factors of the mind, according to one version of the theory. Guilford proposed that intelligence can be understood in terms of a cube that represents the intersection of three dimensions: various operations, contents, and products. According to him, *operations* are simply mental processes, including memory and evaluation (making judgments, such as determining whether a particular statement is a fact or an opinion). *Contents* are the kinds of terms that appear in a problem, like semantic (words) and visual (pictures). *Products* are the kinds of responses required, such as units (single words, numbers, or pictures), classes (hierarchies), and implications.

Some psychologists (e.g., Eysenck, 1967) criticized Guilford's model for having too many factors. A psychological theory is supposed to be at least somewhat parsimonious, but it is not clear that Guilford's is. Other psychologists criticized Guilford's theory on technical grounds. For example, Horn and Knapp (1973) showed that Guilford's method of handling his factor-analytic data was highly likely to make his theory appear to be supported by data even if it was not. In statistical terms, Guilford's inferences were susceptible to false alarms (Type I errors). Perhaps Guilford's most valuable contribution was to suggest that psychologists should consider various kinds of mental operations, contents, and products in their views and assessments of intelligence.

Cattell, Vernon, and Carroll: Hierarchical Models

A more parsimonious way of handling a number of factors of the mind is through a hierarchical model of intelligence. One such model, developed by Raymond Cattell (1971), proposed that general intelligence can be viewed as occurring at the top of a hierarchy. This general factor of intelligence, in turn, comprises two major group factors of intelligence: *fluid ability* (speed and accuracy of abstract reasoning, especially for novel problems) and *crystallized ability* (accumulated knowledge and vocabulary). Subsumed within these two major group factors are other, more specific factors. A similar view was proposed by Philip E. Vernon (1971), who made a general division between practical-mechanical and verbal-educational abilities.

More recently, John B. Carroll (1993) proposed a hierarchical model of intelligence, based on his analysis of more than 460 data sets obtained between 1927 and 1987. Others, such as J. L. Horn (1994), have proposed related theories. Carroll's analysis encompasses more than 130,000 people from diverse walks of life and even countries of origin (although non-English-speaking countries are poorly represented among his data sets). The model Carroll proposed, based on his monumental undertaking, is a hierarchy comprising three strata: Stratum I, which includes many narrow, specific abilities (e.g., spelling ability, speed of reasoning); Stratum II, which includes group-level abilities (e.g., fluid intelligence, crystallized intelligence); and Stratum III, which is a single general intelligence, much like Spearman's *g*. Of these strata, the most interesting is the middle stratum (Stratum II), which is neither too narrow nor all-encompassing.

In addition to fluid intelligence and crystallized intelligence, Stratum II includes learning and memory processes, visual perception, auditory perception, facile production of ideas (similar to verbal fluency), and speed (both sheer speed of response and speed of accurate responding). Although Carroll did not break much new ground, in that many of the abilities in his model have been mentioned in other theories, he masterfully integrated a large and diverse factor-analytic literature, thereby giving great authority to his model. Whereas the factor-analytic approach has tended to emphasize the structures of intelligence, the information-processing approach has tended to emphasize the operations of intelligence.

INFORMATION PROCESSING AND INTELLIGENCE

As previous chapters have shown, information-processing theorists are interested in studying how people mentally manipulate what they learn and know about the world. The ways in which various information-processing investigators study intelligence differ primarily in the complexity of the processes being studied. Among the advocates of this approach have been Ted Nettelbeck, Arthur Jensen, Earl Hunt, Herbert Simon, and Robert Sternberg. Each of these researchers has considered both the speed and the accuracy of information processing to be important factors in intelligence. In addition to speed and accuracy of processing, Hunt has considered verbal versus spatial skill, as well as attentional ability. Both Simon and Sternberg have considered intelligent processing of relatively complex cognitive tasks, such as those related to problem solving. First, we consider speed.

Process-Based Theories

Inspection Time

Ted Nettelbeck and his colleagues (e.g., Nettelbeck 1987; Nettelbeck & Lally, 1976; Nettelbeck & Rabbitt, 1992; see also Deary, 2000; Deary & Stough, 1996) have suggested a psychophysical type of indicator of intelligence, involving the encoding of visual information for brief storage in working memory. The inspection-time paradigm works as follows: For each of a number of trials, the investigator presents a fixation cue (a dot in the area where a target figure will appear) on a computer monitor for 500 milliseconds. Then there is a pause of 360 milliseconds, following which the investigator presents the target stimulus for a particular interval. Finally, the investigator presents a *visual mask* (a stimulus that erases the trace in iconic memory).

The target stimulus comprises two vertical lines of unequal length (e.g., 25 mm versus 35 mm), which are aligned at the top by a horizontal crossbar. The shorter of the two lines may appear on either the right or the left side of the stimulus. The visual mask is a pair of lines that is thicker and longer than the two lines of the target stimulus. The task is to inspect the target stimulus and then indicate the side on which the shorter line appeared by pressing either a left- or a right-hand button on a keypad connected to a computer that records the responses.

The key variable is the duration of the presentation of the target stimulus, not the speed of the participant's response by pressing the button. Nettelbeck operationally defined *inspection time* as the length of time for presentation of the target stimulus after which the participant still responds with at least 90% accuracy in indicating the side on which the shorter line appeared. Nettelbeck (1987) found that shorter inspection times correlate with higher scores on intelligence tests (e.g., various subscales of the WAIS) among differing populations of participants. Other investigators have confirmed this finding (e.g., Deary & Stough, 1996).

Choice Reaction Time

Arthur Jensen (1979) emphasized a different aspect of information-processing speed; specifically, he proposed that intelligence can be understood in terms of the speed of neuronal conduction. In other words, the smart person is someone whose neural circuits conduct information rapidly. When Jensen proposed this notion, direct measures of neural-conduction velocity were not readily available, so he primarily studied a proposed proxy for measuring neural-processing speed: *choice reaction time*—the time it takes to select one answer from among several possibilities.

For example, suppose that you are one of Jensen's participants. You might be seated in front of a set of lights on a board (see Figure 11.2). When one of the lights flashed, you would be expected to extinguish it by pressing as rapidly as possible a button beneath the correct light. The experimenter would then measure your speed in performing this task.

Jensen (1982) found that participants with higher IQs are faster than participants with lower IQs in their *reaction time* (RT), the time between when a light comes on and the finger

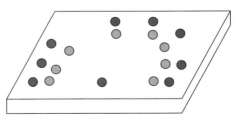

Figure 11.2 Jensen's apparatus.

leaves the home (central) button. In some studies, participants with higher IQs also showed a faster *movement time* (MT), the time between letting the finger leave the home button and hitting the button under the light. On the basis of such tasks, Reed and Jensen (1991, 1993) proposed that their findings may be due to increased central nerve-conduction velocity, although at present this proposal remains speculative.

More recently, it has been suggested that various findings regarding choice reaction time may be influenced by the number of response alternatives and the visual-scanning requirements of Jensen's apparatus, rather than the speed of reaction time alone (Bors, MacLeod, & Forrin, 1993). In particular, Bors and his colleagues found that manipulating the number of buttons and the size of the visual angle of the display could reduce the correlation between IQ and reaction time. Thus, the relation between reaction time and intelligence is unclear. In general, it seems that speed of processing bears multiple relationships with intelligence (Neubauer & Bucik, 1996).

Lexical Access Speed and Speed of Simultaneous Processing

Like Jensen, Earl Hunt (1978, 1980) suggested that intelligence should be measured in terms of speed. However, Hunt was particularly interested in verbal intelligence, so he focused on *lexical-access speed*—the speed with which we can retrieve information about words (e.g., letter names) stored in our long-term memories. To measure this speed, Hunt proposed using a letter-matching, reaction-time task (Posner & Mitchell, 1967).

In the lexical-access task, participants are shown pairs of letters, such as "A A," "A a," or "A b." For each pair, they are asked to indicate whether the letters constitute a match in name (e.g., "A a" match in name of the letter of the alphabet, but "A b" do not). They also are given a simpler task, in which they are asked to indicate whether the letters match physically (e.g., "A A" are physically identical, whereas "A a" are not). The investigator is especially interested in discerning the difference between each participant's speed for the first set of tasks, involving the matching of names, and for the second set, involving the matching of physical characteristics. Hunt would consider the difference in reaction time for each task to indicate a measure of a participant's speed of lexical access. Thus, he would *subtract* from his equation the physical-match reaction time. For Hunt, the response time in indicating that "A A" is a physical match is unimportant. What really matters is a more complex reaction time— that for recognizing names of letters. He and his colleagues have found that students with lower verbal ability take longer to gain access to lexical information than do students with higher verbal ability.

Earl Hunt and Marcy Lansman (1982) also studied people's ability to divide their attention as a function of intelligence. For example, suppose that participants are asked to solve mathematical problems and simultaneously to listen for a tone and press a button as soon as they hear it. We can expect that they would both solve the math problems effectively and respond quickly to hearing the tone. According to Hunt and Lansman, more intelligent people are better able to share time between two tasks and to perform both effectively.

In sum, process timing theories attempt to account for differences in intelligence as caused by differences in the speed of various forms of information processing—inspection time, choice reaction time, and lexical access timing have all been found to correlate with measures of intelligence. These findings suggest that higher intelligence may be related to the speed of various information-processing abilities, including (1) encoding information more rapidly into working memory, (2) gaining access to information in long-term memory more rapidly, and (3) responding more rapidly. Why would more rapid encoding, retrieval, and responding be associated with higher scores on intelligence tests? Do rapid information-processors learn more?

More recent research on learning in aged persons investigated whether there is a link between age-related slowing of information processing and (1) initial encoding and recall of information and (2) long-term retention (Nettelbeck, Rabbitt, Wilson, & Batt, 1996; see also Bors & Forrin, 1995). The findings suggest that the relation between inspection time and intelligence may not be related to learning. In particular, Nettelbeck et al. found that there is a difference between initial recall and actual long-term learning. Whereas initial recall performance is mediated by processing speed (older, slower participants showed deficits), longer-term retention of new information (preserved in older participants) is mediated by cognitive processes other than speed of processing, including rehearsal strategies. Thus, speed of information processing may influence initial performance on recall and inspection-time tasks, but speed is not related to long-term learning. Perhaps faster information processing aids participants in performing aspects of tasks on intelligence tests, rather than its contributing to actual learning and intelligence. Clearly, this area requires more research to determine how information-processing speed relates to intelligence.

The Componential Theory and Complex Problem Solving

In his early work on intelligence, Sternberg (1977, 1983, 1984) used cognitive approaches to study information processing in more complex tasks, such as analogies, series problems (e.g., completing a numerical or figural series), and syllogisms. His goal was to find out what made some people more intelligent processors of information than others. The idea was to take the kinds of tasks used on conventional intelligence tests and to isolate the **components** of intelligence, which are the mental processes used in performing these tasks. Among these components are translating a sensory input into a mental representation, transforming one conceptual representation into another, and translating a conceptual representation into a motor output (Sternberg, 1982).

Componential analysis breaks down people's reaction times and error rates on these tasks in terms of the processes that make up the tasks. This kind of analysis revealed that people may solve analogies and similar tasks by using several component processes. Among these processes are (1) encoding the terms of the problem (what Spearman referred to as apprehension of experience); (2) inferring relations among at least some of the terms (what Spearman referred to as eduction of relations); (3) mapping the inferred relations to other terms, which would be presumed to show similar relations; and (4) applying the previously inferred relations to the new situations (what Spearman referred to as eduction of correlates).

Consider the analogy, LAWYER : CLIENT :: DOCTOR : (a. PATIENT b. MEDICINE), in terms of this theory. To solve this analogy, you need to *encode* each term of the problem, which includes perceiving a term and retrieving information about it from memory. You then need to *infer* the relationship between lawyer and client—that the former provides professional services to the latter. You then need to *map* the relationship in the first half of the analogy to the second half of the analogy, noting that it will involve that same relationship. Finally, you need to *apply* that inferred relationship to generate the final term of the analogy, leading to the appropriate response: PATIENT. (Figure 11.3 shows how componential analysis would be

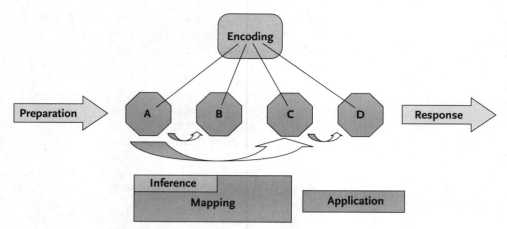

Figure 11.3 Componential analysis of an analogy problem.

applied to an analogy problem, A is to B as C is to D, where D is the solution.) Studying these components of information processing reveals more than the measurement of mental speed alone.

When measuring speed alone, Sternberg (1985) found significant correlations between speed in executing these processes and performance on other, traditional intelligence tests. However, a more intriguing discovery is that participants who score higher on traditional intelligence tests take *longer* to encode the terms of the problem than do those who score lower on the tests, but they make up for the extra time by taking less time to perform the remaining components of the task. In general, more-intelligent participants take longer during **global planning**—encoding the problem and formulating a general strategy for attacking the problem (or set of problems)—but they take less time for **local planning**—forming and implementing strategies for the details of the task (Sternberg, 1981).

The advantage of spending more time on global planning is the increased likelihood that the overall strategy will be correct. Thus, more intelligent people may take longer to do something than will less intelligent people when it is advantageous to take more time. For example, the more intelligent person may spend more time researching and planning for writing a term paper, but less time in actually writing it. This same differential in time allocation has been shown in other tasks, such as solving physics problems (Larkin, McDermott, Simon, & Simon, 1980; see Sternberg, 1979, 1985). In other words, more intelligent people seem to spend more time planning for and encoding the problems they face, but less time engaging in the other components of performing a task. This finding may be related to the previously mentioned metacognitive attribute that many include in their notions of intelligence.

In a similar cognitive approach, Herbert Simon (1976; see also Newell & Simon 1972) studied the intelligent information processing of people who are engaged in **complex problem-solving** situations, such as when playing chess and performing logical derivations. For example, a simple, brief task may require the participant to view an arithmetic or geometric series, figure out the rule underlying the progression, and guess what numeral or geometric figure may come next; more complex tasks may include some tasks like the water-jugs (also known as "water-pitcher") problems, where one has to figure out how to sequence pouring a certain amount of water from one jug to another using intermediate steps (see Estes, 1982).

In Simon's work with Allen Newell and others, computer simulations were created that would solve these complex problems. The idea was to understand intelligence through highly complex problem solving in which solution times may be measured in minutes, rather than seconds. Simon was particularly interested in the limits imposed by working memory and by the ways in which more intelligent people organize and sequence the processes by which they solve problems. Just as more artificially intelligent computer programs can be designed to handle various procedures more efficiently, more intelligent humans should be able to coordinate their handling of mental procedures more efficiently. One way of studying mental efficiency is through biological analysis.

Biological Bases of Intelligence

Although the human brain is clearly the organ responsible for human intelligence, early studies (e.g., those by Karl Lashley and others) that sought to find biological indices of intelligence and other aspects of mental processes were a resounding failure, despite great efforts. As tools for studying the brain have become more sophisticated, however, we are beginning to see the possibility of finding physiological indicators of intelligence. Some investigators (e.g., Matarazzo, 1992) believe that we will have clinically useful psychophysiological indices of intelligence early in this century, although widely applicable indices will be much longer in coming. In the meantime, the biological studies that have been conducted have been largely correlational, showing statistical associations between biological and psychometric or other measures of intelligence. The studies have not established causal relations.

Some of these studies offer some appealing possibilities. For example, it appears that complex patterns of electrical activity in the brain, which are prompted by specific stimuli, correlate with scores on IQ tests (Barrett & Eysenck, 1992). Several studies (e.g., McGarry-Roberts, Stelmack, & Campbell, 1992; P. A. Vernon & Mori, 1992) initially suggested that the speed of conduction of neural impulses may correlate with intelligence, as measured by IQ tests. A follow-up study (Wickett & Vernon, 1994), however, failed to find a strong relationship between neural-conduction velocity (as measured by neural-conduction speeds in a main nerve of the arm) and intelligence (as measured on the Multidimensional Aptitude Battery). A surprising finding was that neural-conduction velocity may be a more powerful predictor of IQ scores for men than for women, so sex differences may account for some of the differences in the data (Wickett & Vernon, 1994). Additional studies on both men and women are needed.

An alternative approach to studying the brain suggests that neural efficiency may be related to intelligence; such an approach is based on studies of how the brain metabolizes *glucose* (simple sugar required for brain activity) during mental activities. Richard Haier and his colleagues (1992) have cited several other researchers who support their own findings that higher intelligence correlates with reduced levels of glucose metabolism during problem-solving tasks—that is, smarter brains consume less sugar (and hence expend less effort) than do less-smart brains doing the same task. Furthermore, Haier and his colleagues found that cerebral efficiency increases as a result of learning on a relatively complex task involving visuospatial manipulations (the computer game *Tetris*). As a result of practice, more intelligent participants show not only lower cerebral glucose metabolism overall, but higher levels of glucose metabolism in selected areas of their brains (believed to be important to the task at hand).

Thus, more-intelligent participants may have learned how to use their brains more efficiently to focus their brains better on given tasks.

More recent research by Haier and his colleagues (Haier et al., 1995; Larson, Haier, La-Casse, & Hazen, 1995), however, suggests that the relationship between glucose metabolism and intelligence may be more complex. Whereas Haier et al. (1995) confirmed the earlier findings of increased glucose metabolism in less intelligent participants (in this case, those who were mildly retarded), Larsen et al. (1995) found, contrary to the earlier findings, that more intelligent participants had increased glucose metabolism relative to their average comparison group.

One problem with earlier studies is that the tasks used were not matched for the level of difficulty across groups of high intelligent and average individuals. Larsen et al. used tasks that were matched to the ability levels of the more intelligent and average participants and found that the more intelligent ones used more glucose. Moreover, the glucose metabolism was highest in the right hemisphere of the more intelligent participants performing the difficult task—again suggesting the selectivity of brain areas. What could be driving the increases in glucose metabolism? Currently, it appears that the key factor may be subjective task difficulty, with more intelligent participants in earlier studies simply finding the tasks too easy. Matching the difficulty of tasks to participants' abilities seems to indicate that the glucose metabolism of more intelligent participants increases when the task demands it. The preliminary findings in this area need to be investigated further before any conclusive answers will be found.

Some neuropsychological research (e.g., Dempster, 1991) suggests that performance on intelligence tests may not indicate a crucial aspect of intelligence: the ability to set goals, to plan how to achieve them, and to implement those plans. Specifically, persons with lesions on the frontal lobe of the brain frequently perform well on standardized IQ tests, which require responses to questions within a highly structured situation but do not require much in the way of goal setting or planning. If intelligence involves the ability to learn from experience and to adapt to the surrounding environment, the ability to set goals and to design and implement plans cannot be ignored. An essential aspect of goal setting and planning is the ability to attend appropriately to relevant stimuli and to ignore or discount irrelevant stimuli.

What makes some responses appropriate or inappropriate and some stimuli irrelevant or relevant? The context in which they occur is key. Specifically, we cannot realistically study a brain or its contents and processes in isolation, without considering the entire human being, including the person's interaction with the entire environmental context within which the person acts intelligently. Hence, many researchers and theorists urge us to take a more contextual view of intelligence. Furthermore, some alternative views of intelligence have attempted to broaden the definition of intelligence to be more inclusive of people's varied abilities.

Some researchers who are interested in the biological approach to intelligence have looked at the relationship of brain size to IQ. Lee Willerman and his colleagues (Willerman, Schultz, Rutledge, & Bigler, 1991) correlated brain size with IQ scores on WAIS-R, controlling for body size. They found that IQ correlated .65 in men and .35 in women and .51 in both sexes combined. A follow-up analysis of the same 40 participants suggested that, in men, a relatively larger left hemisphere better predicted Wechsler Adult Intelligence Scale verbal ability than nonverbal ability, whereas in women, a larger left hemisphere predicted nonverbal ability better than verbal ability (Willerman et al., 1992). These brain-size correlations are suggestive, but it is difficult to say what they mean at this point. For example, greater brain size may lead to higher intellectual functioning, higher intellectual functioning may lead to greater brain size, or both may be dependent on one or more other factors.

Yet another approach that is at least partially biologically based is behavior genetics (see Grigorenko, 2000, and Sternberg & Grigorenko, 1997a, for reviews of this extensive literature). The literature is complex, but it appears that about half the total variance in IQ scores is accounted for by genetic factors (Loehlin, 1989; Plomin, 1997). This figure may be an underestimate because the variance includes error variance and because most studies of heritability have been with children, but we know that heritabilitiy of IQ is higher for adults than for children (Plomin, 1997). In addition, some studies, such as the Texas Adoption Project (Loehlin, Horn, & Willerman, 1997), have suggested higher estimates, generally in the .70s. Keep in mind that heritability is a ratio of genetic variance to phenotypic variance and can vary from one population to another.

At the same time, some researchers have argued that the effects of heredity and environment cannot be clearly and validly separated (Bronfenbrenner & Ceci, 1994; Wahlsten & Gottlieb, 1997). Perhaps the direction for future research is thus to figure out more clearly how heredity and environment work together. In looking at environmental effects, it appears that researchers will want to concentrate not on differences among families, but on differences in what happens to children within families, since the evidence to date suggests that most environmental effects occur within, rather than among families (Jensen, 1997; Plomin, 1997; Scarr, 1997).

ALTERNATIVE APPROACHES TO INTELLIGENCE

According to **contextualists**, intelligence cannot be understood outside its real-world context. The context of intelligence may be viewed at any level of analysis, focusing narrowly, as on the home and family environment, or focusing broadly, as on entire cultures. For example, even cross-community differences have been correlated with differences in performance on intelligence tests; such context-related differences include those of rural versus urban communities, low versus high proportions of teenagers to adults in communities, and low versus high socioeconomic status of communities (see Coon, Carey, & Fulker, 1992). Contextualists have been particularly intrigued by the effects of cultural context on intelligence.

In fact, contextualists consider intelligence so inextricably linked to culture that they view it as something that a culture creates to define the nature of adaptive performance in that culture. Intelligence also accounts for why some people perform better than others on the tasks that the culture happens to value (Sternberg, 1985). Theorists who endorse this model study how intelligence relates to the external world in which the model is being applied and evaluated. In general, definitions and theories of intelligence more effectively encompass cultural diversity when they are broad in scope. Before exploring some of the contextual theories of intelligence, it may help to see what prompted psychologists to believe that culture may play a role in how they define and assess intelligence.

Cultural Context and Intelligence

People in different cultures may have quite different ideas of what it means to be intelligent (Serpell, 2000). For example, an interesting cross-cultural study of intelligence looked at how members of the Kpelle tribe in Africa sort terms (Cole, Gay, Glick, & Sharp, 1971). The investigators asked adult members of the Kpelle tribe to sort terms representing concepts. In Western culture, when adults are given a sorting task on an intelligence test, the more intelligent ones typically sort hierarchically. For example, they may sort names of different kinds of fish together, and then the word "fish" over that, with the name "animal" over "fish" and over "birds," and so on. Less intelligent adults typically sort functionally. That is, they may sort "fish" with "eat," for instance, because we eat fish or "clothes" with "wear" because we wear clothes. The Kpelle sorted functionally—even after the investigators unsuccessfully tried to get them spontaneously to sort hierarchically.

Finally, in desperation, one of the experimenters (Glick) asked a Kpelle to sort concepts as a foolish person would do. In response, the Kpelle quickly and easily sorted hierarchically. The Kpelle had been able to sort this way all along; they just had not done it because they viewed it as foolish—and they probably considered the questioners rather unintelligent for asking such stupid questions.

The Kpelle people are not the only ones who may question Western understandings of intelligence. In the Puluwat culture of the Pacific Ocean, for example, sailors navigate incredibly long distances, using none of the navigational aids that sailors from technologically advanced countries would need to get from one place to another (Gladwin, 1970). If Puluwat sailors were to devise intelligence tests for us, we might not seem intelligent to them. Similarly, the highly skilled Puluwat sailors might not do well on American-crafted tests of intelligence. These and other observations have prompted quite a few theoreticians to recognize the importance of considering cultural context when assessing intelligence.

A study by Seymour Sarason and John Doris (1979) provides an example closer to home regarding the effects of cultural differences on intelligence tests. These researchers tracked the IQs of an immigrant population: Italian Americans. Less than a century ago, first-generation Italian American children had a median IQ of 87 (low average; range 76–100), even when nonverbal measures were used and when so-called mainstream American attitudes were considered. Some social commentators and researchers on intelligence of the day pointed to heredity and other nonenvironmental factors as the basis for the low IQs—much as they do today for other minority groups.

For example, a leading researcher of the day, Henry Goddard, argued that 79% of the immigrant Italians (and about 80% of the immigrant Jews, Hungarians, and Russians) were "feeble-minded" (Eysenck & Kamin, 1981). Believing that moral decadence was associated with this deficit in intelligence, Goddard (1917) recommended that the intelligence tests he used should be administered to all immigrants and that all those he deemed substandard should be excluded from entering the United States. Stephen Ceci (1991) noted that the subsequent generations of Italian American students who take IQ tests today show slightly above-average IQs; other immigrant groups that Goddard denigrated have shown similar "amazing" increases. Even the most fervent hereditarians would be unlikely to attribute such remarkable gains in so few generations to heredity. Cultural assimilation, including integrated education, seems a much more plausible explanation.

The preceding arguments may make it clear why it is so difficult to come up with a test that everyone would consider **culture fair**—equally appropriate and fair for members of all cultures. If members of different cultures have different ideas of what it means to be intelligent, then the very behaviors that may be considered intelligent in one culture may be considered unintelligent in another. Take, for example, the concept of mental quickness. In mainstream U.S. culture, to say someone is "quick" is to say that the person is intelligent, and, indeed, most group tests of intelligence are strictly timed, and even on individual tests of intelligence, the test giver times the responses of the test taker. Many information-processing theorists and even psychophysiological theorists focus on the study of intelligence as a function of mental speed.

In many cultures of the world, however, quickness is not considered an asset. People in these cultures may believe that more intelligent people do not rush into things. Even in our culture, no one will view you as brilliant if you decide on a marital partner, a job, or a place to live in the 20 to 30 seconds you might normally have to solve an intelligence-test problem. Thus, given that there are no perfectly culture-fair tests of intelligence, how should we consider context when assessing and understanding intelligence?

Several researchers (e.g., Baltes, Dittmann-Kohli, & Dixon, 1984; Jenkins, 1979; Keating, 1984) have suggested that it is possible to provide **culture-relevant** tests that assess skills and knowledge that relate to the cultural experiences of the test takers. Designing culture-relevant tests requires creativity and effort but is probably not impossible. For example, Daniel Wagner (1978) investigated memory abilities—one aspect of intelligence as our culture defines it—in the U.S. versus the Moroccan culture. He found that the level of recall depended on the content that was being remembered and that culture-relevant content was remembered more effectively than culture-irrelevant content (e.g., when compared with Westerners, Moroccan rug merchants were better able to recall complex visual patterns on black-and-white photos of Oriental rugs). Wagner further suggested that when tests are not designed to minimize the effects of cultural differences, the key to culture-specific differences in memory may be the knowledge and use of metamemory strategies, rather than actual structural differences in memory (e.g., memory span and rates of forgetting).

In related research in Kenya, Robert Sternberg and his colleagues (Sternberg & Grigorenko,1997b; Sternberg et al., in press) found that rural Kenyan schoolchildren have substantial knowledge about natural herbal medicines they believe fight infection—knowledge that Western children do not have. Furthermore, the Kenyan children's scores on tests of the use of these natural herbal medicines showed significant negative correlations with the children's scores on conventional verbal tests of intelligence. In other words, the better the children did on the indigenous tests, the worse they did on the Western tests. In short, making a test culturally relevant appears to involve much more than just removing specific linguistic barriers to understanding.

Ceci and Roazzi (1994) found similar context effects in children's and adults' performance on a variety of tasks. They suggested that the *social context* (e.g., whether a task is considered masculine or feminine), the *mental context* (e.g., whether a visuospatial task involves buying a home or burgling it), and the *physical context* (e.g., whether a task is presented at the beach or in a laboratory) all affect performance. For example, 14-year-old boys performed poorly on a task when it was couched as a cupcake-baking task but performed well when it was framed as a battery-charging task (Ceci & Bronfenbrenner, 1985). Brazilian maids had no difficulty with proportional reasoning when they were hypothetically purchasing food, but had great difficulty with it when they were hypothetically purchasing medicinal herbs (Schliemann & Magalhües, 1990). Brazilian children whose poverty had forced them to become street vendors showed no difficulty performing complex arithmetic computations when selling things, but had great difficulty performing similar calculations in a classroom (Carraher, Carraher, & Schliemann, 1985; Nuñes, 1994). Thus, performance on tests may be affected by the context in which the test terms are presented. Several investigators have proposed theories that seek explicitly to examine this interaction within an integrated model of many aspects of intelligence. Such theories view intelligence as a complex system and are discussed in the next two sections.

Gardner: Multiple Intelligences

Howard Gardner (1983, 1993) proposed a **theory of multiple intelligences**, in which intelligence is not just a single, unitary construct. However, instead of proposing multiple abilities that together constitute intelligence as did Thurstone (1938), Gardner (1999) proposed eight distinct intelligences that are relatively independent of each other (see Table 11.1). Each is a separate system of functioning, although these systems can interact to produce what we see as intelligent performance. The intelligences are linguistic, logical-mathematical, spatial, musical, bodily-kinesthetic, naturalist, interpersonal, and intrapersonal.

In some respects, Gardner's theory sounds like a factorial one because it specifies multiple abilities that are construed to reflect intelligence of some sort. However, the theory views each intelligence as separate, not just as part of a single whole. Moreover, a crucial difference between Gardner's theory and factorial ones is that to identify the eight intelligences, Gardner used converging operations, gathering evidence from multiple sources and types of data. In particular, Gardner (1983, pp. 63–67) pointed to eight "signs" he used as criteria for detecting the existence of a discrete kind of intelligence:

1. Potential isolation by brain damage, in that the destruction or sparing of a discrete area of the brain (e.g., areas linked to verbal aphasia) may destroy or spare a particular kind of intelligent behavior

2. The existence of exceptional individuals (e.g., musical or mathematical prodigies) who demonstrate extraordinary ability (or deficit) in a particular kind of intelligent behavior

3. An identifiable core operation or set of operations (e.g., detection of relationships among musical tones) that are essential to performing a particular kind of intelligent behavior

TABLE 11.1 Examples of Gardner's Eight Intelligences

Type of Intelligence	Tasks Reflecting This Type of Intelligence
Linguistic intelligence	Used in reading a book; writing a paper, a novel, or a poem; and understanding spoken words
Logical-mathematical intelligence	Used in solving math problems, in balancing a checkbook, in solving a mathematical proof, and in logical reasoning
Spatial intelligence	Used in getting from one place to another, in reading a map, and in packing suitcases in the trunk of a car so that they all fit into a compact space
Musical intelligence	Used in singing a song, composing a sonata, playing a trumpet, or even appreciating the structure of a piece of music

Source: Gardner (1999).

4. A distinctive developmental history leading from novice to master, along with disparate levels of expert performance (i.e., various degrees of expressing this type of intelligence)

5. A distinctive evolutionary history, in which increases in intelligence may be plausibly associated with enhanced adaptation to the environment

6. Supportive evidence from cognitive-experimental research, such as differences in task-specific performance across discrete kinds of intelligence (e.g., visuospatial tasks versus verbal tasks), accompanied by similarities in cross-task performance within discrete kinds of intelligence (e.g., mental rotation of visuospatial imagery and recall memory of visuospatial images)

7. Supportive evidence from psychometric tests indicating discrete intelligences (e.g., differences in the performance on tests of visuospatial abilities versus on tests of linguistic abilities)

8. Susceptibility to encoding in a symbol system (e.g., language, mathematics, musical notation) or in a culturally devised arena (e.g., dance, athletics, theater, engineering, or surgery as culturally devised expressions of bodily-kinesthetic intelligence)

Thus, although Gardner did not dismiss entirely the use of psychometric tests, the base of evidence he used does not rely on the factor analysis of various psychometric tests alone. Indeed, Gardner views psychometric tests as limited because they rely almost exclusively on paper-and-pencil types of items.

Gardner's view of the mind is modular. *Modularity theorists* believe that different abilities—such as Gardner's intelligences—can be isolated as emanating from distinct portions or modules of the brain. Thus, a major task of existing and future research on intelligence is to isolate the portions of the brain that are responsible for each of the intelligences. Gardner (1983) speculated about at least some of these locales, but hard evidence for the existence of these separate intelligences has yet to be produced. Furthermore, Nettelbeck and Young (1996) questioned the strict modularity of Gardner's theory, noting specifically that the preserved specific cognitive functioning in autistic savants (persons with severe social and cognitive deficits, but with a corresponding high ability in a narrow domain) as evidence of modular intelligences may not be justified. According to Nettelbeck and Young, the narrow long-term memory and specific aptitudes of savants is not really intelligent. Thus, there may be reason to question the intelligence of inflexible modules. The question has to be answered empirically, and so far, there has not been even one empirical test of Gardner's theory as a whole, even though the theory was first proposed in 1983. Thus, at this time, the theory must be viewed as speculative.

Sternberg: The Triarchic Theory

Whereas Gardner's theory emphasizes the separateness of the various aspects of intelligence, Sternberg's (1985a, 1988c, 1996, 1999) **triarchic theory of human intelligence** emphasizes the extent to which they work together. According to this theory, intelligence comprises three aspects, dealing with its relation to (1) the internal world of the person, (2) experience, and (3) the external world. Figure 11.4 illustrates the parts of the theory and their interrelationship.

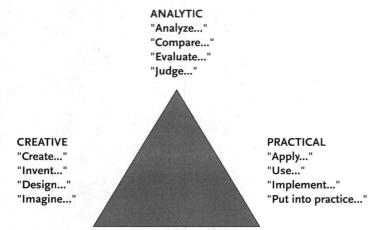

ANALYTIC
"Analyze..."
"Compare..."
"Evaluate..."
"Judge..."

CREATIVE
"Create..."
"Invent..."
"Design..."
"Imagine..."

PRACTICAL
"Apply..."
"Use..."
"Implement..."
"Put into practice..."

Figure 11.4 Sternberg's triarchic theory of intelligence.

How Intelligence Relates to the Internal World

This part of the theory emphasizes the processing of information, which can be viewed in terms of three kinds of components: **metacomponents**—executive processes (i.e., metacognition) used to plan, monitor, and evaluate problem solving; **performance components**—lower-order processes used to implement the commands of the metacomponents; and **knowledge-acquisition components**—the processes used to learn how to solve the problems in the first place. The components are highly interdependent.

Suppose that you were asked to write a term paper. You would use metacomponents to decide on a topic, plan the paper, monitor the writing, and evaluate how well your finished product succeeded in accomplishing your goals for it. You would use knowledge-acquisition components for research to learn about the topic and performance components for the actual writing. In practice, the three kinds of components do not function in isolation. Before you actually wrote the paper, you would have to decide on a topic and then do some research. Similarly, your plans for writing the paper might change as you gathered new information, since you might find that there just is not enough information on particular aspects of the chosen topic and would hence be forced to shift your emphasis. Your plans might also change if particular aspects of the writing went more smoothly than other aspects.

How Intelligence Relates to Experience

In addition, the theory considers how experience may interact with all three kinds of information-processing components. That is, each of us faces tasks and situations with which we have various levels of experience, ranging from a completely novel task, with which we have no experience, to a completely familiar task, with which we have vast, extensive experience. As a task becomes increasingly familiar, many aspects of it may become *automatic*, requiring little conscious effort to determine what step to take next and how to implement it. A novel task makes different demands on intelligence from those of a task for which automatic procedures have been developed.

According to the triarchic theory, relatively novel tasks—such as visiting a foreign country, mastering a new subject, or acquiring a foreign language—demand more of a person's intelligence. On the other hand, a completely unfamiliar task may demand so much of the person as to be overwhelming. For example, if you were visiting a foreign country, you would probably not profit from enrolling in a course with unfamiliar, abstract subject matter, taught in a language you do not understand. The most intellectually stimulating tasks are those that are challenging and demanding but not overwhelming.

How Intelligence Relates to the External World

The triarchic theory also proposes that the various components of intelligence are applied to experience in order to serve three functions in real-world contexts: adapting ourselves to our existing environments, shaping our existing environments to create new environments, and selecting new environments. You use adaptation when you learn the ropes in a new environment and try to figure out how to succeed in it. For example, when you enter college, you probably try to figure out the explicit and implicit rules of college life and how you can use these rules to succeed in the new environment. You also shape your environment, such as by deciding which courses to take and which activities to pursue. You may even try to shape the behavior of those around you. Finally, if you are unable either to adapt yourself or to shape your environment to suit you, you may consider selecting another environment—such as by transferring to a different college.

According to the triarchic theory, people may apply their intelligence to many different kinds of problems. For example, some people may be more intelligent in the face of abstract, academic problems, whereas others may be more intelligent in the face of concrete, practical problems. The theory does not define an intelligent person as someone who necessarily excels in all aspects of intelligence. Rather, intelligent persons know their own strengths and weaknesses and find ways to capitalize on their strengths and either to compensate for or to remediate their weaknesses. For example, a person who is stronger in psychology than in physics may choose as a physics project the creation of a physics aptitude test. The point is to make the most of your strengths and to find ways to improve on or at least to live comfortably with your weaknesses.

In a comprehensive study on the validity of the triarchic theory and its usefulness in improving performance, matching students' instruction and assessment to their abilities did indeed lead to improved performance (Sternberg & Clinkenbeard, 1995; Sternberg, Ferrari, Clinkenbeard, & Grigorenko, 1996; Sternberg, Grigorenko, Ferrari, & Clinkenbeard, 1999). Teaching all the students to use all their analytic, creative, and practical abilities also resulted in improved school acheivement for all the students, whatever their ability pattern (Sternberg, Torff, & Grigorenko, 1998). One important consideration in light of such findings is the need for changes in the assessment of intelligence (Sternberg & Kaufman, 1996). Current measures of intelligence are one-sided, measuring mostly analytic abilities with little or no assessment of the creative and practical aspects of intelligence. A more well-rounded assessment and instructional system could lead to greater benefits of education for a wider variety of students—a nominal goal of education.

Thus far, we have described various models of human intelligence, mentioning only briefly that humans have tried to program computers to simulate various aspects of intelligence. Before we conclude this discussion of intelligence, we discuss artificial intelligence. As this chapter has shown, cognitive psychologists have learned much about human intelligence by attempting to understand and even to create artificial intelligence.

ARTIFICIAL INTELLIGENCE

Much of the early information-processing research centered on work based on computer simulations of human intelligence, as well as on computer systems that use optimal methods to solve tasks. Programs of both kinds can be classified as examples of *artificial intelligence (AI)*. Computers cannot actually think; they must be programmed to behave as though they are thinking, that is, to simulate cognitive processes. In this way, they give us insight into the details of how people process information cognitively. Essentially, computers are just pieces of *hardware*—physical components of equipment—that respond to instructions. Other kinds of hardware (other pieces of equipment) also respond to instructions; for example, if you can figure out how to give the instructions, a VCR will respond to your instructions and will do what you tell it to do.

What makes computers so interesting to researchers is that they can be given highly complex instructions, known as computer programs or even more commonly as *software*, which tell the computer how to respond to new information. The new information may come from various sources:

1. The environment. For example, given the instruction, "When the temperature goes above 75 degrees Fahrenheit (<24 degrees centigrade), turn on the cooling system," a heat-sensing mechanism, and a connection to the cooling system, the program will implement the instruction when it receives environmental information that the temperature has exceeded 75 degrees.

2. Someone interacting with the computer. For instance, given the command to implement a set of instructions, "execute the spell-checking program," the program will do so.

3. The computer's own processes. For example, when implementing an instruction in a program, such as "Repeat this step until reaching a count of 10 iterations and then stop this step and proceed to the next step". Before we consider any AI programs, we need to consider seriously the issue of what, if anything, would lead us to describe a computer program as being "intelligent."

Can a Computer Program Be "Intelligent"?

The Turing Test

Probably the first serious attempt to deal with the issue of whether a computer program can be intelligent was made by Alan Turing (1963), based on ideas he first presented in 1950. Specifically, Turing devised a test by which a human could assess the intelligence of a respondent. The basic idea behind the Turing test is whether an observer can distinguish the performance of a computer from that of a human, whom everyone would agree is intelligent in at least some degree. In the specific form proposed by Turing, the test is conducted with a computer, a human respondent, and an interrogator. The interrogator has two different "conversations" with an interactive computer program. The goal of the interrogator is to figure out which of two parties is a person communicating through the computer and which is the computer itself. The interrogator can ask the two parties any questions at all. However, the computer will try to fool the interrogator into believing that it is human, whereas the human will try to show the interrogator that she or he truly is human. The computer passes the Turing test if an interrogator is unable to distinguish the computer from the human.

The Turing test is commonly used in assessing the intelligence of a computer program, but is not usually performed in quite the way that Turing described. For example, outputs of some kind generated by a computer may be scanned and assessed for their comparability to human performance. In some cases, human data from a problem-solving task are compared to computer-generated data, and the degree of relationship between them is evaluated. For instance, if a computer solves number-series problems, such as 1, 4, 9, 16, . . . (where each number is the next larger perfect square), the response times and error patterns of the computer can be compared to those of human participants who have solved the same problems (e.g., K. Kotovsky & Simon, 1973; Simon & K. Kotovsky, 1963). Of course, the response times of the computer are typically much faster than those of humans, but the researchers are less interested in overall reaction times than in patterns of reaction times. In other words, what matters is not whether computers take more time or less time on each problem than do humans, but whether the problems that take the computer relatively longer to solve also take humans relatively longer.

Sometimes, the goal of a computer model is not to match human performance, but to exceed it. In this case, maximum AI, rather than the simulation of human intelligence, is the program's goal. The criterion of whether computer performance matches that of humans is no longer relevant. Instead, the criterion of interest is that of how well the computer can perform the task assigned it. Computer programs that play chess, for example, typically play in a way that emphasizes "brute force," with the programs evaluating extremely large numbers of possible moves, many of which humans would never even consider evaluating (e.g., Berliner, 1969; Bernstein, 1958). Using brute force, and IBM program, "Deep Blue," beat world champion Gary Kasparov in a 1997 chess match. The same brute force method is used in programs that play checkers (e.g., Samuel, 1963). These programs are generally evaluated in terms of how well they can beat each other or, even more important, human contenders playing against them.

Having considered some issues of what constitutes an intelligent computer program, we now turn to some of the actual programs. The discussion of these programs will give you an idea of how AI research has evolved, as well as of how AI models have influenced the work of cognitive psychologists. As the preceding examples have shown, many early AI programs focused on problem solving.

The Logic Theorist

One of the earliest intelligent programs was formulated by Allen Newell, Clifford Shaw, and Herbert Simon (1957). This program, the Logic Theorist (LT), was designed to discover proofs for theorems in elementary symbolic logic. For example, the program might be asked to prove the theorem, If P or Q is true, then either B is true, or P or Q is true. LT was able to prove this theorem by comparing it to an *axiom* (a logical statement accepted as true): "If A is true, then B or A is true." (For example, "if it will rain, then either it will rain or it will snow" because for a logical *or* statement to be true, it is sufficient that either one—or even both—of its terms is true.)

To prove the original theorem, LT employed the *rule of substitution*. According to this rule, any expression may be substituted for any variable in any theorem, provided that the substitution is made throughout the theorem wherever that variable appears. LT proved the theorem by substituting "P" or "Q" for "A" in the logical axiom. Thus, the statement, If A is true, then B or A is true, becomes, If P or Q is true, then B or P or Q, is true, and the theorem is proved. By using the rule of substitution, LT showed that the theorem was logically equivalent to the axiom.

The example given here is relatively simple. However, using just four rules, including the rule of substitution, LT could prove theorems that were much more complicated. Thus, Newell and his colleagues showed how a machine could be programmed to do a task that formerly required a person with good background knowledge—as well as intelligence—to do. Although LT could prove logical theorems, it could not go beyond its narrow function to address other kinds of problems. Therefore, Newell and his colleagues wrote a program that went beyond the capabilities of LT to solve a broader range of problems.

The General Problem Solver

The new program, the General Problem Solver (GPS), was designed to solve a broader, more general range of kinds of problems than LT could solve (Newell, Shaw, & Simon, 1958). The assumption of this program is that the processing of information is domain general, to a large extent, rather than domain specific. Although GPS uses a number of different methods to solve problems, these methods generally draw on a single heuristic for problem solving. The heuristic GPS uses is *means-ends analysis*, which involves solving problems by successively reducing the difference between the present status (where you are now) and the goal status (where you want to be). Figure 11.5 presents a schematic **flow chart** (a model path for reaching a goal or solving a problem) for how GPS can transform one object (or one problem state) into another using means-ends analysis.

Means-ends analysis can be applied to a wide range of problems (e.g., the Monster Move problems described in Chapter 7). As it was formulated in the 1950s and 1960s, GPS could apply the heuristic to problems, such as proving logic theorems. The GPS program and the LT program were typical of the early work carried out at Carnegie Mellon University, but the Newell-Simon group at Carnegie was not the only group busy trying to create intelligent programs. At MIT, a group led primarily by Marvin Minsky, was also interested in creating AI programs. The MIT programs differed from the Carnegie programs in their greater emphasis

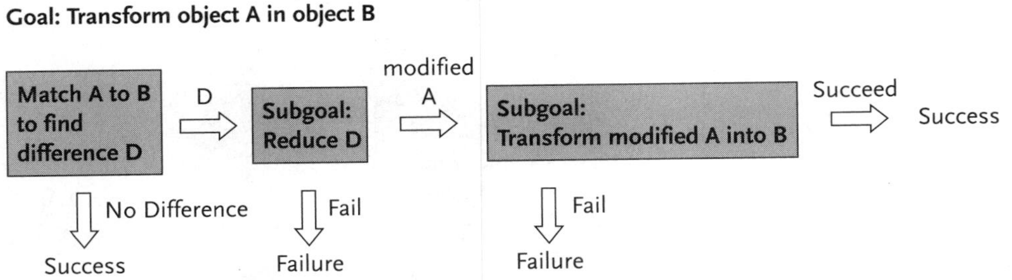

Figure 11.5 Flow chart.

on the retrieval of semantic information—that is, the use of meaningful verbal information (Minsky, 1968).

SHRDLU

By the early 1970s, MIT researcher Terry Winograd (1972) had developed SHRDLU, generally considered a landmark in AI. SHRDLU (named for a basic string of letters on traditional linotype machines used in printing) serves as the basis for operating a robot. Winograd's robot lives in a "block world," in which the tasks of "living" revolve around performing various manipulations on a set of blocks that differ in size, shape, and color (such as a green cube and a red pyramid). The operator of the program might, for example, instruct the robot (through the computer program) to pick up a big red block, which the robot would then pick up. Alternatively, the operator might ask the program how many blocks were not in the box, and the robot would respond with the number of blocks outside the box. Sometimes, the robot could not execute the program because the instructions were ambiguous and required clarification. For example, when asked what supported the pyramid, the robot would ask which of the two pyramids was being referenced. Also, the program would occasionally respond that it did not know an answer, as when asked whether a pyramid can support a pyramid.

SHRDLU processes information in terms of a block world. Other programs, however, operate in different worlds. One of the more interesting is that of a psychotherapist, on the one hand, and a patient, on the other.

Eliza and Parry

Two computer programs that operate in the world of psychotherapy are Eliza and Parry, the former taking on the role of a nondirective psychotherapist, and the latter taking on the role of a paranoid patient of a psychotherapist. The goal of the nondirective therapist is to elicit a patient's feelings, to reflect these feelings back to the patient, and to help the patient understand and figure out what to do about these feelings. Consider, for example, a segment of an interaction between Eliza and a patient shown in Table 11.2. In this segment, Eliza seems to show clinical insight about her patient. However, Eliza is not as bright as she appears here; she uses key words and phrases in the interlocutor's (patient's) remarks to choose her own remarks, without understanding in any larger sense what the patient is saying. Indeed, Joseph Weizenbaum (1966), of MIT, the creator of Eliza, chose the domain of nondirective psychotherapy because he believed it would be relatively easier to simulate the responses of a nondirective psychotherapist than of people in other occupations who more directively show their knowledge and expertise in their interactions with others.

If therapists can be simulated, why not patients? Kenneth Colby (1963), a psychiatrist, created a simulation of a paranoid patient who is especially concerned that the Mafia is after him, as shown in the segment of dialogue reproduced in Table 11.2. Colby's simulation of a paranoid is not just a set of responses that "sounds paranoid." Rather, the simulation is generated from a theory of the neurotic process of a paranoid that the primary intention of the paranoid is to determine another person's intentions. Messages from the other, classified as malevolent, benevolent, or neutral, are scanned to assist in this determination. The interpretation of malevolence, to which the paranoid is particularly susceptible, can emanate from a belief that the other intends either physical or psychological harm to the paranoid.

TABLE 11.2 Programs That Simulate Belief Systems: Eliza and Parry

Eliza	Parry
Men are all alike.	Why are you in the hospital?
IN WHAT WAY?	I SHOULDN'T BE HERE.
They're always bugging us about something or other.	Who brought you here?
CAN YOU THINK OF A SPECIFIC EXAMPLE?	THE POLICE.
Well, my boyfriend made me come here.	What trouble did you have with the police?
YOU'RE BOYFRIEND MADE YOU COME HERE.	COPS DON'T DO THEIR JOB.
He says I'm depressed much of the time.	What do they do instead?
I AM SORRY TO HEAR THAT YOU ARE DEPRESSED.	COPS ARREST THE WRONG PEOPLE.
It's true. I am unhappy.	They arrest the right ones sometimes.
DO YOU THINK COMING HERE WILL HELP YOU NOT TO BE UNHAPPY?	THE LAW SHOULD GET THOSE ITALIAN CROOKS.
I need some help, that much seems certain.	Are you Italian?
WHAT WOULD IT MEAN TO YOU IF YOU GOT SOME HELP?	MY BACKGROUND IS BRITISH, BUT I WAS BORN IN THIS COUNTRY.
Perhaps I could learn to get along with my mother.	Do you know any Italian crooks?
TELL ME MORE ABOUT YOUR FAMILY.	I TRY TO AVOID THE UNDERWORLD.
My mother takes care of me.	Are you afraid of the underworld?
WHO ELSE IN YOUR FAMILY TAKES CARE OF YOU?	THE MAFIA ARE THE WORST GANGSTERS.
My father.	Are you connected with the Mafia?
YOUR FATHER?	YOU KNOW, THEY KNOW ME.
You are like my father in some ways.	How do they know you?
WHAT RESEMBLANCE DO YOU SEE?	THEY SPY ON ME.
You are not very aggressive, but I think you don't want me to notice that.	Why do they?
WHAT MAKES YOU THINK I AM NOT VERY AGGRESSIVE?	THEY WANT TO GET FALSE EVIDENCE TO FRAME ME.
You don't argue with me.	What do they have against you?
WHY DO YOU THINK I DON'T ARGUE WITH YOU?	THEY ARE OUT TO GET ME.
You are afraid of me.	What for?
DOES IT PLEASE YOU TO THINK THAT I AM AFRAID OF YOU?	I HAVE INCRIMINATING EVIDENCE AGAINST THE MAFIA.
My father is afraid of everybody.	Are you sure of all this?
WHAT ELSE COMES TO MIND WHEN YOU THINK OF YOUR FATHER?	YOU DON'T BELIEVE ME?
Bullies.	I am doing my best.
DOES THAT HAVE ANYTHING TO DO WITH THE FACT THAT YOUR BOYFRIEND MADE YOU COME HERE?	(SILENCE ON THE "PATIENT'S" PART)
	(Silence on the psychiatrist's part)
	CAN'T YOU THINK OF A DECENT QUESTION TO ASK?
	You seem hostile to me.
	SOME OF YOUR REMARKS ANNOY ME.
	I am sorry.
	FORGET THE EXCUSES, YOU GUYS ARE ALL ALIKE.

Colby performed a more formal evaluation of his program than is typical. He asked a group of 33 psychiatrists to read transcripts of "interviews" with Parry and with actual paranoid patients. None of the psychiatrists was told that a computer model was involved. Roughly half of them rated the model as more paranoid than actual patients.

Colby's program differs from many other in that it simulates not just abstract cognitive processes, but a belief system. A more recent program by Colby employs cognitive therapy for the treatment of mild depression, using both a text and dialogue mode of interaction with a person (Colby, 1995).

Programs That Simulate Expertise

Unlike the East Coast research at MIT, and Carnegie Mellon, AI research on the West Coast, especially at Stanford, tended to emphasize **expert systems:** computer programs that can perform the way an expert does in a fairly specific domain. No attempt was made to model human intelligence more globally or even to extend the particular expert systems, even in theory. Rather, the researchers attempted to simulate performance in just one domain, often a narrow one, but at a level of expertise that surpasses what would be possible for a program that was fairly domain general.

For example, several programs were developed to diagnose various kinds of medical disorders. Such programs are obviously of enormous potential significance, given the high costs (financial and personal) of incorrect diagnoses. Probably the most well known and certainly the oldest of these programs is MYCIN, which can be used to detect and potentially even to treat certain bacterial infections (Buchanan & Shortliffe, 1984; Shortliffe, 1976). MYCIN processes the results of blood tests, such as the numbers of red and white blood cells or the amount of glucose in the blood. It then proposes a diagnosis of the disease and perhaps a drug treatment and even indicates the relative reliability of its diagnosis. MYCIN, which is based on the use of an organized system of if-then statements, contains roughly 500 rules (if-then statements) and can deal with about 100 different kinds of bacterial infections.

When MYCIN was tested for its validity in making diagnoses and treatment suggestions, it performance compared favorably with that of faculty members at the Stanford School of Medicine, and MYCIN outperformed medical students and residents at that school (Yu et al., 1984). Earlier, it was shown to be effective in prescribing medication for meningitis. Thus, within its relatively narrow domain of expertise, MYCIN is clearly an impressive expert system.

Another expert system that has been created for medical diagnoses is Internist-I (Miller, Pople, & Myers, 1982), which diagnoses a broader spectrum of diseases than does MYCIN, although within its broader domain, its diagnostic powers do not measure up to those of an experienced internist. This program illustrates what is sometimes termed the *bandwidth-fidelity problem.* The broader the bandwidth of a radio or other receiver, the poorer its fidelity (faithfulness, reliability) tends to be. Similarly, the wider the spectrum of problems to which an AI program addresses itself, the less reliable it is likely to be in solving any one of those kinds of problems.

Other expert systems solve other types of problems, including some of those found by scientists. For example, DENDRAL, another early expert system developed at Stanford, helps scientists identify the molecular structure of newly discovered organic compounds, and meta-DENDRAL, an enhanced version, finds new rules for the basic DENDRAL program to use in making these identifications (Buchanan et al., 1976).

Questions About the Intelligence of AI Programs

AI programs, such as the ones described here, are not without their critics, of course. Consider some of the main objections that have been raised to some of the aforementioned programs. Experts differ as to how much credence they give to these various objections. Ultimately, we all need to evaluate the objections for ourselves.

Some of the objections to AI pertain to the limitations of the existing hardware and software designs. For one thing, human brains can process many sources of information simultaneously. However, because of the architectural structure of computer hardware, most computers (virtually all early computers and even most contemporary ones) can handle only one instruction at a time. Hence, models based on computer simulations have tended to depend on *serial processing* (step by step, one at a time) of information. However, by linking various computers into neural networks of computers, it is now possible for computers to simulate *parallel processing* (multiple steps being performed simultaneously). Hence, the serial-processing limitation no longer applies to all computer-based models of AI.

Absence of Intuition

Another limitation of AI is related to a different characteristic of human intelligence: intuition. Hubert Dreyfus and Stuart Dreyfus (1990) argued that whereas computers can be good, competent manipulators of symbols according to prepackaged algorithms, they lack intuition. To these authors, intuition is found in the kinds of hunches that distinguish genuine experts from those with book knowledge, but without the expertise that will enable them to exploit their knowledge maximally when confronted with a difficult situation. Basically, Dreyfus and Dreyfus contended that computers excel in the mathematical and deductive aspect of thinking, but not in the intuitive one.

For example, a United Airlines DC-10 airliner once crash-landed when all three of its hydraulic systems were severed by debris from an engine that was torn off in midair and hit the tail of the plane, where the three hydraulic systems were interlinked. The pilot of the DC-10 radioed to technical headquarters for guidance about what to do when all three hydraulic systems go down. The technical experts were unable to help the crew because they had never encountered the situation before and had no guidelines to follow. Nevertheless, the crew working on intuition, managed to steer the plane roughly by varying the engine thrust. The news media and others applauded the pilot and his crew for their intuitions as to what to do in the face of a problem for which there were no guidelines and for which no computer program had been written. As a result of these intuitions, roughly two thirds of the passengers in the plane survived the crash landing.

The argument that computers cannot show intuitive intelligence has not gone unchallenged. Several researchers who are interested in human problem solving have studied computer simulations of problem solving, and their research has led them to infer that at least some characteristics of intuition can be modeled on computers. For example, Pat Langley, Herbert Simon, Gary Bradshaw, and Jan Zytkow (1987) wrote a set of programs (the "Bacon" programs) simulating the processes involved in various important scientific discoveries in the past. They argued that their programs do display intuition, and moreover, that there is nothing mystical about intuition. Rather, according to these researchers, intuition can be understood in terms of the same information-processing mechanisms that are applied to conventional forms of problem solving.

Along a similar line, John Holland, Keith Holyoak, Richard Nisbett, and Paul Thagard (1986) simulated large parts of a theory of how we reason inductively, going beyond the information given in a problem to come up with a solution that is not deductively determined by the problem's elements. One can easily argue that such a program is intuitive, at least in some sense, in that it goes beyond the information given. Other programs also make inferences that go well beyond the simple facts stored in their data bases.

Intelligence Versus the Appearance of Intelligence

Perhaps a more fundamental challenge to AI came from a philosopher, rather than a cognitive psychologist. John Searle (1980) objected to the basic idea that computers can be considered truly intelligent and used what is known as the "Chinese Room" problem to make his point. Imagine that Searle is locked in a room and is given a large batch of Chinese writing to translate. He knows no Chinese at all. However, suppose that, in addition to the Chinese writing, Searle is given a second batch of Chinese script with a set of rules for translating the Chinese into English. Next, Searle is given a third batch, which contains a set of rules for formulating responses to questions that were raised in the first batch of Chinese writing. Searle then responds to the original, first batch of writing, with a response that makes sense and is in perfect Chinese. Presumably, over time, Searle could become so good at manipulating the rules that his responses would be every bit as good as those of a native Chinese speaker who understood exactly what was being asked. However, in fact, Searle still knows no Chinese at all. He is simply following a set of rules.

According to Searle, programs that seem to understand various kinds of inputs and then to respond in an intelligent way (such as Winograd's SHRDLU) are like Searle in the Chinese room. The computers understand the input being given to them no better than Searle understands Chinese. They are simply operating according to a set of preprogrammed rules. Searle's notion is that the computer does not really see and understand the connections between input and output but, rather, uses preestablished connections that make it seem intelligent on the surface. To Searle, these programs do not demonstrate AI—they only *appear* to show intelligence.

Predictably, AI researchers have not competed with each other to be the first to accept Searle's argument and to acknowledge the folly of their attempts to model AI. A number of them have responded to Searle's charge that the computer is not anything like what it is cracked up to be. Robert Abelson (1980), for example, argued that Searle's use of the rule systems in the second and third batches of input is, in fact, intelligent. He further contended that children who are learning a language also first apply rules blindly, only later coming to understand them and how they are being used. Others have argued that the system as a whole (comprising Searle and the set of instructions) does indeed exhibit understanding. In addition, some computer programs have even shown an ability to simulate at least a modest degree of skill development and knowledge acquisition, although existing computer programs do not begin to approach our human ability to enhance our own intelligence.

TEACHING INTELLIGENCE

Although designers of AI have made great strides in creating programs that simulate the acquisition of knowledge and skills, no existing program even approaches the ability of the human brain to enhance its own intelligence. Human intelligence is highly *malleable*—it can be shaped and even increased through various kinds of interventions (Detterman & Sternberg, 1982; Grotzer & Perkins, 2000; Perkins, 1997; Perkins & Grotzer, 1997; Sternberg et al., 1996; Sternberg, Powell, McGrane, & McGregor, 1997). Moreover, the malleability of intelligence has nothing to do with the extent to which intelligence has a genetic basis (Sternberg, 1997). An attribute (such as height) can be partly or even largely genetically based and yet be environmentally malleable.

The Head Start program was initiated in the 1960s to give preschoolers an edge on intellectual abilities and accomplishments when they started school. Long-term follow-ups have indicated that by midadolescence, children who participated in the program were more than a grade ahead of matched controls who did not receive the program (Lazar & Darlington, 1982; Zigler & Berman, 1983). The children in the program also scored higher on a variety of tests of scholastic achievement, were less likely to need remedial attention, and were less likely to have behavioral problems. Although such measures are not truly measures of intelligence, they show strong positive correlations with intelligence tests.

A number of newer programs have also had some success. One such program, Reuven Feuerstein's (1980) *Instrumental Enrichment* program, involves training in a variety of abstract-reasoning skills and appears to be particularly effective for improving the skills of retarded performers. Another program, the *Odyssey* program (see Adams, 1986), has been found to be effective in raising the intellectual performance of Venezuelan children of junior high school age. The *Philosophy for Children* program (Lipman, Sharp, & Oscanyan, 1980) has been shown to teach logical thinking skills to children throughout the primary and secondary levels of schooling. Aspects of the *Intelligence Applied* program (Sternberg, 1986) for teaching intellectual skills have been shown to improve both insight skills (Davidson & Sternberg, 1984) and the ability to learn meanings of words from context, a primary means of acquiring new vocabulary (Sternberg, 1987a). Practical intelligence can also be taught (Gardner, Krechevsky, Sternberg, & Okagaki, 1994; Sternberg, Okagaki, & Jackson, 1990).

An alternative to intellectual enrichment outside the home may be to provide an enriched home environment. Support for the importance of the home environment in developing the intelligence in young children was found by Robert Bradley and Bettye Caldwell (1984). These researchers found that several factors in the early (preschool) home environment appear to be correlated with high IQ scores: the emotional and verbal *responsivity* of the primary caregiver and the caregiver's *involvement* with the child, *avoidance of restriction* and punishment, *organization* of the physical environment and activity schedule, provision of appropriate play *materials*, and opportunities for *variety* in daily stimulation. Furthermore, Bradley and Caldwell found that these factors more effectively predicted IQ scores than did socioeconomic status or family-structure variables. It should be noted, however, that the Bradley-Caldwell study was correlational and therefore cannot be interpreted as indicating causality. Furthermore, their study pertained to preschool children, and children's IQ scores do not begin to predict adult IQ scores well until age 4. Moreover, before age 7, the scores are not stable (B. S. Bloom, 1964). More recent work (e.g., Pianta & Egeland, 1994) suggested that factors, such as maternal social support and interactive behavior, may play a key role in the instability of scores on tests of intellectual ability between ages 2 and 8.

The Bradley and Caldwell data should not be taken to indicate that demographic variables have little effect on IQ scores. To the contrary, throughout history and across cultures, many groups of people have been assigned pariah status as inferior members of the social order.

Across cultures, the scores of these disadvantaged groups (e.g., native Maoris versus European New Zealanders) have differed on tests of intelligence and aptitude (Steele, 1990; Zeidner, 1990). Such was the case of the Buraku-min tanners in Japan, who, in 1871, were granted emancipation but not full acceptance into Japanese society. Despite their poor performance and underprivileged status in Japan, those who immigrate to America—and are treated like other Japanese immigrants—perform on IQ tests and in school achievement at a level comparable to that of their fellow Japanese Americans (Ogbu, 1986).

Similar positive effects of integration were found on the other side of the world. In Israel, the children of European Jews score much higher on IQ tests than do the children of Yemenite Jews—except when the children are reared on kibbutzim in which the children of all national ancestries are raised by specially trained caregivers in dwellings separate from their parents. When these children shared the same child-rearing environments, there were no national ancestry-related differences in IQ (Smilansky, 1974).

Perhaps the strongest evidence in favor of environmental effects on intelligence comes from work on the so-called *Flynn effect* (Flynn, 1984, 1987, 1994, 1998; Neisser, 1998). The basic phenomenon is that IQ has increased over successive generations around the world through most of the century—at least since 1930. The effect must be environmental because, obviously, a successive stream of genetic mutations could not have taken hold and exerted such an effect over such a short time. The effect is powerful—at least 15 points of IQ per generation for tests of fluid intelligence and 9 points per generation overall. It has occured virtually all over the world. The effect has been shown to be greater for tests of fluid intelligence than for tests of crystallized intelligence. The difference, if linearly extrapolated (a hazardous procedure, at best), would suggest that a person who in 1892 scored at the 90th percentile on the Raven Progressive Matrices, a test of fluid intelligence, in 1982 would, have scored at the 5th percentile in 1992.

There have been no conclusive explanations of the Flynn effect. A symposium dedicated to understanding the cause of the effect (Neisser, 1998) resulted in many possible explanations: increased schooling, increased technology, use of video games, greater educational attainment of parents, better nutrition, and less childhood disease, among others. But it is still an open question as to why the effect occurs and is so strong.

Altogether, there is now abundant evidence that people's environments (e.g., Ceci, Nightingale, & Baker, 1992; T. E. Reed, 1993; Sternberg & Wagner, 1994), motivation (e.g., Collier, 1994; Sternberg & Ruzgis, 1994), and training (e.g., Feuerstein, 1980; Sternberg, 1987b) can profoundly affect their intellectual skills. Thus, the controversial claims made by Herrnstein and Murray (1994) in their book, *The Bell Curve*, regarding the futility of intervention programs, are unfounded when one considers the evidence in favor of the possibility of improving cognitive skills. Likewise, Herrnstein and Murray's appeal to "a genetic factor in cognitive ethnic differences" (p. 270) falls apart in light of the direct evidence against such genetic differences (see Sternberg, 1996) and is a result of the misunderstanding of the heritability of traits in general.

Heredity may set some kind of upper limit on how intelligent a person may become. However, we now know that for any attribute that is partly genetic, there is a *reaction range*—that is, the attribute can be expressed in various ways within broad limits of possibilities. Thus, each person's intelligence can be developed further within this broad range of potential intelligence. We have no reason to believe that people now reach their upper limits in the development of their intellectual skills. To the contrary, the evidence suggests that we can do quite a bit to help people become more intelligent (for further discussion of these issues, see Sternberg, 1995a; see also Neisser et al., 1996).

Ultimately, what we do to help people become more intelligent is to help them to better perceive, learn, remember, represent information, reason, decide, and solve problems. In other words, what we do is to help them improve the cognitive functions that have been the focus of this book. The connection between improving intelligence and improving cognition is not a casual one. On the contrary, complex cognition forms the core of human intelligence, and thus intelligence is a construct that helps us unify all the diverse aspects of cognition. Although cultural and other contextual factors may influence the expression of our intelligence (e.g., behavior that is considered intelligent in one culture may be considered unintelligent in another culture), the cognitive processes underlying behavior are the same: In every culture, people need to learn, to reason, to solve problems, and so on. Thus, when we study complex cognition, we are learning about the fundamental core of human intelligence that helps people the world over to adapt to their environmental circumstances, no matter how different those circumstances may be. No wonder, then, that the study of complex cognition is so fundamental to psychology, in particular, and to the understanding of human behavior, in general.

◆ SUMMARY

From the start of research on intelligence, interest centered on how to conceptualize and measure intelligence. Galton and his followers emphasized the importance of psychophysical acuity, whereas Binet and his followers emphasized judgment. Two common themes that run through the definitions of intelligence proposed by many experts are the capacity to learn from experience and the ability to adapt to the environment. In addition, the importance of metacognition and of cultural context are increasingly recognized by researchers and theorists of intelligence. Nonetheless, psychologists often disagree on the relative importance of context (nurture) versus inheritance (nature) in determining intelligence. Also, different researchers disagree about whether to focus on studying the structures of intelligence (e.g., Spearman, Thurstone, and Cattell) or the processes of intelligence (e.g., Hunt, Jensen, and Simon). Some researchers (e.g., Gardner and Sternberg) have tried to integrate the various approaches to intelligence into comprehensive systems models of intelligence. One approach to intelligence is to understand it in terms of *factor analysis,* a statistical technique that seeks to identify latent sources of individual differences in performance on tests. Some of the principal factor-analytic models of the mind are the *g*-factor model of Spearman, the primary-mental-abilities model of Thurstone, the *structure-of-intellect (SOI)* model of Guilford, and the hierarchical models of Cattell, of Vernon, and of Carroll, among others.

An alternative approach to intelligence is to understand it in terms of information processing. Information-processing theorists have sought to understand intelligence in terms of such constructs as inspection time, choice reaction time, speed of lexical access, the ability to divide attention successfully, the components of reasoning and problem solving, and complex problem solving that can be simulated via computers. A related approach is the biological model, which uses increasingly sophisticated means of viewing the brain while the brain is engaged in intelligent behaviors. Preliminary findings suggest that the speed of neural conduction may play a role in intelligence. Particularly intriguing are findings that neural efficiency and the specialization of cerebral function may be influential in intelligent cognitive processing. Some studies have found a correlation between brain size and intelligence. Intelligence is heritable, at least in part, but genes always express themselves through the environment.

Another main approach to understanding intelligence (based on an anthropological model) is the *contextual approach,* according to which intelligence is viewed as wholly or partly determined by cultural values. Contextual theorists differ in the extent to which they believe that the meaning of intelligence differs from one culture to another. What is considered to be intelligent behavior is, to some extent, *culturally relative:* The same behavior that is considered to be intelligent in one culture may be considered unintelligent in another culture. It is difficult—perhaps impossible—to create a test of intelligence that is *culture fair*—that is, equally fair for members of different cultures—because members of different cultures have different conceptions of what constitutes intelligent behavior.

Systems models of intelligence seek to go beyond cultural content. Gardner's *theory of multiple intelligences* specifies that intelligence is not a unitary construct, but rather that there are multiple intelligences, each relatively independent of the others. Sternberg's *triarchic theory of human intelligence* conceives of intelligence in terms of information-processing components, which are applied to experience to serve the functions of adaptation to the environment, shaping of the environment, and the selection of new environments.

AI research is conducted on the premise that it is both possible and valuable to have machines simulate intelligence. The Turing test is designed to evaluate the extent to which particular AI programs have succeeded in simulating humanlike intelligence. Critics of AI, however, question both the possibility and the worth of trying to get machines to simulate human intelligence, sometimes using the Chinese Room problem to illustrate a distinction between simulated intelligence and true understanding. Arguments can be made to support either perspective. Of the many now-classic AI programs that have been developed, among the earliest ones are the LT, which proves theorems in symbolic logic, and the GPS, which solves various kinds of problems using means-ends analysis. A later program was SHRDLU, which simulated a robot performing various operations in a block world, such as placing one block on top of another or placing a block in a box. Programs that model belief systems include Eliza, designed to simulate a nondirective psychotherapist; and PARRY, designed to simulate the thinking of a paranoid psychiatric patient. *Expert systems*, programs designed to demonstrate expertise, include MYCIN, which diagnoses certain bacterial diseases by analyzing the results of blood tests, and DENDRAL, which analyzes the structure of organic compounds.

Intellectual skills can be taught. Thus, intelligence is malleable rather than fixed. Although researchers largely agree that some improvements are possible, they disagree regarding both the degree to which they believe that such improvements can be achieved, and the means by which to do so. Some studies have shown that people who are taught in ways that take into account their patterns of abilities achieve at higher levels in school. The Flynn effect, by which IQs have been rising at least through most of the twentieth century, demonstrates the importance of the environment for the development of intelligence.

12 Creativity

Creativity is the ability to produce work that is novel (original and unexpected), high in quality, and appropriate (useful and meets the task constraints of tasks) (Lubart, 1994; Ochse, 1990; Sternberg, 1988, 1999b; Sternberg & Lubart, 1995, 1996). Creativity is a topic of wide scope that is important at both the individual and societal levels for a wide range of task domains. At an individual level, it is relevant, for example, when solving problems on the job and in daily life. At a societal level, creativity can lead to new scientific findings, new movements in art, new inventions, and new social programs. The economic importance of creativity is clear because new products or services create jobs. Furthermore, individuals, organizations, and societies must adapt existing resources to the changing demands of tasks to remain competitive.

CREATIVITY AS A NEGLECTED RESEARCH TOPIC

As the first half of the 20th century gave way to the second half, J. P. Guilford (1950), in his Presidential Address to the American Psychological Association (APA), challenged psychol-

This chapter draws on collaborative work with Todd I. Lubart (Sternberg & Lubart, 1996) and with Linda O'Hara (Sternberg & O'Hara, 1999).

ogists to pay attention to what he found to be a neglected but extremely important attribute, namely, creativity. He reported that less than two-tenths of 1% of the entries in *Psychological Abstracts* up to 1950 focused on creativity.

Interest in creativity research began to grow somewhat in the 1950s, and a few research institutes that were concerned with creativity were founded. However, several indicators of work on creativity show that it remained a relatively marginal topic in psychology, at least until recently. Sternberg and Lubart (1996) analyzed the number of references to creativity in *Psychological Abstracts* from 1975 to 1994. To conduct this analysis, they searched the computerized PsychLit database of journal articles using the database keywords of *creativity*, *divergent thinking*, and *creativity measurement.*—terms that are assigned by the database to articles whose content concerns primarily the subject of creativity. They also identified additional entries that contained the word stem "creativ-" somewhere in the title or abstract of the article but were not indexed by one of the keywords for creativity. They examined a random subset of these additional entries and found that they did not concern creativity to any notable extent and should be excluded from the set of articles on creativity. The result of this analysis is that approximately one half of 1% of the articles indexed in *Psychological Abstracts* from 1975 to 1994 concerned creativity. For comparative purposes, articles on reading accounted for approximately 1.5% of the entries in *Psychological Abstracts* during the same 20-year period—three times the proportion for creativity.

If we look at introductory psychology textbooks as another index, we find that creativity is barely covered. Whereas intelligence, for example, gets a chapter or a major part of one, creativity gets a few paragraphs, if that (e.g., Gleitman, 1986). Courses on creativity are rarely given in major psychology programs, although they are sometimes offered in educational psychology programs.

If creativity is so important to society, why has it traditionally been one of psychology's orphans? We believe that, historically, the study of creativity has had several strikes against it. We attempt to elicit what these strikes may be by briefly reviewing some of the history of the study of creativity (see Albert & Runco, 1999, for more details). In the analysis, we consider several of the main approaches to studying creativity, including the mystical, pragmatic, psychoanalytic, psychometric, cognitive, and social-personality approaches. We then consider what we believe to be the most promising approach for future work on creativity: the confluence approach.

MYSTICAL APPROACHES

The study of creativity has always been tinged—some may say tainted—with associations to mystical beliefs. Perhaps the earliest accounts of creativity were based on divine intervention. The creative person was seen as an empty vessel that a divine being would fill with inspiration. The individual would then pour out the inspired ideas, forming an otherworldly product.

In this vein, Plato argued that a poet is able to create only that which the muse dictates, and even today, people sometimes refer to their own muse as a source of inspiration. In Plato's view, one person may be inspired to create choral songs and another, epic poems (Rothenberg & Hausman, 1976). Often, mystical sources have been suggested in creators' introspective reports (Ghiselin, 1985). For example, Kipling (1937/1985, p. 162) referred to the "Daemon" that lives in the writer's pen: "My Daemon was with me in the Jungle Books, Kim, and both Puck books, and good care I took to walk delicately, lest he should withdraw. . . . When your Daemon is in charge, do not think consciously. Drift, wait, and obey."

The mystical approaches to the study of creativity have probably made it harder for scientists to be heard. Many people seem to believe, as they believe regarding love (see Sternberg, 1988), that creativity does not lend itself to scientific study because it is a more spiritual process. We believe that it has been difficult for scientific work to shake the deep-seated view of some that in studying creativity, scientists are treading where they should not.

PRAGMATIC APPROACHES

Equally damaging to the scientific study of creativity, in our view, has been the takeover of the field, in the popular mind, by those who follow what may be called the pragmatic approach. Those who take this approach have been concerned primarily with developing creativity, secondarily with understanding it, but almost not at all with testing the validity of their ideas about it.

Perhaps the foremost proponent of this approach is De Bono, whose work on *lateral thinking*—seeing things broadly and from varied viewpoints—as well as other aspects of creativity has had what appears to be considerable commercial success (e.g., deBono, 1971, 1985, 1992). DeBono's concern is not with theory, but with practice. Thus, for example, he suggests using a tool, such as plus, minus, interesting (PMI) to focus on the aspects of an idea that are pluses, minuses, and interesting. Or he suggests using the word *po*, derived from *hypothesis*, *suppose, possible,* and *poetry,* to provoke, rather than judge, ideas. Another tool, that of "thinking hats," has individuals metaphorically wear different hats, such as a white hat for data-based thinking, a red hat for intuitive thinking, a black hat for critical thinking, and a green hat for generative thinking, to stimulate seeing things from different points of view.

DeBono is not alone in this enterprise. On the basis of his experiences in advertising agencies, Osborn (1953) developed the technique of brainstorming to encourage people to solve problems creatively by seeking many possible solutions in an atmosphere that is constructive, rather than critical and inhibitory. Gordon (1961) developed a method called synectics, which mainly involves seeing analogies, also for stimulating creative thinking.

More recently, authors, such as Adams (1986) and von Oech (1983), have suggested that people often construct a series of false beliefs that interfere with creative functioning (for example, that some people believe that there is only one "right" answer and that ambiguity must be avoided whenever possible). They have also noted that people can become creative by identifying and removing these mental blocks. Von Oech (1986) suggested that we need to adopt the roles of explorer, artist, judge, and warrior to foster our creative productivity.

These approaches have had considerable public visibility, in much the way that Leo Buscaglia gave visibility to the study of love. And they may well be useful. From our point of view as psychologists, however, the approaches lack any basis in serious psychological theory or serious empirical attempts to validate them. Of course, techniques can work in the absence of psychological theory or validation. But the effect of such approaches is often to leave people associating a phenomenon with commercialization and to see it as less than a serious endeavor for psychological study.

THE PSYCHODYNAMIC APPROACH

The psychodynamic approach can be considered the first of the major 20th-century theoretical approaches to the study of creativity. Based on the idea that creativity arises from the tension between conscious reality and unconscious drives, Freud (1908/1959) proposed that writers and artists produce creative work as a way of expressing their unconscious wishes in a publicly acceptable fashion. These unconscious wishes may concern power, riches, fame, honor, or love (P. E. Vernon, 1970). Freud (1910/1964) used case studies of eminent creators, such as Leonardo da Vinci, to support these ideas.

Later, the psychoanalytic approach introduced the concepts of adaptive regression and elaboration for creativity (Kris, 1952). *Adaptive regression*, the primary process, refers to the intrusion of unmodulated thoughts in consciousness. Unmodulated thoughts can occur during active problem solving, but often occur during sleep, intoxication from drugs, fantasies or daydreams, or psychoses. *Elaboration*, the secondary process, refers to the reworking and transformation of primary-process material through reality-oriented, ego-controlled thinking. Other theorists (e.g., Kubie, 1958) emphasized that the preconscious, which falls between conscious reality and the encrypted unconscious, is the true source of creativity because thoughts are loose and vague but interpretable. In contrast to Freud, Kubie claimed that unconscious conflicts actually have a negative effect on creativity because they lead to fixated, repetitive thoughts. Later work recognized the importance of both primary and secondary processes (Noy, 1969; Rothenberg, 1979; Werner & Kaplan, 1963).

Although the psychodynamic approach may have offered some insights into creativity, psychodynamic theory was not at the center of the emerging scientific psychology. The early 20th-century schools of psychology, such as structuralism, functionalism, and behaviorism, devoted practically no resources to the study of creativity. The Gestaltists studied a portion of creativity—insight—but their study never went much beyond labeling, as opposed to characterizing the nature of insight.

Further isolating creativity research, the psychodynamic approach and other early work on creativity relied on case studies of eminent creators. This methodology has been criticized historically because of the difficulty of measuring proposed theoretical constructs (such as primary process thought), and the amount of selection and interpretation that can occur in a case study (Weisberg, 1993). Although there is nothing a priori wrong with case study methods, the emerging scientific psychology valued controlled, experimental methods. Thus, both theoretical and methodological issues served to isolate the study of creativity from mainstream psychology.

PSYCHOMETRIC APPROACHES

When we think of creativity, eminent artists or scientists, such as Michelangelo or Albert Einstein, immediately come to mind. However, these highly creative people are rare and difficult to study in the psychological laboratory. In his APA address, Guilford (1950) noted that the difficulty of studying creativity had limited research on creativity. He proposed that creativity could be studied in everyday subjects using paper-and-pencil tasks, such as the unusual uses test, in which an examinee thinks of as many uses for a common object (such as a brick) as possible. Many researchers adopted Guilford's suggestion, and "divergent thinking" tasks quickly became the main instruments for measuring creative thinking. The tests were a convenient way of comparing people on a standard "creativity" scale.

Building on Guilford's work, Torrance (1974) developed the Torrance Tests of Creative Thinking. These tests consist of several relatively simple verbal and figural tasks that involve divergent thinking plus other problem-solving skills. They can be scored for fluency (total number of relevant responses), flexibility (number of different categories of relevant responses), originality (the statistical rarity of the responses), and elaboration (amount of detail in the responses). Some of the subtests of the Torrance battery are these:

1. Asking questions: The examinee writes out all the questions he or she can think of, based on a drawing of a scene.

2. Product improvement: The examinee lists ways to change a toy monkey so that children will have more fun playing with it.

3. Unusual uses: The examinee lists interesting and unusual uses of a cardboard box.

4. Circles: The examinee expands empty circles into different drawings and titles them.

C. Cox (1926), working with Lewis Terman, believed that exceptionally creative people are also exceptionally intelligent. She published IQ estimates for 301 of the most eminent persons who lived between 1450 and 1850, selected from a list of, 1000 prepared by James McKeen Cattell, who determined eminence by the amount of space allotted in biographical dictionaries. From Cattell's list, they deleted persons from the hereditary aristocracy and nobility unless those individuals distinguished themselves beyond status owing to their birth, those born before 1450, those with ranks over 510 on the original list, and 11 names for whom no records were available. These deletions left 282 persons whose IQs were summarized as Group A. In addition, they discussed a Group B, which consisted of 19 miscellaneous cases from those with ranks over 510 on the original list, bringing the total to 301.

To estimate IQ, Cox, Terman, and Maud Merrill (Cox, 1926) examined biographies, letters, and other writings and records for evidence of the earliest period of instruction; the nature of the earliest learning; the earliest productions; age of first reading and of first mathematical performance; typical precocious activities; unusually intelligent applications of knowledge; the recognition of similarities or differences; the amount and character of the reading; the range of interests; school standing and progress; early maturity of attitude or judgment; the tendency to discriminate, to generalize, or to theorize; and family standing. Their IQ estimates are, of course, necessarily subjective. In a sense, though, the estimates have an ecological validity with regard to real-life intelligence that is not seen in standard IQ tests. The reported IQs were the average of the ratings of three experts—Cox, Terman, and Merrill. Interrater reliability was .90 for the childhood estimate and .89 for the young adulthood estimate (calculated from intercorrelations in Cox, 1926, pp. 67–68).

An example of some of the factors that contributed to their estimates can be seen in a description of Francis Galton (not in the list; he was born in 1822 and published *Hereditary Genius* in 1869), whose IQ Terman estimated to be 200. "Francis knew his capital letters by twelve months and both his alphabets by eighteen months; . . . he could read a little book, *Cobwebs to Catch Flies*, when $2^1/_2$ years old, and could sign his name before 3 years" (quoted in Cox, 1926, pp. 41–42). By age 4 Galton could say all the Latin substantives and adjectives and active verbs, could add and multiply, read a little French, and knew how to tell time. At 5, he was quoting from Walter Scott. By 6, he was familiar with the *Iliad* and the *Odyssey*.

At 7, he was reading Shakespeare for fun and could memorize a page by reading it twice. Clearly, Galton's record was exceptional.

Cox concluded that the average IQs of the group, 135 for childhood and 145 for young adulthood, were probably too low because of instructions to regress toward the mean of 100 for unselected populations (whereas this group's means were 135 and 145) whenever data were unavailable. Also, the unreliability of the data may have caused regression to the mean. One of the problems Cox noted in the data was a strong correlation, .77, between IQ and the reliability of the available data: The more reliable the data, the higher the IQ, and the higher the IQ, the more reliable the data on which it was based. She concluded that if more reliable data had been available, all the IQs would have been estimated to be higher. Therefore, she corrected the original estimates, bringing the group average up to 155 for childhood and 165 for young adulthood.

As Cox was careful to point out, the IQs are estimates not of the actual person's IQ but, rather, of the record of that person. "The IQ of Newton or of Lincoln recorded in these pages is the IQ of the Newton or of the Lincoln of whom we have records. But the records are admittedly incomplete" (Cox, 1926, p. 8).

Cox found the correlation between IQ and rank order of eminence to be .16, plus or minus .039 (Cox, 1926, p. 55), after correcting for unreliability of the data. Simonton (1976) reexamined Cox's data using multiple regression techniques. He showed that the correlation between intelligence and ranked eminence that Cox found was an artifact of the unreliability of the data and, especially, of a time-wise sampling bias—those who were born more recently had both lower estimated IQs and lower ranks of estimated eminence. In Simonton's (1976, pp. 223–224) analysis, the relationship between intelligence and ranked eminence was zero if birth year was controlled for. In any case, Cox (1926, p. 187) recognized the role of factors other than IQ in eminence and concluded that "high but not the highest intelligence, combined with the greatest degree of persistence, will achieve greater eminence than the highest degree of intelligence with somewhat less persistence."

Three basic findings concerning conventional conceptions of intelligence as measured by IQ and creativity are generally agreed upon (see, e.g., Barron & Harrington, 1981; Lubart, 1994). First, creative people tend to have above-average IQs, often higher than 120 (see Renzulli, 1986). This figure is not a cutoff, but an expression of the fact that people with low or even average IQs do not seem to be well represented among the ranks of highly creative individuals. Cox's (1926) geniuses had an estimated average IQ of 165. Barron (1963, p. 242) estimated the mean IQ of his creative writers to be 140 or higher, based on their scores on the Terman Concept Mastery Test. The other groups in the Institute for Personality Assessment Research (IPAR) studies, that is, mathematicians and research scientists, were also above average in intelligence. Roe (1952, 1972), who did similarly thorough assessments of eminent scientists before the IPAR group was set up, estimated IQs for her participants that ranged from 121 to 194, with medians between 137 and 166, depending on whether the IQ test was verbal, spatial, or mathematical.

Second, above an IQ of 120, IQ does not seem to matter as much to creativity as it does below 120. In other words, creativity may be more highly correlated with IQ below an IQ of 120, but only weakly or not at all correlated with it above an IQ of 120. (This relationship is often called the threshold theory. See the contrast with Hayes's, 1989, certification theory discussed below). In the study of architects, in which the average IQ was 130 (significantly above average), the correlation between intelligence and creativity was −.08, not significantly different from zero (Barron, 1969, p. 42). But in the study of military officers, in which the participants were of average intelligence, the correlation was .33 (Barron, 1963, p. 219). These results suggest that extremely highly creative people often have high IQs, but that people with high IQs do not necessarily tend to be extremely creative.

Some investigators (e.g., Simonton, 1994; Sternberg, 1996a) have suggested that very high IQ may actually interfere with creativity. Those who have very high IQs may be so highly rewarded for their IQ-like (analytical) skills that they fail to develop the creative potential within them, which may then remain latent. In a reexamination of the Cox (1926) data, Simonton (1976) found that the eminent leaders showed a significant negative correlation, −.29, between their IQs and eminence. He explained that

> leaders must be understood by a large mass of people before they can achieve eminence, unlike the creators, who need only appeal to an intellectual elite. . . . Scientific, philosophical, literary, artistic, and musical creators do not have to achieve eminence in their own lifetime to earn posterity's recognition, whereas military, political, or religious leaders must have contemporary followers to attain eminence (Simonton, 1976, pp. 220, 222)

Third, the correlation between IQ and creativity is variable, usually ranging from weak to moderate (Getzels & Jackson, 1962; Guilford, 1967; Herr, Moore, & Hasen, 1965; Torrance, 1962; Wallach & Kogan, 1965; Yamamoto, 1964). The correlation depends, in part, on what aspects of creativity and intelligence are being measured and how they are being measured, as well as in what field the creativity is manifested. The role of intelligence is different in art and music, for instance, than it is in mathematics and science (McNemar, 1964).

An obvious drawback to the tests used and assessments done by Roe and Guilford is the time and expense involved in administering them, as well as the subjective scoring of them. In contrast, Mednick (1962) produced a 30-item, objectively scored, 40-minute test of creative ability, called the Remote Associates Test (RAT). The RAT is based on his theory that the creative thinking process is the forming of associative elements into new combinations that either meet specified requirements or that are useful in some way. Elements that are more remote with respect to one another yield more creative solutions (Mednick, 1962). Because the ability to make these combinations and arrive at a creative solution necessarily depends on the existence of the stuff of the combinations, that is, the associative elements, in a person's knowledge base and because the probability and speed of attainment of a creative solution are influenced by the organization of the person's associations, Mednick's theory suggests that creativity and intelligence are overlapping sets.

In the RAT the test taker supplies a fourth word that is remotely associated with three given words. Samples (not actual test items) of given words are as follows:

1. cake   blue   cottage

2. surprise   line   birthday

3. out   dog   cat

(Answers are *1. cheese, 2. party, 3. house.*)

Moderate correlations of .55, .43, and .41 have been shown between the RAT and the WISC (Wechsler Intelligence Scale for Children), the SAT verbal, and the Lorge-Thorndike Verbal intelligence measures, respectively (Mednick & Andrews, 1967). Correlations with quantitative intelligence measures were lower ($r = .20 - .34$). Correlations with other measures of creative performance have been more variable (Andrews, 1975).

This psychometric revolution for measuring creativity had both positive and negative effects on the field. On the positive side, the tests facilitated research by providing a brief, easy to administer, objectively scorable assessment device. Furthermore, research was now possible with "everyday" people (noneminent samples). However, there were some negative effects as well. First, some researchers criticized brief paper-and-pencil tests as trivial, inadequate measures of creativity, stating that larger productions, such as actual drawings or writing samples, should be used instead. Second, other critics suggested that neither fluency, flexibility, originality, nor elaboration scores captured the concept of creativity. In fact, the definition of and criteria for creativity are a matter of ongoing debate, and relying on the objectively defined statistical rarity of a response with regard to all the responses of a subject population is only one of many options. Other possibilities include using the social consensus of judges. Third, some researchers rejected the assumption that noneminent samples could shed light on eminent levels of creativity, which was the ultimate goal for many studies of creativity. Thus, a certain malaise developed and continues to accompany the paper-and-pencil assessment of creativity. Some psychologists, at least, avoided this measurement quagmire in favor of less problematic research topics.

COGNITIVE APPROACHES

The cognitive approach to creativity seeks to understand the mental representations and processes underlying creative thought. By studying, say, perception or memory, one would already be studying the bases of creativity; thus, the study of creativity would merely represent an extension, and perhaps not a large one, of work that is already being done under another guise. For example, in the cognitive area, creativity was often subsumed under the study of intelligence. We do not argue with the idea that creativity and intelligence are related to each other. However, the subsumption has often been so powerful that researchers like Wallach and Kogan (1965), among others, had to write at length on why creativity and intelligence should be viewed as distinct entities. In more recent cognitive work, Weisberg (1986, 1988, 1993, 1999) has proposed that creativity involves essentially ordinary cognitive processes yielding extraordinary products. He attempted to show that the insights depend on subjects using conventional cognitive processes (such as analogical transfer) applied to knowledge already stored in memory. Weisberg did so through the use of case studies of eminent creators and laboratory research, such as studies with Duncker's (1945) candle problem (see also chapter 7). This problem requires participants to attach a candle to a wall using only objects available in a picture (a candle, a box of tacks, and a book of matches). Langley et al. (1987) made a similar claim about the ordinary nature of creative thinking.

As a concrete example of this approach, Weisberg and Alba (1981) had people solve the notorious nine-dot problem (see also chapter 7). In this problem, people are asked to connect all the dots, which are arranged in the shape of a square with three rows of three dots each, using no more than four straight lines, never arriving at a given dot twice, and never lifting their pencil from the page. The problem can be solved only if people allow their line segments to go outside the periphery of the dots. Typically, the solution of this task had been viewed as hinging on the insight that one had to go "outside the box." Weisberg and Alba showed that even when people were given the insight, they still had difficulty solving the problem. In other words, whatever is required to solve the nine-dot problem, it is not just some kind of extraordinary insight.

Studies With Human Participants and Computer Simulations

Approaches based on the study of human participants are perhaps prototypically exemplified by the work of Finke, Ward, and Smith (1992) (see also S. M. Smith, Ward, & Finke, 1995; Sternberg & Davidson, 1994; Ward, Smith, & Finke, 1999). Finke and his colleagues proposed what they call the *Geneplore model*, according to which there are two main processing phases in creative thought: a generative phase and an exploratory phase. In the generative phase, an individual constructs mental representations referred to as preinventive structures, which have properties that promote creative discoveries. In the exploratory phase, an individual uses these properties to come up with creative ideas. A number of mental processes may enter into these phases of creative invention, such as retrieval, association, synthesis, transformation, analogical transfer, and categorical reduction (i.e., mentally reducing objects or elements to more primitive categorical descriptions). In a typical experimental test based on the model (see, e.g., Finke, 1990), participants are shown parts of objects, such as a circle, a cube, a parallelogram, and a cylinder. On a given trial, three parts are named, and the participants are asked to imagine combining the parts to produce a practical object or device. For example, the participants may imagine a tool, a weapon, or a piece of furniture. The objects thus produced are then rated by judges for their practicality and originality.

The goal of computer-simulation approaches, reviewed by Boden (1992, 1999), is to produce creative thought by a computer in a manner that simulates what people do. Langley et al. (1987), for example, developed a set of programs that rediscover basic scientific laws. These computational models rely on heuristics—problem-solving guidelines—for searching a data set or conceptual space and finding hidden relationships between input variables. The initial program, called *BACON*, uses heuristics, such as "if the value of two numerical terms increase together, consider their ratio" to search data for patterns. One of BACON's accomplishments has been to examine observational data on the orbits of planets available to Kepler and to rediscover Kepler's third law of planetary motion. This program is unlike creative functioning, however, in that the problems are given to it in structured form, whereas creative functioning is largely about figuring out what the problems are. Other programs have extended the search heuristics, the ability to transform data sets, and the ability to reason with qualitative data and scientific concepts. There are also models concerning an artistic domain. For example, Johnson-Laird (1988) developed a jazz improvisation program in which novel deviations from the basic jazz chord sequences are guided by harmonic constraints (or tacit principles of jazz) and random choice when several allowable directions for the improvisation exist.

SOCIAL-PERSONALITY APPROACHES

Developing in parallel with work the cognitive approach, work in the social-personality approach has focused on personality variables, motivational variables, and the sociocultural environment as sources of creativity. Researchers, such as Amabile (1983), Barron (1968, 1969), Eysenck (1993), Gough (1979), and MacKinnon (1965), have noted that certain personality traits often characterize creative people. Through correlational studies and research contrasting high- and low-creative samples (at both the eminent and everyday levels), a large set of potentially relevant traits has been identified (Barron & Harrington, 1981). These traits include independence of judgment, self-confidence, attraction to complexity, aesthetic orientation, and risk taking.

Proposals regarding self-actualization and creativity can also be considered within the personality tradition. According to Maslow (1968), boldness, courage, freedom, spontaneity, self-acceptance, and other traits lead a person to realize his or her full potential. Rogers (1954) described the tendency toward self-actualization as having motivational force and being promoted by a supportive, evaluation-free environment.

Focusing on the motivation for creativity, a number of theorists have hypothesized the relevance of intrinsic motivation (Amabile, 1983; Crutchfield, 1962; Golann, 1962), need for order (Barron, 1963), and need for achievement (McClelland, Atkinson, Clark, & Lowell, 1953), among other motives. Amabile (1983) and Hennessey and Amabile (1988) have conducted seminal research on intrinsic and extrinsic motivation. Studies using motivational training and other techniques have manipulated these motivations and observed the effects on creative performance tasks, such as writing poems and making collages.

Finally, the relevance of the social environment to creativity has been an active area of research. At the societal level, Simonton (1984, 1988, 1994, 1999) has conducted numerous studies in which eminent levels of creativity over large spans of time in diverse cultures have been statistically linked to environmental variables. These variables include, among others, cultural diversity, war, availability of role models, availability of resources (such as financial support), and number of competitors in a domain. Cross-cultural comparisons (e.g., Lubart, 1990) and anthropological case studies (e.g., Maduro, 1976; Silver, 1982) have demonstrated cultural variability in the expression of creativity. Moreover, they have shown that cultures differ simply in the amount that they value the creative enterprise.

The cognitive and social-personality approaches have each provided valuable insights into creativity. However, only a handful of studies have investigated both cognitive and social-personality variables at the same time. Cognitive research on creativity has tended to ignore the personality and social system, and the social-personality approaches have tended to have little or nothing to say about the mental representations and processes underlying creativity.

Looking beyond the field of psychology, Wehner, Csikszentmihalyi, and Magyari-Beck (1991) examined 100 recent doctoral dissertations on creativity and found a "parochial isolation" of the various studies concerning creativity. There were relevant dissertations from psychology, education, business, history, history of science, and other fields, such as sociology and political science. However, the different fields tended to use different terms and to focus on different aspects of what seemed to be the same basic phenomenon. For example, dissertations in business used the term *innovation* and tended to look at the organizational level, whereas dissertations in psychology used the term *creativity* and looked at the individual level. Wehner et al. described the situation regarding this research in terms of the fable of the blind men and the elephant. "We touch different parts of the same beast and derive distorted pictures of the whole from what we know: 'The elephant is like a snake,' says the one who only holds its tail; 'The elephant is like a wall,' says the one who touches its flanks" (p. 270).

EVOLUTIONARY APPROACHES

The evolutionary approach to creativity was instigated by Campbell (1960), who suggested that the same kinds of mechanisms that have been applied to the study of the evolution of organisms could be applied to the evolution of ideas. This suggestion has been enthusiastically adopted by a number of investigators (Perkins, 1995; Simonton, 1995, 1998, 1999).

The basic idea underlying this approach is that there are two basic steps in the generation and propagation of creative ideas. The first is *blind variation*, by which the creator generates an idea without any real idea of whether the idea will be successful (selected for) in the world of ideas. Indeed, Simonton (1996) argued that creators do not have the slightest idea which of their ideas will succeed. As a result, their best bet for producing lasting ideas is to go for a large quantity of ideas. The reason is that their hit rate remains relatively constant through their professional life span. In other words, they have a fixed proportion of ideas that will succeed. The more ideas they have in all, the more ideas will achieve success.

The second step is *selective retention*. In this step, the field in which the creator works either retains the idea for the future or lets it die out. Those ideas that are selectively retained are the ones that are judged to be novel and of value, that is, creative. This process, as well as blind generation, are described further by Cziko (1998).

Does an evolutionary model really describe creativity adequately? Sternberg (1997) contended that it does not, and Perkins (1998) also had doubts. Sternberg argued that it seems implausible that great creators, such as Mozart, Einstein, or Picasso, were using nothing more than blind variation to come up with their ideas. Good creators, like experts of any kind, may or may not have more ideas than other people have, but they have better ideas, ones that are more likely to be selectively retained. And the reason the ideas are more likely to be selectively retained is that they were not produced in a blind fashion. This debate is by no means resolved, however, and is likely to continue for some time to come.

If an understanding of creativity required a multidisciplinary approach, the result of a unidisciplinary approach might be that we would view a part of the whole as the whole. At the same time, though, we would have an incomplete explanation of the phenomenon we are seeking to explain, leaving those who do not subscribe to the particular discipline dissatisfied. We believe that traditionally this has been the case for creativity. Recently, theorists have begun to develop confluence approaches to creativity, which we discuss next.

CONFLUENCE APPROACHES

Many recent works on creativity hypothesize that multiple components must converge for creativity to occur (Amabile, 1983; Csikszentmihalyi, 1988; Gardner, 1993; Gruber, 1989; Gruber & Wallace, 1999; Lubart, 1994; Mumford & Gustafson, 1988; Perkins, 1981; Simonton, 1988; Sternberg, 1985; Sternberg & Lubart, 1991a, 1991b, 1995; Weisberg, 1993; Woodman & Schoenfeldt, 1989). Sternberg (1985), for example, examined laypersons' and experts' conceptions of the creative person. He found people's implicit theories contain a combination of cognitive and personality elements, such as "connects ideas," "sees similarities and differences," "has flexibility," "has aesthetic taste," "is unorthodox," "is motivated," "is inquisitive," and "questions societal norms."

At the level of explicit theories, Amabile (1983, 1996; M. A. Collins & Amabile, 1999) described creativity as the confluence of intrinsic motivation, domain-relevant knowledge and abilities, and creativity-relevant skills. The creativity-relevant skills include (1) a cognitive style that involves coping with complexities and breaking one's mental set during problem solving; (2) knowledge of heuristics for generating novel ideas, such as trying a counterintuitive approach; and (3) a work style characterized by concentrated effort, an ability to set aside problems, and high energy.

Gruber and his colleagues (1981, 1989; Gruber & Davis, 1988) proposed a developmental *evolving-systems model* for understanding creativity. A person's knowledge, purpose, and affect grow over time, amplify deviations that an individual encounters, and lead to creative products. Developmental changes in the knowledge system have been documented in cases, such as Charles Darwin's thoughts on evolution. Purpose refers to a set of interrelated goals that also develop and guide an individual's behavior. Finally, the affect or mood system denotes the influence of joy or frustration on the projects undertaken.

Csikszentmihalyi (1988, 1996) has taken a different "systems" approach that highlights the interaction of the individual, domain, and field. An individual draws on information in a domain and transforms or extends it via cognitive processes, personality traits, and motivation. The field, consisting of people who control or influence a domain (e.g., art critics and gallery owners), evaluates and selects new ideas. The domain, a culturally defined symbol system, preserves and transmits creative products to other individuals and future generations. Gardner (1993; see also Policastro & Gardner, 1999) conducted case studies that suggest that the development of creative projects may stem from an anomaly within a system (e.g., tension between competing critics in a field) or moderate asynchronies between the individual, domain, and field (e.g., unusual individual talent for a domain). In particular, he analyzed the lives of seven individuals who made highly creative contributions in the 20th century, with each specializing in one of the multiple intelligences (Gardner, 1983): Sigmund Freud (intrapersonal), Albert Einstein (logical-mathematical), Pablo Picasso (spatial), Igor Stravinsky (musical), T. S. Eliot (linguistic), Martha Graham (bodily kinesthetic), and Mohandas Gandhi (interpersonal). Charles Darwin would be an example of someone with extremely high naturalist intelligence. Gardner pointed out, however, that most of these individuals actually had strengths in more than one intelligence and that they had notable weaknesses as well in others (e.g., Freud's weaknesses may have been in spatial and musical intelligences).

Although creativity can be understood in terms of the uses of the multiple intelligences to generate new and even revolutionary ideas, Gardner's (1993) analysis goes well beyond the intellectual. For example, Gardner pointed out two major themes in the behavior of these creative giants. First, they tended to have a matrix of support at the time of their creative breakthroughs. Second, they tended to drive a "Faustian bargain" whereby they gave up many of the pleasures people typically enjoy in life to attain extraordinary success in their careers. It is not clear, however, that these attributes are intrinsic to creativity, per se; rather, they seem to be associated with those who have been driven to exploit their creative gifts in a way that leads them to attain eminence.

Furthermore, Gardner followed Csikszentmihalyi (1988, 1996) in distinguishing between the importance of the domain (the body of knowledge about a particular subject area) and the field (the context in which this body of knowledge is studied and elaborated, including the persons working with the domain, such as critics, publishers, and other "gatekeepers"). Both are important to the development and, ultimately, the recognition of creativity.

A final confluence theory considered here is Sternberg and Lubart's (1995) *investment theory of creativity*. According to this theory, creative people are willing and able to "buy low and sell high" in the realm of ideas (see also Rubenson & Runco, 1992, for the use of concepts from economic theory). Buying low means pursuing ideas that are unknown or out of favor but that have growth potential. Often, when these ideas are first presented, they encounter resistance. The creative individual persists in the face of this resistance and eventually sells high, moving on to the next new or unpopular idea.

Preliminary research within the investment framework has yielded support for this model (Lubart & Sternberg, 1995). This research has used tasks, such as (1) writing short stories using unusual titles (e.g., the octopus's sneakers), (2) drawing pictures with unusual themes (e.g., the earth from an insect's point of view), (3) devising creative advertisements for boring products (e.g., cufflinks), and (4) solving unusual scientific problems (e.g., how we could tell if someone had been on the moon within the past month). This research showed creative performance to be moderately domain specific and to be predicted by a combination of certain resources, as described next.

According to the investment theory, creativity requires a confluence of six distinct but interrelated resources: intellectual abilities, knowledge, styles of thinking, personality, motivation, and environment. Three intellectual abilities are particularly important (Sternberg, 1985): (1) the synthetic ability to see problems in new ways and to escape the bounds of conventional thinking, (2) the analytic ability to recognize which of one's ideas are worth pursuing and which are not, and (3) the practical-contextual ability to know how to persuade others of—to sell other people on—the value of one's ideas. The confluence of these three abilities is also important. Analytic ability used in the absence of the other two abilities results in powerful critical, but not creative thinking. Synthetic ability used in the absence of the other two abilities results in new ideas that are not subjected to the scrutiny required to make them work. And practical-contextual ability used in the absence of the other two may result in the transmission of ideas not because the ideas are good, but because they have been well and powerfully presented.

On the one hand, one needs to know enough about a field to move it forward. One cannot move beyond where a field is if one doesn't know where it is. On the other hand, knowledge about a field can result in a closed and entrenched perspective, so that a person does not move beyond the way in which he or she has seen problems in the past (Frensch & Sternberg, 1989).

With regard to thinking styles, a legislative style is particularly important for creativity (Sternberg, 1988, 1997), that is, a preference for thinking in new ways. This preference needs to be distinguished from the ability to think creatively: Someone may like to think along new lines, but not think well, or vice versa. To become a major creative thinker, it also helps if one is able to think globally as well as locally, distinguishing the forest from the trees and thereby recognizing which questions are important and which are not.

Numerous research investigations (summarized in Lubart, 1994, and Sternberg & Lubart, 1991, 1995) have supported the importance of certain personality attributes for creative functioning. These attributes include the willingness to overcome obstacles, to take sensible risks, and to tolerate ambiguity and self-efficacy. In particular, buying low and selling high typically mean defying the crowd, so that one has to be willing to stand up to conventions if one wants to think and act in creative ways.

Intrinsic, task-focused motivation is also essential to creativity. The research of Amabile (1983) and others has shown the importance of such motivation for creative work and has suggested that people rarely do truly creative work in an area unless they really love what they are doing and focus on the work, rather than the potential rewards.

Finally, one needs an environment that is supportive and rewarding of creative ideas. One could have all the internal resources needed to think creatively, but without some environmental support (such as a forum for proposing the ideas), the creativity that a person has within him or her may never be displayed.

Concerning the confluence of components, creativity is hypothesized to involve more than a simple sum of a person's level on each component. First, there may be thresholds for some components (e.g., knowledge) below which creativity is not possible, regardless of the levels on other components. Second, partial compensation may occur in which a strength on one component (e.g., motivation) counteracts a weakness on another component (e.g., environment). Third, interactions may also occur between components, such as intelligence and motivation, in which high levels on both components could multiplicatively enhance creativity.

In general, confluence theories of creativity offer the possibility of accounting for diverse aspects of creativity (Lubart, 1994). For example, analyses of scientific and artistic achievements suggest that the median creativity of work in a domain tends to fall toward the lower end of the distribution and the upper—high creativity—tail extends quite far. This pattern can be explained by the need for multiple components of creativity to co-occur for the highest levels of creativity to be achieved. As another example, the partial domain specificity of creativity that is often observed can be explained by the mixture of some relatively domain-specific components for creativity, such as knowledge, and other more domain-general components, such as, the personality trait of perseverance. Creativity, then, is largely something that people show in a particular domain.

TYPES OF CREATIVE CONTRIBUTIONS

Generally, we think of creative contributions as being of a single kind, but several researchers on creativity have questioned this assumption. There are a number of ways of distinguishing among types of creative contributions. It is important to remember, though, that creative contributions can be viewed in different ways at different times. At a given time, the field can never be sure of whose work (such as Mozart's) will withstand the judgments of the field over time and whose work will not (such as Salieri's) (Therivel, 1999).

Theorists of creativity and related topics have recognized that there are different types of creative contributions (for reviews, see Ochse, 1990; Sternberg, 1988; Weisberg, 1993). For instance, Kuhn (1970) distinguished between normal and revolutionary science. Normal science expands or otherwise elaborates upon an already existing paradigm of scientific research, whereas revolutionary science proposes a new paradigm. The same kind of distinction can be applied to the arts and letters. Gardner (1993, 1994) also described different types of creative contributions that individuals can make: the solution of a well-defined problem, the devising of an encompassing theory, the creation of a "frozen work," the performance of a ritualized work, and a "high-stakes" performance.

Other bases for distinguishing among types of creative contributions also exist. For example, psychoeconomic models, such as those of Rubenson and Runco (1992) and Sternberg and Lubart (1991a, 1991b, 1995, 1996), can distinguish different types of contributions in terms of the parameters of the models. In the Sternberg-Lubart model, contributions may differ in the extent to which they "defy the crowd" or in the extent to which they redefine how a field perceives a set of problems.

Simonton's (1997) model of creativity also proposes parameters of creativity, and contributions may be seen as differing in terms of the extent to which they vary from other contributions and are selected for recognition by a field of endeavor (see also Campbell, 1960;

Perkins, 1995; Simonton, 1997). But in no case were these models intended explicitly to distinguish among types of creative contributions.

Maslow (1968) distinguished more generally between two types of creativity, which he referred to as primary and secondary. Primary creativity is the kind of creativity a person uses to become self-actualized—to find self-fulfillment. Secondary creativity is the kind of creativity with which scholars in the field are more familiar—the kind that leads to creative achievements of the kind typically recognized by a field.

Ward et al. (1999) noted that there is evidence in favor of the roles of focusing (Bowers, Regehr, Balthazard, & Parker, 1990; Kaplan & Simon, 1990) and of exploratory thinking (Bransford & Stein, 1984; Getzels & Csikszentmiyalyi, 1976) in creative thinking. In focusing, one concentrates on pursuing a single problem-solving approach, whereas in exploratory thinking one considers many such approaches. A second distinction made by Ward and his colleagues is between domain-specific (J. Clement, 1989; Langley et al., 1987; Perkins, 1981; Weisberg, 1986) and universal (Finke, 1990, 1995; Guilford, 1967; Koestler, 1964) creativity skills. Finally, Ward and his colleagues distinguished between unstructured (Findlay & Lumsden, 1988; Johnson-Laird, 1988) and structured or systematic (Perkins, 1981; Ward, 1994; Weisberg, 1986) creativity.

Sternberg (1999c) presented what he referred to as a propulsion model of creative contributions. The idea is that creative contributions "propel" a field forward in some way—they are the result of creative leadership by their creators. The propulsion model is a descriptive taxonomy of eight types of creative contributions. Although the eight types may differ in the extent of the creative contribution they make, there is no a priori way of evaluating the *amount* of creativity on the basis of the *type* of creative contribution. Certain types of creative contributions probably tend, on average, to be greater in amounts of novelty than are others. For example, replications tend, on average, not to be highly novel. But creativity also involves the quality of work, and the type of creative contribution a work makes does not necessarily predict the quality of that work.

The eight types of creative contributions are as follows:

1. *Replication.* The creative contribution represents an effort to show that a given field is where it should be. The propulsion is intended to keep the field where it is, rather than to move it.

2. *Redefinition.* The creative contribution represents an effort to redefine where the field currently is. The current status of the field is thus seen from a new point of view.

3. *Forward incrementation.* The creative contribution represents an attempt to move the field forward in the direction in which it already is moving, and the contribution takes the field to a point to which others are ready to go.

4. *Advance forward incrementation.* The creative contribution represents an attempt to move the field forward in the direction it is already going, but the contribution moves beyond where others are ready for the field to go.

5. *Redirection.* The creative contribution represents an attempt to move the field from where it is toward a new and different direction.

6. *Reconstruction-redirection.* The creative contribution represents an attempt to move the field back to where it once was (a reconstruction of the past) so that the field may move onward from that point, but in a direction different from the one it took from that point onward.

7. *Reinitiation.* The creative contribution represents an attempt to move the field to a different and as yet not reached starting point and then to move the field in a different direction from that point.

8. *Integration.* The creative contribution represents an attempt to move the field by putting together aspects of two or more past kinds of contributions that were formerly viewed as distinct or even opposed. This type of contribution shows particularly well the potentially dialectical nature of creative contributions, in that it merges into a new Hegelian type of synthesis two ideas that may have formerly been seen as opposed (Sternberg, 1999a).

The eight types of creative contributions described are viewed as qualitatively distinct. However, within each type, there can be quantitative differences. For example, a forward incrementation may represent a fairly small step forward for a given field or a substantial leap. A reinitiation may restart an entire field or just a small area of it. Moreover, a given contribution may overlap categories.

Thus, when people are creative, they can be creative in different ways. Exactly what these ways are depends on the theory of the types of creative contributions one accepts.

◆ SUMMARY

Creativity is the ability to produce novel, high-quality, task-appropriate products. It has been a relatively neglected topic in psychology. Among those who have studied creativity, a number of different approaches have been used. Mystical approaches have suggested that creativity has ineffable properties that are impervious to scientific investigation. Pragmatic approaches generally focus on the use of creativity and how to increase creativity. Psychodynamic approaches focus on the unconscious processes underlying creativity. Psychometric approaches concentrate on how creativity can be measured. Cognitive approaches deal with the information processing and mental representations underlying creativity. Social-personality approaches emphasize the roles of other people and of personality traits, as well as motivation. Evolutionary approaches view creativity as an adaptation that enhances an individual's chances of survival and, hence, of reproduction. And confluence approaches integrate these various other approaches. The contributions of creative individuals can be of different kinds, and different theories partition creative contributions in different ways.

13 Expertise

- ◆ The Nature of Expertise
- ◆ Theories of Expertise
- ◆ Acquisition of Expertise
- ◆ Summary

Many psychologists who are interested in complex cognition are fascinated with expertise. How do experts differ from novices? How does someone become an expert? Can anyone become an expert, or does one have to be born with some innate talent to become one? These kinds of questions have been fundamental to the study of expertise. But before we deal with such questions, we first need to deal with a definitional one.

THE NATURE OF EXPERTISE

What makes someone an expert? The answer is far from straightforward. Sometimes the question, "What is an expert?" is not squarely addressed in the literature on expertise, with the result that it is hard to say whether those being studied as experts are truly experts. There are several conceptions of what would constitute an expert (Sternberg, 1994). Which conception one adopts will determine, in large part, what one studies when one seeks to understand expertise.

Knowledge

One conception is knowledge based. That is, an expert is someone who knows a lot about a given area of endeavor. It seems likely that knowledge is a necessary condition for expertise: No one would want to go to a physician, lawyer, or psychotherapist who lacked knowledge of his or her field. One probably would not wish to pay a lot for a ticket to listen to musicians who knew little or nothing about their chosen instruments. Although knowledge seems to be a necessary condition for expertise, it does not seem to be a sufficient condition. Memorizing vast volumes of medical or legal references would not make one an expert physician or lawyer, or memorizing reams of music would not make one an expert musician.

There is even evidence that knowledge can interfere with expertise, at least the flexible kind of expertise that is needed for success in many pursuits (Adelson, 1984; Frensch & Sternberg, 1989). For example, Frensch and Sternberg compared the performance of expert and novice bridge players in playing bridge against a computer. Predictably, the experts played better than the novices when the game was played in the usual way. However, Frensch and Sternberg modified the game in two ways.

One modification, which they viewed as a *surface-structural modification*, varied the game only by changing the names of the suits. Instead of using the terms *clubs, diamonds, hearts,* and *spades*, the experimenters used different names (neologisms) for the four suits. The playing of both the experts and the novices was initially hurt by this change but quickly recovered.

A second modification was viewed as a *deep-structural modification*. Here a basic rule of the game was changed. Typically, in bridge, the high player on a given round opens the next round of play. In this version of the game, however, the player putting out the low card led off. This change, because it affects the basic way the game is played, disrupts fundamental strategies that experts develop. But novices are less likely to have any fundamental strategies and so are less likely to be disrupted. This result is exactly what the investigators discovered. The experts were actually disrupted more than the novices in their playing, although only initially. Eventually, they recovered and once again started playing better than the novices.

This result makes an important point about flexible expertise. A danger of expertise can be that knowledge interferes with, rather than facilitates, new ways of looking at things. A risk of expertise is entrenchment, or a kind of comfort with old ways of doing things. Flexible experts constantly have to be on guard against letting their knowledge of a domain interfere with their work. Clearly, something more is needed to be an expert than just knowledge.

Utilization of the Knowledge Base

Expertise, as was just suggested, seems to require not just knowledge, but the flexible application of the knowledge base. How the knowledge base is applied seems to depend on the field of expertise. But analytical, creative, and practical skills all seem important (Sternberg, 1994).

Analytical thinking. Experts need to analyze problems that are presented to them. Physicians analyze reports of symptoms and look for diagnostic signs of various illnesses. Musicians need to analyze the pieces they play to meet the pieces' technical requirements. Chess players need to analyze the challenges of each chess game they play. Artists need to analyze the attributes of the persons, scenes, or whatever else they decide to paint or otherwise represent.

Analytical thinking is needed for expertise, but one could argue that it is not enough, anymore than knowledge is. For one thing, someone can be able to analyze and criticize the work of others without being able to do outstanding work oneself. For another thing, there seems to be quite a difference between criticizing ideas and coming up with one's own ideas. For example, an art critic may critique an artistic exhibition or a music critic may critique a work of music or a concert, but the critics may not be able to, nor would they claim to be able to, produce their own expert artistic or musical work. Coming up with one's own ideas and how to implement them require creative thinking.

Creative thinking. Most kinds of expertise require the application of some kind of creative skill. Physicians dealing with difficult cases may soon find themselves in uncharted waters, having to synthesize information that does not fall into any routine pattern they previously encountered. Lawyers devise creative legal strategies to free their clients from legal jeopardy. Musicians do not just play notes, but create unique interpretations of the music they play. Chess players play games and make moves that go beyond any exact situations they have encountered before. And of course, scientists create new theories and experiments to chart the unknown.

Creative thinking is not enough either, though. An expert needs to know how to get people to pay attention to and then accept his or her creative ideas. Such efforts require practical thinking.

Practical thinking. Expertise also requires practical skills. The successful physician needs "patient skills"—ways to reach out to, comfort, and reassure patients that they are getting care in which they can have confidence. Lawyers need to convince their clients to tell them the truth so that the lawyers adequately can represent these clients. Scientists need to convince a frequently skeptical public—scientific or otherwise—that their ideas are not just some hare-brained concoction of fact and fiction but a good representation of the scientific truth. Musicians and artists need to reach out to potential audiences so that these audiences will pay attention to their performances or artworks. The audiences may then label the musicians or artists as experts.

Labeling Phenomena

The importance of practical skills to expertise underscores the fact that, in some sense, expertise may be viewed not just as an attribute of a person but as the way the person is perceived by other persons—as an interaction between a person and a situation. Expertise may be viewed partly as a labeling phenomenon whereby some group of people declares a person an expert. Without that declaration, the person may have difficulty exercising his or her expertise. For example, an individual who is trained in medicine cannot practice without a license; an individual who is trained in the law cannot represent clients without having passed the bar. A scientist can do science without academic credentials, but may have difficulty obtaining an academic job or research funding without those credentials. In chess, expertise is often recognized in terms of a person's numerical rating according to a system of evaluation (discussed later) of how well the person plays chess. So labeling seems to play some role in expertise or, at least, in its recognition.

The Structure of the Definition of Expertise

If one thing should be clear by now, it is that there is no simple definition of expertise that will suffice. Expertise does not seem to be a "classical concept" with a clearly delineated set of defining features. Expertise is perhaps a prototypically defined construct for which it is difficult to specify any one set of characteristics, each of which is singly necessary and all of which are jointly sufficient for a person in any field to be labeled an expert. Or perhaps there are multiple exemplars that serve as bases for the recognition of expertise. But what is clear is that in studying expertise, we cannot simply take for granted that a given person or group of persons is expert.

THEORIES OF EXPERTISE

Having considered definitional issues regarding expertise, let us now consider some of the major theories of expertise delineated by Ericsson and Smith (1991), upon which this account is based.

Theories Focusing on Mental Processing

Some theories of expertise, especially ones proposed when the literature on expertise was just forming, emphasize the role of planning, problem-solving, and reasoning processes. Charness (1981; see also Charness, 1991; Charness, Krampe, & Mayr, 1996), for example, found that chess players with higher levels of skill tended to plan possible sequences of moves in greater depth. That is, more skilled players planned further in advance than did less skilled players.

This account of expertise in chess was compromised by the fact that the findings of other investigators have been different from those of Charness. De Groot (1978), a pioneer in the study of expertise in chess, found no reliable differences in the depth to which experts versus novices planned in advance.

One possibility would be that Charness detected differences that de Groot, with weaker methods, was unable to detect. Or it may be that the differences were so small that they were of no practical importance. Charness (1989) suggested, however, that the difference may be real but nonlinear. In particular, up to a certain level of expertise, the depth of search may increase, after which it stops increasing and other factors become more important in distinguishing who will succeed and who will not in games of chess.

Whatever may be the depth to which expert chess players plan in advance, it is clear that they and other experts need to engage in highly sophisticated information processing. For example, they need to be able to engage in what Sternberg (1985) referred to as metacomponential processing.

Metacomponential processing involves planning, monitoring, and evaluating one's problem solving and decision making. For example, experts, such as physicians, need to be able to define problems and redefine them when they obtain further information (Lesgold et al., 1985; Patel & Groen, 1991). They also need mentally to represent information in an optimal fashion. Indeed, experts and novices do represent information quite differently.

Experts also set up strategies and monitor their performance in sophisticated ways. For example, several teams of investigators have studied expert versus novice physicists as they solve problems or sort them into categories (Chi et al. 1981; Larkin, McDermott, Simon, & Simon, 1980). They found that novices tend to represent problems in terms of their surface structures (e.g., seeing a problem as being about pulleys or inclined planes), whereas experts tend to represent problems in terms of underlying physical principles (e.g., seeing a problem as being one of Newton's first law).

Consider how experts versus novices might go about solving a physics problem or other problem in their domain of expertise. The expert and the novice will both first read the problem, but the expert is likely to spend more time reading the statement of the problem than is the novice, or at least more time relative to the total amounts of time each will spend in problem solving (Larkin et al., 1980; Sternberg, 1981). The expert thus spends relatively more time than does the novice in *global planning*, or strategic planning for solving the problem as a whole. This up-front planning time will save the expert time later on because he or she will be less likely than the novice to misrepresent the problem and hence pursue blind alleys that later will require starting over. The novice, in contrast, is more likely to begin problem solving relatively quickly, but at a later point in problem solving, he or she is more likely to have to restart his or her work. More time spent on global planning is later repaid in less time that needs to be devoted to *local planning*—the tactical planning that needs to be done as one proceeds through the steps of problem solving. In the long run, local planning is likely to drain more time from the problem-solving process when global planning was incomplete or inadequate. In short, experts better balance strategic and tactical thinking than do novices.

The expert is also more likely than the novice to draw some kind of schematic representation of the problem, such as a simple diagram outlining the elements of the problem and their interrelations (Larkin & Simon, 1987). In the verbal domain, such as in writing an essay, the expert may use some kind of outline or map of how the essay will be constructed, rather than a graphical figure.

The expert may write down formulas for quantitative types of problems but only those that are actually needed. The novice, in contrast, may write down or at least consider using a wide range of formulas, trying to figure out which one is appropriate. In other kinds of problem solving as well, experts are likely to zero in quickly on relevant information through selective encoding and selective comparison, while novices seem to muddle through.

Because experts can recognize the deep structure of problems, they are able to solve problems **working forward**, whereas novices are much more likely to solve problems working backward. In other words, experts look at the terms of the problem and then proceed forward from the problem statement to a conclusion. Novices are more likely to start with the known or intended solution and then to work backward to try to figure out how they could get to the terms of the problem, given where they are trying to go.

The persistent difference in representation of problems (Chi et al., 1989) is crucial for understanding an important aspect of the difference between experts and novices. Although the apparent problem being solved by the expert and the novice is the same, the psychological problem being solved, or at least the representation of it, is different. The problem that the expert physicist sees as being about a principle of physics, the novice physicist may see as being about a mechanical device. The problem the layperson may see as being about a person's mood swings, a psychiatrist may see as being about a manic-depressive personality. The differences in representations show how difficult it is to separate knowledge from information processing: The representations that experts construct typically would not be possible without extensive and well-organized knowledge bases.

Experts also need to use sophisticated processes of insightful thinking (Sternberg & Davidson, 1995). They need to be able to engage in *selective encoding*, distinguishing what information is relevant for their purposes. For example, a radiologist needs to know what to look for in an X-ray. A scientist needs to know what to look for in the massive computer outputs that often result from complex data analyses. A lawyer needs to know which facts are relevant to his or her case and which facts, although interesting, are not legally relevant. Experts also need to be able to integrate large amounts of information to make skilled judgments.

Consider a series of studies showing the importance of selective encoding. Lesgold and his colleagues (Lesgold, Feltovich, Glaser, & Wang, 1981; Lesgold et al., 1988) investigated how expert and novice radiologists (residents training to be radiologists) differed in their processing of X-ray data. The participants looked at an X-ray picture for two seconds and then reported any abnormalities they might have noticed. Then, they were allowed to look at the

X-ray picture again for an unlimited amount of time and were asked to think aloud while analyzing the X-ray report. The study found that the experts were better able quickly to detect important patterns in the film and to ignore irrelevant information. In other words, the experts were better at selective encoding.

This is the process Sternberg (1985) called *selective combination*. For example, a physician needs to figure out how to put together the different clues presented by an array of symptoms to reach a diagnosis. A detective needs to put together clues to decide who committed a crime. Finally, they need to be able to do sophisticated *selective comparison*, figuring out which information they already have is relevant for solving problems that are presented to them. Physicians, lawyers, scientists, chess players—all, as we shall see—draw on large-scale knowledge bases to solve problems. Thus, we see again the necessity of knowledge for the work of any expert.

The sophisticated use of these processes typically develops over long periods. But individuals can be taught to use these processes to good effect. For example, Davidson and Sternberg (1984) gave fourth-grade students (roughly age 9) verbal and mathematical insight problems to solve, initially as a pretest and later as a posttest. An example of such a problem might be "Suppose you have black socks and blue socks placed in a dark room and mixed in a drawer in a ratio of 4 to 5. At most how many socks do you need to withdraw from the drawer in order to be sure that you have two socks of the same color?" In this problem, the ratio information is irrelevant and even misleading. Regardless of the ratio, you need to withdraw three socks, because if the first two socks are not of the same color, the third one has to be of the same color (black or blue) as one of the socks that was previously withdrawn. Some children were taught for five weeks how to use the processes of selective encoding, selective combination, and selective comparison to increase their expertise in solving insight problems, but the other children did not receive such instruction. The instructed children gained more from the pretest to the posttest than did the uninstructed children. In a similar study using only verbal problems, in which adults had to learn to use these three processes to figure out meanings of words presented in contexts, those who were instructed in how to use these processes increased more from a pretest to a posttest than did those who were not so instructed (Sternberg, 1987a). In effect, instruction can help speed up processes that are normally learned during the development of various kinds of expertise.

Theories Focusing on the Knowledge Base and Its Organization

Theories that emphasize the role of the knowledge base and its organization often stress the role of stored information in long-term memory as a key to understanding expertise. These theories generally have their origins in the work of de Groot (1978), mentioned earlier, and of Chase and Simon (1973). Because this work is often considered the seminal work in the study of expertise, let us consider it in detail.

De Groot (1978) asked chess players with different levels of expertise to think aloud while they contemplated the next moves they would make from several different presented chess positions. In most cases, grand masters and chess experts who were not at the grand-master level evaluated moves similarly. There was no difference in the number of moves considered by the groups with different levels of expertise. Both groups considered somewhat more than 30 possible moves. But the grand masters arrived at the best move earlier in their consideration of moves than did the more typical experts. De Groot concluded that the grand masters must be relying on a more extensive knowledge base than the more typical chess experts. They recognized that the position presented was similar or identical to one they had seen before and hence were able to zero in rapidly on the optimal move. Knowledge acquired through experience, rather than any special kind of information processing, seemed to be what distinguished the chess experts.

This assessment was further supported by de Groot's asking both the grand masters and the experts to recall a middle-game position shown to them for just a short time. The grand masters were able to recall the positions of 20 to 30 chess pieces perfectly or nearly perfectly, whereas the experts were able to recall with only 50 to 70% accuracy. Why the difference? De Groot attributed it again to differences in knowledge base. The grand masters were recalling a configuration they had seen before and were able to integrate all they were seeing into a single whole. The experts, in contrast, either had not seen the position or had not seen it as often. Hence they were not able to integrate it into a single whole or as easily encode it so they could retrieve it easily.

Chase and Simon (1973) recognized a flaw in the design of de Groot's study. Perhaps the grand masters simply had better memories than did the more common experts. Perhaps the greater knowledge base of the grand masters was due to their exceptional generalized memory skills. Chase and Simon tested this hypothesis by presenting grand masters and experts with chess configurations for five seconds and then asking the two groups to recall them. The critical difference was that Chase and Simon included both configurations of pieces from real games and random configurations of pieces. If the grand masters simply had better memories for pieces than the experts, then their recall should have been better for all chess board configurations, regardless of whether they were real or not. The same applied for experts versus novices. The results were clear: The level of expertise in chess influenced the recall only of sensible (real-game) configurations of chess pieces; it had no influence on the recall of random chess positions. In other words, what distinguished the experts from the novices and the grand masters from the experts was not overall superior recall abilities, but the extent and organization of their knowledge base.

Chase and Simon (1973) took things one step further by observing how individuals at various levels of expertise produced their recall. They noted that recall did not occur in a smooth, ordered progression, but in bursts. In other words, some chess pieces would be rapidly placed on the board, then there would be a pause, then more chess pieces would be rapidly placed on the board, and so on. The sets of pieces placed in a single burst were viewed as chunks, in the sense described by G. Miller (1956). Miller concluded that people were able to hold in their available short-term memory about 7 plus or minus 2 chunks of information, when the chunks were groupings of information encoded by individuals trying to recall the information. A critical feature of Miller's analysis, as well as of Chase and Simon's, was that the chunks could vary in size, depending on how the information was encoded. Chase and Simon found that the size of the chunks of the more-expert players was larger than that of the less-expert players, including novices. In other words, the more-expert players were able to use their knowledge base to retrieve large amounts of information in each burst of recall of chess pieces.

Exactly how many chunks of information did people at various levels of expertise have? Simon and Gilmartin (1973) showed via computer simulation that one could reproduce the performance of chess experts with just 1,000 chunks stored in memory. But they estimated that the experts had stored anywhere from 10,000 to 30,000 chunks in memory. Thus the experts were drawing on huge knowledge bases that were unavailable to the novices in doing the chess-related tasks. These knowledge bases may be organized into **problem schemas**, or organized bodies of knowledge on which people can draw to help them represent and then solve a problem.

If Chase and Simon's (1973) findings applied only to chess, they would be of only modest interest. But the same basic finding regarding the role of the knowledge base has been replicated in a number of other domains, such as the game of Go (Reitman, 1976), diagrams of electronic circuits (Egan & Schwartz, 1979), and bridge (Engle & Bukstel, 1978; Charness, 1979). Thus, the importance of vast and organized knowledge bases and the problem schemas that come with them seem to be fundamental to many different kinds of expertise. Such schemas and their knowledge bases are not rapidly acquired, however. Simon and Chase (1973) estimated that it would take about 3,000 hours of play to become a chess expert and 30,000 hours to become a chess master. But how does one acquire expertise?

ACQUISITION OF EXPERTISE

Expertise takes a long time to acquire. Simon and Chase (1973) proposed that it typically takes a minimum of 10 years to acquire, and the "10-year rule" has become almost a dictum in the study of expertise. It seems to apply across a number of domains (Charness, Krampe, & Mayr, 1996; Ericsson, 1996a; Ericsson, Krampe, & Tesch-Römer, 1993; Simonton, 1996).

The ACT* Theory of Skill Acquisition

A number of theories have been proposed of how people may become experts in skills, whether in music, athletics, art, or whatever (J. R. Anderson, 1987, 1993; Newell, 1990). Here, we briefly consider Anderson's theory, which is embedded in his ACT* theory of cognition.

According to Anderson, skills are acquired in three main stages that represent successive levels in the development of expertise. In the first stage, the kind of situation that evokes the skill and the method of solving problems in that situation are encoded as declarative knowledge. Usually, this declarative knowledge derives from explicit instruction, which may include both an abstract presentation of the type of problem situation and how to solve it and examples of problem solving in action. At this stage, individuals are able to solve problems, but problem solving is relatively slow and deliberate. The more a given problem departs from the exact way in which its solution was taught, the harder the problem is, to the point that even minor levels of transfer may fail to occur.

In the second stage, knowledge comes to be represented procedurally—in the form of *productions rules*, or condition-action statements that can be used in performing a task. For example, one such production rule may be, If you see a dot over a note, play that note in staccato (short and punctuated) fashion.

In the third stage, the production rules are combined into successively more elaborated production systems, or sequences of condition-action statements that can be used to execute a complex series of task requirements. Now the performance of the task becomes more highly automatized and requires less-conscious effort by the individual who is doing the task.

Anderson's model is similar to one proposed earlier by Fitts and Posner (1967). Fitts and Posner also proposed a three-stage model. The first stage, the *cognitive stage*, involves declarative encoding of information. The second stage, the *associative stage*, involves the formation of connections among various elements of the skill. The third stage, the *autonomous stage*, involves the relatively rapid and automatic execution of the skill.

These characterizations of the development of skill apply to many tasks, but they do so in a decontextualized way. Some investigators have proposed models of acquisition that deal with how expertise develops in the course of a person's daily life.

Stages in the Development of Expertise

The development of expertise in many domains seems to go through several stages (B. S. Bloom, 1985). Interviews with exceptional performers in many domains, as well as the parents and teachers of these elite performers, suggest that these experts pass through a number of stages.

In Stage I, the elite performers were initially exposed as children to the domain in which they later became experts under relaxed and playful conditions. At this point, the domain is engaged for pleasure. The future expert musician may be involved in piano playing or the artist in painting. Or the future ice skater may skate just for fun. Sooner or later, the parents or teacher recognize that the child shows promise. This recognition may lead to Stage II.

In Stage II, the parents help the child establish a regular practice schedule and arrange for a teacher or coach to work on a fairly intensive basis with the child. The child typically starts practicing daily, and the amount of practice increases over time. Further signs of promise may lead to Stage III.

In Stage III, a major commitment is made. A nationally or even internationally recognized teacher is sought, and the initial teacher is abandoned. The parents may move to another area to have access to this acclaimed teacher or may make other arrangements for the child to have access to this teacher. This stage represents a major commitment of time and resources to the development of expertise in the child and is, in a sense, the point at which there is no easy turning back: A decision to develop an expert has been made. The parents' investment can be substantial. The parents pay for lessons and perhaps equipment or other material resources, invest time in driving their child to lessons or practice, and give up some of their own activities to support the child's development of expertise. Because of the investment required of them, parents typically do not make such efforts for more than one child in the family.

In Stage IV, the now-expert performer has learned most of what even the internationally acclaimed teacher has to teach him or her. The individual, now an adolescent or adult, moves well beyond being merely a student and creatively defines the kind of expertise that he or she will offer to the world. The individual develops a kind of "signature" that represents his or her particular way of expressing expertise.

Theories of the Acquisition of Expertise

What determines who actually makes it to the level of a world-acclaimed expert and who does not? Opinions in this regard differ. We consider two views, one emphasizing the role of deliberate practice and the other emphasizing the joint roles of deliberate practice and talent.

The Deliberate-Practice View

One view of the development of expertise is that what is required is **deliberate practice**. Deliberate practice is not just any old practice. It is practice in which the task (1) is at an appropriate level of difficulty for the individual, (2) provides informative feedback to the individual, (3) provides for opportunities for repetition, and (4) allows for the correction of errors (Ericsson, 1996a).

Ericsson (1996b) took things a step further. He argued that deliberate practice is not just a necessary condition for the development of expertise, but a sufficient condition as well. In other words, engaging in sufficient deliberate practice will, under normal conditions, produce an expert. This is a strong claim, but there is at least some evidence to back it up. For example, Ericsson et al. (1993) reported that a study of violinists from a music academy in Germany revealed that the primary difference between students at different levels of expertise was the amount of deliberate practice in which they had engaged. The top violinists averaged almost 7,500 hours of deliberate practice by age 18, whereas the good violinists averaged only about 5,300 hours. Sloboda (1991, 1996) also contended that deliberate practice appears to be sufficient for the development of musical expertise.

The claim of those who believe in deliberate practice is not limited to music, but is alleged to apply in all domains, including that of memory. For example, Chase and Ericsson (1982) trained a college student, SF, who had a fairly ordinary digit-span memory, to have an exceptional memory for digits. By the end of an extensive period of training—about 200 hours—SF was able to recall as many as 81 digits at the rate of 1 per second. A typical college student might remember 7 plus or minus 2 digits. How did SF become so adept in memorizing digits? As it turned out, he was a runner, so he used his information about races to facilitate his digit-span memory. He converted sets of digits into race times, thereby increasing the size of his chunks. As one might predict, strings of digits that did not translate into sensible race times gave him more trouble. And when asked to memorize letters, his span of recall was no better than that of the average college student. In other words, he did not transfer the skill to a related domain.

Howe (1999a) did an extensive analysis of great creative writers—individuals whose craft would appear, at least on the surface, to be attributable largely to some innate talent for writing creatively. Howe concluded otherwise. He found that great writers took a great deal of time to learn their craft and that their first efforts were often weak. Many of them, such as John Stuart Mill, John Ruskin, and H. G. Wells, started writing during childhood, so that their adult products represented the culmination of many years of deliberate practice. For many of them, writing did not come easily, and they worked hard to perfect their craft.

The deliberate-practice view has an important implication that is accepted by almost all psychologists who study expertise, regardless of whether they hold to this particular view. This implication is related to inventor Thomas Edison's comment that creative success is 99% perspiration and only 1% inspiration. It is unlikely that one actually could assign percentages to the origins of expertise, but expertise always has its base in extremely substantial amounts of hard work, or what Ericsson called deliberate practice. Many people give up because they are unwilling to engage in these high levels of deliberate practice. Others hope that they will become experts on the basis of sheer talent. Neither those who quit nor those who hope for an easy road to expertise are likely ever to become experts in their fields.

The Deliberate Practice Plus Talent View

Many theorists believe that talent, not just deliberate practice, plays an important role in the development of expertise (B. Bloom, 1985; Shiffrin, 1996; Simonton, 1996; Sternberg, 1996b; Winner, 1996a, 1996b). They argue that although deliberate practice is likely to be a necessary condition for the development of expertise, it is not likely to be a sufficient one. What are some of their main arguments against the sufficiency of deliberate practice?

First, they argue that behavior-genetic studies indicate a role for genetic factors in interaction with environmental ones in the development of various kinds of expertise (Plomin & McClearn, 1993). Many different types of abilities seem to have at least some heritable component as a source of individual differences and the kinds of expertise studied by psychologists seem to be no exception. The counterargument proposed by Ericsson (1996b) is that these studies do not apply at the extremely high levels of deliberate practice that they have studied. Nevertheless, there is no reason to believe that performances at high levels of practice would somehow obey different rules.

Second, advocates of the talent-practice position argue that the deliberate-practice view is not plausible. Is one to believe that anyone could become a Mozart if only he or she put in the time? Or that anyone could reach the level of skill shown by Michael Jordan in basketball if only one worked hard enough at it? Or, for that matter, that becoming an Einstein is just a matter of deliberate practice? Although this argument is one of plausibility, rather than data, on its face it is not a simple matter to refute. Many people have tried to reach the exceptional levels of accomplishment shown by the top people in a given field, and most have given up.

Third, the advocates of the mixed position argue that the demonstrations of deliberate practice have lacked control groups or contained inadequate ones. They speculate that other people who do not become experts or even known may put in the same hours of deliberate practice as the experts. But, because these nonexperts disappear from view, they may never make it into studies of expertise.

Fourth, the advocates of the mixed position argue that deliberate practice is itself a confounded measure, representing talent as well as practice. How could deliberate practice be a function of talent? The idea (Sternberg, 1996b; Winner, 1996) is that only those with high levels of talent continue to put in the deliberate practice it takes to reach high levels of expertise. Their talent motivates them to try harder and thus rack up more hours of deliberate practice. Consider music lessons, for example. Many millions of children have music lessons, but many of them quit. Why? Perhaps because they discover that they lack the talent to become professional or even skilled musicians. So they never put in many hours of practice over the course of their lives. The result is that the correlation between deliberate practice and expertise may be affected, in part, by levels of talent.

An interesting and puzzling kind of instance is that of the *prodigy*, an individual who shows enormous talent at an early age. Prodigies, however, generally are not miniature versions of adult experts (Feldman, 1986; Howe, 1999b). Rather, their work typically tends to have more of an imitative and less of a creative quality than does the work of adult experts. Prodigies need to make a sharp transition from being prodigies to being adult experts, and many fail to do so. Their skills help them do extremely well what others have done, but not to go beyond that point. Moreover, the overwhelming majority of people who become highly expert as adults were never prodigies as children.

At this point, psychologists are unable to decide definitively whether deliberate practice is sufficient or just necessary for the development of expertise. But whatever its role, the findings on deliberate practice should give hope to many individuals who may despair of ever becoming experts. The data suggest that deliberate practice can help a great deal in the development of expertise and may even guarantee it if it is done with sufficient devotion.

◆ SUMMARY

What are the major characteristics of experts in a given field? Experts have large, rich schemas that contain a great deal of declarative knowledge about a domain and procedural knowledge about strategies that are relevant to solving problems in that domain. The knowledge in all their schemas is well organized and highly interconnected. Experts are able to use this knowledge to develop sophisticated representations of problems, based on deep-structural characteristics of and similarities among problems. They also spend proportionately more time than do novices in determining how to represent a problem than in searching for and executing a strategy to solve it.

Experts tend to work forward from given information to implement strategies for finding unknowns, whereas novices tend to work backward. Experts also generally choose a strategy for problem solving based on elaborated schemas of problem strategies. For them, many of the routine steps in problem solving are already automatized and require little conscious effort to perform. This automatization enables experts to be highly efficient in solving problems and generally to solve problems more rapidly than do novices. Experts are usually accurate in predicting the difficulty of solving particular problems and carefully monitor their problem-solving strategies so that they spot errors when they are made or garden paths when they are followed. Experts are highly accurate in reaching appropriate solutions. When they confront unusual problems with atypical structural features, they are careful to represent the problems properly and show flexibility in these representations.

A summary of the distinguishing characteristics of experts and novices is presented in Table 13.1. As you will see, there are many features that distinguish experts from novices. Not all experts have all the characteristics listed in the table, but most have a large number of them, thereby distinguishing themselves from novices.

TABLE 13.1   Characteristics of Experts

Have large, rich schemas containing a great deal of declarative knowledge about a domain

Have well-organized, highly interconnected units of knowledge in schemas

Spend proportionately more time determining how to represent a problem than in searching for and executing a problem strategy

Develop sophisticated representation of problems, based on structural similarities among problems

Work forward from given information to implement strategies for finding unknowns

Generally choose a strategy based on elaborate schemas of problem strategies; use means-ends analysis only as a backup strategy for handling unusual, atypical problems

Schemas contain a great deal of procedural knowledge about problem strategies relevant to a domain

Have automatized many sequences of steps within problem strategies

Show highly efficient problem solving; when time constraints are imposed, solve problems more quickly than novices

Accurately predict the difficulty of solving particular problems

Carefully monitor own problem-solving strategies and processes

Show high accuracy in reaching appropriate solutions

When confronting highly unusual problems with atypical structural features, take relatively more time than novices both to represent the problem and to retrieve appropriate problem strategies

When provided with new information that contradicts initial problem representation, show flexibility in adapting to a more appropriate strategy

14 Development of Complex Cognition

◆ Major Approaches to Cognitive Development

◆ Development of Information-Processing Skills

◆ Cognitive Neuropsychological Changes in Development

◆ Complex Cognitive Development in Adulthood

◆ Summary

Psychologists who seek to understand how thinking changes across the life span study **cognitive development**, the investigation of how mental skills build and change with increasing physiological maturity (maturation) and experience (learning). Thus, they study the differences and similarities among people of different ages, seeking to discover how and why people think and behave differently at different times in their lives, and concentrate on the development of higher-order processes of thought, language, and other aspects of intellectual functioning.

The development of complex cognition involves *qualitative*, as well as *quantitative*, changes in thinking, such as increasing knowledge and ability. Most cognitive psychologists agree that developmental changes occur as a result of the interaction of maturation (nature) and learning (nurture). However, some give much greater emphasis to *maturation*, which refers to any relatively permanent change in thought or behavior that occurs simply as a result of aging, without regard to particular experiences. Others, however, underscore the importance of *learning*, which refers to any relatively permanent change in thinking as a result of experience. Bear this interaction of nature and nurture in mind as you read about the various theoretical perspectives on cognitive development.

The interactive influence of nature and nurture starts in infancy. Young infants appear to be innately predisposed to attend to stimuli that are moderately novel—that is, neither so familiar that the stimuli are uninteresting nor so novel that the infants cannot make sense of the stimuli (McCall, Kennedy, & Appelbaum, 1977). An environment that offers moderately novel stimuli will help infants to make the most of their innate preferences. Some have suggested that infants' preference for moderate novelty explains how infants learn about things when they are ready to do so. Infants do not waste their time attending to completely familiar things or to things that are so new that they are overwhelming. Some researchers (e.g., Bornstein & Sigman, 1986; M. Lewis & Brooks-Gunn, 1981) have suggested that infants who more strongly prefer some degree of novelty are more intelligent than are infants who less strongly prefer novelty. Some findings (e.g., Bornstein, 1989; Fagan, 1984, 1985; Fagan & Montie, 1988) have indicated that young infants with strong preferences for novelty may be more likely to have high scores on intelligence tests at ages 2 to 7, but other researchers (e.g., Humphreys & Davey, 1988; Kagan, 1989; McCall, 1989) advise us not leap to conclusions at this point.

These findings are now an established part of the literature on complex cognition, but they illustrate how a field can change over time. Until the 1970s and even the 1980s, most psychologists viewed intelligence during the first two years of life as involving a different program of intellectual development from that involved after age 2 years of life (e.g., Piaget, 1972). They believed that the first two years involved the development primarily of sensori-motor functioning and that complex processes developed later. But these sensorimotor tests did not correlate with tests of intelligence administered after infancy (see Sternberg & Powell, 1983). The findings on the relation of preference for novelty to later intelligence showed that complex cognition starts early and is involved in intelligence even during infancy.

This chapter opens with some theoretical approaches to cognitive development, in general, and the development of complex cognition, in particular. Then it covers development in specific domains, as well as neurophysiological maturation. Finally, it briefly discusses the development of complex processes in adult cognition, particularly, important cognitive changes that occur after adolescence.

MAJOR APPROACHES TO COGNITIVE DEVELOPMENT

Although this chapter cannot encompass all the many theories of cognitive development, we discuss some of the most influential ones in the field. As you read about the processes involved in cognitive development, think about which ones seem most sensible to you. You may find strengths and weaknesses in each theory and that no single theory has yet explained all aspects of cognitive development. The approaches included here represent psychological theorists' best attempts to explain how human cognition develops. This chapter describes the work of Jean Piaget and the neo-Piagetians, Lev Vygotsky, and the information-processing theorists. After we discuss these cognitive-developmental phenomena of childhood, we consider an additional view of cognitive development, based on neurophysiological research.

General Principles of Cognitive Development

Regardless of the particular theoretical approach—whether Piagetian, Vygotskyan, or information processing—what basic principles crosscut the study of cognitive development and tie it together? A review of the data suggests some possible answers (Sternberg & Powell, 1983). First, over the course of development, people seem to gain more sophisticated control over their thinking and learning and become capable of more complex interactions between thought and behavior. Second, people engage in more thorough information processing with age. Older children encode more information from problems than do younger children and are therefore more likely to solve problems accurately. Even during adulthood, people continue to accumulate knowledge across the life span. Third, people become increasingly able to comprehend successively more complex relationships over the course of development. Finally, over time, people become more and more flexible in using strategies or other information. That is, they become less bound to using information in just a single context and learn how to apply information in a greater variety of contexts. People may even gain greater wisdom—insight into themselves and the world around them.

Maturation of Thought Processes

It would be difficult to overestimate the importance of Swiss psychologist Jean Piaget (1896–1980) to developmental research. His is generally considered the most comprehensive theory of the development of complex cognition. Although aspects of Piaget's theory have been questioned, and, in some cases, disconfirmed, the theory is still enormously influential. Indeed, the contribution of his theory, like that of others, is shown more by its influence on further theory and research than by its ultimate correctness.

In particular, Piaget revolutionized the study of children's concept formation and intelligence by proposing that researchers could learn as much about children's intellectual development from examining their incorrect answers to test items as from examining their correct answers. Through his repeated observations of children, including his own, and especially through investigations of their errors in reasoning, Piaget concluded that coherent logical systems underlie children's thought. These systems, he believed, differ in kind from the logical systems that adults use. If we are to understand development, we must identify these systems and their distinctive characteristics. In this section, we first consider some of Piaget's general principles of development and then Piaget's stages of cognitive development.

Piaget believed that the function of intelligence is to aid in adaptation to the environment. In his view (Piaget, 1972), the means of adaptation form a continuum, ranging from relatively unintelligent means, such as habits and reflexes, to relatively intelligent means, such as those requiring insight, complex mental representation, and the mental manipulation of symbols. In accord with his focus on adaptation, he believed that cognitive development is accompanied by increasingly complex responses to the environment (Piaget, 1972). Piaget further proposed that with increasing learning and maturation, both intelligence and its manifestations become *differentiated*, that is, more highly specialized in various domains.

Piaget believed that development occurs in stages that evolve via **equilibration**, in which children seek a balance (equilibrium) between what they encounter in their environments and what cognitive processes and structures they bring to the encounter, as well as among the cognitive capabilities themselves. Equilibration involves three processes. In some situations, the child's existing mode of thought and existing *schemas* (mental frameworks) are adequate for confronting and adapting to the challenges of the environment; the child is thus in a state of equilibrium. For example, suppose that a 2 year old uses the word *doggie* to embrace all the four-legged furry creatures that are like his own dog; as long as all the four-legged creatures that the child sees are like the dogs he has already seen, he remains in a state of equilibrium.

At other times, however, the child is presented with information that does not fit with his or her existing schemas, so cognitive disequilibrium arises. That is, imbalance occurs when the child's existing schemas are inadequate for new challenges the child encounters. Consequently, the child attempts to restore equilibrium through **assimilation**—the incorporation of the new information into his or her existing schemas. For example, suppose that the 2 year old's dog is a great dane, and that the child goes to the park and sees a poodle, a cocker spaniel, and an Alaskan husky. The child must assimilate the new information into his existing schema for *doggies*—not a big deal.

Suppose, however, that the child visits a small zoo and sees a wolf, a bear, a lion, a zebra, and a camel. On seeing each new animal, the child looks perplexed and asks his mother, "Doggie?" Each time, his mother says, "No, that animal isn't a dog. That animal is a _____ [naming the animal]." Since the child cannot assimilate these diverse creatures into his existing schema for *doggies*, he or she must somehow modify the schemas to allow for the new information, perhaps creating an overarching schema for animals, into which he or she fits the existing schema for dogs. Piaget would suggest that the child modifies existing schemas through **accommodation**—changing the existing schemas to fit the relevant new information about the environment. Together, the processes of assimilation and accommodation result in a more sophisticated level of thought than was possible previously. In addition, they result in the reestablishment of equilibrium, thus offering the individual, such as the 2 year old, higher levels of adaptability.

According to Piaget, the equilibratory processes of assimilation and accommodation account for all the changes associated with cognitive development. In Piaget's view, disequilibrium is more likely to occur during periods of stage transition. That is, although Piaget posited that these processes go on throughout childhood as children continually adapt to their environment, he also thought that development involves discrete, discontinuous stages. In particular, Piaget (1969, 1972) divided cognitive development into the four main stages: the sensorimotor, preoperational, concrete-operational, and formal-operational. Cognition becomes increasingly complex with the increasing age of the child.

The Sensorimotor Stage

The first stage of development, the **sensorimotor stage**, involves increases in the number and complexity of sensory (input) and motor (output) abilities during infancy, roughly from birth to about 2 years. According to Piaget, the infant's earliest adaptations are reflexive. Gradually, infants gain conscious, intentional control over their motor actions. At first, they do so to maintain or to repeat interesting sensations. Later, however, they actively explore their physical world and seek new and interesting sensations.

Throughout the early phases of sensorimotor cognitive development, cognition seems to focus only on what the infants can immediately perceive through their senses. Infants do not conceive of anything that is not immediately perceptible to them and hence do not have a sense of **object permanence**—the sense that objects continue to exist even when they are imperceptible. For example, before about age 9 months, infants who observe an object as it is being hidden from view will not seek the object once it is hidden. If a 4 month old were to watch you hide a rattle beneath a blanket, he or she would not try to find the rattle beneath the blanket, whereas a 9 month old would. Although subsequent research has called into question some of Piaget's interpretations of object permanence, it appears that infants do not have the same concept of the permanence of objects that adults have.

To have a sense of object permanence requires some internal, mental representation of an object even when the object is not seen, heard, or otherwise perceived. The young infant's responses do not require a conception of object permanence or of any other internal mental representations of objects or actions because the infant's thoughts are focused only on sensory perceptions and motor behaviors. By the end of the sensorimotor period (18–24 months), children begin to show signs of **representational thought**—internal representations of external stimuli. In this transition to the preoperational stage, they start to be able to think about people and objects that are not necessarily perceptible at that moment.

Piaget believed that the increasing ability to form internal mental representations continues throughout childhood. Another characteristic pattern of cognitive development is that children move increasingly from a focus on self to an interest in others. That is, as children grow older, they become less **egocentric**—less focused on themselves. Note that Piaget conceived of egocentrism as a cognitive characteristic, not a personality trait. For example, the earliest adaptations that occur during infancy all pertain to the infant's own body (e.g., sucking reflexes may be adapted to include sucking a thumb or a toe). Later adaptations, however, also involve objects in the environment outside the child's body. Similarly, early mental representations involve only the child, but later ones also involve other objects. Piaget viewed this early trend as indicative of a broader trend for children of all ages to become increasingly aware of the outer world and of how others may perceive it.

The Preoperational Stage

In the **preoperational stage**, from about 2 to 6 or 7 years, the child begins actively to develop the internal mental representations that started at the end of the sensorimotor stage. According to Piaget, the arrival of representational thought during the preoperational stage paves the way for the subsequent development of logical thought during the stage of concrete operations. With representational thought comes verbal communication. However, the communication is largely egocentric. That is, a conversation may seem to have no coherence; children say what is on their minds, pretty much without regard to what anyone else has said. As children develop, however, they increasingly take into account what others have said when forming their own comments and replies.

The ability to manipulate verbal symbols for objects and actions, even egocentrically, accompanies the ability to manipulate concepts, and the preoperational stage is characterized by increases in conceptual development. Nonetheless, during this stage, children's ability to manipulate concepts is still limited. For example, children exhibit **centration**—a tendency to focus on only one especially noticeable aspect of a complicated object or situation. Piaget (1946) did a series of experiments on children's centration. He showed children two model trains on two different parallel tracks and, using different starting and stopping times for each train, he ran each train down its track at a different speed. He then asked questions, such as which train traveled longer or faster. He found that the 4- and 5 year olds tended to concentrate on a single dimension, usually the point at which the trains stopped. They said that the train that had traveled farther down the track had also traveled faster and longer, regardless of when the trains had started or stopped. Thus, children in the preoperational stage focus on one particular dimension of a problem—such as the final position of the trains—ignoring other aspects of the situation, even when they are relevant.

Many developmental changes occur during the preoperational stage. Children's active, intentional experimentation with language and with objects in their environments results in tremendous increases in conceptual and language development. These developments help to pave the way for further cognitive development during the stage of concrete operations.

Concrete Operations

In the stage of **concrete operations**, roughly from ages 7 or 8 until 11 or 12, children become able to manipulate mentally the internal representations that they formed during the preoperational stage. In other words, they now not only have thoughts and memories of objects, but they can perform mental operations on these thoughts and memories. However, they can do so only in regard to concrete objects (e.g., thoughts and memories of cars, food, toys, and other tangible things)—hence the term *concrete operations*.

Perhaps the most dramatic evidence of the change from preoperational thought to the representational thought of the concrete-operational stage is seen in Piaget's classic experiments (1952, 1954, 1969) on the **conservation** of quantity. In conservation, the child is able mentally to conserve (keep in mind) a given quantity even though he or she observes changes in the appearance of the objects or substances. These experiments probed children's responses to whether an amount of something (e.g., number of checkers, length of rods, or volume of dough) was conserved despite changes in appearance (see Table 14.1). Initially, children rely on their immediate perceptions of how things appear to be; gradually, they begin to formulate internal rules regarding how the world works and eventually use these internal rules to guide their reasoning, rather than using appearances alone.

Perhaps the most well-known Piagetian conservation experiment demonstrates developmental changes in the *conservation of liquid quantity*. The experimenter shows the child two short, stout beakers with liquid in them and has the child verify that the two beakers contain the same amounts of liquid. Then, as the child watches, the experimenter pours the liquid from one of the short beakers into a third beaker, which is taller and thinner than the other two. In the new beaker, the liquid in the narrower tube rises to a higher level than in the other still-full shorter and wider beaker.

When asked whether the amounts of liquid in the two full beakers are the same or different, the preoperational child says that there is now more liquid in the taller, thinner beaker because the liquid in that beaker reaches a perceptibly higher point. The preoperational child has seen the experimenter pour all the liquid from one to the other, adding none, but the child

TABLE 14.1 Conservation of Quantity

Type	The Child Is Shown:	The Experimenter:	The Child Responds:
Area	two boards with six wooden blocks and agrees that the blocks on both boards take up the same space	scatters the blocks on one board and asks if one board has more unoccupied space or if both are the same	*Preoperational child:* The blocks on the second board take up more space. *Concrete-operational child:* They take up the same amount of space.
Volume	two balls of clay put in two glasses equally full of water and says the level is the same in both	flattens one ball of clay and asks if the water level will be the same in both glasses	*Preoperational child:* The water in the glass with the flat piece won't be as high as the water in the other glass. *Concrete-operational child:* Nothing has changed; the level will be the same in each glass.

does not conceive that the amount is conserved despite the change in appearance. The concrete-operational child, on the other hand, says that the beakers contain the same amount of liquid, on the basis of his or her internal schemas regarding the conservation of matter.

What can the concrete-operational child do that the preoperational child cannot? The concrete-operational child can manipulate internal representations of concrete objects and substances, mentally conserving the notion of amount and concluding that despite different physical appearances, the quantities are identical. Thus, he or she can decenter from the single dimension of the height of the liquid in the container to consider the width of the container as well. Furthermore, concrete-operational thinking is **reversible:** The concrete-operational child can judge the quantities to be identical because the child understands that the liquid could be poured back into the original container (the short beaker), thereby reversing the action. Once the child internally recognizes the possibility of reversing the action and can mentally perform this concrete operation, he or she can grasp the logical implication that the quantity has not changed. Note, however, that the operations are concrete; that is, the cognitive operations act on cognitive representations of actual physical events. The final stage of cognitive development, according to Piaget, involves going beyond these concrete operations and applying the same principles to abstract concepts.

Formal Operations

The **formal-operational stage**, from roughly 11 or 12 years onward, involves mental operations on abstractions and symbols that may not have physical, concrete forms. In addition, children begin to understand some things that they have not directly experienced themselves (Inhelder & Piaget, 1958). During the stage of concrete operations, children begin to be able to see the perspective of others if the alternative perspective can be concretely manipulated. For example, they can guess how another child may view a scene (e.g., depicting a village) when they sit at opposite sides of a table on which the scene is displayed. During formal operations, however, children are finally fully able to take on perspectives other than their own, even when they are not working with concrete objects. Furthermore, persons in the formal-operations stage purposefully seek to create a systematic mental representation of situations they confront.

Piaget used several tasks to demonstrate the entry into formal operations. Consider, for example, the way in which we devise *permutations* (variations in combinations), as elucidated by the following question: What are all the possible permutations of the letters, "A, B, C, D"? A person in the formal-operational stage will devise a system, perhaps first varying the placement of the last letter, then of the second to last, and so on. A formal-operational person's list might start: ABCD, ABDC, ADBC, DABC. . . . The concrete-operational person is more likely just to list combinations randomly, without any systematic plan: ABCD, DCBA, ACBD, DABC, and so forth. Many other aspects of deductive and inductive reasoning also develop during the period of formal operations, as does the ability to use formal logic and mathematical reasoning. In addition, the sophistication of conceptual and linguistic processing continues to increase.

In sum, Piaget's theory of cognitive development involves stages that all children undergo at roughly the same ages, and each stage building on the preceding stage. Thus, stages occur in a fixed order and are irreversible: Once a child enters a new stage, the child thinks in ways that characterize that stage, regardless of the task domain, the specific task, or even the context in which the task is presented. He or she never thinks in ways that characterize an earlier stage of cognitive development. Other theorists (e.g., Beilin, 1971; R. Gelman, 1969), including some neo-Piagetians (e.g., Case, 1992; Fischer, 1980), disagreed with this view, suggesting that there may be greater flexibility in cognitive-developmental progression across tasks and task domains than is suggested by Piagetian theory.

Evaluation of Piaget's Theory

Piaget's theory has been criticized on four fronts. The first is Piaget's assertion that the changes in children's cognition occur chiefly as an outcome of maturational processes. Although Piaget observed that developmental processes result from children's adaptations to their environment, he held that internal maturational processes, rather than environmental contexts or events, determine the sequence of cognitive-developmental progression. However, Piagetian theory is contradicted by evidence (e.g., Ahn, Kalish, Medin, & Gelman, 1995; Blades & Spencer, 1994; Fischer & Bidell, 1991; R. Gelman, 1972; Gottfried, 1984; Kotovsky & Baillargeon, 1994; Oakes & Cohen, 1995) that particular experiences, training, or other environmental factors may alter children's performance on Piagetian tasks.

The second area of criticism is Piaget's fundamental assumption that cognitive development occurs in a fixed sequence of discontinuous spurts across task domains, tasks, and contexts. Many theorists (e.g., Brainerd, 1978), however, believe that cognitive development occurs as a continuous process, rather than in discontinuous stages of development. In addition, accumulating evidence (e.g., Beilin, 1971; see also Bidell & Fischer, 1992; Case, 1992) contradicts the assumption that within a given stage of development, children demonstrate only stage-appropriate levels of performance. It now appears that many aspects of children's physical and social environments, prior experiences with a task and the task materials, and even of the experimenter's presentation of the task may lead to apparent unevenness in cognitive development.

The third point of criticism is Piaget's interpretation of what caused difficulty for children in particular Piagetian tasks. Piaget's theory emphasizes the development of deductive and inductive reasoning, and Piaget held that limitations on children's ability to reason caused their difficulties in solving particular cognitive tasks. Different theorists have suggested that other kinds of limitations may at least partly influence children's performance on Piagetian tasks. Such limitations include children's motor coordination (Mandler, 1990), working-memory capacity (e.g., Bryant & Trabasso, 1971; Kail, 1984; Kail & Park, 1994), memory strategies (Siegler, 1991), or verbal understanding of questions (e.g., Sternberg, 1985). For example, some researchers have suggested that the children might not have understood Piaget's questions, so that his experiments may have failed to elicit their full complement of abilities. In general, Piaget appears to have underestimated the importance of language and its development.

The fourth area of criticism is the accuracy of Piaget's estimates of the ages at which people demonstrate mastery of Piagetian tasks. Piaget underscored the importance of noting the sequence of developments, not the estimated ages at which these developments occurred. In general, the trend has been toward demonstrating that children can do things at ages earlier than Piaget thought possible (see, e.g., Baillargeon, 1987; Brainerd, 1973; R. Gelman, 1969; R. Gelman & Baillargeon, 1983). Piaget's estimates of ages may have been skewed by his use of somewhat loose methods of research.

The evidence cited against stages usually refers to children's inconsistent abilities to perform well on tasks that are believed to be beyond their stage of development. However, Thelen and Smith (1994) presented a new approach to development that encompasses many of these apparent problems in Piaget's theory. In particular, their dynamic systems approach, in which discontinuities occur as part of the natural interaction of nonlinear dynamic systems (systems with highly complex physical properties—in this case, children and their environment), predicts the very kinds of conflicting performance seen in children on the verge of a transition from one stage to another. Indeed, Thelen and Smith pointed out that instability is necessary for new abilities to develop—a system must contain variability in its behavior for new behaviors to be selected. According to them, children move from equilibrium in an ability level to points of instability in performance, in which they inconsistently perform beyond their current stage in some contexts. Furthermore, this disequilibrium is part of the natural interaction of the nonlinear dynamic systems involved in children's interactions with their environment. Thus, the dynamic systems approach to development encompasses conflicting evidence into a new framework: Children do progress through stages, but not strictly via maturation. The discontinuous stages proposed by Piaget and the apparent conflicts in children's performance at transitions to new stages are a result of natural interactions between children and their environment.

At the other end of the spectrum, even adolescents and adults do not demonstrate formal-operational thinking in many circumstances (Dasen & Heron, 1981; Neimark, 1975). They often seem to think associatively, rather than logically (Sloman, 1996). In 1972, Piaget modified his theory to acknowledge that the stage of formal operations may be more a product of an individual's domain-specific expertise, based on experience, than of the maturational processes of cognitive development.

Finally, the variation in the ages at which particular cognitive tasks are mastered shows that most of us have a wide range of performance, so that what we may be optimally capable of doing may often differ from what we actually do much of the time. The context in which we typically demonstrate cognitive performance may not be a true indication of what we are optimally able to achieve, and vice versa. One way of viewing these apparent contradictions is to describe Piaget's theory as primarily a **competence theory**—a theory of what people of various ages are maximally capable of doing. Other theorists prefer to view cognitive development in terms of a **performance theory**—a theory of what people of various ages naturally do in their day-to-day lives (see Davidson & Sternberg, 1985).

Neo-Piagetian Theorists

Neo-Piagetian theorists build on a broad understanding of Piaget's theory of cognitive development. Although each neo-Piagetian is different, most neo-Piagetians (1) accept Piaget's broad notion of developmental stages of cognitive development, (2) concentrate on the scientific or logical aspects of cognitive development (often observing children engage in many of the same tasks as those used by Piaget), and (3) retain some ties with the notion that cognitive development occurs through equilibration. Of the many neo-Piagetian theories, we briefly consider only a few here. First, we describe a few theories that posit a fifth stage of cognitive development.

Fifth-stage theorists do not posit an entirely different theory of cognitive development; instead, they build on Piaget's four stages by suggesting a fifth stage beyond formal operations. Arlin (1975) proposed that a fifth stage of cognitive development is *problem finding*. In this fifth stage, individuals master the tasks of figuring out exactly what problems they face and deciding which problems are the most important and deserving of their efforts to solve.

Several theorists have suggested that logical reasoning beyond Piagetian formal operations may proceed to a fifth stage of *dialectical thinking*. Dialectical thinking recognizes that in much of life, there is no one final, correct answer but, rather, a progression of beliefs whereby we first propose some kind of thesis, then later see its antithesis, and finally effect some kind of synthesis between the two, which then serves as the new thesis for the continuing evolution of thought. For example, adults use dialectical thinking when they consider one extreme and then the other and then incorporate only the best elements of each extreme.

Psychologists, such as Kramer (1990), Labouvie-Vief (1980, 1990), Pascual-Leone (1984, 1990), and Riegel (1973) have stated that after the stage of formal operations, we reach a stage of *postformal thinking*, in which we recognize the constant unfolding and evolution of thought, such as in the dialectic originally proposed by philosopher Georg Hegel. Postformal thought allows adults to manipulate mentally the vagaries and inconsistencies of everyday situations, in which simple, clear answers rarely are available. Through postformal thinking, we can consider and choose among alternatives, recognizing that other alternatives may offer benefits not obtainable from the chosen one. We may also take into account the sociocultural context in which we are making our decisions.

Sociocultural Influences on Thought Processes

Cognitive-developmental theorist Lev Vygotsky (1896–1934) died of tuberculosis at age 37, yet his influence on the field of cognitive development is generally considered to be second only to that of Piaget and has increased in recent years. Whereas Piaget dominated developmental psychology in the 1960s and 1970s, Vygotsky was rediscovered in the late 1970s and 1980s and his ideas continue to be influential today. Although Vygotsky had many fertile ideas, two of them are particularly important for us to consider here: internalization and the zone of proximal development.

In Piaget's theory, cognitive development proceeds largely from the inside out, through maturation. Environments can foster or impede development, but Piaget emphasized the biological and hence the maturational aspect of development. Vygotsky's (1962, 1978) theory takes an entirely different approach by emphasizing the role of the environment in children's intellectual development. Vygotsky suggested that cognitive development proceeds largely from the outside in, through **internalization**—the absorption of knowledge from context. Thus, social, not biological, influences are key in Vygotsky's theory of cognitive development. According to Vygotsky, then, much of children's learning occurs through children's interactions within the environment, which largely determine what the children internalize.

Consider, for example, a young girl on a lurching train. As the train is bumping along, she rises to walk in the aisle. Suppose that her mother simply says authoritatively, "Sit down," without explanation. An opportunity for learning has been lost. The child may neglect to infer the reasoning underlying her mother's demand. However, suppose instead that the mother says, "Sit down because the train may jerk or sway suddenly, and you may fall." The girl now has an opportunity not only to modify her behavior, but to learn how to use this modification in other appropriate circumstances. Thus, parents and others in a child's environment may extend the child's knowledge and may facilitate the child's learning through their interactions with the child.

This interactive form of learning relates to Vygotsky's (1962, 1978) second major contribution to educational and developmental psychology—the construct of the **zone of proximal development (ZPD)** (sometimes termed the *zone of potential development*). The ZPD is the range of potential between a child's observable level of realized ability (performance) and the child's underlying latent capacity (competence), which is not directly obvious. When we observe children, what we typically observe is the ability that they have developed through the interaction of heredity and environment. To a large extent, however, we are truly interested in what children are capable of doing—what their potential would be if they were freed from the confines of an environment that is never truly optimal. Before Vygotsky proposed his theory, people were unsure how to measure this latent capacity.

Vygotsky argued that we need to reconsider not only how we think about children's cognitive abilities, but also how we measure them. A child is typically tested in a **static assessment environment,** in which an examiner asks questions and expects the child to answer them. Whether the child responds correctly or incorrectly, the examiner moves to the next question or task on the list of items in the test. Like Piaget, Vygotsky was interested not only in children's correct responses, but in their incorrect responses to questions.

Thus, Vygotsky recommended children should be tested in a **dynamic assessment environment**, in which the interaction between child and examiner does not end when the child responds, especially if the child responds incorrectly. In static testing, when a child gives a wrong answer, the examiner moves on to the next problem. In dynamic assessment, when the child gives a wrong answer, the examiner gives the child a graded sequence of guided hints to facilitate problem solving. In other words, the examiner serves as both a teacher and a tester.

The literature on dynamic testing is a mixed bag, in that although there is great promise for the technique, many of the studies that have been done are open to alternative interpretations. We report here one study that seems to suggest particular promise for the technique. Grigorenko and Sternberg (2000) devised a dynamic test for use with children aged about 11 to 13 in Tanzania. The 350 tested children—residents of a rural village—did poorly when they were first given IQ-like tasks, such as solving syllogisms and categorization problems. After they completed the tasks, however, they were given a modest amount of instruction on how to complete each of the tasks. They were then retested. What did the investigators find?

The first thing they found was that even after less than one hour of training, the children's scores on the tasks improved significantly and substantially. What is more interesting is that the correlation between pretraining and posttraining scores was only about .3, meaning that the children who performed at a high level before the training were not, for the most part, those who performed at a high level after the training. This finding suggests that one cannot assume a stability of scores among people who are largely unfamiliar with Western modes of testing. It turned out that the best predictor of scores on other cognitive tasks was neither the pretest score nor the posttest score, but the learning score. This result suggests that dynamic testing truly provides information that cannot be gleaned from static testing.

The ability to use instruction or hints is the basis for measuring the ZPD because it indicates the extent to which a child can expand beyond her or his observable abilities at the time of testing. Two children may answer a given question incorrectly. However, a child who can profit from instruction is likely to go far, whereas a child who cannot is unlikely to acquire the skills needed to solve not only the problem being tested, but related ones. Several tests have been created to measure the ZPD (e.g., Brown & French, 1979; Campione, 1989; Campione & Brown, 1990), the most well known of which is Reuven Feuerstein's (1979) *Learning Potential Assessment Device*.

The ZPD is one of the more exciting concepts in cognitive-developmental psychology, since it may enable us to probe beyond a child's observed performance. Moreover, the combination of testing and teaching appeals to many psychologists and educators. Educators, psychologists, and other researchers have been captivated by Vygotsky's notion that we can extend and facilitate children's development of cognitive abilities.

Both Piaget and Vygotsky—arguably the two most influential developmental psychologists to date—urged us not to be content just to note whether children's responses to questions and tasks are accurate. The power of these two developmental psychologists lay in their interest in probing beneath the surface, to try to understand why children behave and respond as they do. As is true of almost any significant contribution to science, Vygotsky's and Piaget's ideas are measured more by how much they prompt us to extend our knowledge than by how nearly perfectly they have represented a complete, final understanding of the developing human mind. Perhaps the most we can ask of a theory is that it be worthy of further exploration. Next, we consider cognitive development as studied in the realm of information-processing skills.

DEVELOPMENT OF INFORMATION-PROCESSING SKILLS

Information-processing theorists seek to understand cognitive development in terms of how people of different ages process (i.e., decode, encode, transfer, combine, store, and retrieve) information, particularly when solving challenging mental problems. We should state at the outset that the available information-processing theories make no claim to providing as comprehensive and well integrated an explanation of cognitive development as did Piaget or even Vygotsky. On the other hand, information-processing theorists, taken as a whole, consider the entire range of cognitive processes that manipulate information in persons of all ages. Any mental activity that involves noticing, taking in, mentally manipulating, storing, combining, retrieving, or acting on information falls within the purview of these approaches: How do our processes, strategies, or ways of representing and organizing information change over time, if at all? If there are changes, what may cause them?

Information-processing theorists take one of two fundamental approaches to studying information processing: a primarily domain-general or a primarily domain-specific approach. Domain-general theorists try to describe, in general terms, how people mentally process information. They want to show how general principles of information processing apply and are used across a variety of cognitive functions, from making perceptual judgments to understanding written text to reading maps to solving calculus problems. Most of these theories emphasize developmental changes in encoding, self-monitoring, and use of feedback. Domain-specific theorists emphasize the role of the development of competencies and knowledge in specific domains, arguing that most development is of this domain-specific kind.

In regard to encoding, as children grow older, they can more fully encode many features of their environment and can organize their encodings more effectively (e.g., Siegler, 1984, 1996; Sternberg, 1982, 1984). Throughout childhood, children increasingly integrate and combine encoded information in more complex ways, forming more elaborate connections with what they already know. In addition, older children just know more than do younger ones, and they can call on increasingly large stores of remembered information.

Metacognitive Skills and Complex Memory Development

It has also been suggested that older children may have greater processing resources (Kail & Bisanz, 1992), such as attentional resources and working memory, which may underlie their overall greater speed of cognitive processing. According to this view, the reason that older children seem able to process information more quickly than younger children may be that they can hold more information for active processing. Hence, in addition to being able to organize information into increasingly large and complex chunks, older children may be able to hold more chunks of information in working memory.

It appears that children increasingly develop and use metamemory skills and various other kinds of *metacognitive skills* (involving the understanding and control of cognitive processes), such as monitoring and modifying their own cognitive processes while they are engaged in tackling cognitive tasks (A. L. Brown, 1978; Flavell & Wellman, 1977). Many information-processing researchers have been interested in the specific metacognitive skills of older children, including understanding appearance and reality. For example, 4- and 5-year-old children were shown imitation objects, such as a sponge that looked exactly like a rock (Flavell, Flavell, & Green, 1983). The researchers encouraged the children to play with the imitations, so it would be clear to the children that the fakes were not what they appeared to be and they could become thoroughly familiar with the objects. The children then had to answer questions about the identity of the objects. Afterward, the children were asked to view the objects through a blue plastic sheet, which distorted the perceived hues of the objects, and to make judgments of the colors of the objects. The children were also asked to judge the sizes of the objects while viewing them under a magnifying glass. The children were fully aware that they were viewing the objects through these intermediaries.

The children made two fundamental kinds of errors. On the one hand, when asked to report reality (the way the object actually was), the children would sometimes report appearance (the way the object looked through the blue plastic or the magnifying glass). On the other hand, when asked to report appearance, they would sometimes report the reality. In other words, these 4- and 5-year-old children did not yet clearly perceive the distinction between appearance and reality.

Actually, many Piagetians would agree with the observation that young children often fail to distinguish appearance from reality; their failure to conserve quantity may also be attributed to their attention to the change in appearance, rather than to the stability of the quantity. Children also increasingly profit from and eventually even seek feedback on the outcomes of their cognitive efforts. These changes in encoding, memory organization and storage, metacognition, and use of feedback seem to affect children's cognitive development across many specific domains. In addition, however, some cognitive-developmental changes seem to be domain specific. The development of memory skills is discussed next.

The use of external memory aids, of rehearsal, and of many other memory strategies seems to come naturally to almost all adults—so much so that we may take for granted that we have always done it; we have not. Appel and her colleagues (1972) designed an experiment to discover the extent to which young children spontaneously rehearse. They showed colored pictures of common objects to children at three grade levels: preschoolers, first graders, and fifth graders and instructed the children either to "look at" the names of 15 pictures or to "remember" the names for a later test.

When the preschool children were instructed just to look at the pictures, very few seemed to know that it would be a good idea to rehearse the information they would later be asked to recall. Moreover, the preschoolers' performance was no better in the memory condition than in the looking condition. The older children performed better. On the basis of these and other data, Flavell and Wellman (1977) concluded that the major difference between the memory of younger and older children (as well as adults) is not in basic mechanisms, but in learned strategies, such as rehearsal. Young children seriously overestimate their ability to recall information and rarely spontaneously use rehearsal strategies when asked to recall items. That is, they seem not to know about many memory-enhancing strategies.

Even when young children do know about such strategies, they do not always use them. For example, when they are trained to use rehearsal strategies in one task, most do not *transfer* the use of that strategy from one task to other tasks (Flavell & Wellman, 1977). Thus, it appears that young children lack not only the knowledge of strategies but the inclination to use them when they do know about them. Older children understand that to retain words in short-term memory, they need to rehearse; younger children do not. In a nutshell, younger children lack metamemory skills.

Whether children rehearse is not just a function of age. A. L. Brown, Campione, Bray, and Wilcox (1973) found that mentally retarded children are much less likely to rehearse spontaneously than are children of normal intelligence. Indeed, if such children are trained to rehearse, their performance can greatly improve (Belmont & Butterfield, 1971; Butterfield, Wambold, & Belmont, 1973). However, the retarded performers do not always spontaneously transfer their learning to other tasks. For example, if the children are taught to rehearse with lists of numbers but then are presented with a list of animals, they may have to be taught all over again to rehearse for the new kinds of items, as well as for the old.

Culture, experience, and environmental demands also affect the use of memory-enhancing strategies. For example, Western children, who generally have more formal schooling than do non-Western children, are given much more practice using rehearsal strategies for remembering isolated bits of information. In contrast, Guatemalan children and Australian aboriginal children generally have many more opportunities to become adept at using memory-enhancing strategies that rely on spatial location and arrangements of objects (Kearins, 1981; Rogoff, 1986).

Another aspect of metamemory skills involves *cognitive monitoring*, in which the individual tracks and, as needed, readjusts an ongoing train of thought. Cognitive monitoring may include several related skills (A. L. Brown, 1978; see also A. L. Brown & DeLoache, 1978). For one thing, you realize "what you know and what you do not know" (A. L. Brown, 1978, p. 82). You learn to be aware of your own mind and the degree of your own understanding (Holt, 1964). More recent work on the development of cognitive monitoring (Nelson & Narens, 1994) proposed a distinction between self-monitoring and self-regulation strategies. Self-monitoring, a bottom-up process of keeping track of current understanding, involves the improving ability to predict memory performance accurately. Self-regulation is a top-down process of central executive control over planning and evaluation. Children benefit from training in using such cognitive monitoring processes to enhance their use of appropriate strategies (see Schneider & Bjorklund, 1998).

Physiological maturation of the brain and increasing knowledge of content may partially explain why adults and older children generally perform better on memory tests than do younger children. These physiological and experience-based changes augment the changes in memory processes, such as increased knowledge about and an inclination to use metamemory strategies. The goal of such strategies is for the child eventually to be able to retrieve stored information, at will.

Quantitative Skills

One approach to understanding quantitative skills has considered computational abilities, as in the ability to solve the addition problem, "2 + 3 = ?" Several information-processing models have proposed how children solve both addition problems (e.g., Groen & Parkman, 1972; Suppes & Groen, 1967) and subtraction problems (Siegler & Shrager, 1984; see also Resnick, 1980). Early models described some type of mental counter that starts at some value (determined by the addition problem) and then adds increments as needed (also determined by the addition problem). Before each *increment* (i.e., addition of one unit), a mental test counts whether the child has already added the needed number of increments. If so, the incremental process stops, and the child has reached the answer. If not, the child adds increments one by one until the required number of increments (in this case, three) have been added.

Siegler's model (1991, 1996; Siegler & Shrager, 1984) enhances the early models by adding a second major component to the process. Specifically, once children encode the problem, they first attempt to retrieve a potential correct answer from memory. If the answer they retrieve exceeds their own preset level of confidence in the accuracy of the answer, they state the retrieved answer. If it does not, they again try to retrieve a correct answer from memory. They repeat this process until they either retrieve a satisfactory answer that exceeds their confidence level or they exceed a preset number of retrieval attempts. If they exceed their preset number of retrieval attempts, they then turn to a *backup strategy* (a more time-consuming but more reliable way of reaching an answer, used when faster methods fail to produce satisfactory results). For addition problems, this backup strategy is the incremental counter mentioned in other models. Siegler has also applied the strategy-choice (retrieval-backup) model to children's other arithmetic computations, such as multiplication (Siegler, 1988).

In a review of the literature on the development of mathematical skills, Ginsburg (1996) proposed various basic principles of mathematical learning. Here, we discuss a few key ideas about the development of quantitative skills. First, even infants have some fundamental notion of quantity within the range of small numbers. Prelinguistic infants seem to know that adding leads to greater quantities and subtracting leaves smaller quantities. Moreover, young children appear to build on this fundamental knowledge to apply more abstract mathematical concepts in counting and to reason about addition and subtraction. Not only do children use the counting and memorization strategies previously discussed, but they derive abstract rules from experience with particular kinds of counting sets. For example, rule learning combined with practice in counting by fives allows children to acquire multiplication principles more easily (Baroody, 1993). Finally, context effects, from the wording of problems to the cultural environment, greatly influence mathematical learning beyond the formulation of informal strategies.

Inductive Reasoning

Inductive reasoning leads not to a single, logically certain solution to a problem, but only to solutions that have different levels of plausibility. In inductive reasoning, the reasoner induces general principles, based on specific observations. Carey (1985; see also Carey & S. A. Gelman, 1991) has done extensive observations of inductive reasoning in children and has detected some developmental trends. For one thing, it appears that 4 year olds do not induce generalized biological principles about animals when they are given specific information about individual animals. By age 10, however, children are much more likely to do so. For example, if 4 year olds are told that both dogs and bees have a particular body organ, they still assume that only animals that are highly similar either to dogs or to bees have this organ and that other animals do not. In contrast, 10 year olds would induce that if animals as dissimilar as dogs and bees have this organ, many other animals are likely to have it, as well. They are also much more likely than 4 year olds to induce biological principles that link humans to other animals. Along the same lines, when 5 year olds learn new information about a specific kind of animal, they seem to add the information to their existing schemas for the particular kind of animal but not to modify their overall schemas for animals or for biology as a whole (see Keil, 1989, 1994). On the other hand, first- and second-graders have shown an ability to choose and even to spontaneously generate appropriate tests for gathering indirect evidence to confirm or disconfirm alternative hypotheses (Sodian, Zaitchik, & Carey, 1991).

S. A. Gelman (1984/1985) and S. A. Gelman & Markman, 1987) noted that even children as young as 3 years old seem to induce some general principles from specific observations, particularly principles that pertain to taxonomic categories for animals. For example, preschoolers were able to induce principles that correctly attribute the cause of phenomena (such as growth) to natural processes, rather than to human intervention (S. A. Gelman, Coley, & Gottfried, 1994; S. A. Gelman & Kremer, 1991; Hickling & Gelman, 1995). In related work, preschoolers were able to reason correctly that a blackbird was more likely to behave like a flamingo than like a bat because blackbirds and flamingos are both birds (S. A. Gelman & Markman, 1987). Note that in this example, the preschoolers were going against their perception that blackbirds look more like bats than like flamingos, basing their judgment instead on the fact that both flamingos and blackbirds are birds (although the effect is admittedly strongest when the term *bird* is also used in regard to both the flamingo and the blackbird).

Another study by S. A. Gelman and Markman (1986) supported the view that preschoolers may make decisions that are based on induced general principles, rather than on perceptual appearances; for example, preschoolers may induce taxonomic categories based on functions (such as means of breathing) instead of on perceptual appearances (such as apparent weight). Furthermore, when given information about the internal parts of objects in one category, preschoolers also induced that other objects in the same category were likely to have the same internal parts (S. A. Gelman & O'Reilly, 1988; see also S. A. Gelman & Wellman, 1991). On the other hand, when inducing principles from discrete information, preschoolers were more likely than older children to emphasize external, superficial features of animals than to give weight to internal structural or functional features. Also, given the same specific information, older children seem to induce richer inferences regarding biological properties than do younger children (S. A. Gelman, 1989).

In a more recent review, Wellman and Gelman (1998) stressed the importance of maintaining both forms of knowledge, appearance-based and principled, for flexible use across dif-

TABLE 14.2 Summary of Cognitive-Development Theories

Theory	Nature or Nurture?	Continuous or Discontinuous (Stages)?	Domain General or Domain Specific?	Process by Which Development Occurs?
Piaget	Biological maturation is crucial; environment plays a secondary but important role.	There are four discontinuous stages.	Development largely occurs simultaneously across domains, although some domains may show change slightly ahead of others.	Equilibratory processes of assimilation and accommodation
Neo-Piagetians	May emphasize role of the environment somewhat more than Piaget did.	May add a fifth stage; may question the ages for particular stages suggested by Piaget.	Same as Piaget (i.e., development largely occurs simultaneously across domains, although some domains may show change slightly ahead of others).	Same as Piaget (i.e., equilibratory processes of assimilation and accommodation)
Vygotsky	Social and physical environment plays a crucial role; maturational readiness may provide the broad parameters (zone of proximal development) within which the social environment determines development.	Continuous	The zone of proximal development may apply to many domains, but the environment may provide sufficient support for development only in specific domains, thus affecting development.	Internalization that results from interactions between the individual and the environment, occurring within the individual's zone of proximal development
Information-processing theorists	Nature provides the physiological structures and functions (e.g., memory capacity), and nurture provides the environmental supports that allow the individual to make the most of the existing structures and functions.	Continuous	Some theorists have been interested in processes that generalize across all domains; others have focused their research and theories on specific domains.	Internal changes in cognitive processing, as a result of physiological maturation, environmental events, and the individual's own shaping of cognitive processes

ferent situations and domains. Knowledge of deep internal functional relationships is important for inducing properties of objects, but similarity in appearance is important under other circumstances. Wellman and Gelman proposed that the acquisition of knowledge develops via the use of framework theories, or models, for drawing inferences about the environment in various domains (such as physics, psychology, and biology). They cited numerous studies that demonstrated children's early and rapid acquisition of expertise in understanding physical objects and causal relations between events, psychological entities and casual-explanatory reasoning, and biological entities and forces. The changes in reasoning about factors in these domains appear to show children's enhanced understanding of the relationship between appearances and deeper functional principles. Thus, children use foundational knowledge within different domains to build framework understandings of the world.

To summarize these findings, it appears that, once again, early developmental psychologists may have underestimated the cognitive capabilities of young children. In addition, a supportive context can greatly enhance children's ability to induce appropriate principles (Keil, 1989, 1994). Nonetheless, there seems to be a developmental trend toward an increasing sophistication in inducing general principles from specific information and toward increasing reliance on more subtle features of the information on which such inductions are based. Furthermore, this sophisticated knowledge may be organized into general frameworks for understanding within the important domains of physics, psychology, and biology.

In this section, we attempted to provide a brief but diverse survey of the abundant research on information-processing theories of cognitive development. These theories greatly elaborate on Piaget's theories, providing details of performance that Piaget did not specify—and show that Piaget's model applies more to ideal competencies than to everyday performances. This vast area of study encompasses far more than can be included in this introduction to cognitive development, but the material covered here provides a good foundation for further investigation.

Finally, it should be noted that the cognitive-developmental perspectives discussed here are not mutually exclusive; some have been pursued simultaneously, some have evolved as reactions to other theories, and some are offshoots of others. Table 14.2 summarizes the ways in which these theories compare, contrast, and relate to one another. All these theories of cognitive development contribute to the ongoing process of understanding how and why we humans think as we do. Yet another view of cognitive development considers the physiological development of the brain and neural apparatus.

COGNITIVE NEUROPSYCHOLOGICAL CHANGES IN DEVELOPMENT

Increasing Neuronal Complexity

Figure 14.1 illustrates some of the striking microlevel (fine) changes in the neural networks of the brain that occur during the first two years of life. In this early period of rapid neural growth, no new neurons are formed; the growth that takes place is the dendritic and axonal growth of existing cells. Here, the "use it or lose it" principle clearly applies—cells that are

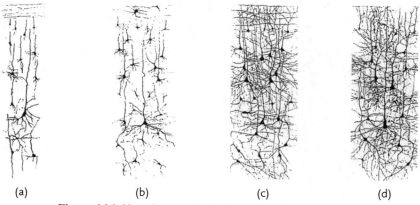

(a)   (b)   (c)   (d)

Figure 14.1 Neural networks in the developing human brain.

not needed and do not form connections to other cells actually die. Likewise, synaptic connections between neurons that are not used become overwhelmed by competing connections that are used. After the first few years, however, the rate of neural growth and development declines dramatically. In fact, 90% of neural growth is complete by age 6. Recall that the evidence for a critical period in language acquisition coincides with this period. Perhaps the complexities of language acquisition (along with other early acquired skills) require the increased plasticity and flexibility of the early developing nervous system. Both the micro- and the macrolevel changes in structure show an increase in complexity over the course of development.

Maturation of Central Nervous System Structures

At birth, the brain stem (which comprises the hindbrain, the midbrain, and part of the forebrain) is almost fully developed. Nonetheless, some subcortical developments continue to influence cognitive development after birth. For example, enhancements in recognition memory seem to correspond to maturation of the hippocampus (Diamond, 1990). Compared with subcortical structures, however, the cerebral cortex is still largely immature.

The areas of the brain that develop most rapidly after birth are those in the sensory and motor cortex; subsequently, the association areas related to problem solving, reasoning, memory, and language develop. The preceding sections of this chapter have already suggested that the physiological material with which we think becomes increasingly complex and that sensorimotor development precedes more sophisticated cognitive processes.

Similarly, physiological changes in the frontal lobes parallel cognitive changes. In infants, maturation of the frontal lobes seems to parallel the significant cognitive developments of this period noted by Piaget (Diamond, 1993; see also Goldman-Rakic, 1993). ERP (event-related potential) studies of electrical waves in the brain have found that later in development, frontal-lobe maturation is linked to reading skills, in that a threshold level of maturation seems to be necessary for effective reading. Above that threshold level of maturation, however, differences in reading skills were correlated with differences in hemispheric specialization for language skill (Segalowitz, Wagner, & Menna, 1992).

Intriguing findings regarding hemispheric specialization may also provide insights into a recurring issue in the study of cognitive development. Studies of the EEG (electroencephalograms) patterns of 577 people who ranged in age from 2 months to early adulthood found different developmental patterns in the right and left cerebral hemispheres (Thatcher, Walker, & Giudice, 1987). In the right hemisphere, there appear to be continuous, gradual changes in EEG patterns associated with age. In the left hemisphere, however, there seem to be abrupt shifts in the EEG patterns, at least through early adulthood.

Additional studies of cerebral architecture development and EEG patterns have found alternations between growth spurts in left and right hemisphere synaptic connections; that is, development in one hemisphere proceeds much more rapidly than in the other during one period, and then the pattern switches to dominance of the other hemisphere. Such alternating asymmetries in hemispheric development could perhaps underlie adult hemispheric differences in abilities—adult left-hemisphere dominance in particular language abilities may reflect the acquisition of those skills during the time of left-hemisphere growth dominance. Likewise, individual differences in relative timing of periods of skill acquisition and periods of hemispheric dominance could be related. Moreover, the anterior portions of the frontal lobes, through connections to posterior areas, appear to regulate the synaptic reorganization of posterior areas.

Thus, there are not only left-right changes in development, but front-back changes as well (Thatcher, 1991, 1992, 1994).

Between the peak in neural growth (in early adulthood) and about age 80, people lose about 5% of their brain weight. Nonetheless, changes in neural connections help to compensate for this loss of cells (Coleman & Flood, 1986). That is, over the life span, people's brains show continually increasing specificity of neural connections (as long as people remain mentally active and do not suffer from abnormal pathologies). Just what those physiological changes may mean in terms of cognitive development during adulthood is the topic of the next section.

COMPLEX COGNITIVE DEVELOPMENT IN ADULTHOOD

Thus far, this chapter has focused primarily on cognitive development in children. Cognitive development does not stop at adolescence, however. Many cognitive psychologists study the changes in abilities that occur over a lifetime. In this final section, we address cognitive development in adults.

Patterns of Growth and Decline

Is cognitive growth never ending? Do scores on cognitive-ability tests continue to increase indefinitely? The available data suggest that they may not. Cognitive psychologists often distinguish between *fluid intelligence*—the cognitive-processing skills that enable us to manipulate abstract symbols, as in mathematics—and *crystallized intelligence*—our stored knowledge, which is largely declarative, such as vocabulary, but may also be procedural, as in the expertise of a master chess player. It turns out that although crystallized intelligence is higher, on average, for older adults than for younger adults, fluid intelligence is higher, on average, for younger adults than for older ones (Horn & Cattell, 1966). For example, the performance of older adults on many information-processing tasks, particularly complex tasks, appears to be slower than that of younger adults (Bashore, Osman, & Hefley, 1989; Cerella, 1990, 1991; Poon, 1987; Salthouse, 1996; Schaie, 1989). In general, crystallized cognitive abilities seem to increase throughout the life span, whereas fluid cognitive abilities seem to increase until the 20s or 30s or possibly the 40s and slowly to decrease thereafter. The preservation of crystallized abilities suggests that long-term memory and the structure and organization of knowledge representation are preserved across the life span (see Salthouse, 1992, 1996).

Although psychometric researchers disagree about the age when fluid intelligence starts to decline, many researchers agree that eventually some decline does occur. The rate and extent of decline varies widely across people. Some cognitive abilities also seem to decline under some circumstances but not others, on average. For example, the effectiveness of performance on some problem-solving tasks appears to decline with age (Denny, 1980), although even brief training appears to improve older adults' scores on problem-solving tasks (Rosenzweig & Bennett, 1996; Willis, 1985).

Not all cognitive abilities decline, however. For example, Cerella, Rybash, Hoyer, and Commons (1993) devoted 20 chapters to describing studies that showed little or no intellectual decline in various areas of cognition, including object and word perception, language comprehension, and problem solving. Some researchers (e.g., Schaie & Willis, 1986) have found that some kinds of learning abilities seem to increase, and others (Graf, 1990; Labouvie-Vief

& Schell, 1982; Perlmutter, 1983) have found that the ability to learn and remember meaningful skills and information shows little decline. In addition, even in a single domain, such as memory, decreases in one kind of performance may not imply decreases in another. For example, although short-term memory performance seems to decline (Hultsch & Dixon, 1990), long-term memory (Bahrick, Bahrick, & Wittlinger, 1975) and recognition memory (Schonfield & Robertson, 1966) remain good.

Some researchers (e.g., Schaie, 1974, 1996) have even questioned much of the evidence for intellectual decline. For one thing, our views of memory and aging may be confounded by reports of pathological changes that occur in some older adults. Such changes are not due to general intellectual decline, but are a result of specific neurophysiological disorders. These neurophysiological disorders, such as Alzheimer's disease, are fairly uncommon even among the most elderly. Preventive screening tools for Alzheimer's disease, which capitalize on differences in the typical abilities of aging adult, are currently being investigated with mixed success (Mirmiran, van Someren, & Swaab, 1996).

Another qualification on findings of decline in older age is the use of *cross-sectional research designs*, which involve testing different cohorts (generations) of individuals at the same time. Such designs tend to overestimate the extent of decline of cognitive abilities because for unknown reasons, more recent generations of individuals show higher cognitive abilities—at least as measured by IQ (J. R. Flynn, 1987; T. M. Flynn, 1978; Neisser, 1998)—than do earlier generations (see chapter 11). Consequently, the lower IQs of the older individuals may be a generational effect, rather than an aging effect. Indeed, studies that have used *longitudinal research designs*, which test the same individuals repeatedly over an extended period, have found less decline in mental abilities with age. These studies, however, may underestimate the extent of decline because the less able participants drop out over the years, perhaps because they find it discouraging or even humiliating to take the cognitive tests.

Although the debate about intellectual decline with age continues, positions have converged somewhat. For one thing, there is a general consensus (e.g., Cerella, 1990, 1991; Kliegl, Mayr, & Krampe, 1994; Salthouse, 1994, 1996) that some slowing of the rate of cognitive processing occurs throughout adulthood, and the evidence of slowing remains even when the experimental methodology and analyses rule out the disproportionate representation of demented adults among the elderly (e.g., Salthouse, Kausler, & Saults, 1990). Among the general factors that have been suggested as contributing to age-related slowing of cognitive processing have been a generalized decline in CNS (central nervous system) functioning (Cerella, 1991), a decline in working-memory capacity (Salthouse, 1993), and a decline in attentional resources (see Horn & Hofer, 1992).

Salthouse (1996) attempted to explain why slowed processing may lead to cognitive deficits by pointing to two speed-related issues in cognitive functioning: limited time and simultaneity. Slowed processing may prevent certain operations from being computed because such operations may need to occur within a limited amount of time, and the operations may need to overlap because of storage limitations. For example, auditory memory decays rapidly, leading to the necessity for the rapid classification of auditory signals. The slowing of upper-level processing can result in incomplete or inaccurate processing of auditory signals. Given the semiparallel nature of much cognitive processing, along with the nature of synaptic transmission, it is not surprising that speed would be an issue, because such processing is time dependent.

In addition to these general factors, many cognitive-developmental psychologists have suggested that specific factors affect age-related changes in cognitive processing and may differentially affect various cognitive tasks. For example, specific factors include the greater slowing of higher-order cognitive processes than of sensory-motor processes (Cerella, 1985), differential slowing of high- versus low-complexity tasks (Kliegl et al., 1994), greater slowing of tasks that require coordinative complexity (simultaneous processing of multiple stimuli) than of tasks that require sequential complexity (sequential processing of multiple stimuli) (Mayr & Kliegl, 1993), and a greater age-related decline in processes of information retrieval than in processes of encoding (see Salthouse, 1992). In addition, priming effects and tasks that require implicit memory seem to show little or no evidence of an age-related decline, but tasks that involve explicit memory do (Salthouse, 1992).

On the basis of the existing research, three basic principles of cognitive development in adulthood have been suggested (Dixon & Baltes, 1986). First, although fluid abilities and other aspects of information processing may decline in late adulthood, this decline is balanced by the stabilization and even advancement of well-practiced and pragmatic aspects of mental functioning (crystallized abilities). Second, despite the age-related decline in information processing, sufficient reserve capacity allows for at least temporary increases in performance, especially if an older adult is motivated to perform well. Third, when adults lose some of the speed and physiology-related efficiency of information processing, they often compensate, in a given task, with other knowledge- and expertise-based information-processing skills (Salthouse, 1991, 1996; see also Salthouse & Somberg, 1982).

Although the evidence regarding age-related differences in the selection of cognitive strategies is mixed, there appear to be no age-related differences in self-monitoring of cognitive processes (see Salthouse, 1992), so it would appear that older adults may be able to utilize information on how to enhance their cognitive performance effectively. Also, when the performance of a task is based more on accuracy than on speed, older adults may at least partly compensate for deficits in speed with greater carefulness and persistence (see Horn & Hofer, 1992). Furthermore, throughout the life span, there is a considerable **plasticity**—modifiability—of abilities (Baltes, 1997; Baltes & Willis, 1979; Mirmiran et al., 1996; Rosenzweig & Bennett, 1996). None of us is stuck at a particular level of performance. Each of us can improve.

Many researchers have come to believe that adult cognition not only does not decline but actually continues to develop and improve. Recall, for example, the characteristics of postformal thought, proposed by some neo-Piagetian fifth-stage theorists. Those who support the notion of postformal thought indicate some ways in which older adults may show a kind of thinking that qualitatively differs from the thinking of adolescents and perhaps even young adults (Moshman, 1998). Although older adults generally do not have the same speed of information processing as do younger adults, they may demonstrate the benefits of taking time to consider alternatives and to reflect on past experiences before making judgments—a skill often termed *wisdom*.

Wisdom and Aging

In recent years, life-span developmental psychologists have become particularly interested in the development of wisdom in adulthood (see Sternberg, 1990). Most theorists have argued that wisdom increases with age, although there are exceptions (Meacham, 1990). Psychologists' definitions of wisdom have been diverse. Some (Baltes & Smith, 1990; Baltes, Staudinger, Maercker, & Smith, 1995, p. 95) defined **wisdom** as "exceptional insight into human development and life matters, exceptionally good judgment, advice, and commentary about difficult life problems." Furthermore, wisdom can be seen as reflecting a positive gain in culture-based cognitive pragmatics (meaningful uses of cognitive skills) in the face of the more physiologically controlled losses in cognitive mechanics (Baltes, 1993). Other research (Sternberg, 1985) found six factors in people's conceptions of wisdom: reasoning ability, sagacity (shrewdness), learning from ideas and from the environment, judgment, expeditious use of information, and *perspicacity* (intensely keen awareness, perception, and insight). Another important factor in wisdom is to know what you do not know (Meacham, 1983, 1990). Whatever the definition, the study of wisdom represents an exciting new direction for discovering which abilities may be developed during later adulthood at the same time that fluid abilities or the mechanical aspects of information processing may be flagging.

Recently, a new theory, called the *balance theory of wisdom*, defined wisdom as the application of informal knowledge for the common good through a balancing of intrapersonal (one's own), interpersonal (others'), and extrapersonal (institutional) interests so that the individual can adapt to, shape, and select environments (Sternberg, 2000). In other words, wisdom involves using one's abilities not only for one's own benefit, but for the benefit of others. Given the state of the world, perhaps we need to place more emphasis in our instruction on wisdom and not so much emphasis simply on intelligence and achievement used only for people's personal and often selfish aims.

◆ SUMMARY

It used to be thought that there were two separate programs for the development of intelligence: one in infancy and one thereafter. Research on infants' preference for novelty, however, has suggested that there may be just a single program—that what constitutes intelligence in infancy is essentially the same as what constitutes intelligence later on. Piaget proposed that cognitive development centers on increasingly complex adaptations to the environment, based primarily on changes that are due to physiological maturation. More specifically, he believed that cognitive development occurs largely through two processes of equilibration: *assimilation* and *accommodation*.

Piaget posited four stages of cognitive development: the *sensorimotor stage,* the *preoperational stage,* the *concrete-operational stage,* and the *formal-operational stage.* At the end of the sensorimotor stage, children start to develop *representational thought,* involving people and objects that they cannot currently see, hear, or otherwise perceive—first clearly noticeable in the achievement of *object permanence,* but later apparent in other cognitive developments as well. Furthermore, as children grow older, they become less *egocentric,* that is, less focused on themselves and better able to see things from the perspective of others. Some theorists have posited a fifth stage beyond Piaget's original four. Such a postformal stage may involve problem finding (rather than problem solving) or a tendency toward dialectical thinking.

Vygotsky's theory of cognitive development emphasizes the importance of the social context, rather than physiological maturation, as a determinant of cognitive development. His theory stresses the importance of *internalization* and of the *zone of proximal development.* In general, development can be seen as the interaction of biological and environmental factors leading to increased cognitive complexity and flexibility.

Information-processing theorists seek to understand cognitive development in terms of how children at different ages process information, particularly in regard to problem solving. Some theorists have formulated general theories of how information processing works, and others have studied information processing within specific domains. In general, the development of many abilities can be related to changes in *metacognitive* skills, particularly knowing the difference between appearance and reality. Furthermore, the development of memory seems to be related to the spontaneous use of rehearsal strategies. Finally, the development of other skills, such as quantitative, visuospatial, and reasoning skills, appear to involve the ability to use rule-based processes and increasingly more subtle strategies.

Overall, cognitive neuropsychological development entails increases in the complexity of neuronal connections with decreases in the actual number of neurons used in the brain. The maturation of the structures of the central nervous system likewise become more complex, and some studies have found cyclical patterns of discontinuous hemispheric development.

It appears that *fluid abilities*—involved in rapid cognitive processing in response to new cognitive tasks—first increase and then start to decline at some point in later life, whereas *crystallized abilities*—represented by the accumulation of knowledge—increase across the life span or at least gradually stabilize in later adulthood. In addition, *wisdom* (broadly defined as extraordinary insight, keen awareness, and exceptional judgment) generally increases with age, although there are exceptions.

15 Teaching Thinking

◆ Domain Generality Versus Domain Specificity

◆ Teaching Thinking From the General to the Specific

◆ Teaching Thinking From the Specific to the General

◆ Promoting a Culture of Thinkers: The Role of Belief Systems and Motivational Factors

◆ Summary

I have never let my schooling interfere with my education.
—MARK TWAIN

Almost all of us know that we cannot divide by zero, but few of us who are not well trained in mathematics can say why we cannot. The disconcerting phenomenon of being able to state facts we know so well without being able to explain their origins is not confined to mathematics. Why are vitamins beneficial? What made Picasso a creative genius? Answers to these and similar questions require an understanding of the underlying principles, the deep structure, of a domain.

In an effort to promote more meaningful learning, researchers and educators have developed programs for teaching thinking. A large part of their efforts have been dedicated to teaching *metacognition*, or thinking about thinking. Metacognitive strategies help learners become aware of their learning strategies and gain more control over the acquisition of substantive knowledge.

We first present a brief history of teaching for thinking and the role of metacognition in promoting meaningful learning. Then we introduce two different philosophical viewpoints on the contributions of cognitive psychology to educational practice. The "cognitivist" view suggests that cognitive psychology can contribute greatly to the understanding of educational practice by examining people's problem-solving behavior in the classroom as well as in the laboratory (J. R. Anderson, Reder, & Simon, 1996, 1997). The "situative" view argues that cognitive psychological studies have limited applications to educational practice because they assume that learning resides in the mind of the individual instead of in the interaction between the individual and his or her environment (Greeno, 1997). The situative view encourages educators to use ethnographic and sociological methods of investigation that do not separate cognition from the social context in which it is embedded.

We next focus on a related debate over whether teaching thinking should occur in specific subject domains, such as mathematics (the **domain-specific view**), or whether thinking should be taught as a separate subject domain, alongside more traditional ones like mathematics and art (the **domain-general view**). In the reminder of the chapter we discuss domain-specific and domain-general programs for teaching thinking and examine their advantages and disadvantages with an emphasis on cognitivist and situative perspectives.

Finally, we discuss the role of motivational factors and belief systems in the success of teaching-for-thinking programs.

Imagine that you are asked to tutor a fourth grader who is in the process of learning to add fractions. Your student is bright and motivated but has made a mistake that is typical of children his age by adding the numerators and denominators of the fractions directly:

$$\frac{1}{3} + \frac{1}{2} = \frac{2}{5}$$

When you question the child, he provides you with the following proof: "Well, if I have a 1/2 then I have one piece of a two-piece pie; I add a 1/3, which is one piece of a three-piece pie; so I get two pieces out of a total of five pieces altogether, which is 2/5" (adapted from Silver, 1986). The child then concludes his proof by drawing pie representations and counting the shaded regions (1 and 2) out of the overall regions of the two pies (1, 2, 3, 4, and 5) (see Figure 15.1). The child uses a correct pie representation for fractions incorrectly, by misunderstanding the relationship between the part and the whole. How would you teach the child the correct algorithm meaningfully in such a way that would convince the child that his proof is faulty? Recently, one of us asked college students in a course on human cognition to do just that. The students found this seemingly simple task to be challenging.

It is clear that accumulating knowledge and facts is a necessary but not sufficient condition for the development of critical reasoning skills (Nisbett, Fong, Lehman, & Cheng, 1987). Viewing knowledge as a collection of information, instead of as a unified structure with purpose and function, may even hamper the achievement of educational goals (e.g., Perkins, 1986). How, then, do we teach for more meaningful thinking? Teaching for thinking as an educational objective in the United States can be traced back to the efforts of John Dewey in the 1920s and 1930s. Dewey (1933, 1938) advocated the cultivation of reflective thinking as the chief aim of primary and secondary education. Reflective thinking is achieved when students learn to transform a situation that is unclear, fragmented, or ambiguous into one that is well defined and unified. Dewey argued that this process involves the general skills of identifying

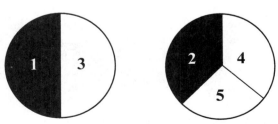

Figure 15.1 An incorrect pie representation of the addition of fractions $\left(\frac{1}{3} + \frac{1}{2} = \frac{2}{5}\right)$.

and formulating a given problem and generating and assessing adequate problem-solving strategies. A curriculum that teaches reflective thinking emphasizes understanding over rote learning, critical thinking over blind acceptance, and concrete experience over abstract materials.

To attain reflective thinking, one needs to achieve a high level of metacognition, or thinking about thinking. Metacognition has been defined in terms of the following three variables and their possible interactions (Flavell, 1981):

1. **Person variables**, which encompass people's beliefs about human cognition, in general, and about their personal thoughts and problem-solving strategies (e.g., learning to assess one's natural tendency to represent information—visual versus verbal)

2. **Task variables**, which relate to understanding the nature of the problem to be solved (e.g., realizing that it is better to space one's learning over a few days before taking an exam, rather than to cram for the test the night before)

3. **Strategy variables**, specific variables that relate to knowing how to approach a given task in multiple ways.

Developing metacognitive skills is important because errors in reasoning and problem solving often arise from what Baron (1993) termed mindless biases. One bias is accepting what may not be an optimal solution because one has deferred to experts in a field without thinking for oneself. Baron argued that one way to assess expert dogmas and opinions is to learn the different methods of inquiry associated with different disciplines. For example, to understand ideas in the social sciences, in general, and psychology, in particular, one needs to develop a metalevel awareness of the process of empirical investigation. Baron argued that this knowledge can be achieved via open-minded instruction that teaches methods of searching for counterexamples and promotes self-criticism. Beyth-Marom (1993) suggested taking Baron's logic one step further by teaching students how experts think in a domain (metacognitive knowledge of normative models); making students aware of their own thinking processes (metacognitive knowledge of descriptive models); and, finally, helping students compare these two models in an attempt to improve their thinking.

Beyth-Marom (1993) raised important questions regarding Baron's conception of open-minded instruction. Two of these questions—What is the role of cognitive psychology in teaching thinking? and Should thinking be taught as a separate subject, alongside other more traditional subjects, like mathematics, science, and art, or should it be integrated into traditional domain-specific classes?—lie at the core of the debate between two opposing camps. On the one hand, the **cognitivist camp** argues that cognitive psychology can contribute greatly to the understanding of educational practices by examining people's problem-solving strategies and representations (J. R. Anderson, Reder, & Simon, 1996, 1998; see also Halpern, 1998). For example, researchers have shown how the nature of worked-out examples leads students to form certain rules or schemas and affects their performance in predictable ways (e.g., Ben-Zeev, 1998; Zhu & Simon, 1988). On the other hand, the **situative camp** claims that cognitive psychology assumes that learning resides in the mind of the individual, instead of in the interaction between the individual and his or her environment (Greeno, 1996). This camp encourages educators to turn to ethnographic and sociological methods of investigation that do not separate cognition from the social context that the individual is a part of (for a critique of this conceptualization of cognitive psychological research, see J. R. Anderson et al., 1998).

Furthermore, the situative view argues that learning is tied to specific contexts and hence that learners have great difficulty transferring what they have learned from one domain to the next. Indeed, there is ample evidence that learning is affected differentially by situational factors. Lave's (1988) study of Orange County homemakers found that those who could calculate the best bargain in the supermarket often did not perform as well on formally equivalent arithmetic problems. In addition, Carraher et al. (1985) showed that Brazilian street children could perform accurate calculations on the job but not in the classroom. Furthermore, Kotovsky, Hayes, and Simon (1985) showed that the transfer of knowledge does not take place even across problems that contain an identical formal structure, including isomorphs of the Tower of Hanoi problem (see chapter 7 for more details). These studies, among others, point to the difficulty of *transferring* knowledge from one context to another (see also Gick & Holyoak, 1980, 1983).

J. R. Anderson and his colleagues (1996, 1998) acknowledged that environmental context is an important factor in the acquisition of skills but suggested that there are also many situations in which knowledge can be transferred between tasks in different domains (see also Fernandez & Glenberg, 1985; Saufley, Otaka, & Baversco, 1985). For example, once reading and writing skills are acquired, they can be used flexibly and almost effortlessly in a variety of domains. The transfer of knowledge can be fostered by giving students hints to use a familiar problem in a new domain (Gick & Holyoak, 1983) and multiple cross-domain examples during learning before they attempt to solve a new task (Catrambone & Holyoak, 1989). Anderson et al. argued that instruction that can help students recognize the relevance of a skill in multiple domains and to form an abstract representation of the underlying structure of surface-structurally different problems may help increase students' ability to generalize across domains.

Other evidence that general rules learned in a particular training environment can be transferred to other domains comes from studies that have shown that people are capable of learning and using formal rule systems to solve real-world problems (Fong et al., 1986; Lehman, Lempert, & Nisbett, 1988; Nisbett et al., 1987). For example, Fong et al. (1986) asked students with different levels of statistical training to generate an answer to a problem about a business woman who is often disappointed with the quality of meals served on repeated visits to a restaurant, although the meal was excellent on her first visit. The students without any statistical education provided nonstatistical, causal explanations for the disparity in the quality of the meals (e.g., "Maybe the chef quit"). Those who had taken one previous statistics course provided statistical answers about 20% of the time (e.g., "She was just lucky the first time"). Graduate psychology students who had taken up to three statistics courses offered correct statistical answers about 40% of the time (e.g., "This is an example of regression to the mean"). Finally, students with postgraduate training provided the correct statistical answers about 80% of the time. The positive effect of statistical training on solving novel problems suggests that people may be able to abstract rules learned in formal domains and transfer them to real-life domains that are surface-structurally different (involve different content).

Greeno (1996, p. 11) argued that the question about the transfer of knowledge can be put in a situative framework as follows: "When someone has become more successful at participating in an activity in one kind of situation, are there other kinds of situations in which that person will also be more adept?" Greeno views learning as improved participation in an interactive system that is subject to situational constraints and environmental affordances. In this framework, the transfer of knowledge depends on the degree of similarity between the affordances and constraints of the original situation and the new situation. If environments are dissimilar, the transfer of knowledge is not expected to occur.

The cognitive versus situative debate has influenced teaching-for-thinking programs in two important ways: the degree to which instruction is created to be domain general or domain specific and the degree to which emphasis is placed on learning individually versus learning in a community. In regard to the first point, cognitivist theorists believe that instruction in general rules would lead to improved performance across more specific domains. Situative theorists argue that formal and everyday types of reasoning are too disparate to allow transfer to take place. This idea can be traced to the earlier writings of Inhelder and Piaget (1958), who suggested that the rules of abstract reasoning are difficult to teach in a formal classroom structure because they are divorced from the way in which people create inductions from everyday experiences with the world. In terms of the second point, both camps encourage individual and group learning, but the situative theorists argue that all learning takes place in a social context that ought to be made explicit in the instructional process.

The cognitivist and situative perspectives tend to lead to different assumptions regarding the nature of learning and the possibilities of transferring knowledge. In the remainder of this chapter we divide programs along the generality-specificity dimension and try and explicate their underlying philosophies. We also focus on the individual-group learning dimension in each program.

DOMAIN GENERALITY VERSUS DOMAIN SPECIFICITY

The domain-general view holds that thinking is a subject domain that should be studied in its own right, alongside such subjects as history and geography. Students who take a course on thinking are expected to acquire general cognitive processes or strategies that, in turn, can be applied to specific content domains. In contrast, the domain-specific view holds that thinking skills are best taught in a specific context or content area. These content-rich strategies can be then applied to other areas, if there is an explicit effort to explicate how these areas are similar. We divide programs along two dimensions:

Dimension 1: *Teaching thinking from the general to the specific*. We discuss teaching-for-thinking programs that embrace the often-cognitivist view that students would benefit from learning general reasoning and problem-solving skills that they can then apply to specific domains. These programs tend to be taught as separate courses and to emphasize both group and individual learning.

Dimension 2: *Teaching thinking from the specific to the general*. We discuss teaching-for-thinking programs that embrace the often-situative view that students would benefit from learning reasoning and problem-solving skills in a rich content domain that they then can apply to similar domains. These programs tend to be part of the regular curriculum, rather than individual programs, and emphasize group over individual learning. These dimensions provide general guidelines that characterize the various approaches to teaching thinking, but they should not be thought of as hard-and-fast boundaries.

TEACHING THINKING FROM THE GENERAL TO THE SPECIFIC

In this section we cover the following programs: Philosophy for Children (Lipman, 1976), CoRT (deBono, 1968, 1970, 1976), Instrumental Enrichment (Feuerstein, 1979; Feuerstein,

Miller, & Jensen, 1980; Feuerstein & Rand, 1974; Feuerstein, Rand, & Hoffman, 1979; Feuerstein, Rand, Hoffman, & Miller, 1980; Feuerstein et al., 1981), Successful Intelligence, (Sternberg, 1996c, 1998a, 1998b; Sternberg & Kaufman, 1998; Sternberg & Spear-Swerling, 1996; Sternberg, Torff, & Grigorenko, 1998; Sternberg & Williams, 1998), Practical Intelligence for Schools (PIFS) (Gardner et al., 1994; Krechevsky & Gardner, 1990; Sternberg, 1994; Sternberg & Williams, 1998; Walters, Blythe, & White, 1993), and Intelligent Tutoring Systems (e.g., J. R. Anderson, 1993; Anderson et al., 1992; Burns & Capps, 1988). In general, these programs are designed as independent units for developing critical thinking skills (note, however, that PIFS is an exception). Each program helps improve reasoning in several specific domains on the basis of a set of core assumptions about the nature of learning and cognition.

The Philosophy for Children Program: Teaching Thinking About Thinking

Lipman (1976) developed the **Philosophy for Children** program to introduce the subject of "mind" into the curriculum explicitly. He believed that teaching thinking was just as important as the more traditional school subjects students are expected to learn. Underlying the Philosophy for Children program is the belief that children are intrinsically interested in philosophical and epistemological issues, that is, they have a "philosophical whimsy," a natural predilection toward exploring the kinds of questions that intrigue philosophers. The instructional materials are embedded in a set of novels. The basic novel, *Harry Stottlemeier's Discovery* (Lippman, 1974), is appropriate for fifth and sixth graders. In this book, Harry and his friends have conversations and experiences that revolve around topics, such as discovery and invention, cause and effect, and inductive reasoning. The scenarios that are depicted in *Harry Stottlemeier's Discovery* and other novels, such as *Tony* (reasoning in science) and *Lisa* (reasoning in ethics), depict children who are deliberating philosophical questions and have to determine how to conduct a scientific analysis of the questions. The children's introspections, experiences, and interactions with others are then discussed in the classroom. The teacher's role is to be an expert questioner who helps facilitate discussion and create a community of inquiry.

For example, in one scenario, Harry formulates the following problem: All planets revolve around the sun, but not everything that revolves around the sun is a planet. Harry then explores the asymmetry of this conditional relation and discovers the nonreversability of the logical "all" (for more details, see the section on the universal affirmative in chapter 5 of this book). Students learn to think deductively by following Harry's logic and examples. By reading and discussing these and similar scenarios, they learn to engage in 30 different thinking skills, such as identifying core concepts, generalizing from instances, and formulating cause-and-effect relationships. Students learn these skills by **identification** with the characters and **simulation** or adaptation of the characters' experiences to their own lives.

In general, the results of the Philosophy for Children program have been favorable. A study conducted by the Educational Testing Service (ETS) from 1976 to 1978 (reported in Nickerson, Perkins, & Smith, 1985) showed that a group of students who were exposed to this program performed better than controls on mathematics and reading tests and had a higher level of creative (as measured by ideational fluency or productivity tests) and formal reasoning skills. However, as Nickerson et al. (1985) pointed out, these results are hard to evaluate because the ETS study focused on statistically significant findings but did not report effect sizes or the magnitude of gains involved and it was unclear what kind of treatment the control participants received. Despite these criticisms, the Philosophy for Children program may serve as an important vehicle for providing students with an opportunity to engage in meaningful thinking.

The CoRT Program: Teaching Vertical and Lateral Thinking

The **CoRT (Cognitive Research Trust)** program was developed by deBono (1968, 1970, 1976) to facilitate the acquisition of a skillful and systematic method of thinking in students of all ages. Underlying the program's specific approaches is the distinction between vertical and lateral thinking. **Vertical thinking** refers to logical deduction that progresses in an orderly and restricted manner from its inception to its conclusion. It is often confined to a particular problem space or frame of reference. On the other hand, **lateral thinking** is often unpredictable and unconventional and tends to restructure the problem space or shift the problem solver's frame of reference. Vertical thinking can be used effectively to evaluate the strength of a particular idea. However, it is the more creative lateral thinking process that generates new ideas to be tested and elaborated on and new approaches to consider. DeBono posited that individuals who confine themselves to vertical thinking may express their ideas prematurely without sufficient consideration of alternatives.

The lessons of the CoRT program are designed to teach lateral and vertical thinking skills to students aged 8 to 22 with a wide range of ability levels. The lessons comprise 6 units, each containing 63 lessons. Each lesson is taught for 35 minutes once a week. The entire three-year program consists of teaching basic processes or mental operations for organizing and structuring one's problem-solving approach. For example, a lesson called APC (alternatives, possibilities, choices) encourages students to consider alternate problem-solving routes before they arrive at an answer. Students learn that the first viable path they discover may not be the only possible solution strategy.

The six CoRT units are as follows:

1. CoRT 1—Breadth—focuses on conceptualizing a situation in alternative ways and considering multiple factors that could affect a given situation. To achieve breadth, students are asked to examine the viewpoints of others that may or may not coincide with their own.

2. CoRT2—Organization—is designed to help students direct their attention without becoming diverted by trivial details. For example, the second lesson of this unit encourages students to pause during the problem-solving process to evaluate the relevance of information they are attending to.

3. CoRT3—Interaction—deals with the process of forming a valid argument and determining the adequate evidence to support it. Errors in the construction of arguments, such as exaggeration and overgeneralization, are explained and exemplified.

4. CoRT4—Creativity—teaches students strategies for generating new ideas, such as using word-association tests.

5. CoRT5—Information and Feeling—is concerned primarily with the affective influences on students' thinking and decision-making processes. The notion of values is discussed in this unit as well.

6. CoRT6—Action—combines the preceding units into an integrative framework.

The CoRT program has been implemented widely. For example, in Venezuela, it was implemented in a program called Aprender a Pensar (Learning to Think), sponsored by the Venezuelan Ministry of Education (Nickerson et al., 1985). An evaluation of the success of this program (deSanchez & Astorga, 1983), reported in Nickerson et al. (1985), showed that CoRT students tended to generate about double the number of ideas as did the controls. For instance, CoRT-trained and untrained groups of middle school students of mixed ability levels were asked, "Is it a good idea for people with more children to pay less taxes?" The CoRT-trained groups tended to generate a larger number of appropriate or relevant responses both in favor of and against the suggestion, provided evidence to support viewpoints other than their own, and were slower to express their judgments, presumably because they spent more time thinking about their answers. In sum, the CoRT strategies seem to provide students with some useful commonsense tactics to apply to solving academic and real-world problems.

Intelligence-Based Programs: Instrumental Enrichment, Successful Intelligence, and Practical Intelligence for Schools

In this subsection we cover three programs that developed from broader theories that have challenged the limited use of IQ for assessing people's intelligence: the **Instrumental Enrichment** program, the **Successful Intelligence** program, and the **Practical Intelligence for Schools** program.

The Instrumental Enrichment Program

The Instrumental Enrichment program is designed to assess a person's potential to learn, rather than his or her previously acquired knowledge. Its underlying idea is that intelligence is malleable—that it is the ability to learn from instructional cues (e.g., hints given by an instructor), via processes of comparing, classifying, and inferring new knowledge. In this framework, intelligence is seen as a dynamic process that can be altered by environmental factors. It was developed in reaction to traditional intelligence tests that heavily emphasize a person's previously acquired knowledge, rather than a person's ability to learn. In the spirit of Vygotsky's (1962, 1978) notion of a zone of proximal development, the belief is that students' intelligence can be assessed best if the children are given cues during the testing process, tapping into their potential for learning.

To assess learning potential, the Instrumental Enrichment program provides what is known as a **mediated learning experience** (MLE), a type of learning that is guided by a mediating agent, such as a parent or teacher. The function of the mediating agent is to provide guidance on how to relate, organize, and categorize information and to help the individual generalize his or her knowledge and skills beyond the immediate learning context. Feuerstein et al. (1979) suggested that lack of early MLEs can produce deleterious effects on cognitive development, but that many of these effects may be reversible with instruction. Specifically, they identified three categories of deficient cognitive functions: (1) **input phase impairments**, such as unplanned, unsystematic, or impulsive behaviors; (2) **elaboration phase impairments**, such as the inability to define a problem adequately; and (3) **output phase impairments**, such as the lack of accuracy or precision in communicating a response.

How are these deficits corrected or mitigated? The program includes 15 instruments, each of which consists of a set of pencil-and-paper exercises that are focused on reversing a particular cognitive deficit. Feuerstein and colleagues use the term *instrument* to mean "a means to an end," or a way of increasing cognitive functioning in the face of a deficit. The instruments are grouped into three clusters according to the level of reading ability required for their completion. The first cluster includes exercises that do not require any reading abilities, such as connecting dots to form a geometric object. The second cluster requires some reading ability or assistance from a teacher to read the instructions and focuses on skills like forming comparisons, understanding family relations, and performing deductive syllogisms. The third cluster, which requires reading and comprehension skills, involves problems of categorization and temporal and transitive relations, for example. For more details on the specifics of these instructional materials, see Feuerstein, Rand et al. (1980).

Overall, the Instrumental Enrichment program is designed to help students acquire basic concepts, terminology, operations, and relationships that are necessary to complete the problem-solving exercises, establish an intrinsic motivation to learn, cultivate metalevel thinking regarding successes and failures in problem-solving tasks, and foster a sense of learning as the active generation of knowledge. The main goal is for students to develop a sense that they are active and responsible for their own learning experiences, not passive recipients of knowledge. Feuerstein and his colleagues believe that it is this latter goal that is the most strongly associated with desired changes in the attitudinal, emotional, and motivational components of learning.

Feuerstein (1979) argued that the conventional means of assessing intelligence create a self-fulfilling prophecy for low-achieving students. A student who receives low scores on a traditional test is often placed in a class composed of other so-called slow learners. In such a class, the student will probably perform relatively poorly, in accordance with the predictions of the intelligence test and the teacher's expectations. On the surface, low-achieving students with low scores on intelligence tests support the predictive validity of intelligence tests. However, a student's poor achievement may be due, in large part, to the effects of his or her environment. That is, an environment composed of other low-achieving students may not give an individual student a chance to perform better, even if he or she has the potential to do so. The Instrumental Enrichment program is designed to help students overcome the self-fulfilling prophecy by advocating the notion that intelligence can be modified.

Evaluations of implementations of the Instrumental Enrichment program have generally yielded positive results (Feuerstein et al., 1981; Rand, Tannenbaum, & Feuerstein, 1979). For example, an evaluation of the effects of the program with low-functioning Israeli youths (aged 12–15) of low socioeconomic status showed that the treatment group outperformed the matched control group in gains on intellectual assessments (e.g., as measured by tests, such as the Thurstone Primary Achievement Abilities Test). The experimental group also showed gains on assessments measuring interpersonal conduct, self-sufficiency, and adaptiveness to work demands. Two years after the program was completed, a large proportion of the students took an army intelligence test (the DAPAR) in preparation for joining the Israeli army. The Instrumental Enrichment group obtained significantly higher scores than did matched controls. On the basis of these long-term gains, Rand et al. (1979) argued that the intervention may be successful in effecting general cognitive change. However, a comprehensive evaluation of the Instrumental Enrichment program, reported by Blagg (1991), showed that the program had either no or moderate effects on the performance of students in Great Britain over a two-year period. In particular, even though the students improved in Instrumental Enrichment-type skills, they did not show evidence that they had transferred these skills to real-life tasks. Nevertheless, the Instrumental Enrichment program has been implemented in several countries, including Canada, Venezuela, and the United States.

The Successful Intelligence Program

The **Successful Intelligence** program stems from Sternberg's (1985, 1988, 1996c) *triarchic theory of human intelligence*. It encompasses three components of human cognition: (1) an information-processing component of how people use internal cognitive mechanisms to plan and execute tasks, which is manifested in **analytical thinking**, or the ability to analyze, judge, evaluate, compare, contrast, and examine information; (2) a novelty component of how people respond to unfamiliar situations that involve **creative thinking**, or the ability to engage in discovery, supposition, and imagination; and (3) a contextual component of how people achieve a good fit between their personal needs and the constraints of a particular situation, which corresponds to **practical thinking**, or the ability to practice, use, apply, and implement information in the learning environment. An important part of practical thinking is **tacit knowledge**— the kind of knowledge that is not explicitly taught, but allows a person to succeed in a given environment (Sternberg & Wagner, 1993; Sternberg et al., 1996).

In general, successful intelligence assesses and promotes students' abilities to adapt to, shape, and select their environments in a way that fulfills their learning goals. Students learn to capitalize on their strengths and compensate for their weaknesses and to behave in a similar way to those who are successful in real-world environments.

Analytical thinking. Analytical thinking allows one to analyze and evaluate alternatives that are available in the environment by defining the existence of problems and the essences of these problems, generating strategies for solving these problems, and evaluating whether the strategies are working well. The triarchic theory describes three kinds of analytical-thinking components: metacomponents, performance components, and knowledge-acquisition components.

Metacomponents are higher-order processes that are used in planning or evaluating performance. They are executive processes that are primarily responsible for generating a strategy to accomplish a task and monitoring whether it is carried out correctly. A key metacomponent is *resource allocation*, or knowledge about which parts of a task require the most attention and time. Often, good problem solvers spend more time thinking about the task before they begin working on it (global resource allocation) and less time actually working on it (local resource allocation), whereas poor problem solvers tend to jump right in and start solving the problem without much foresight. To improve the allocation of resources, students learn to answer questions, such as "How long should it take you to do your [math] homework?"

Performance components are used during the execution of the task. They are the components of intelligence that are often measured in standard IQ tests. Many of these components are involved in inductive reasoning, such as inferring and applying analogical relations. The Successful Intelligence program offers a means of improving performance components via exercises that help students to identify inferential relationships, detect inferential fallacies, and solve verbal and spatial/visual analogies. For example, students are provided with scenarios, such as the following, and are asked to evaluate the logic that is depicted in them.

Jeremy went to his girlfriend's house one evening only to find her very angry at him, for some reason unknown to him. He asked her what he had done to make her angry, and she replied, I don't remember what you did, but I know I'm mad, so you must have done something (Sternberg, 1986, p. 104).

Students learn that this scenario is an example of emotional reasoning that leads to an inferential fallacy that something is true because one feels that it must be true. Sternberg (1986) identified 19 types of fallacies in everyday reasoning and included exercises for students to practice identifying and correcting them.

Knowledge-acquisition components are mechanisms that one uses to learn new information. The Successful Intelligence program distinguishes between knowledge, a measure of achievement and/or experience with a particular area or type of problem, and knowledge acquisition, or how one learns from experience. The program strongly emphasizes the acquisition of vocabulary to improve overall knowledge-acquisition skills, since vocabulary tests are the best predictors of scores on standardized IQ tests. The idea is that the process of enlarging one's vocabulary depends on discerning the meaning of unknown words by making use of the context in which they appear. The program's exercises, therefore, present students with passages containing obscure words and ask students to deduce the meaning of the unknown words from the context provided in the passages.

Creative thinking. Creative thinking requires the ability to deal with novelty. Creative thinkers "buy low and sell high" in the world of ideas (Sternberg & Lubart, 1995). That is, they are willing to embrace unpopular or neglected ideas that are nevertheless of substance and importance and then to convince others of their potential. Dealing with novelty requires students to learn and reason with new kinds of concepts in an unfamiliar context. How can such an ability be assessed or promoted? One way is to give students opportunities to solve problems that require *insight*, which is defined as a sudden understanding of something, or an "Aha!" response, after a period of trying to solve a problem unsuccessfully (e.g., Davidson, 1995; Gick & Lockhart, 1995; Seifert et al., 1995).

Insight problems allow students to enhance their ability to deal with novelty. Specifically, students learn to focus selectively on certain parts of a problem situation and ignore irrelevant information or to combine certain relevant pieces of information to arrive at a solution. The water-pitcher problem described in chapter 7 requires such insight, for example:

The Successful Intelligence program offers exercises to facilitate the use of selective-combination and -comparison processes, which involve taking what may seem to be isolated pieces of information and putting them together in a new and coherent way and relating new information to relevant information that was acquired previously (Davidson & Sternberg, 1984).

Practical thinking. The final component of the triarchic theory examines the relationship between a person's intelligence and the context of his or her environment. This ability requires three kinds of practical thinking. The first kind of practical thinking involves **adaptation**, or engaging in behavior that conforms to the demands of the environment at a particular time. For example, arriving on time for a meeting is intelligent in U.S. culture, but may be maladaptive in other cultures, where it is understood that events do not start on time and that one would be foolish to be punctual. Adaptation involves modifying one's behavior to fit these situational constraints. The second kind of practical thinking involves **shaping**, or changing the environment to fit one's needs. The third kind of practical thinking is **selection**, which occurs when the mismatch between one's needs and the situational constraints is so large that one has to leave the current environment and select a new one. Such a situation may happen when the environment clashes with a person's moral or political viewpoints.

The Successful Intelligence program uses various exercises to develop practical intelligence. One exercise consists of learning to use a decisional balance sheet to decide which course of action, out of several options, one should take, by writing the favorable consequences of each possible decision on one side of the sheet and the unfavorable ones on the other. Students learn to weigh the outcomes of each action in terms of the degree of its favorability or unfavorability. In general, students learn to consider information, avoid acting hastily or impulsively on the basis of incomplete information, and decide whether it would be best to engage in adaptation, shaping, or selection. Learning to increase one's practical intelligence involves taking into account the interaction between the environmental circumstances and oneself as an individual and then determining what choice best fits one's particular needs.

The Successful Intelligence program places equal emphasis on analytic, creative, and practical thinking abilities. However, in schools, teachers tend to favor analytical and memory skills over creative and practical ones, which may lead students who are more creative or practical than analytical in their thinking to seem less academically able than their analytically minded peers. Sternberg et al. (1996) demonstrated this bias experimentally. They recruited 199 high school students from different parts of the United States and assessed them as being either predominately strong analytic, creative, or practical thinkers or as having equal strengths in all or some of these thinking abilities. The students then participated in a Yale summer program, in which they were taught an introductory psychology course that emphasized either analytic, creative, or practical thinking skills. Sternberg et al. found that the students who received instruction that matched their thinking abilities performed significantly better than did those who were placed in a mismatched learning environment. The message for education is clear: Students who are predominantly practical or creative thinkers get penalized in traditional school settings that focus on developing memory and analytical skills at the expense of other skills. It is important to gear instruction in such a way that it will reach students with different abilities.

There is further evidence to suggest that teaching a combination of analytic, creative, and practical thinking skills can improve students' overall performance, even on more traditional, memory-based modes of assessment. Sternberg, Torff, and Grigorenko (1998) conducted a study with 3rd and 8th graders who were taught a unit of instruction (social studies for 3rd graders and psychology for 8th graders) by one of three teaching methods: memory based, analytically based, or *triarchically* based (a combination of analytical, creative, and practical instructional techniques). After the unit was completed, the students' performance was assessed through memory-based multiple-choice items, as well as through items that were designed to assess analytical, creative, and practical achievement. Overall, the students who were taught in a triarchic style outperformed those who were taught by the other two methods. This finding held true for performance on the memory-oriented multiple-choice questions as well, suggesting that even the skills that have traditionally been cultivated in education could be better learned through multidimensional modes of instruction.

The Practical Intelligence for Schools Program

The practical-thinking component of the Successful Intelligence program shows that intelligence is a function of more than just analytical ability. Even though practical reasoning skills tend to be underemphasized in schools, one component of practical thinking is essential for students' success: *tacit knowledge* (described earlier). To do well in school, students need to acquire practical knowledge about themselves as learners, learn to understand and predict the kind of expectations teachers have, and become aware of the values that are upheld by the school system at large.

What kind of knowledge do students need to develop to succeed in a school setting? The Practical Intelligence for Schools (PIFS) program, developed by Robert Sternberg's group at Yale University and Howard Gardner and the Harvard Project Zero group at the Harvard University Graduate School of Education, is designed to promote three main goals: to help students (1) develop a sense of their own intellectual profile, such as understanding their own learning styles and strategies; (2) develop an understanding of the structure and learning of academic tasks; and (3) view the school environment as a complex social system.

PIFS seeks to fulfill these goals by drawing on the theoretical tenets of Sternberg's triarchic theory of human intelligence and the Successful Intelligence program and of Gardner's (1983) theory of multiple intelligences (MI). MI theory suggests that there is no single factor of intelligence but a set of independent intelligences: linguistic, logical-mathematical, spatial, musical, bodily-kinesthetic, interpersonal, intrapersonal, and naturalist (for more discussion of MI, see chapter 11). PIFS incorporates principles from MI and the triarchic theory into a set of lessons that are designed to enable students to assess their strengths and weaknesses on different kinds of intelligences and, more important, to use tacit knowledge to capitalize on their intellectual, academic, and communicative strengths.

PIFS is currently used with sixth- and seventh-grade students—at a time when students make the transition from elementary to middle school. This time may be crucial for receiving an educational intervention because it requires students to start assuming more responsibility for their own learning. PIFS aids in this process by helping students develop an understanding of their own interests and motivations, the aims of various school tasks (the purpose of homework and how engaging in it may be analogous to some of the work situations that adults are in), the particular requirements of different subject domains (how is studying for a math test different from studying for a social studies test?), the importance of organizational skills (allocating resources wisely), and the general practices of self-monitoring and self-awareness.

PIFS is designed to be incorporated into regular subject-matter instruction instead of being taught as a separate course. The PIFS curriculum includes booklets on reading, writing, homework, and test taking that can each be integrated into regular classroom sessions. This curriculum has been used and evaluated successfully in urban schools in the Boston area; in a suburban school in Tewksbury, Massachusetts; and in rural schools in Connecticut.

Finally, we discuss teaching-for-thinking programs that are created on the basis of the ACT-R theory of human cognition.

Intelligent Tutoring Systems: Contributions From ACT-R

The ACT-R theory (J. R. Anderson, 1983, 1993; see also chapter 4) has led to the development of **Intelligent Tutoring Systems (ITSs)**—computer programs designed to be used for individualized instruction. ACT-R proposes that cognitive skills are composed of production rules, which are "if-then" statements that specify the circumstances in which a given rule is applicable and should be executed. The basis for an ITS, therefore, is that knowledge and expertise in a given area can be modeled by programming a computer with the appropriate production rules.

The production rules, in turn, are based on the idea that students learn by induction from examples (see also, Ben-Zeev, 1998; Chi et al., 1989; Pirolli, 1991; Reder, Charney, & Morgan, 1986). In the ACT-R framework, induction proceeds through analogical reasoning, in which features of the familiar example are mapped onto the relevant features of the target problem the person wishes to solve. This analogical procedure creates production rules and stores them in memory (J. R. Anderson & Fincham, 1994). As in other teaching-thinking programs, the tutors' aim is to help students understand and master the deep cognitive structure underlying problems and to apply procedures from one problem to another.

In general, an ITS has three basic requirements: It must (1) "know" the material—to make inferences about the subject and solve problems generated from the information; (2) have some model of the student's grasp of the subject; and (3) use strategies to improve the student's knowledge and/or performance (Burns & Capps, 1988). To accomplish these tasks, the ITS makes use of different modules. The **expert module** represents the knowledge base, or the information that the student is supposed to learn, whereas the **student module** is a representation of the student's current state of knowledge. The mechanism that compares these two modules is known as the **tutor module**. Its main aim is to get the student's knowledge to match that of the Expert Module. The Tutor Module is aimed at enhancing the student's comprehension and skill.

The Expert Module

The expert module is the first component to be designed and programmed. There have been several approaches to designing this module: the *black box*, *glass box*, and *cognitive model*. The black box system is the least compatible with human representation of knowledge (Burns & Capps, 1988), although it makes for simplified programming. In this system, only the correct input and output are encoded for a given problem, so that the system can judge between right and wrong answers. An example of the implementation of this model is the WEST program, designed for tutoring chess skills.

The glass box system represents information in the form of production rules (Anderson et al., 1992). This system has been implemented in more successful programs, such as the GUIDON program by Clancey (1983), designed to help medical students make diagnoses. The expert module consisted of 450 complex if-then rules pointing to a diagnosis in the presence of a specific set of symptoms. For some applications, however, if-then rules do not suffice for representing the knowledge a student has to learn.

The cognitive model is designed to approximate human problem solving and knowledge representation. In these systems, knowledge of procedures is encoded in a similar way to the glass box system, using sets of production rules. Each production rule consists of pairing a situation with a corresponding action. The completion of each production rule results in a new state in which yet another rule might apply. An example would be the solution to a math problem like (5 + 3) * 2. The first production rule would be to add 5 and 3 and get a result. The next production rule would entail multiplying the result by 2. Generalizing these rules would result in a rule that says that one should always perform computations within parentheses first. This rule-based approach has been used successfully to teach a variety of different skills, such as learning the programming languages LISP, Prolog, and Pascal (Anderson et al., 1992).

The Student Module

The student module is designed to assess the amount of knowledge a student has and then use that knowledge as a basis for instruction. The student module must (1) determine when the student is ready to advance to the next instructional level; (2) provide advice on the kinds of strategies the student should use, when needed; (3) generate problems based on the student's responses, on-line; and (4) gear explanations to the student's level of knowledge (VanLehn, 1988).

There are different approaches to developing a student module. The first approach is to generate a list of possible behaviors in response to a problem and compare the student's action to the list. In this fashion, the system continuously updates the internal model of the student's behavior. The second approach is to backtrack at the end of the student's solution to a given problem. The system then assesses what the student did to arrive at the answer, which, in turn, forms the foundation from which to change the student model. A collection of such backtracking procedures produces an algorithm for what the student is doing in a given situation. The third approach is to have the system generate a potential rule that transforms one state of knowledge into the next and then to test that rule against the student's response pattern. This approach may result in a more specific tutorial than the algorithm approach. Finally, a system can be geared toward correcting the mistakes the student makes without trying to model the procedures that the student actually used in generating the mistakes. This approach is referred to as *issue tracing*. Although issue tracing sounds simple, it requires fairly deep access to the student's problem solving (VanLehn, 1988).

The Tutor Module

The instructional interface, or tutor module, is designed to raise a student's level of knowledge to match that of the expert module in a given domain. The tutor module must determine the rate at which the student learns, respond to questions about the goals of a given program, and "know" when to help the student along the way (Burns & Capps, 1988).

The *geometry tutor* (e.g., J. R. Anderson, 1993) exemplifies the utility of the ITS as a teaching-for-thinking tool. It is designed to teach traditional Euclidean proofs based on a search governed by heuristics, or rules of thumb. In any given proof, there could be a voluminous number of appropriate inferential rules that apply, but the tutor is designed to teach students how to choose and apply the rules in a meaningful way that will obtain the correct solution. This goal is achieved through the process of *reasoning backward*, whereby the student must first assess what is being proved and what inferences would allow that proof to be true. The student learns to distinguish which of the correct inferences that follow from the givens are actually relevant to the problem. This approach, along with the step-by-step reasoning and feedback provided by the ITS, has significantly increased both the achievement and motivation of high school students (Schofield & Evans-Rhodes, 1989). (For a review of the effectiveness of ITS, see Psotka, Massey, & Mutter, 1988.)

Teaching Thinking From the General to the Specific: A Brief Summary

The programs we discussed—Philosophy for Children, CoRT, Instrumental Enrichment, Successful Intelligence, the PIFS program, and Intelligent Tutoring Systems—are general programs for promoting critical-thinking skills. Each program can be applied to multiple subject domains and draws on the richness of these domains, but at the base of each program is a core of fundamental reasoning rules and strategies that are independent of a specific domain. These programs share the assumption of the cognitivist view: that by learning general cognitive strategies, students can then apply them to develop a deeper understanding of particular subject domains. Learning can be done either individually, in a group, or both.

In contrast, other programs have emphasized teaching thinking from the specific to the general. These programs share the philosophy of the situative view: that students benefit most from learning reasoning and problem-solving skills within a rich content domain and that these skills can then be applied to similar domains. These programs tend to be part of the regular curriculum and emphasize group over individual learning.

TEACHING THINKING FROM THE SPECIFIC TO THE GENERAL

Baron (1985) argued that good thinking is analogous to choosing a piece of equipment from a carpenter's tool kit. The choice depends on which method provides the best resource to handle the particular job in question. Baron's metaphor suggests that good thinking tends to reflect a rich knowledge base in the domain in question, rather than the acquisition of general strategies. Programs that teach thinking from the specific to the general tend to embrace this belief. In this section we cover four main programs: the earlier Reciprocal Teaching program and the more recent Fostering a Community of Learners, the Computer Supported Intentional Learning Environments project, and the Jasper Woodbury Problem Solving Series. The first two programs focus primarily on the domains of reading and the biological sciences, the third has been used in a variety of domains, and the fourth specifically targets the domain of mathematics.

Reciprocal Teaching and Fostering a Community of Learners

A. L. Brown and colleagues have developed two interrelated educational programs for enhancing critical-thinking skills that heavily emphasize learning in a group setting. These programs are Reciprocal Teaching (A. L. Brown & Campione, 1990; A. L. Brown & Palincsar, 1987, 1989; Palincsar & Brown, 1984, 1988) and the more recent Fostering a Community of Learners (A. L. Brown, 1997; A. L. Brown & Campione, 1994, 1998).

Reciprocal Teaching was developed to enhance children's reading comprehension. In this program, a student-teacher dialogue is created that involves summarizing text, generating questions, clarifying ideas, and predicting what will follow next in a reading comprehension passage. Fostering a Community of Learners capitalized on the success of Reciprocal Teaching and extended it to improving both literacy skills and knowledge of other domain-specific subject matter in environmental science and biology. The program encourages group discussions that build on young children's emergent strategic and metacognitive knowledge along with their intuitive biological theories. The main goal of the program is to lead children to discover the deep principles underlying a specific domain and to develop discovery strategies that would apply to other related domains as well.

Reciprocal Teaching

Reciprocal Teaching (RT) was born out of a need to increase the level of reading comprehension among elementary school students. Reading comprehension is an especially challenging domain because students often have difficulty assessing their understanding of reading passages. In fact, children often have an illusion that they have comprehended even an incomprehensible text. The RT program is designed to train students in methods of questioning, clarifying, and summarizing written text and to help them develop an overall assessment of their level of understanding. This program has been used primarily with at-risk readers in grades 1–9.

In RT reading groups, composed of six members each, are created. Each member takes a turn in leading a discussion on an article that all the members previously read or watched on videotape. The teacher initially serves as the discussion leader and then is followed by a child who has the most reading expertise in the group. Eventually, every group member is expected to lead the discussion. The discussion leader is more of a facilitator than a teacher. The leader's duties include opening the discussion by asking a question and ending it by summarizing the key points of the argument that unfolded over the course of the discussion. At intermediate points, the leader helps to clarify ideas, maintains the organization or structure, and asks the participants to predict what would come next in a reading comprehension passage. In this way, the leader helps to externalize and make explicit the kind of thinking that students engage in during the discussion process. This group interaction allows the novices in the group to model their thought processes after those of the more expert members. It also allows the teacher to assess the level of comprehension and analysis achieved by each student in a dynamic way.

In an RT intervention program that was implemented to increase the reading comprehension of 4th and 5th graders (Brown et al., 1991), the students read simple texts on animal behavior with recurring themes (e.g., camouflage). These themes were emphasized in the oral group discussions and were incorporated into daily written tests of comprehension. To test how well the students understood the main issues, students commonly were asked to solve a new problem and relate it to material that they had previously learned by a process of analogical reasoning. The students' understanding was assessed by how well the students were able to transfer their knowledge from old to new items. The students who received RT intervention outperformed the matched control students in how well they solved the new transfer questions. They also showed more pre- to posttest improvements in their ability to summarize key points and to draw sound inferences. These gains were maintained over the long term, as assessed by a test given one year after the study was completed.

Brown and her colleagues noticed that during the intervention, the students in the RT condition formed their own learning community in which the interpretation of texts became a focus for collaborative learning and shared experience. This spontaneous development of a community of learners prompted Brown and her colleagues to try to design interventions that would develop a view of learning as a collaborative community endeavor. It was through this process that Fostering a Community of Learners was born.

The RT program continues to serve as the reading component of the FCL program. It is helpful in assessing students' use of analogical reasoning and judging the efficacy of the intervention as a whole. Brown and her colleagues have found that with increasing exposure to the RT intervention, students tend to create more deep-structural analogies between surface-structurally different problems. The increased use of analogical reasoning after exposure to RT instruction was corroborated in more controlled laboratory settings as well (A. L. Brown, 1992).

Fostering a Community of Learners

The **Fostering a Community of Learners (FCL)** program is based on the following six key components:

1. Agency refers to a sense of control over one's learning. To promote agency, emphasis is placed on learning as an active and strategic process.

2. Reflection refers to a meta-awareness of one's strengths and weaknesses as a student. This ability is fostered by activities that encourage students to think aloud and become aware of their own mental processes.

3. Collaboration is achieved through the deliberate distribution of expertise in a group. The makeup of the group causes members to be dependent on each other's knowledge and ideas. This interdependence promotes an atmosphere of joint responsibility and mutual respect, as well as a sense of group identity.

4. Culture is based on the values of negotiation and sharing ideas, similarly to the kind of active exchange that is characteristic of a seminar.

5. Deep disciplinary content refers to the choice of content areas that challenge students to reason at the upper bounds of their ability levels.

6. Developmental corridors refer to choosing FCL tasks that match students' cognitive growth in a particular domain.

The metaphor of a developmental corridor comes from the way in which most schools are built, so that students who graduate from one classroom level to the next (e.g., move from the second to the third grade) progress along a physical corridor. The metaphor stands for the ability to learn in a more mature and sophisticated way. FCL traverses the metaphorical corridor by teaching the same concept (e.g., evolution and survival of the species) to 2nd-, 4th-, 6th-, and 8th-grade students. Each time the topic is revisited, it builds further on children's developing biological theories (e.g., Inagaki & Hatano, 1993; Keil, 1992; Wellman & S. A. Gelman, 1992) in conjunction with their previously acquired knowledge.

Although there is some theoretical debate as to when children first develop an intuitive biological theory, it is widely accepted that by age 6, children have some working knowledge of causality and causal agents and tend to overattribute causes to events without including the role of random factors in their explanations. FCL uses the notion of causality in tasks that are designed for younger children, but urges older children to take into account principles of variability and uncertainty as well.

Each FCL task consists of three main parts. In the first part, the participants are involved in both independent and group research projects on a given topic. In the second part, each group shares information with the entire class. In the third part, the members of the group are asked to complete a consequential task. This task may be a traditional form of assessment, such as a question-and-answer test (e.g., what kind of habitat would be appropriate for an endangered species?), or a nontraditional one, such as creating a new environmental design (e.g., designing a habitat to protect an endangered species). Each of the three parts requires a metacognitive approach to learning about the deep structure of a particular discipline.

The FCL project designed for the second grade involves research on the interdependence of animals and their habitats. To tackle this topic, the teacher divides the class into six groups. Each group is responsible for doing research on one of the following subtopics related to survival: defense mechanisms, predator-prey relations, protection from the elements, reproductive strategies, communication, and methods of obtaining food. The end task, which involves the pooled knowledge of the entire class, is to design an animal of the future that has evolved the best possible means of survival.

After each group finishes conducting research on its subtopic, the class divides up into *jigsaw teaching groups*, composed of six representatives of the six original groups. Each representative takes a turn playing the role of the expert and teaches the other members of the jigsaw group about the topic his or her group researched. For example, one child knows more about reproductive strategies while another has acquired more expertise about communication. Each jigsaw group must use its members' pooled information to design the animal of the future. The final product is then evaluated by a panel of visitors who act as reviewers.

Brown found that second graders were able to design an animal whose features fit the six requirements for survival. However, the students seemed to consider each feature as a separate entity when they constructed their animal, ignoring natural correlations between attributes (e.g., most animals that have feathers also have wings and a beak). For example, the second graders were likely to create a carnivorous animal with short legs that also had webbed feet to fit a marshy environment (A. L. Brown, 1997). In contrast, older children (6th- and 8th graders) were guided by the natural-feature correlations in the environment when constructing their animals of the future. However, Brown and her colleagues found that after a year-long intervention, even second graders became sensitive to natural biological constraints and feature correlations (A. L. Brown, Ellery, & Campione, 1998). On the basis of this finding, the second graders' instruction was altered by asking them first to design the habitat and then to generate the animal to fit the environment, allowing them to perform more like sixth- and eigth-graders.

The goals and structure of FCL require active reflection on what one is learning. Children are responsible not only for their own learning, but for teaching other students in their subtopic and jigsaw groups, as well as the class at large. To be successful at teaching others, one must (1) be aware of one's own level of understanding as well as take the perspective of other, more naïve students, and (2) determine what the most relevant information is that one wishes to impart.

To encourage reflective and analytic thinking, FCL uses adult role models. Adult experts are brought into the classroom when a unit is about to begin to introduce the overarching principles and deep concepts of the domain and then return when the class is ready to progress to more advanced levels of learning. The primary purpose of the second visit is to help the class synthesize basic concepts into more complex ones. For example, once the students have discovered the notion of energy as it relates to how much food an organism consumes, the adult can lead a class discussion that promotes an understanding of the metabolic rate of an organism. The adults model how to (1) reason about a topic in a meaningful and rigorous way by helping the children use their existing theories to develop a deep understanding of concepts, such as interdependence, biodiversity, adaptation, and evolution; (2) interact with classmates; (3) force oneself and others to justify assumptions and conclusions with logic and evidence; and (4) set goals for the future on the basis of what is known in a field and what needs to be discovered. Similarly, FCL elicits the help of older students, who are FCL graduates, as part of a process referred to as *cross-age teaching.*

FCL makes students' implicit or intuitive theories explicit and helps students incorporate these theories into the learning process. Students then learn which parts of their intuitive theories they should retain and which part they should discard in favor of more formal reasoning. Concepts that involve a departure from implicit theories (e.g., the concept of statistical randomness) are the most difficult for students to grasp. To promote formal counterintuitive thinking, children learn to use their mistakes in a productive way. In general, students are expected to develop a mature conceptualization of learning as a process that is undergoing constant change.

The Computer Supported Intentional Learning Environments Project

The **Computer Supported Intentional Learning Environments (CSILE)** project is similar in its theoretical orientation to the FCL program. CSILE, which strongly emphasizes collaborative learning and metacognition as vehicles for fostering scientific discovery and hypothesis testing, is designed to promote **intentional learning**, or learning for the sake of learning. Scardamalia, Bereiter, and Lamon (1994) argued that much of early education is focused on encouraging students to provide accurate responses at the expense of developing a deep understanding of what is being taught. Thus, children often adopt strategies that allow them to accomplish tasks while exerting minimal cognitive effort (Scardamalia, 1981; Scardamalia & Bereiter, 1984). For example, elementary school children often use the strategy, of "copy-and-delete" while writing a summary by reading each sentence of the original text, deciding whether or not it is important, and then including or deleting it from their writing (Scardamalia & Bereiter, 1984, 1987). However, they typically fail to read the passage for overall meaning, decide what the main point is, or identify ideas that are implicit.

The tendency to engage in less-demanding and more superficial processing becomes adaptive to succeeding in school, given the endless number of tasks that students are typically required to complete, as well as the rewards they often receive for finishing an assignment early. Unfortunately, what is adaptive in terms of practical success in schoolwork is obviously at odds with the fundamental goals of education. This is a problem that has prompted many educators and researchers to develop ways to "make students think," as we have discussed in the preceding sections. According to Scardamalia, Bereiter, and Lamon, however, these approaches have placed too much emphasis on the cognitive strategies and processes involved in learning, on the way in which knowledge is represented in the individual mind. In the CSILE project, on the other hand, students actively construct their knowledge as a collective unit. The concern is not so much with a particular individual's understanding of evolution or gravity, for example, but with how the class as a whole builds up knowledge in that domain.

CSILE activities have been integrated into such curricular areas as science, social studies, and literature, as well as mathematics to a more limited extent. The program is implemented by creating a computer database for each participating classroom. The students are encouraged to enter all their work on a particular project into the database and access and comment upon the work done by their peers. The database allows the students to look up their classmates' entries, access their own work, and attach notes with comments, questions, and feedback. Thus, a student who works on a special topic gets access to all the notes that other members of the class have attached on that subject. The student, however, does not have the power to edit or delete anything that another student has written.

The use of a computer database as a mode of interaction is designed to foster intentional learning because it provides students with an opportunity to pursue meaningful knowledge for its own sake, rather than for the sake of simply completing a task or getting a good grade. For example, during a sixth-grade CSILE project on biology, each student in the classroom was asked to choose an animal, formulate questions about it, and then conduct research to answer those questions by using the database. One student asked: "How do sponges reproduce?" In the course of doing research, he found that sponges reproduce in three ways: sexually, through budding, and through regeneration. The information he had gathered quickly spread to other users of the database, and a series of notes was generated. In these notes, the classmates speculated on why the sponge has so many ways of reproducing, whereas humans have only one reproductive mechanism. Eventually one student was able to synthesize the information needed to answer the question. He discovered that the structural simplicity of the sponge (versus the complexity of the human body) allows for asexual reproduction. The student reasoned that, "Lungs, a heart, and a brain, etc. could not grow on your finger if it was cut off" (Scardamalia et al., 1994, p. 209). What is important is that this interchange of productive ideas developed spontaneously. The students were not required to read or comment on the work of their classmates and were not graded on the number or quality of their comments.

A main advantage of using CSILE on-line discussions is that they allow for more equal participation among group members. For example, A. Cohen (1992) compared CSILE with face-to-face group discussions in a college physics course and found that there were large discrepancies in the extent to which each group member participated in the face-to-face discussions, whereas nearly all members contributed equally to the CSILE discussions. In general, the computer format provides a more permanent record of information gathering, discussion, and reflection and hence is, accessible to participants over time.

Teaching Mathematical Thinking

A major focus of teaching thinking in specific domains has been concentrated on the enhancement of mathematical thinking. There is a strong need to improve students' mathematical reasoning. A series of distressing reports by the Third International Mathematics and Science Study (TIMSS) (1996, 1997) and by the U.S. Department of Education (1998), showed that out of the 500,000 students in 41 nations, U.S. 12th graders ranked near the bottom of the list of nations in both science and mathematics. Out of the 21 nations that participated in the 12th-grade general assessment of mathematics and science, the scores of U.S. students exceeded those of only 2 nations (Cyprus and South Africa). Although U.S. students performed below the international average in science and math at the 12th-grade level, the same was not true of the younger cohorts. U.S. 4th graders scored above the 26-nation international average in both science and mathematics, outperforming all nations but Korea in tests of scientific knowledge. However, although the U.S. 8th graders, scored above the international average in science, they scored below that average in mathematics. Thus the relative standing of U.S. 12th graders was lower than that of U.S. 8th graders, which was again lower than that of U.S. 4th graders. This downward trend is alarming when one considers the implication that an American student's education becomes comparatively less, rather than more, adequate as she or he progresses through successive levels of schooling.

These results indicate that U.S. secondary schools are failing to equip older students with the higher-order skills that have been attained by their peers around the world. The need for reform in the quality and quantity of instruction received by American high school students is underscored by another finding of the TIMSS study. In international comparisons of advanced students, in which U.S. students were again outranked by students in the majority of the competing nations, it was determined that the U.S. students' performance was related not to the amount of television watched, hours spent working parttime, or amount of homework completed, but to the amount of instructional time spent in advanced mathematics. The United States was significantly below the international average in the proportion of advanced students who received five or more hours of mathematics instruction per week. That is, countries in which a high proportion of students received five or more hours of mathematics instruction per week were likely to outperform those in which the students received fewer hours of instruction. This finding suggests that the discrepancies between the performance of U.S. 12th graders and that of 12th graders in other countries are more closely related to factors located in the classroom than to lifestyle factors that may exert their influence outside the classroom.

In light of these disturbing results, the question that has been central to many investigations of mathematics education has been this: How can we promote students' conceptual learning of underlying principles, rather than of rote algorithmic procedures? This question is especially important, given that students are able to obtain the correct answers for problems they do not understand (Rosnick & Clement, 1980). The goals of teaching for thinking are to help students to represent meaning for mathematical symbols and link procedures by a common organizing principle.

Schoenfeld (1991) contended that one means of teaching for conceptual, rather than rote, knowledge is to connect students' informal mathematical intuitions to the formal mathematics students learn in school. Students learn to view mathematics in the classroom as being divorced from common sense. That is, mathematics is seen as valid if it is internally consistent, regardless of whether its conclusions or premises hold in the real world. Moreover, students learn to regard proofs as ritualistic procedures, in which one is required to prove formally what has already been shown to be true. The process of mathematical reasoning becomes just a matter of executing the right steps instead of a process of invention and discovery.

So how can formal and informal mathematical reasoning be connected? Schoenfeld's (1991) first prescription is that learning should proceed via doing and discussing. For example, students can learn first to use heuristics that are based on a meaningful approach (e.g., identifying subgoals, working backward, and so forth) instead of simply learning the algorithmic procedures that would guarantee a solution. They can then be made to defend their approaches by discussing them with the teacher and students in class.

The **Rightstart** program, developed by Griffin, Case, and Siegler (1994), is designed to bridge the gap between children's intuitive theories of numbers and principles of formal instruction. In particular, Rightstart is concerned with the fact that many low-income children do not enter the first grade with the same intuitive sense of numbers that most middle-income children do. Several neo-Piagetian theorists (Case, 1985; Fischer, 1980; Halford, 1982) have proposed that a cognitive restructuring takes place between ages 5 and 6 in which children go from viewing quantities in dichotomous terms (e.g., big versus small or a lot versus a little) to having a sense of a mental number line in which quantities are represented on a continuum with many intervals between the two poles. This central concept of a number line allows for more meaningful learning of counting and forms the foundation of subsequent addition and subtraction skills.

On the number-knowledge test designed by Case and colleagues (Case & Griffin, 1990; Case & Sandieson 1987; Griffin, Case, & Sandieson; 1992; Okamato, 1992), low-income children can usually correctly answer questions that involve discriminating between a large quantity and a small quantity. However, they are generally unable to make finer distinctions that involve gradations and counting. The goal of Rightstart is to help low-income students develop the concept of a number line so that they can begin the first grade with the same intuitive number sense as their middle-income peers.

Rightstart consists of a series of games that emphasize the mapping of abstract numerical quantities (e.g., a number on a dice) onto physical objects (how many chips you place on a game board). The idea is that concrete representations of the number line that emphasize the one-to-one mapping of numbers onto physical objects will help children abstract a mental number line and understand the principles of counting. More advanced games focus on teaching the cardinal values of numbers and the relationships between quantities. For example, when playing a board game, the children are asked, "Who is closer to the goal and how do you know?"

The idea that correct learning develops by engaging in a process of discovery was proposed earlier by Anzai and Simon (1979), who argued that when students can successfully execute procedures, even in a crude, rote, or inefficient way, they can often use their solution to develop more efficient and meaningful methods of problem solving. In support of this view, Simon and Zhu (1988) demonstrated that students who were given examples of the factorization of polynomials (e.g., $X^2 + 5X + 6 = (X + 2)(X + 3)$) and were asked to solve problems on their own (e.g., $X^2 + 9X + 18 = (\ \ )(\ \ )$), were able to generalize the principles underlying factorization (i.e., $X^2 + aX + b = (X + c)(X + d)$, where $c*d = b$ and $c + d = a$).

In addition to learning by doing, Schoenfeld (1991) suggested that the teacher should become the moderator or facilitator of class-interactive problem solving. The teaching process becomes a negotiation of understanding. It helps uncover students' underlying assumptions and thereby raises their meta-awareness of their beliefs. Schoenfeld argued that teaching for thinking is achieved as a function of group interaction and negotiation.

There seems to be a delicate balance between using one's intuitive theories, which may be correct or incorrect, and learning to suspend one's intuitions. Resnick (1986, p. 191) claimed that "The best high school math students I have talked with also have said that they are quite willing to suspend their need for "sense" for a while while new rules are introduced, because they have found that after a period of just manipulating symbols in accord with the rules, the rules come to make sense to them." It is clear that instruction should help students make use of their intuitive beliefs, but it may also be helpful for students to learn to suspend the need for sense making in the initial execution of a procedure, so they can develop a greater understanding and more rigorous mathematical intuition later on (Ben-Zeev & Star, 2000).

One of the more successful programs for enhancing mathematical thinking in middle school students is the Jasper Woodbury Problem Solving Series. We discuss the specifics of this program and how it attempts to answer the foregoing concerns, next.

The Jasper Woodbury Problem Solving Series

The **Jasper Woodbury Problem Solving Series**, developed by Bransford and his colleagues (e.g., Barron et al., 1995) at the Learning Technology Center (LTC) at Vanderbilt University, is an intervention program aimed at fostering mathematical thinking in middle school students. Members of the LTC were motivated to create this intervention after they became aware of the difficulties that many students have solving simple arithmetic word problems (Charles & Silver, 1988; Silver, 1986; Reusser, 1988), such as the following:

> Tony rides the bus to camp every summer. There are 8 other children on the bus. The bus travels at 9 miles an hour. It takes 4 hours to get there. How far away is the camp? (Bransford, Zech, Schwartz, Barron, & Vye, 1996, p. 206).

Many students who attempted to solve this problem proceeded to add all the given numbers without considering their relevance, resulting in nonsensical solutions (e.g., the camp is 21 miles away). This apparent lack of a meaningful understanding of mathematics, prompted Bransford and his colleagues to look for ways to facilitate correct mental representations of word problems. Their main hypothesis was that since students regard such word problems as artificial or decontextualized, they apply a rote and mechanical approach to solving the problems. Bransford and his colleagues conjectured that to improve their performance, students should learn how to appreciate the context of the problem better—to represent it in a way that is linked with their experiences and intuitions.

Toward this end, Bransford and his colleagues gave students adventure scenarios depicted on videodiscs. Originally, the students were given the first 12 minutes of the movie *Raiders of the Lost Ark*, featuring the brave and cunning Indiana Jones. The students became part of this action adventure by being told that they were to imagine returning with Indiana to the jungle where the adventure began to help him retrieve some gold artifacts that he left behind (the students could rewind the tape to previous scenes). To complete their mission, the students needed to estimate the dimensions of pits, caves, and other key obstacles that they and Indiana would encounter. These dimensions could be determined by using a size standard, in this case, the height of Indiana Jones (the students were told that he was 6 feet tall). By freezing the relevant frames of the video, the students could then conduct on-screen measurements. For example, they could tell that the width of a pit was twice the length of Indiana, which allowed them to estimate the width of the pit and decide how far Indiana would have to jump to avoid falling into it. Throughout this process, the students were encouraged to make visual and symbolic representations of the problems and were then given feedback on the strengths and weaknesses of their approach.

This video-based manipulation led to significant improvements in the students' ability to represent problems visually and to explain their reasoning compared to a control group. The students also exhibited transfer to real-world settings. For example, after solving the Indiana

Jones adventure, one group of students correctly estimated the size of their school flagpole on the basis of each other's height (Bransford et al., 1996).

These results encouraged Bransford and colleagues to develop their own videodisc adventure entitled *The River Adventure*. The students were told that they won a one-week trip on a houseboat and that they had to do all the planning for food, gas, water, docking the boat, and other relevant measures. All the information needed to do this planning (dimensions, fuel efficiency and capacity, cruising speed, and the like) was embedded in the video. For instance, the speed of the boat could be determined by noting the number of minutes required to move from one mile marker on the river to the next. The amount of time needed to arrive at the marina could be calculated on the basis of the speed that was just determined and the distance to the marina. This distance could be found by using a map included in the videodisc. Once again, the results indicated that the students were able to transfer knowledge to posttest problems, demonstrating gains in performance. In addition, students' ability to represent problems visually was markedly improved.

To promote creativity, the second phase of the River Adventure project went beyond problem solving and focused on problem generation and problem formulation as well. College students and both mathematically advanced and delayed fifth graders watched *The River Adventure*. The experimenters paused the videodisc at different points and then asked the students to generate questions about the appropriate goals and subgoals necessary to plan the trip successfully. Only the college students were able to generate the appropriate general planning questions and to come up with the relevant categories for planning. Both groups of fifth graders had trouble generating questions even though they were able to come up with appropriate responses when presented with questions by the experimenters (Furman et al., 1989; Montavon, Furman, Barron, Bransford, & Hasselbring, 1989). These results suggest the importance of fostering skills in generating problems (for an instructional approach that focuses on problem posing, see S. I. Brown & Walter, 1993).

Bransford and his colleagues fostered an active collaboration with classroom teachers. The teachers indicated that the River Adventure was useful but would need to be more attention grabbing and exciting to hold children's attention. This realization led to the creation of the Jasper Woodbury Problem Solving Series. The Jaspers series consists of a sequence of 12 videodiscs, which are designed to improve the mathematical thinking of students in the 5th grade and above. Each disc provides opportunities for problem solving, reasoning, communicating, and making connections to other subject domains, such as science, social studies, literature, and history. The 12 adventures fall into four categories: complex trip planning, statistics and business plans, geometry, and algebra. Each videodisc contains an approximately 17-minute adventure that ends in a complex challenge and includes all the data that are needed to solve the problems. Each disc also comes with analog and extension problems to reinforce and generalize the underlying principles.

For example, the adventure *Blueprint for Success*, which was designed to promote a deep understanding of the uses of geometry, centers on two children, Marcus and Christina, who want to help design a new playground. Creating the blueprints for the playground involves several subgoals, such as finding a way to maximize the area with a given length of fence, determining the optimal height for a swing set on the basis of a survey of the height of students, and deciding what angle the slide should make with ground. Bransford et al. (1996) reported that both the teachers' and students appreciation and uses of geometry dramatically increased after they took part in Blueprint for Success. In several cases, the students went beyond the requirements of the assignment and actually designed and built playhouses, which were then donated to kindergarten classes. Another successful example is the video *The Big Splash*, which involves using sampling methods and statistical inference to determine whether there is enough interest among students in having a dunking booth at the school's fun fair to defray the cost of renting the equipment.

To increase the effectiveness of the videos, Bransford and his colleagues developed a more general multimedia approach, called *SMART* (Special Multimedia Arenas for Refining Thinking), to foster a community of learning. SMART allows students to view work done by other students who are working on the same Jasper problem through the use of telecommunications, television, and the internet. Similar to FCL, SMART gives students an opportunity to discuss their proposed solutions in a group. By presenting ideas to others, critiquing other students' ideas, and comparing these ideas to their own, students are able to improve on the knowledge they received from interacting with the discs individually. The findings have shown that students who use SMART, along with a particular video adventure, demonstrate a better ability to learn and to explain their thinking than do students who do not receive these supplementary materials (Barron et al., 1995).

Bransford and his colleagues' current focus is on promoting a deep understanding of key mathematical concepts, such as rates, proportions, and functions. The goals are to help students construct rich and meaningful approaches to generating and solving problems.

PROMOTING A CULTURE OF THINKERS: THE ROLE OF BELIEF SYSTEMS AND MOTIVATIONAL FACTORS

For teaching-thinking programs to be successful, students must abandon erroneous beliefs about learning. A particularly maladaptive belief is that people are either born with a talent to do well in a particular subject domain or not. This belief is especially prominent in attitudes toward mathematics. If students believe that they are not mathematically inclined, they tend to regard mathematics as a mystical domain that is divorced from common sense and real-world experiences and is therefore available only to a select few. Schoenfeld (1991) lamented the unfortunate division between formal and informal mathematics. He captured this dichotomy extremely well by quoting the following vignette by E. T. Bell (1939, pp. 146–147) of the philosopher Diderot's visit to the court of Catherine the Great:

> Much to her dismay, Diderot earned his keep by trying to convert the courtiers to atheism. Fed up, Catherine commissioned [the great mathematician Leonhard] Euler to muzzle the windy philosopher. This was easy because all mathematics was Chinese to Diderot. Diderot was informed that a learned mathematician was in possession of an algebraical demonstration of the existence of God, and would give it before all the court, if he desired to hear it. Diderot gladly consented. . . . Euler advanced toward Diderot, and said gravely in a tone of perfect conviction: "Sir, $(a + b^n)/n = x$, hence God exists; reply!"
>
> It sounded like sense to Diderot. Humiliated by the unrestrained laughter which greeted his embarrassed silence, the poor man asked Catherine's permission to return at once to France. She graciously gave it.

Schoenfeld pointed out that mathematics (or, for that matter, any domain that one deems independent from common sense) can be used as a great power of intimidation by experts or teachers. In teaching for thinking, it is important to give students the tools to think for themselves and critique the ways in which information is presented to them. Whether God exists or not, students should be able to evaluate the adequacy of Euler's proof.

Baron (1993) also identified unhelpful beliefs that affect students' thinking and their ability to learn:

1. *Changing one's mind is a sign of weakness.* Students want to appear decisive and strongminded and are afraid to appear insecure if they retract a position or viewpoint.

2. *Being open to alternatives leads to confusion and despair.* This belief is often manifested in the way in which students write papers. That is, students often strongly advocate one viewpoint on a given matter, instead of weighing the pros and cons of different viewpoints.

3. *Quick decision making is a sign of strength and wisdom.*

4. *Truth is determined by authority.*

5. *I cannot influence what happens to me by trying to understand the situation.*

The last belief is often reflected in how students respond to failure. Students who endorse this belief consider failure to be evidence of their lack of ability instead of as a challenge to learn from their mistakes and move on.

These detrimental beliefs show that motivational variables play an extremely important role in students' ability to learn and profit from educational interventions. As Halpern (1998) emphasized, it is important to differentiate between a student's disposition to think critically and his or her ability to do so. It is imperative that students develop attitudes that are conducive to learning, such as the willingness to continue working on a difficult task. This idea is illustrated well by Diener and Dweck's (1978) study, in which children were asked to solve a series of arithmetic problems, every fifth one of which was insolvable. The results indicated that there were two groups of students. The *helpless group* failed on the solvable problems that followed the insolvable ones; blamed their failures on intrinsic factors, such as stupidity; and had lower expectation of their success on subsequent problems. The *mastery-oriented group*, on the other hand, performed just as well or better on subsequent solvable problems, had high expectations that they would do well on the next set of problems, and attributed any failure they experienced to a lack of effort. This study shows clearly that the amount of effort that children put into their schoolwork may be due, in a large part, to their sense of mastery and control.

In the second part of Diener and Dweck's study, a trainer (a confederate) sat next to a child during the problem-solving period. After each failure, the trainer told the child that he or she needed to solve a specific number of problems to reach the criterion of success and that the child solved only a certain number of those. The experimenter then told the child explicitly: "That means that you should have tried harder." Following this instruction, more students began attributing their failure to a lack of effort (rather than stupidity), the tendency to become helpless as a result of failure was reduced, and overall performance improved. This teaching technique increased the student's belief in the effectiveness of his or her own thinking. To maximize the efficiency of a given intervention, it is crucial to help students develop a sense of mastery.

For teaching-thinking programs to succeed optimally, the culture of learning in schools would have to change to embrace such values as questioning authority. As Lipman (1976, p. 23) provocatively put it: "Mindlessness does not seem to threaten the established order;

thoughtfulness might. An irrational social order is threatened much more by rationality than by irrationality." Teaching thinking will be the most effective in a culture that values independence of thought.

◆ SUMMARY

Programs for teaching thinking have emphasized the role of metacognitive strategies that help learners become aware of their own learning strategies. Metacognition, or thinking about thinking, encompasses person (people's beliefs about human cognition, in general, and about their own personal task-taking strategies, in particular), task (understanding the nature of the problem to be solved), and strategy variables (knowing how to approach a given task in different ways).

There are two philosophical viewpoints on the best methods for promoting metacognitive and critical thinking skills: the cognitivist and the situative. Researchers and educators who embrace the cognitivist view argue for teaching thinking from the general to the specific. This approach suggests that students should first learn general reasoning strategies and problem-solving principles that can then be applied to specific domains. On the other hand, researchers and educators who tend to embrace the situative view argue for teaching thinking from the specific to the general. They suggest that students benefit most from learning reasoning and problem-solving skills that are specific to a rich content domain that can then be applied to similar domains. Programs of this kind tend to be part of the regular curriculum, rather than stand-alone interventions. They also tend to emphasize the interaction between the student and his or her social environment.

Examples of programs for teaching thinking from the general to the specific are Philosophy for Children, CoRT, Instrumental Enrichment, Successful Intelligence, and PIFS, as well as Intelligent Tutoring Systems. At the core of each program are a host of fundamental reasoning strategies that are independent of a specific domain. The shared assumption is that by learning these strategies, students can then apply them to developing a deeper understanding of particular subject domains. In contrast, programs that emphasize teaching thinking from the specific to the general, such as Reciprocal Teaching, Fostering a Community of Learners, and the Jasper Woodbury Problem Solving Series, share the belief that students benefit most from learning reasoning and problem-solving skills within a rich content domain that can then be applied to similar domains by the processes of analogical reasoning.

For teaching-for-thinking programs to be successful, students must abandon erroneous beliefs or myths about learning. A particularly maladaptive belief is that one is either born with a talent to do well in a particular subject domain or not. This belief is especially prevalent in attitudes toward mathematical ability. To succeed in school, students have to embrace a mastery-oriented approach to learning: the belief that they can learn from their errors and become better problem solvers. Developing the right cognitive skills is just part of the solution to promoting a more meaningful learning environment. Motivational variables and the values of the environment may be just as important for the success of teaching-for-thinking programs.

Glossary

abstract concepts   ideas or events that are not encoded at a perceptual level (e.g., acts of kindness).

accommodation   an equilibratory process by which an individual modifies his or her cognitive schemas to fit relevant new aspects of the environment.

action potential   the firing pulse that a neuron sends down its axon to the synapses, which are connected to dendrites or cell bodies of other neurons.

activation function   in a neural network, the function that determines the final response of a node to a particular pattern of input.

actor-observer effect   the tendency to externalize a negative behavior if it was committed by oneself and to internalize the same behavior if it was committed by someone else.

ACT-R model   a knowledge representation model that assumes that knowledge is realized by production rules.

adaptation   a component of practical thinking in the triarchic theory of intelligence that reflects a person's ability to adapt to his or her environment.

additivity requirement   a requirement that posits that multistep rules are related to the difficulty level of the single-step arguments they are composed of.

ad hoc concepts   concepts that encompass entities (e.g., children, jewelry) that are unified by an underlying principle or explanation (e.g., "things to take out of the house in case of a fire").

affirmation of the antecedent   a valid deduction (including in the event of a biconditional), consisting of two premises "if p, then q" and "p" and the conclusion "q."

affirmation of the consequent   a fallacious deduction (except in the event of a biconditional), consisting of two premises "if p, then q" and "q" and the conclusion "p."

agency   a sense of control over one's learning.

algorithm   a problem-solving method that always produces a solution.

algorithm level   in the ACT-R model, the rules that are actually firing.

Allais paradox   the failure to apply a consistent strategy in decisions among choices involving certain options (the chance of winning nothing, chance of loss, or certain gain).

analogical reasoning a special case of inductive reasoning. In the process of solving a new problem (the "target problem") by analogy, it is suggested that a person retrieves a similar problem that he or she has solved successfully in the past (the "source problem") and then proceeds to perform a mapping between the two problems to reach a solution.

analytical thinking in the triarchic theory of human intelligence, the ability to analyze, judge, evaluate, compare, contrast, and examine information.

anchoring and adjustment heuristic making a first approximation (anchor) and then adjusting that value to fit new information.

and **function** a logic function that is true when each of its components is true. That is, given that (A and B) is true, it follows that both A and B are true.

antecedent in conditional reasoning, the "p" term in the premise, "If p, then q."

argument in a propositional network typically corresponds to nouns, such as times, places, and people.

artifacts human-made objects.

artificial intelligence a field of research that attempts to build systems that demonstrate at least some form (and often the maximum possible) of intelligence.

assimilation an equilibratory process in which an individual incorporates new information into existing cognitive schemas.

associationism a school of psychological thought that examines how humans and other organisms may learn to link particular events or ideas with one another in the mind.

associative priming occurs in a propositional network when a target word is processed faster when it is primed by a word in the same proposition than when it is primed by a word in a different proposition.

associative stage the second stage of acquisition of procedural knowledge in which people practice using explicit rules and, as a result, strengthen the procedures that are instantiated by these rules (e.g., becoming more familiar with which fingers to use to type certain letters).

associative system a system of reasoning that operates on similarity and contiguity, draws on personal experiences with exemplars, and is largely automatic.

atmosphere hypothesis the idea that people are likely to judge a logical conclusion as true if the quantifier type of the conclusion is the same as the quantifier type of the premises.

autonomous stage the third and final stage of acquisition of procedural knowledge, in which people learn to use rules automatically, improving in both speed and accuracy.

availability heuristic a decision-making heuristic that suggests that people's estimation of frequency or probability is affected by the ease of retrieving examples from memory.

axon a neuron's long transmission line that carries an action potential to the synapses.

babbling a prelinguistic preferential production of only the distinct phonemes that are characteristic of the language being acquired.

backpropagation network the most common type of neural network architecture that has at least two layers of weights. The first layer contains weights that connect input to intermediate units called hidden units, and the second contains weights that connect hidden units to output units.

backward-directed rules a main strategy of PSYCOP that evaluates the validity of a conclusion by generating subgoals that are based on the conclusion.

backward pattern-action rules prescribe what goals a person should set to get to a solution.

base-rate neglect in making probability judgments, the tendency to underweigh the importance of how often something occurs in the population and to overemphasize specific information.

basic-level concepts concepts, such as chair and dog, that are at an intermediate level on the hierarchy of concepts, above subordinate concepts, which are more specific, such as bar stool and Dalmatian, but below superordinate concepts, which are more general, such as furniture and animal.

Bayes's theorem a normative theorem of probability that calculates the probability that a hypothesis (H) is true, given the datum (D), denoted P(H/D):

$$P(H \mid D) = \frac{P(H) \cdot P(D \mid H)}{P(H) \cdot P(D \mid H) + P(\sim H) \cdot P(D / \sim H)}$$

behaviorism a school of psychological thought that focuses entirely on the links between environmental contingencies and observed behavior, discounting any mental phenomena that cannot be observed directly.

belief-bias effect a bias that occurs when the content of a syllogism is concrete and causes people to make judgments about the validity of the syllogism on the basis of a presumed relation between the real-world truth of the premises and the conclusion.

biconditional a statement of the form "If and only if (Iff) p then q." In this case the affirmation of the consequent and denial of the antecedent become deductively correct.

bilingual person who can speak two languages.

bounded rationality the idea that people are rational, given their limitations.

cancellation axiom if two options include identical and equally probable outcomes, then the utility of those outcomes should be ignored when deciding between the two options (i.e., the utilities cancel each other out).

candle problem an insight problem, which presents a person with a candle, a box of tacks, and matches and asks the person to mount the candle vertically on a plywood wall, such that the candle will serve as a lamp.

case-based reasoning   an explanation of problem solving that is based on specific examples, or cases, that are stored in memory. These cases are retrieved and adapted to fit a given problem.

categorical perception   the phenomenon in speech perception in which continuously varying sounds are heard as distinct categories and acoustically different members within a category are not distinguished as well as similarly different sounds in different categories.

categorical syllogism   a problem that involves determining which conclusions follow from a set of premises containing quantifiers, such as *some*, *all*, or *none*.

category   a class of objects or entities.

causal essence   an essence that is the causal entity that leads to all other, secondary properties. For example, the essence of water is typically conceived of as being H_2O.

causal models   models that argue that people's judgments are based on their expectations of cause and effect. These models can be divided into two kinds: common cause and common effect.

centration   the tendency of children to center all thought processes on one perceptually salient aspect of an object, situation, or problem, to the exclusion of other relevant aspects.

certainty effect   the tendency of people to choose a sure ($p = 1.0$) over an unsure bet.

change   a schema for solving arithmetic word problems that involves reasoning from a whole to an initial part.

child-directed speech   the characteristic form of speech that adults tend to use when speaking with infants and young children, which usually involves a higher pitch, exaggerated raising and lowering of pitch and volume, and simpler sentence constructions; generally more effective than normal speech in gaining and keeping the attention of infants and young children (formerly termed *motherese*).

classical view   a view that suggests that objects have defining features that are individually necessary and jointly sufficient.

coarticulation   the overlapping in speech production of neighboring phonemes.

cognitive development   the qualitative changes in thinking that occur across the life span in association with increasing physiological maturity (maturation) and experience (learning).

cognitive psychology   the study of how people perceive, learn, remember, and think about information.

cognitive science   a cross-disciplinary science that embraces cognitive psychology, neuroscience philosophy, anthropology, linguistics, and artificial intelligence as means of understanding cognition.

cognitive stage   the first stage in the acquisition of procedural knowledge in which people engage in learning explicit rules for implementing a specific procedure.

cognitivism   a psychological perspective suggesting that the study of how people think will lead to broad insights into much of human behavior.

cognitivist the viewpoint that learning can be understood by studying people's reasoning processes, problem-solving approaches, and mental representations of knowledge. A key element of this viewpoint is that complex tasks and processes can be broken down into subcomponents that can be studied and taught.

collaboration the sharing of knowledge among participants in the Fostering a Community of Learners program to promote an atmosphere of joint responsibility and mutual respect.

combination a schema for solving arithmetic word problems that involves combining parts to form a whole.

common cause model a model that describes a situation in which a single effect (E) is brought about by the presence of multiple causes (C1, C2, and C3).

common effect model a model that describes a situation in which several effects (E1, E2, and E3) are connected by a single cause (C).

communication the exchange of thoughts and feelings that may or may not involve language because it also encompasses such nonverbal forms as gestures, glances, and so on.

comparison a schema for solving arithmetic word problems that involves comparing two given quantities (two parts).

competence model a model that represents the deductions of an ideal reasoner.

competence theory a theoretical approach emphasizing what people are ideally able to do (cf. *performance theory*).

complex cognition the study of how people mentally represent and think about information.

complex concepts concepts that are made up of a combinations of two or more concepts (e.g., pet fish).

component a specific mental process used in performing cognitive tasks, such as encoding, inferring, mapping, or applying.

componential analysis a breakdown of reaction times and error rates on cognitive tasks, to differentiate the various processes that make up each task.

comprehension mechanism a mechanism that decodes the verbal information in a logical argument into the representation used in an inference schema.

Computer Supported Intentional Learning Environments (CSILE) an educational program, which is implemented in the school system by creating a computer database for each participating classroom. The students are encouraged to enter all their work on a particular project into the database and to access and comment on the work done by their peers.

concept a mental representation of a category or class of entities.

concept-identification task a task designed to study concept formation by showing participants a set of stimuli comprising geometric figures on rectangular cards and asking them to discover whether these stimuli follow a predetermined concept or rule.

conclusion a statement that follows from given premises.

concrete operations   the Piagetian stage (roughly ages 7–12 years) during which children become proficient in mentally manipulating their internal representations of concrete objects.

conditional reasoning   making inferences on statements that have an if-then form.

confirmation bias   a bias that occurs in the process of hypothesis testing, when people tend to test cases that would support and strengthen their hypotheses, rather than cases that would weaken their beliefs.

confirmatory questions   questions that are consistent with people's stereotypes.

conflict resolution   in a production system, conflict resolution occurs when more than one production rule provides a match, and the system undergoes a process of deciding which production rules to execute on the basis of different criteria, such as the success with which the rule has performed in the past.

conjunction   a statement in formal logic of the form "p *and* q."

conjunction fallacy   an error in which people judge that the probability that two events will occur together is greater than the probability that one of these events will occur alone.

connection   in a neural network, the weight that links the nodes together.

connectionist network   the term used to refer to a neural network to distinguish it from a biological model.

connotation   an emotional overtone, presupposition, or other nonexplicit meaning of a word.

conservation   the ability to keep in mind the stability of a given quantity despite observed changes in the appearance of the object or substance.

content morpheme   a morpheme that carries the bulk of the meaning of a word.

contextualist   a theorist or researcher who holds that a given psychological construct, such as intelligence, cannot be understood outside its real-world context.

contingent weighting   an explanation of preference reversals in decision making that holds that people treat each gamble as having two (or more) attributes and a preference between choices is contingent on which attribute is the focus of the question being presented.

continuity axiom   the concept that a gamble between the best and worst outcomes should always be preferred to a certain intermediate outcome if the probability of the best outcome is high enough.

contrast model of similarity   a categorization model that assumes that feature sets are independent and can be combined linearly by adding. The contrast rule is given in the following equation (where "I" refers to Instance, and "P" to Prototype):

$$Sim(I,P) = af(I \cap P) - bf(P - I) - cf(I - P)$$

converging operations   evidence from multiple studies with different methodologies that together can show strong support for a particular theory or hypothesis.

conversion hypothesis   a hypothesis that suggests that errors in judgments of syllogisms may be explained by converting "all x are y" into "all y are x" and "some x are y" into "some y are x."

cooing   oral expression that explores the production of all the phones (cf. phonemes) that humans can possibly produce; precedes babbling, which precedes language articulation.

cooperative principle   the principle of conversation in which it is held that people seek to communicate in ways that make it easy for a listener to understand what a speaker means, such as by following the maxims of manner, quality, quantity, and relation proposed by Grice (1967).

CoRT (Cognitive Research Trust)   an educational program designed to facilitate the acquisition of a skillful and systematic method of thinking by promoting the development of both vertical thinking (logical, linear, and ordered) and lateral thinking (creative, nonlinear, and unpredictable).

creative thinking   in the triarchic theory of human intelligence, the ability to engage in discovery, supposition, and imagination and to deal successfully with novel situations.

creativity   the ability to produce work that is novel, high in quality, and task appropriate.

critic   in artificial intelligence, a procedure that monitors a current problem state and signals when a constraint is violated.

critic-related failures   failures that occur when a problem solver does not develop internal mechanisms for detecting violations in the problem-solving process.

culture   in the Fostering a Community of Learners program, the sense of group identity that results from collaborative work and the sharing and evaluating ideas.

culture-fair   an ideal describing something that is equally appropriate and fair for members of all cultures.

culture-relevant   an assessment (or description) that is based on skills and knowledge that relate to the cultural experiences of the test takers and that recognizes that the test givers' definitions of the construct being measured may differ from those of the test takers.

cycle   the sequence of matching production rules, performing conflict resolution, and then executing a production rule in a production system.

decision table   a table used in making decisions in which potential outcomes are generated by crossing the available options with decision states.

declarative memory   in the ACT-R model, memory dedicated to the representation of factual knowledge.

deductive reasoning   the process of making inferences from a specific set of premises to a particular conclusion with certainty.

deductively correct argument   an argument in which the conclusion is true in any state of affairs in which the premises are true.

deep disciplinary content   in the Fostering a Community of Learners program, the selection of content areas that require students to reason at the upper bounds of their ability levels.

deep structure   a level of syntactic analysis, which indicates the relationships among various surface structures by means of transformational rules.

defining features   features that create clear and stable boundaries of categories. That is, all objects, in any given category, share all the defining features of that category. The defining features are individually necessary and jointly sufficient for inclusion in the category.

deliberate practice   practice that is focused and systematic and represents a concerted attempt to analyze errors and improve performance.

dendrites   receptor sites on the receiving neurons that are located in treelike structures.

denial of the antecedent   a fallacious deduction (except in the event of a *biconditional*), consisting of two premises "if p then q" and "not p" and the conclusion "not q."

denial of the consequent   see *modus tollens.*

denotation   the strict dictionary definition of a word (cf. *connotation*).

deontic   involving social contract, obligation, or right.

descriptive model   see *descriptive theory.*

descriptive theory   a theory that specifies how people actually make decisions, as opposed to how they ought to make decisions.

developmental corridors   in the Fostering a Community of Learners program, the study of the same content area at several grade levels, each time with greater depth and complexity.

dialect   a regional variation of a language, characterized by distinctive features, such as differences in vocabulary, syntax, and pronunciation.

difference reduction   a heuristic that prescribes the successive reduction in the greatest difference between the current and goal state until the problem is solved.

direct reasoning   reasoning that is low to moderate in difficulty, often requiring the making of logical inferences in a forward direction.

disconfirmatory questions   questions that are at odds with people's stereotypes.

discourse   the most comprehensive level of linguistic analysis that encompasses language use at the level beyond the sentence, such as in conversations and paragraphs.

discovery problem   the fact that there may be more than one knowledge-representation model that is consistent with the data at the implementation level.

domain-general view   the perspective that thinking should be taught as a separate subject domain, alongside more traditional ones, such as science and social studies. Proponents of this view believe that there are general rules that govern thinking that can be learned and transferred across domains.

domain-specific view   the perspective that the teaching of thinking must be embedded within a particular subject area (or domain), such as mathematics. Adherents of this approach often believe that thinking is dependent on its context and cannot be taught as a separate subject.

dominance axiom   the idea that it is irrational to choose an option that will yield weaker outcomes.

dual-system hypothesis   a view of bilingualism that suggests that the two languages are somehow represented in separate systems of the mind and even in the brain (cf. *single-system hypothesis*).

dynamic assessment environment   a context for examination in which the examiner responds distinctively when a child gives an incorrect answer, offering the child a graded series of hints to guide the child toward the correct answer.

ecological validity   the degree to which particular findings in one context (e.g., a laboratory) may be considered relevant outside that context; based on the notion that human thought processes interact with particular environmental contexts.

egocentric   a characteristic in which children focus largely on themselves and on their own perspective; over the course of development, however, children become decreasingly egocentric and thereby better able to see things from the perspective of others.

elaboration phase impairments   according to Feuerstein, impairments that decrease one's ability to process relevant information about the nature of the problem, for example, the inability to select relevant cues when defining a problem.

electric potential   a neuron's electrical charge when at rest. Incoming neural transmitters change the potential of the receptor neuron.

elimination by aspects (EBA)   a decision-making heuristic that suggests that people eliminate options on the basis of whether or not the alternative choice has certain favorable attributes. This process is done one attribute at a time until only one alternative remains.

Ellsberg paradox   a paradox that shows that in decisions involving multiple attributes, people choose differently in situations in which there is a change in one attribute even though the change affects both choices.

emotional intelligence   the ability to evaluate and express emotions accurately and to regulate emotions in a way that guides both emotional and intellectual development.

empiricist   a person who believes that knowledge is most effectively acquired through observation.

encoding problem   in a neural network, occurs when the network is presented with an input pattern and its job is to output the exact same pattern (also known as an autoassociative problem).

equal weights heuristic (EQW)   a heuristic that calculates the utility of a particular option by (1) breaking it into psychologically independent dimensions, (2) assigning a utility for each dimension, and (3) summing the utilities to arrive at a total utility.

equilibration   the process of cognitively adapting to the environment, whereby the individual works to maintain a state of cognitive equilibrium (balance), even in the face of new information (cf. *accommodation, assimilation*).

error   in a neural network, involves computing the difference between the desired output of the network and its actual output.

essence   the building block of psychological essentialism; a construct that refers to a hidden aspect of an object that determines the object's identity.

exemplar view   of categorization, a similarity-based view that holds that instances of a category are represented mentally by the degree to which they are similar to (have overlapping attributes with) other known instances of the category.

exhaustive search   an algorithm that consists of trying out all possible solution paths to a problem in a brute-force manner.

expected utility   a quantitative value found by multiplying the probability of an option by its utility.

expected utility theory (EUT)   a theory that predicts that people ought to assign subjective utilities to events and then calculate the expected utility of each option.

expected value   a quantitative value found by multiplying the probability of an option by its objective value.

expected value theory (EVT)   a theory that predicts that people ought to make decisions based on their expected value, when outcome values are objective and probabilities are known.

expert module   in Intelligent Tutoring Systems, the representation of the knowledge base, or the information that the student has to learn.

expert system   a computer program designed to perform tasks at a high level of expertise.

expertise   highly skilled, competent performance in one or more task domains.

explanation-based view   a view that suggests that people categorize instances on the basis of principled knowledge that they possess.

factor analysis   a statistical method for discerning various component hypothetical factors within an overall construct.

fallacy of the undistributed middle   a common error in logic that rests on the belief that two terms that are either a subset of or coincident with a third term (All A are B and All C are B) must also be a subset of or coincident with each other (All A are C).

false consensus effect   the tendency to see one's own behaviors and judgments as being more common and appropriate than those of others.

family resemblance   a structure that contains a set of instances (e.g., robin, penguin, blue jay, crow, canary, humming bird) each of which has at least one overlapping attribute with one or more of the other instances in the set (e.g., has wings, flies, sings).

fast-and-frugal heuristics a family of algorithms that involve a simple one-reason decision-making process.

figural effects when people generate conclusions with a particular order of terms on the basis of the order of the premises.

firing 1. executing an action in a production rule.
2. executing an action potential in a neuron.

flow chart a box diagram showing the steps for solving a problem or for implementing a sequence of instructions in a computer program.

focusing an efficient strategy for performing a concept-identification task. In this strategy, a positive exemplar of the correct concept is used as a focus card against which the next card choice is compared. The person selects a card whose features differ from the focus card by either one (in conservative focusing) or several (in focus gambling) attributes at a time.

formal-operational stage the Piagetian stage (starting roughly at age 12) during which children become proficient in mentally manipulating their internal representations not only of concrete objects but of abstract symbols.

forward pattern-action rules provide instructions on what one should do from his or her current problem-solving state.

forward-directed rules the main strategy of PSYCOP, which evaluates the validity of a conclusion working from the outside in.

Fostering a Community of Learners (FCL) an educational program designed to create a collaborative, scientific atmosphere in elementary school classrooms. The program focuses on exploring deep principles of the fields of environmental science and biology.

frame a schema that contains several slots to hold specific information about the situation. The slots specify the general categories that hold true for every instance of the schema.

frequency theory a normative theory of probability that measures probability in terms of the relative frequencies of past events.

function morpheme a morpheme that adds detail and nuance to the meaning of a content morpheme or that helps a content morpheme to fit a particular syntactical context.

functional fixedness the tendency to represent objects as serving traditional problem-solving functions, resulting in the inability to use these objects in novel ways. For example, see *two-string problem*.

functionalist psychologist who holds that the key to understanding the human mind and behavior is to study the processes of how and why the mind works as it does, rather than the structural contents and elements of the mind.

g the general factor of intelligence, originally proposed by Spearman.

Gestalt psychology the school of psychological thought that asserts that many psychological phenomena must be understood as integral wholes and that the analysis of fragmentary elements often destroys the integrity of the phenomena.

global planning an aspect of problem solving during which the individual encodes the problem and formulates a general strategy for attacking the problem.

goal state the solution state that the problem solver tries to achieve.

grammar the study of language in terms of regular patterns that relate to the functions and relationships of words in a sentence, extending as broadly as the level of discourse and as narrowly as the pronunciation and meaning of individual words.

halo effect an inference by a person A that a person B has a favorable trait based on A's experience with B. This inference, in turn, also causes A to think that B has other favorable traits, regardless of whether B does or does not have them.

heuristic a problem-solving method that acts like a rule of thumb. It entails conducting a selective search by looking at selected portions of the problem space that are most likely to produce a solution.

heuristic reasoning program a program that contains routines and strategies for constructing sets of inferences and deciding which schema should be applied at each step of the deductive process.

hidden layer in a neural network, takes weighted input from the input layer, transforms it, and passes a weighted version of that transformation on to the output layer.

hidden units intermediate units in a neural network.

hypothesis a tentative proposal of expected consequences, such as of the outcomes of research.

hypothesis testing a view of language acquisition that asserts that children acquire language by mentally forming tentative assumptions regarding language and then testing these assumptions in the environment, using several operating principles for generating and testing their assumptions.

ideal essence an essence that does not have an objective existence in the world, but is a mental construct (e.g., "romantic love").

idealized cognitive models a theory that argues that concepts appear to be well defined but do not necessarily correspond to real-world attributes.

identification in the Philosophy for Children program, the process whereby students learn to take the viewpoint of the characters they read about.

ill-defined problem a problem that does not have an obvious solution path.

illusory correlation the erroneous belief that two variables are statistically related when they are not.

illusory inference an erroneous inference in logic that results from ignoring information that is false.

impersonal theory a theory that analyzes human rationality by comparing people's reasoning to normative theories that make use of principles of logic and probability without taking personal goals into account.

implementation level   in the ACT-R model, a lower level of processing that specifies exactly when a particular rule will fire and with what speed.

inclusion rule   the probability that two events occur together (A and B), where one is a subset of the other (A is a subset of B), is less than or equal to the probability of the larger set (B).

inclusive disjunction   a statement of the form "p *or* q, or both."

indirect reasoning   as opposed to direct reasoning, requires the making of inferences that lie outside a problem's premises.

indirect request   a form of speech act in which the individual makes a request in an oblique, rather than a direct, manner.

individually necessary   features that an object must have to belong to a given category.

inductive failures   failures that occur when the person overgeneralizes or overspecializes a rule from familiar examples.

inductive reasoning   the process of making a general inference from a set of specific premises to a conclusion, with some but not a complete degree of certainty.

inference schema   a mental representation of logical arguments made up of a set of premises and a conclusion.

information-processing theorists   cognitive psychologists who seek to understand cognitive and cognitive development in terms of how people engage in various cognitive processes, such as decoding, encoding, storing, and retrieving information in various forms (e.g., images, propositions, or symbols).

initial state   of a problem, the state in which the problem solver sorts out the givens of a problem.

input layer   of a neural network, presents a signal that is derived from an external source.

input phase impairments   deficits that create difficulty in correctly diagnosing a student's learning disability, such as unplanned, unsystematic, or impulsive behaviors.

insight   a sudden understanding that arises after a period of trying to solve a problem unsuccessfully; an "Aha!" experience that is the result of taking a new viewpoint on or approach to the problem at hand.

insight problems   problems that require insight.

instance-based models   models that operate on examples instead of on explicit rules.

Instrumental Enrichment   an educational program based on Feuerstein's concept of intelligence. The operating principle is that intelligence is dynamic and can be shaped by environmental influences.

intelligence   the ability to learn from experience and to adapt to the surrounding environment.

Intelligent Tutoring System (ITS)   computer programs that are designed to provide individualized instruction in domains such as geometry, chess, or computer programming.

intentional learning   learning for the sake of learning.

internalization   a process proposed by Vygotsky in which individuals incorporate knowledge that they gain through their interactions within a social context.

invariance axiom   the idea that it is irrational for a decision to be affected by the way alternatives are presented or framed.

inventory requirement   a requirement that posits that for a person to reason correctly, he or she must possess all the relevant rules. Incorrect reasoning indicates the lack of knowledge of at least one rule.

Jasper Woodbury Problem Solving Series   an intervention program developed by Bransford and his colleagues with the aim of fostering mathematical thinking for middle school students. The program is based on a series of interactive videodiscs and follow-up projects that place mathematical principles in real-world settings.

jointly sufficient   features that together define a particular category.

knowledge-acquisition components   in the triarchic theory of human intelligence, mechanisms that one uses to learn new information.

knowledge-lean problem   a problem that requires little specific knowledge about a given domain.

knowledge-rich problem   a problem that requires specialized domain knowledge, such as the ability to carry out mathematical procedures.

language   an organized means of combining words to communicate (cf. *communication*).

language-acquisition device (LAD)   the hypothetical construct of an innate human predisposition to acquire language; not yet found as a specific physiological structure or function.

lateral thinking   see *CoRT*.

law of large numbers   large samples are more representative of the population from which they were selected than are small samples.

lemma   an auxiliary proposition used in the demonstration of another proposition.

lexicon   the entire set of morphemes in a given language or in a given person's linguistic repertoire (cf. *vocabulary*).

linear decomposition   a process by which people apply an operator to each subpart of a problem independently and then combine the partial results from each operation to form the solution.

linear syllogism   a syllogism involving a comparison between terms in which each term shows either more or less of a given quantity or quality.

linearly separable categories categories for which there is a clear dividing line between members of one category and members of another category.

linearly separable function a function in two dimensions that produces a line that divides the vertices of a square into two separate classes. For example, see *and function, or function*.

linguistic relativity hypothesis a proposition regarding the relationship between thought and language that asserts that the speakers of different languages have different cognitive systems, based on the languages they use, and that these different cognitive systems influence the ways in which people speaking the various languages think about the world.

linguistic universals characteristic patterns of language that apply across all the languages of various cultures.

link the arrow in a propositional network that stands for an association between nodes or concepts.

local planning aspect of problem solving during which the individual carries out globally planned strategies and devises detailed tactics.

logical theory a normative theory of probability that suggests that one can specify a set of events or propositions that are exchangeable and thus have independent and identical probabilities. The probability of a proposition is the proportion of exchangeable possible worlds in which that proposition is true.

loose view of reasoning a view that assumes that inductive reasoning does not require a special logical structure, abstract specifications, or discrete inference steps.

meaning-based representations representations that maintain the semantics of an object or event and discard many of its surface-structural or perceptual details.

means-end analysis a problem-solving heuristic in which (1) the goal state is determined, (2) the distance between the current problem-solving state and the desired goal state is assessed, and (3) the problem solver chooses an operator for reducing the greatest difference between these states.

mediated learning experience (MLE) in the Instrumental Enrichment program, a type of learning experience that is guided by a mediating agent, such as a parent or a teacher.

mental model a knowledge structure that represents information contained in the premises by relating it to available examples and real-life knowledge, leading to the formation of a possible conclusion.

mental proof the generation of a set of sentences in working memory that link the premises of an argument with its conclusion via inference rules.

metacognition the act of thinking about thinking; an awareness of one's own thought processes.

metacomponents in the triarchic theory of human intelligence, higher-order processes used in planning or evaluating performance.

metaphor   the juxtaposition of two unlike nouns, thereby asserting their similarities, but not disconfirming their dissimilarities.

metaphysical essentialism   the philosophical view that an object has an essence by virtue of being that object.

micro inferences   in a neural network, hidden units that learn to represent the knowledge of relationships between inputs and outputs, rather than directly encode stimulus-response patterns.

middle term   the term that is used in each of the premises of a categorical syllogism.

mind-body dualism   the view that the body is composed of physical substance, whereas the mind is not.

modus ponens   an inference consisting of two premises "if p, then q" and "p" and the conclusion "q."

modus tollens   an inference consisting of two premises "if p, then q" and "not q" and the conclusion "not p."

monolingual   person who can speak only one language.

more-important-dimension hypothesis   the idea that when people are given a choice between two equally valued options, they will choose the option with the greater value on what they perceive to be the most important dimension involved.

morpheme   the smallest unit of single or combined sounds that denotes meaning within a given language.

multi-attribute utility theory (MAUT)   a decision-making theory that calculates the utility of a particular option by (1) breaking it into psychologically independent dimensions, (2) assigning each dimension a numerical weight relative to the others, and (3) assigning the option a utility along each dimension.

natural kinds   concepts that are first "discovered" and then labeled.

necessary conclusion   a statement that must be true if it holds in all the models of the premises.

neural networks   a class of computational models that is inspired by neural processing in the brain. These models are knowledge structures in which events and concepts are linked by weighted connections that can change with experience.

neuron   a cell that comprises the basic unit of the nervous system and conducts information.

NewAbacus   a new number system based on the Chinese abacus.

node   1. a proposition, relation, or argument in a propositional network.
   2. a simple processing unit in a neural network, linked to other units by connections or weights. A node approximately corresponds to a neuron's cell body.

nominal concepts   entities that are defined by convention.

noun phrase   a syntactic structure that often serves as a subject of a sentence but that may also act as an object of a verb phrase or of a prepositional phrase.

object permanence   the cognitive awareness that objects continue to exist even when the objects are not immediately perceptible through the senses.

or **function**   a logic function that is true when either one of its components is true. That is, given that (A *or* B) is true, it follows that either A or B or both are true.

ordering of alternatives axiom   the idea that it is rational to compare any two alternatives and have a preference for one over the other.

output layer   in a neural network, displays the time-dependent explicit "behavior" of the network.

output phase impairments   problems in communicating responses with accuracy or precision.

outside view   perceiving the possible relationship between a subset and a superset.

overconfidence   overestimation of how accurate one's judgments are.

overextension error   overapplication of the meaning of a given word to more things, ideas, and situations than is appropriate for the denotation and the defining features of the word; usually made by children or other persons when acquiring a language.

overregularization   an error that commonly occurs during language acquisition, in which the novice language user has gained an understanding of how a language usually works and then overapplies the general rules of the language to the exceptional cases for which the rules do not apply.

parallel distributed processing   connectionist networks that combine parallel processing with distributed representations.

parallelism   in a connectionist network, the idea that knowledge flows through the entire system simultaneously, rather than in a step-by-step fashion.

partial matching   occurs when a solver encounters a new problem state and then searches for a familiar example or rule that shares some of the features of the current problem and has successfully worked in the past. Once the familiar example is found, its procedure is then executed.

particular affirmative   consists of statements, such as "Some A are B," in which some members of the first category (A) are members of the second category (B).

particular negative   consists of statements, such as "Some A are not B," in which some members of the first category (A) are not members of the second category (B).

pattern matching   in a production system, a process in which the system determines whether a production rule's conditions match the contents of a rule stored in memory.

pattern-action rules   condition-action rules of the form, "If C, then A." See also *backward pattern-action rules*, *forward pattern-action rules*.

perception-based representations representations that preserve the original perceptual experiences of people in a fairly accurate way.

perceptron convergence theorem a learning rule that guarantees that a neural network will arrive at a correct solution.

performance components in the triarchic theory of human intelligence, the components of intelligence used during the execution of a task.

performance model outlines the constraints on the competence model imposed by the cognitive system, such as working-memory capacity.

performance theory a theoretical perspective emphasizing what people typically do (cf. *competence theory*).

person variables in Flavell's conception of metacognition, the variables that encompass people's beliefs about human cognition, in general, and about their own thoughts and task-taking strategies, in particular.

personal theory a theory that assumes that a probability estimate is a subjective judgment of the likelihood of an event.

perspective effect in the Wason selection task, when people choose either the "p and not-q" cards or the "not-p and q cards," depending on their a priori viewpoints.

Philosophy for Children an educational program that is designed to promote children's thinking by teaching children principles of logic, philosophy, and formal reasoning through a series of novels.

phoneme the smallest unit of speech sound that distinguishes one utterance from another in a given language.

phrase-structure grammars a form of syntactic analysis that analyzes sentences in terms of the superficial sequence of words in sentences without considering relationships among sentences.

Pi function a descriptive model of decision making in which utilities are multiplied by a function of probability.

plasticity a characteristic of human cognition, whereby we appear to be limitlessly able to modify our cognitive processes and products, improving our effectiveness in the tasks we face.

positive test strategy a situation in which people test cases that are positive instances of their hypothesized rules that may or may not lead to falsification.

possible conclusion a statement that may be true if it holds in at least some model of the premises.

Practical Intelligence for Schools (PIFS) an educational program that combines elements of multiple intelligences and the triarchic theory of human intelligence for enhancing students' practical thinking.

practical thinking   in the triarchic theory of human intelligence, the ability to practice, use, apply, and implement information in the learning environment.

pragmatic approach   an approach to studying inductive reasoning that emphasizes the role of the system's goals and the context in which reasoning takes place.

pragmatic reasoning schemas   abstract knowledge structures that incorporate a set of rules that are sensitive to context and are goal directed.

pragmatics   the study of how people use language, emphasizing the contexts in which language is used, as well as the nonverbal communication that augments verbal communication.

pragmatist   a proponent of a school of psychological thought that evaluates the merits of knowledge in terms of the usefulness of that knowledge.

predicate term   the second term in the minor premise of a syllogism.

preference reversal   a person's preference for one of two options can be reversed depending on contextual factors.

premise   one of two statements (the major and minor premise), which along with a conclusion, comprise a syllogism.

preoperational stage   the Piagetian stage (roughly ages 2–7) during which children begin actively to develop internal mental representations and to use language as a means of cognitive manipulation, as well as communication.

principle of truth   the tendency to avoid placing heavy demands on working memory by representing explicitly only what is true and not what is false about a deductive argument.

probabilistic view   a similarity-based view that holds that instances of a category are represented mentally by the degree to which they are similar to (have overlapping attributes with) an abstract representation of the category.

probability estimation   a quantitative measure of the strength of or confidence in a particular proposition or belief.

probable conclusion   a statement that is likely to be true if it holds in most of the models of the premises.

problem   a set of initial states, goal states, and path constraints.

problem schemas   mental representations of the structure of a problem production.

problem space   a mental space consisting of symbolic representations of states and a set of operators. Each operator takes a state as input and produces a state as output. The sequences of applying operators create a solution path.

procedural memory   in the ACT-R model, memory dedicated to the representation of knowledge about operations and procedures.

production rule a rule consisting of an *if* clause followed by a *then* clause. The *if* clause specifies the condition or conditions that must be met for the action specified in the *then* clause to be executed or fired.

production system a knowledge-representation system that embeds a large number of production rules. The production rules are structured around a set of goals and subgoals, in which there is always one goal active. To satisfy the goals, the condition of a production rule responds to information stored in working memory.

proposition the smallest unit of knowledge about which one can make true or false judgments.

propositional network a knowledge structure in which each proposition is represented by a circle, connected by labeled arrows to the relation and argument terms.

propositional structures meaning-based representations that preserve specific information about an event (e.g., what kind of food you ate today for breakfast).

prospect theory a descriptive theory that suggests that people make decisions using values (gains or losses from a reference point) and subjective probabilities.

prototype an instance that shares the most family resemblance to, or overlapping attributes with, other members of its set.

prototype theory a class of probabilistic models, which argues that people create a representation of a category's central tendency in the form of a prototype.

psycholinguistics study of language as it interacts with the human mind.

psychological essentialism the view that people *believe* that concepts have essences that play a role in determining what instances will be classified as members of a concept.

PSYCOP (psychology of proof) a theory that states that people solve deduction problems by constructing mental proofs.

radial categories categories that require the formation of multiple related models.

rarity assumption the assumption that when p and q are each unlikely to occur, then their intersection is even more unlikely, making it beneficial to flip over the p and q cards on the Wason selection task.

rational analysis an attempt to understand human cognition based on the idea that it has been optimized to fit the structure of the environment over time.

rationalist a person who believes that the route to knowledge is through the use of logical analysis.

reception paradigm a version of the concept-identification task, in which the participants are shown cards, in succession, that are either positive or negative exemplars of a particular concept. After each card is presented, the participants are asked to provide a tentative hypothesis about the correct concept it represents, without receiving any feedback from the experimenter.

Reciprocal Teaching   an instructional program designed to enhance reading comprehension by using discussion groups in which each member must take a turn as the discussion leader.

recursive procedure   a procedure that repeats itself until a goal is reached.

reflection   meta-awareness of one's own strengths and weaknesses as a student.

regret theory   a descriptive theory that suggests that people overweigh anticipated feelings of regret (or rejoicing) when the difference between possible outcomes is large.

relatedness effect   manifested when people's response times slow down on a test as a result of similarities between two given concepts.

relation   in a propositional network, corresponds to a verb, adjective, or another term that helps form connections between the arguments.

repair theory   a theory of arithmetic errors that suggests that when a student attempts to solve a problem that requires adding new rules to his or her knowledge base, the student reaches an impasse, or a state of being deadlocked. The student then selects a repair, or a set of actions that modifies the current knowledge base and gets the student "unstuck."

representational thought   cognitive processes by which children form internal representations (symbolic or imaginal depictions) of external stimuli.

representativeness heuristic   a decision-making heuristic that suggests that a sample looks representative if it has important characteristics that are similar to the population from which it was taken.

resolution of ambiguity   the knowledge that social events tend to be ill defined and subject to multiple interpretations.

resource allocation   knowledge about which parts of a task one should focus more attention and time on than others.

reversible   a characteristic of processes that can be undone, once they have been done (e.g., pouring from one container to another and then back again).

Rightstart   an educational program that is designed to incorporate children's intuitive theories into classroom instruction.

robust finding   a finding that has been replicated many times.

rule-based system   a system of inductive reasoning that operates by manipulating symbols that have a logical structure and a set of variables; draws on language, culture, and formal systems (such as formal logic and mathematics); and is largely conscious or strategic.

rule-based theories   theories that suggest that people generate a variety of mistakes but may still have a "mental logic" that requires a special logical structure, abstract specifications of rules and discrete inference steps that derive a conclusion from a delimited set of premises.

ruleless theories   theories that suggest that people have not evolved special structures for deductive reasoning and link reasoning more directly to a person's available experience and the context of the reasoning.

rule-plus-exception model (RULEX)   a theory that suggests that ill-defined categories (categories that cannot be formed by individually necessary and jointly sufficient rules) can be learned by forming "imperfect" rules and then storing exceptions to these rules.

St. Petersburg paradox   in a gamble in which the expected value is infinite, shows that the subjective value is limited because it does not follow a linear function.

satisficing   a process in which people select a choice that fulfills their goals in an acceptable, rather than an optimal, way.

schema   general knowledge structures that aid in comprehending information.

script   a kind of schema that provides a template for the ordered sequences of events that characterize certain everyday situations, such as going to a restaurant, grocery store, or physician's office. Scripts differ from schemas and frames in that they are applicable only to a limited number of stereotyped situations and are structured as an ordered series of causally linked events.

selection   in the triarchic theory of human intelligence, choosing a new environment because of an irreconcilable mismatch between individual needs and environmental constraints.

selection paradigm   a version of the concept-identification task in which a participant is provided with a card that is a positive exemplar of a particular concept from the whole available stimulus array. The participant is then asked to decide what the concept is by choosing cards, one at a time. As each card is chosen, the experimenter provides feedback on whether the card is a positive or a negative exemplar of the concept. The participant is then asked to guess what the concept is.

selective combination   in the triarchic theory of human intelligence, the component of creative thinking that deals with the combination of isolated pieces of information in a new and coherent way.

selective comparison   in the triarchic theory of human intelligence, the component of creative thinking that relates new information to relevant information that has been previously acquired.

selective encoding   in the triarchic theory of human intelligence, the component of creative thinking that deals with sifting out relevant information from the total information provided.

selective exposure   the reality that people usually have access only to biased samples of the population because they tend to socialize with people who are similar to themselves.

semantic induction   the process of forming analogical mappings to real-life examples or concepts to solve unfamiliar problems.

semantic network   organizes general knowledge into categories of information. Semantic networks are structured similarly to propositional networks in that they consist of nodes (concepts) and links (associations) and that the concepts separated by the fewest links are predicted to be the most strongly associated with each other.

semantics   the study of meanings in language.

sensorimotor stage   The Piagetian stage (roughly from birth to 2 years) during which the infant gradually adapts motor output (e.g., reflexes) in response to sensory input to serve his or her intentional goals; involves increases in both the number and the complexity of sensory and motor abilities.

set effect   a situation in which a solver becomes prone toward using a certain problem-solving operator because it is more available, at the expense of using simpler and more efficient operators. For example, see *water-pitcher problem.*

shaping   in the triarchic theory of human intelligence, changing the environment to fit one's needs.

Sierra   a theory that adds a learning component to repair theory by computationally modeling how people select the set of actions that forms the solution strategy by a process of induction from worked-out examples.

sigmoid function   a logistic function in a neural network that usually has a nonlinear S-shape. This function tends to squash either very small or very large responses and behaves like a linear function for medium responses to limit the output range of a network.

similarity-based view   a view that suggests that people categorize instances on the basis of their similarity to old and familiar instances.

simile   the juxtaposition of two unlike nouns, in which the word *like* or *as* is used to suggest similarities between the two.

simple concepts   concepts made up of one object or entity (e.g., fish).

simulation   in the Philosophy for Children program, the process that enables students to adapt a character's experiences to their own lives.

simulation heuristic   the estimation of the frequency or probability of an event on the basis of the ease of simulating (or imagining) the event.

single-layer network   a neural network with direct connections between its input and output.

single-system hypothesis   a view of bilingualism that suggests that both languages are represented in just one system of the mind and in the brain (cf. *dual-system hypothesis*).

situated theory   the perspective that learning cannot be localized to the human mind, but, rather, takes place within the interaction between the learner and her or his environment.

slip   an unintentional overlooking of a problem-solving step.

slips of the tongue   inadvertent errors in what is said, usually as a result of the phonological or semantic confusion of phonemes, morphemes, or even larger units of language.

social concepts   concepts of a social kind, such as introvert and extrovert.

social-contract theory   a theory that proposes that people have evolved domain-specific skills for reasoning in situations of social exchange.

soma   the cell body of the neuron, which accumulates and integrates input signals.

sortal essence   an essence that is made up of defining characteristics that are common to all members of a category.

speech act   any of five basic categories of speech, analyzed in terms of the purposes accomplished by the given act.

spreading activation   the idea that a concept (e.g., red) will first activate strongly linked concepts in a knowledge-representation structure (e.g., fire), followed by slightly weaker associations (e.g., roses).

state   a situation that has a certain likelihood of being true.

static assessment environment   the typical context for examination in which the examiner makes no effort to respond distinctively when a child gives an incorrect answer, proceeding instead to the next question in the test.

strategy variables   in Flavell's theory of metacognition, the more specific variables that are related to knowing how to approach a given task in multiple ways, such as being able to represent a problem both spatially and linguistically.

straw-man argument   an argument in which the results are bound to disconfirm the null hypothesis because the null hypothesis is known to be untrue.

strict view of reasoning   the view that deductive reasoning has a special structure that involves processes and representations that operate in the abstract, without regard to real-life or pragmatic constraints.

structural mapping theory   a theory that suggests that analogical reasoning relies primarily on relational or structural similarity and not so much on the actual object attributes involved.

structuralism   a psychological perspective that sought to analyze consciousness into its constituent components of elementary sensations, using the reflective self-observational technique of introspection.

structure   a constraint on analogical reasoning that states that strong analogs are ones that share a deep-structural similarity (the same underlying principles).

structure-of-intellect (SOI)   Guilford's model for a three-dimensional structure of intelligence, embracing various contents, operations, and products of intelligence.

student module   in an Intelligent Tutoring System, the representation of the student's current state of knowledge.

subgoaling the process that results from a problem-solving situation in which an operator is applied and an obstacle occurs, forcing the problem solver to set a subgoal of removing that obstacle. Subgoaling is a recursive procedure.

subject term the term that is used uniquely in the first premise of a categorical syllogism.

subjective expected utility theory (SEUT) an extension of expected utility theory that uses subjective instead of objective probabilities.

subordinate concepts specific concepts, such as bar stool and Dalmatian, that lie below basic-level and superordinate concepts.

Successful Intelligence an educational program, based on the triarchic theory of human intelligence, that is designed to improve students' analytic, creative, and practical thinking through a series of problems, lessons, and exercises.

successive scanning a strategy that most people use for performing the concept-identification task by testing cards that confirm a single hypothesis, one at a time.

superordinate concepts general concepts, such as furniture and animal, that lie above subordinate and basic-level concepts.

sure-thing principle a principle that suggests that if a person prefers option A to option B, whether the event occurs or not, then option A should always dominate over B.

surface structure a level of syntactic analysis that indicates just the specific syntactical sequence of words in a sentence.

syllogism an argument with exactly two premises followed by a conclusion (see *categorical syllogism*).

syllogistic reasoning reasoning that involves evaluating or generating statements with exactly two premises followed by a conclusion.

synapse the area in the gap between one neuron's axon and the dendrites or soma of another neuron or neurons.

synaptic transmission the propagation of particular neural transmitters from a presynaptic neuronal junction to a postsynaptic neuronal junction.

syntactic induction a process by which people overgeneralize or overspecialize algorithms from the surface-structural features of familiar examples.

syntactic view of reasoning a view that advocates that inductive reasoning has a special structure with abstract representations.

syntax a level of linguistic analysis that centers on the patterns by which users of a particular language put words together at the level of the sentence.

systematicity principle a principle of structural mapping theory that suggests that people interpret an analogy, such as "The hydrogen atom is like our solar system" by observing which relationships are preserved (the electron *revolves around* the nucleus in the same way that the planets *revolve around* the sun).

tacit knowledge in the triarchic theory of human intelligence, the component of practical intelligence that refers to knowledge that is not taught explicitly to the individual, but allows the person to succeed in a given environment.

task variables according to Flavell's definition of metacognition, the variables related to understanding the nature of the particular problem that is to be solved.

telegraphic speech rudimentary syntactical communications of two or more words that are characteristic of very early language acquisition and seem more like telegrams than like conversation because function morphemes are usually omitted.

thematic roles the semantic relationships among words in a sentence, particularly in regard to how the words relate to the verb; roles may include agents, patients, beneficiaries, locations, sources, goals, and instruments.

theory an organized body of general explanatory principles regarding a phenomenon.

theory of multiple intelligences a theoretical perspective in which intelligence is seen as a set of discrete abilities, each of which is a distinct kind of intelligence, not merely a component of a unitary construct of intelligence.

theory-based accounts a subset of explanation-based models that suggest that explanatory structures are derived from global theories.

threshold the point at which a neuron's electrical potential is raised to the necessary degree to send an action potential.

transformational grammar a form of syntactical analysis that centers on the transformational rules that guide the relationships among various surface structures of phrases.

transitivity axiom an axiom that suggests that if choice A is preferred to B and choice B is preferred to C, then it is rational to prefer choice A to C.

triarchic theory of human intelligence a theoretical perspective that integrates features of the internal world, the external world, and the experience of an individual, which the person uses in addressing tasks requiring analytical, practical, and creative intelligence.

triggering conditions conditions that cue people to learn new associations, such as when a change in someone's behavior triggers an inference about the cause of that behavior.

tutor module the element of Intelligent Tutoring Systems that compares the student module with the expert module and provides a means for the student's knowledge to match that of the expert module.

two-string problem a problem that presents a person with the task of tying together two strings that are hanging from the ceiling, given that the strings are so far apart that the person cannot grasp both at once and among the objects in the room are a chair and a pair of pliers.

two-tier approach a theory of categorization that distinguishes between the base concept representation (BCR) and the inferential concept interpretation (ICI). The BCR involves both specific and general information stored in long-term memory. The ICI interprets knowledge in the BCR by using background information and context that is specific to the BCR.

typicality effects   experimental effects (such as faster reaction times) that result from responding to typical or common members of a category.

universal affirmative   statements, such as "All A are B," in which members of the first category (A) are members of the second category (B).

universal negative   a statement, such as "All A are not B" or "No A are B," in which no members of the first category (A) are members of the second category (B).

utility   a quantitative value based on how well an outcome helps a person reach a goal.

verb phrase   one of the two key parts of a statement (also termed a *predicate*; cf. *noun phrase*); the part of the sentence that tells something about the subject of the sentence, usually including a verb and whatever the verb acts on, but sometimes including a linking verb (e.g., *is*, *are*) and a descriptor.

verbal comprehension   the ability to comprehend written and spoken linguistic input, such as words, sentences, and paragraphs.

verbal fluency   the ability to produce written and spoken linguistic output, such as words, sentences, and paragraphs.

verification bias   a bias that occurs in the concept-identification task when people tend to try to confirm their initial hypotheses rather then to seek disconformation.

vertical thinking   see *CoRT*.

vocabulary   a repertoire of words, formed by combining morphemes (cf. *lexicon*).

Wason selection task (WST)   a conditional-reasoning task that presents people with a rule of the form, "If p, then q," and four cards (p, not-p, q, and not-q). People are asked to determine which card(s) must be turned over to determine whether the rule is true or not.

water-pitcher problem   a problem that presents a person with the goal of measuring out an exact number of units of water from an unlimited source of water by using three pitchers that can hold a given number of units each.

weights   in a neural network, carry information about the strength of connection between nodes.

well-defined problem   a problem that has a clear solution path.

wisdom   broadly defined as extraordinary insight, keen awareness, and exceptional judgment.

working backward   a heuristic that is commonly used when there are too many operators that can apply to the initial state of the problem. The person then starts at the desired end state and examines the possible conditions that would have to be true if the desired end state were true. This process is then continued for each identified "prior-to-the-goal" state.

working forward   a heuristic whereby an individual solves a problem by starting with the givens and then trying to solve the problem from the beginning.

working memory   a portion of memory that contains only the most recently activated knowledge that a person or computational system is attending to at a given time.

XOR function   a logic function that is true when either one of its components is true but not both. That is, given that (A OR B) is true, it follows that either A is true, or that B is true, but that both cannot be true at the same time.

zone of proximal development (ZPD)   the range of ability between a child's existing undeveloped potential ability (competence) and the child's observed ability (performance).

References

Abelson, R. P. (1980). Searle's argument is just a set of Chinese symbols. *Behavioral and Brain Sciences, 3,* 424–425.

Adams, M. J. (Ed.). (1986). *Odyssey: A curriculum for thinking* (Vols. 1–6). Watertown, MA: Charlesbridge.

Adelson, B. (1984). When novices surpass experts: The difficulty of a task may increase with expertise. *Journal of Experimental Psychology: Learning, Memory, and Cognition, 10,* 483–495.

Adler, J. (1991, July 22). The melting of a mighty myth. *Newsweek,* p. 63.

Agnoli, F., & Krantz, D. H. (1989). Suppressing natural heuristics by formal instruction: The case of the conjunction fallacy. *Cognitive Psychology, 21,* 515–550.

Ahn, W.-K. (1999). Effect of causal structure on category construction. *Memory & Cognition, 27,* 1008–1023.

Ahn, W.-K., Kalish, C. W., Medin, D. L., & Gelman, S. A. (1995). The role of covariation versus mechanism information in causal attribution. *Cognition, 54,* 299–352.

Ahn, W.-K., & Medin, D. L. (1992). A two-stage model of category construction. *Cognitive Science, 16,* 81–121.

Albert, M. L., & Obler, L. (1978). *The bilingual brain: Neuropsychological and neurolinguistic aspects of bilingualism.* New York: Academic Press.

Albert, R. S., & Runco, M. A. (1999). A history of research on creativity. In R. J. Sternberg (Ed.), *Handbook of creativity* (pp. 16–31). New York: Cambridge University Press.

Allais, M. (1953). Le comportement de l'homme rationnel devant le risque: Critique des postulates et axioms de l'ecole americaine [The behavior of the rational human confronted to risk: A critical view of the postulates and axioms of the American school]. *Econometrica, 21,* 503–546.

Almor, A., & Sloman, S. A. (1996). Is deontic reasoning special? *Psychological Review, 103,* 374–380.

Amabile, T. M. (1983). *The social psychology of creativity.* New York: Springer.

Amabile, T. M. (1996). *Creativity in context.* Boulder, CO: Westview.

Anderson, J. A. (1995). *An introduction to neural networks.* Cambridge, MA: MIT Press.

Anderson, J. R. (1976). *Language, memory, and thought.* Hillsdale, NJ: Lawrence Erlbaum Associates.

Anderson, J. R. (1980). Concepts, propositions, and schemata: What are the cognitive units? *Nebraska Symposium on Motivation, 28,* 121–162.

Anderson, J. R. (1983). *The architecture of cognition.* Cambridge, MA: Harvard University Press.

Anderson, J. R. (1987). Skill acquisition: Compilation of weak-method problem solutions. *Psychological Review, 94,* 192–210.

Anderson, J. R. (1990). *The adaptive character of thought.* Hillsdale, NJ: Lawrence Erlbaum Associates.

Anderson, J. R. (1991). The adaptive nature of human categorization. *Psychological Review, 98,* 409–429.

Anderson, J. R. (1993). *Rules of the mind.* Hillsdale, NJ: Lawrence Erlbaum Associates.

Anderson, J. R., & Bower, G. H. (1973). *Human associative memory.* Washington, DC: V. H. Winston.

Anderson, J. R., Corbett, A. T., Fincham, J. M., Hoffman, D., & Pelletier, R. (1982). General principles for an intelligent architecture. In J. W. Regian & V. J. Shute (Eds.), *Cognitive approaches to automated instruction* (pp. 81–103). Hillsdale, NJ: Lawrence Erlbaum Associates

Anderson, J. R., Farrell, R., & Sauers, R. (1984). Learning to program in LISP. *Cognitive Science, 8,* 87–129.

Anderson, J. R., & Fincham, J. M. (1994). Acquisition of procedural skills from examples. *Journal of Experimental Psychology: Learning, Memory, and Cognition, 20,* 1–20.

Anderson, J. R., Simon, H. A., & Reder, L. M. (1996). Situated learning and education. *Educational Researcher, 25,* 5–11.

Anderson, J. R., Simon, H. A., & Reder, L. M. (1997). Situative versus cognitive perspectives: Form versus substance. *Educational Researcher, 26,* 18–21.

Anderson, R. C., & Pichert, J. W. (1978). Recall of previously unrecallable information following a shift in perspective. *Journal of Verbal Learning and Verbal Behavior, 17,* 1–12.

Andrews, F. M. (1975). Social and psychological factors which influence the creative process. In I. A. Taylor & J. W. Getzels (Eds.), *Perspectives in creativity* (pp. 117–145). Chicago, IL: Aldine.

Angell, J. R. (1907). The province of functional psychology. *Psychological Review, 14,* 61–91.

Anzai, Y., & Simon, H. A. (1979). The theory of learning by doing. *Psychological Review, 86,* 124–140.

Appel, L. F., Cooper, R. G., McCarrell, N., Sims-Knight, J., Yussen, S. R., & Flavell, J. H. (1972). The development of the distinction between perceiving and memorizing. *Child Development, 43,* 1365–1381.

Arkes, H. R., & Harkness, A. R. (1983). Estimates of contingency between two dichotomous variables. *Journal of Experimental Psychology: General, 112,* 117–135.

Arlin, P. K. (1975). Cognitive development in adulthood: A fifth stage? *Developmental Psychology, 11,* 602–606.

Asher, J. J., & Garcia, R. (1969). The optimal age to learn a foreign language. *Modern Language Journal, 53,* 334–341.

Ashlock, R. B. (1976). *Error patterns in computation.* Columbus, OH: Bell & Howell.

Bahrick, H. P., Bahrick, P. O., & Wittlinger, R. P. (1975). Fifty years of memory for names and faces: A cross-sectional approach. *Journal of Experimental Psychology: General, 104,* 54–75.

Bahrick, H. P., Hall, L. K., Goggin, J. P., Bahrick, L. E., & Berger, S. A. (1994). Fifty years of language maintenance and language dominance in bilingual hispanic immigrants. *Journal of Experimental Psychology: General, 123,* 264–283.

Baillargeon, R. L. (1987). Young infants' reasoning about the physical and spatial properties of a hidden object. *Cognitive Development 2,* 179–200.

Baltes, P. B. (1993). The aging mind: Potential and limits. *The Gerontologist, 33,* 580–594.

Baltes, P. B. (1997). On the incomplete architecture of human ontogeny: Selection, optimization, and compensation as foundation of developmental theory. *American Psychologist, 52,* 366–380.

Baltes, P. B., Dittmann-Kohli, F., & Dixon, R. A. (1984). New perspectives on the development of intelligence in adulthood: Toward a dual-process conception and a model of selective optimization with compensation. In P. B. Baltes & O. G. Brim, Jr. (Eds.), *Life-span development and behavior* (Vol. 6, pp. 33–76). New York: Academic Press.

Baltes, P. B., & Smith, J. (1990). Toward a psychology of wisdom and its ontogenesis. In R. J. Sternberg (Ed.), *Wisdom: Its nature, origins, and development* (pp. 87–120). New York: Cambridge University Press.

Baltes, P. B., Staudinger, U. M., Maercker, A., & Smith, J. (1995). People nominated as wise: A comparative study of wisdom-related knowledge. *Psychology and Aging, 10,* 155–166.

Baltes, P. B., & Willis, S. L. (1979). Toward psychological theories of aging and development. In J. E. Birren & K. W. Schaie (Eds.), *Handbook of the psychology of aging.* New York: Van Nostrand Reinhold.

Banks, S. M., Salovey, P., Greener, S., Rothman, A. J., Moyer, A., Beauvais, J., & Epel, E. (1995). The effects of message framing on mammography utilization. *Health Psychology, 14,* 178–184.

Bar-Hillel, M., & Falk, R. (1982). Some teasers concerning conditional probabilities. *Cognition, 11,* 109–122.

Bar-Hillel, M., & Fischhoff, B. (1981). When do base rates affect predictions? *Journal of Personality and Social Psychology, 41,* 671–680.

Baron, J. (1985). *Rationality and intelligence.* New York: Cambridge University Press.

Baron, J. (1988). *Thinking and deciding.* Cambridge, MA: Cambridge University Press.

Baron, J. (1993). Why teach thinking? An essay. *Applied Psychology: An International Review, 42,* 191–214.

Baron, J. (1994). Nonconsequentialist decisions. *Behavioral and Brain Sciences, 17,* 1–42.

Baron, J. (1995). A theory of social decisions. *Journal for the Theory of Social Behaviour, 25,* 103–114.

Baroody, A. J. (1993). Early mental multiplication performance and the role of relational knowledge in mastering combinations involving "two." *Learning & Instruction, 3,* 93–111.

Barrett, P. T., & Eysenck, H. J. (1992). Brain evoked potentials and intelligence: The Hendrickson paradigm. *Intelligence, 16*(3–4), 361–381.

Barron, B., Vye, N. J., Zech, L., Schwartz, D., Bransford, J. D., Goldman, S. R., Pellegrino, J., Morris, J., Garrison, S., & Kantor, R. (1995). Creating contexts for community-based problem solving: The Jaspers challenge series. In C. N. Hedley, P. Antonacci, & M. Rabinowitz (Eds.), *Thinking and literacy: The mind at work* (pp. 47–71). Mahwah, NJ: Lawrence Erlbaum Associates.

Barron, F. (1963). *Creativity and psychological health.* Princeton, NJ: D. Van Nostrand.

Barron, F. (1968). *Creativity and personal freedom.* New York: Van Nostrand.

Barron, F. (1969). *Creative person and creative process.* New York: Holt, Rinehart & Winston.

Barron, F., & Harrington, D. M. (1981). Creativity, intelligence, and personality. *Annual Review of Psychology, 32,* 439–476.

Barsalou, L. W. (1982). Context-independent and context-dependent information in concepts. *Memory and Cognition, 10,* 82–93.

Barsalou, L. W. (1983). Ad hoc categories. *Memory and Cognition, 11,* 211–227.

Barsalou, L. W. (1989). Intraconcept similarity and its implications for interconcept similarity. In S. Vosniadou & A. Ortony (Eds.), *Similarity and analogical reasoning* (pp. 76–121). New York: Cambridge University Press.

Bartlett, F. C. (1932). *Remembering: A study in experimental and social psychology.* New York: Cambridge University Press.

Bashore, T. R., Osman, A., & Hefley, E. F. (1989). Mental slowing in elderly persons: A cognitive psychophysiological analysis. *Psychology and Aging, 4,* 235–244.

Basseches, J. (1984). *Dialectical thinking and adult development.* Norwood, NJ: Ablex.

Bassok, M., Wu, L., & Olseth, K. L. (1995). Judging a book by its cover: Interpretative effects of content on problem-solving transfer. *Memory and Cognition, 23,* 354–367.

Beardsley, M. (1962). The metaphorical twist. *Philosophical Phenomenological Research, 22,* 293–307.

Beck, I. L., Perfetti, C. A., & McKeown, M. G. (1982). Effects of long-term vocabulary instruction on lexical access and reading comprehension. *Journal of Educational Psychology, 74,* 506–521.

Bedard, J., & Chi, M. T. H. (1992). Expertise. *Current Directions in Psychological Science, 1,* 135–139.

Begg, I., & Denny, J. P. (1969). Empirical reconciliation of atmosphere and conversion interpretations of syllogistic reasoning errors. *Journal of Experimental Psychology, 81,* 351–354.

Beilin, H. (1971). Developmental stages and developmental processes. In D. R. Green, M. P. Ford, & G. B. Flamer (Eds.), *Measurement and Piaget* (pp. 172–197). New York: McGraw-Hill.

Bell, D. E. (1982). Regret in decision making under uncertainty. *Operations Research, 30,* 961–981.

Bell, E. T. (1937). *Men of mathematics.* New York: Simon & Schuster.

Bellezza, F. S. (1984). Reliability of retrieval from semantic memory: Noun meanings. *Bulletin of the Psychonomic Society, 22,* 377–380.

Belmont, J. M., & Butterfield, E. C. (1971). Learning strategies as determinants of memory deficiencies. *Cognitive Psychology, 2,* 411–420.

Ben-Zeev, T. (1995). The nature and origin of rational errors in arithmetic thinking: Induction from examples and prior knowledge. *Cognitive Science, 19,* 341–376.

Ben-Zeev, T. (1996). When erroneous mathematical thinking is just as "correct": The oxymoron of rational errors. In R. J. Sternberg & T. Ben-Zeev (Eds.), *The nature of mathematical thinking* (pp. 55–79). Mahwah, NJ: Lawrence Erlbaum Associates.

Ben-Zeev, T. (1998). Rational errors and the mathematical mind. *Review of General Psychology, 2,* 366–383.

Ben-Zeev, T., Dennis, M., Stibel, J. M., & Sloman, S. A. (2000). *Increasing working memory demands improves probabilistic choice but not judgment on the Monty Hall dilemma.* Manuscript submitted for publication.

Ben-Zeev, T., & Star, J. (2000). Intuitive mathematics: Theoretical and educational implications. In B. Torff & R. J. Sternberg (Eds.), *Understanding and teaching the intuitive mind* (pp. 29–56). Mahwah, NJ: Lawrence Erlbaum Associates.

Berlin, B., & Kay, P. (1969). *Basic color terms: Their universality and evolution.* Los Angeles: University of California Press.

Berliner, H. J. (1969, August). Chess playing program. *SICART Newsletter, 19,* 19–20.

Bernoulli, D. (1954). Exposition of a new theory of the measurement of risk (L. Sommer, Trans.). *Econometrica, 22,* 23–26. (Original work published 1738)

Bernstein, A. (1958, July). A chess-playing program for the IBM-704. *Chess Review,* pp. 208–209.

Berry, J. W. (1974). Radical cultural relativism and the concept of intelligence. In J. W. Berry & P. R. Dasen (Eds.), *Culture and cognition: Readings in cross-cultural psychology* (pp. 225–229). London: Methuen.

Bertoncini, J. (1993). Infants' perception of speech units: Primary representation capacities. In B. B. De Boysson-Bardies, S. De Schonen, P. Jusczyk, P. MacNeilage, & J. Morton (Eds.), *Developmental neurocognition: Speech and face processing in the first year of life.* Dordrecht, the Netherlands: Kluwer.

Beth, E. W., & Piaget, J. (1966). *Mathematical epistemology and psychology.* Dordrecht, the Netherlands: D. Reidel.

Beyth-Marom, R. (1993). Teaching thinking: What, when, where, who and how. *Applied Psychology: An International Review, 42,* 220–223.

Bialystok, E., & Hakuta, K. (1994). *In other words: The science and psychology of second-language acquisition.* New York: Basic Books.

Bickerton, D. (1969). Prolegomena to a linguistic theory of metaphor. *Foundations of Language, 5,* 36–51.

Bickerton, D. (1990). *Language and species.* Chicago: University of Chicago Press.

Bidell, T. R., & Fischer, K. W. (1992). Beyond the stage debate: Action, structure, and variability in Piagetian theory and research. In R. J. Sternberg & C. A. Berg (Eds.), *Intellectual development* (pp. 100–140). New York: Cambridge University Press.

Billman, D., & Heit, E. (1988). Observational learning from internal feedback: A simulation of an adaptive learning method. *Cognitive Science, 12,* 587–625.

Billman, D., & Knutson, J. (1996). Unsupervised concept learning and value systematicitiy: A complex whole aids learning the parts. *Journal of Experimental Psychology: Learning, Memory, and Cognition, 22,* 458–475.

Binet, A., & Simon, T. (1916). *The development of intelligence in children* (E. S. Kite, Trans.). Baltimore: Williams & Wilkins.

Black, M. (1962). *Models and metaphors.* Ithaca, NY: Cornell University Press.

Blades, M., & Spencer, C. (1994). The development of children's ability to use spatial representations. *Advances in Child Development and Behavior* (Vol. 25). San Diego, CA: Academic Press.

Blagg, N. (1991). *Can we teach intelligence? A comprehensive evaluation of Feuerstein's Instrumental Enrichment Program.* Hillsdale, NJ: Lawrence Erlbaum Associates.

Blessing, S. B., & Ross, B. H. (1996). Content effects in problem categorization and problem solving. *Journal of Experimental Psychology: Learning, Memory, and Cognition, 22,* 792–810.

Bloom, B. S. (1964). *Stability and change in human characteristics.* New York: John Wiley & Sons.

Bloom, B. S. (Ed.). (1985). *Developing talent in young people.* New York: Ballantine.

Bloom, P. (1996). Intention, history, and artifact concepts. *Cognition, 60,* 1–29.

Bock, K. (1990). Structure in language: Creating form in talk. *American Psychologist, 45,* 1221–1236.

Bock, K., Loebell, H., & Morey, R. (1992). From conceptual roles to structural relations: Bridging the syntactic cleft. *Psychological Review, 99,* 150–171.

Boden, M. (1992). *The creative mind: Myths and mechanisms.* New York: Basic Books.

Boden, M. (Ed.). (1994). *Dimensions of creativity.* Cambridge, MA: MIT Press.

Boden, M. A. (1994). Precis of the creative mind: Myths and mechanisms. *Behavioral and Brain Sciences, 17,* 519–570.

Boden, M. A. (1999). Computer models of creativity. In R. J. Sternberg (Ed.), *Handbook of creativity* (pp. 351–372). New York: Cambridge University Press.

Boring, E. G. (1923, June 6). Intelligence as the tests test it. *New Republic,* pp. 35–37.

Bornstein, M. H. (1989). Stability in early mental development: From attention and information processing in infancy to language and cognition in childhood. In M. H. Bornstein & N. K. Krasnege (Eds.), *Stability and continuity in mental development: Behavioural and biological perspectives* (pp. 147–170). Hillsdale, NJ: Lawrence Erlbaum Associates.

Bornstein, M. H., & Sigman, M. D. (1986). Continuity in mental development from infancy. *Child Development, 57,* 251–274.

Bors, D. A., & Forrin, B. (1995). Age, speed of information processing, recall, and fluid intelligence. *Intelligence, 20,* 229–248.

Bors, D. A., MacLeod, C. M., & Forrin, B. (1993). Eliminating the IQ–RT correlation by eliminating an experimental confound. *Intelligence, 17,* 475–500.

Boshuizen, H. P., & Schmidt, H. G. (1992). On the role of biomedical knowledge in clinical reasoning by experts, intermediates and novices. *Cognitive Science, 16,* 153–184.

Bowden, R. J. (1994). *Factor analysis of predictive curves, with applications to the term structure of interest rates.* Parkville, Australia: The Department.

Bower, G. H., Black, J. B., & Turner, T. J. (1979). Scripts in memory for text. *Cognitive Psychology, 11,* 177–220.

Bower, G. H., Karlin, M. B., & Dueck, A. (1975). Comprehension and memory for pictures. *Memory and Cognition, 3,* 216–220.

Bowers, K. S., Regehr, G., Balthazard, C., & Parker, K. (1990). Intuition in the context of discovery. *Cognitive Psychology, 22,* 72–109.

Bradley, R. H., & Caldwell, B. M. (1984). 174 children: A study of the relationship between home environment and cognitive development during the first 5 years. In A. W. Gottfried (Ed.), *Home environment and early cognitive development: Longitudinal research.* San Diego, CA: Academic Press.

Braine, M. D. S., Reiser, B. J., & Rumain, B. (1984). Some empirical justification for a theory of natural propositional logic. In G. H. Bower (Ed.), *The psychology of learning and motivation* (Vol. 18). Orlando, FL: Academic Press.

Brainerd, C. J. (1973). Neo-Piagetian training experiments revisited: Is there any support for the cognitive developmental hypothesis? *Cognition, 2,* 349–370.

Brainerd, C. J. (1978). The stage question in cognitive-developmental theory. *Behavioral and Brain Sciences, 1,* 173–182.

Brand, C. (1996). Doing something about g. *Intelligence, 22,* 311–326.

Bransford, J. D., & Franks, J. J. (1971). The abstraction of linguistic ideas. *Cognitive Psychology, 2,* 331–350.

Bransford, J. D., & Johnson, M. K. (1972). Contextual prerequisites for understanding: Some investigations of comprehension and recall. *Journal of Verbal Learning and Verbal Behavior, 11,* 717–726.

Bransford, J. D., & Stein, B. S. (1984). *The IDEAL problem solver.* New York: W. H. Freeman.

Bransford J. D., Zech, L., Schwartz, D., Barron, B., & Vye, N. (1996). Fostering mathematical thinking in middle school students: Lessons from research. In R. J. Sternberg, & T. Ben-Zeev, (Eds.), *The nature of mathematical thinking* (pp. 55–79). Mahwah, NJ: Lawrence Erlbaum Associates.

Bresnan, J. W. (Ed.). (1982). *The mental representation of grammatical relations.* Cambridge, MA: MIT Press.

Brian, C. R., & Goodenough, F. L. (1929). The relative potency of color and form perception at various ages. *Journal of Experimental Psychology, 12,* 197–213.

Bronfenbrenner, U., & Ceci, S. J. (1994). Nature-nurture reconceptualized in developmental perspective: A bioecological model. *Psychological Review, 101,* 568–586.

Brooks, L. R. (1978). Nonanalytic concept formation and memory for instances. In E. Rosch & B. B. Lloyd (Eds.), *Cognition and categorization* (pp. 169–211). Hillsdale, NJ: Lawrence Erlbaum Associates.

Brown, A. L. (1978). Knowing when, where, and how to remember: A problem of metacognition. In R. Glaser (Ed.), *Advances in instructional psychology* (Vol. 1, pp. 77–165). Hillsdale, NJ: Lawrence Erlbaum Associates.

Brown, A. L. (1992). Design experiments: Theoretical and methodological challenges in creating complex interventions in classroom settings. *Journal of the Learning Sciences, 2,* 141–178.

Brown, A. L. (1997). Transforming schools into communities of thinking and learning about serious matters. *American Psychologist, 52,* 399–413.

Brown, A. L., & Campione, J. C. (1990). Communities of learning and thinking: Or a context by any other name. *Contributions to Human Development, 21,* 108–126.

Brown, A. L., & Campione, J. C. (1994). Guided discovery in a community of learners. In K. McGilly (Ed.), *Classroom lessons: Integrating cognitive theory and classroom practice* (pp. 229–270). Cambridge, MA: MIT Press.

Brown, A. L., Campione, J. C., Bray, N. W., & Wilcox, B. L. (1973). Keeping track of changing variables: Effects of rehearsal training and rehearsal prevention in normal and retarded adolescents. *Journal of Experimental Psychology, 101,* 123–131.

Brown, A. L., & DeLoache, J. S. (1978). Skills, plans, and self-regulation. In R. Siegler (Ed.), *Children's thinking: What develops?* (pp. 3–35). Hillsdale, NJ: Lawrence Erlbaum Associates.

Brown, A. L., Ellery, S., & Campione, J. C. (1998). Creating zones of proximal development electronically. In J. G. Greeno & S. Goldman (Eds.), *Thinking practices: A symposium in mathematics and science education.* (pp. 341–367). Mahwah, NJ: Lawrence Erlbaum Associates.

Brown, A. L., & French, A. L. (1979). The zone of potential development: Implications for intelligence testing in the year 2000. In R. J. Sternberg & D. K. Detterman (Eds.), *Human intelligence: Perspectives on its theory and measurement* (pp. 217–235). Norwood, NJ: Ablex.

Brown, A. L., & Palincsar, A. S. (1987). Reciprocal teaching of comprehension strategies: A natural history of one program for enhancing learning. In J. D. Day & J. G. Borkowski, (Eds.), *Intelligence and exceptionality: New directions for theory, assessment, and instructional practices* (pp. 81–132). Norwood, NJ: Ablex.

Brown, A. L., & Palincsar, A. S. (1989). Guided, cooperative learning and individual knowledge acquisition. In L. B. Resnick (Ed.), *Knowing, learning, and instruction: Essays in honor of Robert Glaser* (pp. 393–451). Hillsdale, NJ: Lawrence Erlbaum Associates.

Brown, J. S., & VanLehn, K. (1980). Repair theory: A generative theory of bugs in procedural skills. *Cognitive Science, 4,* 379–426.

Brown, R. (1965). *Social psychology.* New York: Free Press.

Brown, R., Cazden, C. B., & Bellugi, U. (1969). The child's grammar from 1 to 3. In J. P. Hill (Ed.), *Minnesota Symposium on Child Psychology* (Vol. 2). Minneapolis: University of Minnesota Press.

Brown, S. I., & Walter, M. I. (1993). Problem posing in mathematics education. In S. I. Brown, & M. I. Walter, (Eds.), *Problem posing: Reflections and applications* (pp. 16–27). Hillsdale, NJ: Lawrence Erlbaum Associates.

Bruner, J. S., Goodnow, J. J. & Austin, G. A. (1956). *A study of thinking.* New York: John Wiley & Sons.

Bryant, P. E., & Trabasso, T. (1971). Transitive inferences and memory in young children. *Nature, 232,* 456–458.

Buchanan, B. G., & Shortliffe, E. H. (1984). *Rule-based expert systems: The MYCIN experiments of the Stanford Heuristic Programming Project.* Reading, MA: Addison-Wesley.

Buchanan, B. G., Smith, D. H., White, W. C., Gritter, R., Feigenbaum, E. A., Lederberg, J., & Djerassi, C. (1976). Applications of artificial intelligence for chemical inference: XXII. Automatic rule formation in mass spectrometry by means of the meta-dendral program. *Journal of the American Chemistry Society, 98,* 6168–6178.

Burns, H. L., & Capps, C. G. (1988). Foundations of intelligent tutoring systems: An introduction. In M. C. Polson, C. Martha, & J. J. Richardson (Eds.), *Foundations of intelligent tutoring systems* (pp. 1–19). Hillsdale, NJ: Lawrence Erlbaum Associates.

Buswell, G. T. (1926). *Diagnostic studies in arithmetic.* Chicago: University of Chicago Press.

Butterfield, E. C., Wambold, C., & Belmont, J. M. (1973). On the theory and practice of improving short-term memory. *American Journal of Mental Deficiency, 77,* 654–669.

Butterworth, B., & Howard, D. (1987). Paragrammatisms. *Cognition, 26,* 1–37.

Cabeza, R., & Nyberg, L. (1997). Imaging cognition: An empirical review of PET studies with normal subjects. *Journal of Cognitive Neuroscience, 9,* 1–26.

Campbell, D. T. (1960). Blind variation and selective retention in creative thought as in other knowledge processes. *Psychological Bulletin, 67,* 380–400.

Campione, J. C. (1989). Assisted assessments: A taxonomy of approaches and an outline of strengths and weaknesses. *Journal of Learning Disabilities, 22,* 151–165.

Campione, J. C., & Brown, A. L. (1990). Guided learning and transfer: Implications for approaches to assessment. In N. Frederiksen, R. Glaser, A. Lesgold, & M. Shafto (Eds.), *Diagnostic monitoring of skill and knowledge acquisition* (pp. 141–172). Hillsdale, NJ: Lawrence Erlbaum Associates.

Cantor, N., & Mischel, W. (1979). Prototypicality and personality: Effects on free recall and personality impressions. *Journal of Research in Personality, 13,* 187–205.

Cappa, S. F., Perani, D., Grassli, F., Bressi, S., et al. (1997). A PET follow-up study of recovery after stroke in acute aphasics. *Brain & Language, 56,* 55–67.

Carey, S. (1985). *Conceptual change in childhood.* Cambridge, MA: MIT Press.

Carey, S., & Gelman, R. (Eds.). (1991). *The epigenesis of mind: Essays on biology and cognition.* Hillsdale, NJ: Lawrence Erlbaum Associates.

Carlson, E. R. (1995). Evaluating the credibility of sources: A missing link in the teaching of critical thinking. *Teaching of Psychology, 22,* 39–41.

Carnap, R. (1950). *Logical foundations of probability.* Chicago: University of Chicago Press.

Carraher, T. N., Carraher, D., & Schliemann, A. D. (1985). Mathematics in the streets and in the schools. *British Journal of Developmental Psychology, 3,* 21–29.

Carroll, D. W. (1986). *Psychology of language.* Monterey, CA: Brooks/Cole.

Carroll, J. B., & Casagrande, J. B. (1958). The function of language classification in behavior. In E. E. Maccoby, T. Newcomb, & E. L. Hartley (Eds.), *Readings in social psychology* (3rd ed., pp. 18–31). New York: Holt, Rinehart & Winston.

Case, R. (1985). *Intellectual development: Birth to adulthood.* New York: Academic Press.

Case, R. (1992). Neo-Piagetian theories of child development. In R. J. Sternberg & C. A. Berg (Eds.), *Intellectual development* (pp. 161–196). New York: Cambridge University Press.

Case, R., & Griffin, S. (1990). Child cognitive development: The role of central conceptual structures in the development of scientific and social thought. In C. A. Hauert (Ed.), *Developmental psychol-*

ogy: Cognitive, perceptuo-motor and psychological perspectives (pp. 193–230). New York: Elsevier North Holland.

Case, R., & Sandieson, R. (1987, April). *General developmental constraints on the acquisition of special procedures (and vice versa).* Paper presented at the annual meeting of the American Educational Research Association, Baltimore.

Catrambone, R. (1994). Improving examples to improve transfer to novel problems. *Memory and Cognition, 22,* 606–615.

Cattell, R. B. (1971). *Abilities: Their structure, growth, and action.* Boston: Houghton Mifflin.

Ceci, S. J. (1991). How much does schooling influence general intelligence and its cognitive components? A reassessment of the evidence. *Developmental Psychology, 27,* 703–722.

Ceci, S. J., & Bronfenbrenner, U. (1985). Don't forget to take the cupcakes out of the oven: Strategic time-monitoring, prospective memory and context. *Child Development, 56,* 175–190.

Ceci, S. J., Nightingale, N. N., & Baker, J. G. (1992). The ecologies of intelligence: Challenges to traditional views. In D. K. Detterman (Ed.), *Current topics in human intelligence: Vol. 2. Is mind modular or unitary?* (pp. 61–82). Norwood, NJ: Ablex.

Ceci, S. J., & Roazzi, A. (1994). The effects of context on cognition: Postcards from Brazil. In R. J. Sternberg & R. K. Wagner (Eds.), *Mind in context: Interactionist perspectives on human intelligence* (pp. 74–111). New York: Cambridge University Press.

Ceraso, J., & Provitera, A. (1971). Sources of error in syllogistic reasoning. *Cognitive Psychology, 2,* 400–410.

Cerella, J. (1985). Information processing rates in the elderly. *Psychological Bulletin, 98,* 67–83.

Cerella, J. (1990). Aging and information-processing rate. In J. E. Birren & K. W. Schaie (Eds.), *Handbook of the psychology of aging* (3rd ed., pp. 201–221). San Diego, CA: Academic Press.

Cerella, J. (1991). Age effects may be global, not local: Comment on Fisk and Rogers (1991). *Journal of Experimental Psychology: General, 120,* 215–223.

Cerella, J., Rybash, J. M., Hoyer, W., & Commons, M. L. (1993). *Adult information processing: Limits on loss.* San Diego, CA: Academic Press.

Chapman, L. J., & Chapman, J. P. (1959). Atmosphere effect re-examined. *Journal of Experimental Psychology, 58,* 220–226.

Chapman, L. J., & Chapman, J. P. (1967). Genesis of popular but erroneous psychodiagnostic observations. *Journal of Abnormal Psychology, 72,* 193–204.

Chapman, L. J., & Chapman, J. P. (1969). Illusory correlation as an obstacle to the use of valid psychodiagnostic signs. *Journal of Abnormal Psychology, 74,* 271–280.

Charles, R., & Silver, E. A. (Eds.). (1988). *The teaching and assessing of mathematical problem solving.* Hillsdale, NJ: Lawrence Erlbaum Associates.

Charness, N. (1979). Components of skill in bridge. *Canadian Journal of Psychology, 33,* 1–16.

Charness, N. (1981). Search in chess: Age and skill differences. *Journal of Experimental Psychology: Human Perception and Performance, 7,* 467–476.

Charness, N. (1989). Expertise in chess and bridge. In D. Klahr & K. Kotovsky (Eds.), *Complex information processing: The impact of Herbert A. Simon* (pp. 183–208). Hillsdale, NJ: Lawrence Erlbaum Associates.

Charness, N. (1991). Expertise in chess: The balance between knowledge and search. In K. A. Ericsson & J. Smith (Eds.), *Toward a general theory of expertise* (pp. 39–63). New York: Cambridge University Press.

Charness, N., Krampe, R., & Mayr, U. (1996). The role of practice and coaching in entrepreneurial skill domains: An international comparison of life-span chess skill acquisition. In K. A. Ericsson (Ed.), *The road to excellence: The acquisition of expert performance in the arts and sciences, sports, and games* (pp. 51–80). Mahwah, NJ: Lawrence Erlbaum Associates.

Chase, W. G., & Ericsson, K. A. (1982). Skill and working memory. In G. H. Bower (Ed.), *The psychology of learning and motivation* (Vol. 16, pp. 1–58). New York: Academic Press.

Chase, W. G., & Simon, H. A. (1973). The mind's eye in chess. In W. G. Chase (Ed.), *Visual information processing* (pp. 215–281). New York: Academic Press.

Chen, M. J. (1994). Chinese and Australian concepts of intelligence. *Psychology and Developing Societies, 6,* 101–117.

Cheng, P. W., & Holyoak, K. J. (1985). Pragmatic reasoning schemas. *Cognitive Psychology, 17,* 391–416.

Cheng, P. W., & Holyoak, K. J. (1995). Complex adaptive systems as intuitive statisticians: Causality, contingency, and prediction. In H. L. Roitblat & J. A. Meyer (Eds.), *Comparative approaches to cognitive science* (pp. 271–302). Cambridge, MA: MIT Press.

Chi, M. T. H., Bassok, M., Lewis, M. W., Reimann, P., & Glaser, R. (1989). Self-explanations: How students study and use examples in learning to solve problems. *Cognitive Science, 13,* 145–182.

Chi, M. T. H., de Leeuw, N., Chiu, M.-H., & LaVancher, C. (1994). Eliciting self-explanations improves understanding. *Cognitive Science, 18,* 439–477.

Chi, M. T. H., Feltovich, P. J., & Glaser, R. (1981). Categorization and representation of physics problems by experts and novices. *Cognitive Science, 5,* 121–152.

Chi, M. T. H., Glaser, R., & Farr, M. J. (Eds.). (1988). *The nature of expertise.* Hillsdale, NJ: Lawrence Erlbaum Associates.

Chi, M. T. H., & Slotta, J. D. (1993). The ontological coherence of intuitive physics. *Cognition and Instruction, 10,* 249–260.

Chomsky, N. (1965). *Aspects of the theory of syntax.* Cambridge, MA: MIT Press.

Chomsky, N. (1972). *Language and mind* (2nd ed.). New York: Harcourt Brace Jovanovich.

Christensen-Szalanski, J. J., & Beach, L. R. (1982). Experience and the base-rate fallacy. *Organizational Behavior and Human Decision Processes, 29,* 270–278.

Christensen-Szalanski, J. J. J., Beck, D. E., Christensen-Szalanski, C. M., & Koepsell, T. D. (1983). Effects of expertise and experience on risk judgments. *Journal of Applied Psychology, 68,* 278–284.

Christensen-Szalanski, J. J. J., & Bushyhead, J. B. (1981). Physicians' use of probabilistic information in a real clinical setting. *Journal of Experimental Psychology: Human Perception and Performance, 7,* 928–935.

Christensen-Szalanski, J. J. J., & Willham, C. F. (1991). The hindsight bias: A meta-analysis. *Organizational Behavior and Human Decision Processes, 48,* 147–168.

Clancey. W. J. (1983). GUIDON. *Journal of Computer-Based Instruction, 10,* 8–15.

Clapper, J. P., & Bower, G. H. (1994). Category invention in unsupervised learning. *Journal of Experimental Psychology: Learning, Memory, and Cognition, 20,* 443–460.

Clark, E. V. (1973). What's in a word? On the child's acquisition of semantics in his first language. In T. E. Moore (Ed.), *Cognitive development and the acquisition of language.* New York: Academic Press.

Clark, H. H., & Brennan, S. E. (1991). Grounding in communication. In L. B. Resnick, J. M. Levine, & S. P. Tansley (Eds.), *Perspectives on socially shared cognition* (pp. 127–149). Washington, DC: American Psychological Association.

Clark, H. H., & Clark, E. V. (1977). *Psychology and language: An introduction to psycholinguistics.* New York: Harcourt Brace Jovanovich.

Clark, H. H., & Lucy, P. (1975). Understanding what is meant from what is said: A study in conversationally conveyed requests. *Journal of Verbal Learning and Verbal Behavior, 14,* 56–72.

Clement, C. A., & Falmagne, R. J. (1986). Logical reasoning, world knowledge, and mental imagery: Interconnections in cognitive processes. *Memory and Cognition, 14,* 299 307.

Clement, J. (1989). Learning via model construction and criticism: Protocol evidence on sources of creativity in science. In G. Glover, R. Ronning, & C. Reynolds (Eds.), *Handbook of creativity* (pp. 341–381). New York: Plenum.

Cohen, A. (1992, April). *Using CSILE in a progressive discourse in physics.* Paper presented at the annual meeting of the American Educational Research Association, San Francisco.

Cohen, L. J. (1981). Can human irrationality be experimentally demonstrated? *Behavioral and Brain Sciences, 4*, 317–370.

Colby, K. M. (1963). Computer simulation of a neurotic process. In S. S. Tomkins & S. Messick (Eds.), *Computer simulation of personality: Frontier of psychological research* (pp. 165–180). New York: John Wiley & Sons.

Colby, K. M. (1995). A computer program using cognitive therapy to treat depressed patients. *Psychiatric Services, 46*, 1223–1225.

Cole, M., Gay, J., Glick, J., & Sharp, D. W. (1971). *The cultural context of learning and thinking.* New York: Basic Books.

Cole, M., & Scribner, S. (1974). *Culture and thought: A psychological introduction.* New York: John Wiley & Sons.

Coleman, P. D., & Flood, D. G. (1986). Dendritic proliferation in the aging brain as a compensatory repair mechanism. In D. F. Swaab, E. Fliers, M. Mirmiram, W. A. Van Gool, & F. Van Haaren (Eds.), *Progress in brain research* (Vol. 20). New York: Elsevier.

Collier, G. (1994). *Social origins of mental ability.* New York: John Wiley & Sons.

Collins, A. M., & Loftus, E. F. (1975). A spreading-activation theory of semantic processing. *Psychological Review, 82*, 407–428.

Collins, A. M., & Quillian, M. R. (1969). Retrieval time from semantic memory. *Journal of Verbal Learning and Verbal Behavior, 8*, 240–247.

Collins, A. M., & Qullian, M. R. (1972). Experiments on semantic memory and language comprehension. In L. W. Gregg (Ed.), *Cognition and Learning,* (pp. 117–147). New York: John Wiley & Sons.

Collins, M. A., & Amabile, T. M. (1999). Motivation and creativity. In R. J. Sternberg (Ed.), *Handbook of creativity* (pp. 297–312). New York: Cambridge University Press.

Coon, H., Carey, G., & Fulker, D. W. (1992). Community influences on cognitive ability. *Intelligence, 16*, 169–188.

Cosmides, L. (1989). The logic of social exchange: Has natural selection shaped how humans reason? Studies with the Wason selection task. *Cognition, 31*, 187–276.

Cosmides, L., & Tooby, J. (1996). Are humans good intuitive statisticians after all? Rethinking some conclusions from the literature on judgment under uncertainty. *Cognition, 58*, 1–73.

Cox, C. M. (1926). *The early mental traits of three hundred geniuses.* Stanford, CA: Stanford University Press.

Cox, L. S. (1975). Diagnosing and remediating systematic errors in addition and subtraction computation. *The Arithmetic Teacher, 22*, 151–157.

Craik, K. (1943). *The nature of exploration.* Cambridge, England: Cambridge University Press.

Crocker, J. (1981). Judgment of covariation by social perceivers. *Psychological Bulletin, 90*, 272–292.

Crutchfield, R. (1962). Conformity and creative thinking. In H. Gruber, G. Terrell, & M. Wertheimer (Eds.), *Contemporary approaches to creative thinking* (pp. 120–140). New York: Atherton Press.

Crystal, D. (Ed.). (1987). *The Cambridge encyclopedia of language.* New York: Cambridge University Press.

Csikszentmihalyi, M. (1988). Society, culture, and person: A systems view of creativity. In R. J. Sternberg (Ed.), *The nature of creativity* (pp. 325–339). New York: Cambridge University Press.

Csikszentmihalyi, M. (1996). *Creativity: Flow and the psychology of discovery and invention.* New York: HarperCollins.

Cummins, D. D., Lubart, T., Alksnis, O., & Rist, R. (1991). Conditional reasoning and causation. *Memory & Cognition, 19*, 274–282.

Cummins, J. (1976). The influence of bilingualism on cognitive growth: A synthesis of research findings and explanatory hypothesis. *Working Papers on Bilingualism, 9*, 1–43.

Cziko, Gary A. (1998) From blind to creative: In defense of Donald Campbell's selectionist theory of human creativity. *Journal of Creative Behavior, 32*, 192–208.

Daniel, M. H. (1997). Intelligence testing: Status and trends. *American Psychologist, 52*, 1038–1045.

Daniel, M. H. (2000). Interpretation of intelligence test scores. In R. J. Sternberg (Ed.), *Handbook of intelligence*. New York: Cambridge University Press.

Dasen, P. R., & Heron, A. (1981). Cross-cultural tests of Piaget's theory. In H. C. Triandis & A. Heron (Eds.), *Handbook of cross-cultural psychology* (Vol. 4). Boston: Allyn & Bacon.

Davidson, J. E. (1995). The suddenness of insight. In R. J. Sternberg & J. E. Davidson (Eds.), *The Nature of insight* (pp. 125–155). Cambridge, MA: MIT Press.

Davidson, J. E., & Sternberg, R. J. (1984). The role of insight in intellectual giftedness. *Gifted Child Quarterly, 28,* 58–64.

Davidson, J. E., & Sternberg, R. J. (1985). Competence and performance in intellectual development. In E. Neimark, R. deLisi, & J. H. Newman (Eds.), *Moderators of competence* (pp. 43–76). Hillsdale, NJ: Lawrence Erlbaum Associates.

Davies, T. R. (1988). Determination, uniformity, and relevance: Normative criteria for generalization and reasoning by analogy. In D. H. Helman (Ed.), *Analogical Reasoning* (pp. 227–250). Dordrecht, the Netherlands: Kluwer.

Davis, R. B., & Vinner, S. (1986). The notion of limit: Some seemingly unavoidable misconception stages. *Journal of Mathematical Behavior, 5,* 281–303.

Dawes, R. M. (1998). Behavioral decision making and judgment. In D. T Gilbert & S. T. Fiske (Eds.), *The handbook of social psychology* (Vol. 2, pp. 497–548). New York: McGraw-Hill.

Dawes, R. M., & Mulford, M. (1996). The false consensus effect and overconfidence: Flaws in judgment or flaws in how we study judgment? *Organizational Behavior & Human Decision Processes, 65,* 201–211.

Deary, I. J. (2000). Simple information processing. In R. J. Sternberg (Ed.), *Handbook of intelligence* (pp. 267–284). New York: Cambridge University Press.

Deary, I. J., & Stough, C. (1996). Intelligence and inspection time: Achievements, prospects, and problems. *American Psychologist, 51*(6), 599–608.

de Bono, E. (1968). *New think. The use of lateral thinking in the generation of new ideas.* New York: Basic Books.

de Bono, E. (1970). *Lateral thinking: Creativity step by step.* New York: Harper & Row.

de Bono, E. (1971). *Lateral thinking for management.* New York: McGraw-Hill.

de Bono, E. (1976). *Teaching thinking.* New York: Penguin Books.

de Bono, E. (1985). *Six thinking hats.* Boston: Little, Brown.

de Bono, E. (1992). *Serious creativity: Using the power of lateral thinking to create new ideas.* New York: HarperCollins.

DeCasper, A. J., & Fifer, W. P. (1980). Of human bonding: Newborns prefer their mothers' voices. *Science, 208,* 1174–1176.

De Groot, A. D. (1965). *Thought and choice in chess.* The Hague, the Netherlands: Mouton.

De Groot, A. D. (1978). *Thought and choice in chess.* The Hague, the Netherlands: Mouton. (Original work published 1946)

Dell, G. S. (1986). A spreading-activation theory of retrieval in sentence production. *Psychological Review, 93,* 283–321.

Dempster, F. N. (1991). Inhibitory processes: A neglected dimension of intelligence. *Intelligence, 15,* 157–173.

Dennett, D. (1991). *Consciousness explained.* Boston: Little, Brown.

Denny, N. W. (1980). Task demands and problem-solving strategies in middle-aged and older adults. *Journal of Gerontology, 35,* 559–564.

Descartes, R. (1972). *The treatise of man.* Cambridge, MA: Harvard University Press. (Original work published 1662)

Detterman, D. K., & Sternberg, R. J. (Eds.). (1982). *How and how much can intelligence be increased.* Norwood, NJ: Ablex.

Dewey, J. (1910). *How we think.* Boston: D. C. Heath.

Dewey, J. (1913). *Interest and effort in education.* New York: Houghton Mifflin.

Dewey, J. (1922). *Human nature and conduct: An introduction to social psychology.* New York: Henry Holt.

Dewey, J. (1933). *How we think.* Boston: D. C. Heath.

Dewey, J. (1938). *Logic: The theory of inquiry.* New York: Henry Holt.

Diamond, A. (1990). Rate of maturation of the hippocampus and the developmental progression of children's performance on the delayed non-matching to sample and visual paired comparison tasks. *Annals of the New York Academy of Sciences, 608,* 394–433.

Diamond, A. (1993). Neuropsychological insights into the meaning of object concept development. In M. H. Johnson (Ed.), *Brain development and cognition: A reader* (pp. 208–247). Oxford, England: Blackwell.

Diener, C. I., & Dweck, C. S. (1978). An analysis of learned helplessness: Continuous changes in performance, strategy, and achievement cognitions following failure. *Journal of Personality and Social Psychology, 36,* 451–462.

diSessa, A. A. (1982). Unlearning Aristotelian physics: A study of knowledge-based learning. *Cognitive Science, 6,* 37–75.

diSessa, A. A. (1993). Toward an epistemology of physics. *Cognition and Instruction, 10,* 105–225.

Dixon, R. A., & Baltes, P. B. (1986). Toward life-span research on the functions and pragmatics of intelligence. In R. J. Sternberg & R. K. Wagner (Eds.), *Practical intelligence: Nature and origins of competence in the everyday world* (pp. 203–235). New York: Cambridge University Press.

Dreyfus, H. L., & Dreyfus, S. E. (1990). Making a mind versus modeling the brain: Artificial intelligence back at a branch-point. In M. A. Boden (Ed.), *The philosophy of artificial intelligence: Oxford readings in philosophy* (pp. 309–333). Oxford, England: Oxford University Press.

Duffin, J. M., & Simpson, A. P., (1993). Natural, conflicting and alien. *Journal of Mathematical Behavior, 12,* 313–328.

Dugdale, S. (1993). Functions and graphs—Perspectives on student thinking. In T. A. Romberg, E. Fennema, & T. Carpenter (Eds.), *Integrating research on the graphical representation of functions* (pp. 101–130). Mahwah, NJ: Lawrence Erlbaum Associates.

Dunbar, K. (1993). Concept discovery in a scientific domain. *Cognitive Science, 17,* 397–434.

Duncker, K. (1945). On problem solving. *Psychological Monographs, 58* (whole No. 270).

Eddy, D. M. (1982). Probabilistic reasoning in clinical medicine: Problems and opportunities. In D. Kahneman, P. Slovic, & A. Tversky (Eds.), *Judgment under uncertainty: Heuristics and biases* (pp. 249–267). Cambridge, England: Cambridge University Press.

Edwards, W. (1982). Conservatism in human information processing. In D. Kahneman, P. Slovic, & A. Tversky (Eds.), *Judgment under uncertainty: Heuristics and biases* (pp. 359–369). Cambridge, MA: Cambridge University Press.

Egan, D. E., & Schwartz, B. J. (1979). Chunking in recall of symbolic drawings. *Memory and Cognition, 7,* 149–158.

Eimas, P. D. (1985). The perception of speech in early infancy. *Scientific American, 252,* 46–52.

Einhorn, H. J., & Hogarth, R. M. (1978). Confidence in judgment: Persistence of the illusion of validity. *Psychological Review, 85,* 395–416.

Ellsberg, D. (1961). Risk, ambiguity, and the Savage axioms. *Quarterly Journal of Economics, 75,* 643–699.

Elman, J. L., Bates, E. A, Johnson, M. H., Karmiloff-Smith, A., Parisi, D., & Plunkett, K. (1996). *Rethinking innateness: A connectionist perspective on development.* Cambridge, MA: MIT Press.

Engle, R. W., & Bukstel, L. (1978). Memory processes among bridge players of differing expertise. *American Journal of Psychology, 91,* 673–679.

Erickson, J. R. (1974). A set analysis theory of behavior in formal syllogistic reasoning tasks. In R. Solso (Ed.), *Theories of cognitive psychology: The Loyola Symposium* (Vol. 2). Hillsdale, NJ: Lawrence Erlbaum Associates.

Ericsson, K. A. (Ed.). (1996a). *The road to excellence.* Mahwah, NJ: Lawrence Erlbaum Associates.

Ericsson, K. A. (1996b). The acquisition of expert performance. In K. A. Ericsson (Ed.), *The road to excellence* (pp. 1–50). Mahwah, NJ: Lawrence Erlbaum Associates.

Ericsson, K. A., Krampe, R. T., & Tesch-Römer, C. (1993). The role of deliberate practice in the acquisition of expert performance. *Psychological Review, 100,* 363–406.

Ericsson, K. A., & Simon, H. A. (1980). Verbal reports as data. *Psychological Review, 87,* 215–251.

Ericsson, K. A., & Smith, J. (1991). Prospects and limits in the empirical study of expertise: An introduction. In K. A. Ericsson & J. Smith (Eds.), *Toward a general theory of expertise: Prospects and limits* (pp. 19–38). Cambridge, England: Cambridge University Press.

Estes, W. K. (1982). Learning, memory, and intelligence. In R. J. Sternberg (Ed.), *Handbook of intelligence* (pp. 170–224). New York: Cambridge University Press.

Evans, J. St. B. T. (1977). Linguistic factors in reasoning. *Quarterly Journal of Experimental Psychology, 29,* 297–306.

Evans, J. St. B. T. (1989). *Bias in human reasoning: Causes and consequences.* Hove, England: Lawrence Erlbaum Associates.

Evans, J. St. B. T., & Over, D. E. (1996). Rationality in the selection task: Epistemic utility versus uncertainty reduction. *Psychological Review, 103,* 356–363.

Eysenck, H. J. (1967). Intelligence assessment: A theoretical and experimental approach. *British Journal of Educational Psychology, 37,* 81–98.

Eysenck, H. J. (1993). Creativity and personality: A theoretical perspective. *Psychological Inquiry, 4,* 147–178.

Eysenck, H. J., & Kamin, L. (1981). *The intelligence controversy: H. J. Eysenck vs. Leon Kamin.* New York: John Wiley & Sons.

Fagan, J. F. (1984). The intelligent infant: Theoretical implications. *Intelligence, 8,* 1–9.

Fagan, J. F. (1985). A new look at infant intelligence. In D. K. Detterman (Ed.), *Current topics in human intelligence: Vol 1. Research methodology* (pp. 223–246). Norwood, NJ: Ablex.

Fagan, J. F., III, & Montie, J. E. (1988). Behavioral assessment of cognitive well-being in the infant. In J. Kavanagh (Ed.), *Understanding mental retardation: Research accomplishments and new frontiers.* Baltimore: Paul H. Brookes.

Falk, R. (1992). A closer look at the probabilities of the notorious three prisoners. *Cognition, 43,* 197–223.

Falkenhainer, B., Forbus, K. D., & Gentner, D. (1990). The structure-mapping engine. *Artificial Intelligence, 41,* 1–63.

Feldman, D. H. (1986). *Nature's gambit: Child prodigies and the development of human potential.* New York: Basic Books.

Fernald, A. (1985). Four-month-old infants prefer to listen to motherese. *Infant Behavior and Development, 8,* 118–195.

Fernald, A., Taeschner, T., Dunn, J., Papousek, M., De Boysson-Bardies, B., & Fukui, I. (1989). A cross-cultural study of prosodic modification in mothers' and fathers' speech to preverbal infants. *Journal of Child Language, 16,* 477–501.

Fernandez, A., & Glenberg, A. M. (1985). Changing environmental context does not reliably affect memory. *Memory and Cognition, 13,* 333–345.

Feuerstein, R. (1979). *The dynamic assessment of retarded performers.* Baltimore: University Park Press.

Feuerstein, R., Miller, R., Hoffman, M. B., Rand, Y., Mintzer, Y., & Jensen, M. R. (1981). Cognitive modifiability in adolescence: Cognitive structure and the effects of intervention. *Journal of Special Education, 15,* 269–286.

Feuerstein, R., Miller, R., & Jensen, M. R. (1980). Can evolving techniques better measure cognitive change? *Journal of Special Education,* Symposium Edition.

Feuerstein, R., & Rand, Y. (1974). Mediated learning experiences: An outline of the proximal etiology for differential development of cognitive functions. *International Understanding, 9,* 7–37.

Feuerstein, R., Rand, Y., Hoffman, M., & Miller, R. (1980). *Instrumental enrichment.* Baltimore: University Park Press.

Feynman, R. (1985). *Surely you're joking, Mr. Feynman.* New York: Norton.

Fiedler, K. (1988). The dependence of the conjunction fallacy on subtle linguistic factors. *Psychological Research, 50,* 123–129.

Field, T. (1978). Interaction behaviors of primary versus secondary caregiver fathers. *Developmental Psychology, 14,* 183–184.

Fienberg, S. E., & Schervish, M. J. (1986). The relevance of Bayesian inference for the presentation of evidence and for legal decision making. *Journal of Boston University Law Review, 66,* 771–798.

Findlay, C. S., & Lumsden, C. J. (1988). The creative mind: Toward an evolutionary theory of discovery and invention. *Journal of Social and Biological Structures, 11,* 3–55.

Finke, R. (1990). *Creative imagery: Discoveries and inventions in visualization.* Hillsdale, NJ: Lawrence Erlbaum Associates.

Finke, R. (1995). Creative insight and preinventive forms. In R. J. Sternberg & J. E. Davidson (Eds.), *The nature of insight* (pp. 255–280). Cambridge, MA: MIT Press.

Finke, R. A., Ward T. B., & Smith, S. M. (1992). *Creative cognition: Theory, research, and applications.* Cambridge, MA: MIT Press.

Finkelstein, M. O. (1978). *Quantitative methods in law.* New York: Free Press.

Fischer, K. W. (1980). A theory of cognitive development: The control and construction of hierarchies of skill. *Psychological Review, 87,* 477–531.

Fischer, K. W., & Bidell, T. R. (1991). Constraining nativist inferences about cognitive capacities. In S. Carey & R. Gelman (Eds.), *Structural constraints on knowledge in cognitive development.* Hillsdale, NJ: Lawrence Erlbaum Associates.

Fischhoff, B., & Beyth-Marom, R. (1983). Hypothesis evaluation from a Bayesian perspective. *Psychological Review, 90,* 239–260.

Fischhoff, B., Slovic, P., & Lichtenstein, S. (1977). Knowing with certainty: The appropriateness of extreme confidence. *Journal of Experimental Psychology: Human Perception and Performance, 3,* 552–564.

Fitts, P. M., & Posner, M. I. (1967). *Human performance.* Belmont, CA: Brooks-Cole.

Flavell, J. H. (1981). Cognitive monitoring. In W. P. Dickson (Ed.), *Children's oral communication skills* (pp. 35–60). New York: Academic Press.

Flavell, J. H., Flavell, E. R., & Green, F. L. (1983). Development of the appearance-reality distinction. *Cognitive Psychology, 15,* 95–120.

Flavell, J. H., & Wellman, H. M. (1977). Metamemory. In R. V. Kail, Jr., & J. W. Hagen (Eds.), *Perspectives on the development of memory and cognition* (pp. 3–33). Hillsdale, NJ: Lawrence Erlbaum Associates.

Flege, J. (1991). The interlingual identification of Spanish and English vowels: Orthographic evidence. *Quarterly Journal of Experimental Psychology: Human Experimental Psychology, 43,* 701–731.

Flescher, I. (1963). Anxiety and achievement of intellectually gifted and creatively gifted children. *Journal of Psychology, 56,* 251–268.

Flynn, J. R. (1984). The mean IQ of Americans: Massive gains 1932 to 1978. *Psychological Bulletin, 95,* 29–51.

Flynn, J. R. (1987). Massive IQ gains in 14 nations: What IQ tests really measure. *Psychological Bulletin, 95,* 29–51.

Flynn, J. R. (1994). Giving g a fair chance: How to define intelligence, survive falsification, and resist behaviorism. *Psychological Inquiry, 5,* 204–208.

Flynn, J. R. (1998). WAIS-III and WISC-III gains in the United States from 1972 to 1995: How to compensate for obsolete norms. *Perceptual & Motor Skills, 86,* 1231–1239

Fodor, J. A. (1975). *The language of thought.* New York: Crowell.

Fodor, J. A., & Pylyshyn, Z. W. (1988). Connectionism and cognitive architecture: A critical analysis. *Cognition, 28,* 3–71.

Fogel, A. (1991). *Infancy: Infant, family, and society* (2nd ed.). St. Paul, MN: West.

Fong, G. T., Krantz, D. H., & Nisbett, R. E. (1986). The effects of statistical training on thinking about everyday problems. *Cognitive Psychology, 18,* 253–292.

Forbus, K. D., Gentner, D., & Law, K. (1995). MAC/FAC: A model of similarity-based retreival. *Cognitive Science, 19,* 141–205.

Fox, R., & McDaniel, C. (1982). The perception of biological motion by human infants. *Science, 218,* 486–487.

Franks, J. J., & Bransford, J. D. (1971). Abstraction of visual patterns. *Journal of Experimental Psychology, 90,* 65–74.

Frazier, L. (1995). Issues of representation in psycholinguistics. In J. L. Miller & P. D. Eimas (Eds.), *Speech, language, and communication* (pp. 1–27). San Diego, CA: Academic Press.

Frederiksen, C. H. (1975). Representing logical and semantic structure of knowledge acquired from discourse. *Cognitive Psychology, 7,* 371–458.

Frensch, P. A. & Sternberg, R. J. (1989). Expertise and intelligent thinking: When is it worse to know better? In R. J. Sternberg (Ed.), *Advances in the psychology of human intelligence* (Vol. 5, pp. 157–158). Hillsdale, NJ: Lawrence Erlbaum Associates.

Freud, S. (1908/1959). The relation of the poet to day-dreaming. In *Collected papers* (Vol. 4, pp. 173–183). London: Hogarth Press.

Freud, S. (1908/1964). *Leonardo da Vinci and a memory of his childhood.* New York: Norton. (Original work published in 1910)

Fromkin, V., & Rodman, R. (1988). *An introduction to language* (4th ed.). Fort Worth, TX: Holt, Rinehart & Winston.

Furman, L., Barron, B., Montavon, E., Vye, N. J., Bransford, J. D., & Shah, P. (1989, April). *The effects of problem formulation training and type of feedback on math handicapped students' problem solving abilities.* Paper presented at the meeting of the American Educational Research Association, San Francisco.

Galton, F. (1883). *Inquiry into human faculty and its development.* London: Macmillan.

Garcia-Madruga, J. A., Moreno, S., Carriedo, N, & Gutierrez, F. (2000). Task, premise order, and strategies in Rip's conjunction-disjunction and conditionals problems. In W. Schaeken & G. De Vooght (Eds.), *Deductive reasoning and strategies* (pp. 49–71). Mahwah, NJ: Lawrence Erlbaum Associates.

Gardner, H. (1983). *Frames of mind: The theory of multiple intelligences.* New York: Basic Books.

Gardner, H. (1993). *Multiple intelligences: The theory in practice.* New York: Basic Books.

Gardner, H. (1994). The creator's patterns. In D. H. Feldman, M. Csikszentmiyhalyi, & H. Gardner (Eds.), *Changing the world: A framework for the study of creativity* (pp. 69–84). Westport, CT: Praeger.

Gardner, H. (1999). Are there additional intelligences? The case for naturalist, spiritual, and existential intelligences. In J. Kane (Ed.), *Education, information, and transformation* (pp. 111–131). Upper Saddle River, NJ: Prentice-Hall.

Gardner, H., Krechevsky, M., Sternberg, R. J., & Okagaki, L. (1994). Intelligence in context: Enhancing students' practical intelligence for school. In K. McGilly (Ed.), *Classroom lessons: Integrating cognitive theory and classroom practice* (pp. 105–127). Cambridge, MA: MIT Press.

Garrett, M. (1992). Disorders of lexical selection. *Cognition, 42*(1–3), 143–180.

Garrett, M. F. (1980). Levels of processing in sentence production. In B. Butterworth (Ed.), *Language production: Vol. 1. Speech and talk* (pp. 177–210). London: Academic Press.

Gati, I., & Tversky, A. (1984). Weighting common and distinctive features in perceptual and conceptual judgments. *Cognitive Psychology, 16,* 341–370.

Gelman, R. (1969). Conservation acquisition: A problem of learning to attend to relevant attributes. *Journal of Experimental Child Psychology, 7,* 167–187.

Gelman, R. (1972). Logical capacity of very young children: Number invariance rules. *Child Development, 43,* 75–90.

Gelman, R., & Baillargeon, R. (1983). A review of some Piagetian concepts. In P. H. Mussen (Series Ed.), & J. Flavell & E. Markman (Vol. Eds.), *Handbook of child psychology: Cognitive development* (Vol. 3, 4th ed., pp. 167–230). New York: John Wiley & Sons.

Gelman, S. A. (1985). Children's inductive inferences from natural kind and artifact categories. (Doctoral dissertation, Stanford University, 1984). *Dissertation Abstracts International, 45*(10–B), 3351–3352.

Gelman, S. A. (1988a). Children's expectations concerning natural kind categories. *Human Development, 31,* 28–34.

Gelman, S. A. (1988b). The development of induction within natural kind and artifact categories. *Cognitive Psychology, 20,* 65–95.

Gelman, S. A. (1989). Children's use of categories to guide biological inferences. *Human Development, 32,* 65–71.

Gelman, S. A., Coley, J. D., & Gottfried, G. M. (1994). Essentialist beliefs in children: The acquisition of concepts and theories. In L. A. Hirschfeld & S. A. Gelman (Eds.), *Mapping the mind: Domain specificity in cognition and culture* (pp. 341–365). New York: Cambridge University Press.

Gelman, S. A., & Hirschfeld, L. A. (1999). How biological is essentialism? In D. L. Medin & S. Atran (Eds.), *Folkbiology* (pp. 403–446). Cambridge, MA: MIT Press.

Gelman, S. A., & Kremer, K. E. (1991). Understanding natural causes: Children's explanations of how objects and their properties originate. *Child Development, 62,* 396–414.

Gelman, S. A., & Markman, E. M. (1986). Categories and induction in young children. *Cognition, 23,* 183–209.

Gelman, S. A., & Markman, E. M. (1987). Young children's inductions from natural kinds: The role of categories and appearances. *Child Development, 58,* 1532–1541.

Gelman, S. A., & O'Reilly, A. W. (1988). Children's inductive inferences within superordinate categories: The role of language and category structure. *Child Development, 59,* 876–887.

Gelman, S. A., & Wellman, H. M. (1991). Insides and essence: Early understandings of the non-obvious. *Cognition, 38,* 213–244.

Gentner, D. (1983). Structure-mapping: A theoretical framework for analogy. *Cognitive Science, 7,* 155–170.

Gentner, D. (1989). The mechanisms of analogical reasoning. In S. Vosniadou & A. Ortony (Eds.), *Similarity and analogical reasoning* (pp. 199–241). Cambridge, England: Cambridge University Press.

Gentner, D., & Rattermann, M. J. (1991). Language and the career of similarity. In S. A. Gelman & J. P. Byrnes (Eds.), *Perspectives on language and thought: Interrelations in development* (pp. 225–277). New York: Cambridge University Press.

Gentner, D., Rattermann. M. J., & Forbus, K. D. (1993). The roles of similarity in transfer: Separating retrievability from inferential soundness. *Cognitive Psychology, 25,* 524–575.

Gernsbacher, M. A. (1985). Surface information loss in comprehension. *Cognitive Psychology, 17,* 324–363.

Gerrig, R., & Banaji, M. R., (1994). Language and thought. In R. J. Sternberg (Ed.), *Handbook of perception and cognition* (Vol. 12). New York: Academic Press.

Gerrig, R. J., & Healy, A. F. (1983). Dual processes in metaphor understanding: Comprehension and appreciation. *Journal of Experimental Psychology: Learning, Memory, & Cognition, 9,* 667–675.

Geschwind, N. (1970). The organization of language and the brain. *Science, 170,* 940–944.

Getzels, J. W., & Csikszentmihalyi, M. (1976). *The creative vision: A longitudinal study of problem finding in art.* New York: John Wiley & Sons.

Getzels, J. W., & Jackson, P. W. (1962). *Creativity and intelligence: Explorations with gifted students.* New York: John Wiley & Sons.

Ghiselin, B. (Ed.). (1985). *The creative process: A symposium.* Berkeley, CA: University of California Press.

Gibbs, R. W. (1979). Contextual effects in understanding indirect requests. *Discourse Processes, 2,* 1–10.

Gibbs, R. W. (1986). What makes some indirect speech acts conventional? *Journal of Memory and Language, 25,* 181–196.

Gibson, E. J., & Walker, A. S. (1984). Development of knowledge of visual-tactual affordances of substance. *Child Development, 55,* 453–460.

Gick, M. L., & Holyoak, K. J. (1980). Analogical problem solving. *Cognitive Psychology, 12,* 306–355.

Gick, M. L., & Holyoak, K. J. (1983). Schema induction and analogical transfer. *Cognitive Psychology, 15,* 1–38.

Gick, M. L., & Lockhart, R. S. (1995). Cognitive and affective components of insight. In R. J. Sternberg & J. E. Davidson (Eds.), *The nature of insight* (pp. 197–228). Cambridge, MA: MIT Press.

Gigerenzer, G. (1991). From tools to theories: A heuristic of discovery in cognitive psychology. *Psychological Review, 98,* 254–267.

Gigerenzer, G. (1996). On narrow norms and vague heuristics: A reply to Kahneman and Tversky. *Psychological Review, 103,* 592–596.

Gigerenzer, G., & Goldstein, D. G. (1996). Reasoning the fast and frugal way: Models of bounded rationality. *Psychological Review, 103,* 650–669.

Gigerenzer, G., Hell, W., & Blank, H. (1988). Presentation and content: The use of base rates as a continuous variable. *Journal of Experimental Psychology: General, 4,* 513–525.

Gigerenzer, G., Hoffrage, U., & Kleinboelting, H. (1991). Probabilistic mental models: A Brunswikian theory of confidence. *Psychological Review, 98,* 506–528.

Gigerenzer, G., & Hug, K. (1992). Domain specific reasoning: Social contracts, cheating, and perspective change. *Cognition, 43,* 127–171.

Gigerenzer, G., & Todd, P. M. (1999). *Simple heuristics that make us smart.* New York: Oxford University Press.

Gilhooly, K. J. (1988). *Thinking: Directed, undirected, and creative.* New York: Academic Press.

Gilovich, T., Medvec, V. H., & Chen, S. (1995). Commission, omission, and dissonance reduction: Coping with regret in the Monty Hall problem. *Personality and Social Psychology Bulletin, 21,* 182–190.

Ginsburg, H. (1996). Toby's math. In R. J. Sternberg & T. Ben-Zeev (Eds.), *The nature of mathematical thinking* (pp. 175–202). Mahwah, NJ: Lawrence Erlbaum Associates.

Gladwin, T. (1970). *East is a big bird.* Cambridge, MA: Harvard University Press.

Glaser, R., & Chi, M. T. H. (1988). Overview. In M. T. H. Chi, R. Glaser, & M. Farr (Eds.), *The nature of expertise* (pp. xv–xxxvi). Hillsdale, NJ: Lawrence Erlbaum Associates.

Gleitman, H. (1986). *Psychology.* (2nd ed.). New York: W.W. Norton & Co.

Glucksberg, S. (1988). Language and thought. In R. J. Sternberg & E. E. Smith (Eds.), *The psychology of human thought* (pp. 214–241). New York: Cambridge University Press.

Glucksberg, S., & Danks, J. H. (1975). *Experimental psycholinguistics.* Hillsdale, NJ: Lawrence Erlbaum Associates.

Glucksberg, S., & Keysar, B. (1990). Understanding metaphorical comparisons: Beyond similarity. *Psychological Review, 97,* 3–18.

Goddard, H. H. (1917). Mental tests and immigrants. *Journal of Delinquency, 2,* 243–277.

Golann, S. E. (1962). The creativity motive. *Journal of Personality, 30,* 588–600.

Goldman, S. R., Pellegrino, J. W. & Bransford, J. (1994). Assessing programs that invite thinking. In E. L. Baker & H. F. O'Neil, Jr. (Eds.). *Technology assessment in education and training* (pp. 199–230). Hillsdale, NJ: Lawrence Erlbaum Associates.

Goldman-Rakic, P. S. (1993). Specification of higher cortical functions. *Journal of Head Trauma Rehabilitation, 8,* 13–23.

Goldstein, W. M. (1990). Judgments of relative importance in decision making: Global vs. local interpretations of subjective weight. *Organizational Behavior and Human Decision Processes, 47,* 313–336.

Goldstone, R. L. (1994). The role of similarity in categorization: Providing a groundwork. *Cognition, 52,* 125–157.

Goodman, N. (1955). *Fact, fiction, and forecast.* Cambridge, MA: Harvard University Press.

Goodman, N. (1972). Seven strictures on similarity. In N. Goodman (Ed.), *Problems and projects.* Indianapolis, IN: Bobbs-Merrill.

Gordon, D. & Lakoff, G. (1971). Conversational postulates. In *Papers from the Seventh Regional Meeting, Chicago Linguistic Society* (pp. 63–84). Chicago: Chicago Linguistic Society.

Gordon, W. J. J. (1961). *Synectics: The development of creative capacity.* New York: Harper & Row.

Gottfried, A. W. (Ed.). (1984). *Home environment and early cognitive development: Longitudinal research.* San Diego, CA: Academic Press.

Gough, H. G. (1979). A creativity scale for the Adjective Check List. *Journal of Personality and Social Psychology, 37,* 1398–1405.

Graesser, A. C., & Kreuz, R. J. (1993). A theory of inference generation during text comprehension. *Discourse Processes, 16,* 145–160.

Graf, P. (1990). Life-span changes in implicit and explicit memory. *Bulletin of the Psychonomic Society, 28,* 353–358.

Green, D. W. (1995). Externalization, counter-examples, and the abstract selection task. *The Quarterly Journal of Experimental Psychology, 48,* 424–446.

Green, D. W., & Larking, R. (1995). The locus of facilitation in the abstract selection task. *Thinking and Reasoning, 1,* 183–199.

Greeno, J. G. (1974). Hobbits and orcs: Acquisition of a sequential concept. *Cognitive Psychology, 6,* 270–292.

Greeno, J. G. (1980). Some examples of cognitive task analysis with instructional implications. In R. E. Snow, P. Federico, & W. E. Montague (Eds.), *Aptitude, learning, and instruction* (Vol. 2, pp. 1–21). Hillsdale, NJ: Lawrence Erlbaum Associates.

Greeno, J. G. (1997). On claims that answer the wrong questions. *Educational Researcher, 26,* 5–17.

Greeno, J. G. (1998). The situativity of knowing, learning, and research. *American Psychologist, 53,* 5–26.

Gregory, W. L., Cialdini, R. B., & Carpenter, K. M. (1982). Self-relevant scenarios as mediators of likelihood estimates and compliance: Does imagining make it so? *Journal of Personality and Social Psychology, 43,* 89–99.

Grice, H. P. (1967). William James Lectures, Harvard University, published in part as "Logic and conversation." In P. Cole & J. L. Morgan (Eds.), *Syntax and semantics: Vol. 3. Speech acts* (pp. 41–58). New York: Seminar Press.

Griffin, D., & Tversky, A. (1992). The weighing of evidence and the determinants of confidence. *Cognitive Psychology, 24,* 411–435.

Griffin, D. W., & Ross, L. (1991). Subjective construal, social inference, and human misunderstanding. In M. P. Zanna (Ed.), *Advances in Experimental Social Psychology* (Vol. 24, pp. 319–359). New York: Academic Press.

Griffin, S. A., Case, R., & Sandieson, R. (1992). Synchrony and asynchrony in the acquisition of everyday mathematical knowledge: Towards a representational theory of children's intellectual growth. In R. Case (Ed.), *The mind's staircase: Exploring the central conceptual underpinnings of children's theory and knowledge.* Hillsdale, NJ: Lawrence Erlbaum Associates.

Griffin, S. A., Case, R., & Siegler, R. S. (1994). Rightstart: Providing the central conceptual prerequisites for first formal learning of arithmetic for students at risk for school failure. In K. McGilly (Ed.), *Classroom lessons: Integrating cognitive theory and classroom practice* (pp. 25–49). Cambridge, MA: MIT Press.

Griggs, R. A., & Cox, J. R. (1982). The elusive thematic-materials effect in Wason's selection task. *British Journal of Psychology, 73,* 407–420.

Grigorenko, E. L., & Sternberg, R. J. (1998). Dynamic testing. *Psychological Bulletin, 124,* 75–111.

Grigorenko, E. L., & Sternberg, R. J. (2000). Elucidating the etiology and nature of beliefs about parenting styles. *Developmental Science, 3,* 93–112.

Groen, G. J., & Parkman, J. M. (1972). A chronometric analysis of simple addition. *Psychological Review, 79,* 329–343.

Grosz, B. J., Pollack, M. E., & Sidner, C. L. (1989). Discourse. In M. I. Posner (Ed.), *Foundations of cognitive science* (pp. 437–468). Cambridge, MA: MIT Press.

Grotzer, T. A., & Perkins, D. A. (2000). Teaching of intelligence: A performance conception. In R. J. Sternberg (Ed.), *Handbook of intelligence* (pp. 492–515). New York: Cambridge University Press.

Gruber, H. (1981). *Darwin on man: A psychological study of scientific creativity* (2nd ed.). Chicago: University of Chicago Press. (Original work published 1974)

Gruber, H. E. (1989). The evolving systems approach to creative work. In D. B. Wallace & H. E. Gruber (Eds.), *Creative people at work: Twelve cognitive case studies* (pp. 3–24). New York: Oxford University Press.

Gruber, H. E., & Davis, S. N. (1988). Inching our way up Mount Olympus: The evolving-systems approach to creative thinking. In R. J. Sternberg (Ed.), *The nature of creativity* (pp. 243–270). New York: Cambridge University Press.

Gruber, H. E., & Wallace, D. B. (1999). The case study method and evolving systems approach for understanding unique creative people at work. In R. J. Sternberg (Ed.), *Handbook of creativity* (pp. 93–115). New York: Cambridge University Press.

Guilford, J. P. (1950). Creativity. *American Psychologist, 5,* 444–454.

Guilford, J. P. (1967). *The nature of human intelligence.* New York: McGraw-Hill.

Guilford, J. P. (1968). Intelligence has three facets. *Science, 160,* 615–620.

Guilford, J. P. (1982). Cognitive psychology's ambiguities: Some suggested remedies. *Psychological Review, 89,* 48–59.

Guilford, J. P. (1988). Some changes in the structure-of-intellect model. *Educational & Psychological Measurement, 48,* 1–4.

Guyote, M. J., & Sternberg, R. J. (1981). A transitive-chain theory of syllogistic reasoning. *Cognitive Psychology, 13,* 461–525.

Hacking, I. (1965). *Logic of statistical inference.* Cambridge, England: Cambridge University Press.

Haier, R. J., Chueh, D., Touchette, R., Lott, I., Buchbuam, M. S., MacMillan, D., Sandman, C, LaCase, L., & Sosa, E. (1995). Brain size and cerebral glucose metabolic rate in nonspecific mental retardation and Down syndrome. *Intelligence, 20,* 191–210.

Hakuta, K. (1986). *Mirror of language.* New York: Basic Books.

Halford, G. S. (1982). *The development of thought.* Hillsdale, NJ: Lawrence Erlbaum Associates.

Hall, E. T. (1966). *The hidden dimension.* Garden City, NY: Doubleday.

Halpern, D. F. (1998). Teaching critical thinking for transfer across domains: Dispositions, skills, structure training, and metacognitive monitoring. *American Psychologist, 53,* 449–455.

Hampton, J. (1993). Prototype models of concept representation. In I. Van Mechelen & J. Hampton (Eds.), *Categories and concepts: Theoretical views and inductive data analysis. Cognitive science series* (pp. 67–95). London: Academic Press.

Hampton, J. A. (1998). Similarity-based categorization and fuzziness of natural categories. *Cognition, 65,* 137–165

Haviland, S. E., & Clark, H. H. (1974). What's new? Acquiring new information as a process in comprehension. *Journal of Verbal Learning and Verbal Behavior, 13,* 512–521.

Hawkins, S. A., & Hastie, R. (1990). Hindsight: Biased judgments of past events after the outcomes are known. *Psychological Bulletin, 107,* 311–327.

Hayes, J. R. (1989). *The complete problem solver* (2nd ed.). Hillsdale, NJ: Lawrence Erlbaum Associates.

Hayes Roth, B., & Hayes Roth, F. (1977). Concept learning and the recognition and classification of exemplars. *Journal of Verbal Learning and Verbal Behavior, 16,* 321–338.

Hegel, G. W. F. (1931). *The phenomenology of mind* (2nd ed.; J. B. Baillie, Trans.). London: Allen & Unwin. (Original work published 1807)

Heit, E. (1992). Categorization using chains of examples. *Cognitive Psychology, 24,* 341–380.

Henle, M. (1962). On the relation between logic and thinking. *Psychological Review, 69,* 366–378.

Hennessey, B. A., & Amabile, T. M. (1988). The conditions of creativity. In R. J. Sternberg (Ed.), *The nature of creativity* (pp. 11–38). New York: Cambridge University Press.

Hennessy, S. (1993). The stability of children's mathematical behavior: When is a bug really a bug? *Learning and Instruction, 3,* 315–338.

Herr, E. L., Moore, G. D., & Hasen, J. S. (1965). Creativity, intelligence, and values: A study of relationships. *Exceptional Children, 32,* 114–115.

Herrnstein, R. J., & Murray, C. (1994). *The bell curve.* New York: Free Press.

Hesse, M. (1966). *Models and analogies in science.* Notre Dame, IN: University of Notre Dame Press.

Hickling, A. K., & Gelman, S. A. (1995). How does your garden grow? Early conceptualization of seeds
and their place in plant growth cycle. *Child Development, 66,* 856–876.

Hilgard, E. R. (1987). *Psychology in America.* Orlando, FL: Harcourt Brace Jovanovich.

Hinsley, D., Hayes, J. R., & Simon, H. A. (1977). From words to equations. In M. Just and P. Carpenter (Eds.), *Cognitive processes in comprehension* (pp. 89–106). Hillsdale, NJ: Lawrence Erlbaum
Associates.

Hinton, G. E. (1989). Learning distributed representations of concepts. In R. G. M. Morris (Ed.), *Parallel distributed processing: Implications for psychology and neurobiology* (pp. 46–61). Oxford,
England: Clarendon Press.

Hintzman, D. L. (1986). "Schema abstraction" in a multiple-trace memory model. *Psychological Review,
93,* 411–428

Hintzman, D. L., & Ludlam, G. (1980). Differential forgetting of prototypes and old instances: Simulation by an exemplar-based classification model. *Memory and Cognition, 8,* 378–382.

Hirsh-Pasek, K., Kemler Nelson, D. G., Jusczyk, P. W., Cassidy, K. W., Druss, B., & Kennedy, L. (1987).
Clauses are perceptual units for young infants. *Cognition, 26,* 269–286.

Hoffman, C., Lau, I., & Johnson, D. R. (1986). The linguistic relativity of person cognition: An Eng-
lish-Chinese comparison. *Journal of Personality and Social Psychology, 51,* 1097–1105.

Holland, J. H., Holyoak, K. J., Nisbett, R. E., & Thagard, P. (1986). *Induction: Processes of inference,
learning and discovery.* Cambridge, MA: MIT Press

Holt, J. (1964). *How children fail.* New York: Pitman.

Holyoak, K. J., & Koh, K. (1987). Surface and structural similarity in analogical transfer. *Memory and
Cognition, 15,* 332–340.

Holyoak, K. J., & Thagard, P. (1989a). Analogical mapping by constraint satisfaction. *Cognitive Science, 13,* 295–355.

Holyoak, K. J., & Thagard, P. (1989b). A computational model of analogical problem solving. In
S. Vosniadou & A. Ortony (Eds.), *Similarity and analogical reasoning* (pp. 242–266). Cambridge,
MA: Cambridge University Press.

Holyoak, K. J., & Thagard, P. (1995). *Mental leaps.* Cambridge, MA: MIT Press.

Homa, D. (1984). On the nature of categories. In G. H. Bower (Ed.), *The psychology of learning and
motivation* (pp. 49–94). Orlando, FL: Academic Press.

Horn, J. L. (1994). Theory of fluid and crystallized intelligence. In R. J. Sternberg (Ed.), *The encyclopedia of human intelligence* (Vol. 1, pp. 443–451). New York: Macmillan.

Horn, J. L., & Cattell, R. B. (1966). Refinement and test of the theory of fluid and crystallized ability
intelligences. *Journal of Educational Psychology, 57,* 253–270.

Horn, J. L., & Hofer, S. M. (1992). Major abilities and development in the adult period. In R. J. Sternberg & C. A. Berg (Eds.), *Intellectual development* (pp. 44–99). New York: Cambridge University
Press.

Horn, J. L., & Knapp, J. R. (1973). On the subjective character of the empirical base of Guilford's structure-of-intellect model. *Psychological Bulletin, 80,* 33–43.

Howe, M. J. A. (1999a). *Genius explained.* Cambridge, England: Cambridge University Press.

Howe, M. J. A. (1999b). Prodigies and creativity. In R. J. Sternberg (Ed.), *Handbook of creativity*
(pp. 431–446). New York: Cambridge University Press.

Hughlings-Jackson, J. (1932). In J. Taylor (Ed.), *Selected writings of John Hughlings Jackson.* London:
Hodder & Stoughton. (Original work published 1866)

Hull, C. L. (1952). *A behavior system: An introduction to behavior theory concerning the individual organism.* New Haven, CT: Yale University Press.

Hultsch, D. F., & Dixon, R. A. (1990). Learning and memory in aging. In J. E. Birren & K. W. Schaie (Eds.), *Handbook of the psychology of aging: The handbooks of aging* (3rd ed., pp. 356–368). San Diego, CA: Academic Press.

Hummel, J. E., & Holyoak, K. J. (1997). Distributed representations of structure: A theory of analogical access and mapping. *Psychological Review, 104,* 427–466.

Humphreys, L. G., & Davey, T. C. (1988). Continuity in intellectual growth from 12 months to 9 years. *Intelligence, 12,* 183–197.

Hunt, E. B. (1978). Mechanics of verbal ability. *Psychological Review, 85,* 109–130.

Hunt, E. B. (1980). Intelligence as an information-processing concept. *British Journal of Psychology, 71,* 449–474.

Hunt, E. B. (1994). Problem solving. In R. J. Sternberg (Ed.), *Thinking and problem soloving* (pp. 215–231). San Diego, CA: Academic Press.

Hunt, E. B., & Banaji, M. (1988). The Whorfian hypothesis revisited: A cognitive science view of linguistic and cultural effects on thought. In J. W. Berry, S. H. Irvine, & E. Hunt (Eds.), *Indigenous cognition: Functioning in cultural context* (pp. 57–84). Dordrecht, the Netherlands: Martinus Nijhoff.

Hunt, E. B., & Lansman, M. (1982). Individual differences in attention. In R. J. Sternberg (Ed.), *Advances in the psychology of human intelligence* (Vol. 1, pp. 207–254). Hillsdale, NJ: Lawrence Erlbaum Associates.

Hunt, E. B., & Lansman, M. (1986). A unified model of attention and problem solving. *Psychological Review, 93,* 446–461.

Hunt, E. B., Lunneborg, C., & Lewis, J. (1975). What does it mean to be high verbal? *Cognitive Psychology, 7,* 194–227.

Inagaki, K., & Hatana, G. (1993). Young children's spontaneous personification as analogy. *Child Development, 58,* 1013–1020.

Inhelder, B., & Piaget, J. (1958). The growth of logical thinking from childhood to adolescence. New York: Basic Books.

"Intelligence and its measurement": A symposium (1921). *Journal of Educational Psychology, 12,* 123–147, 195–216, 271–275.

International Association for the Evaluation of Educational Achievement (1996). *Mathematics achievement in middle school years, science achievement in middle school years: IEA's third international mathematics and science study (TIMMS).* Boston: Author.

International Association for the Evaluation of Educational Achievement (1997). *Mathematics achievement in primary school years, science achievement in primary school years: IEA's third international mathematics and science study (TIMMS).* Boston: Author.

Jackendoff, R. (1991). Parts and boundaries. *Cognition, 41*(1–3), 9–45.

James, W. (1983). *Principles of psychology* (Vol. 1). Cambridge, MA: Harvard University Press. (Original work published 1890)

Janis, I., & Frick, P. (1943). The relationship between attitudes toward conclusions and errors in judging logical validity of syllogisms. *Journal of Experimental Psychology, 33,* 73–77.

Jeffries, R., Polson, P. G., Razran, L., & Atwood, M. E. (1977). A process model for missionaries-cannibals and other river-crossing problems. *Cognitive Psychology, 9,* 412–440.

Jenkins, J. J. (1979). Four points to remember: A tetrahedral model of memory experiments. In L. S. Cermak & F. I. M. Craik (Eds.), *Levels of processing in human memory* (pp. 429–446). Hillsdale, NJ: Lawrence Erlbaum Associates.

Jennings, D. L., Amabile, T. M., & Ross, L. (1982). Informal covariation assessment: Data-based vs. theory-based judgments. In D. Kahneman, P. Slovic, & A. Tversky (Eds.), *Judgment under uncertainty: Heuristics and biases* (pp. 211–230).

Jensen, A. R. (1979). g: Outmoded theory or unconquered frontier? *Creative Science and Technology, 2,* 16–29.

Jensen, A. R. (1982). The chronometry of intelligence. In R. J. Sternberg (Ed.), *Advances in the psychology of human intelligence.* (Vol. 1, pp. 255–310). Hillsdale, NJ: Lawrence Erlbaum Associates.

Jensen, A. R. (1997). The puzzle of nongenetic variance. In R. J. Sternberg & E. L. Grigorenko (Eds.), *Intelligence, heredity, and environment* (pp. 42–88). New York: Cambridge University Press.

Jensen, A. R. (1998). *The g factor: The science of mental ability.* Westport, CT: Praeger/Greenwood.

Johnson, J. S., & Newport, E. L. (1989). Critical period effects in second language learning: The influence of maturational state on the acquisition of English as a second language. *Cognitive Psychology, 21,* 60–99.

Johnson, J. S., & Newport, E. L. (1991). Critical period effects on universal properties of language: The status of subjacency in the acquisition of a second language. *Cognition, 39,* 215–258.

Johnson-Laird, P. N. (1983). *Mental models.* Cambridge, MA: Harvard University Press.

Johnson-Laird, P. N. (1988). Freedom and constraint in creativity. In R.J. Sternberg (Ed.), *The nature of creativity* (pp. 202–219). New York: Cambridge University Press.

Johnson-Laird, P. N. (1989). Mental models. In M. I. Posner (Ed.), *Foundations of cognitive science* (pp. 469–499). Cambridge, MA: MIT Press.

Johnson-Laird, P. N. (1993). Jazz improvisation: A theory at the computational level. In P. Howell, R. West, & I. Cross (Eds.), *Representing musical structure* (pp. 291–326). London: Academic Press.

Johnson-Laird, P. N. (1997). Rules and illusions: A critical study of Rips's *The Psychology of Proof*: *Minds and Machines, 7,* 387–407.

Johnson-Laird, P. N., & Bara, B. G. (1984). Syllogistic inference. *Cognition, 16,* 1–61.

Johnson-Laird, P. N., & Barres, P. E. (1994). When "or" means "and": A study in mental models. *Proceedings of the Sixteenth Annual Conference of the Cognitive Science Society* (pp. 475–478). Mahwah, NJ: Lawrence Erlbaum Associates.

Johnson-Laird, P. N., & Byrne, R. M. J. (1991). *Deduction.* Hove, England: Lawrence Erlbaum Associates.

Johnson-Laird, P. N., & Byrne, R. M. J. (1993). Multiple book review of *Deduction. Behavioral and Brain Sciences, 16,* 323–380.

Johnson-Laird, P. N., Byrne, R. M. J., & Schaeken, W. (1992). Propositional reasoning by model. *Psychological Review, 99,* 418 439.

Johnson-Laird, P. N., Legrenzi, P., Girotto, V., Legrenzi, M. S., & Caverni, J. P. (1999). Naive probability: A model theory of extensional reasoning. *Psychological Review 106,* 62–88.

Johnson-Laird, P. N., Legrenzi, P, & Legrenzi, M. (1972). Reasoning and a sense of reality. *British Journal of Psychology, 63,* 395–400.

Johnson-Laird, P. N., & Savary, F. (1999) Illusory inferences: A novel class of erroneous deductions. *Cognition, 71,* 191–229.

Johnson-Laird, P. N., & Steedman, M. (1978). The psychology of syllogisms. *Cognitive Psychology, 10,* 64–99

Jones, E. E., & Davis, K. E. (1965). From acts to dispositions: The attribution process in person perception. In L. Berkowitz (Ed.), *Advances in experimental social psychology* (Vol. 2). New York, NY: Academic Press.

Jones, E. E., & Nisbett, R. (1971). *The actor and the observer: Divergent perceptions of the causes of behavior.* Morristown, NJ: General Learning Press.

Jones, E. E., & Nisbett, R. (1987). The actor and the observer: Divergent perceptions of causality. In E. E. Jones, D. E. Kanouse, H. H. Kelley, & R. E. Nisbett (Eds.), *Attribution: Perceiving the causes of behavior* (pp. 79–94). Morristown, NJ: General Learning Press.

Joyce, E., & Biddle, G. (1981). Are auditors' judgments sufficiently regressive? *Journal of Accounting Research, 19,* 323–349.

Jusczyk, P. W. (1995). Language acquisition: Speech sounds and the beginning of phonology. In J. L. Miller & P. D. Eimas (Eds.), *Speech, language, and communication* (pp. 263–301). San Diego, CA: Academic Press.

Jusczyk, P. W. (1997). *The discovery of spoken language*. Cambridge, MA: MIT Press.

Just, M. A., & Carpenter, P. A. (1992). A capacity theory of comprehension: Individual differences in working memory. *Psychological Review, 99,* 122–149.

Kagan, J. (1989). Commentary [Special topic: Continuity in early cognitive development—conceptual and methodological challenges]. *Human Development, 32,* 172–176.

Kahneman, D., & Tversky, A. (1972). Subjective probability: A judgment of representativeness. *Cognitive Psychology, 3,* 430–454.

Kahneman D., & Tversky, A. (1973). On the psychology of prediction. *Psychological Review, 80,* 237–251.

Kahneman, D., & Tversky, A. (1979). On the interpretation of intuitive probability: A reply to Jonathan Cohen. *Cognition, 7,* 409–411.

Kahneman, D., & Tversky, A. (1982). The psychology of preferences. *Scientific American, 246,* 160–173.

Kahneman, D. & Tversky, A. (1996). On the reality of cognitive illusions. *Psychological Review, 103,* 582–591.

Kail, R. V. (1984). *The development of memory in children* (2nd ed.). New York: W. H. Freeman.

Kail, R., & Bisanz, J. (1992). The information-processing perspective on cognitive development in childhood and adolescence. In R. J. Sternberg & C. A. Berg (Eds.), *Intellectual development* (pp. 229–260). New York: Cambridge University Press.

Kail, R., & Park, Y-S. (1994). Processing time, articulation time, and memory span. *Journal of Experimental Child Psychology, 57,* 281–291.

Kalmar, D. A., & Sternberg, R. J. (1988). Theory knitting: An integrative approach to theory development. *Philosophical Psychology, 1,* 153–170.

Kant, I. (1987). The critique of pure reason. In *Great books of the Western world: Vol. 42. Kant.* Chicago: Encyclopaedia Britannica. (Original work published 1781)

Kaplan, C. A., & Simon, H. A. (1990). In search of insight. *Cognitive Psychology, 22,* 374–419.

Karmiloff-Smith, A. (1986). From meta-processes to conscious access: Evidence from children's metalinguistic and repair data. *Cognition, 23,* 95–147.

Katz, J. J. (1972). *Semantic theory*. New York: Harper & Row.

Katz, J. J., & Fodor, J. A. (1963). The structure of a semantic theory. *Language, 39,* 170–210.

Kay, P. (1975). Synchronic variability and diachronic changes in basic color terms. *Language in Society, 4,* 257–270.

Kaye, D. H. (1989). The probability of an ultimate issue: The strange case of paternity testing. *Iowa Law Review, 75,* 75–109.

Kearins, J. M. (1981). Visual spatial memory in Australian aboriginal children of the desert regions. *Cognitive Psychology, 13,* 434–460.

Keating, D. P. (1984). The emperor's new clothes: The "new look" in intelligence research. In R. J. Sternberg (Ed.), *Advances in the psychology of human intelligence* (Vol. 2, pp. 1–45). Hillsdale, NJ: Lawrence Erlbaum Associates.

Keating, D. P., & Bobbitt, B. L. (1978). Individual and developmental differences in cognitive-processing components of mental ability. *Child Development, 49,* 155–167.

Keil, F. C. (1979). *Semantic and conceptual development*. Cambridge, MA: Harvard University Press.

Keil, F. C. (1986). Conceptual domains and the acquisition of metaphor. *Cognitive Development, 1,* 73–96.

Keil, F. C. (1989). *Concepts, kinds, and cognitive development*. Cambridge, MA: MIT Press.

Keil, F. C. (1992). The origins of autonomous biology. In M. R. Gunnan & M. Maratsos (Eds.), *Minnesota Symposium on Child Psychology: Modularity and constraints on language and cognition* (pp. 103–137). Hillsdale, NJ: Lawrence Erlbaum Associates.

Keil, F. C. (1994). The birth and nurturance of concepts by domains: The origins of concepts of living things. In L. A. Hirschfeld & S. A. Gelman (Eds.), *Mapping the mind: Domain specificity in cognition and culture.* New York: Cambridge University Press.

Keil, F. C., Smith, W. C., Simons, D. J., & Levin, D. T. (1998). Two dogmas of conceptual empiricism: Implications for hybrid models of the structure of knowledge. *Cognition, 65,* 103–135.

Kelemen, D., & Bloom, P. (1994). Domain-specific knowledge in simple categorization tasks. *Psychonomic Bulletin and Review, 1,* 390–395.

Keller, E. (1976). Gambits. *TESL Talk, 7*(2), 18–21.

Kihlstrom, J. F. (1990). The psychological unconscious. In L. A. Pervin (Ed.), *Handbook of personality: Theory and research* (pp. 445–464). New York: Guilford Press.

Kimura, D. (1981). Neural mechanisms in manual signing. *Sign Language Studies, 33,* 291–312.

Kimura, D. (1987). Are men's and women's brains really different? *Canadian Psychology, 28,* 133–147.

Kintsch, W. (1974). *The representation of meaning in memory.* Hillsdale, NJ: Lawrence Erlbaum Associates.

Kintsch, W. (1988). The role of knowledge in discourse comprehension: A construction-integration model. *Psychological Review, 95,* 163–182.

Kintsch, W. (1990). The representation of knowledge and the use of knowledge in discourse comprehension. In C. Graumann & R. Dietrich (Eds.), *Language in the social context.* Amsterdam: Elsevier.

Kintsch, W., & Keenan, J. (1973). Reading rate and retention as a function of the number of propositions in the base structure of sentences. *Cognitive Psychology, 5,* 257–274.

Kintsch, W., & van Dijk, T. A. (1978). Toward a model of text comprehension and production. *Psychological Review, 85,* 363–394.

Kipling, R. (1985). Working-tools. In B. Ghiselin (Ed.), *The creative process: A symposium* (pp. 161–163). Berkeley, CA: University of California Press. (Original article published 1937)

Kirby, K. N. (1994). Probabilities and utilities of fictional outcomes in Wason's four-card selection task. *Cognition, 51,* 1–28.

Klahr, D., Langley, P., & Neches, R. (1987). *Production-system models of learning and development.* Cambridge, MA: MIT Press.

Klayman, J., & Ha, Y. (1987). Confirmation, disconfirmation, and information in hypothesis testing. *Psychological Review, 94,* 211–228.

Kliegl, R., Mayr, U., & Krampe, R. T. (1994). Time-accuracy functions for determining process and person differences: An application to cognitive aging. *Cognitive Psychology, 26,* 134–164.

Knapp, A. G., & Anderson, J. A. (1984). Theory of categorization based on distributed memory storage. *Journal of Experimental Psychology: Learning, Memory, & Cognition, 10,* 616–637.

Koehler, J. J. (1996). The base rate of fallacy reconsidered: Descriptive, normative, and methodological challenges. *Behavioral & Brain Sciences, 19,* 1–53.

Koestler, A. (1964). *The act of creation.* New York: Dell.

Kolb, B., & Whishaw, I. Q. (1990). *Fundamentals of human neuropsychology* (3rd ed.). New York: W. H. Freeman.

Kolodner, J. L. (1993). *Case-based reasoning.* San Mateo, CA: Morgan Kaufmann.

Komatsu, L. K. (1992). Recent views of conceptual structure. *Psychological Bulletin, 112,* 500–526.

Kotovsky, K., Hayes, J. R., & Simon, H. A. (1985). Why are some problems hard? Evidence from the Tower of Hanoi. *Cognitive Psychology, 17,* 248–294.

Kotovsky, K., & Simon, H. A. (1973). Empirical tests of a theory of human acquisition of concepts for sequential events. *Cognitive Psychology, 4,* 399–424.

Kotovsky, L., & Baillargeon, R. (1994). Calibration-based reasoning about collision events in 11–month-old infants. *Cognition, 51,* 107–129.

Kramer, D. A. (1990). Conceptualizing wisdom: The primacy of affect-cognition relations. In R. J. Sternberg (Ed.), *Wisdom: Its nature, origins, and development* (pp. 279–313). New York: Cambridge University Press.

Krechevsky, M., & Gardner, H. (1990). Approaching school intelligently: An infusion approach. In D. Kuhn (Ed.), *Developmental perspectives on teaching and learning thinking skills* (pp. 79–94). Basel, Switzerland: Karger.

Kris, E. (1952). *Psychoanalytic exploration in art*. New York: International Universities Press.

Krueger, J. (1998). On the perception of social consensus. In M. P. Zanna (Ed.), *Advances in Experimental Social Psychology* (Vol. 30, pp. 163–239). New York: Academic Press.

Kubie, L. S. (1958). *The neurotic distortion of the creative process*. Lawrence, KS: University of Kansas Press.

Kuhn, T. S (1970). *The structure of scientific revolutions* (2nd ed.). Chicago: University of Chicago Press.

Kutas, M., & Hillyard, S. A. (1980). Reading senseless sentences: Brain potentials reflect semantic incongruity. *Science, 207,* 203–205.

Kutas, M., & Van Patten, C. (1994). Psycholinguistics electrified: Event-related brain potential investigations. In M. A. Gernsbacher (Ed.), *Handbook of psycholinguistics* (pp. 83–143). San Diego, CA: Academic Press.

Labouvie-Vief, G. (1980). Beyond formal operations: Uses and limits of pure logic in life span development. *Human Development, 23,* 141–161.

Labouvie-Vief, G. (1990). Wisdom as integrated thought: Historical and developmental perspectives. In R. J. Sternberg (Ed.), *Wisdom: Its nature, origins, and development* (pp. 52–83). New York: Cambridge University Press.

Labouvie-Vief, G., & Schell, D. A. (1982). Learning and memory in later life. In B. B. Wolman (Ed.), *Handbook of developmental psychology* Englewood Cliffs, NJ: Prentice-Hall.

Ladefoged, P., & Maddieson, I. (1996). *The sounds of the world's languages*. Cambridge, MA: Blackwell.

Lakoff, G. (1987a). Cognitive models and prototype theory. In U. Neisser (Ed.), *Concepts and conceptual development: Ecological and intellectual factors in categorization. Emory symposia in cognition* (Vol. 1, pp. 63–100). New York: Cambridge University Press.

Lakoff, G. (1987b). *Women, fire, and dangerous things: What categories reveal about the mind*. Chicago: University of Chicago Press.

Landau, B. (1982). Will the real grandmother please stand up? The psychological reality of dual meaning representations. *Journal of Psycholinguistic Research, 11,* 47–62.

Langley, P., Simon, H. A., Bradshaw, G. L., & Zytkow, J. M. (1987). *Scientific discovery: Computational explorations of the creative process*. Cambridge, MA: MIT Press.

Larkin, J. H. (1983). *Mechanisms of effective problem representation in physics*. C. I. P. 434. Department of Psychology, Carnegie-Mellon University, Pittsburgh, PA.

Larkin, J. H., McDermott, J., Simon, D. P., & Simon, H. A. (1980). Expert and novice performance in solving physics problems. *Science, 208,* 1335–1342.

Larkin, J. H., & Simon, H. A. (1987). Why a diagram is (sometimes) worth ten thousand words. *Cognitive Science, 11,* 65–100.

Larson, G. E., Haier, R. J., LaCasse, L., & Hazen, K. (1995). Evaluation of a "mental effort" hypothesis for correlation between cortical metabolism and intelligence. *Intelligence, 21,* 267–278.

Lassaline, M. E., & Murphy, G. L. (1996). Induction and category coherence. *Psychonomic Bulletin and Review, 3,* 95–99.

Lave, J. (1988). *Cognition in practice: Mind, mathematics, and culture in everyday life*. New York: Cambridge University Press.

Lazar, I., & Darlington, R. (1982). Lasting effects of early education: A report from the consortium for longitudinal studies. *Monographs of the Society for Research in Child Development, 47*(2–3, Serial No. 195).

Lederer, R. (1991). *The miracle of language*. New York: Pocket Books.

LeFevre, J. A., & Dixon, P. (1986). Do written instructions need examples? *Cognition and Instruction, 3,* 1–30.

Lefford, A. (1946). The influence of emotional subject matter on logical reasoning. *Journal of General Psychology, 34,* 127–151.

Lehman, D. R., Lempert, R. O., & Nisbett, R. E. (1988). The effect of graduate training on reasoning: Formal discipline and thinking about everyday-life events. *American Psychologist, 43,* 431–442.

Lesgold, A., Rubinson, H., Feltovich, P., Glaser, R., Klopfer, D., & Wang, Y. (1988). Expertise in a complex skill: Diagnosing x-ray pictures. In M. T. H. Chi, R. Glaser, & M. Farr (Eds.), *The nature of expertise.* Hillsdale, N.J.: Lawrence Erlbaum Associates.

Lesgold, A. M., Feltovich, P. J., Glaser, R., & Wang, Y. (1981). *The acquisition of perceptual diagnostic skill in radiology.* (Technical Report No. PDS-1). Pittsburgh, PA: University of Pittsburgh, Learning Research and Development Center.

Leslie, A. M. (1995a). Pretending and believing: Issues in the theory of ToMM. In J. Mehler & S. Franck (Eds.), *Cognition on cognition special series* (pp. 193–220). Cambridge, MA: MIT Press.

Leslie, A. M. (1995b). A theory of agency. In D. Sperber & D. Premack (Eds.), *Causal cognition: A multidisciplinary debate. Symposia of the Fyssen Foundation* (pp. 121–149). Oxford, England: Clarendon Press.

Lewis, C., & Anderson, J. R. (1985). Discrimination of operator schemata in problem solving: Learning from examples. *Cognitive Psychology, 17,* 26–65.

Lewis, M., & Brooks-Gunn, J. (1981). Visual attention at three months as a predictor of cognitive functioning at two years of age. *Intelligence, 5,* 131–140.

Lichtenstein, S., & Slovic, P. (1971). Reversals of preference between bids and choices in gambling decisions. *Journal of Experimental Psychology, 89,* 46–55.

Lichtenstein, S., & Slovic, P. (1973). Response-induced reversals of preference in gambling: An extended replication in Las Vegas. *Journal of Experimental Psychology, 101,* 16–20.

Lipman, M. (1974). *Harry Stottlemeier's discovery.* Upper Montclair, NJ: Institute for the Advancement of Philosophy for Children.

Lipman, M. (1976). Philosophy for children. *Metaphilosophy, 1,* 17–19.

Lipman, M., Sharp, A. M., & Oscanyan, F. S. (1980). *Philosophy in the classroom.* Philadelphia: Temple University Press.

Locke, J. (1690/1961). Essays concerning human understanding. In *Great books of the Western world: Vol. 35. Locke, Berkeley, Hume.* Chicago: Encyclopedia Britannica.

Locke, J. L. (1994). Phases in the child's development of language. *American Scientist, 82,* 436–445.

Loehlin, J. C. (1989). Partitioning environmental and genetic contributions to behavioral development. *American Psychologist, 44,* 1285–1292.

Loftus, E. F. (1997). Memories for a past that never was. *Current Directions in Psychological Science, 6,* 60–65.

Loftus, E. F., & Palmer, J. C. (1974). Reconstruction of automobile destruction: An example of the interaction between language and memory. *Journal of Verbal Learning and Verbal Behavior, 13,* 585–589.

Lonner, W. J. (1989). The introductory psychology text: Beyond Ekman, Whorf, and biased IQ tests. In D. M. Keats, D. Munro, & L. Mann (Eds.), *Heterogeneity in cross-cultural.* Amsterdam: Swets & Zeitlinger.

Loomes, G. (1987). Testing for regret and disappointment in choice under uncertainty. *Economic Journal, 97,* 118–129.

Loomes, G., & Sugden, R. (1982). Regret theory: An alternative theory of rational choice under uncertainty. *Economic Journal, 92,* 805–824.

Loomes, G., & Sugden, R. (1987). Testing for regret and disappointment in choice under uncertainty. *Economic Journal, 97,* 118–129.

Lubart, T. I. (1990). Creativity and cross-cultural variation. *International Journal of Psychology, 25,* 39–59.

Lubart, T. I. (1994). Creativity. In R. J. Sternberg (Ed.), *Thinking and problem solving* (pp. 290–332). San Diego, CA: Academic Press.

Lubart, T. I., & Sternberg, R. J. (1995). An investment approach to creativity: Theory and data. In

S. M. Smith, T. B. Ward, & R. A. Finke (Eds.), *The creative cognition approach* (pp. 269–302). Cambridge, MA: MIT Press.

Luchins, A. S. (1942). Mechanization in problem solving. *Psychological Monographs, 54,* No. 248.

Luchins, A. S., & Luchins, E. H. (1950). New experimental attempts at preventing mechanization in problem solving. *Journal of General Psychology, 42,* 279–297.

Lyons, J. (1977). *Semantics.* New York: Cambridge University Press.

MacKinnon, D. W. (1965). Personality and the realization of creative potential. *American Psychologist, 20,* 273–281.

Maduro, R. (1976). Artistic creativity in a Brahmin painter community. *Research monograph 1.* Berkeley, CA: Center for South and Southeast Asia Studies, University of California.

Mahoney, M. J. (1977). Publication prejudices. *Cognitive Therapy and Research, 1,* 161–175.

Maier, N. R. F. (1931). Reasoning in humans II. The solution of a problem and its appearance in consciousness. *Journal of Comparative Psychology, 12,* 181–194.

Malgady, R., & Johnson, M. (1976). Modifiers in metaphors: Effects of constituent phrase similarity on the interpretation of figurative sentences. *Journal of Psycholinguistic Research, 5,* 43–52.

Malt, B. C. (1990). Features and beliefs in the mental representation of categories. *Journal of Memory and Language, 29,* 289–315.

Malt, B. C. (1995). Category coherence in cross-cultural perspective. *Cognitive Psychology, 29,* 85–148.

Malt, B. C., & Smith, E. E. (1984). Correlated properties in natural categories. *Journal of Verbal Learning and Verbal Behavior, 23,* 250–269.

Mandler, J. M. (1990). A new perspective on cognitive development in infancy. *American Scientist, 78,* 236–243.

Manis, M., Dovalina, I., Avis, N. E., & Cardoze, S. (1980). Base rates can affect individual predictions. *Journal of Personality and Social Psychology, 38,* 287–298.

Manktelow, K. I., & Over, D. E. (1991). Social roles and utilities in reasoning with deontic conditionals. *Cognition, 39,* 85–105.

Marcus, D., & Overton, W. (1978). The development of gender constancy and sex role preferences. *Child Development, 49,* 434–444.

Marcus, G., Pinker, S., Ullman, M., Hollander, M., Rosen, T., & Xu, F. (1992). Overregularization in language acquisition. *Monographs of the Society for Research in Child Development, 57.*

Marcus, S. L., & Rips, L. J. (1979). Conditional reasoning. *Journal of Verbal Leaming and Verbal Behavior, 18,* 199–224.

Markman, E. M. (1977). Realizing that you don't understand: A preliminary investigation. *Child Development, 48,* 986–992.

Markman, E. M. (1979). Realizing that you don't understand: Elementary school children's awareness of inconsistencies. *Child Development, 50,* 643–655.

Markman, E. M. (1989). *Categorization and naming in children: Problems of induction.* Cambridge, MA: MIT Press.

Markovits, H. (1988). Conditional reasoning, representation and empirical evidence on a concrete task. *Quarterly Journal of Experimental Psychology: Human Experimental Psychology, 45,* 483–495.

Márquez, P. C. (1999). *The street is my home.* Stanford, CA: Stanford University Press.

Marr, D. (1982). *Vision: A computational investigation into the human representation and processing of visual information.* San Francisco: W. H. Freeman.

Martin, J. A. (1981). A longitudinal study of the consequences of early mother-infant interaction: A microanalytic approach. *Monographs of the Society for Research in Child Development, 46*(203, Serial No. 190).

Martin, L. (1986). Eskimo words for snow: A case study in the genesis and decay of an anthropological example. *American Psychologist, 88,* 418–423.

Maslow, A. (1967). A theory of metamotivation: The biological rooting of the value-life. *Journal of Humanistic Psychology, 7,* 93–127.

Maslow, A. (1968). *Toward a psychology of being.* New York: Van Nostrand.

Matarazzo, J. D. (1992). Biological and physiological correlates of intelligence. *Intelligence, 16*(3–4), 257–258.

Matz, M. (1982). Towards a process model for high school algebra errors. In D. Sleeman & J. S. Brown (Eds.), *Intelligent tutoring systems* (pp. 25–49). New York: Academic Press.

Mayer, R. E. (1982). Memory for algebra story problems. *Journal of Educational Psychology, 74,* 199–216.

Mayr, U., & Kliegl, R. (1993). Sequential and coordinative complexity: Age-based processing in figural transformations. *Journal of Experimental Psychology: Learning, Memory, & Cognition, 19*(6), 1297–1320.

McArthur, T. (Ed.). (1992). *The Oxford companion to the English language.* New York: Oxford University Press.

McCall, R. B. (1989). The development of intellectual functioning in infancy and the prediction of later IQ. In S. D. Osofsky (Ed.), *The handbook of infant development* (pp. 707–741). New York: John Wiley & Sons.

McCall, R. B., Kennedy, C. B., & Appelbaum, M. I. (1977). Magnitude of discrepancy and the distribution of attention in infants. *Child Development, 48,* 772–786.

McClelland, D. C., Atkinson, J. W., Clark, R. A., & Lowell, E. L. (1953). *The achievement motive.* New York: Appleton-Century-Crofts, Inc.

McCloskey, M. (1980). The stimulus familiarity problem in semantic memory research. *Journal of Verbal Learning and Verbal Behavior, 19,* 485–502.

McCloskey, M., Caramazza, A., & Green, B. (1980). Curvilinear motion in the absence of external forces: Naive beliefs about the motion of objects. *Science, 210,* 1139–1141.

McCloskey, M. & Glucksberg, S. (1978). Natural categories: Well defined or fuzzy sets? *Memory & Cognition, 6,* 462–472.

McCord, M., & de Neufville, R. (1985). *Eliminating the certainty effect problem in utility assessment: Theory and experiment.* Unpublished manuscript, Ohio State University, Columbus.

McGarry-Roberts, P. A., Stelmack, R. M., & Campbell, K. B. (1992). Intelligence, reaction time, and event-related potentials. *Intelligence, 16*(3–4), 289–313.

McKoon, G., & Ratcliff, R. (1992). Inference during reading. *Psychological Review, 99,* 440–466.

McNamara, T. P., & Sternberg, R. J. (1983). Mental models of word meaning. *Journal of Verbal Learning and Verbal Behavior, 22,* 449–474.

McNemar, Q. (1964). Lost our intelligence? Why? *American Psychologist, 19,* 871–882.

Meacham, J. A. (1983). Wisdom and the context of knowledge: Knowing that one doesn't know. In D. Kuhn & J. A. Meacham (Eds.), *On the development of developmental psychology* (pp. 111–134). Basel, Switzerland: Karger.

Meacham, J. A. (1990). The loss of wisdom. In R. J. Sternberg (Ed.), *Wisdom: Its nature, origins, and development* (pp. 181–211). New York: Cambridge University Press.

Medin, D. L. (1989). Concepts and conceptual structure. *American Psychologist, 44,* 1469–1481.

Medin, D. L., Altom, M. W., Edelson, S. M., & Freko, D. (1982). Correlated symptoms and simulated medical classification. *Journal of Experimental Psychology: Learning, Memory, & Cognition, 8,* 37–50.

Medin, D. L., Dewey, G., & Murphy, T. (1983). Relationships between item and category learning: Evidence that abstraction is not automatic. *Journal of Experimental Psychology: Learning, Memory, & Cognition, 9,* 607–625.

Medin, D. L., & Edelson, S. M. (1988). Problem structure and the use of base-rate information from experience. *Journal of Experimental Psychology: General, 117,* 68–85.

Medin, D. L., Goldstone, R. L., & Gentner, D. (1993). Respects for similarity. *Psychological Review, 100,* 254–278.

Medin, D. L., & Heit, E. (1994). Categorization. In D. E. Rumelhart & B. O. Martin (Eds.), *Handbook of cognition and perception: Cognitive science.* San Diego, CA: Academic Press.

Medin, D. L., Lynch, E. B., Coley, J. D., & Atran, S. (1997). Categorization and reasoning among tree experts: Do all roads lead to Rome? *Cognitive Psychology, 32,* 49–96.

Medin, D. L., & Ortony, A. (1989). Psychological essentialism. In S. Vosniadou & A. Ortony (Eds.), *Similarity and analogical reasoning* (pp. 179–195). Cambridge, England: Cambridge University Press.

Medin, D. L., & Ross, B. H. (1992). *Cognitive psychology*. Ft Worth, TX: Harcourt Brace Jovanovich.

Medin, D. L., & Schaffer, M. M. (1978). A context theory of classification learning. *Psychological Review, 85*, 207–238.

Medin, D. L., & Schwanenflugel, P. J. (1981). Linear separability in classification learning. *Journal of Experimental Psychology: Human Learning and Memory, 7*, 355–368.

Medin, D. L., & Smith, E. E. (1981). Strategies and classification learning. *Journal of Experimental Psychology: Human Learning and Memory, 7*, 241–253.

Medin, D. L., & Smith E. E. (1984). Concepts and concept formation. *Annual Review of Psychology, 35*, 113–138.

Medin, D. L., Wattenmaker, W. D., & Hampson, S. E. (1987). Family resemblance, conceptual cohesiveness, and category construction. *Cognitive Psychology, 19*, 242–279.

Mednick, M. T., & Andrews, F. M. (1967). Creative thinking and level of intelligence. *Journal of Creative Behavior, 1*, 428–431.

Mednick, S. A. (1962). The associative basis of the creative process. *Psychological Review, 69*, 220–232.

Meehl, P. E., & Rosen, A. (1955). Antecedent probability and the efficiency of psychometric signs, patterns, or cutting scores. *Psychological Bulletin, 52*, 194–216.

Mehler, J., Dupoux, E., Nazzi, T., & Dehaene-Lambertz, G. (1996). Coping with linguistic diversity: The infant's viewpoint. In J. L. Morgan & K. Demuth (Eds.), *Signal to syntax: Bootstrapping from speech to grammar in early acquisition* (pp. 101–116). Mahwah, NJ: Lawrence Erlbaum Associates.

Meier, R. P. (1991). Language acquisition by deaf children. *American Scientist, 79*, 60–76.

Mervis, C. B., & Rosch, E. (1981). Categorization of natural objects. *Annual Review of Psychology, 32*, 89–115.

Metcalfe, J., & Fisher, R. P. (1986). The relation between recognition memory and classification learning. *Memory and Cognition, 14*, 164–173.

Metcalfe, J. & Wiebe, D. (1987). Intuition in insight and noninsight problem solving. *Memory and Cognition, 15*, 238–246.

Meyerowitz, B. E., & Chaiken, S. (1987). The effect of message framing on breast self-examination attitudes, intentions, and behavior. *Journal of Personality and Social Psychology, 52*, 500–510.

Michalski, R. S. (1989). Two-tiered concept meaning, inferential matching, and conceptual cohesiveness. In S. Vosniadou & A. Ortony (Eds.), *Similarity and analogical reasoning* (pp. 122–145). New York: Cambridge University Press.

Mill, J. S. (1843). *A system of logic, ratiocinative and inductive*. London: J. W. Parker.

Miller, G. (1956). The magical number seven, plus or minus two: Some limits on our capacity for processing information. *Psychological Review, 63*, 81–97.

Miller, G. A. (1979). Images and models, similes and metaphors. In A. Ortony (Ed.), *Metaphor and thought* (pp. 202–250). New York: Cambridge University Press.

Miller, G. A., Galanter, E. H., & Pribram, K. H. (1960). *Plans and the structure of behavior*. New York: Holt, Rinehart & Winston.

Miller, G. A., & Gildea, P. M. (1987). How children learn words. *Scientific American, 257*(3), 94–99.

Miller, R. A., Pople, H., & Myers, J. (1982). Internist-I, an experimental computer-based diagnostic consultant for general internal medicine. *New England Journal of Medicine, 307*, 494.

Minsky, M. (Ed.). (1968). *Semantic information processing*. Cambridge, MA: MIT Press.

Minsky, M. (1975). A framework for representing knowledge. In P. H. Winston (Ed.), *The psychology of computer vision* (pp. 211–277). New York: McGraw-Hill.

Minsky, M. L., & Papert, S. (1969). *Perceptrons: An introduction to computational geometry*. Cambridge, MA: MIT Press.

Mirmiran, M., van Someren, E. J. W., & Swaab, D. F. (1996). Is brain plasticity preserved during aging and in Alzheimer's disease? *Behavioural Brain Research, 78,* 43–48.

Montavon, E., Furman, L., Barron, B., Bransford, J. D., & Hasselbring, T. S. (1989, April). *The effects of varied context training and irrelevant information training on the transfer of math problem solving skills.* Paper presented at the meeting of the American Educational Research Association, San Francisco.

Morgan, J. J. B. (1945). Attitudes of students towards the Japanese. *Journal of Social Psychology, 21,* 219–227.

Morgan, J. J. B., & Morton, J. T. (1944). The distortion of syllogistic reasoning produced by personal convictions. *Journal of Social Psychology, 20,* 39–59.

Morton, T. U. (1978). Intimacy and reciprocity of exchange: A comparison of spouses and strangers. *Journal of Personality and Social Psychology, 36,* 72–81.

Moshman, E. (1998). Cognitive development beyond childhood. In W. Damon (Ed.-in-chief) & D. Kuhn & R. S. Siegler (Vol. Eds.), *Handbook of child psychology* (Vol. 2, pp. 947–978). New York: John Wiley & Sons.

Mumford, M. D., & Gustafson, S. B. (1988). Creativity syndrome: Integration, application, and innovation. *Psychological Bulletin, 103,* 27–43.

Murphy, G. L. (1993). Theories and concept formation. In I. Van Mechelen, J. Hampton, R. Michalski, & P. Theuns (Eds.), *Categories and concepts: Theoretical views and inductive data analysis* (pp. 173–200). London: Academic Press.

Murphy, G. L., & Allopenna, P. D. (1994). The locus of knowledge effects in concept learning. *Journal of Experimental Psychology: Learning, Memory, and Cognition, 20,* 904–919.

Murphy, G. L., & Brownell, H. H. (1985). Category differentiation in object recognition: Typicality constraints on the basic category advantage. *Journal of Experimental Psychology: Learning, Memory, and Cognition, 11,* 70–84.

Murphy, G. L., & Medin, D. L. (1985). The role of theories in conceptual coherence. *Psychological Review, 92,* 289–316.

Murphy, G. L., & Wisniewski, E. J. (1989). Categorizing objects in isolation and in scenes: What a superordinate is good for. *Journal of Experimental Psychology: Learning, Memory, and Cognition, 15,* 572–586.

Mynatt, C. R., Doherty, M. E., & Tweney, R. D. (1977). Confirmation bias in a simulated research environment: An experimental study of scientific inference. *Quarterly Journal of Experimental Psychology, 29,* 85–95.

Mynatt, C. R., Doherty, M. E., & Tweney, R. D. (1978). Consequences of confirmation and disconfirmation in a simulated research environment. *Quarterly Journal of Experimental Psychology, 30,* 395–406.

Nakamura, G. V. (1985). Knowledge-based classification of ill-defined categories. *Memory and Cognition, 13,* 377–384.

National Center for Educational Statistics, National Assessment of Educational Progress. (1997). *NAEP 1996 trends in academic progress.* Washington, DC: U.S. Department of Education.

Neimark, E. D. (1975). Intellectual development during adolescence. In F. D. Horowitz (Ed.), *Review of child development research* (Vol. 4). Chicago: University of Chicago Press.

Neisser, U. (1967). *Cognitive psychology.* New York: Appleton-Century-Crofts.

Neisser, U. (1987). From direct perception to conceptual structure. In U. Neisser (Ed.), *Concepts and conceptual development: Ecological and intellectual factors in categorization. Emory symposia in cognition* (Vol. 1, pp. 11–24). New York: Cambridge University Press.

Neisser, U. (Ed.). (1998). *The rising curve.* Washington, DC: American Psychological Association.

Neisser, U., Boodoo, G., Bouchard, T. J. Jr., Boykin, A. W., Brody, N., Ceci, S. J, Halpern, D. F., Loehlin, J. C., Perloff, R., Sternberg, R. J., Urbina, S. (1996). Intelligence: Knowns and unknowns. *American Psychologist, 51,* 77–101.

Nelson, D. G. K. (1995). Principle-based inferences in young children's categorization: Revisiting the impact of function on the naming of artifacts. *Cognitive Development, 10,* 347–380.

Nelson, K. (1973). Structure and strategy in learning to talk. *Monograph of the Society for Research in Child Development, 38* (Serial No. 149).

Nelson, T. O., & Narens, L. (1994). Why investigate metacognition? In J. Metcalfe & A. P. Shimamura (Eds.), *Metacognition—Knowing about knowing.* Norwood, NJ: Ablex.

Nettelbeck, T. (1987). Inspection time and intelligence. In P. A. Vernon (Ed.), *Speed of information-processing and intelligence* (pp. 295–346). Norwood, NJ: Ablex.

Nettelbeck, T., & Lally, M. (1976). Inspection time and measured intelligence. *British Journal of Psychology, 67,* 17–22.

Nettelbeck, T., & Rabbitt, P. M. A. (1992). Aging, cognitive performance, and mental speed. *Intelligence, 16,* 189–205.

Nettelbeck, T., Rabbitt, P. M. A., Wilson, C., & Batt, R. (1996). Uncoupling learning from initial recall: The relationship between speed and memory deficits in old age. *British Journal of Psychology, 87,* 593–607.

Nettelbeck, T., & Young, R. (1996). Intelligence and savant syndrome: Is the whole greater than the sum of the fragments? *Intelligence, 22,* 49–67.

Neubauer, A. C., & Bucik, V. (1996). The mental speed–IQ relationship: Unitary or modular. *Intelligence, 22,* 23–48.

Newell, A. (1990). *Unified theories of cognition.* Cambridge, MA: Harvard University Press.

Newell, A., Shaw, J. C., & Simon, H. A. (1957). Problem solving in humans and computers. *Carnegie Technical, 21*(4), 34–38.

Newell, A., & Simon, H. A. (1972). *Human problem solving.* Englewood Cliffs, NJ: Prentice-Hall

Newport, E. L. (1990). Maturational constraints on language learning. *Cognitive Science, 14,* 11–28.

Nickerson, R. S., Perkins, D. N., & Smith, E. E. (1985). *The teaching of thinking.* Hillsdale, NJ: Lawrence Erlbaum Associates.

Nisbett, R. E., & Borgida, E. (1975). Attribution and the psychology of prediction. *Journal of Personality and Social Psychology, 32,* 932–943.

Nisbett, R. E., Fong, G. T., Lehman, D. R., & Cheng, P. W. (1987). Teaching reasoning. *Science, 238,* 625–631.

Nisbett, R. E., Krantz, D. H., Jepson, D., & Kunda, Z. (1983). The use of statistical heuristics in everyday inductive reasoning. *Psychological Review, 90,* 339–363.

Nisbett, R. E., & Ross, L. (1980). *Human inference: Strategies and shortcomings of social judgment.* Englewood Cliffs, NJ: Prentice-Hall.

Nisbett, R. E., & Wilson, T. D. (1977). Telling more than we can know: Verbal reports on mental processes. *Psychological Review, 84,* 231–259.

Norman, D. A. (1981). Categorization of action slips. *Psychological Review, 88,* 1–15.

Norman, D. A., & Rumelhart, D. E. (1975). *Explorations in cognition.* San Francisco: W. H. Freeman.

Norman, G. R., & Schmidt, H. G. (1992). The psychological basis of problem-based learning: A review of the evidence. *Academic Medicine, 67,* 557–565.

Nosofsky, R. M. (1986). Attention, similarity, and the attention-categorization relationship. *Journal of Experimental Psychology: General, 115,* 39–57.

Nosofsky, R. M. (1988). Exemplar-based accounts of relations between classification, recognition, and typicality. *Journal of Experimental Psychology: Learning, Memory, and Cognition, 14,* 700–708.

Nosofsky, R. M. (1989). Further tests of an exemplar-similarity approach to relating identification and categorization. *Perception and Psychophysics, 45,* 279–290.

Nosofsky, R. M. (1991). Tests of an exemplar model for relating perceptual classification and recognition memory. *Journal of Experimental Psychology: Human Perception and Performance, 17,* 3–27.

Nosofsky, R. M., Palmeri, T. J., & McKinley, S. C. (1994). Rule-plus-exception model of classification learning. *Psychological Review, 101,* 53–79.

Novick, L. R. (1988). Analogical transfer, problem similarity, and expertise. *Journal of Experimental Psychology: Learning, Memory, & Cognition. 14*, 510–520.

Novick, L. R., & Holyoak, K. J. (1991). Mathematical problem solving by analogy. *Journal of Experimental Psychology: Learning, Memory, & Cognition, 17*, 398–415.

Noy, P. (1969). A revision of the psychoanalytic theory of the primary process. *International Journal of Psychoanalysis, 50*, 155–178.

Nuñes, T. (1994). Street intelligence. In R. J. Sternberg (Ed.), *Encyclopedia of human intelligence* (Vol. 2, pp. 1045–1049). New York: Macmillan.

Oakes, L. M., & Cohen, L. B. (1995). Infant causal perception. In C. Rovee-Collier & L. P. Lipsitt (Eds.), *Advances in infancy research* (Vol. 9). Norwood, NJ: Ablex.

Oaksford, M., & Chater, N. (1994). A rational analysis of the selection task as optimal data selection. *Psychological Review, 101*, 608–631.

Ochse, R. (1990). *Before the gates of excellence.* New York: Cambridge University Press.

Ogbu, J. U. (1986). The consequences of the American caste system. In U. Neisser (Ed.), *The school achievement of minority children.* Hillsdale, NJ: Lawrence Erlbaum Associates.

Ojemann, G. A. (1975). The thalamus and language. *Brain and Language, 2*, 1–120.

Ojemann, G. A. (1982). Models of the brain organization for higher integrative functions derived with electrical stimulation techniques. *Human Neurobiology, 1*, 243–250.

Ojemann, G. A., & Mateer, C. (1979). Human language cortex: Localization of memory, syntax, and sequential motor–phoneme identification systems. *Science, 205*, 1401–1403.

Ojemann, G. A., & Whitaker, H. A. (1978). The bilingual brain. *Archives of Neurology, 35*, 409–412.

Okagaki, L., & Sternberg, R. J. (1993). Parental beliefs and children's school performance. *Child Development, 64*, 36–56.

Okamato, Y. (1992, April). *Implications of the notion of central conceptual structures for assessment.* Paper presented at the annual meeting of the American Education Research Association, San Francisco.

Ortony, A. (1979). The role of similarity in similes and metaphors. In A. Ortony (Ed.), *Metaphor and thought* (pp. 186–201). New York: Cambridge University Press.

Osborn, A. F. (1953). *Applied imagination* (rev. ed.). New York: Charles Scribner's Sons.

Osherson, D. (1975). Logic and models of logical thinking. In R. J. Falmagne (Ed.), *Reasoning: Representation and process in children and adults.* Hillsdale, NJ: Lawrence Erlbaum Associates.

Osherson, D. N. (1976). *Logical abilities in children* (Vol. 4). Hillside, NJ: Lawrence Erlbaum Associates.

Osherson, D. N., Smith, E. E., & Shafir, E. B. (1986) Some origins of belief. *Cognition, 24*, 197–224.

Osherson, D. N., Smith, E. E., Wilkie, O., Lopez, A., & Shafir, E. B. (1990). Category-based induction. *Psychological Review, 97*, 185–200.

Oyama, S. (1976). A sensitive period for the acquisition of a nonnative phonological system. *Journal of Psycholinguistic Research, 5*, 261–283.

Paige, J. M., & Simon, H. A. (1966). Cognitive processes in solving algebra word problems. In B. Kleinmuntz (Ed.), *Problem solving: Research, method, and theory* (pp. 51–118). New York: John Wiley & Sons.

Palinscar, A. S., & Brown, A. L. (1984). Reciprocal teaching of comprehension-fostering and monitoring activities. *Cognition and Instruction, 1*, 117–175.

Palincsar, A. S., & Brown, A. L. (1988). Teaching and practicing thinking skills to promote comprehension in the context of group problem solving. *Remedial and Special Education, 9*, 53–59.

Paradis, M. (1977). Bilingualism and aphasia. In H. A. Whitaker & H. Whitaker (Eds.), *Studies in neurolinguistics* (Vol. 3). New York: Academic Press.

Paradis, M. (1981). Neurolinguistic organization of a bilingual's two languages. In J. E. Copeland & P. W. Davis (Eds.), *The seventh LACUS forum.* Columbia, SC: Hornbeam Press.

Pascual-Leone, J. (1984). Attentional, dialectic, and mental effort. In L. M. Commons, F. A. Richards, & C. Armon (eds.), *Beyond formal operations* (pp. 182–215). New York: Plenum.

Pascual-Leone, J. (1990). An essay on wisdom: Toward organismic processes that make it possible. In R. J. Sternberg (Ed.), *Wisdom: Its nature, origins, and development* (pp. 244–278). New York: Cambridge University Press.

Patel, V. L. & Groen, G. J. (1991). The general and specific nature of medical expertise: A critical look. In A. Ericsson, & J. Smith, (Eds.), *Toward a general theory of expertise: Prospects and limits* (pp. 93–125). New York: Cambridge University Press.

Pauker, S. G., & Kopelman, R. I. (1992). Clinical problem solving. *New England Journal of Medicine, 326,* 40–43.

Pavlov, I. P. (1955). *Selected works.* Moscow: Foreign Languages Publishing House.

Payne, J. W., Bettman, J. R., & Johnson, E. J. (1993). The use of multiple strategies in judgment and choice. In N. J. Castellan, Jr. (Ed.), *Individual and group decision making: Current issues* (pp. 19–39). Mahwah, NJ: Lawrence Erlbaum Associates.

Payne. S., & Squibb, H. (1990). Algebra mal-rules and cognitive accounts of error. *Cognitive Science, 14,* 445–481.

Penfield, W., & Roberts, L. (1959). *Speech and brain mechanisms.* Princeton, NJ: Princeton University Press.

Penrose, R. (1989). *The emperor's new mind: Concerning computers, minds, and the laws of physics.* New York: Oxford University Press.

Perkins, D. N. (1981). *The mind's best work.* Cambridge, MA: Harvard University Press.

Perkins, D. N. (1986). *Knowledge as design: Critical and creative thinking for teachers and learners.* Hillsdale, NJ: Lawrence Erlbaum Associates.

Perkins, D. N. (1995). *Outsmarting IQ: The emerging science of learnable intelligence.* New York: Free Press.

Perkins, D. N. (1997). Creativity's camel: The role of analogy in invention. In T. B. Ward, S. M. Smith, & J. Vaid (Eds.), *Creative thought: An investigation of conceptual structures and processes* (pp. 523–538). Washington, DC: American Psychological Association.

Perkins, D. N. (1998). In the country of the blind: An appreciation of Donald Campbell's vision of creative thought. *Journal of Creative Behavior, 32,* 177–191.

Perkins, D. N., & Grotzer, T. A. (1997). Teaching intelligence. *American Psychologist, 52,* 1125–1133.

Perlmutter, D. (Ed.). (1983). *Studies in relational grammar* (Vol. 1). Chicago: University of Chicago Press.

Petersen, S. E., Fox, P. T., Posner, M. I., & Mintun, M. (1989). Positron emission tomographic studies of the processing of single words. *Journal of Cognitive Neuroscience, 1,* 153–170.

Petersen, S. E., Fox, P. T., Posner, M. I., Mintun, M., & Raichle, M. E. (1988). Positron-emission tomographic studies of the cortical anatomy of single-word processing. *Nature, 331,* 585–589.

Petitto, L., & Marentette, P. F. (1991). Babbling in the manual mode: Evidence for the ontogeny of language. *Science, 251,* 1493–1499.

Piaget, J. (1946). *The development of children's concept of time.* Paris: Presses Universitaires de France.

Piaget, J. (1952). *The origins of intelligence in children.* New York: International Universities Press.

Piaget, J. (1954). *The construction of reality in the child.* New York: Basic Books.

Piaget, J. (1965). *The child's conception of number.* New York: W. W. Norton.

Piaget, J. (1969). *The child's conception of physical causality.* Totowa, NJ: Littlefield, Adams.

Piaget, J. (1972). *The psychology of intelligence.* Totowa, NJ: Littlefield, Adams.

Pianta, R. C., & Egeland, B. (1994). Predictors of instability in children's mental test performance at 24, 48, and 96 months. *Intelligence, 18,* 145–163.

Pichert, J. W., Anderson, R. C. (1977). Taking different perspectives on a story. *Journal of Educational Psychology, 69,* 309–315.

Pinker, S. (1994). *The language instinct.* New York: William Morrow.

Pirolli, P. L., & Anderson, J. R. (1985). The role of practice in fact retrieval. *Journal of Experimental Psychology: Learning, Memory, & Cognition, 11,* 136–153.

Pirolli, P. (1991). Effects of examples and their explanations in a lesson on recursion: A production system analysis. *Cognition and Instruction, 8,* 207–259.

Pirolli, P., & Recker, M. (1994). Learning strategies and transfer in the domain of programming. *Cognition & Instruction, 12,* 235–275.

Plomin, R. (1997). Identifying genes for cognitive abilities and disabilities. In R. J. Sternberg & E. L. Grigorenko (Eds.), *Intelligence, heredity, and environment* (pp. 89–104). New York: Cambridge University Press.

Plomin, R., & McClearn, G. E. (Eds.) (1993). *Nature, nurture and psychology.* Washington D.C.: APA Books.

Plous, S. (1993). *The psychology of judgment and decision making.* New York: McGraw-Hill Book Company.

Policastro, E., & Gardner, H. (1999). From case studies to robust generalizations: An approach to the study of creativity. In R. J. Sternberg (Ed.), *Handbook of creativity* (pp. 213–225). New York: Cambridge University Press.

Poon, L. W. (1987). *Myths and truisms: Beyond extant analyses of speed of behavior and age.* Address to the Eastern Psychological Association Convention.

Posner, M. I., & Keele, S. W. (1967). Decay of visual information from a single letter. *Science, 158,* 137–139.

Posner, M. I., & Keele, S. W. (1968). On the genesis of abstract ideas. *Journal of Experimental Psychology, 77*(3, 1), 353–363.

Posner, M. I., & Mitchell, R. F. (1967). Chronometric analysis of classification. *Psychological Review, 74,* 392–409.

Priest, A. G., & Lindsay, R. O. (1992). New light on novice and expert differences in physics problem solving. *British Journal of Psychology, 83,* 389–405.

Psotka, J., Massey, L. D., & Mutter, S. A. (1988). *Intelligent tutoring systems: Lessons learned.* Hillsdale, NJ: Lawrence Erlbaum Associates.

Pullum, G. K. (1991). *The great Eskimo vocabulary hoax and other irreverent essays on the study of language.* Chicago: University of Chicago Press.

Putnam, H. (1988). *Representation and reality.* Cambridge, MA: MIT Press.

Quillian, M. R. (1966). *Semantic memory.* Cambridge, MA: Bolt, Beranak, & Newman.

Rand, Y., Tannenbaum, A. J., & Feuerstein, R. (1979). Effects of Instrumental Enrichment on the pseudo-educational development of low-functioning adolescents. *Journal of Educational Psychology, 71,* 751–763.

Ratcliff, R., & McKoon, G. (1978). Priming in item recognition: Evidence for the propositional structure of sentences. *Journal of Verbal Learning and Verbal Behavior, 17,* 403–417.

Reder, L. M., Charney, D. H., & Morgan, K. I. (1986). The role of elaborations in learning a skill from an instructional text. *Memory and Cognition, 14,* 64–78.

Reed, S. K. (1972). Pattern recognition and categorization. *Cognitive Psychology, 3,* 382–407.

Reed, S. K., Dempster, A., & Ettinger, M. (1985). Usefulness of analogous solutions for solving algebra word problems. *Journal of Experimental Psychology: Learning, Memory, and Cognition, 11,* 106–125.

Reed, T. E. (1993). Effect of enriched (complex) environment on nerve conduction velocity: New data and review of implications for the speed of information processing. *Intelligence. 17,* 533–540.

Reed, T. E., & Jensen, A. R. (1991). Arm nerve conduction velocity (NCV), brain NCV, reaction time, and intelligence. *Intelligence, 15,* 33–47.

Reed, T. E., & Jensen, A. R. (1993). Choice reaction time and visual pathway nerve conduction velocity both correlate with intelligence but appear not to correlate with each other: Implications for information processing. *Intelligence, 17,* 191–203.

Reeves, L. M., & Weisberg, R. W. (1993). On the concrete nature of human thinking: Content and context in analogical transfer. *Educational Psychology, 13,* 245–258.

Rehder, B., & Hastie, R. (1996). The moderating influence of variability on belief revision. *Psychonomic Bulletin & Review, 3,* 499–503.

Reitman, J. (1976). Skilled perception in GO: Deducing memory structures from interresponse times. *Cognitive Psychology, 8,* 336–356.

Renzulli, J. S. (1986). The three-ring conception of giftedness: A developmental model for creative productivity. In R. J. Sternberg & J. E. Davidson (Eds.), *Conceptions of giftedness* (pp. 53–92). New
York: Cambridge University Press.

Resnick, L. B. (1980). *The role of invention in the development of mathematical competence.* Unpublished manuscript.

Resnick, L. B. (1986). The development of mathematical intuition. In M. Perlmutter (Ed.), *Perspectives
on intellectual development: The Minnesota Symposia on child psychology* (Vol. 19, pp. 159–194).
Minneapolis: University of Minnesota Press.

Resnick, L. B., Nesher, P., Leonard, F., Magone M., Omanson, S. F., & Peled, I. (1989). Conceptual
bases of arithmetic errors: The case of decimal fractions. *Journal for Research in Mathematics Education, 20,* 8–27.

Reusser, K. (1988). Problem solving beyond the logic of things: Contextual effects on understanding and
solving word problems. *Instructional Science, 17,* 309–338.

Revlin, R. & Leirer, V. O. (1978). The effect of personal biases on syllogistic reasoning: Rational decisions from personalized representations. In R. Revlin & R. E. Mayer (Eds.), *Human reasoning.*
Washington, DC: Winston.

Revlis, R. (1975). Two models of syllogistic reasoning: Feature selection and conversion. *Journal of
Verbal Learning and Verbal Behavior, 14,* 180–195.

Rice, M. L. (1989). Children's language acquisition. *American Psychologist, 44,* 149–156.

Riegel, K. F. (1973). Dialectical operations: The final period of cognitive development. *Human Development, 16,* 346–370.

Riley, M. S., Greeno, J. G., & Heller, J. (1983). The development of children's problem solving ability
in arithmetic. In H. P. Ginsburg (Ed.), *The development of mathematical thinking* (pp. 153–196).
New York: Academic Press.

Rips, L. J. (1975). Inductive judgments about natural categories. *Journal of Verbal Learning and Verbal Behavior, 14,* 665–681.

Rips, L. J. (1983). Cognitive processes in propositional reasoning. *Psychological Review, 90,* 38–71.

Rips, L. J. (1989a). The psychology of knights and knaves. *Cognition, 31,* 85–116.

Rips, L. J. (1989b). Similarity, typicality, and categorization. In S. Vosniadou & A. Ortony (Eds.), *Similarity and analogical reasoning* (pp. 21–59). New York: Cambridge University Press.

Rips. L. J. (1990). Reasoning. *Annual Review of Psychology, 41,* 321–353.

Rips, L. J. (1994). *The psychology of proof: Deductive reasoning in human thinking.* Cambridge, MA:
MIT Press.

Rips, L. J., Shoben, E. J., & Smith, E. E. (1973). Semantic distance and the verification of semantic relations. *Journal of Verbal Learning and Verbal Behavior, 12,* 1–20.

Rissland, E. L. (1985). Artificial intelligence and the learning of mathematics: A tutorial sampling. In
E. A. Silver (Ed.), *Teaching and learning mathematical problem solving: Multiple research perspectives* (pp. 147–176). Hillsdale, NJ: Lawrence Erlbaum Associates.

Robinson, D. N. (1995*). An intellectual history of psychology* (3rd ed.). Madison: University of Wis-
consin Press.

Roe, A. (1952). *The making of a scientist.* New York: Dodd, Mead.

Roe, A. (1972). Patterns of productivity of scientists. *Science, 176,* 940–941.

Rogers, C. R. (1954). Toward a theory of creativity. *ETC: A Review of General Semantics, 11,* 249–260.

Rogoff, B. (1986). The development of strategic use of context in spatial memory. In M. Perlmutter
(Ed.), *Perspectives on intellectual development.* Hillsdale, NJ: Lawrence Erlbaum Associates.

Roitblat, H. L., & Meyer, J.-A. (Eds.) (1995). *Comparative approaches to cognitive science.* Cambridge,
MA: MIT Press.

Rosch, E. (1975). Cognitive representations of semantic categories. *Journal of Experimental Psychology: General, 104,* 192–233.

Rosch, E. (1978). *Principles of categorization in cognition and categorization.* Hillsdale, NJ: Lawrence
Erlbaum Associates.

Rosch, E., & Mervis, C. B. (1975). Family resemblances: Studies in the internal structure of categories. *Cognitive Psychology, 7,* 573–605.

Rosch, E. H., Mervis, C. B., Gray, W D., Johnson, D. M., & Boyes-Braem, P. (1976). Basic objects in natural categories. *Cognitive Psychology, 8,* 382–439.

Rosenblatt, F. (1958). *The perceptron, a theory of statistical separability in cognitive systems* (Project PARA). Washington, DC: U.S. Department of Commerce, Office of Technical Services.

Rosenzweig, M. R., & Bennett, E. L. (1996). Psychobiology of plasticity: Effects of training and experience on brain and behavior. *Behavioral Brain Research, 78,* 57–65.

Rosnick, P., & Clement, J. (1980). Learning without understanding: The effect of tutoring strategies on algebra misconceptions. *Journal of Mathematical Behavior, 3,* 3–27.

Ross, B. H. (1984). Reminders and their effects in learning a cognitive skill. *Cognitive Psychology, 16,* 371–416.

Ross, B. H. (1996). Category representations and the effects of interacting with instances. *Journal of Experimental Psychology: Learning, Memory, and Cognition, 22,* 1249–1265.

Ross, B. H., & Spalding, T. L. (1994). Concepts and categories. In R. J. Sternberg (Ed.), *Handbook of perception and cognition* (Vol. 12, pp. 119–148). San Diego, CA: Academic Press.

Ross, L. (1977). The intuitive psychologist and his shortcomings: Distortions in the attribution process. In L. Berkowitz (Ed.), *Advances in experimental psychology* (Vol. 10, pp. 173–200). New York: Academic Press.

Ross, L., Greene, D., & House, P. (1977). The "false consensus effect": An egocentric bias in social perception and attribution processes. *Journal of Experimental Social Psychology, 13,* 279–301.

Roth, E. M., & Mervis, C. B. (1983). Fuzzy set theory and class inclusion relations in semantic categories. *Journal of Verbal Learning and Verbal Behavior, 22,* 509–525.

Roth, E. M., & Shoben, E. J. (1983). The effect of context on the structure of categories. *Cognitive Psychology, 15,* 346–378.

Rothenberg, A. (1979). *The emerging goddess.* Chicago: University of Chicago Press.

Rothenberg, A., & Hausman, C. R. (Eds.). (1976). *The creativity question.* Durham, NC: Duke University Press.

Rubenson, D. L., & Runco, M. A. (1992). The psychoeconomic approach to creativity. *New Ideas in Psychology, 10,* 131–147.

Rubin, Z., Hill, C. T., Peplau, L. A., & Dunkel-Schetter, C. (1980). Self-disclosure in dating couples: Sex roles and the ethic of openness. *Journal of Marriage and the Family, 42,* 305–317.

Rumelhart, D. E., McClelland, J. L., & University of California–San Diego PDP Research Group. (1986). *Parallel distributed processing: Explorations in the microstructure of cognition.* Cambridge, MA: MIT Press.

Rumelhart, D. E., & Ortony, A. (1977). The representation of knowledge in memory. In R. C. Anderson, R. J. Spiro, & W. E. Montague (Eds.), *Schooling and the acquisition of knowledge* (pp. 99–135). Hillsdale, NJ: Lawrence Erlbaum Associates.

Sacks, H., Schegloff, E. A., & Jefferson, G. (1974). A simplest systematic for the organization of turn-taking for conversation. *Language, 50,* 696–735.

Salthouse, T. A. (1991). Expertise as the circumvention of human processing limitations. In K. A. Ericsson & J. Smith (Eds.), *Toward a general theory of expertise: Prospects and limits* (pp. 286–300). New York: Cambridge University Press.

Salthouse, T. A. (1992). The information-processing perspective on cognitive aging. In R. J. Sternberg & C. A. Berg (Eds.), *Intellectual development* (pp. 261–277). New York: Cambridge University Press.

Salthouse, T. A. (1993). Influence of working memory on adult age differences in matrix reasoning. *British Journal of Psychology, 84,* 171–199.

Salthouse, T. A. (1994). The nature of the influence of speed on adult age differences in cognition. *Developmental Psychology, 30,* 240–259.

Salthouse, T. A. (1996). Constraints on theories of cognitive aging. *Psychonomic Bulletin and Review, 3,* 287–299.

Salthouse, T. A., Kausler, D. H., & Saults, J. S. (1990). Age, self-assessed health status, and cognition. *Journal of Gerontology, 45,* 156–160.

Salthouse, T. A., & Somberg, B. L. (1982). Skilled performance: Effects of adult age and experience on elementary processes. *Journal of Experimental Psychology: General, 111,* 176–207.

Samuel, A. L. (1963). Some studies in machine learning using the game of checkers. In E. A. Feigenbaum & J. Feldman (Eds.), *Computers and thought* (pp. 71–105). New York: McGraw-Hill.

Sapir, E. (1964). *Culture, language and personality.* Berkeley: University of California Press. (Original work published 1941)

Sarason, S. B., & Doris, J. (1979). *Educational handicap, public policy, and social history.* New York: Free Press.

Saufley, W. H., Otaka, S. R., & Bavaresco, J. L. (1985). Context effects: Classroom tests and context independence. *Memory and Cognition, 13,* 522–528.

Savage, L. J. (1954). *The foundations of statistics.* New York: Wiley.

Scardamalia, M. (1981). How children cope with the cognitive demands of writing. In C. H. Fredriksen, & J. F. Dominic (Eds.), *Writing: The nature, development, and teaching of written communication* (Vol. 2, pp. 81–103). Hillsdale, NJ: Lawrence Erlbaum Associates.

Scardamalia, M., & Bereiter, C. (1984). Development of strategies in text processing. In H. Mandl, N. L. Stein, & T. Trabasso (Eds.), *Learning and comprehension of text* (pp. 379–406). Hillsdale, NJ: Lawrence Erlbaum Associates.

Scardamalia, M., & Bereiter, C. (1987). Knowledge telling and knowledge transforming in written composition. In S. Rosenberg (Ed.), *Advances in applied psycholinguistics: Vol. 2. Reading, writing, and language learning* (pp. 142–175). Cambridge, England: Cambridge University Press.

Scardamalia, M., Bereiter, C., & Lamon, M. (1994). The CSILE project: Trying to bring the classroom into World 3. In K. McGilly (Ed.), *Classroom lessons: Integrating cognitive theory and classroom practice* (pp. 201–228). Cambridge, MA: MIT press.

Scarr, S. (1997). Behavior-genetic and socialization theories of intelligence: Truce and reconciliation. In R. J. Sternberg & E. L. Grigorenko (Eds.), *Intelligence, heredity and environment* (pp. 3–41). New York: Cambridge University Press.

Schacter, D. L. (Ed.). (1995). *Memory distortions: How minds, brains, and societies reconstruct the past.* (Vol. 11). Cambridge, MA: Harvard University Press.

Schaffer, H. R. (1977). *Mothering.* Cambridge, MA: Harvard University Press.

Schaie, K. W. (1974). Translations in gerontology—From lab to life. *American Psychologist, 29,* 802–807.

Schaie, K. W. (1989). Perceptual speed in adulthood: Cross-sectional and longitudinal studies. *Psychology and Aging, 4,* 443–453.

Schaie, K. W. (1996). *Intellectual development in adulthood: The Seattle Longitudinal Study.* New York: Cambridge University Press.

Schaie, K. W., & Willis, S. L. (1986). Can decline in intellectual functioning in the elderly be reversed? *Developmental Psychology, 22,* 223–232.

Schank, R. C. (1982). *Dynamic memory: A theory of reminding and learning in computers and people.* New York: Cambridge University Press.

Schank, R. C., & Abelson, R. P. (1977). *Scripts, plans, goals and understanding: An inquiry into human knowledge structures.* Hillsdale, NJ: Lawrence Erlbaum Associates.

Schank, R. C., Collins, G. C., & Hunter, L. E. (1986). Transcending inductive category formation in learning. *Behavioral and Brain Sciences, 9,* 639–651.

Schliemann, A. D., & Magalhües, V. P. (1990). *Proportional reasoning: From shops, to kitchens, laboratories, and, hopefully, schools.* (Proceedings of the 14th International Conference for the Psychology of Mathematics Education, Oaxtepec, Mexico).

Schneider, W., & Bjorklund, D. F. (1998). Memory. In W. Damon (Ed.-in-Chief) & D. Kuhn & R. S. Siegler (Vol. Eds.), *Handbook of child psychology* (Vol. 2, pp. 467–521). New York: John Wiley & Sons.

Schoenfeld, A. H. (1988). When good teaching leads to bad results: The disasters of "well-taught" mathematics courses. *Educational Psychologist, 23,* 145–166.

Schoenfeld, A. H. (1991). On mathematics as sense making: an informal attack on the unfortunate divorce of formal and informal mathematics. In J. F. Voss, D. N Perkins, & J. W. Segal (Eds.), *Informal reasoning and education* (pp. 311–343). Hillsdale, NJ: Lawrence Erlbaum Associates.

Schofield, J. W., & Evans-Rhodes, D. (1989). Artificial intelligence in the classroom. In D. Bierman, J. Greuker, & J. Sandberg (Eds.), *Artificial intelligence and education: Synthesis and reflection* (pp. 238–243). Springfield, VA: IOS.

Schonfield, D., & Robertson, D. A. (1966). Memory storage and aging. *Canadian Journal of Psychology, 20,* 228–236.

Schooler, J. W., & Engstler-Schooler, T. Y. (1990). Verbal overshadowing of visual memories: Some things are better left unsaid. *Cognitive Psychology, 22,* 36–71.

Schooler, J. W., & Melcher, J. (1994). The ineffability of insight. In S. M. Smith, T. B. Ward, & R. A. Finke (Eds.). *The creative cognition approach* (pp. 97–133). Cambridge, MA: MIT Press.

Schooler, J. W., Ohlsson, S., & Brooks, K. (1993). Thoughts beyond words: When language overshadows insight. *Journal of Experimental Psychology: General, 122,* 166–183.

Schraagen, J. M. (1993). How experts solve a novel problem in experimental design. *Cognitive Science. 17,* 285–309.

Schultz, D. (1981). *A history of modern psychology* (3rd ed.). New York: Academic Press.

Schustack, M. W., & Sternberg, R. J. (1981). Evaluation of evidence in causal inference. *Journal of Experimental Psychology: General, 110,* 101–120.

Scribner, S. (1975). Recall of classical syllogisms: A cross-cultural investigation of error on logical problems. In R. J. Falmagne (Ed.), *Reasoning: Representation and process in children and adults* (pp. 153–173). Hillsdale, NJ: Lawrence Erlbaum Associates.

Searle, J. R. (1975a). Indirect speech acts. In P. Cole & J. L. Morgan (Eds.), *Syntax and semantics: Speech acts* (Vol. 3, pp. 59–82). New York: Seminar Press.

Searle, J. R. (1975b). A taxonomy of elocutionary acts. In K. Gunderson (Ed.), *Minnesota studies in the philosophy of language* (pp. 344–369). Minneapolis: University of Minnesota Press.

Searle, J. R. (1979). *Expression and meaning: Studies in the theory of speech acts.* Cambridge, England: Cambridge University Press.

Searle, J. R. (1980). Minds, brains, and programs. *Behavioral and Brain Sciences, 3,* 417–424.

Segalowitz, S. J., Wagner, W. J., & Menna, R. (1992). Lateral versus frontal ERP predictors of reading skill. *Brain and Cognition, 20,* 85–103.

Seifert, C. M., Meyer, D. E., Davidson, N., Palatano, A. L., & Yaniv, I. (1995). Demystification of cognitive insight: Opportunistic assimilation and the prepared-mind perspective. In R. J. Sternberg & J. E. Davidson (Eds.), *The nature of insight* (pp. 65–124). Cambridge, MA: MIT Press.

Sells, S. B. (1936). The atmosphere effect: an experimental study of reasoning. *Archives of Psychology, 200,* 1–72.

Sells, S. B., & Koob, H. E. (1937). A classroom demonstration of "atmosphere effect" in reasoning. *Journal of Educational Psychology, 72,* 197–200.

Sera, M. D. (1992). To be or to be: Use and acquisition of the Spanish copulas. *Journal of Memory and Language, 31,* 408–427.

Serpell, R. (2000). Intelligence and culture. In R. J. Sternberg (Ed.), *Handbook of intelligence* (pp. 549–580). New York: Cambridge University Press.

Shafir, E. (1993). Choosing versus rejecting: Why some options are both better and worse than others. *Memory and Cognition, 21,* 546–556.

Shaywitz, B. A., Pugh, K. R., Constable, R. T., Shaywitz, S. E., Bronen, R. A., Fulbright, R. K., Shankweiler, D. P., Katz, L., Fletcher, J. M., Skudlarski, P., & Gore, J. C. (1995). Localization of semantic processing using functional magnetic resonance imaging. *Human Brain Mapping, 2,* 149–158.

Shiffrin, R. M. (1996). Laboratory experimentation on the genesis of expertise. In K. A. Ericsson (Ed.), *The road to excellence* (pp. 337–345). Mahwah, NJ: Lawrence Erlbaum Associates.

Shimojo, S., & Ichikawa, S. (1989). Intuitive reasoning about probability: Theoretical and experimental analyses of the problem of three prisoners. *Cognition, 32,* 1–24.

Shortliffe, E. H. (1976). *Computer-based medical consultations: MYCIN.* New York: American Elsevier.

Shweder, R. A. (1977). Likeness and likelihood in everyday thought: Magical thinking in judgments about personality. *Current Anthropology, 18,* 637–638.

Shweder, R. A., & D'Andrade, R. G. (1979). Accurate reflection or systematic distortion? A reply to Block, Weiss, and Thorne. *Journal of Personality and Social Psychology, 37,* 1075–1084.

Siegler, R. S. (1981). Developmental sequences within and between concepts. *Monographs of the Society for Research in Child Development, 46* (Serial No. 189).

Sieger, R. S. (1984). Mechanisms of cognitive growth: Variation and selection. In R. J. Sternberg (Ed.), *Mechanisms of cognitive development* (pp. 142–162). New York: Freeman.

Siegler, R. S. (1986). *Children's thinking.* Englewood Cliffs, NJ: Prentice-Hall.

Siegler, R. S. (1988). Individual differences in strategy choices: Good students, not-so-good students, and perfectionists. *Child Development, 59,* 833–851.

Siegler, R. S. (1991). Strategy choice and strategy discovery. *Learning and Instruction, 1,* 89–102.

Siegler, R. S. (1996). *Emerging minds: The process of change in children's thinking.* New York: Oxford University Press.

Siegler, R. S. & Shrager, J. (1984). Strategy choices in addition and subtraction: How do children know what to do? In C. Sophian (Ed.), *Origins of cognitive skills* (pp. 229–293). Hillsdale, NJ: Lawrence Erlbaum Associates.

Silver, E. A. (1982). Problem perception, problem schemata, and problem solving. *Journal of Mathematical Behavior, 3,* 169–181.

Silver, E. A. (1986). Using conceptual and procedural knowledge: A focus on relationships. In J. Hiebert (Ed.), *Conceptual and procedural knowledge: The case of mathematics* (pp. 181–189). Hillsdale, NJ: Lawrence Erlbaum Associates.

Silver, E. A. (1996). Moving beyond learning alone and in silence: Observations from the QUASAR project concerning communication in mathematics classrooms. In L. Schauble & R. Glaser (Eds.), *Innovations in learning: New environments for education* (pp. 127–159). Mahwah, NJ: Lawrence Erlbaum Associates.

Simon, H. A. (1957). *Administrative behavior* (2nd ed.). Totowa, NJ: Littlefield, Adams.

Simon, H. A., & Chase, W. G. (1973). Skill in chess. *American Scientist, 61,* 394–403.

Simon, H. A., & Gilmartin, K. (1973). A simulation of memory for chess positions. *Cognitive Psychology, 8,* 165–190.

Simon, H. A., & Kotovsky, K. (1963). Human acquisition of concepts for sequential patterns. *Psychological Review, 70,* 534–546.

Simon, H. A., & Zhu, X. (1988). Learning mathematics from examples and by doing. *Cognition and Instruction, 4,* 137–166.

Simonton, D. K. (1976). Biographical determinants of achieved eminence: A multivariate approach to the Cox data. *Journal of Personality and Social Psychology, 33,* 218–226.

Simonton, D. K. (1984). *Genius, creativity, and leadership.* Cambridge, MA: Harvard University Press.

Simonton, D. K. (1988). Age and outstanding achievement: What do we know after a century of research? *Psychological Bulletin, 104,* 251–267.

Simonton, D. K. (1994). *Greatness: Who makes history and why?* New York: Guilford.

Simonton, D. K. (1995). Foresight in insight: A Darwinian answer. In R. J. Sternberg & J. E. Davidson (Eds.), *The nature of insight* (pp. 495–534). Cambridge, MA: MIT Press.

Simonton, D. K. (1996). Creative expertise: A life-span developmental perspective. In K. A. Ericsson (Ed.), *The road to excellence: The acquisition of expert performance in the arts and sciences, sports, and games* (pp. 227–253). Mahwah, NJ: Lawrence Erlbaum Associates.

Simonton, D. K. (1997). Creative productivity: A predictive and explanatory model of career trajectories and landmarks. *Psychological Review, 104,* 66–89.

Simonton, D. K. (1998). Donald Campbell's model of the creative process: Creativity as blind variation and selective retention. *Journal of Creative Behavior, 32,* 153–158.

Simonton, D. K. (1999). Creativity from a historiometric perspective. In R. J. Sternberg (Ed.), *Handbook of creativity* (pp. 116–133). New York: Cambridge University Press.

Sincoff, J. B., & Sternberg, R. J. (1988). Development of verbal fluency abilities and strategies in elementary-school-age children. *Developmental Psychology, 24,* 646–653.

Skinner, B. F. (1948). *Walden II.* New York: Macmillan.

Skyrms, B. (1966). *Choice and chance: An introduction to inductive logic.* Belmont, CA: Dickenson Publishers.

Sleeman, D. (1984). An attempt to understand students' understanding of basic algebra. *Cognitive Science, 8,* 387–412.

Slobin, D. I. (1971). Cognitive prerequisites for the acquisition of grammar. In C. A. Ferguson & D. I. Slobin (Eds.), *Studies of child language development.* New York: Holt, Rinehart & Winston.

Slobin, D. I. (Ed.). (1985). *The cross-linguistic study of language acquisition.* Hillsdale, NJ: Lawrence Erlbaum Associates.

Sloboda, J. A. (1991). Musical expertise. In K. A. Ericsson & J. Smith (Eds.), *Toward a general theory of expertise: Prospects and limits* (pp. 153–171). New York: Cambridge University Press.

Sloboda, J. A. (1996). The acquisition of musical performance expertise: Deconstructing the "talent" account of individual differences in musical expressivity. In K. A. Ericsson (Ed.), *The road to excellence: The acquisition of expert performance in the arts and sciences, sports, and games* (pp. 347–354). Mahwah, NJ: Lawrence Erlbaum Associates.

Sloman, S. A. (1996). The empirical case for two systems of reasoning. *Psychological Bulletin, 119,* 3–22.

Sloman, S. A. (1998). Categorical inference is not a tree: The myth of inheritance hierarchies. *Cognitive Psychology, 35,* 1–33.

Sloman, S. A., & Rips, L. J. (1998). Similarity as an explanatory construct. *Cognition, 65*(2–3), 87–101.

Slovic, P. (1975). Choice between equally valued alternatives. *Journal of Experimental Psychology: Human Perception & Performance. 1,* 280–287.

Slovic, P., & Fischhoff, B. (1977). On the psychology of experimental surprises. *Journal of Experimental Psychology: Human Perception and Performance, 3,* 544–551.

Slovic, P., Fischhoff, B., & Lichtenstein, S. (1982). Response mode, framing, and information processing effects in risk assessment. In R. Hogarth (Ed.), *New directions for methodology of social and behavioral science: Question framing and response consistency.* San Francisco: Jossey-Bass.

Slovic, P., & Lichtenstein, S. (1971). Comparison of Bayesian and regression approaches to the study of information processing in judgment. *Organizational Behavior and Human Decision Processes, 6,* 649–744.

Smedslund, J. (1963). The concept of correlation in adults. *Scandinavian Journal of Psychology, 4,* 165–173.

Smilansky, B. (1974). Paper presented at the meeting of the American Educational Research Association, Chicago.

Smith, E. E. (1989). Concepts and induction. In M. I. Posner (Ed.), *Foundations of Cognitive Science* (pp. 501–526). Cambridge, MA: MIT Press.

Smith, E. E., Langston, C., & Nisbett, R. (1992). The case for rules in reasoning. *Cognitive Science, 16,* 1–40.

Smith, E. E., & Medin, D. L. (1981). *Categories and concepts.* Cambridge, MA: Harvard University Press.

Smith, E. E., Shoben, E. J., & Rips, L. J. (1974). Structure and process in semantic memory: A featural model for semantic decisions. *Psychological Review, 81,* 214–241.

Smith, E. E. & Sloman, S. A. (1994). Similarity-versus rule-based categorization. *Memory and Cognition, 22,* 377–386.

Smith, E. R., & Zarate, M. A. (1992). Exemplar-based model of social judgment. *Psychological Review, 99,* 3–21.

Smith, L. B., Jones, S. S., & Landau, B. (1996). Naming in young children: A dumb attentional mechanism? *Cognition, 60,* 143–171.

Smith, S. M., Ward, T. B., & Finke, R. A. (Eds.). (1995). *Creativity and the mind: Discovering the genius within.* Cambridge, MA: MIT Press.

Smullyan, R. (1978). *What is the name of this book: The riddle of Dracula and other logical puzzles.* Englewood Cliffs, NJ: Prentice-Hall.

Snodgrass, J. G., & Vanderwart, M. (1980). A standardized set of 260 pictures: Norms for name agreement, image agreement, familiarity, and visual complexity. *Journal of Experimental Psychology: Human Learning & Memory, 6,* 174–215.

Snow, C. E. (1977). The development of conversation between mothers and babies. *Journal of Child Language, 4,* 1–22.

Snyder, M. & Swann, W. B. (1978). Behavioral confirmation in social interaction: From social perception to social reality. *Journal of Experimental Social Psychology, 14,* 148–162.

Sodian, B., Zaitchik, D., & Carey, S. (1991). Young children's differentiation of hypothetical beliefs from evidence. *Child Development, 62,* 753–766.

Sommer, R. (1969). *Personal space.* Englewood Cliffs, NJ: Prentice-Hall.

Spearman, C. (1927). *The abilities of man.* New York: Macmillan.

Spelke, E. S., von Hofsten, C., & Kestenbaum, R. (1989). Object perception in infancy: Interaction of spatial and kinetic information for object boundaries. *Developmental Psychology, 25,* 185–196.

Sperber, D., Cara, F., & Girotto, V. (1995). Relevance theory explains the selection task. *Cognition, 57,* 31–95.

Staller, A., Sloman S. A., & Ben-Zeev, T. (2000). *Perspective effects in non-deontic versions of the Wason selection task. Memory and Cognition, 28,* 396–405.

Staudenmayer, H. (1975). Understanding conditional reasoning with meaningful propositions. In R. J. Falmagne (Ed.), *Reasoning: Representation and process in children and adult.* Hillsdale, NJ: Lawrence Erlbaum Associates.

Steele, C. (1990, May). A conversation with Claude Steele. *APS Observer,* pp. 11–17.

Stern, D. (1977). *The first relationship: Mother and infant.* Cambridge, MA: Harvard University Press.

Stern, W. (1912). *Psychologische Methoden der Intelligenz-Prüfung.* Leipzig, Germany: Barth.

Sternberg, R. J. (1977). *Intelligence, information processing, and analogical reasoning: The componential analysis of human abilities.* Hillsdale, NJ: Lawrence Erlbaum Associates.

Sternberg, R. J. (1979, September). Beyond IQ: Stalking the IQ quark. *Psychology Today,* pp. 42–54.

Sternberg, R. J. (1981). Intelligence and nonentrenchment. *Journal of Educational Psychology, 73,* 1–16.

Sternberg, R. J. (Ed.). (1982). *Handbook of human intelligence.* New York: Cambridge University Press.

Sternberg, R. J. (1983). Components of human intelligence. *Cognition, 15,* 1–48.

Sternberg, R. J. (1984). Toward a triarchic theory of human intelligence. *Behavioral and Brain Sciences, 7,* 269–287.

Sternberg, R. J. (1985). *Beyond IQ: A triarchic theory of human intelligence.* New York: Cambridge University Press.

Sternberg, R. J. (1986). *Intelligence applied: Understanding and increasing your intellectual skills.* San Diego, CA: Harcourt Brace Jovanovich.

Sternberg, R. J. (1987a). Most vocabulary is learned from context. In M. McKeown (Ed.), *The nature of vocabulary acquisition* (pp. 89–105). Hillsdale, NJ: Lawrence Erlbaum Associates.

Sternberg, R. J. (1987b). Teaching intelligence: The application of cognitive psychology to the improvement of intellectual skills. In J. B. Baron & R. J. Sternberg (Eds.), *Teaching thinking skills: Theory and practice* (pp. 182–218). New York: W. H. Freeman.

Sternberg, R. J. (1988). *The triarchic mind.* New York: Viking.

Sternberg, R. J. (Ed.). (1990). *Wisdom: Its nature, origins, and development.* New York: Cambridge University Press.

Sternberg, R. J. (1994). La theorie triarchique de l'intelligence [A triarchic theory of human intelligence]. *Orientation-Scolaire et Professionnelle, 23,* 119–136.

Sternberg, R. J. (1995a). For whom the bell curve tolls: A review of *The bell curve. Psychological Science, 6* (5), 257–261.

Sternberg, R. J. (1995b). *In search of the human mind.* Orlando: Harcourt Brace College Publishers.

Sternberg, R. J. (1996). Matching abilities, instruction, and assessment: Reawakening the sleeping giant of ATI. In I. Dennis & P. Tapsfield (Eds.), *Human abilities: Their nature and measurement* (pp. 167–181). Mahwah, NJ: Lawrence Erlbaum Associates.

Sternberg, R. J. (1997). *Successful intelligence.* New York: Plume.

Sternberg, R. J. (1998a). Applying the triarchic theory of human intelligence in the classroom. In R. J. Sternberg & W. M. Williams (Eds.), *Intelligence, instruction, and assessment: Theory into practice* (pp. 1–15). Mahwah, NJ: Lawrence Erlbaum Associates.

Sternberg, R. J. (1998b). The dialectic as a tool for teaching psychology. *Teaching of Psychology, 25*(3), 177–180.

Sternberg, R. J. (1999a). A dialectical basis for understanding the study of cognition. In R. J. Sternberg (Ed.), *The nature of cognition* (pp. 51–78). Cambridge, MA: MIT Press.

Sternberg, R. J. (Ed.). (1999b). *Handbook of creativity.* New York: Cambridge University Press.

Sternberg, R. J. (Ed.). (1999c). *The nature of cognition.* Cambridge, MA: MIT Press.

Sternberg, R. J., & Clinkenbeard, P. R. (1995). A triarchic model of identifying, teaching, and assessing gifted children. *Roeper Review, 17,* 255–260.

Sternberg, R. J., Conway, B. E., Ketron, J. L., & Bernstein, M. (1981). People's conceptions of intelligence. *Journal of Personality and Social Psychology, 41,* 37–55.

Sternberg, R. J., & Davidson, J. E. (Eds.). (1994). *The nature of insight.* Cambridge, MA: MIT Press.

Sternberg, R. J., & Detterman, D. K. (Eds.). (1986). *What is intelligence? Contemporary viewpoints on it nature and definition.* Norwood, NJ: Ablex.

Sternberg, R. J., Ferrari, M., Clinkenbeard, P. R., & Grigorenko, E. L. (1996). Identification, instruction, and assessment of gifted children: A construct validation of a triarchic model. *Gifted Child Quarterly, 40,* 129–137.

Sternberg, R. J., & Grigorenko, E. L. (1997a). The cognitive costs of physical and mental ill health: Applying the psychology of the developed world to the problems of the developing world. *Eye on Psi Chi, 2,* 20–27.

Sternberg, R. J., & Grigorenko, E. L. (1997b). *Intelligence, heredity, and environment.* New York: Cambridge University Press.

Sternberg, R. J., Grigorenko, E. L., Ferrari, M., & Clinkenbeard, P. (1999). A triarchic analysis of an aptitude-treatment interaction. *European Journal of Psychological Assessment, 15,* 1–11

Sternberg, R. J., & Kaufman, J. C. (1996). Innovation and intelligence testing: The curious case of the dog that didn't bark. *European Journal of Psychological Assessment, 12,* 175–182.

Sternberg, R. J., & Kaufman J. C. (1998). Human abilities. *Annual Review of Psychology, 49,* 479–502.

Sternberg, R. J., & Lubart, T. I. (1995). *Defying the crowd: Cultivating creativity in a culture of conformity.* New York: Free Press.

Sternberg, R. J., & Lubart, T. I. (1996). Investing in creativity. *American Psychologist, 51,* 677–688.

Sternberg, R. J., & Lubart, T. I. (1999). The concept of creativity: Prospects and paradigms. In R. J. Sternberg (Ed.), *Handbook of creativity* (pp. 3–15). New York: Cambridge University Press.

Sternberg, R. J., & Nigro, G. (1983). Interaction and analogy in the comprehension and appreciation of metaphors. *Quarterly Journal of Experimental Psychology, 35A,* 17–38.

Sternberg, R. J., Nokes, K., Geissler, P. W., Prince, R., Okatcha, F., Bundy, D. A., & Grigorenko, E. L. (in press). The relationship between academic and practical intelligence: A case study in Kenya. *Intelligence.*

Sternberg, R. J., & O'Hara, L. (1999). Creativity and intelligence. In R. J. Sternberg (Ed.), *Handbook of creativity* (pp. 251–272). New York: Cambridge University Press.

Sternberg, R. J., Okagaki, L., & Jackson, A. (1990). Practical intelligence for success in school. *Educational Leadership, 48,* 35–39.

Sternberg, R. J., Powell, C., McGrane, P. A., & McGregor, S. (1997). Effects of a parasitic infection on cognitive functioning. *Journal of Experimental Psychology: Applied, 3,* 67–76.

Sternberg, R. J., & Powell, J. S. (1983). Comprehending verbal comprehension. *American Psychologist, 38,* 878–893.

Sternberg, R. J., & Ruzgis, P. (Eds.). (1994). *Personality and intelligence.* New York: Cambridge University Press.

Sternberg, R. J., & Spear-Swerling, L. (1996). *Teaching for thinking.* Washington, DC: American Psychological Association.

Sternberg, R. J., Torff, B., & Grigorenko, E. L. (1998). Teaching triarchically improves school achievement. *Journal of Educational Psychology, 90,* 374–384.

Sternberg, R. J., & Wagner, R. K. (1993). The g-ocentric view of intelligence and job performance is wrong. *Current Directions in Psychological Science, 2,* 1–5.

Sternberg, R. J., & Wagner, R. K. (Eds.). (1994). *Mind in context: Interactionist perspectives on human intelligence.* New York: Cambridge University Press.

Sternberg, R. J., & Williams, W. M. (1997). Does the Graduate Record Examination predict meaningful success in the graduate training of psychologists? *American Psychologist, 52,* 630–641.

Sternberg, R. J., & Williams, W. M. (1998). *Intelligence, instruction, and assessment: Theory into practice* (pp. 1–15). Mahwah, NJ: Lawrence Erlbaum Associates.

Suh, S., & Trabasso, T. (1993). Inferences during reading: converging evidence from discourse analysis, talk-aloud protocols, and recognition priming. *Journal of Memory and Language, 32,* 279–300.

Suppes, P. & Groen, G. (1967). Some counting models for first-grade performance data on simple addition facts. In J. M. Scandura (Ed.), *Research in mathematics education.* Washington, DC: National Council of Teachers of Mathematics.

Tanenhaus, M., Spivey-Knowlton, M., Eberhard, K., & Sedivy, J. (1995). Integration of visual and linguistic information in spoken language comprehension. *Science, 268,* 1632–1634.

Tanenhaus, M. K., & Trueswell, J. C. (1995). Sentence comprehension. In J. L. Miller & P. D. Eimas (Eds.), *Speech, language, and communication* (pp. 217–262). San Diego, CA: Academic Press.

Tannen, D. (1986). *That's not what I meant! How conversational style makes or breaks relationships.* New York: Ballantine.

Tannen, D. (1990). *You just don't understand: Women and men in conversation.* New York: Ballantine.

Tannen, D. (1994). *Talking from 9 to 5: How women's and men's conversational styles affect who gets heard, who gets credit, and what gets done at work.* New York: Morrow.

Taplin, J. E. (1971). Reasoning with conditional sentences. *Journal of Verbal Learning and Verbal Behaviour, 10,* 219–225.

Taplin, J. E., & Staudenmayer, H. (1973). Interpretation of abstract conditional sentences in deductive reasoning. *Journal Verbal Learning and Verbal Behavior, 12,* 530–542.

Tatsuoka, K. K., & Baillie, R. (1982). *Rule space, the product space of two score components in signed-number subtraction: An approach to dealing with inconsistent use of erroneous rules* (Tech. Rep. 82–3–ONR). Urbana-Champaign: Computer-based Education Laboratory, University of Illinois.

Terman, L. M., & Merrill, M. A. (1937). *Measuring intelligence.* Boston: Houghton Mifflin.

Terman, L. M., & Merrill, M. A. (1973). *Stanford-Binet Intelligence Scale: Manual for the third revision.* Boston: Houghton Mifflin.

Thagard, P. (1996). *Mind: An introduction to cognitive science.* Cambridge, MA: MIT Press.

Thatcher, R. W. (1991). Maturation of the human frontal lobes: Physiological evidence for staging. *Developmental Neuropsychology, 7,* 397–419.

Thatcher, R. W. (1992). Cyclic cortical reorganization during early childhood. *Brain and Cognition, 20,* 24–50.

Thatcher, R. W. (1994). Psychopathology of early frontal lobe damage: Dependence on cycles of development. *Development and Psychopathology, 6,* 565–596.

Thatcher, R. W., Walker, R. A., & Giudice, S. (1987). Human cerebral hemispheres develop at different rates and ages. *Science, 236,* 1110–1113.

Thelen, E., & Smith, L. B. (1994). *A dynamic systems approach to the development of cognition and action.* Cambridge, MA: MIT Press.

Therivel, W. A. (1999). Why Mozart and not Salieri? *Creativity Research Journal, 12,* 67–76.

Thomas, J. C., Jr. (1974). An analysis of behavior in the hobbits-orcs problem. *Cognitive Psychology, 6,* 257–269.

Thorndike, E. L. (1905). *The elements of psychology.* New York: Seiler.

Thorndike, R. L., Hagen, E. P., & Sattler, J. M. (1986). *Stanford-Binet Intelligence Scale: Guide for administering and scoring the fourth edition.* Chicago: Riverside.

Thurstone, L. L. (1938). *Primary mental abilities.* Chicago: University of Chicago Press.

Titchener, E. B. (1910). *A text-book of psychology.* New York: Macmillan.

Torrance, E. P. (1962). *Guiding creative talent.* Englewood Cliffs, NJ: Prentice-Hall.

Torrance, E. P. (1974). *Torrance tests of creative thinking.* Lexington, MA: Personnel Press.

Tourangeau, R., & Sternberg, R. J. (1981). Aptness in metaphor. *Cognitive Psychology, 13,* 27–55.

Tourangeau, R., & Sternberg, R. J. (1982). Understanding and appreciating metaphors. *Cognition, 11,* 203–244.

Trabasso, T., & Suh, S. (1993). Understanding text: Achieving explanatory coherence through on-line inferences and mental operations in working memory. *Discourse Processes, 16,* 3–34.

Trager, J. (1992). *The people's chronology.* New York: Holt.

Tversky, A. (1972). Elimination by aspects: A theory of choice. *Psychological Review, 79,* 281–299.

Tversky, A. (1977). Features of similarity. *Psychological Review, 84,* 327–352.

Tversky, A., & Gati, I. (1982). Similarity, separability, and the triangle inequality. *Psychological Review, 89,* 123–154.

Tversky, A., & Kahneman, D. (1971). Belief in the law of small numbers. *Psychological Bulletin, 76,* 105–110.

Tversky, A., & Kahneman, D. (1973). Availability: A heuristic for judging frequency and probability. *Cognitive Psychology, 5,* 207–232.

Tversky, A., & Kahneman, D. (1974). Judgment under uncertainty: Heuristics and biases. *Science, 185,* 1124–1131.

Tversky, A., & Kahneman, D. (1981). The framing of decisions and the psychology of choice. *Science, 211,* 453–458.

Tversky, A., & Kahneman, D. (1982). Evidential impact of base rates. In D. Kahneman, P. Slovic, & A. Tversky (Eds.), *Judgment under uncertainty: Heuristics and biases* (pp. 153–160). Cambridge, MA: Cambridge University Press.

Tversky, A., & Kahneman, D. (1983). Extensional versus intuitive reasoning: The conjunction fallacy in probability judgment. *Psychological Review, 90,* 293–315.

Tversky, A., Sattath, S., & Slovic, P. (1988). Contingent weighting in judgment and choice. *Psychological Review, 95,* 371–384.

Tweney, R. D., Doherty, M. E., Warner, W. J., Pliske, D. B., Mynatt, C. R., Gross, K. A., & Arkkezin, D. L. (1980). Strategies of rule discovery in an inference task. *Quarterly Journal of Experimental Psychology , 32,* 109–124.

U.S. Department of Education, National Center for Educational Statistics, National Assessment of Educational Progress. (1998). *Pursuing Excellence: A Study of U.S. Twelfth-Grade Mathematics and Science Achievement in International Context.* Washington, DC: Author.

van Daalen-Kapteijns, M., & Elshout-Mohr, M. (1981). The acquisition of word meanings as a cognitive learning process. *Journal of Verbal Learning and Verbal Behavior, 20,* 386–399.

van Dijk, T. (1975). Formal semantics of metaphorical discourse. *Poetics, 4,* 173–198.

VanLehn, K. (1983). On the representation of procedures in repair theory. In H. P. Ginsburg (Ed.), *The development of mathematical thinking* (pp. 201–252). Hillsdale, NJ: Lawrence Erlbaum Associates.

VanLehn, K. (1986). Arithmetic procedures are induced from examples. In J. Hiebert (Ed.), *Conceptual and procedural knowledge: The case of mathematics* (pp. 133–179). Hillsdale, NJ: Lawrence Erlbaum Associates.

VanLehn, K. (1987). Learning one subprocedure per lesson. *Artificial Intelligence, 31,* 1–40.

VanLehn, K. (1988). Student modeling. In M. C. Polson & J. J. Richardson (Eds.), *Foundations of intelligent tutoring systems* (pp. 55–78). Hillsdale, NJ: Lawrence Erlbaum Associates.

VanLehn, K. (1989). Problem solving and cognitive skill acquisition. In M. I. Posner (Ed.), *Foundations of cognitive science* (pp. 527–579). Cambridge, MA: MIT Press.

VanLehn, K. (1990). *Mind bugs: The origins of procedural misconceptions.* Cambridge, MA: MIT Press.

VanLehn, K., & Brown, J. S. (1980). Planning nets: A representation for formalizing analogies and semantic models of procedural skills. In R. E. Snow, P. A. Federico, & W. Montague (Eds.), *Aptitude, learning, and instruction: Cognitive process analyses* (Vol. 2). Hillsdale, NJ: Lawrence Erlbaum Associates.

Vernon, P. A., & Mori, M. (1992). Intelligence, reaction times, and peripheral nerve conduction velocity. *Intelligence, 16*(3–4), 273–288.

Vernon, P. E. (Ed.). (1970). *Creativity: Selected readings* (pp. 126–136). Baltimore, MD: Penguin Books.

Vernon, P. E. (1971). *The structure of human abilities.* London: Methuen.

Vicente, K., & de Groot, A. D. (1990). The memory recall paradigm: Straightening out the historical record. *American Psychologist, 45,* 285–287.

Von Neumann, J., & Morgenstern, O. (1947). *Theory of games and economic behavior* (2nd rev. ed.). Princeton, NJ: Princeton University Press.

von Oech, R. (1983). *A whack on the side of the head.* New York: Warner.

von Oech, R. (1986). *A kick in the seat of the pants.* New York: Harper & Row.

von Winterfeldt, D., & Edwards, W. (1986). *Decision analysis and behavioral research.* Cambridge, England: Cambridge University Press.

Voss, J. F., Wolfe, C. R., Lawrence, J. A., & Engle, R. A. (1991). From representation to decision: An analysis of problem solving in international relations. In R. J. Sternberg & P. A. Frensch (Eds.), *Complex problem solving: Principles and mechanisms* (pp. 119–158). Hillsdale, NJ: Lawrence Erlbaum Associates.

Vygotsky, L. S. (1962). *Thought and language.* Cambridge, MA: MIT Press.

Vygotsky, L. S. (1978). *Mind in society: The development of higher psychological processes.* Cambridge, MA: Harvard University Press.

Vygotsky, L. S. (1986). *Thought and language.* Cambridge, MA: MIT Press.

Wagner, D. A. (1978). Memories of Morocco: The influence of age, schooling and environment on memory. *Cognitive Psychology, 10,* 1–28.

Wahlsten, D., & Gottlieb, G. (1997). The invalid separation of effects of nature and nurture: Lessons from animal experimentation. In R. J. Sternberg & E. L. Grigorenko (Eds.), *Intelligence, heredity, and environment* (pp. 163–192). New York: Cambridge University Press.

Waldmann, M. R., & Holyoak, K. J. (1992). Predictive and diagnostic learning within causal models: Asymmetries in cue competition. *Journal of Experimental Psychology: General, 121,* 222–236.

Waldmann, M. R., Holyoak, K. J., & Fratianne, A. (1995). Causal models and the acquisition of category structure. *Joumal of Experimental Psychology: General, 124,* 181–206.

Walker, S. J. (1992). Supernatural beliefs, natural kinds, and conceptual structure. *Memory and Cognition, 20,* 655–662.

Wallach, M., & Kogan, N. (1965). *Modes of thinking in young children.* New York: Holt, Rinehart, & Winston.

Walters, J., Blythe, T., & White, N. (1993). PIFS: Everyday cognition goes to school. In H. Reese & J. Puckett (Eds.), *Advances in lifespan development* (pp. 137–153). Mahwah, NJ: Lawrence Erlbaum Associates.

Ward, T. B. (1994). Structured imagination: The role of conceptual structure in exemplar generation. *Cognitive Psychology, 27,* 1–40.

Ward, T. B., Smith, S. M., & Finke, R. A. (1999). Creative cognition. In R. J. Sternberg (Ed.), *Handbook of creativity* (pp. 189–225). New York: Cambridge University Press.

Wason, P. C. (1960). On the failure to eliminate hypotheses in a conceptual task. *Quarterly Journal of Experimental Psychology, 12,* 129–140.

Wason, P. C. (1966). Reasoning. In B. M. Foss (Ed.), *New horizons in psychology.* Harmondsworth, England: Penguin.

Wason, P. C. (1968). Reasoning about a rule. *Quarterly Journal of Experimental Psychology, 20,* 273–281.

Wason, P. C., & Johnson-Laird, P. N. (1972). *Psychology of reasoning: Structure and content.* London: Batsford.

Wasow, T. (1989). Grammatical theory. In M. I. Posner (Ed.), *Foundations of cognitive science* (pp. 208–243). Cambridge, MA: MIT Press.

Watson, J. B. (1930). *Behaviorism* (rev. ed.). New York: W. W. Norton.

Watson, J. B., & McDougall, W. (1929). *The battle of behaviorism.* New York: W. W. Norton.

Watson, O. M. (1970). *Proxemic behavior: A cross-cultural study.* The Hague, the Netherlands: Mouton.

Wattenmaker, W. D. (1992). Relational properties and memory-based category construction. *Journal of Experimental Psychology: Learning, Memory, and Cognition, 18,* 1125–1138.

Wattenmaker, W. D. (1993). Incidental concept learning, feature frequency, and correlated properties. *Journal of Experimental Psychology: Learning, Memory, and Cognition, 19,* 203–222.

Wattenmaker, W. D., Dewey, G. I., Murphy, T. D., & Medin, D. L. (1986). Linear separability and concept learning: Context, relational properties, and concept naturalness. *Cognitive Psychology, 18,* 158–194.

Wattenmaker, W. D., Nakamura, G. V., & Medin, D. L. (1988). Relationships between similarity-based and explanation-based categorization. In D. J. Hilton (Ed.), *Contemporary science and natural explanation: Commonsense conceptions of causality* (pp. 204–240). New York: New York University Press.

Weber, E. U., Boeckenholt, U., Hilton, D. J., & Wallace, B. (1993). Determinants of diagnostic hypothesis generation: Effects of information, base rates, and experience. *Journal of Experimental Psychology: Learning, Memory, and Cognition, 19,* 1151–1164.

Wechsler, D. (1939). *The measurement of adult intelligence.* Baltimore: Williams & Wilkins.

Wehner, L., Csikszentmihalyi, M., & Magyari-Beck, I. (1991). Current approaches used in studying creativity: An exploratory investigation. *Creativity Research Journal, 4,* 261–271.

Weiller, C., Isansee, C., Rijntgis, M., Huber, W. et al. (1996). Recovery from Wernicke's aphasia: A positron emission tomography study. *Annals of Neurology, 37,* 723–732 .

Weisberg, R. W. (1969). Sentence processing assessed through intrasentence word associations. *Journal of Experimental Psychology, 82,* 332–338.

Weisberg, R. W. (1986). *Creativity, genius and other myths.* New York: Freeman.

Weisberg, R. W. (1988). Problem solving and creativity. In R. J. Sternberg (Ed.), *The nature of creativity* (pp. 148–176). New York: Cambridge University Press.

Weisberg, R. W. (1993). *Creativity: Beyond the myth of genius.* New York: Freeman.

Weisberg, R. W. (1999). Creativity and knowledge: A challenge to theories. In R. J. Sternberg (Ed.), *Handbook of creativity* (pp. 226–250). New York: Cambridge University Press.

Weisberg, R. W. & Alba, J. W. (1981). An examination of the alleged role of "fixation in the solution of several "insight" problems. *Journal of Experimental Psychology: General, 110,* 169–192.

Weizenbaum, J. (1966). ELIZA—A computer program for the study of natural language communication between man and machine. *Communications of the Association for Computing Machinery, 9,* 36–45.

Wellman, H. M., & Gelman, S. A. (1992). Cognitive development: Foundational theories of core domains. *Annual Review of Psychology, 43,* 337–375.

Werker, J. F., & Tees, R. L. (1984). Cross-language speech perception: Evidence for perceptual reorganization during the first year of life. *Infant Behavior & Development, 7,* 49–63.

Werner, H., & Kaplan, B. (1963). *Symbol formation.* Hillsdale, NJ: Lawrence Erlbaum Associates.

Werner, H., & Kaplan, E. (1952). The acquisition of word meanings: A developmental study. *Monographs of the Society for Research in Child Development,* No. 51.

Whittlesea, B. W. (1987). Preservation of specific experiences in the representation of general knowledge. *Journal of Experimental Psychology: Learning, Memory, and Cognition, 13,* 3–17.

Whorf, B. L. (1956). In J. B. Carroll (Ed.), *Language, thought and reality: Selected writings of Benjamin Lee Whorf.* Cambridge, MA: MIT Press.

Wickelgren, W. A. (1974). How to solve problems: Elements of a theory of problems and problem solving. San Fransisco: W. H. Freeman.

Wickett, J. C., & Vernon, P. (1994). Peripheral nerve conduction velocity, reaction time, and intelligence: An attempt to replicate Vernon and Mori. *Intelligence, 18,* 127–132.

Wilkins, M. C. (1928). The effect of changed material on ability to do formal syllogistic reasoning. *Archives of Psychology, 16,* No. 102.

Willerman, L., Schultz, R., Rutledge, J. N., & Bigler, E. D. (1991). In vivo brain size and intelligence. *Intelligence, 15,* 223–228.

Willerman, L., Schultz, R., Rutledge, J. N., & Bigler, E. D. (1992). Hemisphere size asymmetry predicts relative verbal and nonverbal intelligence differently in the sexes: An MRI study of structure function relations. *Intelligence, 16,* 315–328.

Willis, S. L. (1985). Towards an educational psychology of the older adult learner: Intellectual and cognitive bases. In J. E. Birren & K. W. Schaie (Eds.), *Handbook of the psychology of aging* (2nd ed.). New York: Van Nostrand Reinhold.

Winner, E. (1996a). *Gifted children: Myths and realities.* New York: Basic Books.

Winner, E. (1996b). The rage to master: The decisive role of talent in the visual arts. In K. A. Ericsson (Ed.), *The road to excellence: The acquisition of expert performance in the arts and sciences, sports and games* (pp. 271–301). Mahwah, NJ: Lawrence Erlbaum Associates.

Winograd, T. (1972). *Understanding natural language.* New York: Academic Press.

Wisniewski, E. J. (1995). Prior knowledge and functionally relevant features in concept learning. *Journal of Experimental Psychology: Learning, Memory, & Cognition, 21,* 449–468.

Wisniewski, E. J., & Medin, D. L. (1994). On the interaction of theory and data in concept learning. *Cognitive Science, 18,* 221–281.

Wissler, C. (1901). The correlation of mental and physical tests. *Psychological Review, Monograph Supplement 3.*

Woodman, R. W., & Schoenfeldt, L. F. (1989). Individual differences in creativity: An interactionist perspective. In J. A. Glover, R. R. Ronning, & C. R. Reynolds (Eds.), *Handbook of creativity* (pp. 77–91). New York: Plenum.

Woodworth, R. S., & Sells, S. B. (1935). An atmosphere effect in formal syllogistic reasoning. *Journal of Experimental Psychology, 18,* 451–460.

Wright, G. (1984). *Behavioral decision theory*. Harmondsworth, England: Penguin.

Yamamoto, K. (1964). Creativity and sociometric choice among adolescents. *Journal of Social Psychology, 64,* 249–261.

Yang, S., & Sternberg, R. J. (1997). Taiwanese Chinese people's conceptions of intelligence. *Intelligence, 25,* 21–36.

Young, R. M., & O'Shea, T. (1981). Errors in students' subtraction. *Cognitive Science, 5,* 153–177.

Yu, V. L., Fagan, L. M., Bennet, S. W., Clancey, W. J., Scott, A. C., Hannigan, J. F., Blum, R. L., Buchanan, B. G., & Cohen, S. N. (1984). An evaluation of MYCIN's advice. In B. G. Buchanan & E. H. Shortliffe, *Rule-based expert systems.* Reading, MA: Addison-Wesley.

Zbrodoff, N. J., & Logan, G. D. (1986). On the autonomy of mental processes: A case study of arithmetic. *Journal of Experimental Psychology: General, 115,* 118–130.

Zeidner, M. (1990). Perceptions of ethnic group modal intelligence scores: Reflections of cultural stereotypes or intelligence test scores? *Journal of Cross-Cultural Psychology, 21,* 214–231.

Zhu, X., & Simon, H. A. (1988). Learning mathematics from examples and by doing. *Cognition and Instruction, 4,* 137–166.

Zigler, E., & Berman, W. (1983). Discerning the future of early childhood intervention. *American Psychologist, 38,* 894–906.

Zurif, E. B. (1990). Language and the brain. In D. N. Osherson & H. Lasnik (Eds.), *Language* (pp. 177–198). Cambridge, MA: MIT Press.

Author Index

Note: Page numbers followed by an f indicate a reference to a figure; page numbers followed by a t indicate a reference to a table.

Abelson, R. P., 66, 67, 155, 271
Adams, M. J., 272, 278
Adelson, B., 293
Adler, J., 219
Agnoli, F., 190
Ahn, W.-K., 45, 51, 311
Alba, J. W., 283
Albert, M. L., 224
Albert, R. S., 277
Allais, M., 174
Allen, W., 90
Allopenna, P. D., 53
Almor, A., 101, 115
Amabile, T. M., 139, 284, 285, 286, 288
Anderson, J. A., 42, 77n1
Anderson, J. R., 37, 54, 59, 60, 61, 62, 69, 70, 71, 72, 73, 77n1, 150, 162, 163, 165, 299, 328, 330, 333, 341, 342
Anderson, R. C., 67, 238
Andrews, F. M., 282
Angell, J. R., 23, 24
Anzai, Y., 350
Appel, L. F., 316
Appelbaum, M. I., 304
Aquinas, T., 17
Aristotle, 15–16, 17, 18, 19, 25, 30
Arkes, H. R., 140
Arlin, P. K., 313
Asher, J. J., 223
Ashlock, R. B., 158
Atkinson, J. W., 285
Atran, S., 55
Augustine of Hippo, 17
Austin, G. A., 13, 34
Avis, N. E., 135

Bacon, F., 18, 19
Bahrick, H. P., 212, 223, 324

Bahrick, L. E., 212
Bahrick, P. O., 324
Baillargeon, R., 311
Baillie, R., 73
Baker, J. G., 273
Baltes, P. B., 259, 325, 326
Balthazard, C., 290
Banaji, M. R., 218, 219
Banks, S. M., 183
Bara, B. G., 93, 107, 109
Bar-Hillel, M., 130, 135
Baron, J., 129, 130, 131, 133, 141, 184, 185, 192, 193, 330, 343, 354
Baroody, A. J., 318
Barres, P. E., 110
Barrett, P. T., 255
Barron, B., 351, 352, 353
Barron, F., 281, 282, 284, 285
Barsalou, L. W., 33, 44, 45
Bartlett, F. C., 66, 69, 155
Bashore, T. R., 323
Basseches, J., 22
Bassok, M., 153, 157
Batt, R., 253
Baversco, J. L., 331
Beach, L. R., 135
Beardsley, M., 227
Beck, D. E., 187
Beck, I. L., 235
Bedard, J., 157
Begg, I., 93
Beilin, H., 311
Bell, D. E., 185, 195
Bell, E. T., 353
Bellezza, F. S., 34
Bellugi, U., 214
Belmont, J. M., 317
Bennett, E. L., 323, 325

Ben-Zeev, T., 73, 101, 102f, 137, 138, 158, 161, 162, 163, 164, 330, 341, 351
Bereiter, C., 347
Berger, S. A., 212
Berlin, B., 220
Berliner, H. J., 265
Berman, W., 272
Bernoulli, D., 170
Bernstein, A., 265
Bernstein, M., 244
Berry, J. W., 244
Bertoncini, J., 210
Beth, E. W., 104
Bettman, J. R., 173
Beyth-Marom, R., 126, 127, 133, 330
Bialystok, E., 223
Bickerton, D., 224, 227
Biddle, G., 133
Bidell, T. R., 311
Bigler, E. D., 256
Billman, D., 54
Binet, A., 159, 245–46, 247
Bisanz, J., 316
Bjorklund, D. F., 317
Black, J. B., 67
Black, M., 227, 228
Blades, M., 311
Blagg, N., 336
Blank, H., 135
Blessing, S. B., 165
Bloom, B. S., 272, 300, 301
Bloom, P., 48, 49
Blythe, T., 333
Bobbitt, B. L., 215
Bock, K., 203, 204, 208, 226
Boden, M., 150, 284
Boeckenholt, U., 187
Borgida, E., 192

Subject Index